Comprehensive Stress Management

TENTH EDITION

Jerrold S. Greenberg
University of Maryland

Boston   Burr Ridge, IL   Dubuque, IA   Madison, WI   New York   San Francisco   St. Louis
Bangkok   Bogotá   Caracas   Kuala Lumpur   Lisbon   London   Madrid   Mexico City
Milan   Montreal   New Delhi   Santiago   Seoul   Singapore   Sydney   Taipei   Toronto

The McGraw·Hill Companies

 **Higher Education**

COMPREHENSIVE STRESS MANAGEMENT

Published by McGraw-Hill, a business unit of The McGraw-Hill Companies, Inc., 1221 Avenue of the Americas, New York, NY 10020. Copyright © 2008, 2006, 2004, 2002, 1999, 1996, 1993, 1990, 1987, 1983 by The McGraw-Hill Companies, Inc. All rights reserved. No part of this publication may be reproduced or distributed in any form or by any means, or stored in a database or retrieval system, without the prior written consent of The McGraw-Hill Companies, Inc., including, but not limited to, in any network or other electronic storage or transmission, or broadcast for distance learning.

Some ancillaries, including electronic and print components, may not be available to customers outside the United States.

This book is printed on acid-free paper.

1 2 3 4 5 6 7 8 9 0 CCI/CCI 0 9 8 7 6

ISBN-13: 978-0-07-352962-2
ISBN-10:   0-07-352962-1

Vice President and Editor-in-Chief: *Emily Barrosse*
Publisher: *William R. Glass*
Sponsoring Editor: *Joseph Diggins*
Executive Marketing Manager: *Pamela S. Cooper*
Director of Development: *Kathleen Engelberg*
Developmental Editor: *Kelly Wagner, Carlisle Publishers Services*
Development Editor for Technology: *Julia D. Ersery*
Editorial Coordinator: *Sarah B. Hill*
Media Producer: *Michele Borrelli*
Managing Editor: *Jean Dal Porto*
Project Manager: *Ruth Smith*
Art Editor: *Katherine McNab*
Designer: *Srdjan Savanovic*
Cover Designer: *Pam Verros, images are © Master file.*
Photo Research Coordinator: *Natalia C. Peschiera*
Production Supervisor: *Janean A. Utley*
Composition: *10.5/12 Minion, by Techbooks*
Printing: *45 # Pub Matte, Courier*

Credits: The credits section for this book begins on page C and is considered an extension of the copyright page.

Library of Congress Cataloging-in-Publication Data

Greenberg, Jerrold S.
    Comprehensive stress management / Jerrold S. Greenberg.—10th ed.
      p. cm.
    Includes bibliographical references.
    ISBN-13: 978-0-07-352962-2 (softcover : alk. paper)
    ISBN-10: 0-07-352962-1 (softcover : alk. paper)
    1. Stress (Psychology) 2. Stress (Physiology) 3. Stress (Psychology)—Prevention. 4. Stress management. I.
Title.
BF575.S75G66 2008
155.9'042—dc22

                                   2006044909

The Internet addresses listed in the text were accurate at the time of publication. The inclusion of a Web site does not indicate an endorsement by the authors or McGraw-Hill, and McGraw-Hill does not guarantee the accuracy of the information presented at these sites.

www.mhhe.com

If I were asked to choose the best way to manage stress, I would probably choose communicating with other people and obtaining social support from them. For this to occur, though, people have to make themselves available to provide that support, meaning they have to sacrifice a good deal of their own time, effort, and energy. That is why this book is dedicated to my wife, Karen. Karen is social support incarnate. She is caring, concerned, considerate, loving, and available to friends, family, and even acquaintances. That is why she is sought out by people in her world who encounter problems and need a sympathetic ear to listen. To recognize this extraordinary person, whom I am fortunate to have in my life, and to acknowledge that sympathetic ear, that loving person, that stress-buster, I dedicate this book with love.

brief table of contents

brief table of contents

table of contents

table of contents

part 3

General Applications: Relxation Techniques **169**

part 4

General Applications: Physiological Arousal and Behavior Change Intervention 231

CHAPTER 13

CHAPTER 14

CHAPTER 15

part 5

Specific Applications 299

CHAPTER 16

CHAPTER 17

The first edition of this book evolved out of two needs. The first pertained to my discussions with students, colleagues, friends, and relatives who, as I listened more carefully, seemed to be crying out for help in dealing with the stress of life. Upon closer scrutiny, I realized that the only cries I was deaf to were my own. I, too, needed help managing stress. The second need related to the nature of texts on this subject. I thought they were informative or interesting but seldom both. Furthermore, I didn't think stress management was presented as the complex subject I envision it to be. I thought books on this subject explored parts of stress management but omitted several key components. Both of these needs continue to exist and cry out for this, the tenth edition of *Comprehensive Stress Management.*

This book, then, is written in a more personal, informal manner than most and is organized to consider stress as a function of situations in life that, when perceived as distressing, result in emotional and physiological arousal. There is an abundance of scientific and statistical information in this book, but it hangs on to anecdote, humor, and personal experience to breathe life into its content. In addition, numerous means of self-evaluation are provided in the form of Laboratory Assessments at the end of all chapters so that content takes on personal meaning for each reader.

New to This Edition

We all learn from our experiences, and I am no exception. Consequently, this tenth edition of *Comprehensive Stress Management* incorporates changes recommended by readers of the first nine editions while maintaining the elements valued by those readers. Revisions include the following:

- Boxed content has been added at the end of the chapters. Entitled "Coping in Today's World," these boxes present current and interesting additional material related to the chapter's content for the student to consider. Among the "Coping in Today's World" boxes are discussions of environmental noise and stress, life satisfaction, effects of brain neuroplasticity and stress, laughter clubs to cope with stress, complementary and alternative medicine, new technology and stress, hospital clowns to help patients cope with their illnesses, the Health Belief Model, health disparities, American workers' vacation days and lunch times compared with those of other countries' workers, ethical violations by college students, and marriage and stress.

- Ten new Lab Assessments have been added at the end of the chapters. Now, each chapter has at least one Lab Assessment.

- The new USDA MyPyramid replaces the previous Food Guide Pyramid in Chapter 5. The Web site address for the new pyramid is provided. Maintained, though, are the discussions and references to ethnic food guide pyramids.

- The discussion of women and social support appearing in Chapter 6 has been replaced with updated content and references from studies published in 2005.

- A new scale has been added that helps students identify how satisfied they are with their lives. This scale appears in Chapter 6 and is entitled the *Satisfaction with Life Scale.* By completing this scale, students are challenged to take action to improve their lives so they are more satisfied. The result will be less stress.

- Current research findings related to locus of control have been added in Chapter 7. These studies demonstrate the relationship between locus of control and breast cancer, chronic fatigue syndrome, sick leave from work, and response to a diagnosis of human papillomavirus.

- A new scale, the Spirituality Assessment Scale has been added to Chapter 8. This scale allows students to measure their perceptions of their purpose and meaning in life, innerness (or inner resources) unifying interconnectedness, and transcendence.

- Current research findings related to autogenics and cancer, multiple sclerosis, coronary angioplasty, anxiety, drug abuse, menstrual discomfort, scoliosis, and dyspnea (painful breathing) have been added in Chapter 10.

- Updated statistics and an expanded discussion regarding caregiving and stress are presented in Chapter 19.

- Statistics have been revised to present the latest available data. These data have been acquired through credible sources, mostly U.S. governmental data repositories.

- References have been updated throughout the book. More than 120 current references—most from the year 2000 and later—have been added, and outdated references omitted.

- Web sites presented at the end of each chapter allow students to explore the chapter's content in more detail. All of these references have been checked, and those no longer operational have been replaced with current Web sites.

- New color photographs replace less relevant and outdated images throughout the book.

- A new full-color format and design provide a fresh look to the text.

The sum of these changes assures the student of the most current and accurate content, presented in an interesting and educational format.

Pedagogial Features

- The workbook icon appears alongside content that relates to sections in the accompanying online workbook, *Your Personal Stress Profile and Activity Workbook,* giving instructors the option of integrating coursework with workbook content.

- The stress portfolio icon appears with related content in the text to better enable students to organize their materials into one source and to develop their own stress portfolio.

- Lab Assessments are included at the end of each chapter, enabling students to specifically relate the chapter content to their personal lives.

- The boxed feature "Getting Involved in Your Community," appearing in selected chapters, challenges students to apply the chapter content to a related community project to assist in decreasing stress levels in their communities.

- Bulleted chapter summaries are provided at the end of every chapter to reinforce the content and assist students with test preparation.

- The extensive bibliography is updated and included at the back of the book so students can delve further into the topics discussed.

Organization

Part 1 of this book contains a complete discussion of the stress reaction and its relationship to specific illnesses and diseases. Parts 2, 3, and 4 teach you how to intervene—to step between the stressor and physiological arousal. Consequently, you should be able to limit the harmful effects of the stressors you encounter. In brief, you will learn how to adjust your life situations, perceive events differently, react less emotionally, and use the products of stress to limit their duration. In addition, you should be able to recognize the relationship between spirituality and stress. Part 5 discusses the particular stress needs of homemakers, workers outside the home, children and youths, college students, and older adults. The stress management procedures presented in Parts 2, 3, and 4 are applied to each of these specific populations to demonstrate their use in alleviating the harmful effects of stress.

The major theme of this book is that people usually have greater control over their lives and their environments than they realize. Unfortunately, many of us do not exercise this control and become rudderless in a rapidly changing and stressful society. Stress management is learning to recapture control of ourselves, and this book describes how to do that.

Online Learning Center for *Comprehensive Stress Management* (www.mhhe.com/greenberg10e)

The **Online Learning Center** for *Comprehensive Stress Management* offers resources for both instructors and students.

For the instructor:

- **Course Integrator Guide**   This instructor's guide includes learning objectives, suggested lecture outlines, classroom activities, media resources, and Web links. It also describes how to integrate other supplementary materials into lectures and assignments for each chapter.

- **Test bank**   The text bank includes multiple choice, true-false, and fill-in-the-blank questions for each chapter. It is available as Word files and with EZ Test computerized testing software. EZ Test provides a powerful, easy-to-use test maker to create printed quizzes and exams. For secure online testing, exams created in EZ Test can be exported to WebCT, Blackboard, PageOut, and EZ Test Online. EZ Test comes with a Quick Start Guide, and once the program is installed, users have access to a User's Manual and Flash tutorials. Additional help is available online at www.mhhe.com/eztest.

- **PowerPoint slides**   These slides includes key lecture points and provide a tool you can add to or change to meet the needs of your course.

For the student:

- **Y*our Personal Stress Profile and Activity Workbook,* 4th edition, by Jerrold Greenberg. Referenced at appropriate places in the text with a special icon, the workbook shows students how to evaluate their current level of stress, develop a personal stress profile, and use the tools and activities to become active participants in managing their own stress.

- **Chapter reviews**

- **Interactive quizzes**

- **Glossary flashcards**

- **PowerPoint slide presentation**

Acknowledgments

There are many people who have helped bring this project to completion. They can never be adequately thanked, but perhaps a mention here will let them know that their help has been appreciated.

First are my students, who have taught me as much about stress management as I have ever taught them. Not only do I learn from their term papers and other assignments, but the way in which they live their lives teaches me much about managing stress.

Then there are my professional colleagues, who encourage, stimulate, and provoke me to be as competent and as qualified as I can—if for no other reason than to keep pace with them. In particular, I wish to thank Robert Feldman, the author of Chapter 14, whose contribution to this book is obvious, albeit immeasurable.

And, of course, there are the academic reviewers, whose comments sometimes exasperated, bewildered, or angered me but who also encouraged me and provided important guidance for revision. Because of them, this book is better than it otherwise would have been. These reviewers include

Dr. Edward Baker
Chesapeake College

Guy E. Cunningham
Grand View College

Danna Ethan
Borough of Manhattan Community College, CUNY

Rebecca A. Glass
Austin Peay State University

Gary Guyot
Regis University

Loeen M. Irons
Baylor University

Dr. Mary L. Jones
Glendale Community College

Martin J. Loy
University of Wisconsin–Stevens Point

Joanne Marrow
California State University–Sacramento

Steven J. Radlo
Western Illinois University

Mary Ellen Rose
American University

Janet L. Sholes
Frederick Community College

Gayle Lynn Westberg
University of Utah

I would be remiss not to acknowledge the support of Kelly Wagner, my developmental editor for the tenth edition of *Comprehensive Stress Management,* for helping to guide this edition through the sometimes confusing production process. Her support, competence, and encouragement are very much appreciated.

Most important, there is my family. They not only respected my need for quiet time to write but also provided much of the inspiration I needed. Karen, Keri, and Todd—I don't tell you often enough how much you contribute to my work and productivity, but you do, and I recognize your support and value it.

part 1

Scientific Foundations

It was a pleasant spring day—about seventy degrees, with the sun shining and a slight breeze. It was the kind of day I would have enjoyed celebrating by playing tennis, jogging, and helping my son learn how to ride his bicycle (an aggravating but necessary task). Instead, I was on the shoulder of a country road in upstate New York with my hands on my knees, vomiting. The story of how I wound up on such a glorious day in such an inglorious position serves as an important lesson.

At the time, I was an assistant professor, imposing my know-it-all attitude upon unsuspecting and innocent college students at the State University of New York at Buffalo. I had become quite successful in each of the three areas the university established as criteria for promotion and tenure: teaching, research and other publications, and university and community service. The student evaluations of my classes were quite flattering. I had published approximately fifteen articles in professional journals and was contracted to write my first book. So much for teaching and the proverbial "publish or perish" syndrome. It is on the community-service criteria that I need to elaborate.

To meet the community-service standards of acceptance for promotion and tenure, I made myself available as a guest speaker to community groups. I soon found that I was able to motivate groups of people through speeches and workshops on numerous topics, both directly and tangentially related to my area of expertise—health education. I spoke to the local Kiwanis Club on the topic "Drug Education Techniques" and to the Green Acres Cooperative Nursery School's parents and teachers on "Drug Education for Young Children." I was asked to present the senior class speech at Medaille College on "Sex Education" and wound up conducting workshops for local public school districts on such concerns as "Why Health Education?" "Values and Teaching," "Group Process," and "Peer Training Programs for Cigarette-Smoking Education." Things started to take shape, and I expanded my local presentations to state and national workshops and to presenting papers at various state and national meetings.

My life changed rapidly and repeatedly. I went to Buffalo as an assistant professor and was promoted twice, leaving as a full professor with tenure and administrative responsibility for the graduate program in health education. When I left Buffalo, I had published more than forty articles in professional journals, and my second book was soon to come off the presses. During my tenure at SUNY/Buffalo, I appeared on radio and television programs and was the subject of numerous newspaper articles. In Buffalo I bought my first house, fathered my two children, and won my first tennis tournament. In short, I became a success.

So why the vomiting? I was experiencing too much change in too short a period of time. I wondered if I was as good as others thought I was or if I was just lucky. I worried about embarrassing myself in front of other people and became extremely anxious when due to speak in front of a large group—so anxious that on a nice spring day, about seventy degrees, with the sun shining and a slight breeze, as I was on my way to address a group of teachers, school administrators, and parents in Wheatfield, New York, I became sick to my stomach. I pulled the car off the road, jumped out, vomited, jumped back in, proceeded to Wheatfield, and presented a one-hour speech that is long since forgotten by everyone who was there.

What I didn't know then, but know now, is that I was experiencing stress—too much stress. I also didn't know what to do. Everything seemed to be going very well; there seemed to be no reason to become anxious or ill. I think I understand it all now and want to explain it to you. I want to help you learn about stress and how to manage it so that your life will be better and you will be healthier.

The Pioneers

I don't know about you, but I found that the history courses I was required to take as an undergraduate were not as interesting as they might have been. On the other hand, the information included in those classes was important to learn—not for the facts per se, but for the general concepts. For example, although I long ago forgot the specific economic factors preceding the World Wars, I have remembered that wars are often the result of economic realities and not just conflicts of ideology. That is an important concept that I would not have appreciated had I not enrolled in History 101.

This wordy introduction to the history of stress management somewhat assuages my conscience but won't help you much unless I make this discussion interesting. Accepting this challenge, and with apologies for my failures to meet it, let's wander through the past and meet some of the pioneers in the field of stress (see Table 1.1).

The first person we meet is Walter Cannon. In the early part of the twentieth century, Walter Cannon was a noted physiologist employed at the Harvard Medical School. It was he who first described the body's reaction to stress.[1] Picture this: You're walking down a dark alley at night, all alone, and you forgot your glasses. Halfway through the alley (at the point of no return) you spot a big, burly figure carrying a club and straddling your path. Other than thinking "Woe is me," what else happens within you? Your heart begins to pound and speed up, you seem unable to catch your breath, you begin to perspire, your muscles tense, and a whole array of changes occur within your body. Cannon was the researcher who first identified this stress reaction as the **fight-or-flight response.** Your body prepares itself, when confronted by a threat, to either stand ground and fight or run away. In the alley, that response is invaluable because you want to be able to mobilize yourself quickly for some kind of action. We'll soon see, though, that in today's society the fight-or-flight response has become a threat itself—a threat to your health.

fight-or-flight response
The body's stress reaction that includes an increase in heart rate, respiration, blood pressure, and serum cholesterol.

Curious about the fight-or-flight response, a young endocrinologist studied it in detail. Using rats and exposing them to **stressors**—factors with the potential to cause stress—Hans Selye was able to specify the changes in the body's physiology. Selye concluded that, regardless of the source of the stress, the body reacted in the same manner. His rats developed a "substantial enlargement of the cortex of the adrenal glands; shrinkage or atrophy of the thymus, spleen, lymph nodes, and other lymphatic structures; an almost total disappearance of eosinophil cells (a kind of white blood cell); and bleeding ulcers in the lining of the stomach and duodenum."[2] His research was first published in his classic book *The Stress of Life.*[3] Selye summarized stress reactivity as a three-phase process termed the **general adaptation syndrome:**

stressor
Something with the potential to cause a stress reaction.

general adaptation syndrome
The three stages of stress reaction described by Hans Selye.

> *Phase 1: Alarm reaction.* The body shows the changes characteristic of the first exposure to a stressor. At the same time, its resistance is diminished and, if the stressor is sufficiently strong (severe burns, extremes of temperature), death may result.
>
> *Phase 2: Stage of resistance.* Resistance ensues if continued exposure to the stressor is compatible with adaptation. The bodily signs characteristic of the alarm reaction have virtually disappeared, and resistance rises above normal.
>
> *Phase 3: Stage of exhaustion.* Following long-continued exposure to the same stressor, to which the body has become adjusted, eventually adaptation energy is exhausted. The signs of the alarm reaction reappear, but now they are irreversible, and the individual dies.

Hans Selye defined stress as "the nonspecific response of the body to any demand made upon it."[4] That means good things (e.g., a job promotion) to which we must adapt (termed **eustress**) and bad things (e.g., the death of a loved one) to which we must adapt (termed **distress**); both are experienced the same physiologically.

eustress
Good things to which one has to adapt and that can lead to a stress reaction.

distress
Bad things to which one has to adapt and that can lead to a stress reaction.

Table 1.1

PIONEERS IN STRESS AND STRESS MANAGEMENT

Pioneer	Date	Area of Study/Influence
Oskar Vogt	1900	Hypnosis
Walter Cannon	1932	The fight-or-flight response
Edmund Jacobson	1938	Progressive relaxation
Johannes Schultz	1953	Autogenic training
Stewart Wolf/Harold Wolff	1953	Stress and headaches
George Engel	1955	Stress and ulcerative colitis
Hans Selye	1956	The physiological responses to stress
A. T. W. Simeons	1961	Psychosomatic disease
Stewart Wolf	1965	Stress and the digestive system
Wolfgang Luthe	1965	Autogenic training
Lawrence LeShan	1966	Stress and cancer
Richard Lazarus	1966	Stress and coping/hassles
Thomas Holmes/Richard Rahe	1967	Stress/life change/illness
Robert Keith Wallace	1970	Transcendental meditation
Thomas Budzynski	1970	Stress and headaches
Meyer Friedman/Ray Rosenman	1974	Type A behavior pattern
Carl Simonton	1975	Stress and cancer
Herbert Benson	1975	The relaxation response/meditation
Daniel Goleman	1976	Meditation
Gary Schwartz	1976	Meditation/biofeedback
Anita DeLongis	1982	Hassles and illness

Selye was really onto something. His research proved so interesting and important that he drew a large number of followers. One of these was A. T. W. Simeons, who related evolution to psychosomatic disease in his classic work, *Man's Presumptuous Brain*.[5] Simeons argued that the human brain (the diencephalon, in particular) had failed to develop at the pace needed to respond to symbolic stressors of twentieth-century life. For example, when our self-esteem is threatened, Simeons stated, the brain prepares the body with the fight-or-flight response. If the threat to self-esteem stems from fear of embarrassment during public speaking, neither fighting nor running away is an appropriate reaction. Consequently, the body has prepared itself physiologically to do something our psychology prohibits. The unused stress products break down the body, and psychosomatic disease may result.

Other researchers have added to the work of Cannon, Selye, Simeons, and others to shed more light on the relationship of stress to body processes. With this understanding has come a better appreciation of which illnesses and diseases are associated with stress and how to prevent these conditions from developing. For example, Dr. Harold Wolff became curious why only 1 in 100 prisoners of war held by the Germans during World War II died before their release, while 33 in 100 held in Japanese camps died before their release. Keeping nutrition and length of time held captive constant, Wolff found that emotional stress, much greater in Japanese prisoner-of-war camps than in German ones, was the cause of much of this difference.[6]

Others also helped clarify the effects of stress: Stewart Wolf demonstrated its effects on digestive function;[7] Lawrence LeShan studied its effects on the development of cancer;[8] George Engel studied stress and ulcerative colitis;[9] Meyer Friedman and Ray Rosenman and more recent researchers[10–17] identified the relationship between stress and coronary heart disease; and Wolf and Wolff studied stress and headaches.[18]

Others have found ways of successfully treating people with stress-related illnesses. For example, Carl Simonton, believing personality to be related to cancer, has added a component to the standard cancer therapy: It consists of visualizing the beneficial effects of the therapy upon the malignancy.[19] For some headache sufferers, Thomas Budzynski has successfully employed biofeedback for relief.[20] Herbert Benson, a cardiologist, first became interested in stress when he studied transcendental meditation (TM) with Robert Keith Wallace.[21] Benson then developed a relaxation technique similar to TM and has used it effectively to treat people with high blood pressure.[22–25]

Relaxation techniques have also been studied in some detail. In addition to Benson's **relaxation response,** some of the more noteworthy methods include **autogenic training** and **progressive relaxation.** Around 1900, a physiologist, Oskar Vogt, noted that people were capable of hypnotizing themselves. A German psychiatrist, Johannes Schultz, combined this knowledge with specific exercises to bring about heaviness and warmth in the limbs—that is, a state of relaxation.[26] This autohypnotic relaxation method became known as autogenic training and was developed and studied further by Schultz's student Wolfgang Luthe.[27]

Another effective and well-studied relaxation technique involves the tensing and relaxing of muscles so as to recognize muscle tension and bring about muscular relaxation when desired. This technique, progressive relaxation, was developed by Dr. Edmund Jacobson when he noticed his bedridden patients were still muscularly tense in spite of their restful appearance.[28] Their muscular tenseness (**bracing**), Jacobson reasoned, was a function of nerve impulses sent to the muscles, and it was interfering with their recovery. Progressive relaxation, sometimes termed **neuromuscular relaxation,** involves a structured set of exercises that trains people to eliminate unnecessary muscular tension.

Although Benson's relaxation response, a form of meditation, became popular in the 1970s, meditation has been around for a long time. In fact, records of meditation date back 2,000 years. Indian yogis and Zen monks were the first meditators to be scientifically studied. The results of these studies demonstrated the slowing-down effect (hypometabolic state) of meditation upon many body processes: heart rate, breathing, and muscle tension to name but a few. For example, Therese Brosse reported Indian yogis able to control their heart rates;[29] Anand and colleagues showed changes in brain waves during meditation;[30] Kasamatsu and Hirai confirmed and expounded upon Anand's findings;[31] and Goleman and Schwartz found meditators more psychologically stable than nonmeditators.[32]

Lastly, a whole area of study regarding life changes to which we must adapt and their effect upon health has emerged. Thomas Holmes and Richard Rahe showed that, the more significant the changes in one's life, the greater the chance of the onset of illness.[33] Based on these conclusions, researchers are working toward a better understanding of this relationship. For example, Lazarus,[34] DeLongis,[35] and their colleagues have found that everyday hassles are even more detrimental to one's health than major life changes.

This brief overview, which brings us to the early 1980s, is painted with a broad brush. Subsequent chapters refer to these pioneers and their work, providing you with an even better understanding of the significance of managing stress and tension. When we discuss stress-related illnesses and diseases, for example, you will once again read about Friedman and Rosenman, Simonton, Wolff, and others. When we discuss life-situation stressors, reference will be made to Lazarus and to Holmes and Rahe. When we discuss relaxation techniques, we will elaborate upon the work of Benson, Schultz, Luthe, Jacobson, and others. Obviously, there have been other stress

relaxation response
A series of bodily changes that are the opposite of the stress reaction.

autogenic training
A relaxation technique that involves a sensation of heaviness, warmth, and tingling in the limbs.

progressive relaxation
A relaxation technique that involves contracting and relaxing muscle groups throughout the body.

bracing
The contraction of muscles for no obvious purpose.

neuromuscular relaxation
Another term for progressive relaxation.

Muscle Tension

As you begin to read this, FREEZE. Don't move a bit! Now pay attention to your body sensations and position.

Can you drop your shoulders? If so, your muscles were unnecessarily raising them.

Are your forearm muscles able to relax more? If so, you were unnecessarily tensing them.

Is your body seated in a position in which you appear ready to do something active? If so, your muscles are probably unnecessarily contracted.

Can your forehead relax more? If so, you were tensing those muscles for no useful purpose.

Check your stomach, buttocks, thigh, and calf muscles. Are they, too, contracted more than is needed?

Unnecessary muscular contraction is called *bracing.* Many of us are guilty of bracing and suffer tension headaches, neck aches, or bad backs as a result.

Take a moment for yourself now. Place this book aside, and concentrate on just letting as many of your muscles relax as possible. Notice how that feels.

When we discuss deep muscle relaxation, and progressive relaxation in particular, you'll learn skills enabling you to bring about this sensation more readily.

researchers since the early 1980s. However, the researchers listed in Table 1.1 are the pioneers. Subsequent research has built on their findings.

For now, I hope you come away from this brief history of the stress field understanding that stress may be not just bothersome but downright unhealthy, and that stress may lead to other negative consequences such as poor relationships with loved ones or low academic achievement. There are, however, means of lessening these unhealthy and negative effects. Stress management is serious business to which some very fine minds have devoted their time and effort. As you'll find out in this book, this study has paid off and is continuing to do so.

Stress Theory

Now let's get down to business. What causes stress? There are several different theories about what causes stress and its effects on illness and disease.

Life-Events Theory

One theory developed by Holmes and Rahe[36] proposes that stress occurs when a situation requires more resources than are available. For example, if you are taking a test for which you are unprepared, you might experience stress. To measure this type of stress, some researchers have compiled lists of major stressful life events such as the death of a loved one. The rationale is that the more of these events a person experiences, the greater is his or her stress.

DeLongis and her colleagues[37] are supporters of this general approach, but they consider routine stressful life events more significant than major ones that happen infrequently. They argue that daily *hassles,* though appearing less important by themselves, add up and therefore are more stressful than major events. Furthermore, when computing the formula for stress, they consider daily *uplifts,* such as someone saying something nice about you, as counteracting some hassles.

Hardiness Theory

Other researchers conceive of stress somewhat differently. They focus not on how many stressful events you experience but on your attitude toward those events. For example, Kobasa and her colleagues[38] argue that if you perceive potentially stressful events as a *challenge* instead of as a *threat,* less stress will result. This buffering effect—buffering between stress and the development of illness and disease—is termed *hardiness* and is discussed in detail in Chapter 7.

Social Support Theory

Still other stress experts, such as Overholser and colleagues,[39] envision stress occurring when there is not enough social support available to respond to the event effectively. Social support may take many forms. For example, it could be emotional support to help you feel better about yourself or about the event as you cope with it, or it could take the form of financial assistance. In any case, social support helps you cope with the event and therefore decreases your level of stress. Social support is discussed in detail in Chapters 6 and 8.

There are many other ways to conceptualize stress and its effects. Each, though, consists of at least two components: a stressor and stress reactivity.

The Stressor

A stressor is a stimulus with the *potential* for triggering the fight-or-flight response. The stressors for which our bodies were evolutionarily trained were threats to our safety. The caveman who saw a lion looking for its next meal needed to react quickly. Cavemen who were not fast enough or strong enough to respond to this threat didn't have to worry about the next threat. They became meals for the lions. The fight-or-flight response was necessary, and its rapidity was vital for survival.

Modern men and women also find comfort and safety in the fight-or-flight response. We periodically read of some superhuman feat of strength in response to a stressor, such as a person lifting a heavy car off another person pinned under it. We attribute this strength to an increase in adrenaline, and it is true that adrenaline secretion does increase as part of the fight-or-flight response. However, there are less dramatic examples of the use the fight-or-flight response has for us. When you step off a curb not noticing an automobile coming down the street, and you hear the auto's horn, you quickly jump back onto the curb. Your heart beats fast, your breathing changes, and you perspire. These are all manifestations of your response to a stressor, the threat of being hit by a car. They indicate that your body has been prepared to do something active and to do it immediately (jump back onto the curb).

So far, these examples of stressors have all required immediate action to prevent physical harm. Other stressors you encounter have the potential for eliciting this same fight-or-flight response, even though it would be inappropriate to respond immediately or with some action. These stressors are symbolic ones—for example, loss of status, threats to self-esteem, work overload, or overcrowding. When the boss overloads you with work, it is dysfunctional to fight with him or her and equally ridiculous to run away and not tackle the work. When you encounter the stressors associated with moving to a new town, either fighting with new people you meet or shying away from meeting new people is an inappropriate means of adjustment.

Stressors come in many forms.

We encounter many different types of stressors. Some are environmental (toxins, heat, cold), some psychological (threats to self-esteem, depression), others sociological (unemployment, death of a loved one), and still others philosophical (use of time, purpose in life). In any case, as Selye discovered, regardless of the stressor, the body's reaction will be the same. The pituitary, thyroid, parathyroid, and adrenal glands, as well as the hypothalamus and other parts of the brain, are activated by stressors.

The point is, our bodies have evolved to respond to stressors with an immediate action by altering their physiology for greater speed and strength. When we encounter symbolic stressors, our bodies are altered in the same manner, although we do not use the changed physiology by responding with some action. Therefore, we build up stress products, which include elevated blood pressure and increased muscular contractions, serum cholesterol, and secretions of hydrochloric acid in the stomach. We do not use these stress products but rather "grin and bear" the situation. The results are illness and disease when the stress reaction is chronic, is prolonged, or goes unabated.

This need not be the case. We can learn to take control of ourselves and our bodies to prevent the fight-or-flight response from developing when we encounter symbolic threats.[40] We can also learn how to use stress products once our physiology has changed to prevent them from resulting in illness, disease, or other negative consequences. Remember, stressors are stimuli with the *potential* for triggering the fight-or-flight response; they need not lead to such a response. As our computer programs sometimes need updating, so do our responses to stressors. Reprogramming ourselves in this way means that we learn to perceive events as less stressful, and we choose responses that are healthier and more life-enhancing. With this book and the practice of the skills it describes, you can learn to manage stress better.

Stress Reactivity

The fight-or-flight response is termed *stress reactivity*. This reaction, described in more detail in the next chapter, includes increased muscle tension; increased heart rate, stroke volume, and output; elevated blood pressure; increased neural excitability; less saliva in the mouth; increased sodium retention; increased perspiration; change in respiratory rate; increased serum glucose; increased release of hydrochloric acid in the stomach; changes in brain waves; and increased urination. This reaction prepares us for swift action when such a response is warranted. When we build up stress products that we don't use, this stress reaction becomes unhealthy.

The longer our physiology varies from its baseline measures (duration) and the greater the variance from that baseline (degree), the more likely we are to experience ill effects from this stress reactivity. Of the two, duration and degree, duration is the more important. For example, if you awaken to realize your alarm clock didn't go off and you'll be late for work, you become physiologically aroused from that stressor. If in your haste you accidentally pour too much milk into your cereal, that stressor will result in further physiological arousal. Next, you get into the car, only to learn you're out of gas. Ever have a day like that? Although each of those stressors will probably result in less arousal than having to jump back from a car bearing down on you, it is the length of time that these stressors are with you that makes them more harmful.

People who have learned stress management skills often respond to a greater degree to a stressor but return to their resting rate sooner than those not trained in stress management. An analogy can be made with joggers, whose heart rate may increase tremendously when they exercise but returns to normal sooner than that of out-of-shape exercisers. Try the exercise in Figure 1.1 to demonstrate the effects of a stressor upon your physiology.

Gender Differences in Reactivity

Interestingly, there are some differences between the way males and females cope with stress. Shelly Taylor and her colleagues[41] have found that females tend to exhibit

Figure 1.1

Stress reactivity

While seated in a comfortable position, determine how fast your heart beats at rest using one of the following methods. (Use a watch that has a second hand.)

1. Place the first two fingers (pointer and middle finger) of one hand on the underside of your other wrist, on the thumb side. Feel for your pulse and count the number of pulses for thirty seconds. (See the drawing.)

2. Place the first two fingers of one hand on your lower neck, just above the collarbone; move your fingers toward your shoulder until you find your pulse. Count the pulses for thirty seconds.

3. Place the first two fingers of one hand in front of your ear near your sideburn, moving your fingers until you find your pulse. Count the pulses for thirty seconds. Multiply your thirty-second pulse count by two to determine how many times your heart beats each minute while at rest.

Now close your eyes and think of either someone you really dislike or some situation you experienced that really frightened you. If you are recalling a person, think of how that person looks, smells, and what he or she does to incur your dislike. Really feel the dislike, don't just think about it. If you recall a frightening situation, try to place yourself back in that situation. Sense the fright, be scared, vividly recall the situation in all its detail. Think of the person or situation for one minute, and then count your pulse rate for thirty seconds, as you did earlier. Multiply the rate by two, and compare your first total with the second.

Most people find that their heart rate increases when experiencing the stressful memory. This increase occurs despite a lack of any physical activity; just thoughts increase heart rate. This fact demonstrates two things: the nature of stressors and the nature of stress reactivity. The stressor is a stimulus with the potential of eliciting a stress reaction (physiological arousal).

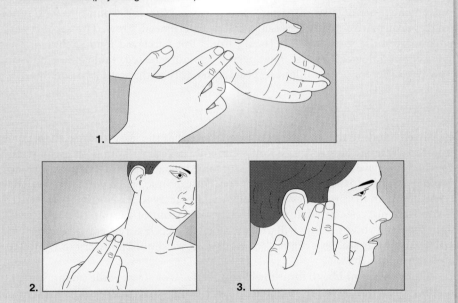

nurturing activities designed to protect themselves and others in coping with stress. These activities are termed "tend-and-befriend." The authors argue that females use social groups more than do males as a response to stress, and that males, in contrast, tend to exhibit more of a flight-or-fight response to stress. Gender differences are discussed in detail later in Chapter 16.

A Definition of Stress

Now that you know what a stressor is and what stress reactivity is, it is time to define stress itself.

Although Lazarus offered a definition of stress that encompasses a whole spectrum of factors (stimulus, response, cognitive appraisal of threat, coping styles, psychological defenses, and the social milieu),[42] for our purposes that may be too encompassing.

Defining stress becomes a problem even for the experts. Mason aptly described this problem by citing several different ways the term *stress* is used:[43]

1. *The stimulus.* This is our definition of stressor.
2. *The response.* This is our definition of stress reactivity.
3. *The whole spectrum of interacting factors.* This is Lazarus' definition.
4. *The stimulus-response interaction.*

Still another view of stress conceptualizes it as the difference between pressure and adaptability—that is, stress = pressure − adaptability.[44]

For our purposes, we will operationally define *stress* as the term is used in number 4: the combination of a stressor and stress reactivity. Without both of these components there is no stress. A stressor has only the *potential* for eliciting a stress reaction.

To illustrate this point, imagine two people fired from their jobs. One views being fired as catastrophic: "How will I support my family? How will I pay my rent? What do I do if I get ill without health insurance in force?" The other views being fired as less severe and says, "It's not good that I was fired, but I never really liked that job. This will give me the impetus to find a job I'll enjoy. I've been working too hard, anyhow. I needed a vacation. Now I'll take one." As you can see, the stressor (being fired) had the potential of eliciting physiological arousal, but only the thought processes employed by the first person would result in such a reaction. The first person encountered a stressor, perceived it as stressful, and wound up with physiological arousal. By definition, that person experienced stress. The second person encountered the same stressor (being fired) but perceived it in such a way as to *prevent* physiological arousal. That person was not stressed. Table 1.2 demonstrates how two different people might respond differently to the same stressors.

Stress Management Goals

Before concluding this chapter, we should note that the goal of stress management is not to eliminate all stress. Life would certainly be dull without both joyful stressors to which we have to adjust and distressors needing a response. Furthermore, stress is often a motivator for peak performance. For example, when you are experiencing stress about an upcoming test, you will be more likely to study more intensely than if you were not concerned. If you are to speak in front of a group of people and are apprehensive, you probably will prepare a better speech. Stress can be useful, stimulating, and welcome. So, even if it were possible, we should not want to eliminate all stress from our lives.

Our goal should be to limit the harmful effects of stress while maintaining life's quality and vitality. Some researchers have found that the relationship between stress and illness can be plotted on a U-shaped curve, as shown in Figure 1.2. The curve illustrates that, with a great deal of stress, a great deal of illness occurs. However, it also indicates that, with only a minute amount of stress, a great deal of illness can still occur. These researchers found that there is an optimal amount of stress—not too much and not too little—that is healthy and prophylactic.[45] We will keep that important finding to the fore as we proceed toward taking control of our stress.

The Way to Use This Book

Your instructor will help you decide the best way to use this book. There are many options, and he or she is an expert on whom you should rely. Some of these options follow.

Your Personal Stress Profile and Activity Workbook

In my stress management classes, each student completes the accompanying *Your Personal Stress Profile and Activity Workbook.* This is done throughout the semester at the

Table 1.2 A DAY IN THE LIVES OF JOE AND ROSCOE

Stressor	Joe (Chronic Stress Pattern)	Roscoe (Healthy Stress Pattern)
Oversleeps—awakes at 7:30 instead of 6:30	Action: Gulps coffee, skips breakfast, cuts himself shaving, tears button off shirt getting dressed	Action: Phones professor to let her know he will be late; eats a good breakfast
	Thoughts: I can't be late again! The professor will be furious! I just know this is going to ruin my whole day.	Thoughts: No problem. I must have needed the extra sleep.
	Result: Leaves home anxious, worried, and hungry	Result: Leaves home calm and relaxed
Stuck behind slow driver	Action: Flashes lights, honks, grits teeth, curses, bangs on dashboard with fist; finally passes on blind curve and nearly collides with oncoming car	Action: Uses time to do relaxation exercises and to listen to his favorite radio station
	Thoughts: What an idiot! Slow drivers should be put in jail! No consideration of others!	Thoughts: Here's a gift of time—how can I use it?
Meeting with classmates	Action: Sits back and ignores everyone, and surreptitiously works on running log.	Action: Listens carefully and participates actively.
	Thoughts: What a waste of time. Who cares about all of my classmates' views? I work better alone anyhow.	Thoughts: It's really good to hear my classmates' thoughts. I can learn a lot if I understand various points of view.
	Results: Misses important input; is later reprimanded by professor	Results: His professor compliments him on his suggestions.
Noon—behind on term paper	Action: Skips lunch; has coffee at desk; spills coffee over important papers	Action: Eats light lunch and goes for short walk in park
	Thoughts: That's the last straw! Now I'll have to have this whole term paper typed over. I'll have to stay and work late.	Thoughts: I'll be in better shape for a good afternoon with a little exercise and some time out of my room.
Evening	Action: Arrives home 9 p.m., family resentful; ends up sleeping on couch; does not fall asleep until long into the morning	Action: Arrives home at usual time; quiet evening with family; to bed by 11 p.m., falls asleep easily
	Thoughts: What a life! If only I could run away and start over! It's just not worth it. I'll never amount to anything.	Thoughts: A good day! I felt really effective at school, and it was nice spending time talking with the family tonight.
	Results: Wakes up late again, feeling awful; decides to cut class.	Results: Wakes up early, feeling good

Source: "Dealing with Potential Stress," in *Medical Self-Care*, no. 5 (1978): 11. Reprinted by permission of the publisher.

student's own pace. Each student submits a two-page paper when the workbook is turned in near the end of the semester. This paper consists of three paragraphs:

1. A listing of each scale completed and the student's score.
2. An interpretation of the scores (which were satisfactory and which needed improvement).
3. A summary of what was learned by completing the workbook and a plan for remedying those variables on which the student scored low.

My students tell me this is an extremely valuable experience that supplements and complements the content presented in the textbook.

Your instructor may conclude that you, too, would benefit from completing *Your Personal Stress Profile and Activity Workbook*. In the event your instructor makes that decision, we let you know when it is appropriate to go to the workbook on the Online Learning Center for the text (www.mhhe.com/greenberg10e). We do this through the use of a logo alongside content in the textbook that pertains to a

Figure 1.2

The relationship between stress and illness is a complex one. Illness may result from too *little* stress, just as it might from too much stress.

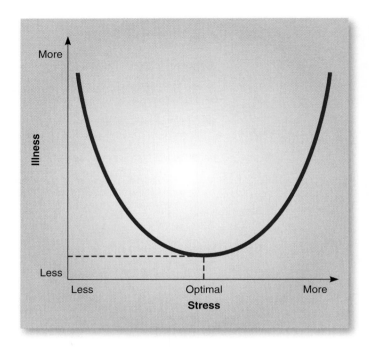

section of the workbook. If your instructor decides not to use *Your Personal Stress Profile and Activity Workbook,* you can just ignore this logo.

The Stress Portfolio

In this book, we help you develop a stress portfolio. A portfolio is a grouping of all material you have produced, similar to an artist's portfolio consisting of drawings and paintings or a model's portfolio comprised of past modeling photographs and letters of reference. In your stress portfolio, you will include the results of all of the scales completed in the text or workbook, thoughts you have during particular class sessions or while reading this book, your responses to all of the boxed material in this text, other assignments you may have been expected to complete, the results of all examinations and quizzes in this class, descriptions and accompanying materials that show any ways you have taught others how to manage stress, and any other materials that relate to you and your expertise in stress and stress management (e.g., stress workshops you took outside of this class). By the end of this course, then, you will have a complete summary of how you have come to interact with stress, how much expertise you have developed in managing stress, and evidence to demonstrate this to others (e.g., future employers and graduate or professional schools to which you may apply).

Materials that should be included in your stress portfolio are identified by this logo and should be removed or photocopied from the text or printed from the on-line workbook. Then these materials should be placed in a folder in which you will add other material throughout this course. At the end of this class, you might want to share your portfolio with several of your classmates. That might give you additional ideas on how to expand your own portfolio and thereby make it even more impressive to anyone who might see it.

"Getting Involved in Your Community" Boxes

We all live in several different communities that can be envisioned as concentric circles. In the middle circle stand you and your immediate family. In the next circle is your extended family. As the circles expand, we find your campus, then your county or city, next the state, then the country, and eventually the world. It is my belief that all of us, in addition to intervening in our own stress, have an obligation to respond

Health, Wellness, And Stress

In another publication,[a] I describe the difference between health and wellness. I define **health** as consisting of five dimensions: physical health, social health, mental health, emotional health, and spiritual health:

- **Physical health**—the ability of the body to function daily with energy remaining to respond to emergencies; the absence of disease; the level of physical fitness.
- **Social health**—the ability to interact well with people and the environment, to have satisfying interpersonal relationships.
- **Mental health**—the ability to learn and grow intellectually.
- **Emotional health**—the ability to control emotions so that you feel comfortable expressing them and can express them appropriately.
- **Spiritual health**—a belief in some unifying force, which varies from person to person but has the concept of faith at its core. Faith is feeling connected to other humans, believing one's life has purpose and meaning.

I wish I had added **environmental health**—a healthy, supportive setting in which to function. It includes the quality of the air you breathe, the purity of the water you drink, the amount of noise to which you are subjected, and the amount of space in which you are able to function. Environmental health also includes the effectiveness of the institutions with which you interact regularly: schools, health care facilities, places of work, recreational facilities, and others.

The extent and degree to which you possess these components of health determine how healthy you are. **Wellness** is the degree to which these components of health are *in balance*. Imagine meeting a friend you haven't seen in some time. You ask how he has been, and he tells you that he never felt better. He started running marathons and devotes most of his day to training and reading about running. His blood pressure is down, his heart rate is lower, he has more stamina, and his blood cholesterol is even better than normal. He appears to be healthy.

Then you ask about his family, and he tells you that he is divorced. He spent so much time running that he had little left for his family (poor social health). Next, you ask about his job, and he tells you that he was fired because he did not spend enough time learning new skills to do the job better (poor mental health). When you ask about his work with the charitable organization he was devoted to, he tells you that he gave that up when he got into running seriously (poor spiritual health). Do you get the point? Your friend may be more physically healthy, but he developed that degree of physical health by ignoring other aspects of his health.

When you achieve wellness, you have the components of health in balance. Imagine *health* as a tire divided into segments, the components of health. If one segment of that tire is too large and others are too small, the tire is "out-of-round" and will not provide a smooth ride. If your health segments are "out-of-round," you will not have a smooth ride down the road of life, and stressful consequences are likely to occur.

Both *health* and *wellness* are important considerations in the management of stress, and we will refer to them in various ways throughout this book.

[a]Jerrold S. Greenberg, George B. Dintiman, and Barbee Myers Oakes, *Physical Fitness and Wellness,* 3rd ed. (Champaign, IL: Human Kinetics, 2004).

to the stress our communities experience. To encourage you to contribute to the health of the communities in which you live, a box entitled "Getting Involved in Your Community" appears in most chapters. It is suggested that you use the knowledge, attitudinal development, skills, and behaviors learned in each chapter not only to limit the stress you experience but also to help your family, friends, classmates, neighbors, and others to be less stressed. Your instructor may suggest still other ways for you to contribute to your community.

The interesting thing about helping others is that you cannot but help yourself in the process. As Ralph Waldo Emerson wrote, "It is one of the most beautiful compensations of this life that no man can sincerely try to help another without helping himself." If you get involved in your community, you, too, will learn the truth of Emerson's observation. My students have. They are required to participate in a service-learning project in which they use what they learn in their stress management class to help others to be less stressful. One group of students worked with several cancer patients to help them better manage the stress associated with their illness. Other students worked with children in local schools to help them manage the stress of moving from one level of schooling to another (e.g., from middle school to senior high school). Still others worked with volunteer firefighters, nursery school teachers, elderly residents of nursing homes, and youths in local community centers. The interesting thing is that even those students who did not initially want to engage in this assignment reported tremendous benefits at the conclusion of the course. It is not unusual for my students to state that they learned more about stress by having to teach the course content to others, that they felt good about helping other people, and that they now want to contribute to their communities in still other ways.

Now, you may decide not to contribute to your community. That is your option (unless, like me, your instructor decides this is such a valuable experience that enhances learning and has other benefits that it becomes a course requirement). Before you make that decision, however, remember the words of Marion Wright Edelman, the executive director of the Children's Defense Fund:

> Service is the rent we pay for living. If you see a need, don't ask, "Why doesn't someone do something?" Ask, "Why don't I do something?" . . . We are not all equally guilty but we are all equally responsible.[46]

Getting Involved In Your Community

You are naturally concerned with your own health. When you experience stress, you want to know how to alleviate it. This book is devoted to helping you intervene between stress and its negative consequences, yet you not only "receive" stress but you also "emit stress." When you are unnecessarily argumentative or intolerant, for example, others with whom you interact may experience stress from your behavior. When you drive aggressively, other drivers may get "all stressed out." And when you make too much noise or play your stereo too loudly, students in your dormitory, who may require quiet to study, may develop a stress response.

To limit the stress you create for others in your community (your campus, your home, your city), list three people about whom you care and the ways in which you cause them stress. Next, list three ways you can cause each of these people less stress. Then commit yourself to following through on some of these ways to cause others less stress.

How I Cause Three People Stress

1. A Relative:
   a. _____
   b. _____
   c. _____
2. A Friend:
   a. _____
   b. _____
   c. _____
3. Someone Else:
   a. _____
   b. _____
   c. _____

How I Can Cause These People Less Stress

1. A Relative:
   a. _____
   b. _____
   c. _____
2. A Friend:
   a. _____
   b. _____
   c. _____
3. Someone Else:
   a. _____
   b. _____
   c. _____

I commit to make the following changes to cause people less stress:

summary

- Physiologist Walter Cannon first described the stress response. Cannon called this the fight-or-flight response.

- Endocrinologist Hans Selye was able to specify the changes in the body's physiology that resulted from stress.

- Selye found rats that he stressed developed substantial enlargement of the adrenal cortex; shrinkage of the thymus, spleen, lymph nodes, and other lymphatic structures; a disappearance of the eosinophil cells; and bleeding ulcers in the lining of the stomach and duodenum.

- Selye summarized stress reactivity as a three-phase process: alarm reaction, stage of resistance, and stage of exhaustion. He defined stress as the nonspecific response of the body to any demand made upon it.

- Cardiologist Herbert Benson studied transcendental meditation and developed a similar meditative technique that he successfully employed to help reduce his patients' levels of high blood pressure.

- A stressor is a stimulus with the potential of triggering the fight-or-flight response. Stressors can be biological, psychological, sociological, or philosophical in origin.

- The longer one's physiology varies from its baseline measures (duration) and the greater the variance (degree), the more likely one is to experience ill effects from stress reactivity.

- Stress has been defined differently by different experts. Some define stress as the stimulus, others as the response, and still others as the whole spectrum of interacting factors. This book defines stress as the combination of a stressor and stress reactivity.

notes

1. Walter B. Cannon, *The Wisdom of the Body* (New York: W. W. Norton, 1932).

2. Kenneth R. Pelletier, *Mind as Healer, Mind as Slayer* (New York: Dell Publishing Co., 1977), 71.

3. Hans Selye, *The Stress of Life* (New York: McGraw-Hill Book Co., 1956).

4. Hans Selye, *Stress Without Distress* (New York: J. B. Lippincott, 1974), 14.

5. A. T. W. Simeons, *Man's Presumptuous Brain: An Evolutionary Interpretation of Psychosomatic Disease* (New York: E. P. Dutton, 1961).

6. Harold G. Wolff, *Stress and Disease* (Springfield, IL: Charles C. Thomas, 1953).

7. Stewart Wolf, *The Stomach* (Oxford: Oxford University Press, 1965).

8. Lawrence LeShan, "An Emotional Life-History Pattern Associated with Neoplastic Disease," *Annals of the New York Academy of Sciences,* 1966.

9. George L. Engel, "Studies of Ulcerative Colitis—III: The Nature of the Psychologic Processes," *American Journal of Medicine,* August 1955.

10. Meyer Friedman and Ray H. Rosenman, *Type A Behavior and Your Heart* (Greenwich, CT: Fawcett, 1974).

11. H. Bosma, M. G. Marmot, H. Hemingway, A. C. Nicholson, E. Brunner, and S. A. Stansfeld, "Low Job Control and Risk of Coronary Heart Disease in Whitehall II (Prospective Cohort) Study," *British Medical Journal* 314(1997): 558–65.

12. S. A. Everson et al., "Interaction of Workplace Demands and Cardiovascular Reactivity in Progression of Carotid Atherosclerosis: Population Based Study," *British Medical Journal* 314(1997): 553–58.

13. C. M. Stoney, R. Niaura, and L. Bausserman, "Temporal Stability of Lipid Responses to Acute Psychological Stress in Middle-Aged Men," *Psychophysiology* 34(1997): 285–91.

14. C. M. Stoney, "Plasma Homocysteine Levels Increase in Women During Psychological Stress," *Life Sciences* 64(1999): 2359–65.

15. C. M. Stoney, R. Niaura, L. Bausserman, and M. Matacin, "Lipid Reactivity to Stress: I. Comparison of Chronic and Acute Stress Responses in Middle-Aged Pilots," *Health Psychology* 18(1999): 241–50.

16. C. M. Stoney, L. Bausserman, R. Niaura, B. Marcus, and M. Flynn, "Lipid Reactivity to Stress: II. Biological and Behavioral Influences," *Health Psychology* 18(1999): 251–61.

17. T. G. Plante and M. Ford, "The Association Between Cardiovascular Stress Responsivity and Perceived Stress Among Subjects with Irritable Bowel Syndrome and Temporomandibular Joint Disorder: A Preliminary Analysis," *International Journal of Stress Management* 7(2000): 103–19.

18. Stewart Wolf and Harold G. Wolff, *Headaches: Their Nature and Treatment* (Boston: Little, Brown, 1953).

19. Carl O. Simonton and Stephanie Matthews-Simonton, "Belief Systems and Management of the Emotional Aspects of Malignancy," *Journal of Transpersonal Psychology* 7(1975): 29–48.

20. Thomas Budzynski, Johann Stoyva, and C. Adler, "Feedback-Induced Muscle Relaxation: Application to Tension Headache," *Journal of Behavior Therapy and Experimental Psychiatry* 1(1970): 205–11.

21. Robert Keith Wallace, "Physiological Effects of Transcendental Meditation," *Science* 167(1970): 1751–54.

22. Herbert Benson, *The Relaxation Response* (New York: Avon Books, 1975).

23. R. K. Peters, Herbert Benson, and John Peters, "Daily Relaxation Response Breaks in a Working Population: II. Effects on Blood Pressure," *American Journal of Public Health* 67(1977): 954–59.

24. H. Benson and W. Proctor, *Beyond the Relaxation Response: How to Harness the Healing Power of Your Personal Beliefs* (East Rutherford, NJ: Berkley Publishing Group, 1994).

25. H. Benson and E. M. Stuart, *The Wellness Book: The Comprehensive Guide to Maintaining Health and Treating Stress-Related Illness* (New York: Simon & Schuster, 1992).

26. Johannes Schultz, *Das Autogene Training* (Stuttgart, Germany: Georg-Thieme Verlag, 1953).

27. Wolfgang Luthe, ed., *Autogenic Training* (New York: Grune & Stratton, 1965).

28. Edmund Jacobson, *Progressive Relaxation,* 2nd ed. (Chicago: University of Chicago Press, 1938).

29. Therese Brosse, "A Psychophysiological Study of Yoga," *Main Currents in Modern Thought* 4(1946): 77–84.

30. B. K. Anand et al., "Studies on Shri Ramananda Yogi During His Stay in an Air-Tight Box," *Indian Journal of Medical Research* 49(1961): 82–89.

31. A. Kasamatsu and T. Hirai, "Studies of EEG's of Expert Zen Meditators," *Folia Psychiatrica Neurologica Japonica* 28(1966): 315.

32. Daniel J. Goleman and Gary E. Schwartz, "Meditation as an Intervention in Stress Reactivity," *Journal of Consulting and Clinical Psychology* 44(1976): 456–66.

33. Thomas H. Holmes and Richard H. Rahe, "The Social Readjustment Rating Scale," *Journal of Psychosomatic Research* 11(1967): 213–18.

34. Richard S. Lazarus, "Puzzles in the Study of Daily Hassles," *Journal of Behavioral Medicine* 7(1984): 375–89.

35. Anita DeLongis, James C. Coyne, Gayle Dakof, Susan Folkman, and Richard Lazarus, "Relationship of Daily Hassles, Uplifts, and Major Life Events to Health Status," *Health Psychology* 1(1982): 119–36.

36. Holmes and Rahe, "The Social Readjustment Rating Scale."

37. DeLongis et al., "Relationship of Daily Hassles."

38. Suzanne C. Kobasa et al., "Effectiveness of Hardiness, Exercise, and Social Support as Resources Against Illness," *Journal of Psychosomatic Research* 29(1985): 525–33.

39. J. C. Overholser, W. H. Norman, and I. W. Miller, "Life Stress and Support in Depressed Patients," *Behavioral Medicine,* Fall 1990, 125–31.

40. Alfred A. Keltner and Paul M. B. Young, "Control and Maintenance Effects of Long-Term Relaxation Training in a Case of Hypertension," *International Journal of Stress Management* 1(1994): 75–79.

41. Shelly E. Taylor, Laura Copusino Klein, Brian P. Lewis, Tara L. Gruenewald, Regan A. Gurung, and John A. Updegraff, "Biobehavioral Response to Stress in Females: Tend-and-Befriend, Not Fight-or-Flight," *Psychological Review* 107(2000): 411–29.

42. Richard S. Lazarus, *Psychological Stress and the Coping Process* (New York: McGraw-Hill Book Co., 1966).

43. James W. Mason, "A Historical View of the Stress Field," *Journal of Human Stress* 1(1975): 22–36.

44. Robert Dato, "Letter to the Editor: The Law of Stress," *International Journal of Stress Management* 3(1996): 181–82.

45. Clinton G. Weiman, "A Study of Occupational Stressors and the Incidence of Disease/Risk," *Journal of Occupational Medicine* 19(1977): 119–22.

46. Marion Wright Edelman, *The Measure of Our Success: A Letter to My Children and Yours* (Boston: Beacon Press, 1992).

internet resources

Stress Management and Emotional Wellness Links
imt.net/~randolfi/StressLinks.html
Contains numerous links to stress-related topics, such as relaxation techniques, workplace stress, time management, as well as commercial resources to contact for aids to cope with stress.

The American Institute of Stress
www.stress.org
The AIS is a nonprofit organization that is committed to helping advance knowledge of the role of stress in health and disease. It is a clearinghouse for information on all stress-related subjects.

Stress Education Center
www.dstress.com/
A site devoted to stress management and information to enhance health/wellness and productivity. A resource for tapes, books, seminars, and online classes.

Coping in Today's World

We have become a society that increasingly expresses its stress through anger. The American Automobile Association's Foundation for Traffic Safety reported that aggressive driving increased 7 percent in the 1990s. Airlines report more outbursts of sky rage than before. And we have all read of parents who go "berserk" on the sidelines as their children are playing soccer or baseball. In fact, rough play during his son's ice hockey practice at a Massachusetts ice rink led a father to beat another father to death, as their children looked on. Not even celebrities are immune to this phenomenon. Sean "Puff" Daddy Combs and Courtney Love have both been sentenced by a judge to attend anger management programs.

The reasons for Americans becoming so angry are complicated. Certainly, the fact that we are always moving quickly, available 24/7 on our cell phones or PDAs, and striving for more and more make us extraordinarily tense and impatient. That can manifest itself in anger and rage. Technology contributes to these feelings as well. Technology was supposed to make our lives more relaxing and efficient and easier. Tell that to anyone whose computer has crashed or whose cell phone is repeatedly ringing.

Having recognized all of these stressful influences that result in anger, we need to embrace the realization that no one forces anyone else to be angry. People choose to be angry and, as such, can choose not to be. This book will teach you how much you can be in control of your life and, unfortunately, how often you give up that control. For example, too many of us respond to someone who yells at us by yelling right back. That is dysfunctional. It is unhealthy. It is stressful. Whereas you cannot control someone else's behavior, you can control your own.

LAB ASSESSMENT 1.1

Why Do Some of Your Stressors Result in a Stress Response?

You, like the rest of us, have experienced *stressors* with the potential to elicit a stress reaction. Some of these stressors have resulted in an increased heart rate, tense muscles, perspiration, and other stress reactions. Other stressors, though, seem not to produce those effects. Have you ever wondered why some stressors elicit a stress response, while others do not? To explore this question, start by listing three stressors you have encountered that have resulted in a stress reaction:

1. _____

2. _____

3. _____

Now list three stressors you have encountered that did not result in a stress reaction:

1. _____

2. _____

3. _____

What did the stressors that did lead to a stress reaction have in common? Were they all threats to your self-esteem? Were they all threats to your physical health? List three commonalities among these stressors:

1. _____

2. _____

3. _____

What did the stressors that *did not* lead to a stress reaction have in common? Did they all involve someone whose opinion of you was unimportant? Was the threat minimal? Did you perceive the threat differently? List three commonalities among these stressors:

1. _____

2. _____

3. _____

Now, describe how you can you use this insight to respond to stressors/threats in ways to minimize the likelihood they will result in a stress reaction?

_____

_____

_____

_____

Whenever I walk through a large shopping mall with my children, Todd and Keri, my shrewdness is put to the test. I kid them by saying that I should have had two more children so I could have named them "the four me's": Buy Me, Give Me, Take Me, and Show Me. If it isn't a soft pretzel they want, it's a new baseball bat, or a new doll, or a new doll holding a new baseball bat. Before leaving our neighborhood shopping mall, we are bombarded by a cacophony of noise (bings, bongs, rings, buzzes, and crashes) and a rainbow of colors and lights. If you haven't guessed yet, our mall is "blessed" with an arcade. Arcade games were probably invented by a malicious child who was punished so often that revenge was foremost in his or her mind. The object of this revenge was parents; the means of revenge was the arcade.

As we walk past the arcade, I start talking about the last soccer game my daughter played in or one she is anticipating. Sometimes I'll discuss a movie they both enjoyed or a vacation we're planning. Do you get the picture? Anything to divert their attention from the arcade and those money-hungry machines. I know my diversion has been successful when I have left the mall without having my arm tugged out of its socket or my pants yanked below my waist. More often than not, I leave the mall with fewer dollars than when I entered.

Computer games are the most popular at these arcades. There are several reasons for this: The sounds and noises are rewarding, and the player can fantasize a trip or battle in space and vent some aggression in a socially acceptable manner. There are probably other reasons as well, and I'm willing to bet one of these is with the future and the influence of the computer on that future. Little do we realize, though, that, in a sense, we have always had computers. You and I even program computers. Our programs instruct our computers to bing, bong, ring, buzz, and crash and to project rainbows and lights. We have, in other words, our own arcade!

Our computers are our brains, our programs are our minds, and our arcades are our bodies. Enter this arcade with us now and learn how our machines operate, especially when stressed.

The Brain

When we are talking about stress management, we are really talking about managing psychological or sociological stressors. Although stress can be caused by biological agents (e.g., viruses), the environment (e.g., temperature), and other sources, the focus of this book is on threats to our self-esteem, the loss of a loved one and the resultant loneliness, and other such stressors. These psychological and sociological stressors are perceived by the mind and translated by the brain. The brain, in turn, instructs the rest of the body how to adjust to the stressor.

The brain includes two major components: the **cerebral cortex** (the upper part) and the **subcortex** (the lower part). Figure 2.1 shows the structures of the brain and their locations. The subcortex includes the **cerebellum** (coordinates body movements), the **medulla oblongata** (regulates heartbeat, respiration, and other such basic physiological processes), the **pons** (regulates the sleep cycle), and the **diencephalon.** The diencephalon has many purposes, including the regulation of the emotions. It is made up of the **thalamus** and **hypothalamus.** The thalamus relays sensory impulses from other parts of the nervous system to the cerebral cortex. The hypothalamus, a key structure in stress reactivity, is the primary activator of the **autonomic nervous system,** which controls basic body processes such as hormone balance, temperature, and the constriction and dilation of blood vessels.

cerebral cortex
The upper part of the brain responsible for thinking functions.

subcortex
The lower part of the brain responsible for various physiological processes necessary to stay alive.

cerebellum
Part of the subcortex responsible for coordination.

medulla oblongata
Part of the subcortex responsible for the regulation of the heartbeat and breathing.

pons
Part of the subcortex responsible for regulating sleep.

diencephalon
Part of the subcortex responsible for regulation of the emotions.

thalamus
Part of the diencephalon that relays sensory impulses to the cerebral cortex.

hypothalamus
Part of the diencephalon that activates the autonomic nervous system.

autonomic nervous system
Controls such body processes as hormone balance, temperature, and width of blood vessels.

Figure 2.1

The brain.

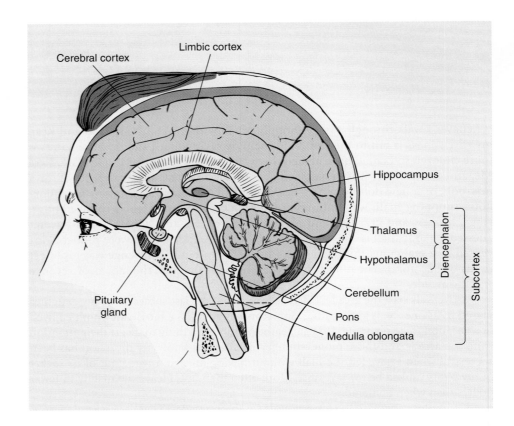

The brain diagram labels: Cerebral cortex, Limbic cortex, Hippocampus, Thalamus, Hypothalamus, Cerebellum, Pons, Medulla oblongata, Pituitary gland, Diencephalon, Subcortex

limbic system
Produces emotions; the "seat of emotions."

gray matter
The cerebral cortex.

reticular activating system (RAS)
A network of nerves that connects the mind and the body.

The **limbic system,** called the "seat of emotions," consists of the thalamus and hypothalamus (the diencephalon) and other structures important in stress physiology. The limbic system is connected to the diencephalon and is primarily concerned with emotions and their behavioral expression. The limbic system is thought to produce such emotions as fear, anxiety, and joy in response to physical and psychological signals. As you might expect, since emotions play a big role in the stress response, the limbic system is an important structure when discussing stress psychophysiology.

The cerebral cortex (called the **gray matter**) controls higher-order abstract functioning, such as language and judgment. The cerebral cortex can also control more primitive areas of the brain. When the diencephalon recognizes fear, for instance, the cerebral cortex can use judgment to recognize the stimulus as nonthreatening and override the fear.

Last, there is the **reticular activating system (RAS).** In the past, cortical and subcortical functions were considered dichotomized—that is, human behavior was thought to be a function of one area of the brain or the other. Now, brain researchers believe that neurological connections between the cortex and subcortex feed information back and forth. This network of nerves, the RAS, can be considered the connection between mind and body. The "reticular system is a kind of two-way street, carrying messages perceived by the higher awareness centers to the organs and muscles and also relaying stimuli received at the muscular and organic levels up to the cerebral cortex. In this manner, a purely physical stressor can influence the higher thought centers, and a mentally or intellectually perceived stressor can generate neurophysiological responses."[1]

Now that the brain's key structures have been outlined, let's see how a stressor affects the brain and how the brain functions to prepare the rest of the body to react. When we encounter a stressor, the body part (eyes, nose, muscles, etc.) that first notes the stressor passes a message along nerves to the brain. These messages pass

Figure 2.2 Stress and its pathways.

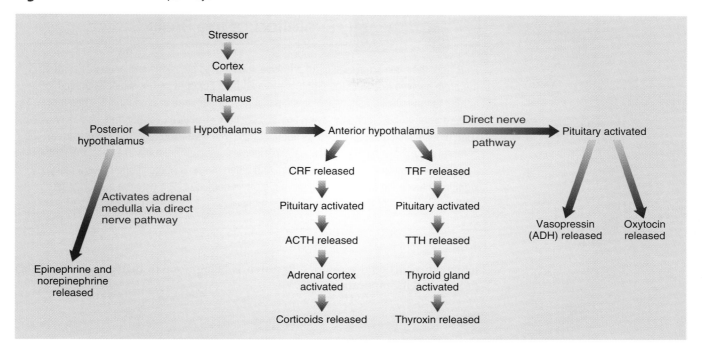

through the reticular activating system either from or to the limbic system and the thalamus. The limbic system is where emotion evolves, and the thalamus serves as the switchboard, determining what to do with the incoming messages. The hypothalamus then comes into play.

When the hypothalamus experiences a stressor, it activates the two major stress reactivity pathways: the **endocrine system** and the autonomic nervous system. To activate the endocrine system, the anterior portion of the hypothalamus releases **corticotropin releasing factor (CRF),** which instructs the pituitary gland at the base of the brain to secrete **adrenocorticotropic hormone (ACTH).** ACTH then activates the adrenal cortex to secrete corticoid hormones. To activate the autonomic nervous system, a message is sent by the posterior part of the hypothalamus via a nerve pathway to the adrenal medulla. Figure 2.2 diagrams stress's pathways in the body.

The hypothalamus performs other functions as well. One of these is the releasing of **thyrotropic hormone releasing factor (TRF)** from its anterior portion, which instructs the pituitary to secrete **thyrotropic hormone (TTH).** TTH then stimulates the thyroid gland to secrete the hormone thyroxin. The anterior hypothalamus also stimulates the pituitary gland to secrete **oxytocin** and **vasopressin (ADH).**[2] The functions of these hormones (adrenal medulla and cortex secretions, thyroxin, oxytocin, and vasopressin) are discussed in the next section.

Now that you have an understanding of the relationship between stress and the brain, you might be interested in some research that indicates stress may result in irreversible brain damage.[3] Several pieces of information are important to know to understand these findings. First, you need to know that the **hippocampus** is the part of the brain that "sounds the alarm" that stress is present. Next you need to know that glucocorticoids are hormones released by the adrenal glands. The presence of these glucocorticoids is detected by receptors on the cells of the hippocampus. Prolonged stress has been found to damage these receptors and the cells of the hippocampus themselves. Brain cells do not regenerate, so their death means we have lost these cells forever. The net effects of this process are not completely understood, but it probably means we do not respond as well to stress, since we do not have as

endocrine system
Comprised of hormones that regulate physiological functions.

corticotropin releasing factor (CRF)
Released by hypothalamus and results in the release of adrenocorticotropic hormone.

adrenocorticotropic hormone (ACTH)
Activates the adrenal cortex to secrete corticoid hormones.

thyrotropic hormone releasing factor (TRF)
Released by hypothalamus and stimulates the pituitary gland to secrete thyrotropic hormone.

thyrotropic hormone (TTH)
Stimulates the thyroid gland to secrete thyroxin.

oxytocin
A hormone secreted by the pituitary gland.

vasopressin (ADH)
A hormone secreted by the pituitary gland.

Evolution of the Brain

Eons ago, the brain stem was quite primitive. It governed decisions and actions. Eventually, the brain evolved to create the limbic system and the cerebral cortex, which is unique to human beings. Unlike fish, which developed a new appendage or component—fins and gills—the brain developed by laying one evolutionary structure over another. That is why we sometimes have conflicting feelings about stress. When we experience little or no stress, the cerebral cortex is in charge. When we experience significant amounts of stress, the limbic system is interpreting what is happening. And when stress is perceived to be especially significant, even life threatening, the brain stem is dominant. The way the human brain evolved accounts for many of our stress responses.

many glucocorticoid receptors. Research is being done to better understand this process and its implications.

The Endocrine System

One of the most important systems of the body that is related to stress is the endocrine system. The endocrine system includes all the glands that secrete hormones. These hormones alter the function of other bodily tissues and are carried through the circulatory system to various targets. The endocrine system includes the pituitary, thyroid, parathyroid, and adrenal glands, as well as the pancreas, ovaries, testes, pineal gland, and thymus gland. The locations of these endocrine glands are shown in Figure 2.3.

When the anterior hypothalamus releases CRF, and the pituitary then releases ACTH, the outer layer of the adrenal glands, the **adrenal cortex,** secretes **glucocorticoids** and **mineralocorticoids** (see Figure 2.4). Chemically classified as steroid molecules, glucocorticoids regulate metabolism of glucose, and mineral corticoids regulate the balance between sodium and potassium. The primary glucocorticoid is the hormone **cortisol,** and the primary mineralocorticoid is **aldosterone.**

Cortisol provides the fuel for battle (fight-or-flight). Its primary function is to increase the blood glucose so we have the energy for action. It does this by the conversion of amino acids to glycogen, which occurs in the liver. When glycogen is depleted, the liver can produce glucose from amino acids. This process is termed **gluconeogenesis.** In addition, cortisol mobilizes free fatty acids from fat (adipose) tissue, breaks down protein, and increases arterial blood pressure. All of this is designed to prepare us to fight or run from the stressor. Cortisol also causes other physiological changes. One of the more significant changes is the decrease of lymphocytes released from the thymus gland and lymph nodes. The lymphocytes, in their role of destroying invading substances (e.g., bacteria), are important for the effectiveness of the immunological system. Consequently, an increase in cortisol decreases the effectiveness of the immune response, and we are more likely to become ill. Salivary cortisol increases have been found within thirty minutes of waking in people who are under considerable stress because of work or family concerns.[4]

Aldosterone also prepares us for action. Its major purpose is to increase blood pressure so we can transport food and oxygen to the active parts of our bodies—limbs as well as organs. The manner in which aldosterone raises blood pressure is to increase blood volume. This is accomplished in two ways: a decrease in urine production and an increase in sodium retention. Both of these mechanisms result in less elimination of body fluids, greater blood volume, and a subsequent increase in blood pressure.

hippocampus
The part of the brain that "sounds the alarm" that stress is present.

adrenal cortex
The part of the adrenal gland that secretes corticoids.

glucocorticoids
Regulate metabolism of glucose.

mineralocorticoids
Regulate the balance between sodium and potassium.

cortisol
The primary glucocorticoid.

aldosterone
The primary mineralocorticoid.

gluconeogenesis
The producing of glucose from amino acids by the liver.

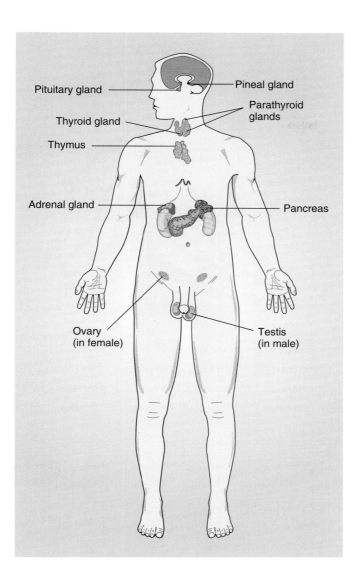

Figure 2.3

Locations of major endocrine glands.

Blood pressure is measured as systolic and diastolic. Systolic blood pressure is the amount of pressure on the arterial walls when blood is pumped from the heart. Diastolic blood pressure is the pressure of blood against the walls of the arteries when the heart is relaxed. An average blood pressure for a young adult is 120/80; the higher number is the systolic reading (120mm Hg), and the lower is the diastolic reading (80mm Hg). Aldosterone can raise systolic blood pressure 15mm–20mm Hg. Although health scientists are not in total agreement regarding the point at which hypertension (high blood pressure) begins, generally a systolic reading consistently above 140 or a diastolic reading consistently above 90 is considered harmful.

In addition to the involvement of the adrenal cortex in stress reactivity, the **adrenal medulla** (the inner portion of the adrenal gland) is activated through a direct nerve connection from the posterior portion of the hypothalamus. The adrenal medulla then secretes the catecholamines **epinephrine** (commonly called *adrenalin*) and **norepinephrine** (commonly called *noradrenaline*). These hormones lead to various changes within the body, which remain ten times longer than the effects of adrenal corticoids,[5] including the following:

1. Acceleration of heart rate.
2. Increase in force at which blood is pumped out of the heart.

adrenal medulla
The inner portion of the adrenal gland that secretes catecholamines.

epinephrine
A catecholamine secreted by the adrenal medulla.

norepinephrine
A catecholamine secreted by the adrenal medulla.

Figure 2.4

An adrenal gland consists of an outer cortex and an inner medulla, which secrete different hormones.

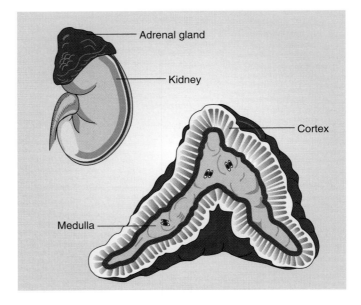

thyroid gland
An endocrine gland that secretes the hormone thyroxin.

3. Dilation (widening) of coronary arteries.
4. Dilation of bronchial tubes (through which air passes to and from the lungs).
5. Increase in the basal metabolic rate (i.e., most body processes speed up).
6. Constriction (narrowing) of the blood vessels in the muscles and skin of the arms and legs.
7. Increase in oxygen consumption.

The **thyroid gland** is also involved in the stress reaction. Activated by TTH from the pituitary, it secretes thyroxin, which performs the following functions:

1. Increases the basal metabolic rate.
2. Increases free fatty acids.
3. Increases rate of gluconeogenesis.
4. Increases gastrointestinal motility (often resulting in diarrhea).
5. Increases the rate and depth of respiration.
6. Accelerates the heart rate.
7. Increases blood pressure.
8. Increases anxiety.
9. Decreases feelings of tiredness.

In addition, through a direct nerve pathway, the hypothalamus instructs the pituitary to secrete vasopressin, also known as antidiuretic hormone (ADH), and oxytocin. Vasopressin acts on the kidneys to promote water retention, which in turn decreases urine production resulting in more water being retained in the blood. Oxytocin secretion results in contraction of the walls of the blood vessels. Taken together, the physiological changes resulting from the secretion of vasopressin and oxytocin help explain the relationship between stress and high blood pressure.

To sum up so far, during stress the hypothalamus activates the adrenal and thyroid glands (either through the pituitary or direct nerve innervation), which in turn secrete cortisol, aldosterone, epinephrine, norepinephrine, and thyroxin. These hormones affect numerous body processes to prepare the stressed person to respond in a physically active manner.

Using Lab 2.1, at the end of the chapter, assess how much you now know about stress psychophysiology.

The Autonomic Nervous System

Some people have suggested that you've been feeling terrible for several centuries. Well, maybe not you personally, but the collective you (us)—that is, human beings. The argument goes that human beings viewed themselves as having major importance until Copernicus demonstrated that the earth is but one of many planets revolving about the sun rather than being the center of the universe. We could no longer command the "center of attention" (get it?). Another major blow to *Homo sapiens* was Darwin's theory of evolution. To think that we come from apes! Though only a theory, Darwin's ideas became widely accepted, and human beings were relegated to just one rung on the ladder of life. Lastly, when Galen, da Vinci, and other notables described the structure and function of the human body, it became apparent that much of that function was involuntary—beyond our control. Here was one more blow to our self-esteem; we had less free will than we previously believed.

Hearken, brothers and sisters, good news is just ahead. As we shall see, stress research has demonstrated that we are in greater control than we thought. The involuntary functions of the body are controlled by the autonomic (involuntary) nervous system. A general view of the nervous system appears in Figure 2.5. Examples of involuntary functions are heart rate, blood pressure, respiratory rate,

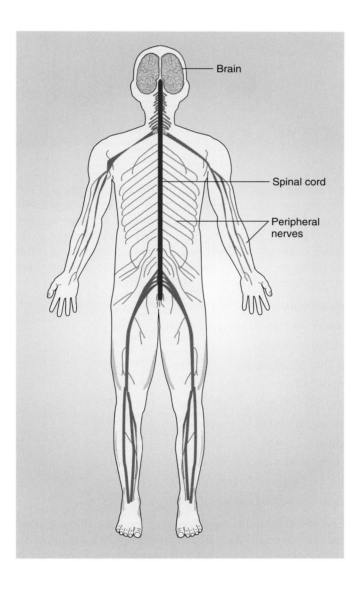

Figure 2.5

The nervous system consists of the brain, spinal cord, and numerous peripheral nerves.

Figure 2.6

Visceral organs are usually innervated from fibers from both the parasympathetic and sympathetic divisions.

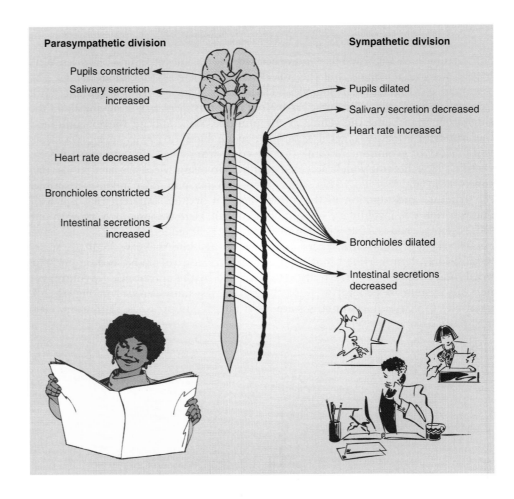

Parasympathetic division

- Pupils constricted
- Salivary secretion increased
- Heart rate decreased
- Bronchioles constricted
- Intestinal secretions increased

Sympathetic division

- Pupils dilated
- Salivary secretion decreased
- Heart rate increased
- Bronchioles dilated
- Intestinal secretions decreased

and body fluid regulation. This control is maintained by the two components of the autonomic nervous system: the sympathetic and the parasympathetic nervous systems (see Figure 2.6). Generally, the **sympathetic nervous system** is in charge of expending energy (e.g., increasing respiratory rate), and the **parasympathetic nervous system** is in charge of conserving energy (e.g., decreasing respiratory rate).

When you encounter a stressor, the sympathetic nervous system, activated by the hypothalamus, regulates the body to do the following:

1. Increase heart rate.
2. Increase force with which heart contracts.
3. Dilate coronary arteries.
4. Constrict abdominal arteries.
5. Dilate pupils.
6. Dilate bronchial tubes.
7. Increase strength of skeletal muscles.
8. Release glucose from liver.
9. Increase mental activity.
10. Dilate arterioles deep in skeletal muscles
11. Increase basal metabolic rate significantly.

Because of these physiological changes, people have been able to perform incredible feats in emergencies. A relatively frail person who pulls a car off of a child pinned beneath it is an example of the power of this fight-or-flight response. The parasympathetic nervous system is generally responsible for returning us to a relaxed state when the stressor has passed.

Now to my earlier promise of better things to come. It has been suggested that the first major scientific finding that improves, rather than diminishes, the self-esteem of human beings is the discovery that the involuntary functions of the human body are not totally involuntary. The development of biofeedback equipment, which instantaneously measures and reports what is occurring in the body, has allowed research studies of the voluntary control of "involuntary" body processes. For instance, people have been taught to control their blood pressure, to regulate their heart and respiratory rates, to emit particular brain waves, and to dilate and constrict blood vessels in various parts of their bodies. In other words, people now know they can be more in control of themselves (and their bodies) than they ever believed possible. It is suggested that this knowledge is a major influence on the level of esteem in which people hold themselves.

What some consider to be even more significant is the understanding that we often control our physiology and often allow ourselves to become ill. Once we understand that, we can stop viewing ourselves as helpless and hopeless victims of illnesses and diseases; we can consider ourselves capable of preventing them.

Here is one last word about the sympathetic and parasympathetic nervous systems. Although these two systems are generally counteractive, this is not always the case. Certain things are influenced by the sympathetic system only (e.g., sweat glands and blood glucose), and others are influenced by the parasympathetic system alone (e.g., the ciliary muscles of the eye). Generally, however, the parasympathetic nervous system is responsible for the relaxation response.

The Cardiovascular System

My family and I have recently moved into a new house and have experienced a most frustrating situation. It seems that every few weeks I have to dismantle the faucet to clean out debris. The builder tells me this is to be expected in a new house, but I've had a house built before and never experienced that problem. You can imagine the discussions we have had over this situation! In any case, every few weeks the screen in the faucet gets clogged, and I have to take it out and clean it.

The reason I relate this story is that my problem is analogous to that of your body's fluid system, which includes your heart, blood, and blood vessels (see Figure 2.7). This circulatory system can also become clogged—although this takes a lot of years. When your blood vessels get clogged (not at one end—more like rusting throughout), several things may happen: Organs awaiting the oxygen and food in the blood may die if not enough of these substances is received; blood vessels may burst due to increased pressure on their walls; or other blood vessels may sprout to provide alternative routes to the waiting organs and cells.

The effects of stress upon the circulatory system are pronounced. When the hypothalamus reacts to a stressor, it signals the pituitary to release oxytocin and vasopressin. Both of these hormones cause contraction of the smooth muscles, resulting in constriction in the walls of the blood vessels. Vasopressin also increases the permeability of the kidney's blood vessels to water, resulting in greater blood volume. Coupled with the sodium retention brought about by aldosterone, the constriction of blood vessels and the increased permeability to water result in an increase in blood pressure caused by stress.

In addition, the heart itself is affected by stress. It increases its force of contraction and pumps out more blood when stressed due to the effects of the sympathetic nervous system and the aforementioned hormones. Further, serum cholesterol and other free fatty acids increase during stress. This increases the possibility of clogging of the arteries supplying the heart and death of a part of the heart resulting from a lack of blood supply to that part. Last, severe stressors can shock the heart to such an extent that sudden death occurs.

Figure 2.7

The cardiovascular system transports blood between the body cells and organs that communicate with the external environment.

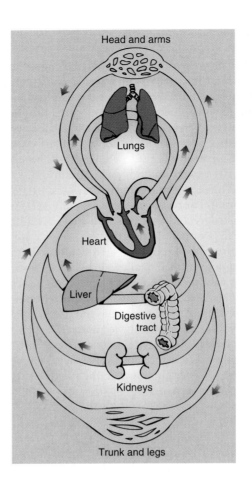

Stress Phrases

The stress reaction, as we have come to realize, results in numerous changes in our physiology. These physiological changes often lead to emotional interpretations, as witnessed by our use of phrases such as *cold feet*. We get cold feet when we are stressed because there is a constriction of blood vessels in the arms and legs. When we are stressed we may feel *uptight*. Of course we do! We have increased muscle tension.

Can you think of other "stress phrases" that have a physiological basis? Write them below.

Phrase	Physiological Basis
1.	1.
2.	2.
3.	3.
4.	4.
5.	5.

The Gastrointestinal System

I began this book by describing myself vomiting by the side of a road. You now know that my condition was a function of stress overload. It is obvious, then, that the **gastrointestinal (GI) system** is a component of the stress response.

Some years back, Woody Allen made a movie titled *Everything You Wanted to Know About Sex but Were Afraid to Ask.* In that movie, a scene of the inside of a male's reproductive system includes actors as sperm. Let's use a similar approach in describing the structure and function of the GI system. The purpose of this system is to accept, break down, and distribute food and to eliminate waste products resulting from this process.

"Hey, Harry, here comes another shipment," says Joe *Saliva* to his brother. The Salivas live in the mouth and, when food enters, they help break it down to small, manageable pieces. These pieces are then mailed by pneumatic tube (the *esophagus*) to Phil *Hydrochloric Acid,* who lives in *Stomach*ville. Hydrochloric acid (HCl) activates enzymes that break the food down even further so it can pass into the small intestine. Another town, *Liver,* sends Bobby *Bile* to help break down the fatty shipments. Once these shipments (food) are made small, they can be placed in local post offices for delivery to various other cities (body parts). The pieces without zip codes are unusable and are discarded by being sent via the large intestine through the anus into space (i.e., flushed into another galaxy).

To make sure my attempt at levity hasn't been more confusing than motivating, let me summarize: Food enters the mouth, where it is broken down by chewing and **saliva.** It then passes down the food pipe (the **esophagus**) into the *stomach,* where a number of substances break the food down further. Two of these substances are **hydrochloric acid** and protein-splitting enzymes. The food substances then pass into the **small intestine,** where they are broken down further. The usable food then passes through the walls of the small intestine into the bloodstream for passage to various body parts. The unusable food substances (waste) are transported through the small intestine to the **large intestine,** finally making their way out of the body through the **anal opening.**

Stress has a very significant effect upon the GI system. Because stress decreases the amount of saliva in the mouth, people are often so nervous before speaking in public that their mouths are too dry to speak. Because stress may result in uncontrollable contractions of the muscles of the esophagus, swallowing may be difficult. Because stress increases the amount of hydrochloric acid in the stomach, constricts blood vessels in the digestive tract, and reduces the gastric mucus that protects the lining of the stomach, ulcers (small fissures in the stomach wall) may develop. Because stress may alter the rhythmic movements (*peristalsis*) of the small and large intestines necessary for the transport of food substances, diarrhea (if peristalsis is too fast) or constipation (if peristalsis is too slow) may result. "Constipation goes with depression and dullness, diarrhea with panic."[6] Even blockage of the bile and pancreatic ducts, as well as pancreatitis (inflammation of the pancreas), have been associated with stress,[7] along with irritable bowel syndrome.[8]

The Muscles

To hold yourself in a certain posture or position, or to move, you send messages to your muscles. These messages result in muscular contraction. The absence of these messages results in muscular relaxation. Interacting systems in your body feed back the results of muscular contraction to the brain so you don't contract a muscle group too much or too little for your purposes. To demonstrate this point, place an empty gallon paint can on the floor and tell someone it is full of paint and very heavy. Then ask that person to pick up the "full" can. You will notice how quickly and how high the can is lifted before the muscles adjust to a lighter load. What really happened is that the brain perceived a can full of paint and sent that message to the muscles. Based on past experience, the muscles were instructed that *x* amount of contraction

gastrointestinal (GI) system
The body system responsible for digestion.

saliva
Substance in the mouth that starts to break down food.

esophagus
The food pipe.

hydrochloric acid
A substance found in the digestive system that helps break down food for digestion.

small intestine
Part of the digestive system into which the esophagus empties.

large intestine
Part of the digestive system that receives unusable food substances from the small intestine.

anal opening
The exit point for unusable food substances.

was needed to lift the full can. When the can was lifted, a message (visual and kinesthetic) was sent to the brain ("Hey, dummy, this can ain't full; it's empty!"), which resulted in an adjustment to make the amount of muscular contraction more appropriate to the task.

Stress results in muscles contracting—tensing. Some people appear as if they are always ready to defend themselves or to be aggressive. They seem "at the ready." This type of muscle tension is called **bracing**.[9] As we shall discuss in the next chapter, this muscular bracing can lead to numerous states of poor health, such as tension headaches and backaches. How many times have you heard someone say, "I've got a knot in my shoulders"? When people say they are "uptight," they mean their muscles are bracing and fatiguing.

Many of us never realize our muscles are tensed. We squeeze our pens when writing letters of complaint. We sit on the edges of our chairs ("on edge") during a scary movie. We hold our steering wheels more tightly than necessary during a traffic jam. Or we clench our jaws when angered. Intermittent muscle tension is not the problem; it is the frequent stressor to which we react with bracing that is harmful. When a new stressor is introduced while muscle tension is present, even greater muscle tension is the result.

The previous examples involved **skeletal muscles**—muscles attached to bones (see Figure 2.8). In addition, we have **smooth muscles** that control the contraction of the internal organs. The stress response results in these muscles being contracted as well. For example, when we experience a stressor, the pituitary hormones oxytocin and vasopressin result in increased blood pressure due to their contracting the smooth muscles in the walls of the blood vessels. No wonder that chronic stress can lead to hypertension. When the smooth muscles in the stomach walls contract, we might get stomachaches; when the smooth muscles of the intestines contract, we might wind up with diarrhea; and so on throughout the body.

The Skin

Linda was a doctoral student advisee of mine several years ago. One September, she surprised me by saying, "This year I'm not breaking out." When asked to explain what she meant, she told me that each summer she would leave campus and return home to a relatively unstressful existence. During the summer, her skin was very smooth, but when September rolled around and school began, she "broke out" with acne. Linda was telling me several things besides "You guys put too much pressure on us students." She was saying that she manifested her stress in "the window to her body"—her skin—and that she believed she could control that response.

Although there is no definitive relationship between stress and acne, the skin is involved in our stress response. The skin's ability to conduct electrical currents and the skin's temperature are both affected. During stress, perspiration increases. Even though this increased perspiration may be imperceptible, it will increase electrical conductance and can be measured by a galvanometer. This measure is called your **galvanic skin response (GSR)**—sometimes referred to as the electrodermal response—and is a major part of the lie detector test. One of the reasons that the lie detector test is not infallible and is viewed with caution is that people can control their nervousness (and, therefore, their level of skin moisture), thereby affecting their GSR. A good liar may have a lower GSR than a nervous innocent suspect, although a well-trained, experienced lie detector administrator will often (but not always) be able to distinguish between the two.

During stress, the surface temperature of the skin decreases. Because nor-epinephrine constricts the blood vessels of the skin of the arms and legs, for example, fingers and toes feel colder during stress than otherwise. The skin may also appear pale due to this vasoconstriction. We often hear of people described as appearing "white as a ghost." Now you know why the skin of nervous, anxious, stressed people is described as cold, clammy, and pale.

bracing
Unnecessary muscle tension.

skeletal muscles
Muscles attached to bones.

smooth muscles
Muscles that control the contraction of internal organs.

galvanic skin response (GSR)
The electrodermal response or the electrical conductance of the skin.

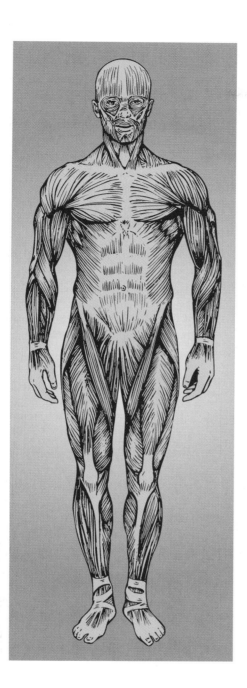

Symptoms, Stress, and You

Now that you have an idea of how your body reacts to stress, you are in a better position to be more specific. Using Lab 2.2, at the end of this chapter, assess how often each of the physical symptoms happens to you. If you score between 40 and 75, the chances of becoming physically ill as a result of stress are minimal. If you score between 76 and 100, you have a slight chance of becoming physically ill from the stress in your life. If you score between 101 and 150, it is likely you will become ill from the stress you experience. If you score over 150, you may very well already be ill from the stress you have experienced. Luckily, you are reading this book and will find out how to better manage the stress you encounter and how to eliminate some stressors in the first place.

summary

- The brain includes two major components: the cerebral cortex and the subcortex. The subcortex includes the cerebellum, medulla oblongata, pons, and diencephalon. The diencephalon is made up of the thalamus and the hypothalamus.

- When the hypothalamus experiences a stressor, it releases corticotropin releasing factor, which instructs the pituitary to secrete adrenocorticotropic hormone. In addition, the hypothalamus directly activates the adrenal medulla.

- Once instructed by the hypothalamus and pituitary, the adrenal cortex secretes glucocorticoids and mineralocorticoids. The primary glucocorticoid is cortisol, and the primary mineralocorticoid is aldosterone. In addition, the hypothalamus instructs the adrenal medulla to secrete the catecholamines epinephrine and norepinephrine.

- Adrenal hormones cause a number of physiological changes that include accelerated heart rate, dilation of coronary arteries, dilation of bronchial tubes, increased basal metabolic rate, constriction of blood vessels in the limbs, increased oxygen consumption, increased blood sugar, and increased blood pressure.

- In addition to the adrenal gland response to stress, the thyroid gland releases thyroxin, and the pituitary secretes oxytocin and vasopressin. These hormones also help prepare the body for a physical response to the stressor.

- Stress results in secretions of oxytocin and vasopressin, which cause contractions of smooth muscles (such as in the walls of the blood vessels). Therefore, blood vessel constriction occurs. Vasopressin secretion also results in a greater blood volume. The combination of these effects leads to increased blood pressure, which can threaten the cardiovascular system.

- The autonomic nervous system is made up of the sympathetic nervous system (generally in charge of expending energy—such as during stress) and the parasympathetic nervous system (generally in charge of conserving energy—such as during relaxation).

- Stress decreases the amount of saliva in the mouth, leaving a feeling of cotton mouth. It may also lead to uncontrollable contractions of the esophagus, making swallowing difficult. Stress also causes greater secretions of hydrochloric acid, which can result in ulcers.

- The contraction of skeletal muscle that results from stress can lead to tension headaches, backaches, and fatigue. The smooth muscle contractions of the walls of blood vessels can lead to hypertension.

- The skin's ability to conduct electrical currents and the skin's temperature are both affected by stress.

notes

1. Kenneth R. Pelletier, *Mind as Healer, Mind as Slayer* (New York: Dell Publishing Co., 1977), 51.

2. G. Makara, M. Palkovits, and J. Szentagothal, "The Endocrine Hypothalamus and the Hormonal Response to Stress," in *Selye's Guide to Stress Research,* ed. Hans Selye (New York: Van Nostrand Rinehold, 1980), 280–337.

3. "Of Rats and Men," *Psychology Today,* July 1985, 21.

4. Bruce S. McEwen, "Protective and Damaging Effects of Stress Mediators," *The New England Journal of Medicine* 338(1998):171–78.

5. Stuart Ira Fox, *Human Physiology,* 4th ed. (Dubuque, IA: Wm. C. Brown, 1993), 272.

6. Walter McQuade and Ann Aikman, *Stress* (New York: Bantam Books, 1974), 52.

7. Daniel A. Girdano, George S. Everly, and Dorothy E. Dusek, *Controlling Stress and Tension* (Boston: Allyn and Bacon, 1997), 39.

8. Thomas G. Plante and Maire Ford, "The Association Between Cardiovascular Stress Responsivity and Perceived Stress Among Subjects with Irritable Bowel Syndrome and Temperomandibular Joint Disorder: A Preliminary Study," *International Journal of Stress Management* 7(2000): 103–19.

9. Barbara B. Brown, *Stress and the Art of Biofeedback* (New York: Harper & Row, 1977), 28.

internet resources

Job Stress Network
www.workhealth.org/
Information related to job strain and work stress, by the Center for Social Epidemiology, a private nonprofit foundation whose purpose is to promote public awareness of the role of environmental and occupational stress in the etiology of cardiovascular disease.

The Medical Basis of Stress, Depression, Anxiety, Sleep Problems, and Drug Use
www.teachhealth.com/
An easy-to-understand presentation of how the brain responds to stress.

Coping in Today's World

Do you or someone you know live near an airport? Do you or someone you know live in or near a flight path to the airport with planes flying overhead frequently? These conditions can lead to physiological arousal and a stress response. Some people are fearful of a plane crashing into their neighborhood, as occurred in 2001 in Queens, New York, killing 260 people, 5 of whom were on the ground. That fear is accompanied by increased heart rate, blood pressure, and muscle tension; perspiration; and other evidence of physiological arousal and a stress response. Others are affected by the noise of planes flying in and out throughout the day. A study[a] of the environmental effects of airport noise found that 80 percent of people who lived near the airport were more likely to have high blood pressure than those who did not. Researcher Mats Rosenlund and colleagues hypothesized that the erratic cycle of take-offs and landings affected cognitive functions, caused emotional arousal, and interfered with sleep and relaxation. As a result, those who live in flight paths should regularly be checked for hypertension.

[a]Rosenlund, M., Berglind, N., Pershagen, G., Jarup, L., and Bluhm, G. "Increased Prevalence of Hypertension in a Population Exposed to Aircraft Noise." *Occupational and Environmental Medicine* 58(2001):769–773.

How Much Do You Know About Stress Psychophysiology?

Directions: Stop for a moment to test your recall of the stress psychophysiology presented so far. See if you can match the numbered items in the column on the left with the lettered items in the column on the right.

_____ 1. Limbic system

_____ 2. Subcortex

_____ 3. Diencephalon

_____ 4. Cerebral cortex

_____ 5. Adrenal medulla

_____ 6. Adrenal cortex

_____ 7. Hypothalamus

_____ 8. Aldosterone

_____ 9. Pituitary

_____ 10. Norepinephrine

a. Thalamus and hypothalamus

b. Upper part of brain

c. Activated by ACTH

d. "Seat of emotions"

e. Cerebellum, medulla oblongata, pons, and diencephalon

f. Secreted by adrenal cortex

g. Activated by nerves from hypothalamus

h. Releases ACTH

i. Gluconeogenesis

j. Releases CRF

k. Vasopressin

l. Secreted by adrenal medulla

Check your answers with the key below. If you didn't answer at least seven correctly, you might be wise to review the beginning of this chapter before proceeding further.

Answer key: 1. d, 2. e, 3. a, 4. b, 5. g, 6. c, 7. j, 8. f, 9. h, 10. l

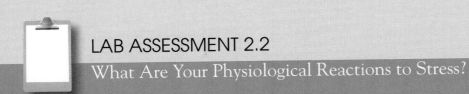

LAB ASSESSMENT 2.2
What Are Your Physiological Reactions to Stress?

Directions: Circle the number that best represents the frequency of occurrence of the following physical symptoms, and add up the total number of points.

	Never	Infrequently (More Than Once in Six Months)	Occasionally (More Than Once per Month)	Very Often (More Than Once per Week)	Constantly
1. Tension headaches	1	2	3	4	5
2. Migraine (vascular) headaches	1	2	3	4	5
3. Stomachaches	1	2	3	4	5
4. Increase in blood pressure	1	2	3	4	5
5. Cold hands	1	2	3	4	5
6. Acidic stomach	1	2	3	4	5
7. Shallow, rapid breathing	1	2	3	4	5
8. Diarrhea	1	2	3	4	5
9. Palpitations	1	2	3	4	5
10. Shaky hands	1	2	3	4	5
11. Burping	1	2	3	4	5
12. Gassiness	1	2	3	4	5
13. Increased urge to urinate	1	2	3	4	5
14. Sweaty feet/hands	1	2	3	4	5
15. Oily skin	1	2	3	4	5
16. Fatigue/exhausted feeling	1	2	3	4	5
17. Panting	1	2	3	4	5
18. Dry mouth	1	2	3	4	5
19. Hand tremor	1	2	3	4	5
20. Backache	1	2	3	4	5
21. Neck stiffness	1	2	3	4	5
22. Gum chewing	1	2	3	4	5
23. Grinding teeth	1	2	3	4	5
24. Constipation	1	2	3	4	5
25. Tightness in chest or heart	1	2	3	4	5
26. Dizziness	1	2	3	4	5
27. Nausea/vomiting	1	2	3	4	5
28. Menstrual distress	1	2	3	4	5
29. Skin blemishes	1	2	3	4	5
30. Heart pounding	1	2	3	4	5
31. Colitis	1	2	3	4	5
32. Asthma	1	2	3	4	5
33. Indigestion	1	2	3	4	5
34. High blood pressure	1	2	3	4	5
35. Hyperventilation	1	2	3	4	5
36. Arthritis	1	2	3	4	5
37. Skin rash	1	2	3	4	5
38. Bruxism/jaw pain	1	2	3	4	5
39. Allergy	1	2	3	4	5

Source: H. Ebel et al., eds., *Presidential Sports Award Fitness Manual,* 197–98. Copyright © 1983 FitCom Corporation, Havertown, PA.

Interpretation
40–75 Low physiological symptoms of stress response
76–100 Moderate physiological symptoms of stress response

101–150 High physiological symptoms of stress response
Over 150 Excessive physiological symptoms of stress response

If stress were only discomforting—that is, if it led only to increased muscle tension, perspiration, rapid and shallow breathing, or a general psychological state of uneasiness—it would be bad enough. Unfortunately, chronic stress also leads to poor health. Numerous examples of the relationship between stress and ill health abound. Perhaps among the more dramatic examples is the breakup of the Soviet Union. During that stressful period, cardiovascular disease was a major contributor to an almost 40 percent increase in the death rate among Russian men.[1] We all have also heard of traumatic events (e.g., war experiences, traffic accidents, or sexual assaults) resulting in ill health (both psychological and physiological) for many years after the event itself. As a result, stress researchers have recommended that physicians and other health care providers help patients "learn coping skills, recognize their own limitations, and relax."[2]

Hot Reactors

Are you a hot reactor? Some people tend to react to stressors with an all-out physiological effort that takes a toll on their health.[3,4] In a sense, their bodies are overreacting to the stressful situation. We call these people **hot reactors.**[5] If you notice you anger easily, you are often anxious or depressed, you urinate frequently, you experience constipation or diarrhea more than usual, or you experience nausea or vomiting, you may be a hot reactor. In that case, you may want to obtain regular medical examinations to identify illnesses when they can be easily cured or contained and learn and use stress management techniques and strategies such as those in this book. This chapter presents the body's responses to stress, and you should therefore be better able to understand why it is so important to learn to cope with stress. We identify specific illnesses, diseases, and other negative consequences that are stress related and discuss ways to prevent these from developing.

hot reactors
People who react to stress with an all-out physiological reaction.

Psychosomatic Disease

Bill's wife died last year, and Bill grieved long and hard over her death. He felt it unfair (she was such a kind person), and a sense of helplessness crept over him. Loneliness became a part of his every day, and tears became the companions of his late evening hours. There were those who were not even surprised at Bill's own death just one year after his wife's. They officially called it a heart attack, but Bill's friends, to this day, know he died of a "broken heart."

You probably know some Bills yourself—people who have died or have become ill from severe stress, with seemingly little physically wrong with them. Maybe you have even been guilty of telling these people, "It's all in your mind," or at least thinking that. Well, in Bill's case it was not "all in his mind"—it was, obviously, partially in his heart. Some illnesses are easily seen as being physical (e.g., a skin rash), while others are assuredly recognized as being mental (e.g., neuroses), yet it is impossible to deny the interaction between the mind and the body and the effects of one upon the other.

Why is it, for example, that when we are infected with a cold-causing virus we do not always come down with the common cold? We shall soon discuss numerous diseases and illnesses to which the mind makes the body susceptible. These conditions are called **psychosomatic** (*psyche* for mind; *soma* for body). Psychosomatic disease is not "all in the mind" but involves both mind and body. In fact, the term **psychophysiological** is now sometimes used in place of psychosomatic. Psychosomatic disease is real, can be diagnosed, and is manifested physically. However, it also has a component in the mind, although it is not easily measured. That common cold may be a function of psychological

psychosomatic
Conditions that have both a mind and body component.

psychophysiological
Synonymous with psychosomatic.

Doctors can go a long way in helping people respond to illness and disease, but approximately half of all deaths in the United States are a result of poor lifestyle choices such as poor nutrition, lack of physical activity, smoking, and the inability to manage stress.

stress, which decreases the effectiveness of the immunological system and results in the body being more vulnerable to cold viruses. That cold may also be caused by psychological stress using up particular vitamins in the body and leading to decreased effectiveness in combating cold viruses.

Psychosomatic disease may be psychogenic or somatogenic. **Psychogenic** refers to a physical disease caused by emotional stress. Asthma is an example of a psychogenic psychosomatic disease. In this case, there is no invasion of disease-causing microorganisms; the mind changes the physiology so that parts of the body break down. **Somatogenic** psychosomatic disease occurs when the mind increases the body's susceptibility to some disease-causing microbes or some natural degenerative process. Examples of diseases suspected of being somatogenic are cancer and rheumatoid arthritis, although there are other causes of these conditions as well.

Stress and the Immunological System

There is a field of scientific inquiry that studies the chemical basis of communication between the mind and the body—in particular, the link between the nervous system and the immune system.[6,7] In 1980, psychologist Robert Ader of the University of Rochester medical school named this scientific field **psychoneuroimmunology.** The focus of researchers in this field is on both the illness-causing and the healing effects the mind can have upon the body. Robert Ornstein and David Sobel summarized data linking the social world to a decrease in the effectiveness of the immunological system.[8] They cite studies that have found the following: Bereaved people have immunological systems functioning below par; rats exposed to stress develop larger cancerous tumors than other rats; West Point cadets who develop mononucleosis come disproportionately from families with fathers who were overachievers; and reoccurrences of oral herpes simplex are associated with stress and the person's emotional reaction to the disease.

On the other hand, you may be able to enhance the functioning of your immunological system by becoming less stressed. College students who watched humorous videotapes,[9] elderly people who practiced progressive relaxation,[10] and others who used biofeedback[11] and imagery[12] to relax were found to have a strengthened immune response (e.g., greater natural killer cell activity—NKA).

psychogenic

A physical disease caused by emotional stress without a microorganism involved.

somatogenic

A psychosomatic disease that results from the mind increasing the body's susceptibility to disease-causing microbes or natural degenerative processes.

psychoneuroimmunology

The study of the illness-causing and healing effects of the mind on the body.

Stressing and Unstressing

Two newspaper articles highlight the mind-body potential for causing illness and for alleviating it. The first one concerns "whistleblower stress"—the stress experienced by government employees who report wrongdoings and misuse of funds to people of authority. It seems that these whistleblowers are subsequently subjected to harassment and strain. They often become suicidal or manifest other signs of mental or physical disease.[a]

The second article describes the research of psychologist Paul Ekman, who found that facial expressions elicit specific bodily responses. Facial expression of anger leads to an increased heart rate and skin temperature. Expression of fear, however, results in increased heart rate but a decrease in skin temperature. These changes occur even when the person does not feel these emotions but only acts them out facially.[b]

Could treatment for whistleblowers someday include acting class? Will the rest of us also learn how to mimic emotion facially to make our bodies healthier?

[a]Jack Anderson, "Whistleblower Stress," *Washington Post,* 24 March 1985, C7.
[b]Sally Squires, "When You're Smiling, the Whole Immune System Smiles with You," *Washington Post,* 9 January 1985, 16.

To understand the relationship between stress and these findings requires an understanding of the immunological system. The most important component of this system is the white blood cell; we each have about 1 trillion of these cells. White blood cells fall into three groups: the **phagocytes** and two kinds of lymphocytes—**T cells** and **B cells.** These three groups all share one function—to identify and destroy all substances foreign to the body.

When a foreign substance—for example, a virus—invades your body, some of it is initially consumed by the most important phagocytes—the *macrophages.* Macrophages surround and engulf invading substances while summoning *helper T cells.* Helper T cells identify the invader and stimulate the multiplication of *killer T cells* and *B cells.* Killer T cells puncture the membranes of body cells invaded by the foreign substance, thereby killing the cell and the substance. B cells produce antibodies that travel to the site of invasion and either neutralize the enemy or tag it for attack by other cells and chemicals. As the invasion becomes contained, **suppressor T cells** are produced that halt the immune response and **memory T and B cells** are left in the bloodstream and in the lymphatic system to recognize and respond quickly to a future attack by the same invader. Anything that decreases your number of white blood cells, or any of their component parts, threatens your health. Stress has that effect.

Several researchers have studied personality and health status and have concluded that stress and related constructs can indeed lead to ill health. In an interesting article entitled "The 'Disease-Prone Personality,'" researchers Howard Friedman and Stephanie Booth-Kewley[13] cite evidence that a disease-prone personality exists that involves depression, anger/hostility, and anxiety. Psychologist Hans Eysenck,[14] entitling his article "Health's Character," presents evidence for a cancer-prone personality (unassertive, overpatient, avoiding conflicts, and failing to express negative emotions) and a coronary heart disease–prone personality (angry, hostile, and aggressive).

The specific effects of stress on immunity have also been researched. In one study,[15] college students' levels of an antibody that fights infections (salivary IgA) were tested five days before, on the day of, and two weeks after their final exams. As expected, S-IgA levels were lowest during the exam period, the most stressful time tested. In another interesting study,[16] positive moods were induced in subjects by asking them to

phagocytes
A type of white blood cell whose purpose is to destroy substances foreign to the body.

T cells
A type of lymphocyte whose purpose is to destroy substances foreign to the body by puncturing invaded body cells and killing the cells and the foreign substances.

B cells
A type of lymphocyte that produces antibodies.

suppressor T cells
Cells whose purpose is to halt the immune response.

memory T and B cells
Cells left in the bloodstream and the lymphatic system to recognize and respond to future attacks to the body by the same invader.

"experience care and compassion." When the researchers measured S-IgA levels during these positive states, they found them to be increased. The researchers concluded that, whereas negative moods (stress) could decrease S-IgA levels thereby making people more susceptible to disease, positive moods could increase S-IgA levels and, consequently, enhance immunosuppressive effects.

Dr. Candace Pert, a neuroscientist and the former section chief of brain biochemistry at the National Institute of Mental Health, has investigated chemicals that send messages between cells to various parts of the brain and between the brain and other parts of the body. Hundreds of these brain message transmitters (called *neuropeptides*) have been found that are produced by the brain itself. The aspect pertinent to our discussion of the mind-body connection is that Pert believes some of these neuropeptides are also produced in small amounts by the macrophages—white blood cells that ingest and destroy bacteria and viruses.[17] In addition, the macrophages are attracted to neuropeptides produced by the brain. If neuropeptides are produced by the brain to fight off an invasion of bacteria, for instance, macrophages will also travel to help combat the invasion. Since relaxation and some forms of visualization result in the production of neuropeptides (e.g., beta-endorphins), it may be possible to purposefully cause the brain to produce more of these substances, thereby making the immunological system more effective. The result may be less disease.

Other evidence of the importance of the mind to physical illness also exists. For example, dental students who had depressed moods were also found to have lowered antibody production and thereby were more susceptible to foreign substances.[18] Women experiencing marital separation had 40 percent fewer natural killer cells (cells that fight viruses and tumors) and 20 percent fewer T cells than married women of similar age and social background.[19] Men's recoveries from heart attacks are also affected by their minds. When men recovering from a heart attack were given an illusion of some control over their health (such as very simple exercises to do), they encountered fewer complications and shorter stays in the cardiac care unit.[20] The suspicion is that feeling in control alleviated the stress experienced from helplessness. Emotions have also been found to play an important role in preventing a second heart attack. Some experts have even suggested that no illness is completely free from the influence of stress.[21]

Stress and Serum Cholesterol

Cholesterol roaming about your blood can accumulate on the walls of your blood vessels, blocking the flow of blood to various parts of your body. When it is the heart that is blocked, you may develop coronary heart disease or die of a heart attack caused by an insufficient supply of oxygen to the heart. When it is the brain that is blocked, you may develop a stroke or die from an insufficient supply of oxygen to the brain. Researchers have attempted to determine the causes of increased levels of serum cholesterol so they can help people avoid this condition; they have found stress to be one of the culprits. Friedman, Rosenman, and Carroll conducted one of the early investigations of the relationship between stress and serum cholesterol.[22] They studied accountants during times of the year when they had deadlines to meet—for example, when tax returns had to be prepared—and found average serum cholesterol increased dramatically. Other researchers have verified these results. For example, when medical students were studied just before and just after their final examinations, 20 of 21 of them had higher serum-cholesterol levels before this stressful event.[23] In another investigation, military pilots at the beginning of their training showed increased serum-cholesterol levels, and the levels were highest during examination periods.[24] Clarifying the relationship between stress and serum cholesterol is the study of 7,000 men by Tucker, Cole, and Friedman in which they conclude that "when it comes to differences in serum-cholesterol levels, the perceptions people have of their problems play a more significant role than the problems themselves."[25] They go on to recommend that "given this finding and the supporting results of related research,[26] increased efforts to determine the impact of managing perceptions of stress to alter serum-cholesterol levels would appear warranted and worthwhile."

Specific diseases and illnesses are discussed next, but the important concept here is that a person is an interconnected whole. A separation, even just for discussion or research purposes, of the mind from the body is inappropriate. The mind is ultimately affected by what the body experiences, and the body is ultimately affected by what the mind experiences.

Specific Conditions

Now that you understand the concept of psychosomatic disease, we can look at specific diseases and their relationship to stress. As you will discover, stress can lead to both psychogenic and somatogenic psychosomatic diseases.

Hypertension

Hypertension (high blood pressure) is excessive and damaging pressure of the blood against the walls of the arterial blood vessels. Blood pressure is measured with a **sphygmomanometer,** an instrument consisting of an inflatable cuff placed around the upper arm and a stethoscope. The cuff cuts off the blood flow in the brachial artery until it is deflated to the point where the blood pressure forces the blood through. That measure is called the **systolic blood pressure,** and 120mm Hg is considered average (normal). At the point where the cuff is deflated further and the blood is not impeded at all, another measure is taken. That measure is termed the **diastolic blood pressure,** and 80mm Hg is considered average. The total blood pressure is given in this formula: systolic/diastolic (120/80). Systolic blood pressure represents the force against the arterial blood vessel walls when the left ventricle contracts and blood is pumped out of the heart. Diastolic blood pressure represents the force against the arterial walls when the heart is relaxed.

High blood pressure is a relative term. Health scientists disagree as to its exact beginning, but generally a systolic pressure greater than 140mm Hg or a diastolic pressure greater than 90mm Hg is considered hypertension. Because average blood pressure tends to be higher in the elderly than in others, measures slightly above 140/90 are not unusual for this age group. However, that is not to say they are inevitable. Increased blood pressure may be related more to lifestyle than to age.

There are several causes of hypertension. Excessive sodium (salt) intake may cause hypertension in those genetically susceptible. Since we can't determine who is genetically susceptible, dietary guidelines in the United States suggest no more than a 5,000mg daily ingestion of salt. The average diet has been estimated to consist of 10g–20g (10,000mg–20,000mg) of salt daily. The problem with monitoring salt in our diets is that it is hidden in many processed foods. Those who just eliminate the saltshaker may still be ingesting too much salt.

Hypertension may also be caused by kidney disease, too narrow an opening in the aorta (main blood vessel through which blood exits the heart), Cushing's syndrome (oversecretion of cortisol hormones), obesity, and the use of oral contraceptives. However, these conditions cause only an estimated 10 percent of all hypertension. Approximately 90 percent of hypertension is termed **essential hypertension** and has no known cause.

Forty-one percent of the United States population aged twenty to seventy-four is hypertensive, although many of these people do not even know it, since hypertension occurs without signs and symptoms. Even though many people believe high blood pressure is a condition that affects only older adults, in actuality slightly over 16 percent of twenty- to twenty-four-year-olds are hypertensive. More men than women are hypertensive, and the likelihood of developing hypertension increases with age. Proportionately more blacks than whites are hypertensive. The lowest incidence is found in white women and the highest incidence in black women.

Imagine, for a moment, the Alaska pipeline. Through that tube, oil is pumped that passes through Alaska. When that pipeline works correctly, oil is provided in sufficient quantity without any breaks in the pipeline. What would happen, though, if so much oil were pumped through that it created too great a pressure against the metal tube? The tube would probably rupture. The same thing happens with blood pressure,

sphygmomanometer
An instrument used to measure blood pressure.

systolic blood pressure
The pressure of the blood as it leaves the heart.

diastolic blood pressure
The pressure of the blood against the arterial walls when the heart is relaxed.

essential hypertension
Hypertension with no known cause.

cerebral hemorrhage
A rupture of a blood vessel in the brain.

myocardial infarction
When a part of the heart dies because of a lack of oxygen.

plaque
Debris that clogs coronary arteries.

apoplexy
A lack of oxygen to the brain resulting from a blockage or rupture of a blood vessel; also called stroke.

stroke
A lack of oxygen to the brain resulting from a blockage or rupture of a blood vessel; also called apoplexy.

blood, and blood vessels. Blood is analogous to oil, and blood vessels (in particular, arteries) are analogous to the pipeline. If blood creates too great a pressure upon the arterial walls, they will rupture, and the blood intended for some destination beyond the point of rupture will not reach its goal. If the rupture is in the brain, we call that a **cerebral hemorrhage.** If a coronary artery ruptures, and part of the heart dies from lack of oxygen usually transported to it by the blood, we call that a **myocardial infarction.** Blood can also be prevented from reaching its destination by a blockage of the blood vessels or a narrowing of the vessels by debris (**plaque**) collecting on their inner walls.

Since blood pressure as well as serum cholesterol increase during stress (plaque is made up of cholesterol), the relationship between stress and hypertension has long been suspected. Emotional stress is generally regarded as a major factor in the etiology of hypertension.[27] Recognizing this relationship, educational programs for hypertensives have included stress management.[28] Although hypertension can be controlled with medication, the possibility of disturbing side effects from these drugs has led to attempts to control hypertension in other ways. Since obesity, cigarette smoking, and lack of exercise are correlates to hypertension, programs involving weight control, smoking withdrawal, and exercise, as well as decreased ingestion of salt, have all been used to respond to high blood pressure.

Stress management has also been employed to control high blood pressure. Unfortunately, too many health care providers tell a hypertensive person that he or she needs to "relax" without providing instruction in how to do so. A notable exception is Dr. Herbert Benson, a cardiologist who has used meditation to reduce blood pressure in hypertensive patients. His patients are instructed in how to meditate and do so in the clinical setting with instructions to meditate between hospital visits. Described in his books *The Relaxation Response,*[29] *Beyond the Relaxation Response,*[30] *Timeless Healing,*[31] and *The Wellness Book,*[32] Dr. Benson's technique has been quite successful.[33]

Further evidence of the relationship between stress and essential hypertension appears in the massive study of 1,600 hospital patients by Flanders Dunbar in the 1940s.[34] Dunbar found that certain personality traits were characteristic of hypertensive patients. For example, they were easily upset by criticism or imperfection, possessed pent-up anger, and lacked self-confidence. One can readily see the role stress might play in "setting off" these susceptible people.

Stroke

Apoplexy (also termed **stroke**) is a lack of oxygen in the brain resulting from a blockage or rupture of one of the arteries that supply it. Depending on the exact location of the brain tissue dying from this lack of oxygen and the amount of time oxygen was denied, paralysis, speech impairment, motor-function impairment, or death may result. Stroke is related to hypertension, which may also result in a cerebral hemorrhage (rupture of a major blood vessel supplying the brain). Cardiovascular disorders, of which apoplexy is one, kill more Americans each year than any other disorder. Stroke has been related to high blood pressure, diet, and stress.[35]

Coronary Heart Disease

Heart attacks kill more Americans than any other single cause of death. That stress is related to coronary heart disease is not surprising when we consider the physiological mechanisms that stress brings into play: accelerated heart rate, increased blood pressure, increased serum cholesterol, and fluid retention resulting in increased blood volume. Further, the stereotypical heart attack victim has been the highly stressed, overworked, overweight businessman with a cigarette dangling from his lips and a martini in his hand.

Coronary heart disease has been associated with diets high in saturated fats, a lack of exercise, obesity, heredity, and even maleness and baldness. However, the three major risk factors generally agreed to be most associated with coronary heart disease are *hypercholesterolemia* (high serum cholesterol), hypertension, and cigarette smoking; and yet, two researchers state:

> Largely unquestioned, however, has been the repeated finding that these factors are completely absent in more than half of all the new cases of coronary heart disease encountered in clinical practice. Indeed, most patients do not have high blood cholesterol, and only a fraction have high blood pressure. Data from pooled prospective studies in the United States actually show that of men with two or more of these alleged risks, only about 10 percent develop coronary heart disease over a ten-year period, while the remainder do not.... Almost twenty years ago we discovered that young coronary patients could be differentiated from healthy control subjects far more readily by the dimensions of occupational stress than by differences in heredity, diet, obesity, tobacco consumption, or exercise. In our study it was found that at the time of their attack 91 percent of 100 patients as compared with only 20 percent of healthy controls had been holding down two or more jobs, working more than sixty hours per week, or experiencing unusual insecurity, discontent, or frustration in relation to employment.[36]

Those researchers go on to present data from studies in which various professionals ranked the specialties within their professions by stress level. Next, the prevalence of coronary heart disease by specialty was determined. The more stressful the specialty, the more prevalent was coronary heart disease. For example, within the practice of medicine, dermatology was found to be the least stressful specialty and the general medical practice the most stressful. Consistent with the theory that stress is related to coronary heart disease, dermatologists had a lower prevalence of heart disease than general practitioners during their younger years (40–49) as well as later in life (60–69). Similarly, periodontists were the least stressful of the dentists, with general practitioner dentists being the most stressful. As with the physicians, the least stressful dentists (periodontists) had a lower prevalence of coronary heart disease than the most stressful dentists (the general practitioners). The same held true for attorneys. The least stressful (patent attorneys) had the lowest prevalence of coronary heart disease, and the most stressful (the general practice attorneys who handle a variety of cases) had the highest rate of coronary heart disease. When we add to this our knowledge that heart attack deaths for men in the United States are most prevalent on Mondays and least prevalent on Fridays, we can consider stress in general, and occupational stress in particular, a major cause of coronary heart disease.

Further evidence of the relationship between stress and coronary heart disease was presented in the studies of Meyer Friedman and Ray Rosenman. These two cardiologists and their work are discussed in more detail in Chapter 7. For purposes of this discussion, suffice it to say that Friedman and Rosenman identified a **Type A** behavior pattern disproportionately represented among heart attack patients. These patients were aggressive, competitive, time-urgent, and hostile; often found themselves doing things quickly; were overly concerned with numbers (quantity rather than quality); and often did more than one thing at a time (e.g., read the newspaper over breakfast).[37] A comprehensive review of studies of the Type A behavior pattern has verified the relationship between these stress-related behaviors and coronary heart disease;[38] however, other researchers have found conflicting results, some finding hostility to be the prime culprit.[39] We discuss the Type A behavior pattern in greater detail in Chapter 7.

The physiological mechanisms that appear to lead from chronic stress down the road to coronary heart disease seem to be related to the increased serum cholesterol, blood pressure, blood volume, and accelerated heart rate associated with stress reactivity. The last three make the heart work harder, and the first (hypercholesterolemia) leads to clogging of arteries (**atherosclerosis**) and eventual loss of elasticity of the coronary and other arteries (**arteriosclerosis**). Both of these conditions also result in an excessive workload for the heart muscle, as well as a decreased supply of oxygen to the heart itself. Not to be disregarded, however, is the interaction between other coronary risk factors and stress. One might expect a person who is overstressed not to have time to exercise, to overeat as a reward for "hard work," or to smoke cigarettes to relax (actually, nicotine is physiologically a stimulant). Consequently, the negative

Type A
A behavior pattern associated with the development of coronary heart disease.

atherosclerosis
Clogging of the coronary arteries.

arteriosclerosis
Loss of elasticity of the coronary arteries.

effects of stress upon the heart are often multiplied by the introduction of other heart-damaging behaviors.

Another physiological mechanism explaining the relationship between stress and coronary heart disease relates to production of plasma homocysteine. Homocysteine is an amino acid formed during the metabolism of plasma methionine, an amino acid derived from dietary proteins. Increased levels of homocysteine have been associated with an increased risk of coronary heart disease.[40] In a study of the effects of anger and hostility on homocysteine levels, Stoney[41] found a positive association between these variables. As anger and hostility increased, so did the level of homocysteine in the blood. Stoney concluded that "it is possible that one mechanism for the increased risk of CHD as a function of psychological stress is through a stress-associated elevation in homocysteine."[42]

Other researchers have found additional factors explaining the relationship between stress and coronary heart disease. For example, Everson and her colleagues found stress to exacerbate the effects of socioeconomic status on carotid artery atherosclerosis.[43] As one stress investigator put it:

> . . . low SES may have indirect influence on lipid and hemostatic profiles through smoking and lack of exercise. For example, the neuroendocrine response to a stressful psychosocial environment may be determined by the person's cognitive appraisal of the severity of environmental demands in relation to his or her own coping resources. A lack of balance between demands (e.g., job stress) and buffering resources (e.g., social network) evokes negative emotions (such as hopelessness). Negative emotions may lead to smoking, lack of exercise, and poor diet, which may in part be reflected by obesity and poor lipid and hemostatic profiles. Another hypothesis is that psychosocial stress may have direct effects on physiological systems independent of effects on health behaviors. For example, psychosocial stress may result in pathogenic physiological mechanisms, through nervous and endocrine processes. Stress hormones, including catecholamines, have pronounced effects on hemodynamics, lipid metabolism, hemostasis, and other aspects of metabolism.[44]

Hostility may be one of these psychosocial stressors changing physiological mechanisms resulting in heart disease. A study by Iribarren and his colleagues demonstrated a two times greater prevalence in coronary calcification in young adult subjects who scored above the median in hostility.[45] Iribarren concludes that "Our results are consistent with the hypothesis that hostility might contribute to the development of coronary atherosclerosis not only through poor health habits. . . but via other physiological mechanisms." He then goes on to cite some possible physiological mechanisms such as cardiovascular reactivity, blood pressure morning surge, increased platelet activation, increased catecholamine levels, and prolonged neuroendocrine responses.

Another physiological mechanism researchers have found related to stress and coronary heart disease pertains to the heart's rhythm. McCraty and colleagues conducted studies of the variability in heart rhythm and concluded that it is modified by the autonomic nervous system and emotional state. The heart beats faster and less rhythmically during stress and "when a person is in a state of deep peace and inner harmony the heart shifts to a very regular and coherent rhythm."[46]

Ulcers

Ulcers are fissures or cuts in the wall of the stomach, duodenum, or other parts of the intestines. For many years, it was thought that stress led to the production of excessive amounts of hydrochloric acid in the stomach and the intestines. There was ample evidence for this conclusion. Selye reported that ulcers developed in the stomach and duodenum of rats exposed to stress.[47] When studying grief reactions, Lindemann reported thirty-three out of forty-one ulcer patients "developed their disease in close relationship to the loss of an important person."[48] Others have noted a sense of utter helplessness among ulcer patients and believe this feeling preceded, rather than resulted from, the development of ulcers.[49] Even unemployment has been shown to result in ulcers in men laid off from their jobs *and in the wives* of those men.[50]

One theory explaining the effects of stress on the development of ulcers pertains to the mucous coating that lines the stomach. The theory states that, during chronic stress, norepinephrine secretion causes capillaries in the stomach lining to constrict. This, in turn, results in a shutting down of mucosal production, and the mucous protective barrier for the stomach wall is lost. Without the protective barrier, hydrochloric acid breaks down the tissue and can even reach blood vessels, resulting in a bleeding ulcer.

However, it has since been discovered that many cases of ulcers—in particular, peptic ulcers—are caused by a bacteria called *Helicobacter pylori* (termed *H. pylori*). Although the exact mechanism by which it causes ulcers is unknown, it is believed that *H. pylori* inflames the gastrointestinal lining, stimulates acid production, or both. A panel convened by the National Institutes of Health has advised doctors to treat ulcers with a two-week course of antibiotics in combination with nonprescription bismuth. This is in contrast to the long-standing treatment by costly drugs used to block acid secretion. These drugs—called histamine blockers, or H2 blockers, such as Tagamet, Zantac, and Pepcid—are no longer necessary in many ulcer cases, although they are still helpful when ulcers are caused by something other than *H. pylori*.

Another major cause of ulcers is the ingestion of aspirin and other nonsteroidal anti-inflammatory drugs (*ibuprofen* such as in brand names Advil, Motrin, and Nuprin; *naproxen* such as in the brand name Naprosyn; and *piroxicam* such as in the brand name Feldene). These drugs promote bleeding in the stomach and can wear away its protective lining.

Still, stress can exacerbate the conditions in the digestive tract to make ulcers more likely to occur. Stress results in an increase in hydrochloric acid in the intestinal tract and stomach, and a decreased effectiveness of the immunological system that is marshaled to combat the invasion by *H. pylori*.

Migraine Headaches

Terry was a very busy and productive woman. She had two adorable boys and an equally adorable dentist husband (whom the boys greatly resembled). Because she felt her roles as mother and wife were not fulfilling enough, and because she had a special talent, Terry painted most afternoons and eventually entered a master's degree program in art. She did so well in her graduate work that, upon the awarding of her master's degree, she was asked to join the faculty. All of this wasn't enough, so she served on committees for local museums and civic organizations.

It was clear to everyone but Terry herself that she was doing too much. She had been having headaches. Soon, the headaches came more frequently and became more severe. Many a time Terry's neighbors had to watch her children while her husband drilled teeth and she hibernated in a bedroom darkened by drawn shades, waiting out the migraine. I know because I was one of Terry's neighbors.

Migraine headaches are the result of a constriction and dilation of the carotid arteries of one side of the head. The constriction phase, called the **preattack** or **prodrome**, is often associated with light or noise sensitivity, irritability, and a flushing or pallor of the skin. When the dilation of the arteries occurs, certain chemicals stimulate adjacent nerve endings, causing pain.

Over the years, extreme measures have been taken to treat migraines. Among these "treatments" are tiny holes bored into the skull, bleeding of the scalp, and the ingestion of mercury (which cured the headache by killing the patient). English physicians even applied a mixture of dried houseflies and hot vinegar to the scalp and, when blisters appeared, punctured them in the hopes of finding an outlet for the pain.

The migraine is not just a severe headache. It is a unique type of headache with special characteristics, and it usually involves just one side of the head. The prodrome consists of warning signs, such as flashing lights, differing patterns, or some dark spaces. The prodrome usually occurs one or two hours prior to the headache itself. The actual headache usually involves a throbbing pain that lasts approximately six hours (although this varies greatly from person to person). An interesting point about migraine attacks is that they usually occur after a pressure-packed situation is over,

preattack
Synonymous with prodrome.

prodrome
The constriction phase of a migraine headache; also called preattack.

rather than when the pressure is being experienced. Consequently, attacks often occur on weekends. Many of Terry's weekends were spent waiting out a migraine.

Migraines are quite prevalent. They plague approximately 28 million Americans,[51] more women than men.[52] They can also be quite costly to employers when their workers are prone to them. It is estimated that migraines cost businesses $13 billion a year.[53]

Diet may precipitate migraine headaches for some people. Chocolate, aged cheese, and red wine are implicated culprits. However, predominant thought on the cause of migraine focuses on emotional stress and tension. "Feelings of anxiety, nervous tension, anger, or repressed rage are associated with migraine. . . . An attack may be aborted when the individual gives vent to underlying hostility."[54] A typical migraine sufferer is a perfectionist, "ambitious, rigid, orderly, excessively competitive, and unable to delegate responsibility."[55] Sound like someone you know?

Although migraines most often occur between the ages of sixteen and thirty-five and are greatly reduced in frequency by age fifty, migraine sufferers aren't willing to wait years for relief. Medications of various sorts are available for migraine sufferers, most of which contain ergotamine tartrate and are taken during the prodrome to constrict the carotid arteries. Migraine medication, however, may produce side effects: weakness in the legs, muscle pain, numbness, and heart-rate irregularity.

Other relief that does not produce disturbing side effects is available to sufferers of migraine headaches. Since the major problem is the dilation of blood vessels in the head, any method of preventing an increased blood flow to the head would help prevent or treat migraine. Relaxation techniques that are discussed later in this book (biofeedback, meditation, and autogenic training) result in an increased blood flow in the peripheral blood system (arms and legs). This increased flow comes from several areas, of which the head is one. As you might imagine, these techniques have been found successful in the prevention and treatment of migraine.[56]

An important point needs to be made here. Migraines are a sign and symptom of a lifestyle gone awry. Treating signs and symptoms with either medication or meditation without eliminating the underlying cause (one's lifestyle) reminds me of the following poem:

> Twas a dangerous cliff, as they freely confessed,
> Though to walk near its crest was so pleasant;
> But over its terrible edge there had slipped
> A duke, and full many a peasant.
> The people said something would have to be done,
> But their projects did not at all tally.
> Some said, "Put a fence 'round the edge of the cliff";
> Some, "An ambulance down in the valley."
> The lament of the crowd was profound and was loud,
> As their hearts overflowed with their pity;
> But the cry for the ambulance carried the day
> As it spread through the neighboring city,
> A collection was made to accumulate aid,
> And the dwellers in highway and alley
> Gave dollars or cents—not to finish a fence—
> But an ambulance down in the valley.
> The story looks queer as we've written it here,
> But things oft occur that are stranger,
> More humane, we assert, than to succor the hurt,
> Is the plan of removing the danger.
> The best possible course is to safeguard the source;
> Attend to things rationally.
> Yes, build up the fence, and let us dispense
> With the ambulance down in the valley.

Courtesy American Chiropractic Association, Arlington, VA.

Rather than care for the migraine after it occurs or during the prodrome, why not prevent it in the first place by changing your lifestyle? Help in doing that is available in subsequent chapters of this book.

Tension Headaches

Headaches are serious business—yes, business. Not only do many pharmaceutical companies and health care providers make a good deal of money treating headache sufferers, but businesses also suffer their consequences. Pain from headaches can affect a worker's ability to do physical work (e.g., lift, walk, or even sit) and his or her cognitive work performance (e.g., ability to think, concentrate, or effectively interact with others). One study found that 36 percent of people who suffered from moderate to severe headache pain were unable to obtain or keep full-time work at some time during the three-year study period.[57]

Headaches may be caused by muscle tension accompanying stress. This muscle tension may affect the forehead, jaw, or neck. I'm often amazed at the numbers of students who come to my classes, especially the early or late evening ones, with tension headaches. Perhaps a whole day of work or school is the instigator, but we all have control over our own muscles. If we only knew how to relax them prior to the onset of a tension headache! Once the headache occurs, it tends to fuel itself. It is difficult to relax when you're in pain.

Stress can lead to tension headaches, which can be quite debilitating.

Treatment for tension headaches may include medication (aspirin or a tranquilizer), heat on tense muscles, or massage. However, just as I'm amazed at the number of students entering my classes with tension headaches, I'm also amazed (actually, I've long since stopped being amazed about the potency of stress management) at the numbers of students who leave my classes without headaches when we've been practicing a relaxation technique. Others have also reported on the effectiveness of relaxation training (in particular, biofeedback) for control and prevention of tension headaches.[58–60] As with migraines, however, an ounce of prevention is worth a pound of cure.

Cancer

Although many people do not realize it, both the prevention and the treatment of cancer are suspected of being related to stress. Cancer is really several diseases, some of which may be caused by ingested **carcinogens** (cancer-causing agents), some by inhaled carcinogens (in the environment or in cigarette smoke), and some by viruses. In any case, cancer is the unbridled multiplication of cells that leads to tumors and, eventually, organ damage.

When a viral cancer occurs, the immunological system—particularly its lymphocytesis—is called into play.[61] The number of **T-lymphocytes** that normally destroy mutant cells prior to their multiplying and causing damage is reduced during stress. Consequently, some researchers believe that chronic stress results in a chronic inability of the immune response to prevent the multiplication of mutant cells, which some believe are present but normally controlled in most people.

The role of stress in the development of cancer is still being debated, but because cancer is the second leading cause of death in the United States, research in this area has been and is presently being conducted. Support for the role of stress in the development of malignancy has been found in these studies. When experimental mice whose mothers had a cancerous virus were divided into two groups (one stressed and one not), 90 percent of the stressed mice as compared with only 7 percent of the mice not stressed developed cancer.[62] Further, some support has been provided for a cancer-prone personality type. The cancer-prone person has been described as (1) holding resentment, with the inability to forgive; (2) using self-pity; (3) lacking the ability to

carcinogens
Cancer-causing agents.

T-lymphocytes
A part of the immune system that destroys mutant cells.

develop and maintain meaningful interpersonal relationships; and (4) having a poor self-image.[63] Cancer patients were also found to have experienced severe emotional disturbances in childhood (parents divorced, death in the family, etc.), resulting in their feeling lonely, anxious, and rejected.[64] The classic study by Lawrence LeShan in the 1950s of the psychological characteristics of cancer patients found that these patients differed from healthy controls. The patients more frequently

1. Reported a lost relationship prior to the cancer diagnosis.
2. Were unable to express hostility in their own defense.
3. Felt unworthy and disliked themselves.
4. Had a tense relationship with one or both parents.[65]

Even the treatment of cancer has included the recognition that the mind can affect the body. Cancer patients have been taught to imagine the T-lymphocytes attacking the cancerous cells. These visualization skills and other relaxation techniques are utilized because it seems sensible to conclude that if T-lymphocytes are decreased during the stress response, they will be increased during the relaxation response. The immunological system will then be more potent in controlling the cancerous cells. It should be recognized, however, that this type of treatment for cancer is controversial and experimental. Further, visualization therapy always includes more treatment modalities as well—for example, X-ray, chemical, and surgical methods.

Allergies, Asthma, and Hay Fever

Allergies—asthma and hay fever are but two examples—are the body's defense against a foreign, irritating substance called an **antigen.** In response to this antigen, the body produces **antibodies.** Among their other functions, antibodies stimulate the release of chemicals. Histamine, one of these chemicals, causes tissues to swell, mucous secretions to increase, and air passages in the lungs to constrict. Now you know why the drug of choice for allergy sufferers is an antihistamine.

Some medical scientists, unable to identify any antigen in many asthmatics, have argued that allergies are emotional diseases. Supporting this theory is the result of an experiment in which a woman who was allergic to horses began to wheeze when shown only a picture of a horse; another woman who was allergic to fish had an allergic reaction to a toy fish and empty fishbowl; and others reacted to uncontaminated air when suspecting it contained pollen.[66] Crying-induced asthma, brought on during stressful events, is another example.[67]

In support of the relationship between emotional factors (in particular, stress) and allergic reactions, recall the decrease in the effectiveness of the immunological system discussed previously. The reduced number of T-lymphocytes that results during stress means decreased effectiveness in controlling antigens, since it is these T cells that destroy the antigens (either by direct contact or by secreting toxins). Further, we know that the cortisol secreted by the adrenal cortex during the stress response decreases the effectiveness of histamine.

Some have concluded, therefore, that the effects of stress on the immunological system either decrease our ability to withstand an antigen (meaning a decreased allergic threshold) or, even in the absence of an antigen, can lead to an allergiclike response (see Figure 3.1). Some allergy sufferers—in particular, asthmatics—are being taught relaxation techniques and breathing-control exercises to enable them to control their physiology during allergic reactions. As you will learn in the next chapter, such an approach to stress management is incomplete if it doesn't also include adjustments in the life situation to avoid stressors in the first place or change our perceptions of the stressors we encounter.

Rheumatoid Arthritis

Rheumatoid arthritis afflicts a large number of U.S. citizens (three times as many women as men) with inflammation and swelling in various body joints, which may proceed developmentally to be extremely painful and debilitating. The exact cause of this condition

antigen
A foreign substance irritating to the body.

antibodies
Substances produced by the body to fight antigens.

Figure 3.1

Stress and the immune response.

is unknown, though it is suspected of being related to the faulty functioning of the immune response.

The normal joint is lined with a synovial membrane, which secretes fluid to lubricate the joint. In rheumatoid arthritis, this synovial membrane multiplies exceedingly fast and creates swelling. This swelling can cause the membrane to enter the joint itself, eventually to deteriorate the cartilage covering the ends of the bones, and perhaps even to erode the bone itself. The last stages of this disease process may be the development of scar tissue that immobilizes the joint and makes for knobbiness and deformity. The beginning of rheumatoid arthritis may be an infection of the synovial cells. For some reason, antibodies produced to fight this infection may attack healthy as well as unhealthy cells, leading to multiplication to replace the healthy cells. Then the process described above occurs.

It also appears that some people are hereditarily susceptible to rheumatoid arthritis. Approximately half of the sufferers of this condition have a blood protein called the **rheumatoid factor,** which is rare in nonarthritic people.

Since rheumatoid arthritis involves the body's turning on itself (an **autoimmune response**), it was hypothesized that a self-destructive personality may manifest itself through this disease. Although the evidence to support this hypothesis is not conclusive, several investigators have found personality differences between rheumatoid arthritis sufferers and others. Those afflicted with this disease have been found to be perfectionists who are self-sacrificing, masochistic, self-conscious, shy, and inhibited. Female rheumatoid patients were found to be nervous, moody, and depressed, with a history of being rejected by their mothers and having strict fathers.[68] It has been suggested that people with the rheumatoid factor who experience chronic stress become susceptible to

rheumatoid factor
A blood protein associated with rheumatoid arthritis.

autoimmune response
A physiological response in which the body turns on itself.

rheumatoid arthritis. Their immunological system malfunctions, and their genetic predisposition to rheumatoid arthritis results in their developing the condition. We know, for instance, that stress can precipitate arthritic attacks. Because the standard treatment of cortisone brings with it the possible side effects of brittle bones, fat deposits, loss of muscular strength, ulcers, and psychosis, it would be very significant if stress management techniques were found to be effective in reducing the amount of cortisone needed.

Backache

Like headaches, backaches affect people's abilities to do physical and cognitive work. Stang and his colleagues found that 48 percent of people who suffered from moderate-to-severe back pain were unable to obtain or keep full-time work at some time during the three-year study period.[69] Millions of people suffer backache and erroneously bemoan their posture or jobs. Certainly, backache may result from lifting a heavy object incorrectly or from structural problems.[70] The vast majority of backache problems, however, are the result of muscular weakness or muscular bracing. One of the experts on backache, Dr. Henry Feffer, suggests exercise as the best preventive measure.[71]

As with tension headaches, bracing causes muscle to lose its elasticity and fatigue easily. Bracing may lead to muscle spasms and back pain. This constant muscular contraction is found in people who are competitive, angry, and apprehensive. Backaches have been found more frequently in people who have experienced a good deal of stress.[72]

TMJ Syndrome

The temporomandibular joint, which connects the upper to the lower jaw, is a complex structure requiring the coordination of five muscles and several ligaments. When something interferes with the smooth operation of this joint, **temporomandibular (TMJ) syndrome** may develop (see Figure 3.2). TMJ syndrome sufferers may have facial pain, clicking or popping sounds when they open or close their mouths, migraine headaches, earaches, ringing in the ears, dizziness, or sensitive teeth. It is most often women between the ages of twenty and forty who develop TMJ syndrome, although estimates vary widely as to how many in the population experience this condition (from 28 percent to 86 percent—obviously, it is difficult to diagnose).[73] TMJ syndrome has many causes. It can develop as a result of malocclusion of the teeth, a blow to the head, gum chewing, nail biting, or jaw jutting. However, the most common cause is clenching or grinding of the teeth (termed *bruxism*) due to stress.[74] Treatment often consists of wearing an acrylic mouthpiece (an orthodontic splint)—either twenty-four hours a day or only while asleep—the dentist adjusting the bite by selectively grinding the teeth, using crowns and bridges, or orthodontia. In addition, stress reduction techniques such as biofeedback are taught to TMJ sufferers to relax the jaw and to limit teeth grinding (especially when done during the waking hours).[75]

temporomandibular (TMJ) syndrome
The interference with the smooth functioning of the jaw.

Figure 3.2

The disc separating the bones of the temporomandibular joint may pop loose, causing discomfort. Grinding the teeth as a result of stress can also lead to muscular pain and/or misalignment of the upper and lower jawbones.

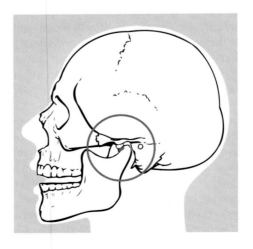

It seems clear from the research literature that illness and disease may be stress related. Such conditions as TMJ syndrome, hypertension, stroke, heart disease, ulcers, migraines, tension headaches, cancer, allergies, asthma, hay fever, rheumatoid arthritis, and backache may develop because the body has changed its physiology because of what the mind has experienced. Recognizing the vast physiological changes associated with the stress response, it should not be surprising that poor health can result from stress. Likewise, that poor health is itself stressful and further aggravates the condition is only common sense. The conclusion that can be drawn from all of this is that managing stress can help prevent disease and illness and can be a valuable adjunct to therapy once they have developed. The wonders of the mind-body relationship are only beginning to be realized. The fruits of this knowledge are only beginning to be harvested. There are, though, some insights that you can use immediately to improve the quality of your life. These are presented in Part 2 of this book.

Posttraumatic Stress Disorder

Posttraumatic stress disorder (PTSD) is a condition that develops in people who have experienced an extreme psychological or physical event that is interpreted as particularly distressing. The American Psychiatric Association's *Diagnostic and Statistical Manual*[76] describes PTSD as involving

1. A threat to one's life or serious injury or being subject to horror with intense fear and helplessness.

2. Recurrent flashbacks, repeated memories and emotions, dreams, nightmares, illusions, or hallucinations related to traumatic events from which one is often amnesic.

PTSD first appeared as a diagnosis in the American Psychiatric Association's *Diagnostic and Statistical Manual* in 1980. The diagnosis was revised in 1987 and appears in the latest version of the *Manual* (1994). The *International Classification of Disease,* published by the World Health Organization, added PTSD in 1992.[77] In the year 2000, a committee of the International Consensus Group on Depression and Anxiety refined the definition of PTSD:

> PSTD is often a chronic and recurring condition associated with an increased risk of developing secondary comorbid disorders, such as depression. Selective serotonin reuptake inhibitors are generally the most appropriate choice of first-line medication for PTSD, and effective therapy should be continued for 12 months or longer. The most appropriate psychotherapy is exposure therapy, and it should be continued for 6 months, with follow-up therapy as needed.[78]

PTSD is more prevalent than many of us realize. Epidemiologists report that most people will experience a traumatic event and that up to 25 percent of them will develop PTSD.[79, 80] Some experts believe PTSD is as prevalent as any other mental disorder, yet only a minority of people obtain treatment.[81] A history of mental illness in oneself or one's family increases the likelihood of developing PTSD.[82] Being prone to anxiety attacks or depression also increases this likelihood.[83] However, not everyone who experiences trauma develops posttraumatic stress disorder. Furthermore, if you can anticipate a traumatic event, you can decrease the likelihood of that event's resulting in PTSD. This was demonstrated in a study of 106 British soldiers returning from United Nations peacekeeping duties in the former Yugoslavia.[84] In anticipation of the trauma they would experience, they received an Operational Stress Training Package. As a result, very low rates of PTSD were experienced by these soldiers. The researchers concluded that "a high incidence of psychiatric morbidity is not an inevitable consequence of military conflict."

Among the characteristics of those who have successfully managed PTSD are that they had supportive relationships with family and friends, they did not dwell on the trauma,

Current Research in Complementary and Alternative Medicine

In 1993, Congress created the Office of Alternative Medicine within the National Institutes of Health to explore the value of unconventional modalities in the treatment of illness and disease. The rationale behind funding such an office was related to the large number of Americans who were turning to these treatments. The government decided to fund the testing of these unconventional medical treatments to provide guidance regarding which ones were effective and which were a waste of money or, worse, unsafe. In 1997, approximately 42 percent of Americans spent $27 billion on these forms of therapy. In recognition of this increasing trend, the government elevated the office, creating the National Center for Complementary and Alternative Medicine (NCCAM), and allowed it to determine the projects it would research. During his March 28, 2000, testimony to the Senate Appropriations Committee on Labor, HHS, and Related Agencies, NCCAM Director Stephen Straus cited the research the center was engaged in as of that date:

- Efficacy of relaxation/guided imagery and chamomile tea for treating bowel disorders in children.
- Self-hypnosis, acupuncture, and osteopathic manipulation for children with cerebral palsy.
- Palliative benefits of hatha yoga on cognitive and behavioral changes associated with aging and neurological disorders in multiple sclerosis patients and in the healthy elderly.
- Reducing hypertension and other cardiovascular disease risk factors through meditation.
- A combination of relaxation training, hypnosis, and guided imagery employed during radiologic procedures to reduce the need for intravenous drugs and improve patient safety.
- Improvement in well-being and immune function as a result of self-transcendence in members of a breast-cancer support group.
- Biofeedback and yoga to treat asthma.
- Tai chi, compared to Western exercise, in preventing frailty in the elderly.

they had personal faith/religion/hope, and they had a sense of humor.[85] As you will note as you read further in this book, these are all effective means of managing stress in general.

Stress is associated with a variety of psychosocial illnesses besides posttraumatic stress disorder. Anxiety and depression are two of the most common. They are discussed in detail in Chapter 7. However, mention is made of them here so that you are not left with the impression that it is only the physical health consequences of stress with which we need be concerned. In fact, it is nearly impossible to separate physical consequences from psychological or sociological ones. We know this from research involving placebos.

A placebo is a substance that looks like a medication but is not. A placebo has no effect on the condition that a researcher is studying. Still, people who are told that a placebo is a drug that will improve their health often report feeling better. Why? The only explanation is that their minds perceive a benefit and convince their bodies that the substance is working. So it is with many other conditions.

Earlier in this chapter we discussed the relationship between stress, the immune system, and allergies. If we assume that allergies interfere with your ability to be productive at work—not an unrealistic assumption—we have a sociological effect of stress to add to its physical and psychological effects.

Do you know people who have one or more of the conditions discussed in this chapter? Perhaps a relative has tension headaches, a roommate has allergies, or someone else you know has TMJ syndrome. Identify this person and the condition below:

Person: _____

Condition: _____

This person should seek the help of a health professional (e.g., a physician or dentist), but since we know stress can make this condition worse, knowing how to manage stress might also help. List ways in which you can help this person alleviate the stress component of this condition. If you need to, consult Chapters 4 through 14.

1. _____
2. _____
3. _____
4. _____
5. _____

Posttraumatic Stress Disorder: the 9/11 Effects

On September 11, 2001, Americans witnessed or experienced firsthand four horrific attacks. In 2005, Americans witnessed or experienced three hurricanes in succession; Katrina, Rita, and Wilma—leaving many homeless and without electricity or water or food. Some of the effects of these events were specifically stress related. Fewer people traveled, and large numbers of people vowed to move out of the path of storms and hurricanes. Many experienced symptoms of posttraumatic stress disorder that included sleeplessness, fear and helplessness, flashbacks, and dreams and nightmares. Even those not directly experiencing these events knew someone who did or watched as the news was reported on television and in newspapers and other media outlets throughout the United States and the world.

It would be extremely satisfying if in this book I could offer solutions to these stress-related effects and to posttraumatic stress disorder. Unfortunately, that is not possible. There are no easy ways to cope with such traumatic events. Professional counseling and the passage of time can help, but the reality is that the events of 9/11 and major hurricanes will be etched in the minds and behaviors of thousands—maybe millions—of Americans forever. The information and skills presented in this text are intended to help Americans live productive, satisfying lives as a testament to those who perished on September 11, 2001, and in defiance of challenging weather and other traumatic occurrences.

Stress and Other Conditions

Stress has been shown to affect other health conditions as well. For example, stress can lead pregnant women to miscarry. In one study, 70 percent of women who had a miscarriage had at least one stressful experience four to five months before the miscarriage, as compared with 52 percent of women who did not have a miscarriage.[86] This is true, in particular, for women who are older and are carrying their first pregnancy.[87] Stress has also been associated with premature delivery.[88]

Even sports injuries can be caused by stress.[89] It has been known for some time that sports injuries occur more frequently in athletes who have experienced recent stressors and who do not have the resources and skills to cope well with stress. One explanation for this observation is the stress-injury model first described by Anderson and Williams.[90] According to this model, during sports events that are inherently stressful, the athlete's history of stressors, personality characteristics, and coping resources contribute interactively to the stress response. With high stress and poor coping resources, the result is increased muscle tension and attention redirected toward the stress and away from the event. Anderson and Williams hypothesized that increases in muscle tension, narrowing of the field of vision, and increased distractibility were the primary causes of sports injury. Evidence for this hypothesis also comes from the studies of Smith, Smoll, and Ptacek, who found that athletes who scored low in social support and psychological coping skills experienced more sports injuries.[91, 92] It might be reasonable to assume that stress also plays a part in traffic accidents, given that it narrows the field of vision and results in distractibility.

summary

- Psychosomatic disease involves the mind and the body; it is a real disease and not "just in the mind."
- Psychogenic psychosomatic disease is a physical disease caused by emotional stress. There is no invasion of disease-causing microorganisms; the mind changes the physiology so that parts of the body break down.
- Somatogenic psychosomatic disease occurs when the mind increases the body's susceptibility to disease causing microbes or a natural degenerative process.
- Stress-related diseases include hypertension, stroke, coronary heart disease, ulcers, migraine headaches, tension headaches, cancer, allergies, asthma, hay fever, rheumatoid arthritis, backache, TMJ syndrome, and posttraumatic stress disorder.
- Stress increases blood pressure and serum cholesterol, so it is no surprise that studies have found it associated with hypertension, stroke, and coronary heart disease.
- Stress decreases the effectiveness of the immunological system by decreasing the number of T-lymphocytes. A less effective immunological system is suspected of resulting in allergic reactions, asthma attacks, and even cancer.
- Stress results in increased muscle tension and bracing. It is this phenomenon that is thought to be the cause of tension headaches, backaches, and neck and shoulder pain.

notes

1. M. Bobak and M. Marmot, "East-West Mortality Divide and Its Potential Explanations: Proposed Research Agenda," *British Medical Journal* 312(1996): 421–25.

2. Bruce S. McEwen, "Protective and Damaging Effects of Stress Mediators," *The New England Journal of Medicine* 338(1998): 171–78.

3. K. C. Light, C. A. Dolan, M. R. Davis, and A. Sherwood, "Cardiovascular Responses to an Active Coping Challenge as Predictors of Blood Pressure Patterns 10 to 15 Years Later," *Psychosomatic Medicine* 54(1992): 217–30.

4. S. B. Manuck, A. L. Kasprowicz, and M. F. Muldoon, "Behaviorally-Evoked Cardiovascular Reactivity and Hypertension: Conceptual Issues and Potential Associations," *Annals of Behavioral Medicine* 12(1990): 17–29.

5. Cleveland Clinic Heart Center, "Angry Young Men Become Angry Old Men—With Heart Attacks," *Health Extra.* November 2002. http://www.clevelandclinic.org/heartcenter/pub/guide/prevention/stress/anger.htm

6. A. E. Ganesh-Kumar, J. Bienenstock, Edward J. Goetzl, and Michael G. Blennerhassett, *Autonomic Neuroimmunology* (London: Taylor & Francis, 2003).

7. R. Ader, D. L. Felten, and N. Cohen (eds.). *Psychoneuroimmunology,* 3rd ed. (San Diego: Academic Press, 2001).

8. Robert Ornstein and David Sobel, *The Healing Brain: A New Perspective on the Brain and Health* (New York: Simon & Schuster, 1987).

9. K. M. Dillon, F. Minchoff, and K. H. Baker, "Positive Emotional States and Enhancement of the Immune System," *International Journal of Psychiatry in Medicine* 15(1985): 13–18.

10. J. K. Kiecolt-Glaser, R. Glaser, D. Williger, J. Stout, G. Messick, S. Sheppard, D. Ricker, S. C. Romisher,

W. Briner, G. Bonnell, and R. Donnerberg, "Psychosocial Enhancement of Immunocompetence in a Geriatric Population," *Health Psychology* 4(1990): 25–41.

11. B. Peavey, F. Lawlis, and A. Goven, "Biofeedback-Assisted Relaxation: Effective on Phagocytic Capacity," *Biofeedback and Self-Regulation* 11(1985): 33–47.

12. M. S. Rider and J. Achterberg, "Effects of Music-Assisted Relaxation: Effects on Phagocytic Capacity," *Biofeedback and Self-Regulation* 14(1989): 247–57.

13. Howard S. Friedman and Stephanie Booth-Kewley, "The 'Disease-Prone Personality': A Meta-Analytic View of the Construct," *American Psychologist* 42(1987): 539–55.

14. Hans J. Eysenck, "Health's Character," *Psychology Today,* December 1988, 28–35.

15. "Princeton Study: Student Stress Lowers Immunity," *Brain Mind Bulletin* 14(1989): 1, 7.

16. Glen Rein, Mike Atkinson, and Rollin McCraty, "The Physiological and Psychological Effects of Compassion and Anger: Part 1 of 2," *Journal of Advancement in Medicine* 8(1995): 87–105.

17. Sally Squires, "The Power of Positive Imagery: Visions to Boost Immunity," *American Health,* July 1987, 56–61.

18. Arthur A. Stone et al., "Evidence That Secretory IgA Antibody Is Associated with Daily Mood," *Journal of Personality and Social Psychology* 52(1987): 988–93.

19. "Women's Health: More Sniffles in Splitsville," *American Health,* July/August 1986, 96, 98.

20. "Putting the Heart in Cardiac Care," *Psychology Today,* April 1986, 18.

21. C. A. Paternak, "Molecular Biology of Environmental Stress," *Impact of Science on Society* 41(1991): 49–57.

22. Meyer Friedman, Ray Rosenman, and V. Carroll, "Changes in the Serum Cholesterol and Blood Clotting Time in Men Subjected to Cycle Variation of Occupational Stress," *Circulation* 17(1958): 852–64.

23. F. Dreyfuss and J. Czaczkes, "Blood Cholesterol and Uric Acid of Healthy Medical Students Under Stress of an Examination," *Archives of Internal Medicine* 103(1959): 708–11.

24. N. Clark, E. Arnold, and E. Foulds, "Serum Urate and Cholesterol Levels in Air Force Academy Cadets," *Aviation and Space Environmental Medicine* 46(1975): 1044–48.

25. Larry A. Tucker, Galen E. Cole, and Glenn M. Friedman, "Stress and Serum Cholesterol: A Study of 7,000 Adult Males," *Health Values* 11(1987): 34–39.

26. L. van Doornen and K. Orlebeke, "Stress, Personality and Serum Cholesterol Level," *Journal of Human Stress* 8(1982): 24–29.

27. Eric R. Braverman, *The Amazing Way to Reverse Heart Disease: Beyond the Hypertension Hype: Why Drugs Are Not the Answer* (North Bergen, NJ: Basic Health Publications, 2004).

28. Lawrence W. Green, David M. Levine, and Sigrid Deeds, "Clinical Trials of Health Education for Hypertensive Outpatients: Design and Baseline Data," *Preventive Medicine* 4(1975): 417–25.

29. Herbert Benson and Miriam Z. Klipper, *The Relaxation Response* (New York: William Morrow, 2000).

30. Herbert Benson and William Proctor, *Beyond the Relaxation Response* (East Rutherford, NJ: Berkley Publishing Group, 1985).

31. Herbert Benson and Marg Stark, *Timeless Healing: The Power and Biology of Belief* (New York: Simon & Schuster, 1996).

32. Herbert Benson and Eileen M. Stuart, *The Wellness Book: The Comprehensive Guide to Maintaining Health and Treating Stress-Related Illness* (New York: Simon & Schuster, 1992).

33. Ruanne K. Peters, Herbert Benson, and John M. Peters, "Daily Relaxation Response Breaks in a Working Population: II. Effects on Blood Pressure," *American Journal of Public Health* 67(1977): 954–59.

34. Flanders Dunbar, *Psychosomatic Diagnosis* (New York: Harper, 1943).

35. S. B. Manuck et al., "Does Cardiovascular Reactivity to Mental Stress Have Prognostic Value in Post-Infarction Patients? A Pilot Study," *Psychosomatic Medicine* 54(1992): 102–8.

36. Henry I. Russek and Linda G. Russek, "Is Emotional Stress an Etiological Factor in Coronary Heart Disease?" *Psychosomatics* 17(1976): 63.

37. Meyer Friedman and Ray H. Rosenman, *Type A Behavior and Your Heart* (Greenwich, CT: Fawcett, 1974).

38. Jack Sparacino, "The Type A Behavior Pattern: A Critical Assessment," *Journal of Human Stress* 5(1979): 37–51.

39. Markku Koskenvuo, Jaakko Kaprio, Richard J. Rose, Antero Kesaniemi, and Seppo Sarna, "Hostility as a Risk Factor for Mortality and Ischemic Heart Disease in Men," *Psychosomatic Medicine* 50(1988): 330–40.

40. H. Turhan, A. R. Erbay, A. S. Yasar, A. Bicer, O. Sahin, N. Basar, and E. Yetkin, "Plasma Homocysteine Levels in Patients with Isolated Coronary Artery Ectasia." *International Journal of Cardiology* 104(2005): 158–62.

41. Catherine M. Stoney, "Plasma Homocysteine Levels Increase in Women During Psychological Stress," *Life Sciences* 64(1999): 2359–65.

42. Catherine M. Stoney and Tilmer O. Engebretson, "Plasma Homocysteine Concentrations Are Positively Associated with Hostility and Anger," *Life Sciences* 66(2000): 2267–75.

43. Susan A. Everson, George A. Kaplan, Riitta Salonen, and Jukka T. Salonen, "Does Low Socioeconomic Status Potentiate the Effects of Heightened Cardiovascular Responses to Stress on the Progression of Carotid

Atherosclerosis?" *American Journal of Public Health* 88(1998): 389–94.

44. Sarah P. Wamala, Murray A. Mittleman, Karen Schenck-Gustafson, and Kristina Orth-Gomer, "Potential Explanations for the Educational Gradient in Coronary Heart Disease: A Population-Based Case-Control Study of Swedish Women," *American Journal of Public Health* 89(1999): 315–21.

45. Carlos Iribarren, Stephen Sidney, Diane E. Bild, Kiang Liu, Jerome H. Markovitz, Jeffrey M. Roseman, and Karen Matthews, "Association of Hostility with Coronary Artery Calcification in Young Adults," *Journal of the American Medical Association* 283(2000): 2546–51.

46. Rollin McCraty, Mike Atkinson, and William A. Tiller, "New Electrophysiological Correlates Associated with Intentional Heart Focus," *Subtle Energies* 4(1995): 251–62.

47. Hans Selye, *The Stress of Life* (New York: McGraw-Hill Book Co., 1956).

48. Erich Lindemann, "Symptomatology and Management of Acute Grief," in *Stress and Coping: An Anthology,* ed. Alan Monet and Richard S. Lazarus (New York: Columbia University Press, 1977), 342.

49. Walter McQuade and Ann Aikman, *Stress* (New York: Bantam Books, 1974), 56.

50. B. Fier, "Recession Is Causing Dire Illness," *Moneysworth,* 23 June 1975.

51. "Economic Impact of Migraine Headaches on American Businesses is Staggering," *Medical Study News* (December 2004). http://www.news-medical.net/?id=7068.

52. F. D. Sheftell, S. D. Silberstein, A. M. Rapoport, and R. W. Rossum, "Migraine and Women: Diagnosis, Pathophysiology, and Treatment," *Journal of Women's Health* 1 (1992): 5–19.

53. Anne D. Walling, "Update on the Management of Migraine Headaches," *American Family Physician* (October 1, 2004). http://www.findarticles.com/p/articles/mi_m3225/is_7_70/ai_n8570254.

54. Kenneth R. Pelletier, *Mind as Healer, Mind as Slayer* (New York: Dell Publishing Co., 1977), 171.

55. Ibid., 171–72.

56. P. S. Sandor and J. Afra, "Nonpharmacologic Treatment of Migraine," *Current Pain and Headache Report* 9(2005): 202–5.

57. Paul Stang, Michael Von Korff, and Bradley S. Galer, "Reduced Labor Force Participation Among Primary Care Patients with Headache," *Journal of General Internal Medicine* 13(1998): 296–302.

58. Thomas H. Budzynski, Johann Stoyva, and C. Adler, "Feedback-Induced Muscle Relaxation: Application to Tension Headache," *Journal of Behavior Therapy and Experimental Psychiatry* 1(1970): 205–11.

59. Thomas H. Budzynski et al., "EMG Biofeedback and Tension Headache: A Controlled Outcome Study," *Psychosomatic Medicine* 35(1973): 484–96.

60. Ricky Fishman, "Headache Cures," *Medical Self-Care,* November/December 1989, 24–29, 64.

61. Steven F. Maier and Mark Laudenslager, "Stress and Health: Exploring the Links," *Psychology Today,* August 1985, 44–49.

62. V. Riley, "Mouse Mammary Tumors: Alternation of Incidence as Apparent Function of Stress," *Science* 189(1975): 465–67.

63. Carl O. Simonton and Stephanie Simonton, "Belief Systems and Management of the Emotional Aspects of Malignancy," *Journal of Transpersonal Psychology* 7(1975): 29–48.

64. Pelletier, *Mind as Healer,* 134.

65. Lawrence LeShan and R. E. Worthington, "Some Recurrent Life-History Patterns Observed in Patients with Malignant Disease," *Journal of Nervous and Mental Disorders* 124(1956): 460–65.

66. McQuade and Aikman, *Stress,* 69.

67. A. Steptoe, "The Link Between Stress and Illness," *Journal of Psychosomatic Research* 35(1991): 633–44.

68. R. H. Moos and George F. Solomon, "Psychologic Comparisons Between Women with Rheumatoid Arthritis and Their Nonarthritic Sisters," *Psychosomatic Medicine* 2(1965): 150.

69. Paul Stang, Michael Von Korff, and Bradley S. Galer, "Reduced Labor Force Participation Among Primary Care Patients with Headaches," *Journal of General Internal Medicine* 13(1998): 296–302.

70. L. R. Prado-Leon, A. Celis, and R. Avila-Chaurand, "Occupational Lifting Tasks as a Risk Factor in Low Back Pain: A Case-Control Study in a Mexican Population," *Work* 25(2005): 107–14.

71. "How to Prevent Back Trouble," *U.S. News & World Report,* 14 April 1975, 45–48.

72. F. S. Violante, F. Graziosi, R. Bonfiglioli, S. Curti, and S. Mattioli, "Relations between Occupational, Psychosocial and Individual Factors and Three Different Categories of Back Disorder among Supermarket Workers," *International Archives of Occupational and Environmental Health* (2005): 1–12

73. Robin Marantz Henig, "The Jaw out of Joint," *Washington Post, Health,* 9 February 1988, 16.

74. T. Fujii, T. Torisu, and S. Nakamura, "A Change of Occlusal Conditions after Splint Therapy for Bruxers with and without Pain in the Masticatory Muscles," *Craniology* 23(2005): 113–18.

75. K. Wahlund, T. List, and B. Larsson, "Treatment of Temporomandibular Disorders among Adolescents: A Comparison between Occlusal Appliance, Relaxation

Training, and Brief Information," *Acta Odontology Scandinavia* (2003): 203–11.

76. American Psychiatric Association, *Diagnostic and Statistical Manual of Mental Disorders,* 4th ed. (Washington, DC: American Psychiatric Association, 1994).

77. G. J. Turnbull, "A Review of Post-Traumatic Stress Disorder. Part I: Historical Development and Classification," *Injury* 29(1998): 87–91.

78. J. C. Ballenger, J. R. Davidson, Y. Lecrubier, D. J. Nutt, E. B. Foa, R. C. Kessler, A. C. McFarlane, and A. Y. Shalev, "Consensus Statement on Posttraumatic Stress Disorder from the International Consensus Group on Depression and Anxiety," *Journal of Clinical Psychiatry* 61(2000): 60–66.

79. R. B. Hidalgo and J. R. Davidson, "Posttraumatic Stress Disorder: Epidemiology and Health-Related Considerations," *Journal of Clinical Psychiatry* 61(2000): 5–13.

80. D. J. Nutt, "The Psychobiology of Posttraumatic Stress Disorder," *Journal of Clinical Psychiatry* 61(2000): 24–29.

81. R. C. Kessler, "Posttraumatic Stress Disorder: The Burden to the Individual and to Society," *Journal of Clinical Psychiatry* 61(2000): 4–12.

82. Hidalgo and Davidson, "Posttraumatic Stress Disorder."

83. G. C. Davis, "Post Traumatic Stress Disorder in Victims of Civilian Trauma and Criminal Violence," *Psychiatric Clinics of North America* 17(1994): 289–99.

84. M. Deahl, M. Srinivasan, N. Jones, J. Thomas, C. Neblett, and A. Jolly, "Preventing Psychological Trauma in Soldiers: The Role of Operational Stress Training and Psychological Debriefing," *British Journal of Medical Psychology* 73(2000): 77–85.

85. E. Eliot Benezra, "Personality Factors of Individuals Who Survive Traumatic Experiences Without Professional Help," *International Journal of Stress Management* 3 (1996): 147–53.

86. R. Neugebauer et al., "Association of Stressful Life Events with Chromosomally Normal Spontaneous Abortion," *American Journal of Epidemiology* 143(1996): 588–96.

87. L. Fenster et al., "Psychological Stress in the Workplace and Spontaneous Abortion," *American Journal of Epidemiology* 142(1995): 1176–83.

88. M. Nordentoft et al., "Intrauterine Growth Retardation and Premature Delivery: The Influence of Maternal Smoking and Psychological Factors," *American Journal of Public Health* 86(1996): 347–54.

89. S. A. Galambos, P. C. Terry, G. M. Moyle, S. A. Locke, and A. M. Lane, "Psychological Predictors of Injury among Elite Athletes," *British Journal of Sports Medicine* 39(2005): 351–54.

90. M. B. Anderson and J. M. Williams, "A Model of Stress and Athletic Injury: Prediction and Prevention," *Journal of Sport Psychology of Injury* 10(1988): 294–306.

91. R. E. Smith, F. L. Smoll, and J. T. Ptacek, "Conjunctive Moderator Variables in Vulnerability and Resiliency Research: Life Stress, Social Support and Coping Skills, and Adolescent Sport Injuries," *Journal of Personality and Social Psychology* 58(1990): 360–69.

92. R. E. Smith, J. T. Ptacek, and F. L. Smoll, "Sensation Seeking, Stress, and Adolescent Injuries: A Test of Stress-Buffering, Risk-Taking, and Coping Skills Hypotheses," *Journal of Personality and Social Psychology* 62(1992): 1016–24.

internet resources

Stress Management for the Health of It
www.cdc.gov/niosh/nasd/docs4/sc98011.html
Examines the causes of and responses to stress, as well as lifestyle changes that can be made to help prevent stress.

National Center for Post Traumatic Stress Disorder
www.ncptsd.org
This Web site provides information on the science, diagnosis, and treatment of PTSD and stress-related disorders.

Stress Management for Patient and Physician
www.mentalhealth.com/mag1/p51-str.html
An article that lists ten practical techniques for reducing stress.

Coping in Today's World

Being ill is not funny! Especially if you are a kid. Then why are there so many clowns roaming around hospitals throughout the United States? There they are, dressed in their clown outfits, with bulbous noses and clown makeup. They suddenly appear in sick children's rooms blowing bubbles, singing songs, and showing up with irremovable bandages and invisible strings to pull. At Washington, DC's Children's Hospital they are members of the *Clown Care Unit*,[a] which originated with the Big Apple Circus in New York in 1986. There are 17 hospitals around the United States that are affiliated with the Clown Care Unit. In these 17 hospitals, there are more than 90 clowns who make 250,000 visits to sick children each year. These clowns are the same ones who perform at children's birthday parties, magic shows, and other such events. Yet, when they are performing in hospitals, the only pay they receive is the reward of knowing they made a child feel better, even if for only a short period of time.

After having read this chapter and learning about the mind–body connection, it should not be surprising that clowns can not only make children feel better, but they may also be contributing to the health of the children for whom they perform. We would expect positive changes in the immunological system, and in emotional and mental health when children laugh and forget about their illnesses for a while. What other health benefits do you think result from visits of members of the Clown Care Unit?

Hospitals are always looking for volunteers. Are you interested in offering your services to make children or other patients feel better? Perhaps you can be trained to become a clown. Check with your local hospital if you are interested in helping to alleviate some of the stress experienced by its patients.

[a]"Is There a Clown in the House? The Art of Medical Slapstick." *Washington Post Magazine* May 9, 2004: 13.

LAB ASSESSMENT 3.1

Do You Know What to Do for Posttraumatic Stress Disorder?

Many of us have experienced a traumatic event. For some, it is an automobile accident, and they report seeing their lives flash before their eyes. For others, it is the sudden death of a loved one, and the memory of how they were told is forever etched in their minds. For still others, it is a sexual assault by a stranger, relative, or date/acquaintance, and the violation seems like it occurred yesterday, even though it was some time ago. Many of these traumatic events will manifest themselves in symptoms of posttraumatic stress disorder such as fear, nightmares, limitation on where one goes or what one does, or impaired relationships. If you have experienced a traumatic event with the potential to elicit these symptoms, describe that event here. If you have not, describe a traumatic event that someone you know has experienced.

_____
_____
_____

What were/are the symptoms that resulted from this event? Be sure to list physical, psychological, and social/relationship symptoms.

1. _____
2. _____
3. _____
4. _____
5. _____
6. _____

How can you or this other person receive help with these symptoms? Cite *from whom* help should be solicited and *what type* of help that source can provide. Include family members, professionals, and others such as professors/teachers, coaches, friends, and clergy.

1. _____
2. _____
3. _____
4. _____

Of course, just listing sources will not help with these symptoms. These sources have to actually be accessed for assistance to be provided. If it is you who experienced the traumatic event, write in your calendar when you will contact each source, and adhere to that schedule. If it is someone else who experienced the traumatic event, encourage that person to specify when assistance will be sought, and offer to help that person to remember to do so.

part 2

General Applications
Life-Situation and Perception Interventions

A young boy asked his older brother where babies come from. The older brother told him that babies come from the stork. Seeking verification of this shocking revelation, the young boy asked his father where babies come from. The father said that babies come from the stork. Not wanting to be impolite but still not completely satisfied, the boy approached the wise old sage of the family, his grandfather, and asked him where babies come from. The grandfather, following the party line, told him that babies come from the stork. The next day in school, the young boy related his conversations with his brother, father, and grandfather to the teacher and his classmates, concluding that there hadn't been normal sexual relations in his family for at least three generations.

Obviously, there was miscommunication in this family. To prevent any miscommunication regarding stress management, Part 1 of this book has provided you with information about the nature of stress, examples of stressors, the manner in which the body reacts to stressors, and illnesses and diseases associated with stress. You are, therefore, more prepared to see stress management as a complex of activities rather than something accomplished simply by following some guru. There are no simple, "storklike" answers to coping with stress. There is, however, a comprehensive stress management system that you can employ to control stress and tension. This chapter presents a model of stress and its relationship to illness, and stress management techniques are seen as interventions within this model. **Interventions** are activities to block a stressor from resulting in negative consequences, such as psychological discomfort, anxiety, illness, and disease. You'll soon see that comprehensive stress management is sensible, logical, and possible and that you can manage your own stress.

A Model of Stress

Stress begins with a *life situation* that knocks you (gently or abruptly) out of balance. You are nudged or shoved into disequilibrium and need to right yourself. This life situation could be a change in temperature, a threat from another person, the death of a loved one, or some other change in your life to which you need to adapt.

We all know, however, that the same situation presented to different people may result in different reactions. That is because different people will interpret the situation differently. This is termed their **cognitive appraisal** and, as we will see later, it can be controlled.

Some people may view the death of a loved one, for example, as terrible and dwell on that loss. Others may also view the death of a loved one as terrible but think about the nice times experienced with the one who died. A life situation to which you must adapt is therefore a necessary but not sufficient component of stress. What is also necessary is your perception of that life situation as stressful.

So far, then, we have a life situation that is *perceived* (or cognitively appraised) as distressing. This is represented in Figure 4.1. What occurs next is an *emotional reaction* to the distressing life event. Such feelings as fear, anger, and insecurity or feelings of being rushed, overwhelmed, frustrated, or helpless may be results of perceiving a life situation as stressful.

These feelings lead to *physiological arousal.* As described in detail in Chapter 2, stress reactivity includes increases in serum cholesterol, respiratory and heart rates, muscle tension, blood pressure, and blood glucose, along with decreases in the effectiveness of the immunological system, strength of the cardiac muscle, digestion, and histamine effectiveness. If physiological arousal is chronic or prolonged, illness or

Interventions
Activities to prevent a stressor from resulting in negative consequences.

cognitive appraisal
Interpretation of a stressor.

Figure 4.1

Perception of a life situation.

disease may result. In addition to illness or disease (be it physical or psychological), stress can lead to other *consequences* (poor performance in school or on the job, poor interpersonal relationships, or other such negative effects). The stress model is now complete and appears in Figure 4.2.

Let's follow a person down this road to the consequences of prolonged stress to demonstrate the functioning of this model. Suppose you work for the automobile industry and are relatively well adjusted. Your job is pleasing, and you've been employed at the same location for eight years. You have become comfortable interacting with your fellow workers, and you know when the coffee breaks occur, the best routes to travel to and from work, and to whom to be especially nice. Unfortunately, the economy takes a turn for the worse. Credit becomes tight and interest rates rise. People stop buying cars, and your company decides to lay off several hundred employees. Your pink slip appears in the envelope with your paycheck. Thus, a life situation has presented itself to which you need to adapt.

You consider this situation earth-shattering! How will you pay the rent, buy food, pay medical bills? How will you occupy your time? What will people think of you? Can you get another job? How should you begin to look for one? Questions, questions, concerns, concerns. You have now progressed to the second component of the model: You perceive being fired as distressing. Recognize, though, that not everyone will perceive this same event as distressing. Some of your fellow employees may be saying:

1. It's not good being fired, but I really do need a rest. I've been working too hard lately.

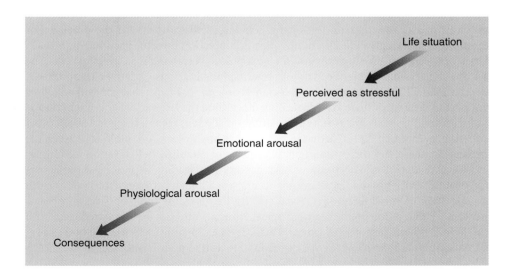

Figure 4.2

Stress model.

2. I'm going to use this opportunity to spend more time with my children.

3. I think I'll take advantage of this situation by going back to school. I always wanted the time to be able to do that.

These people have set up a roadblock between the life situation and their perceptions of that situation. They have changed their cognitive appraisal of being fired. They are not perceiving the event as a major catastrophe, and therefore it will not become one.

You, however, have perceived being fired as traumatic and subsequently are aroused emotionally. You feel *fear* about the future. You become *unsure* of your self-worth. You are *angry* at the boss for choosing you as one of those fired. You are *frustrated* at the whole situation and *confused* about what to do next. These feelings result in physiological arousal. You wind up with more blood fats roaming within your blood vessels. You perspire more, breathe differently, brace your muscles, secrete more hydrochloric acid in your stomach, and have fewer lymphocytes in your blood to combat infectious agents. If you don't use these built-up stress products in some way, and if this situation and your reaction to it remain the same, you may contract a stress-related illness.

Feedback Loops in the Stress Model

The stress model presented in Figure 4.2 is fairly simple. One part of the model leads to the next, and the next part leads further down the model. This conceptualization is helpful when we consider how to manage stress better, later in this chapter. In reality, however, stress and our reaction to it are much more complex, and the stress model can have many feedback loops. For example, when an illness results from stress—a negative consequence—that illness is a life situation that starts down the road of stress all over again. If it is perceived as distressing, emotional and physiological arousal result, and still other negative consequences occur. Or emotional arousal, such as anger, may lead to arguing at work. The result may be losing your job. Job loss then becomes a life situation you need to manage. Keep in mind that the way we interact with stressors and stress is quite complicated. Still, the simple conceptualization of the stress model (in Figure 4.2), and of how we can set up roadblocks on that model makes stress management more easily understood.

Setting Up Roadblocks

Once the progression from a life situation through perception, emotion, physiological arousal, and vulnerability to disease and other consequences is understood, it is then possible to intervene short of these consequences. Intervention entails setting up roadblocks at various points on the stress theory model (see Figure 4.3). Because this model includes sequential phases, with each phase dependent upon the full development of the previous phase, any interruption of this sequence will short-circuit the process. For example, even though a life situation requiring adaptation presents itself to you, a roadblock between that life situation and the next phase (perceiving it as stressful) could be set up. This roadblock might consist of prescribed medications (sedatives, tranquilizers, depressants), illicit drugs (marijuana, cocaine), or your insistence that you will not allow yourself to view this situation as disturbing. Regarding the last option, you might decide to focus upon the positive aspect of the situation (there is something good about *every* situation, even if that "good" is that things can't get any worse). A roadblock between the perception phase and the emotion phase can also be established. Relaxation techniques are also excellent ways to keep emotional reactions from leading to prolonged physiological arousal. Once physiological arousal occurs, a roadblock between it and poor health must consist of some form of physical activity that uses the built-up stress products. Remember that at the point of physiological arousal your body has prepared itself with the fight-or-flight response. A physical activity (e.g., jogging) will use the body's preparedness rather than allow the state of arousal to lead to poor health.

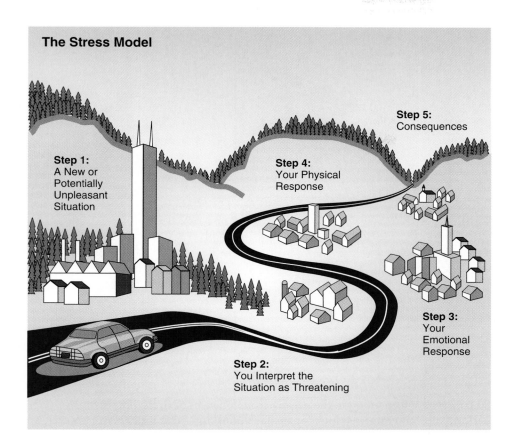

The Stress Model

Step 1:
A New or
Potentially
Unpleasant
Situation

Step 2:
You Interpret the
Situation as Threatening

Step 3:
Your
Emotional
Response

Step 4:
Your Physical
Response

Step 5:
Consequences

Figure 4.3

Think of the stress model as a map
that goes through different towns. As
with all roads, you can set up
roadblocks along the way.

Comprehensive Stress Management

Some *incomplete* stress management programs teach participants only one or just a few stress management skills. Consequently, they are prepared to set up a roadblock at only one location on the stress theory model. Some programs teach people meditation, yoga, or time management. To understand the reason these programs are incomplete, you must first be introduced to the sievelike aspect of the stress theory model.

At each level on the model, it is possible to filter out only a portion of the stress experience. Consequently, a roadblock (intervention technique) employed at only one place on the road will not stop *all* the "bad guys" from getting through. Each roadblock will stop some "bad guys," but no *one* roadblock will stop all it encounters. Each roadblock, then, is like a sieve that sifts and filters out some stress but allows some to pass through to the next phase of the stress theory model. It follows, then, that programs teaching only one or just a few stress management skills are helping their participants to some extent but not to the greatest degree possible.

Complete, comprehensive stress management includes intervention at *all* phases of the stress theory model and *several* means of intervening at *each* of these locations. As you can see from the table of contents of this book, Chapters 5 through 14 give us means to do just that. Each of those chapters focuses upon one phase of the stress theory model and describes several ways to sift out some of the stress experienced at that phase. Your goal, however, will not be to eliminate all of your stress. Remember from our earlier discussion that there is an optimum amount of stress. It is impossible, and undesirable, to eliminate all stress. Complete stress management does not subscribe to that goal but conveys the nature of eustress to its participants.

Getting away from your normal routine and focusing on something other than your stressors can be a very effective roadblock on the stress model.

Eustress and the Model

So far, we have focused upon the negative consequences of stress: illness, disease, poor performance, and impaired interpersonal relationships—that is **distress.** However, we can use the same stress model to better understand the positive consequences of stress. Stress that results in good consequences, such as producing personal growth, is called **eustress.** Stress that leads to actions that are beneficial to a person is also eustress. And stress that encourages optimum performance is eustress.

.   An example of eustress will make it more understandable. When I teach stress management, the class is conducted informally but includes most of the topics discussed in this book. A glance at the table of contents will show the array and number of topics studied. It would be easy for these topics to be lost and for their interconnectedness to be overlooked. My dilemma is how to keep the class interesting yet encourage students to study the content so as to realize how, for example, time management and biofeedback (two seemingly unrelated subjects) are cousins in the same stress management family.

I decided on a final examination as the vehicle by which students are required to deal with the array of topics studied as a meaningful whole. The test, then, serves as a eustressor—it leads to stress for the students who seek to do well on the exam and results in more learning than would have otherwise been accomplished. The stress is beneficial and useful (more learning occurs) and is, therefore, positive—eustress.

Using the stress model to explain the positive consequences in this example, the test is the life situation. Next, my students interpret the test as a threat and perceive it as stressful. That perception results in such emotions as fear, self-doubt, and worry, which lead to physiological arousal. However, because of this stress, my students study longer and consequently learn more. The positive outcome is that they know more about stress and how to manage it than they would have known if they hadn't experienced this situation, and they do better on the test than they might have done otherwise. So, you see, the stress model can be used to explain both the negative and the positive consequences of stress.

I'll bet you have experienced stress that, when it was over, made you consider yourself better for the experience. Either it was a positive life event that required significant adjustment (a move to a grass shack in Hawaii) or a more threatening event that led you to make important changes in your life (a brush with death that made you

distress
Stress that results in negative consequences such as decreased performance and growth.

eustress
Stress that results in positive consequences such as enhanced performance or personal growth.

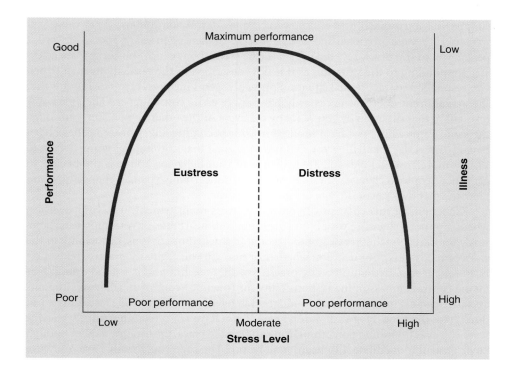

Figure 4.4

The Yerkes-Dodson Curve

The Yerkes-Dodson Curve is an excellent way to envision the difference between distress and eustress. Stress can be productive and have positive consequences— increase performance, as depicted to the left of the midpoint. This is *eustress*. However, stress can also have negative consequences— interfere with performance, as depicted to the right of the midpoint. This is *distress*.

Source: R. M. Yerkes, J. D. Dodson, "The Relation of Strength of Stimulus to Rapidity of Habit Formation," *Journal of Comparative Neurology and Psychology* 18(1908): 459–82.

reorganize your priorities). In any case, you were stressed "for the better." That is eustress. The following are some other examples of eustressors:

1. Having to make a presentation before a group of people and preparing better because of the stress.

2. Asking someone out on a date and rehearsing a better way of doing it because of the stress.

3. Having someone you love tell you the things he or she dislikes about you and using that information to make you a better you.

Taking Control

If there is only one concept by which you remember this book, I'd like it to be that *you are in much greater control over yourself than you have ever realized*. Managing stress is really just exercising that control rather than giving it up to others or to your environment. Let me give you an example of the kind of control you have over yourself. Recall an occasion when you became angry with someone. As vividly as you can, remember what preceded your anger. What happened earlier that day? What was the weather like? What were you anticipating? What was your previous relationship with that person? What did that person do that made you angry? Also recall your angry response in all its detail: How did you feel, what did you want to do, what did you actually do, and how did it all work out?

So often we hear others say, "So-and-so made me angry!" No one can make you angry. Rather, you *allow* yourself to be angered by what so-and-so has said or done. When you describe your behavior as dependent upon another's, you have given up control of that behavior *to* that other person. To demonstrate this point for yourself, manipulate the variables in the situation you just recalled.

Instead of a rainy day, imagine it to have been warm and sunny. Instead of a person with whom you have had a bad relationship doing or saying the thing about which you became angry, imagine it to have been the person you love most. Further, imagine that you received word of getting straight A's in school, a promotion, a salary raise, or some other nice event just prior to the situation about which you became angered. To summarize: You awakened to a nice, warm, sunny day. When you arrived at work, you were told you were promoted and given a substantial increase in salary. Soon afterward, a person whom you dearly love did or said X (the event about which you became angered).

Responding to the situation as it is now described in the same manner in which you responded to the original situation probably seems incongruous. The point is that the actual event does not necessarily have anger as its consequence. The anger was brought to that situation by you—not by the event or the other person. On some days, the same event would not have resulted in your becoming angry. You may have been having a great day and telling yourself it was so great that nothing was going to ruin it. What's more, nothing did! You are in charge of your behavior. You may not be able to get other people to change what they say or do, but certainly you can change how you react to what they say or do. *You are in charge of you.*

Generalizing this concept of control to stress management, it is your decision whether or not to increase your blood pressure, your heart rate, or your muscle tension. It is your decision whether or not to become frightened or anxious, or to vomit at the sides of roads. It is your decision whether or not you will regularly practice relaxation techniques (e.g., meditation). The practice of these techniques is a good example of taking control and assuming responsibility for (owning) your own behavior. Students and participants in workshops I conduct often tell me they would like to meditate but don't have the time. Hogwash. I don't care if you have ten screaming, unruly teenage werewolves at home and don't think you can find the place, the time, or a quiet-enough environment to meditate. I've heard it all before. The time you already have. You have chosen to use it for something else. The quiet you can get. I recall meditating in a car in the garage of the apartment house in which my parents lived, because their two-bedroom apartment with four adults, two children, and several neighbor children creating dissonance (one screeching violin strings and the other hammering the keys of an irreparably out-of-tune piano) was not conducive to relaxation.

The *place* is also available, since you can meditate anywhere. I've meditated on airplanes, under a tree on a golf course in the Bahamas, and once in the front seat of a car my wife was driving at sixty miles per hour on a highway in Florida.

Demonstrating You can Take Charge

In the space provided, rewrite each of the statements to indicate that *you* are really in control. The first statement serves as an example.

1. You make me upset.

   When you do that, I allow myself to become upset.

2. It was my insecurity that forced me to do that.

   _____

3. I was so frightened, I was helpless.

   _____

4. It's just a rotten habit that I can't break.

   _____

5. I'm just destined to be a failure.

   _____

6. If I were articulate, I'd be better at my job.

   _____

7. I was successful because I work well under pressure.

   _____

8. I'm the way I am because of my upbringing and parents.

   _____

In any case, you are in charge of what you do or do not do to manage your stress. Further, you are responsible for that decision and must accept its consequences. The intervention skills presented in this book can help you to control the stress and tension you experience. Whether they do that depends on whether you learn these skills, practice them, and incorporate them into your daily routine.

It would be dysfunctional to employ stress management techniques in a stressful way—yet that is not uncommon. Trying very hard to control stress will, in and of itself, create stress. If you have not bothered to use comprehensive stress management for the many years of your life, don't rush into it now. Read slowly and carefully. Try the skills; use those that work for you, and discard the others. If you are under medical care, check the appropriateness of these techniques and skills with your physician. You may need less medication, or certain procedures may be contraindicated for someone with your condition. Enjoy managing stress rather than making it one more thing to do. Use comprehensive stress management to free up, rather than clutter up, your day.

A change of scenery and physical activity can help intervene between stressors and their negative consequences.

Making a Commitment

While you are advised not to rush into this stress management system, a beginning should be made immediately. This beginning may consist only of a commitment to read this book so as to learn more about stress and its control. That first step is significant, however, because subsequent steps depend on it. Since stress reactivity that is chronic or prolonged may result in your becoming ill, the longer you wait to begin controlling your stress, the less healthy you can expect to be. If you're healthy now, you want to maintain that status. If you're presently ill and that illness is exacerbated by stress, you can move toward health by managing that stress. Are you willing to begin? How much are you willing to do? Behaviorists know that behavior that is reinforced is repeated, whereas behavior that is punished tends to be eliminated. Determine your commitment to managing your stress by completing a contract with yourself; you can use the contract presented here. Notice that it contains a reward for accomplishing what you contract to do and a punishment for not living up to the contract.

Don't make this contract too stressful. Try to be realistic. Here are some examples of rewards you might use:

Buying tickets to the theater.

Buying a new coat.

Restringing your tennis racket with gut.

Eating dinner with your fingers.

Asking someone you love to pamper you.

Here are some possible punishments:

Not watching television for one week.

Not eating ice cream for three weeks.

Not playing bridge for one month.

Eating alone for four days.

There's no time like the present; a stitch in time saves nine; he who hesitates is lost; the early bird . . . *the sooner the better.*

Contract of Commitment

I, _____, am concerned about the effects of stress upon my health and have decided to learn how to better manage the stress I encounter. Therefore, I commit myself to completely reading this book, practicing the skills presented, and incorporating at least two of these skills into my daily routine.

If I have met this commitment by _____

(two months from now)

I will reward myself by _____

(buying something you would not ordinarily buy or

_____ .

doing something you would not ordinarily do)

If I have not met this commitment by the date above, I will punish myself by

_____ .

(depriving yourself of something you really enjoy)

_____ .

_____   _____

(Signature)   (Date)

Getting Involved In Your Community

Are there life situations that occur on your campus that can cause stress? Perhaps there is not a sufficient study period between the end of classes and the beginning of final examinations. Perhaps the library is not open late enough. Maybe because there is no place on campus to gather, students mingle at local bars that serve alcohol. Identify these life situations below.

Life Situations: 1. _____

2. _____

3. _____

4. _____

5. _____

What can you do that would result in a change in these life situations? What can you do to either eliminate the stressor altogether or adjust the situation to make it less stressful? List these below.

1. _____

2. _____

3. _____

4. _____

5. _____

Will you commit to work on these changes to make your campus less stressful? If so, remember to be tactful, polite, and cooperative. Belligerence might result only in others being resistant to change.

summary

- Interventions are activities designed to block a stressor from resulting in negative consequences such as illness or disease. Stress management consists of the use of these interventions.

- Stress begins with a life situation that knocks you out of balance. However, for the stress response to develop, this situation has to be perceived and cognitively appraised as distressing.

- When life situations are perceived and cognitively appraised as distressing, emotional reactions such as fear, anger, and insecurity develop. These emotional reactions then lead to physiological arousal.

- Physiological arousal that is chronic or prolonged can lead to negative consequences such as illness or disease, poor performance, and impaired interpersonal relationships.

- Stress management involves "setting up roadblocks" on the road leading from life situations through perception, emotional arousal, and physiological arousal and ending at negative consequences.

- Incomplete stress management programs teach only one or a few stress management skills. Comprehensive programs teach means of intervening at each level of the stress model.

- Stress that leads to positive consequences is called eustress. Eustress involves change that still requires adaptation but is growth producing and welcome. A test can be an example of a eustressor when concern for a good grade results in your studying and learning more.

- You are in much greater control of yourself than you have ever realized. Managing stress is really just exercising that control, rather than giving it up to others or to your environment.

internet resources

MEDLINE Plus—Stress
www.nlm.nih.gov/medlineplus/stress.html
A National Institute of Health site that provides links to stress-related sites.

How to Master Stress
www.mindtools.com/smpage.html
A "how to" site on understanding stress and its effects, and stress management techniques.

Stress Cure
www.stresscure.com/
Contains a Health Resource Network for general stress information as well as strategies for coping with stress.

Coping in Today's World

Researchers have found that eustress has significant healthful effects. For example, when fifty-two healthy men viewed a humorous video for one hour, they produced increased levels of natural killer cells, immunoglobulin, T cells, and other changes that lasted twelve hours.[a] In a similar study,[b] twenty-seven healthy volunteers watched a cheerful, comical video for thirty minutes. It was found that their levels of free radical-scavenging capacity significantly increased, indicating better health. Recognizing these healthful effects, those in stressful jobs are particularly advised to use humor as a eustressor. For example, this advice has been recommended to nurses[c] and, in particular, to nurses who work in the Operating Room.[d] When nurses used humor, their bodies reacted in ways that indicated they were healthier. So, make a point of smiling, finding the humor in situations, and clowning it up. You will be happier and healthier if you embrace eustress.

[a]L. S. Berk, D. L. Felton, S. A. Tan, B. B. Bittman, and J. Westengard, "Modulation of Neuroimmune Parameters During the Eustress of Humor-Associated Mirthful Laughter," *Alternative Therapies in Health and Medicine* 7(2001): 62–72, 74–76.
[b]T. Atsumi, S. Fujisawa, Y. Nakabayashi, T. Kawarai, T. Yasui, and K. Tonosaki, "Pleasant Feeling from Watching a Comical Video Enhances Free Radical-Scavenging Capacity in Human Saliva," *Journal of Psychosomatic Research* 56(2004):377–379.
[c]B. A. D'Anna, "Nurse Clowns in the OR: An Interview with Barbara D'Anna," *Today's OR Nurse* 15(1993):25–27.
[d]B. L. Simmons, and D. L. Nelson, "Eustress at Work: The Relationship between Hope and Health in Hospital Nurses," *Health Care Management Review* 26(2001): 7–18.

LAB ASSESSMENT 4.1

What Eustressors Have You Experienced?

Eustress is the result of a threat that is encountered, that elicits a response, and that results in beneficial outcomes. For example, the fear of failing an exam results in your studying extra long, and the result is an "A" on the exam. Or, the fear of approaching your boss for a raise in salary leads you to prepare extra well for that discussion, and the result is you getting the raise. List three occasions when you experienced eustress:

1. _____

2. _____

3. _____

Why did you classify those instances as eustress? What were the beneficial outcomes? For the three eustress occasions above, list three of these beneficial outcomes:

1. _____

2. _____

3. _____

What did you do that resulted in eustress on these occasions, when it could have turned out badly and resulted in distress? In these examples, the student studied longer than otherwise, and the worker prepared for a discussion the worker might not have prepared for otherwise. For each of the eustress occasions listed, identify what you did that resulted in eustress instead of distress:

1. _____

2. _____

3. _____

What can you learn from this insight about managing stressors? Draw three conclusions:

1. _____

2. _____

3. _____

Whenever I get to thinking too much of myself, I recall a story told by Richard Feynman. Feynman won the Nobel prize in physics, but his curiosity was not limited to science. He describes his adventures in the book *Surely You're Joking, Mr. Feynman!: Adventures of a Curious Character.*[1] These adventures include learning to play drums in Brazil and courting showgirls in Las Vegas. However, it is the story of a conference he attended that I want to relate here. Feynman writes:

> At this conference, *every word* that every guy said at the plenary session was so important that they had a stenotypist there, typing every goddamn thing. Somewhere on the second day the stenotypist came up to me and said, "What profession are you? Surely not a professor."
>
> "I *am* a professor," I said.
>
> "Of what?"
>
> "Of physics—science."
>
> "Oh, *that* must be the reason," he said.
>
> "Reason for what?"
>
> He said, "You see, I'm a stenotypist and I type everything that is said here. Now when the other fellas talk, I type what they say, but I don't understand what they're saying. But every time *you* get up to ask a question or to say something, I understand exactly what you mean—what the question is, and what you're saying—so I thought you *can't* be a professor!"

Now, not all professors are confusing. I hope to prove that in this chapter. This chapter relates the various aspects of stress management at the life-situation phase to each other in a cohesive, sensible manner. The topics all relate to intrapersonal matters—that is, what is between you and you rather than between you and others. Rather than bits and pieces of ways to control stress and tension, a management system for adjusting your life is described—a system that will be meaningful and relevant for you and that can actually make you healthier and happier.

Eliminating Unnecessary Stressors

The higher on the stress theory model you can siphon off stressors, the more likely it is that you will be able to manage the stress in your life. You would think that if you could eliminate all stressors from your life, you would never experience stress and therefore would never become ill from it. Because that goal is both impossible and undesirable, your attempt at stress management at the top level of the model (life situation) should be to eliminate as many distressors as is feasible. To accomplish this end, this chapter presents you with introspective activities for identifying unnecessary stressors in your life and eliminating them.

In my course "Controlling Stress and Tension," students keep a diary for three weeks. Why don't you keep a diary as well? A sample page appears in Figure 5.1. This diary must include seven components for each day:

1. Stressors for that day:
   a. Routine stressors (experienced often).
   b. Unique stressors (seldom encountered).
2. Reactions to *each* stressor encountered:
   a. Physiological reactions (e.g., perspiration, increased pulse rate, muscle tension).
   b. Psychological reactions (e.g., fear, anxiety, confusion).

Figure 5.1

The stress diary.

Stressor	Reactions		Means of coping	Means of coping better
	Physiological	Psychological		
1. Routine				
a.				
b.				
2. Unique				
a.				
b.				

Relaxation techniques tried	Effectiveness of technique
1.	
2.	
3.	

Sensations	
Bodily sensations	Mind sensations

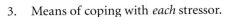

3. Means of coping with *each* stressor.
4. Better means of coping that might have been attempted.
5. Relaxation techniques tried that day.
6. Effectiveness of these relaxation techniques.
7. Sensations during that day:
   a. Bodily sensations (e.g., headache, stomach discomfort, backache).
   b. Mind sensations (e.g., anxiety attack, feelings of insecurity, sense of being rushed).

In addition to reporting how tedious it becomes to keep a diary for three weeks, students say they value this learning experience highly among others with which they have ever been presented. To understand this reaction requires an explanation of how we use the diary once the three-week period is concluded. The contents of the diary are considered data from which generalizations (or patterns) about each student and each student's life can be gleaned. Rather than focusing on one occurrence or even one day, we try to identify consistent features that will provide insight into how each student interacts with the stress of his or her life. To accomplish this end, we ask the following questions:

1. What stressors do you frequently experience?
2. Do you need or want to continue experiencing these stressors?
3. If you do not, which routine stressors can you eliminate? How?
4. How does your body typically react to stressors?
5. How does your psyche typically react to stressors?
6. Can your body's or mind's reactions to stress teach you ways to identify stress early in its progression so as to make it less harmful?
7. Are there any coping techniques that you use more than others?

8. Do these techniques work for you or against you?

9. Are there any coping techniques that you believe would be helpful but you don't use often enough?

10. How can you get yourself to use these infrequently used coping techniques more often?

11. Are any particular relaxation techniques more effective for you than others?

12. Are you experiencing difficulty in employing a relaxation technique? No time? No place? No quiet?

13. How can you better organize your life to obtain periods of relaxation?

14. Are there any bodily sensations that you usually experience either preceding or following stressful events?

15. Are there any mind sensations that you usually experience either preceding or following stressful events?

16. Are there ways to prevent either bodily or mind sensations developing from your stress?

17. Summarize what you will *do* as a result of recording and analyzing this diary. Be as specific as you can; for example, rather than state that you will relax more, describe the time of day, place, and method of relaxation.

After three weeks, ask and answer the previous seventeen questions. You will probably gain much insight into your stress experience and be able to adjust your life to experience fewer stressors. What you will be doing is taking charge of your life to prevent stressors from leading to poor health by eliminating unnecessary stressors before they even begin their journey down the stress road. The more stressors you can eliminate in this fashion, the less likely it is that stress will cause illness or disease for you. The importance of eliminating unnecessary stressors will become even more evident in the next section.

Nutrition and Stress

The relationship between nutrition and stress remains unclear. This is definitely one stress-related area fertile for research. However, we do know that certain food substances can produce a stresslike response, that other substances provided by foods can be depleted by stress, and that certain stress-related illnesses can be exacerbated by dietary habits. We also know that feelings of stress can lead to poor nutritional habits. People who have low self-esteem—in particular, those who feel badly about their physical selves—may take drastic measures to improve their bodies. Some of these measures turn into eating disorders, such as *anorexia nervosa* and *bulimia,* and cause stress in and of themselves. *Anorexia nervosa* is a condition in which a person takes in so few calories as to basically starve him or her self. *Bulimia* is binge eating followed by the purging of consumed foods by induced vomiting, use of laxatives, or some other method. Both of these eating disorders are discussed in detail later in this section. For now, recognize that they sometimes result when a person feels distressed about his or her body.

Before ways to eliminate nutrition stressors are recommended, a discussion of nutrition per se seems in order. To be nutritionally healthy, you need to maintain a balanced diet. A balanced diet is one that contains a variety of foods that will provide you with a variety of nutrients (proteins, carbohydrates, fats, minerals, vitamins, and water). To ensure that you get the appropriate variety of foods, you should eat foods in the amounts consistent with the food pyramid described in Figure 5.2. The pyramid is designed to be used by individuals via the internet. If you go to http://www.mypyramid.gov, you will be able to find your recommended balance between food and physical activity, learn how to make smart choices in every food group, and how to get the most nutrition out of your calories. After all,

Figure 5.2

MyPyramid
STEPS TO A HEALTHIER YOU
MyPyramid.gov

1% MILK

GRAINS	VEGETABLES	FRUITS	MILK	MEAT & BEANS
Make half your grains whole	Vary your veggies	Focus on fruits	Get your calcium-rich foods	Go lean with protein
Eat at least 3 oz. of whole-grain cereals, breads, crackers, rice, or pasta every day 1 oz. is about 1 slice of bread, about 1 cup of breakfast cereal, or ½ cup of cooked rice, cereal, or pasta	Eat more dark-green veggies like broccoli, spinach, and other dark leafy greens Eat more orange vegetables like carrots and sweet potatoes Eat more dry beans and peas like pinto beans, kidney beans, and lentils	Eat a variety of fruit Choose fresh, frozen, canned, or dried fruit Go easy on fruit juices	Go low-fat or fat-free when you choose milk, yogurt, and other milk products If you don't or can't consume milk, choose lactose-free products or other calcium sources such as fortified foods and beverages	Choose low-fat or lean meats and poultry Bake it, broil it, or grill it Vary your protein routine — choose more fish, beans, peas, nuts, and seeds

For a 2,000-calorie diet, you need the amounts below from each food group. To find the amounts that are right for you, go to MyPyramid.gov.

Eat 6 oz. every day	Eat 2½ cups every day	Eat 2 cups every day	Get 3 cups every day; for kids aged 2 to 8, it's 2	Eat 5½ oz. every day

Find your balance between food and physical activity

- Be sure to stay within your daily calorie needs.
- Be physically active for at least 30 minutes most days of the week.
- About 60 minutes a day of physical activity may be needed to prevent weight gain.
- For sustaining weight loss, at least 60 to 90 minutes a day of physical activity may be required.
- Children and teenagers should be physically active for 60 minutes every day, or most days.

Know the limits on fats, sugars, and salt (sodium)

- Make most of your fat sources from fish, nuts, and vegetable oils.
- Limit solid fats like butter, stick margarine, shortening, and lard, as well as foods that contain these.
- Check the Nutrition Facts label to keep saturated fats, *trans* fats, and sodium low.
- Choose food and beverages low in added sugars. Added sugars contribute calories with few, if any, nutrients.

MyPyramid.gov
STEPS TO A HEALTHIER YOU

U.S. Department of Agriculture
Center for Nutrition Policy and Promotion
April 2005
CNPP-15

USDA

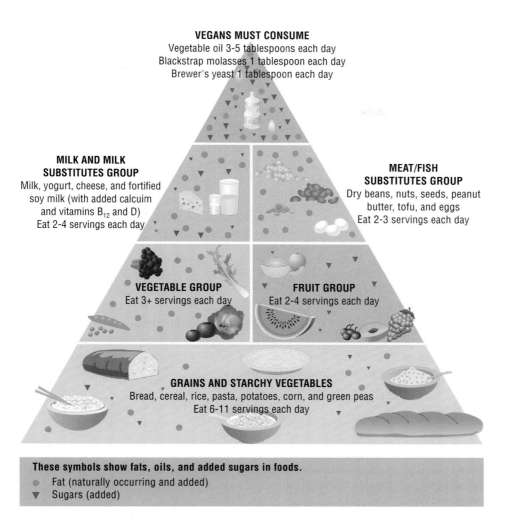

VEGANS MUST CONSUME
Vegetable oil 3-5 tablespoons each day
Blackstrap molasses 1 tablespoon each day
Brewer's yeast 1 tablespoon each day

MILK AND MILK SUBSTITUTES GROUP
Milk, yogurt, cheese, and fortified soy milk (with added calcuim and vitamins B_{12} and D)
Eat 2-4 servings each day

MEAT/FISH SUBSTITUTES GROUP
Dry beans, nuts, seeds, peanut butter, tofu, and eggs
Eat 2-3 servings each day

VEGETABLE GROUP
Eat 3+ servings each day

FRUIT GROUP
Eat 2-4 servings each day

GRAINS AND STARCHY VEGETABLES
Bread, cereal, rice, pasta, potatoes, corn, and green peas
Eat 6-11 servings each day

These symbols show fats, oils, and added sugars in foods.
● Fat (naturally occurring and added)
▼ Sugars (added)

no one wants to be *malnourished*. Being malnourished means you eat either too little or too much of the recommended foods, or you ingest some nutrients in inappropriate amounts.

Although following the food pyramid guidelines is appropriate for many people, there are exceptions. For example, vegetarians may not want to eat meat; some people may be lactose intolerant and cannot drink milk; others may come from cultures that make following the general pyramid impractical. For this reason, food pyramids, based on the original food guide pyramid, have been devised to reflect individual concerns. Figure 5.3 provides an example, a pyramid for vegetarians. Ethnic food pyramids can be found in the "Ethnic Food Pyramids" box.

In addition to resulting in malnourishment, ingesting too much or too little of particular nutrients can lead to illnesses that in and of themselves can cause a great deal of stress. The relationship of nutrition to heart disease and cancer are discussed as examples here because of the prevalence of those conditions in our society. However, many other illnesses are also related to nutrition.

Coronary heart disease results when the arteries supplying the heart with oxygen are so clogged that blood cannot pass through and the heart does not get needed oxygen. As a result, parts of the heart may die, and if those parts are in certain places in the heart or are extensive throughout the heart, the victim may die. Over time, diets high in saturated fats (derived from red meats, whole milk, butter) increase the amount of cholesterol in the blood. The cholesterol then accumulates on the walls of the arteries, and coronary heart disease develops. That is why the

Ethnic Food Pyramids

1. *Food Guide Pyramid with a Mexican Flavor.* University of California Agriculture and Natural Resources. (800) 994-8849.

2. *Puerto Rican Food Guide Pyramid.* Hispanic Health Council, the University of Connecticut Department of Nutrition, the COOP Extension, and the Connecticut State Department of Social Services.

3. *East African Eating Guide for Good Health, Native American Food Guide, Southeast Asian Food Guide, Pacific Northwest Native American Food Guide.* Washington State Department of Health Warehouse Materials Management. (360) 664-9046 or fax: (360) 664-2929.

4. *Multicultural Pyramid Packet* from the Penn State Nutrition Center, with eight different cultural pyramids: African American, Chinese, Jewish, Puerto Rican, Navajo, Mexican, Indian, and Vietnamese for $10 at (814) 865-6323 or fax: (814) 865-5870; Penn State Nutrition Center, 5 Henderson Building, University Park, PA 16802.

5. *Asian, Latin American, Mediterranean, and Vegetarian Pyramids.* Oldways Preservation & Exchange Trust, 25 First Street, Cambridge, MA 02141. (617) 621-3000; fax: 617-621-1230; www.oldways@tiac.net.

amount of saturated fats in a person's diet should be restricted. One way to do this is to substitute monounsaturated fats (e.g., peanut and olive oils) or polyunsaturated fats (e.g., liquid vegetable oils such as corn, soybean, or safflower oils) for saturated fats.

Cancer has also been associated with diet. The data indicate that people are more prone to developing certain cancers if their diets are low in fiber (e.g., whole-grain bread, cereal, and flour, fruits, vegetables, nuts, and popcorn) or high in saturated fats. To prevent certain cancers, the American Cancer Society recommends diets low in fats (to prevent breast, colon, and prostate cancers), high in fiber (to prevent colon cancer), and high in vitamins A and C (to prevent larynx, esophagus, stomach, and lung cancers). The American Cancer Society also recommends the consumption of cruciferous vegetables such as broccoli, cauliflower, and brussels sprouts (to prevent digestive-tract cancers) and limited use of alcohol (to prevent mouth, larynx, throat, esophagus, and liver cancers).[2] In addition, obesity in women increases the risk of uterine, cervical, and breast cancers. It seems that, with more body fat, women produce more estrogen and thereby increase their chances of contracting one of these forms of cancer.[3]

Although it is desirable to control your body weight, an overemphasis on dieting can itself be unhealthy. Sometimes, for example, obesity can be in the mind of the beholder. We are bombarded with media images of the ideal body type as being thin with all the curves in the right places. Consequently, when our bodies differ from this ideal, we become distressed and vow to diet that extra weight off. The popularity and abundance of diet books attest to our desire to lose weight. Unfortunately, some diets are unhealthy and therefore can lead to even more stress. Table 5.1 presents what we know about how to lose weight effectively and also healthfully. Nutrition experts now recommend paying more attention to body mass than to weight alone. This gauge seems to more accurately reflect a person's risk of ill health as a result of too much weight. Table 5.2 helps you calculate your body

Table 5.1 BEHAVIORAL PRINCIPLES OF WEIGHT LOSS

Principles

I. STIMULUS CONTROL

   A. Shopping
1. Shop for food after eating.
2. Shop from a list.
3. Avoid ready-to-eat foods.
4. Don't carry more cash than needed for items on shopping list.

   B. Plans
1. Plan to limit food intake.
2. Substitute exercise for snacking.
3. Eat meals and snacks at scheduled times.
4. Don't accept food offered by others.

   C. Activities
1. Store food out of sight.
2. Eat all food in the same place.
3. Remove food from inappropriate storage areas in the house.
4. Keep serving dishes off the table.
5. Use smaller dishes and utensils.
6. Avoid being the food server.
7. Leave the table immediately after eating.
8. Don't save leftovers.

   D. Holidays and Parties
1. Drink fewer alcoholic beverages.
2. Plan eating habits before parties.
3. Eat a low-calorie snack before parties.
4. Practice polite ways to decline food.
5. Don't get discouraged by an occasional setback.

II. EATING BEHAVIOR
1. Put fork down between mouthfuls.
2. Chew thoroughly before swallowing.
3. Prepare foods one portion at a time.
4. Leave some food on the plate.
5. Pause in the middle of the meal.
6. Do nothing else while eating (read, watch television).

III. REWARD
1. Solicit help from family and friends.
2. Help family and friends provide this help in the form of praise and material rewards.
3. Utilize self-monitoring records as basis for rewards.
4. Plan specific rewards for specific behaviors (behavioral contracts).

IV. SELF-MONITORING

   Keep diet diary that includes
1. Time and place of eating.
2. Type and amount of food.
3. Who is present/how you feel.

V. NUTRITION EDUCATION
1. Use diet diary to identify problem areas.
2. Make small changes that you can continue.
3. Learn nutritional values of foods.
4. Decrease fat intake; increase complex carbohydrates.

VI. PHYSICAL ACTIVITY

   A. Routine Activity
1. Increase routine activity.
2. Increase use of stairs.
3. Keep a record of distance walked each day.

   B. Exercise
1. Begin a very mild exercise program.
2. Keep a record of daily exercise.
3. Increase the exercise very gradually.

VII. COGNITIVE RESTRUCTURING
1. Avoid setting unreasonable goals.
2. Think about progress, not shortcomings.
3. Avoid imperatives such as "always" and "never."
4. Counter negative thoughts with rational restatements.
5. Set weight goals.

Source: Reprinted with permission from *American Journal of Clinical Nutrition* 41 (1985): 823. Copyright © 1985, American Society for Clinical Nutrition Inc.

mass. The desirable body mass index (BMI) for females is between 21–23; the desirable range for males is 22–24.[4] Recognize, though, that people with high muscle mass—such as weight trainers—may have a BMI out of range but actually be the right weight and have a healthy percentage of body fat. Lab 5.1 (at the end of this chapter) presents another way to determine how much weight you should lose.

For some people, the obsession with being thin takes the form of excessive weight loss through self-imposed starvation (anorexia nervosa) or binge eating followed by purging through self-induced vomiting, fasting, abuse of laxatives, diuretics or enemas, or excessive exercise (bulimia).[5] Although males also experience eating disorders, approximately 2 percent of young American females are affected by serious eating disorders,[6] and they often have obsessional, perfectionistic, and anxious personality styles[7] that lead them to want to maintain total control over what they perceive to be ideal weight. Interestingly, eating disorders are prevalent in Western cultures where food is plentiful and attractiveness for females is associated with thinness. They are rare in countries where food is scarce, such as India.[8] Although individual and family

Table 5.2 BODY MASS INDEX TABLE

To use this table, find the appropriate height in the left-hand column. Move across to a given weight. The number at the top of the column is the BMI at the height and weight. Pounds have been rounded off.

Height (Inches)	19	20	21	22	23	24	25	26	27	28	29	30	31	32	33	34	35	36
								Body Weight (Pounds)										
58	91	96	100	105	110	115	119	124	129	134	138	143	148	153	158	162	167	172
59	94	99	104	109	114	119	124	128	133	138	143	148	153	158	163	168	173	178
60	97	102	107	112	118	123	128	133	138	143	148	153	158	163	168	174	179	184
61	100	106	111	116	122	127	132	137	143	148	153	158	164	169	174	180	185	190
62	104	109	115	120	126	131	136	142	147	153	158	164	169	175	180	186	191	196
63	107	113	118	124	130	135	141	146	152	158	163	169	175	180	186	191	197	203
64	110	116	122	128	134	140	145	151	157	163	169	174	180	186	192	197	204	209
65	114	120	126	132	138	144	150	156	162	168	174	180	186	192	198	204	210	216
66	118	124	130	136	142	148	155	161	167	173	179	186	192	198	204	210	216	223
67	121	127	134	140	146	153	159	166	172	178	185	191	198	204	211	217	223	230
68	125	131	138	144	151	158	164	171	177	184	190	197	203	210	216	223	230	236
69	128	135	142	149	155	162	169	176	182	189	196	203	209	216	223	230	236	243
70	132	139	146	153	160	167	174	181	188	195	202	209	216	222	229	236	243	250
71	136	143	150	157	165	172	179	186	193	200	208	215	222	229	236	243	250	257
72	140	147	154	162	169	177	184	191	199	206	213	221	228	235	242	250	258	265
73	144	151	159	166	174	182	189	197	204	212	219	227	235	242	250	257	265	272
74	148	155	163	171	179	186	194	202	210	218	225	233	241	249	256	264	272	280
75	152	160	168	176	184	192	200	208	216	224	232	240	248	256	264	272	279	287
76	156	164	172	180	189	197	205	213	221	230	238	246	254	263	271	279	287	295

psychotherapies are often successful in treating eating disorders, there is generally a lack of adequate training of practicing therapists to deliver these treatments.[9]

Since anorexia nervosa and bulimia can eventually lead to severe illness or death, if you know someone with one of these conditions, you ought to encourage him or her to seek professional help as soon as possible. If you find you are obsessive about your own weight and you really needn't be, you might want to consult with a counselor at your campus health center or with your personal physician.

Furthermore, certain food *substances* have particular relationships with stress. For example, a group of food substances can actually produce a stresslike response. These substances are called **pseudostressors,** or **sympathomimetics.** They mimic sympathetic nervous system stimulation. Colas, coffee, tea, and chocolate that contain caffeine are examples of sympathomimetic agents. Tea also contains theobromine and theophylline, which are sympathomimetics. These substances increase metabolism, make one highly alert, and result in the release of stress hormones, which elevate the heart rate and blood pressure. In addition to creating a pseudostress response, sympathomimetics make the nervous system more reactive and thereby more likely to have a stressor elicit a stress response. Nicotine (found in tobacco) is also a sympathomimetic agent.

pseudostressors

Food substances that produce a stresslike response; also called sympathomimetics.

sympathomimetics

Synonymous with pseudostressors.

Table 5.2 (Continued)

To use this table, find the appropriate height in the left-hand column. Move across to a given weight. The number at the top of the column is the BMI at the height and weight. Pounds have been rounded off.

Height (Inches)	37	38	39	40	41	42	43	44	45	46	47	48	49	50	51	52	53	54
									Body Weight (Pounds)									
58	177	181	186	191	196	201	205	210	215	220	224	229	234	239	244	248	253	258
59	183	188	193	198	203	208	212	217	222	227	232	237	242	247	252	257	262	267
60	189	194	199	204	209	215	220	225	230	235	240	245	250	255	261	266	271	276
61	195	201	206	211	217	222	227	232	238	243	248	254	259	264	269	275	280	285
62	202	207	213	218	224	229	235	240	246	251	256	262	267	273	278	284	289	295
63	208	214	220	225	231	237	242	248	254	259	265	270	278	282	287	293	299	304
64	215	221	227	232	238	244	250	256	262	267	273	279	285	291	296	302	308	314
65	222	228	234	240	246	252	258	264	270	276	282	288	294	300	306	312	318	324
66	229	235	241	247	253	260	266	272	278	284	291	297	303	309	315	322	328	334
67	236	242	249	255	261	268	274	280	287	293	299	306	312	319	325	331	338	344
68	243	249	256	262	269	276	282	289	295	302	308	315	322	328	335	341	348	354
69	250	257	263	270	277	284	291	297	304	311	318	324	331	338	345	351	358	365
70	257	264	271	278	285	292	299	306	313	320	327	334	341	348	355	362	369	376
71	265	272	279	286	293	301	308	315	322	329	338	343	351	358	365	372	379	386
72	272	279	287	294	302	309	316	324	331	338	346	353	361	368	375	383	390	397
73	280	288	295	302	310	318	325	333	340	348	355	363	371	378	386	393	401	408
74	287	295	303	311	319	326	334	342	350	358	365	373	381	389	396	404	412	420
75	295	303	311	319	327	335	343	351	359	367	375	383	391	399	407	415	423	431
76	304	312	320	328	336	344	353	361	369	377	385	394	402	410	418	426	435	443

Source: National Heart, Lung, and Blood Institute, 2000.

Another way nutrition is related to stress is by the effect of stress on *vitamins*. The production of cortisol (the stress hormone produced by the adrenal cortex) requires the use of vitamins.[10] Consequently, chronic stress can deplete the vitamins we take into our bodies. In particular, the B complex vitamins (thiamine, riboflavin, niacin, pantothenic acid, and pyridoxine hydrochloride) and vitamin C seem to be the most affected. A deficiency in these vitamins can result in anxiety, depression, insomnia, muscular weakness, and stomach upset. Not only may stress deplete these vitamins, but, because these vitamins are used to produce adrenal hormones, their depletion makes one less able to respond satisfactorily to stress. Thereby, a vicious cycle develops. Vitamin B can be obtained by eating cereals, green leafy vegetables, liver, and fish. Vitamin C is contained in citrus fruits, tomatoes, cabbage, and potatoes.

In addition, stress can interfere with calcium absorption in the intestines and can increase calcium excretion, as well as increase the excretion of potassium, zinc, copper, and magnesium. This is of particular concern to women who are trying to prevent the development of osteoporosis (a condition in which the bones become weak and brittle and the woman is at increased risk of fractures), since osteoporosis is a result of a decalcification of the bones.[11] Although postmenopausal women are most prone to osteoporosis (decalcification is related to decreased levels of estrogens), it appears that long-term lifestyle habits (diet and exercise, in particular) affect one's susceptibility to this condition. Eating a diet sufficient in calcium, exercising regularly, and managing stress—all begun at a young age—are the best ways to prevent or postpone the development of osteoporosis.

Sugar is another stress culprit. To break down sugar, the body must use some of its B complex vitamins. We now know what that means. This results in the symptoms described previously and a diminished ability to produce adrenal hormones in response to stressors. *Processed flour* also requires the body to use B complex vitamins (as well as other nutrients) and, unless enriched with vitamins and minerals, can have the same effect as sugar.

Sugar ingestion has other stress implications. Ingestion of a large amount of sugar in a short period of time or missing meals and then ingesting sugar over a period of time can result in a condition called **hypoglycemia** in susceptible individuals. Hypoglycemia is low blood sugar that is preceded by elevated levels of blood sugar. This condition may be accompanied by symptoms of anxiety, headache, dizziness, trembling, and irritability. Subsequent stressors are likely to provoke an unusually intense stress response.

Furthermore, the stress response and accompanying cortisol production cause an elevation in the level of blood glucose. To respond to the blood glucose, the beta cells of the islets of Langerhans produce insulin. Stress that is chronic can burn out these beta cells. These cells are not replaceable, thus, the body's ability to produce insulin is compromised. The result might be the development of diabetes in genetically susceptible individuals.

Another food substance that has a relationship to stress is *salt.* Some people are genetically susceptible to sodium and develop high blood pressure when they ingest too much of it. The federal government recommends no more than 5,000 milligrams of salt (sodium chloride), which translates to 2,000 milligrams of sodium, daily. On a short-term basis, sodium ingestion can raise blood pressure by retaining body fluids. When a person whose blood pressure is elevated encounters stress, his or her blood pressure may be further elevated to a dangerous level.

Now that you have an appreciation for the relationship of nutrition to stress, it is time to study ways of using this information to manage stress better. Here are some ways to reduce stressors in your diet:

1. Eat a balanced diet that includes the amounts recommended in the food pyramid.

2. Limit the amount of saturated fats in your diet, and increase the amount of fiber.

3. Add cruciferous vegetables (such as broccoli, cauliflower, and brussels sprouts) to your diet, and limit the amount of alcohol you ingest.

4. Be more realistic about your weight. Lose weight if you need to, but don't expect to measure up to the ideal projected by the media. Remember, obsession about weight can lead to anorexia nervosa or bulimia.

5. Limit your intake of cola, coffee, tea, and chocolate and other products containing caffeine. Also, do not smoke cigarettes or use other tobacco products (snuff, chewing tobacco).

6. During particularly stressful times, you might want to consider supplementing your diet with vitamins. In particular, focus on vitamin C and the B complex vitamins. However, many experts believe that eating a balanced diet that includes a wide variety of foods will ensure a sufficient amount of vitamins.

7. Limit foods containing sugar. If ingesting sugar, do not take in large amounts in a short period of time, and do not skip meals.

hypoglycemia
A condition of low blood sugar.

8. Limit intake of processed flour. However, some experts believe that if the flour is enriched with vitamins and minerals, it need not be avoided.

9. Limit your intake of sodium.

Part of eliminating unnecessary stressors includes eliminating those food substances that either make us more prone to stress or create a stresslike response. This is another area of our lives we need to take charge of.

Noise and Stress

Anyone who has roomed with a noisy person, worked in a noisy office, or tried to study with a party going on in the next room can attest to the effect of noise on one's level of stress. Noise can raise blood pressure, increase heart rate, and lead to muscle tension. Noise has been found to be related to job dissatisfaction and to result in irritation and anxiety.[12] One expert describes noise as the most troublesome of all stressors in our environment.[13] Noise can result in sleep disturbance, headaches, and hypertension.[14]

Most disturbing is noise that constantly changes in pitch, intensity, or frequency. We may become used to more common and stable noise and almost ignore it. People who live near airports, for example, seem to not hear the planes after a while. However, just because you become accustomed to a noise or are able to tune it out doesn't mean you are not being affected by it.

Noise is measured in decibels. At 85 decibels, stress responses usually develop, and prolonged exposure to sounds above 90 decibels can result in hearing damage. Of course, depending on one's level of concentration and the task being performed, even low levels of noise can be bothersome. Figure 5.4 lists decibel ratings for some common sounds. To reduce noise levels, you can

1. Use cotton or ear plugs if your job requires constant exposure to loud noises.
2. Sit as far away as possible from the performers at loud rock, symphony, or band concerts.
3. Learn to enjoy listening to music at home at a moderate volume.
4. Put drapes over windows to reduce street noise.
5. Choose acoustical tile for ceilings and walls when building a house or adding a room.
6. Use carpeting or select an apartment with carpeting in all rooms adjacent to other units.
7. Keep noise-making appliances away from bedrooms, den, and living room.
8. Select home sites or apartments away from truck routes, airports, businesses, and industrial areas.

In spite of its potential for stress, noise can at times be soothing. In fact, on many stress management audiotapes, you will find noise to help you relax. This is called "white noise," and its purpose is to drown out other sounds that may interfere with relaxation. Sounds such as the surf rolling onto the shore, birds chirping, or the wind rustling through the leaves can serve as comforting sounds. In addition, some sounds are used to focus upon to bring about relaxation. For example, some forms of meditation use a word (called a **mantra**) for focusing, and other methods of relaxation employ chanting.

So you can see that *noise* can be stressful but certain *sounds* can be relaxing. You can take greater control of your life by limiting disturbing noises and seeking out relaxing sounds. Walk through the woods; recline on a beach. Noise or relaxing sound— it's up to you.

mantra
A word that is the focus of meditation.

Figure 5.4

Common sounds and their decibel ratings.

Source: National Institute on Deafness and Other Communication Disorders, NIH, Bethesda, Jan. 1990

NOISE LEVELS AND HUMAN RESPONSE

COMMON SOUNDS	DECIBELS	EFFECTS
Normal breathing	10	Just audible
Whisper	30	Very quiet
Normal conversation	50–65	Comfortable under 60
Vacuum cleaner	70	Intrusive, interferes with telephone use
Garbage disposal	80	Annoying, interferes with conversation. Constant exposure may cause damage.
Television	70–90	Very annoying, 85—noise level at which hearing damage begins after eight hours' exposure
Lawn mower	85–90	
Motorcycle at 25 ft.	90	
Snowmobile	105	Regular exposure of more than one minute risks permanent loss over 100 decibels.
Power saw, chain saw	110	
Thunderclap, boom box	120	Threshold of sensation is 120 decibels.
Stereos (over 120 watts)	110–125	
Jet takeoff	130	Beyond threshold of pain—125 decibels
Shotgun firing	130	
Rock concerts	110–140	

Life Events and Stress

The information in this section will have more meaning for you if you follow these instructions: If you are presently a college student, determine which events you have experienced by completing Lab 5.2, a life-events scale developed by G. E. Anderson.

If you are older than the typical college student, assess the amount of life events you have experienced within the past year by completing Lab 5.3, a life-events scale developed by Thomas Holmes and Richard Rahe.

Labs 5.2 and 5.3 will help you assess the amount of significant changes in your life to which you have had to adjust. In other words, your life change units (LCU) is a measure of the stressors you encountered this past year. The original research in this field was conducted by Holmes and Rahe, who developed the *Social Readjustment Rating Scale* appearing in Lab 5.3. They argued that if stress results in illness and disease, then people experiencing a great deal of stress should report more illness than people reporting only a little stress. Their theory was subsequently supported by their research. Lab 5.2 is an adaptation of the Social Readjustment Rating Scale specific to college students.

Many other researchers have supported the findings of Holmes and Rahe.[15–18] However, not all studies measuring life-change units have been so supportive of this theory. The inconsistency of these research findings should not be surprising. If you'll recall the stress theory model, all that these life-events scales measure is the top phase (life situation). We know, though, that changes in life situations alone are not enough to cause illness and disease. These changes must be perceived as distressing and result in emotional and, subsequently, physiological arousal that is chronic, prolonged, or unabated. We also now know that it is possible to establish roadblocks (intervention techniques) to inhibit the development of illness or disease from stressors we experience. Researchers have found one such roadblock to be **social support.**[19] People who experienced a great deal of life change but had family or friends with whom to discuss their problems contracted no more illness than people who experienced less life change. However, people who experienced a great deal of life change but *did not* have family or friends with whom to discuss their problems contracted much more illness than the others. Suffice it to say that life change does not, in and of itself, lead to poor health.

What should you do if your score on the life-events scale concerns you? First, let's look at how people typically react to a stressful period of time. We often hear people say, "I've been under a lot of stress lately. I need a vacation." If you have too many life-change units, why add more? Vacation is worth 13 points! Rather than add to your stress, you'd be better advised to make your life more routine to reduce your need to adapt to changes. Rather than taking a vacation, maintain your daily routine (perhaps eliminating some events but *not* substituting others). I'm often asked how such pleasant events as a vacation and Christmas or Hanukkah can be stressors. Remember that stress occurs when we are knocked out of balance. We are in equilibrium when suddenly something occurs requiring us to use energy to adapt. All of the adjustments required prior to, during, and returning from a vacation are the reasons why a vacation can be a stressor.

Another interesting revelation can be inferred from the Holmes and Rahe scale. If you have a marital separation, you accumulate 65 stressor points. That event requires you to adjust from being married and the routines you have established within your marriage to being single again. The functions your spouse performed now need your attention. The time you spent together now needs to be used for another purpose. You need to adjust to aloneness or loneliness or both. You need to spend time meeting new people. It is evident that this separation requires a great deal of adaptation energy and can be quite stressful. Let's assume that you have spent six months adjusting to your marital separation and have finally adapted to your new routines and way of living. Lo and behold, the old flame flickers once again, and you and your spouse decide to try a reconciliation. Notice, though, that marital reconciliation is worth 45 stressor points. Once again, you are requiring yourself (mind and body) to adapt to being married just after you have finally adapted to being single. Your daily routines need changing, your associations and affiliations may need to be readjusted, and you must develop your marital relationship more effectively than before.

The moral of this story is to be sure of your need for marital separation (and other breaks in your relationships with loved ones) prior to the separation and, once you have made that decision, do not easily revert to that old relationship. Of course, there are intervening variables associated with these decisions. For some people, the separation can be so stressful and the adaptation so difficult that the

social support
The presence of significant others with whom to discuss stressors.

It's the daily hassles that might be more threatening to your health than major life events. Having a parking meter expire and getting a ticket, or searching for a job, can create chronic stress and its accompanying negative consequences.

stress associated with reconciliation would be less than the stress of continuing the separation. Others may be willing to tolerate the threat to their health in order to re-establish their marriage (or other relationship). You can probably think of other considerations that enter into this decision. However, recognize that the more your life situation requires adaptation, the more likely you are to become ill. Some stressors you may not be able to eliminate (e.g., the death of a spouse or close friend), but others you can control. You can, therefore, decide that they will no longer be a part of your life; to do so would be to improve your health.

Hassles and Chronic Stress

Carrying the life change–stress relationship further, Kanner[20] and his colleagues hypothesized that everyday **hassles** would be even more detrimental to health than major life events. They defined hassles as daily interactions with the environment that were essentially negative and, because of their chronic nature, could take a significant toll on health. Losing a wallet, smoking too much, and having troublesome neighbors are examples of these hassles. Furthermore, Lazarus[21] proposed that the absence of **uplifts**—positive events that make us feel good—would also be related to ill health.

Although the absence of uplifts has not been found to be related to ill health, the presence of hassles has. Hassles have been shown to be predictive of psychological distress[22] and the dynamics of stress and aging[23] and to be related to poorer mental and physical health.[24,25] In general, Lazarus's theory has been shown to be correct in asserting that hassles are related to subsequent illness and disease to a greater degree than are major life events.[26] One major difference between these scales is that the hassles scale asks respondents to judge the severity of the event. This is important because an event can occur but be perceived as inconsequential. In that case, it might not have much effect on the respondent's health.

You can assess the amount and intensity of the hassles you experience by completing Lab 5.4. When a group of adults completed the hassles scale,[27] they reported experiencing a mean of 20.6 hassles per month over a nine-month period of time. The mean intensity of these hassles was 1.47. Once you have identified your hassles, try to eliminate as many of them as you can while recognizing that many others will either take a long time to change or are unchangeable (you will have to learn to live with these).

Success Analysis

A friend of mine wrote a book that I recommend to you. Its title reflects both her personality and her reality: *Success: You Can Make It Happen.*[28] You really can make it happen. Success need not be left to chance. As gambling casinos give themselves an edge to ensure a profit, you can give yourself an edge to ensure being successful. Giving yourself success (don't miss the importance of this phrasing) will result in your thinking better of yourself. Stated more pedantically, success will lead to improved self-esteem. The converse, of course, is that lack of success (failure) will lead to diminished self-esteem, resulting in a very significant stressor.

At this point, you need some information about yourself to infer personal meaning from our discussion. Complete the success chart shown in Table 5.3. Divide your life into three equal time periods, beginning at age five. If you are fifty years old, your three time periods will be five to twenty, twenty-one to thirty-five, and thirty-six to fifty; if you are twenty years old, they'll be five to ten, eleven to fifteen, and sixteen to twenty. Next, think of three of your successes during each period and the reasons you consider these experiences successes. Place these successes and reasons within the success chart. Lastly, write in what you consider to be the most successful experience of your life and the least successful one, along with the reasons you consider them such. The last part of this data-gathering procedure requires you to list, on a separate sheet of paper, ten strengths of yours—your most positive characteristics and talents. Please do this before reading further.

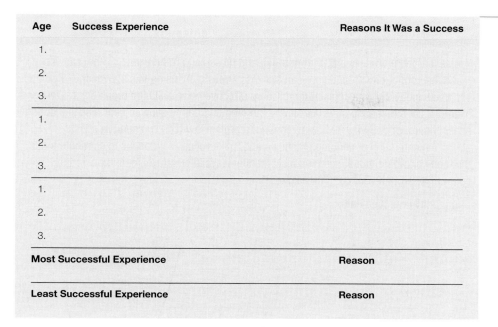

Age	Success Experience	Reasons It Was a Success
1.		
2.		
3.		
1.		
2.		
3.		
1.		
2.		
3.		

Most Successful Experience	Reason
Least Successful Experience	Reason

Table 5.3

YOUR SUCCESS CHART

Source: From Lila Swell, *Success: You Can Make It Happen.* © 1976 by Lila Swell. Reprinted by permission of Lila Swell.

Success is multifaceted and, like beauty, is in the eyes of the beholder. What you view as successful, others might not. Some consider themselves successful when they achieve independence, and their success charts reflect this viewpoint, with successes such as owning their first car, getting their first job, or moving into their own apartment. Their reasons for regarding these as successes might be "Didn't have to rely on others" or "Now I had money to do my own thing."

Others view success as competing and winning. Their success charts include successes such as playing on a championship team, winning a trophy, and competing with other students and winning a scholarship to college. The reasons given might be "The competition was intense" or "A lot of people tried to do this, but only I succeeded." Still others define success in other ways:

1. Being chosen (or elected) by others.
2. Pleasing others (parents, teachers, friends).
3. Being helpful.
4. Achieving academically.
5. Achieving in sports activities.
6. Being the best.
7. Achieving in spite of great obstacles and difficulty (if too easy, the achievement is not viewed as a success).
8. Learning a skill.
9. Getting recognition from others.
10. Being happy.

How do you define success? Scan your success chart and list at least four patterns that emerge. Make sure that your patterns are just that—patterns. They must appear several times within the chart. You should conclude with a sentence that begins "Success to me is . . . ."

Now that you know your own view of success, how can you achieve it? The best way is to use the strengths you listed previously. Try to maximize those strengths and minimize any weaknesses you have in order to "fix the deck" and increase your chances of being successful. Prescribe life experiences for yourself that use those strengths; shy

Getting Involved in Your Community

You've learned in this chapter that nutrition and noise can produce stress. How can you make the community around your campus less stressful by using this knowledge? Perhaps you could lobby the local legislature for more effective noise pollution regulations—for example, construction to start later in the morning and not be allowed near a school during school hours. Or you may be able to conduct a project in which you analyze a local school's lunch menu or vending machines and make recommendations to eliminate foods that can contribute to a stress response. Identify ways in which you can improve the community around your campus below.

Community Improvements:

1. _____
2. _____
3. _____
4. _____
5. _____

Will you commit to working on one of these projects to make the community around your campus less stressful? Ask your instructor for advice if you decide to "make a difference."

away from experiences that rely on talents, skills, or characteristics that you lack. For example, if you perceive success as achieving independence, don't seek success occupationally by working on an assembly line. If you don't have the "gift of gab," you should not become a salesperson. You might try to be successful as an author if you view success as recognition from others and have a talent for writing. If you also have *helping others* as a component of your success definition, the books you write should present information that can be used to help others.

With the data you have acquired regarding your definition of success and your list of strengths, you are now able to give *yourself* success. You are now in control of one more possible stressor. You are now better able to maintain your health and improve the quality of your life. *But* you will do this only if you use this information to make your life situation consistent with what you have learned.

summary

- Good nutrition may help in managing stress. Foods should be eaten from a variety of sources. Eating the recommended amounts of foods from the food pyramid groups is one way of ensuring that you eat a balanced diet.

- Maintaining nutritional health by practices such as eating less saturated fat and alcohol and eating more fiber and cruciferous vegetables may also reduce stressors in your diet.

- Food substances that produce a stresslike response are called pseudostressors or sympathomimetics, since they mimic sympathetic nervous system stimulation. Foods containing caffeine are examples of these substances.

- Stress may deplete the B complex and C vitamins; in the case of chronic stress, the diet may require supplementation with vitamins and minerals. Ingestion of sugar and processed flour may make this situation even worse, since both of these use up valuable nutrients when the body metabolizes them.

- To manage stress better, limit intake of caffeine, sugar, and foods containing processed flour that has not been enriched. During stressful times, consider vitamin supplementation.

- Noise can be either distressing or relaxing. Noises louder than 85 decibels usually elicit a stress response, and prolonged exposure to sounds above 90 decibels can result in hearing damage. White noise is used to drown out disturbing noises while one is trying to relax.

- Thomas Holmes and Richard Rahe found that the more significant changes a person has in his or her life, the greater is the chance that he or she will contract some physical or psychological illness. Since they conceptualized stress as adapting to change, Holmes and Rahe viewed more change as equivalent to more stress and, consequently, to more illness and disease.

- Richard Lazarus found that the daily hassles a person experiences are more harmful to his or her health than are the significant life changes that concerned Holmes and Rahe. Lazarus believes these daily events are so damaging to health because of how frequently they occur, as compared with the major life events that Holmes and Rahe researched, which were usually encountered only rarely.

notes

1. R. P. Feynman, *Surely You're Joking, Mr. Feynman!: Adventures of a Curious Character* (New York: W. W. Norton, 1985).

2. American Cancer Society, *American Cancer Society Guidelines on Diet and Cancer Prevention.* 2005. http://www.cancer.org/docroot/MED/content/MED_2_1X_American_Cancer_Society_guidelines_on_diet_and_cancer_prevention.asp

3. American Cancer Society. *Nutrition and Cancer Risk.* http://www.cancer.org/docroot/NWS/content/NWS_2_1X_Nutririon_and_Cancer_Risk.asp

4. National Heart, Lung, and Blood Institute, "Aim for a Healthy Weight," *Patient and Public Education Materials,* 2000. www.nhlbi.nih.gov/health/public/heart/obesity/lose_wt/risk.htm

5. American Psychiatric Association, *Diagnostic and Statistical Manual of Mental Disorders,* 4th ed. (Washington, DC: American Psychiatric Association, 1994).

6. P. H. Robinson, "Review Article: Recognition and Treatment of Eating Disorders in Primary and Secondary Care," *Alimentary Pharmacological Therapy* 14(2000): 367–77.

7. W. H. Kaye, K. L. Klump, G. K. Frank, and M. Strober, "Anorexia and Bulimia Nervosa," *Annual Review of Medicine* 51(2000): 299–313.

8. D. R. Patel, E. L. Phillips, and H. D. Pratt, "Eating Disorders," *Indian Journal of Pediatrics* 65(1998): 487–94.

9. B. A. Arnow, "Why Are Empirically Supported Treatments for Bulimia Nervosa Underutilized and What Can We Do About It?" *Journal of Clinical Psychology* 55(1999): 769–79.

10. J. W. Hole, *Human Anatomy and Physiology,* 6th ed. (Dubuque, IA: Wm. C. Brown Publishers, 2002), 505.

11. Rod R. Seeley, Trent D. Stephens, and Philip Tate, *Anatomy & Physiology* (Boston: McGraw-Hill, 2003), 190–91.

12. M. Boudarene, J. J. Legros, and M. Timsit-Berthier, "Study of the Stress Response: Role of Anxiety, Cortisol and DHEAs," *Encephale* 28 (2002): 139–46.

13. Sheldon Cohen, "Sound Effects on Behavior," *Psychology Today,* October 1981, 38–49.

14. Rebecca J. Donatelle and Lorraine G. Davis, *Access to Health,* 6th ed. (Boston: Allyn and Bacon, 2000), 567.

15. D. J. Lynch, A. McGrady, E. Alvarez, and J. Forman, "Recent Life Changes and Medical Utilization in an Academic Family Practice," *Journal of Nervous and Mental Disorders* 193 (2005): 633–35.

16. A. J. Costa, S. Labuda Schrop, G. McCord, and C. Ritter, "Depression in Family Medicine Faculty," *Family Medicine* 37 (2005): 271–75.

17. D. Clarke and R. Singh, "Life Events, Stress Appraisals, and Hospital Doctors' Mental Health," *New Zealand Medical Journal* 117 (2004): U1121.

18. Y. Yamada, K. Tatsumi, T. Yamaguchi, N. Tanabe, Y. Takiguchi, T. Kuriyama, and R. Mikami, "Influence of Stressful Life Events on the Onset of Sarcoidosis," *Respirology* 8 (2003): 186–91.

19. Thomas Stachnik et al., "Goal Setting, Social Support and Financial Incentives in Stress Management Programs: A Pilot Study of Their Impact on Adherence," *American Journal of Health Promotion* 5(1990): 24–29.

20. A. D. Kanner et al., "Comparison of Two Modes of Stress Management: Daily Hassles and Uplifts Versus Major Life Events," *Journal of Behavioral Medicine* 4(1981): 1–39.

21. Richard S. Lazarus, "Puzzles in the Study of Daily Hassles," *Journal of Behavioral Medicine* 7(1984): 375–89.

22. C. K. Holahan, C. J. Holahan, and S. S. Belk, "Adjustment in Aging: The Roles of Life Stress, Hassles, and Self-Efficacy," *Health Psychology* 3(1984): 315–28.

23. Richard S. Lazarus and A. DeLongis, "Psychological Stress and Coping in Aging," *American Psychologist* 38(1983): 245–54.

24. Kanner et al., "Comparison of Two Modes," 1–39.

25. J. J. Zarski, "Hassles and Health: A Replication," *Health Psychology* 3(1984): 243–51.

26. Nancy Burks and Barclay Martin, "Everyday Problems and Life Change Events: Ongoing Versus Acute Sources of Stress," *Journal of Human Stress* 11(1985): 27–35.

27. Anita DeLongis, James C. Coyne, Gayle Dakof, Susan Folkman, and Richard S. Lazarus, "Relationship of Daily Hassles, Uplifts, and Major Life Events to Health Status," *Health Psychology* 1(1982): 119–36.

28. Lila Swell, *Success: You Can Make It Happen* (New York: Simon & Schuster, 1976).

internet resources

Stress Management Links
www.pp.okstate.edu/ehs/links/stress.htm
Links to articles on managing stress.

Food and Nutrition Information Center
www.nal.usda.gov/fnic/
A USDA site that provides access to a variety of nutrition-related databases.

Stress Management
www.md-phc.com/education/stress.html
An article on how to identify the symptoms and sources of stress, and how to effectively manage it.

Stress Less
www.stressless.com
Offers a wide selection of stress reduction products and programs for use in coping with the effects of excess stress.

Coping in Today's World

Researchers have uncovered some interesting findings regarding the life event they define as marital discord.[a] Married couples were admitted twice to a hospital research unit for twenty-four hours each admission. During the first admission, couples had a social support interaction that would result in greater marital accord. During the second hospital admission, couples discussed marital disagreement and how to resolve several marital problems. During each admission, researchers inflicted blisters wounds on the subjects and measured the pace at which these wounds healed. They also measured the level of cytokine production since cytokine facilitates healing. Researchers found that wounds healed more slowly, and local cytokine production was lower at wound sites, following marital conflicts than after social support interactions. Furthermore, couples who demonstrated consistently high levels of hostile behaviors healed 60 percent more slowly than low-hostile couples. It seems that supporting one another and limiting hostility is not only emotionally healthy but is also physically healthy. And, this is probably true in other relationships as well.

[a]J. K. Kiecolt-Glaser, T. J. Loving, J. R. Stowell, W. B. Malarkey, S. Lemeshow, S. L. Dickinson, and R. Glaser, "Hostile Marital Interactions, Proinflammatory Cytokine Production, and Wound Healing," *Archives of General Psychiatry* 62(2005):1377–84.

LAB ASSESSMENT 5.1
What Is Your Resting Metabolic Rate (RMR)?

Everyone's caloric needs are determined by the calories expended during physical activities, as well as during nonactivity. Approximately one-third of calories burned each day are a result of regular metabolic activity. This includes calories to maintain body temperature, heartbeat, breathing, organ repair, and basic chemical reactions. This is your Resting Metabolic Rate, or RMR. The other two-thirds of the calories expended each day are a function of activities engaged in that particular day. It stands to reason that if you desire to lose weight, you want to keep your RMR high and increase your other activities (assuming your caloric intake remains constant). One way to keep RMR high is to maintain a high level of physical fitness. A physically fit body burns more calories at rest than does an unfit one. RMR also decreases with age, about 2 percent per decade, because of muscle loss. Therefore, to keep RMR high, weight training is recommended.

If you want to lose weight, a first step might be to calculate your RMR. The formula to do so is one that was developed many years ago but is still the preferred method, short of laboratory procedures. It was developed in 1919 by Francis G. Benedict and J. Arthur Harris and is called the Harris-Benedict equation.

Directions: Calculate your RMR by completing the sections below, depending on whether you are female or male.

Women		Men	
1. Begin with a base of 655 calories	655	1. Begin with a base of 655 calories	655
2. Multiply your weight in pounds by 4.3	____	2. Multiply your weight in pounds by 6.3	____
3. Multiply your height in inches by 4.7	____	3. Multiply your height in inches by 12.7	____
4. Add the totals from #1, #2, #3	____	4. Add the totals from #1, #2, #3	____
5. Multiply your age by 4.7	____	5. Multiply your age by 6.8	____
6. Subtract #5 from #4 to find your RMR	____	6. Subtract #5 from #4 to find your RMR	____
7. To maintain your current weight, multiply #6 by your Physical Activity Factor (see below)	____	7. To maintain your current weight, multiply #6 by your Physical Activity Factor (see below)	____
8. For a weight-loss diet, subtract 250 calories	____	8. For a weight-loss diet, subtract 250 calories	____

Physical Activity Factor: 1.2 for low activity (sedentary); 1.4 for moderate activity (light exercise); 1.6 for high levels of activity

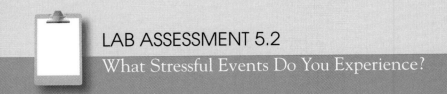

LAB ASSESSMENT 5.2

What Stressful Events Do You Experience?

Directions: Determine which events you have experienced in the past year.

Mean Value	Event
(50)	Entered college
(77)	Married
(38)	Had either a lot more or a lot less trouble with your boss
(43)	Held a job while attending school
(87)	Experienced the death of a spouse
(34)	Experienced a major change in sleeping habits (sleeping a lot more or a lot less, or a change in part of the day when asleep)
(77)	Experienced the death of a close family member
(30)	Experienced a major change in eating habits (a lot more or a lot less food intake, or very different meal hours or surroundings)
(41)	Made a change in or choice of a major field of study
(45)	Had a revision of your personal habits (friends, dress, manners, associations, etc.)
(68)	Experienced the death of a close friend
(22)	Have been found guilty of minor violations of the law (traffic tickets, jaywalking, etc.)
(40)	Have had an outstanding personal achievement
(68)	Experienced pregnancy or fathered a child
(56)	Had a major change in the health or behavior of a family member
(58)	Had sexual difficulties
(42)	Had trouble with in-laws
(26)	Had a major change in the number of family get-togethers (a lot more or a lot less)
(53)	Had a major change in financial state (a lot worse off or a lot better off than usual)
(50)	Gained a new family member (through birth, adoption, older person moving in, etc.)
(42)	Changed your residence or living conditions
(50)	Had a major conflict in or change in values
(36)	Had a major change in church activities (a lot more or a lot less than usual)
(58)	Had a marital reconciliation with your mate
(62)	Were fired from work
(76)	Were divorced
(50)	Changed to a different line of work
(50)	Had a major change in the number of arguments with spouse (either a lot more or a lot less than usual)
(47)	Had a major change in responsibilities at work (promotion, demotion, lateral transfer)
(41)	Had your spouse begin or cease work outside the home
(74)	Had a marital separation from your mate
(57)	Had a major change in usual type and/or amount of recreation
(52)	Took a mortgage or loan *less* than $10,000 (such as purchase of a car, TV, school loan, etc.)
(65)	Had a major personal injury or illness
(46)	Had a major change in the use of alcohol (a lot more or a lot less)
(48)	Had a major change in social activities
(38)	Had a major change in the amount of participation in school activities
(49)	Had a major change in the amount of independence and responsibility (for example, for budgeting time)
(33)	Took a trip or a vacation
(54)	Were engaged to be married
(50)	Changed to a new school
(41)	Changed dating habits
(44)	Had trouble with school administration (instructors, advisors, class scheduling, etc.)
(60)	Broke or had broken a marital engagement or a steady relationship
(57)	Had a major change in self-concept or self-awareness

Source: G. E. Anderson, "College Schedule of Recent Experience." *Master's thesis,* North Dakota State University, 1972.

Scoring: Multiply the number of times an event occurred by its mean value. Then total all of the scores. The result is your life-change unit (LCU) score. Although there are no norms for scoring this scale as there are for Lab 5.3, the greater the number of LCUs, the greater is the chance of a resulting illness or disease. Based on research of the *Social Readjustment Rating Scale* (presented in Lab 5.3), LCUs between 150–199 lead to a 37 percent chance of these stressors leading to illness or disease, LCUs between 200–299 lead to a 51 percent chance, and LCUs over 300 increase the chance to 79 percent.

LAB ASSESSMENT 5.3

Are Your Life Events Unhealthy?

Directions: Determine which events you have experienced in the past year.

Mean Value	Event
(100)	Death of spouse
(73)	Divorce
(65)	Marital separation
(63)	Jail term
(63)	Death of close family member
(53)	Personal injury or illness
(50)	Marriage
(47)	Fired at work
(45)	Marital reconciliation
(45)	Retirement
(44)	Change in health of family member
(40)	Pregnancy
(39)	Sex difficulties
(39)	Gain of new family member
(39)	Business readjustment
(38)	Change in financial state
(37)	Death of close friend
(36)	Change to different line of work
(35)	Change in number of arguments with spouse
(31)	Mortgage or loan for major purchase (home, etc.)
(30)	Foreclosure of mortgage or loan
(29)	Change in responsibilities at work
(29)	Son or daughter leaving home
(29)	Trouble with in-laws
(28)	Outstanding personal achievement
(26)	Spouse begins or stops work
(25)	Change in living conditions
(24)	Revision of personal habits
(23)	Trouble with boss
(20)	Change in work hours or conditions
(20)	Change in residence
(19)	Change in recreation
(19)	Change in church activities
(18)	Change in social activities
(17)	Mortgage or loan for lesser purchase (car, TV, etc.)
(16)	Change in sleeping habits
(15)	Change in number of family get-togethers
(15)	Change in eating habits
(13)	Vacation
(12)	Christmas or Chanukah
(11)	Minor violations of the law

Source: Thomas H. Holmes and Richard H. Rahe, "The Social Readjustment Rating Scale," *Journal of Psychosomatic Research* 11(1967): 213–18.

Scoring: Multiply the number of times an event occurred by its mean value. Then total all of the scores. The result is your life change unit (LCU) score. If you scored between 150–199, there is a 37 percent chance of these stressors leading to illness or disease. If you scored 200–299, there is a 51 percent chance of these stressors leading to illness or disease. Over 300 and the chance increases to 79 percent.

LAB ASSESSMENT 5.4

What Hassles Do You Encounter?

Directions: Hassles are irritants that can range from minor annoyances to major pressures, problems, or difficulties. They can occur few or many times. Listed here are ways in which a person can feel hassled. First, circle the hassles that have happened to you *in the past month*. Then look at the numbers to the right of the items you circled. Indicate by circling 1, 2, or 3 how often each of the *circled* hassles has occurred in the past month. If a hassle did not occur in the past month, do not circle it.

	How Often				How Often				How Often		
	1 = Somewhat Often				1 = Somewhat Often				1 = Somewhat Often		
	2 = Moderately Often				2 = Moderately Often				2 = Moderately Often		
Hassles	3 = Extremely Often			**Hassles**	3 = Extremely Often			**Hassles**	3 = Extremely Often		
Misplacing or losing things	1	2	3	Too many interruptions	1	2	3	Concerns about meeting high			
Troublesome neighbors	1	2	3	Unexpected company	1	2	3	standards	1	2	3
Social obligations	1	2	3	Too much time on hands	1	2	3	Financial dealing with friends or			
Inconsiderate smokers	1	2	3	Having to wait	1	2	3	acquaintances	1	2	3
Troubling thoughts about				Concerns about accidents	1	2	3	Job dissatisfactions	1	2	3
your future	1	2	3	Being lonely	1	2	3	Worries about decisions to			
Thoughts about death	1	2	3	Not enough money for				change jobs	1	2	3
Health of a family member	1	2	3	health care	1	2	3	Trouble with reading, writing,			
Not enough money for clothing	1	2	3	Fear of confrontation	1	2	3	or spelling abilities	1	2	3
Not enough money for housing	1	2	3	Financial security	1	2	3	Too many meetings	1	2	3
Concerns about owing money	1	2	3	Silly practical mistakes	1	2	3	Problems with divorce or			
Concerns about getting credit	1	2	3	Inability to express yourself	1	2	3	separation	1	2	3
Concerns about money for				Physical illness	1	2	3	Trouble with arithmetic skills	1	2	3
emergencies	1	2	3	Fear of rejection	1	2	3	Gossip	1	2	3
Someone owes you money	1	2	3	Difficulties with getting pregnant	1	2	3	Legal problems	1	2	3
Financial responsibility for				Sexual problems that result				Concerns about weight	1	2	3
someone who doesn't live				from physical problems	1	2	3	Not enough time to do the			
with you	1	2	3	Concerns about health				things you need to do	1	2	3
Cutting down on electricity,				in general	1	2	3	Television	1	2	3
water, etc.	1	2	3	Not seeing enough people	1	2	3	Not enough personal energy	1	2	3
Smoking too much	1	2	3	Friends or relatives too far away	1	2	3	Concern about inner conflicts	1	2	3
Use of alcohol	1	2	3	Preparing meals	1	2	3	Feel conflicted over what to do	1	2	3
Personal use of drugs	1	2	3	Wasting time	1	2	3	Regrets over past decisions	1	2	3
Too many responsibilities	1	2	3	Auto maintenance	1	2	3	Menstrual (period) problems	1	2	3
Decisions about having children	1	2	3	Filling out forms	1	2	3	The weather	1	2	3
Nonfamily members living in				Neighborhood deterioration	1	2	3	Nightmares	1	2	3
your home	1	2	3	Financing children's education	1	2	3	Concerns about getting ahead	1	2	3
Care for pet	1	2	3	Problems with employees	1	2	3	Hassles from boss or supervisor	1	2	3
Planning meals	1	2	3	Problems on job due to being				Difficulties with friends	1	2	3
Concerned about the				a woman or a man	1	2	3	Not enough time for family	1	2	3
meaning of life	1	2	3	Declining physical abilities	1	2	3	Transportation problems	1	2	3
Trouble relaxing	1	2	3	Being exploited	1	2	3	Not enough money for			
Trouble making decisions	1	2	3	Concerns about bodily functions	1	2	3	transportation	1	2	3
Problems getting along				Rising prices of common goods	1	2	3	Not enough money for			
with fellow workers	1	2	3	Not getting enough rest	1	2	3	entertainment and recreation	1	2	3
Customers or clients give				Not getting enough sleep	1	2	3	Shopping	1	2	3
you a hard time	1	2	3	Problems with aging parents	1	2	3	Prejudice and discrimination			
Home maintenance (inside)	1	2	3	Problems with your children	1	2	3	from others	1	2	3
Concerns about job security	1	2	3	Problems with persons younger				Property, investments, or taxes	1	2	3
Concerns about retirement	1	2	3	than yourself	1	2	3	Yard work or outside home			
Laid-off or out of work	1	2	3	Problems with your lover	1	2	3	maintenance	1	2	3
Don't like current work duties	1	2	3	Difficulties seeing or hearing	1	2	3	Concerns about news events	1	2	3
Don't like fellow workers	1	2	3	Overload with family				Noise	1	2	3
Not enough money for				responsibilities	1	2	3	Crime	1	2	3
basic necessities	1	2	3	Too many things to do	1	2	3	Traffic	1	2	3
Not enough money for food	1	2	3	Unchallenging work	1	2	3	Pollution	1	2	3

Source: A. D. Kanner et al., "Comparison of Two Modes of Stress Management: Daily Hassles and Uplifts Versus Major Life Events," *Journal of Behavioral Medicine* 4(1981): 1–39.

Scoring: The mean score is 20.6 hassles per month. The mean intensity of these hassles is 1.47. If your scores are higher, you experience more hassles, or more intense hassles, than the average person. If that is the case, you are more susceptible than is the average person to negative consequences, such as illness and disease, because of this increased level of stress.

Life-Situation Interventions

While some life-situation interventions can be successfully employed when no one else is directly involved, this chapter presents life-situation interventions that are useful when the situation involves other people as well as yourself. The topics we will consider include assertiveness; resolving conflicts; communicating effectively with others; and managing time wisely and coordinating it with coworkers, family, and friends. We will also consider how to develop a network of supporters to serve as a buffer between stress and its negative consequences.

Because other people are involved, you might want to consider teaching these stress management techniques to the people you interact with often. In that way, when a situation presents itself that calls for one of the stress management strategies discussed in this chapter and you forget to use it, the other person might remember. The result can be more effective interactions for you, and that can only mean less stress.

Asserting Yourself

> Ring! Gladys picks up the telephone to hear the dulcet voice of her friend Sue. "Gladys, I have an appointment for lunch. Can you watch Billy from noon until three?"
>
> "Sure, Sue. Take your time and enjoy yourself. I'll expect you at noon." But in Gladys' mind another conversation is being recorded: "I don't believe that Sue! She's always asking me to watch her kid. What am I, a babysitter? I was looking forward to scheduling a tennis match with Joan today. Well, there goes that idea."

This scenario is not atypical and not exclusive to women. Men and women who find it difficult to say no when asked by the boss if they can handle one other chore or responsibility and youths who can't say no to friends when teased into trying a mood-altering substance (alcohol or other drugs) have the same problem as Gladys does. Training programs have been mushrooming throughout the country and world to help people say no when they should, say yes when they want to, and, in general, behave in a self-actualizing manner. These training programs teach assertive behavior. Several definitions are necessary at this point:

1. *Assertive behavior:* Expressing yourself and satisfying your own needs. Feeling good about this and not hurting others in the process.

2. *Nonassertive behavior:* Denying your own wishes to satisfy someone else's. Sacrificing your own needs to meet someone else's needs.

3. *Aggressive behavior:* Seeking to dominate or to get your own way at the expense of others.

To assess your general pattern of behavior regarding assertiveness, complete Lab 6.1 at the end of this chapter.

In the phone conversation just described, Gladys's response was **nonassertive**. She gave up her need for scheduling recreation time and did not express her feelings of being used and taken advantage of by Sue. If she had been **aggressive,** Gladys might have said, "How dare you ask me to watch that brat of yours? I have more important things to do. You're selfish and self-centered. You never even asked if you could watch my children." Acting aggressively, Gladys would have denied Sue's right to ask a favor of her. Gladys would have gone about fulfilling her needs, but she would have done so in a manner that was unfair to Sue. Sue has the right to ask, and Gladys should not deny her that right. However, Gladys owns her own behavior. She

Interpersonal

nonassertive
Giving up what one is entitled to, one's rights, in order not to upset another person.

aggressive
Acting in a way to get what one is entitled to, one's rights, but at the expense of someone else's rights.

assertive

Acting in a way to get what one is entitled to, one's rights, but not at the expense of someone else's rights.

has the right to say no. In a more **assertive** response to Sue's request, Gladys might have replied, "I can appreciate your need for someone to watch Billy, but I've been so busy lately that I promised myself today I wouldn't take on any such commitments. I really need some recreation time, so I'm going to play tennis with Joan. Perhaps Mary is free to watch Billy. Do you have her phone number?" It would also be appropriate during this response, or sometime soon after, for Gladys to express to Sue her feelings of being used. If these feelings are expressed, they can be dealt with, and Sue will have the information she needs to change her behavior. However, if Gladys never lets Sue know how she feels, Sue will continue to make the same request, and Gladys's feelings will persist, diminishing the quality of their relationship. Soon we will discuss how Gladys can express these feelings assertively—both verbally and nonverbally.

The relationship of assertive behavior to stress lies in satisfaction of needs. If you generally act assertively, you are usually achieving your needs while maintaining effective interpersonal relationships. If you generally act nonassertively, you are not satisfying your needs, and those unsatisfied needs will become stressors. If you generally behave aggressively, your needs are met but at the expense of your relationships with others. Poor interpersonal relationships will become stressors. You can see that, to siphon off stressors at the life-situation level, you need to learn, practice, and adopt assertive behavior as your general pattern of satisfying needs.

You may understand that you have a right to act assertively, and even know how to do so, but decide not to. There could be several reasons for that decision. You might decide that acting nonassertively in a particular situation is in your best interest. Or you might decide to act nonassertively because you lack confidence and have low self-esteem. Self-esteem, discussed in detail in Chapter 7, is regard for oneself. Do you think you are smart enough to make good decisions? Do you believe you are worthy of being treated with respect and dignity? If you have low regard for yourself—low self-esteem—you might not believe you are worthy of having your rights met, and you might decide not to act assertively. If this is the case, the recommendations for improving self-esteem in Chapter 7 should help.

Assertion theory is based on the premise that every person has certain basic rights. Unfortunately, we are often taught that acting consistently with these rights is socially or morally unacceptable. We are taught some traditional assumptions as children—which stay with us as adults—that interfere with basing our behavior on these basic rights. These assumptions violate our rights, and we need to dispense with them. Table 6.1 lists some basic human rights, along with the assumptions we have been taught, and often use, to deny these rights. Which of these assumptions do you use? Which do you want to give up? How will you behave differently if you dispense with your traditional assumptions?

Table 6.1 SAMPLE OF BASIC HUMAN RIGHTS AND RELATED ASSUMPTIONS VIOLATING THESE RIGHTS

Mistaken Traditional Assumptions	Your Legitimate Rights
It is selfish to put your needs before others' needs.	You have a right to put yourself first, sometimes.
It is shameful to make mistakes. You should have an appropriate response for every occasion.	You have a right to make mistakes.
If you can't convince others that your feelings are reasonable, then they must be wrong, or maybe you are going crazy.	You have a right to be the final judge of your feelings and accept them as legitimate.
You should respect the views of others, especially if they are in a position of authority. Keep your differences of opinion to yourself. Listen and learn.	You have a right to have your own opinions and convictions.

Source: Martha Davis, Matthew McKay, and Elizabeth Robbins Eshelman, *The Relaxation and Stress Reduction Workbook.* © 1980 New Harbinger Publications, Richmond, California. Reprinted by permission.

Nonverbal Assertiveness

Unwilling to deny your basic human rights, you may choose to become more assertive. Behaving assertively is more difficult for some than others, but the hints in this section should allow everyone to begin moving in the assertive direction. Assertiveness is not only a matter of *what* you say but also a function of *how* you say it. Even if you make an assertive verbal response, you will not be believed if your body's response is nonassertive. Those who express themselves assertively

1. Stand straight, remain steady, and directly face the people to whom they are speaking, while maintaining eye contact.
2. Speak in a clear, steady voice, loud enough for the people to whom they are speaking to hear them.
3. Speak fluently, without hesitation and with assurance and confidence.

In contrast, nonassertive body language includes

1. Lack of eye contact; looking down or away.
2. Swaying and shifting of weight from one foot to the other.
3. Whining and hesitancy when speaking.

Aggressive behavior can also be recognized without even hearing the words; it includes

1. Leaning forward, with glaring eyes.
2. Pointing a finger at the person to whom you are speaking.
3. Shouting.
4. Clenching the fists.
5. Putting hands on hips and wagging the head.

If you want to act assertively, then you must pay attention to your body language. Practice and adopt assertive nonverbal behavior while concentrating on eliminating signs of nonassertive and aggressive behavior.

Verbal Assertiveness

A formula I have found effective in helping people verbally express themselves assertively is the **DESC form.** The verbal response is divided into four components:

1. *Describe:* Paint a verbal picture of the other person's behavior or the situation to which you are reacting: "When . . . "
2. *Express:* Relate your feelings regarding the other person's behavior or the situation you have just described. Use "I" statements here: "I feel . . . "
3. *Specify:* Be specific by identifying several ways you would like the other person's behavior or the situation to change. Rather than saying, "You should . . . ," use "I" statements: "I would prefer . . . ," "I would like . . . ," "I want . . . "
4. *Consequence:* Select the consequences you have decided to apply to the behavior or situation. What will you do if the other person's behavior or the situation changes to your satisfaction? "If you do _____, I will . . . " What will be the consequences if nothing changes, or if the changes do not meet your needs? "If you don't _____, I will . . . "*

To demonstrate the DESC form of organizing assertive responses, let's assume Jim and Kathy are dating. Jim wants Kathy to date him exclusively. Kathy believes she's too young to eliminate other men from her love life. Jim's assertive response to this situation might take this form:

> (Describe) When you go out with other men, (Express) I feel very jealous and have doubts about the extent of your love for me. (Specify) I would prefer that we date only each other. (Consequence) If you only date me, I'll make a sincere effort to offer you a

DESC form

A formula for verbally expressing assertiveness consisting of a description of the situation, expression of feelings, specification of preferred change, and consequences of whether or not a change is made.

*Source: S. Bower and G. A. Bower, *Asserting Yourself,* 2nd ed. (p. 126). © 1976 by Susan Anthony Bower and Gordon A. Bower. Reprinted by permission of Perseus Book Publishers, a member of Perseus Books, L.L.C.

variety of experiences so that you do not feel you've missed anything. We'll go to nice restaurants, attend plays, go to concerts, and whatever else you'd like that I can afford and that is reasonable. If you do not agree to date me exclusively, I will not date you at all. The pain would just be more than I'm willing to tolerate.

A woman in my class whose boss required that she work Monday through Friday *and* Saturdays organized the following DESC form assertive response:

(Describe) When I am expected to work six days a week, (Express) I feel tired and abused. (Specify) I would prefer working only Monday through Friday. (Consequence) If I can work only those five days, I will be conscientious about doing all my work well and on time. If need be, I'll work through some lunch hours, stay later when necessary, or even be willing to take some work home. However, if I'm required to work on Saturdays, I will resign and look for another job. That is how strongly I feel about my right to have a total weekend for myself.

Organize your own assertive response! Think of a situation that has been of concern to you for which an assertive response would be helpful. For example, one of my students recalled having invited a friend to dinner. While dinner was cooking, the friend received a call from a man she was longing to see. Before the telephone conversation was too old, he asked her out for dinner that night, and she accepted. Upon hanging up, this "friend" apologized to my student as she left to have dinner with her male acquaintance. Another student was anticipating her son's return from college with his girlfriend for a Christmas vacation. She knew he would want to sleep in the same room as his girlfriend, since they shared a room while away at school. Believing that these sleeping arrangements would violate her rights, she chose to prepare an assertive response to convey to her son. She prepared a response, stated it to her son and his girlfriend, and reported that things worked out marvelously.

Is there a situation in your life crying out for assertive behavior? Can you give up the assumptions preventing you from claiming your basic human rights in this situation? Write what you would say if you responded assertively.

_____

_____

_____

How does that feel to you? Will you do it? If so, remember to have your body language be assertive as well.

Conflict Resolution

If you become effective in resolving conflict, your interpersonal relationships will be improved. The result of this improvement will be a decrease in the number of stressors you experience. Less conflict of shorter duration resolved to your satisfaction will mean a less-stressed and healthier you.

Before we proceed with suggestions for effectively resolving conflict, you might be interested in an identification of your typical modus operandi—that is, how you usually deal with conflict situations. To make this determination, complete Lab 6.2 at the end of this chapter.

Resolving conflict can be relatively simple. What confounds the situation are usually a lack of listening, an attempt at winning, an inability to demonstrate an understanding of the person with whom you are in conflict, and a rigidity that prevents you from considering alternative solutions. Consider the following extended example from *Sexuality Education: Theory and Practice* (Bruess and Greenberg, 2004).*

Paul: Well, Barbara, as you know, Thanksgiving vacation is soon, and I'd like you to come home with me and spend it with my family.

Barbara: Now you ask! I've already told my folks to expect us for Thanksgiving dinner!

*Source: Clint E. Bruess and Jerrold S. Greenberg, *Sexuality Education: Theory and Practice*, 4th ed. (Sudbury, MA: Jones and Bartlett, 2004), 107–8.

Paul: You've got some nerve! You didn't even ask me if I wanted to go to your house for Thanksgiving.

Barbara: Ask you? You've been hitting the books so much lately that I've hardly seen you long enough to say hello, much less ask you to Thanksgiving dinner.

Paul: What would you rather I do, fail my courses? You're pretty selfish, aren't you?

Barbara: I've had it! Either we're going to my house for Thanksgiving or you can say goodbye right now.

Paul: In that case, GOODBYE!

Some arguments could be avoided if couples would listen to each other.

In this situation, both Paul and Barbara are trying to win. Each is trying to get the other to spend Thanksgiving vacation at the family home. However, neither Paul nor Barbara can win! You see, there are several choices presented by them, either overt or implied:

1. Spend the vacation at Paul's house.
2. Spend the vacation at Barbara's house.
3. Break up their relationship.

If they decide to spend the vacation at Paul's, Barbara will be required to cancel her plans with her family and put up with the hassle that would entail. Further, she will feel that her wishes are not very important in the relationship. The bottom line is that she will resent being at Paul's for Thanksgiving. But if they spend the vacation at Barbara's house, Paul will resent having to be *there*. He might feel that, since he asked first, they should be at his house. Further, he objects to Barbara's assuming she can make plans that include him without even bothering to consult him. It becomes evident, then, that regardless of whose house they visit for the vacation, one or the other will be resentful. This resentment will probably result in the Thanksgiving vacation being uncomfortable and unenjoyable for all concerned. In other words, no matter who wins, both really lose. They both wind up with a miserable vacation. The third possibility, dissolving the relationship, is also obviously a no-win solution.

How might the issue be better decided? Consider the following communication.

Paul: Well, Barbara, as you know, Thanksgiving vacation is soon, and I'd like you to come home with me and spend it with my family.

Barbara: Now you ask! I've already told my folks to expect us for Thanksgiving dinner!

Paul: You thought we would go to your house for Thanksgiving vacation?

Barbara: Yes, and my parents have made preparations already.

Paul: Your parents would be upset if we canceled Thanksgiving dinner with them?

Barbara: You bet! And I wouldn't want to be the one to have to tell them either!

Paul: You think that your parents would really hassle you if you didn't spend Thanksgiving with them?

Barbara: Yes.

Paul: Would you also feel some embarrassment in having to change plans that your parents thought were definite?

Barbara: Yes, I guess I would.

Paul: It sounds like you were really looking forward to our being together at your house and with your family this vacation.

Barbara: Yes, I really was.

Paul: I'm glad that you included me in your Thanksgiving plans, but I really was looking forward to spending this vacation together with you and with my family. I haven't seen my family for a while and, further, I know that they would really like you. And I'm a little bothered that you didn't consult me before making plans for the vacation.

Barbara: Gee, I guess you have some rights, too. I'm sorry.

Paul: Well, let's see if there are some alternatives that we haven't considered.

Barbara: Maybe we could spend half the vacation at my house and half at yours.

Paul: Or perhaps we could invite your family to my house.

Barbara: How about staying here and not spending Thanksgiving with either of our families?

Paul: It seems like we have several possibilities. We could divide the vacation in half at each of our houses, but that would mean that we waste a good part of the vacation in travel.

Barbara: It's not very realistic, either, to expect that my whole family could cancel their plans to go to your house.

Paul: At the same time, if we stayed here, both sets of parents and family would be disappointed. That would be cutting off our noses to spite our faces.

Barbara: Would it make sense to agree to spend Thanksgiving vacation at one of our houses and the next vacation at the other's?

Paul: That seems sensible, and since you've already made plans, let's spend Thanksgiving at your house.

Barbara: Okay. Remember, though, the next vacation will be at your house.

In this example, Paul followed a simple procedure to resolve interpersonal conflict. The steps of this communication process consist of the following:

1. Active listening (reflecting back to the other person his or her *words* and feelings)
2. Identifying your position (stating your *thoughts* and *feelings* about the situation)
3. Exploring alternative solutions (brainstorming other possibilities)

active listening
Paraphrasing the speaker's words and feelings; also called reflective listening.

reflective listening
Paraphrasing the speaker's words and feelings; also called active listening.

Paul began by employing a technique known as **active listening,** or **reflective listening.** This technique requires the listener to paraphrase the speaker's words so the speaker knows that his or her meaning has been received. Further, it requires the listener to go beyond the speaker's words to paraphrase the *feelings* left unspoken. Note that Paul understood Barbara would be embarrassed to have to cancel Thanksgiving vacation with her family, even though she never explicitly stated that she would. By reflecting the speaker's *words* and *thoughts,* the listener creates an awareness on the speaker's part that the listener cares enough to really understand his or her views. Once the speaker appreciates this fact, he or she is more receptive to hearing and understanding the listener's viewpoint. The net result will be both people understanding each other's point of view better; each will also be less insistent that his or her way is the only way.

The next step is to explore alternative solutions by "brainstorming"—that is, listing all possible solutions prior to evaluating their appropriateness. Once all possible solutions are listed, evaluate each proposed solution until both people agree upon one. With this technique, it initially appears that no one wins. However, in fact, everyone wins. In the previous example, Paul will accompany Barbara to her house for Thanksgiving without being resentful. He will know that she now understands his need to be involved in their planning and that the next vacation is going to be spent with his family. Consequently, he will be better able to enjoy being with Barbara and her family. The vacation will be fun, and everyone will win.

I can tell you that many people to whom I have taught this technique have dealt with their conflicts more successfully. Remember, though, that the purpose of this technique is *not* to convince someone that your point of view is correct. It is not a technique to manipulate anyone. The intention is to end up at an *alternative* solution that makes both you and the other person happy. If you are not willing to end up at some solution other than the one you had in mind, do not use this method of resolving conflict. If you are not willing to give up your power over the other person (e.g., parent over child or boss over employee), then don't use this technique.

A student of mine asked, "What happens if I use the steps you outlined and my daughter says, 'There you go with that psychology crap again.' What do I do then?" I told her to tell her daughter, "You're right. This is something I learned at school to help resolve conflict. I love you so much and place such a high value on our relationship that I felt I would try this technique. I hope we can both use it so, when we disagree, we come to a solution both of us are happy with. Would you like me to teach it to you?" How can anyone object to the use of a system designed to help them arrive at a solution satisfactory to them both and maintain their relationship?

I'll bet there are some conflicts that you can anticipate. Why not try achieving a positive resolution of those conflicts rather than generally giving in or being so stubborn that, although you get your way, you're not happy? Why not try a system that lets both you and the other person win? Try it; you'll like it.

Communication

In addition to learning to be more assertive and to resolve conflicts well, other communication skills will help you get along better with friends, family, and coworkers, with the result being less stress.

Nonverbal Communication

Notice the body posture of your classmates. During an interesting lecture or activity, most of them will probably be leaning or looking toward the lecturer or the center of the group, indicating that they are involved in what is going on. During a boring class, they will probably be leaning away from the lecturer or group. We call this physical behavior *body language.* Communication by body posture often says as much as the spoken word. When people feel uncomfortable about expressing their thoughts or feelings verbally, body language is sometimes the only form of communication they participate in.

We all recognize the importance of communicating nonverbally, since we smile when we say hello, scratch our heads when perplexed, and hug a friend to show affection. We also have an array of body terms to describe our nonverbal behavior: "Keep a stiff upper lip," "I can't stomach him," "She has no backbone," "I'm tongue-tied," "He caught her eye," "I have two left feet," and "That was spine-tingling." We show appreciation and affection, revulsion, and indifference with expressions and gestures. We tell people we are interested in them by merely making eye contact and, like the male peacock displaying his feathers, we display our sexuality by the way we dress, by the way we walk, and even by how we stand.[1]

Verbal Communication

Unfortunately, the nonverbal expression of feelings and thoughts is easy to misinterpret. Consequently, depending on nonverbal communication alone to express yourself is to risk being misunderstood. Furthermore, if another person is depending on nonverbal communication to express feelings to you, it is up to you to ask—verbally— whether you are getting the right message. Without such a *reality check,* the other person, while totally failing to connect, might assume that he or she is communicating effectively. For example, imagine that a man and woman on their first date begin hugging, kissing, and caressing each other after a movie. The woman's breathing speeds up and the man, taking this as a sign of sexual arousal and interest, presses onward. When the woman suddenly pushes free and complains that the man is too impatient, he is confused. The problem here is one of interpretation rather than incompatibility. The rapid breathing that the man took as a sign of arousal was really a sign of nervousness. If these people had been more effective verbal communicators, they would have been able to clarify the situation in the beginning. Instead, they reached a silent impasse, with him confused and her resentful. Check out your impressions of someone's nonverbal communication, and improve your communication by making your nonverbal and verbal messages as consistent as you can.

Planning Time to Talk

One common barrier to communication is the television set. We are often so busy watching it that we don't take the time to talk with those around us. To improve your communication with others, you may need to plan time for discussions. In setting up such times, it is wise to do the following:

1. Make sure you allow sufficient time to have a meaningful discussion.
2. Disconnect the phone and don't allow other people to barge in on you.
3. Accept all feelings and the right for the verbal expression of these feelings. For example, it is just as appropriate to say, "I feel angry when . . . " as it is to say, "I feel terrific when. . . ."
4. Take a risk and really describe your thoughts and feelings. Don't expect the other person to guess what they are.
5. Approach your discussions with both of you understanding that the goal is to improve your relationship.

Listening

This hint seems obvious, yet, as demonstrated in our discussion of conflict resolution, it is often ignored. Listening and paraphrasing (active or reflective listening) are effective in regular conversation as well as during conflict. All of us can do a better job at listening. Try to pay more attention to this aspect of your communications.

Beginning with Agreement

You would be surprised at how much better you can communicate with someone with whom you disagree if you start your message with a point on which you do agree. Of course, this requires you to listen carefully so you can identify something with which you can agree. For example, if you are disagreeing about who should do the dishes, you might begin by saying, "I agree that it is important the dishes be cleaned." If you look and listen intently, you can always find a point of agreement.

"And," Not "But"

The word "but" is like an eraser; it erases everything that precedes it. When someone says, "Yes, your needs are important but . . . " they are saying, "Your needs may be important, but let's forget about them because I'm about to tell you what's *really* important." In other words, the importance of your needs is being erased and now we can focus on the real issue. Listen to how people use the word "but" and you will get a real insight into how people communicate. Listen to how *you* use "but"!

Substituting the word "and" for "but" is so simple yet so significant. "And" leaves what preceded it on the table and *adds* something to it. "Your needs are important and . . ." means that we will not discount (erase) your needs; we will consider them in addition to considering what will be presented next. Use more "ands" and fewer "buts."

"I" Statements

Too often we try to get other people to behave or believe as we do. Others naturally resent that, just as we resent it when others try to get us to behave or believe as they do. Part of this problem relates to the words we use when communicating. Remember the DESC form example of the student who was expected to work on Saturdays? If not, reread it now and notice that the wording of her assertive response includes many "I" statements. For example, she doesn't say, "When *you* expect me to work on Saturdays. . . . " She says, "When *I* am expected to work on Saturdays. . . . " In this manner, she places the focus not on the boss's behavior but on the situation. Consequently, the boss need not get defensive, and they can better discuss and resolve the situation. When we say "you," we are making the other person feel that he or she is being criticized and needs to defend himself or herself. When we say "I," we are focusing on our feelings, beliefs, and interpretations. Feeling less defensive, the other person is more likely to listen to us, and the result is more effective communication.

Using time management techniques will help you with one of life's most precious possessions—your time.

Avoid "Why" Questions

As with statements that include "you" instead of "I," questions that begin with "why" make the other person defensive. "Why did you leave so early?" makes the other person have to justify leaving early. In addition, "why" questions are often veiled criticisms. "Why don't you spend more time with me?" may be asked to get an answer, but, more often than not, it is a statement ("You don't spend enough time with me!") rather than a question. Avoid "why" questions.

Time Management

One of the tasks we are often unsuccessful at is managing our time well. There really is no reason for this, since there are effective time management techniques. These techniques can help you with your most precious possession—your time. Time spent is time gone forever. In spite of what we often profess, we cannot save time. Time moves continually and it is used—one way or another. If we waste time, there is no bank where we can withdraw time we previously saved to replace the time wasted. To come to terms with our mortality is to realize that our time is limited. Given this realization and the probability that you would like to better organize your time (I've never met anyone who didn't profess that need), some techniques that can help are presented next.

Assessing How You Spend Time

As a first step in managing time better, you might want to analyze how you spend your time now. To do this, divide your day into fifteen-minute segments. Then record what you are doing every fifteen minutes (see Table 6.2). Afterward, review this time diary

Table 6.2 DAILY RECORD OF ACTIVITY

Time (a.m.)	Activity	Time (a.m.)	Activity	Time (p.m.)	Activity	Time (p.m.)	Activity
12:00		6:00		12:00		6:00	
12:15		6:15		12:15		6:15	
12:30		6:30		12:30		6:30	
M		M		M		M	
M		M		M		M	

and total the time spent on each activity throughout the day (see Table 6.3). For example, you might find you spent three hours watching television, one hour exercising, one hour studying, and two hours shopping. Next, evaluate that use of time. You might decide you spent too much time watching television and too little time studying. Based upon this evaluation, decide on an adjustment, but make it specific. For example, I will watch only one hour of television and will study two hours. A good way to actually make this change is to draw up a contract with yourself that includes a reward for being successful.

Setting Goals

The most important thing you can do to manage time is to set goals: daily, weekly, monthly, yearly, and long-range. If you don't have a clear sense of where you are headed, you will not be able to plan how to get there. Your use of time should be organized to maximize the chances of achieving your goals.

Prioritizing

Once you have defined your goals, you need to prioritize them and your activities. Not all of your goals will be equally important. Focus on goals of major importance to you, and work on the other goals secondarily. Likewise, focus on activities most important to the achievement of your highest goals and on other activities afterward. To help with this, develop **A,B,C lists.**

On the A list are those activities that must get done; they are so important that not to do them would be very undesirable. For example, if your term paper is due next week and today is the only day this week you can get to the library to do the research required for that paper, going to the library goes on your A list today.

A,B,C lists
A time management technique in which tasks are prioritized.

Table 6.3
SUMMARY OF ACTIVITIES
(SAMPLE)

Activity	Total Time Spent on Activity
Talking on the telephone	2 hours
Socializing	2 hours
Studying	1 hour
Watching television	3 hours
Exercising	1 hour
Shopping	2 hours
Housework	2 hours
In class	5 hours
Sleeping	6 hours

On the B list are those activities you'd like to do today and that need to be done. However, if they don't get done today, it wouldn't be too terrible. For example, if you haven't spoken to a close friend and have been meaning to telephone, you might put that on your B list. Your intent is to call today, but, if you don't get around to it, you can always call tomorrow or the next day.

On the C list are those activities you'd like to do if you get all the A and B list activities done. If the C list activities *never* get done, that would be just fine. For example, if a department store has a sale and you'd like to go browse, put that on your C list. If you do all of the A's and B's, then you can go browse; if not, no big loss.

In addition, you should make a list of things *not to do*. For example, if you tend to waste your time watching television, you might want to include that on your not-to-do list. In that way, you'll have a reminder not to watch television today. Other time wasters should be placed on this list as well.

Scheduling

Once you've prioritized your activities, you can then schedule them into your day. When will you go to the library? When will you grocery-shop? Don't forget to schedule some relaxation and recreation as well.

Maximizing Your Rewards

In scheduling your activities, remember what some time management experts say: We get 80 percent of our rewards from only 20 percent of our activities and, conversely, get only 20 percent of our rewards from 80 percent of the time we spend. What that tells us is that we need to make sure we identify and engage in the 20 percent of the activities that give us 80 percent of our rewards *before* we move to the other activities. Maximize your rewards by organizing your time.

Saying No

I have a friend who says, "You mean that I don't have to do everything I want to do?" What he means is that there are so many activities he would love to engage in that he overloads himself and winds up enjoying them less and feeling overburdened. Because of guilt, concern for what others might think, or a real desire to engage in an activity, we have a hard time saying no. The A,B,C lists and the scheduled activities will help identify how much time remains for other activities and will make saying no easier.

Delegating

When possible, get others to do those things that need to be done but that do not need your personal attention. Conversely, avoid taking on chores that others try to delegate to you. A word of caution: This advice does not mean that you use other people to do work you should be doing or that you do not help out others when they ask. What I am suggesting is that you be more *discriminating* about the delegation of activities. In other words: Do not hesitate to seek help when you are short on time and are overloaded, and help others only when they really need help and you have the time available.

Evaluating Tasks Once

Many of us open our mail, read through it, and set it aside. For example, I often receive a questionnaire from some graduate student doing a study on stress. My tendency is to put the questionnaire aside and fill it out later. However, that is a waste of time. If I pick it up later, I have to once again familiarize myself with the task. As much as possible, look things over only once. That means, when you first pick something up, be prepared to complete working on it *then*.

Using the Circular File

Another way of handling questionnaires is to file them—in the garbage can. How many times do we receive junk mail that is obvious from its envelope—you know, the kind addressed to "Resident"? In spite of knowing what is enclosed in that envelope and that after we read its contents we will throw it out, we still take the time to open it and read the junk inside. We would be better off bypassing the opening and reading part and going directly to the throwing-out part.

Limiting Interruptions

Throughout the day, we are likely to be interrupted from what we have planned to do. Recognizing this fact, we should actually schedule in times for interruptions. On the one hand, don't make your schedule so tight that interruptions would throw you into a tizzy. On the other hand, try to keep these interruptions to a minimum. There are several ways you can accomplish that. You can refuse to accept phone calls between certain hours. Ask your roommate or assistant to take messages and call back later. Do the same with visitors. Anyone who visits should be asked to return at a more convenient time, or you should schedule a visit with him or her for later. If you are serious about making better use of your time, you will need to adopt some of these means of limiting interruptions. Adhere to your schedule as much as you can.

Investing Time

The bottom line of time management is that you need to invest time *initially* in order to benefit by the good use of your time subsequently. Those who attend my classes or workshops often say, "I don't have the time to organize myself the way you suggest. That would put me further in the hole." This is an interesting paradox. Those who feel they don't have time to plan the better use of their time probably need to take the time more than those who feel they do have the time. Confusing enough? Well, let me state it this way: If you are so pressed for time that you believe you don't even have sufficient time to get yourself organized, that in itself tells you that you are in need of applying time management skills. The investment in time devoted to organizing yourself will pay dividends by allowing you to achieve more of what is really important to you.

Social Support Networking

As mentioned earlier, one of the protective factors suspected of preventing stress-related illness or disease is social support. Social support is belonging, being accepted, being loved, or being needed "all for oneself and not for what one can do."[2] In different words, it is having people you can really talk to, to whom you feel close, and with whom you share your joys, problems, apprehensions, and love. Social support comes in many different forms. Matich and Sims[3] distinguish between three different types of social support: (1) tangible support (e.g., money or the use of a car); (2) emotional support (e.g., love or caring concern); and (3) informational support (e.g., facts or advice). House adds a fourth type of social support, appraisal support, that provides information about the person being supported to help in a self-evaluation.[4] Social support can be provided by family members, friends, lovers, or anyone else who provides what is described above.

The manner in which social support helps manage stress is hypothesized to occur in one of two ways.[5] One hypothesis, the *direct effect theory,* views social support as a means of preventing stressors from occurring in the first place. For example, support received in the form of information and advice might prevent you from losing your job and experiencing the stress associated with that event. Another theory, the *stress buffering theory,* states that social support helps after a stressor is encountered to help prevent that stressor from resulting in negative consequences. For example, you may lose your job, but your family and friends may help you feel worthwhile nonetheless. Caplan puts it another way: "Significant others help an individual mobilize his psychological resources and master his emotional burdens; they share his tasks, and they provide him with extra supplies of money, materials, tools, skills, and cognitive guidance to improve his handling of the situation."[6] They help you deal with and feel better about stressors.

Common sense dictates that social support can help prevent stressors from leading to negative consequences. I volunteer to conduct a monthly stress management workshop for parents residing at the Washington, D.C., Ronald McDonald House. The

Ronald McDonald House is a residence for families of seriously ill children who are being treated in local hospitals and whose parents and siblings need a place to stay during the time of the treatment. Most of the families staying at the house are in the military and travel great distances—often from other countries in which they are stationed—to have their children treated. Other families are from states across the United States, far away from relatives and friends. The social support provided to families residing at the house by the staff and by other families is obviously invaluable. In fact, when we evaluate the stress management workshops I conduct there, parents state that what they value most is the opportunity to interact with other families experiencing a similar stressful situation. You have probably also found value in talking over your problems and stressors with friends and relatives. You may not have known it at the time, but what you were experiencing was social support.

Social support has been found to be related to several indices of health and illness. For example, in a study of women in a depressed mood, it was found that the loss of social support was related to poor quality of life.[7] African American women's psychological and physical health functioning was found to be related to the quality of their intimate relationships, as well as to how connected they felt to their neighborhood. The better the quality of the relationship and the more connected to the neighborhood, the better their health.[8] In a study of youth in an urban community, social support emerged as the strongest predictor of life satisfaction.[9]

Other studies concur with these earlier findings. For example, when students' class schedules were changed to encourage attachment to a home-room teacher and to peers, the social support that resulted led to improved academic performance.[10] The support obtained from others has also been found to help Type A people postpone or prevent the occurrence of coronary heart disease.[11] Melanoma patients who participated in a six-week support group experienced only half as many recurrences as similar patients who did not.[12] Conversely, a lack of social support experienced by men with AIDS led them to report feeling more distress.[13] An interesting observation was made by Solomon and colleagues.[14] They reported that soldiers who were lonely were more apt to develop combat stress. Solomon recommended that lonely soldiers be identified early on and their officers and buddies encouraged to provide social support. It only makes sense that the same early identification of loneliness be made with college students so social support interventions can be organized. Perhaps the university health center, the counseling center, or the student's major department can be recruited in this effort.

There appears to be a difference between males and females when it comes to social support. Researchers have found that whereas males prepare to use fight-or-flight when encountering a stressor, females tend to employ the "tend and befriend" response.[15] When encountering a stressor, females are likely to "tend" after their children and loved ones (to protect them) and seek the support of other females through social networks. This strategy seems to be learned at a young age. Boys report having fewer people they feel comfortable turning to for support than do girls. Boys seek the support of friends less, instead turning to exercise, watching television, and spending time on the computer as a means of coping.[16] To assess your level of social support, complete Lab 6.3 at the end of this chapter.

The development of a social support system is complex and would require a whole book to describe. Certainly, the conflict-resolution technique and the assertiveness skills discussed in this chapter contribute to improved relationships. However, one of the keys to developing social support networks is being open and caring with others. It's often easier and less threatening to stay aloof and detached from others. Fear prevents us from getting close to others. We fear that if we show love for another person, we will be rejected by that person. We fear that we will be embarrassed. We fear that we will be ridiculed. We even fear that we will find within ourselves an inability to be intimate, caring, and loving. To develop social support systems, however, requires an overcoming of these fears.

I vividly recall listening to a colleague whom I had known casually for several years give a speech upon the occasion of being awarded a professional honor. His speech was very uplifting and quite emotional. At its conclusion, my colleague was

Positive healthy relationships are within your reach. The social support obtained from these relationships can help prevent illness or disease resulting from stress.

greeted with a standing ovation and hordes of well-wishers. As I was waiting to get close enough to congratulate him on the speech and the honor bestowed upon him, I noticed most women hugged him after their congratulations, whereas *all* the men shook his hand. At that time, I felt very close to my colleague. I wanted very much to grab him and hug his guts out, but fear entered my mind. What would other colleagues of mine think? What if Bob reached out with his hand, thereby rejecting my hug? Do I dare? Will I be embarrassed? Well, I rejected that fear and, when I got close enough, hugged my colleague and told him how much I had enjoyed his speech and how deserving I believed he was of his honor. Do you know what? He hugged me harder than I hugged him! He turned out to be the "hugger" and I the "huggee"! That small incident remains with me always. If I had not taken a chance, I would have always regretted not hugging Bob. The chance taken resulted in our being closer than before. I now realize that these fleeting moments have great meaning in our lives and that they present us with opportunities that are removed only too quickly. If we don't take advantage of them when they are presented to us, we probably will never have another chance.

Why don't you take a chance? Tell someone that you love him or her. Get involved with those around you. Show people you care about them. By doing so, you will be improving your social support network. You can expect this love, involvement, and care to rebound to you, allowing you to be more effective in managing the stress in your life.

Getting Involved in Your Community

Many communities have after-school recreation or community centers. These are usually open on weekdays from when public schools let out to approximately 10 p.m. and on weekends. Children and youths of all ages attend these centers, which offer sports competition (e.g., soccer or basketball leagues), classes (e.g., arts and crafts, photography, or dance), and open recreation time (e.g., shooting pool or playing Ping Pong). These centers provide an excellent vehicle for educating youths about conflict-resolution techniques so as to help prevent fights and other aggressive behavior that can cause a great deal of stress. Why not volunteer to teach a conflict-resolution class at a local community center, YMCA, Jewish community center, or other after-school program? You can really make a difference in the lives of young people in your community if you choose to.

summary

- Assertiveness is expressing yourself and satisfying your own needs while not hurting others in the process. People who cannot have their needs satisfied or who perceive that their basic human rights are violated will be stressed by that situation. The use of the DESC form can help you organize a verbal assertive response. Standing straight and speaking clearly, fluently, and without hesitation can convey assertiveness nonverbally.

- Conflicts resolved to only one person's satisfaction are not effectively resolved. A three-step approach to resolve conflict is effective in satisfying both people. This approach entails active listening, identifying the points of view, and exploring alternative solutions.

- To improve communication, check out your impressions of someone's nonverbal messages, plan time to have discussions, listen better, begin disagreeing by stating a point of agreement, substitute the word "and" for the word "but," use "I" statements, and avoid "why" questions.

- Time management skills involve setting goals and prioritizing them, making schedules, saying no when that is appropriate, delegating tasks, reviewing materials only once, limiting interruptions, and assessing how time is now spent.

- Social support is belonging, being accepted, being loved, or being needed all for oneself and not for what one can do. It is having people to whom you feel close and with whom you share your joys, problems, apprehensions, and love. Social support can help protect you from the negative consequences of stress.

notes

1. Jerrold S. Greenberg, Clint E. Bruess, and Debra W. Haffner, *Exploring the Dimensions of Human Sexuality* (Boston: Jones and Bartlett, 2004).

2. G. E. Moss, *Illness, Immunity and Social Interaction* (New York: John Wiley & Sons, 1973), 237.

3. J. Matich and L. Sims, "A Comparison of Social Support Variables Between Women Who Intend to Breast or Bottle Feed," *Social Science Medicine* 34(1992): 919–27.

4. J. S. House, *Work Stress and Social Support* (Reading, MA: Addison-Wesley, 1981), 39.

5. J. C. Overholser, W. H. Norman, and I. W. Miller, "Life Stress and Support in Depressed Patients," *Behavioral Medicine*, Fall 1990, 125–31.

6. G. Caplan, *Support Systems and Community Mental Health* (New York: Behavioral Publications, 1974), 6.

7. L. C. Friedman, A. E. Brown, C. Romero, M. F. Dulay, L. E. Peterson, P. Wehrma, D. J. Whisnand, L. Laufman, and J. Lomax, "Depressed Mood and Social Support as Predictors of Quality of Life in Women Receiving Home Health Care," *Quality of Life Research* 14(2005): 1925–29.

8. A. R Black, J. L. Cook, V. M. Murry, and C. E. Cutrona, "Ties That Bind: Implications of Social Support for Rural, Partnered African American Women's Health Functioning," *Womens Health Issues* 15(2005): 216–23.

9. P. Bramston, H. Chipuer, and G. Pretty, "Conceptual Principles of Quality of Life: An Empirical Exploration," *Journal of Intellectual Disability Research* 49(2005): 728–33.

10. R. D. Feiner, S. S. Farber, and J. Primavera, "Transitions in Stressful Life Events: A Model of Primary Prevention," in *Preventive Psychology: Theory, Research and Practice,* ed. R. D. Feiner, L. A. Jason, J. N. Moritsugu, and S. S. Farber (New York: Plenum, 1983).

11. J. A. Blumenthal, M. M. Burg, J. Barefoot, R. B. Williams, T. Haney, and G. Zimet, "Social Support, Type A Behavior, and Coronary Artery Disease," *Psychosomatic Research* 49(1987): 331–40.

12. "Stress," *Newsweek,* 14 June 1999, 61.

13. J. Zich and L. Temoshok, "Perceptions of Social Support in Men with AIDS and ARC: Relationships with Distress and Hardiness," *Journal of Applied Social Psychology* 17(1987): 193–215.

14. Z. Solomon, M. Mikulincer, and S. E. Hobfoll, "Objective Versus Subjective Measurement of Stress and Social Support: Combat Related Reactions," *Journal of Consulting and Clinical Psychology* 55(1987): 557–83.

15. Curt Suplee, "Stressed Women Turn to Mother Nurture, Study Says," *Washington Post,* 9 May, 2000, A2.

16. "Coping with Stress," *Washington Post Health,* 9 September 1998, 5.

internet resources

Time Management
www.muskingum.edu/cal/database/time.html#Strategies
A discussion of time management with practical suggestions for improving time management skills.

Assertiveness Training Web Sites
www.selfgrowth.com/assert.html
Links to assertiveness Web sites, including numerous articles.

Conflict Resolution Resource Center
www.conflict-resolution.net/
Resources, articles, organizations, and much more related to conflict resolution.

Stress and Communication
http://www.cdc.gov/nasd/docs/d000001-d000100/d000012/d000012.html
An article on stress and communication, including steps to effective conflict resolution.

Coping in Today's World

Have you arranged to have a satisfying life? The *Satisfaction with Life* scale[a] presented here helps you determine whether you need to improve your level of satisfaction with your life. If you do, there is still time to do that. Once completing the scale and analyzing the results, elaborate on your answers—why did you answer as you did? Then, write down the things you can change to increase the satisfaction with your life. The results should be placed in your Stress Portfolio.

Satisfaction with Life Scale

Here are five statements that you may agree or disagree with. Using the 1–7 scale below, indicate your agreement with each statement.

7 = strongly agree   6 = agree   5 = slightly agree

4 = neither agree nor disagree   3 = slightly disagree

2 = disagree   1 = strongly disagree

_____ In most ways my life is close to ideal.

_____ The conditions of my life are excellent.

_____ I am satisfied with my life.

_____ So far I have gotten the important things I want in life.

_____ If I could live my life over, I would change almost nothing.

Scoring:

31–35	Extremely satisfied
26–30	Satisfied
21–25	Slightly satisfied
20	Neutral
15–19	Slightly dissatisfied
10–14	Dissatisfied
5–9	Extremely dissatisfied

[a]Pavot, W. & Deiner, E. "Review of the Satisfaction with Life Scale." *Psychological Assessment* 5(1993): 164–172.

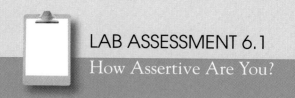

Directions: To determine your general pattern of behavior, indicate how characteristic or descriptive each of the following statements is of you by using the code that follows. This scale was developed by Spencer Rathus.

+3 = very characteristic of me, extremely descriptive
+2 = rather characteristic of me, quite descriptive
+1 = somewhat characteristic of me, slightly descriptive
−1 = somewhat uncharacteristic of me, slightly nondescriptive
−2 = rather uncharacteristic of me, quite nondescriptive
−3 = very uncharacteristic of me, extremely nondescriptive

_____ 1. Most people seem to be more aggressive and assertive than I am.
_____ 2. I have hesitated to make or accept dates because of "shyness."
_____ 3. When the food served at a restaurant is not done to my satisfaction, I complain about it to the waiter or waitress.
_____ 4. I am careful to avoid hurting other people's feelings, even when I feel that I have been injured.
_____ 5. If a salesperson has gone to considerable trouble to show me merchandise that is not quite suitable, I have a difficult time in saying no.
_____ 6. When I am asked to do something, I insist upon knowing why.
_____ 7. There are times when I look for a good, vigorous argument.
_____ 8. I strive to get ahead as well as most people in my position.
_____ 9. To be honest, people often take advantage of me.
_____ 10. I enjoy starting conversations with new acquaintances and strangers.
_____ 11. I often don't know what to say to attractive persons of the opposite sex.
_____ 12. I will hesitate to make phone calls to business establishments and institutions.
_____ 13. I would rather apply for a job or for admission to a college by writing letters than by going through with personal interviews.
_____ 14. I find it embarrassing to return merchandise.
_____ 15. If a close and respected relative were annoying me, I would smother my feelings rather than express my annoyance.
_____ 16. I have avoided asking questions for fear of sounding stupid.
_____ 17. During an argument I am sometimes afraid that I will get so upset that I will shake all over.
_____ 18. If a famed and respected lecturer makes a statement that I think is incorrect, I will have the audience hear my point of view as well.
_____ 19. I avoid arguing over prices with clerks and salespeople.
_____ 20. When I have done something important or worthwhile, I manage to let others know about it.
_____ 21. I am open and frank about my feelings.
_____ 22. If someone has been spreading false and bad stories about me, I see him (her) as soon as possible to "have a talk" about it.
_____ 23. I often have a hard time saying no.
_____ 24. I tend to bottle up my emotions rather than make a scene.
_____ 25. I complain about poor service in a restaurant and elsewhere.
_____ 26. When I am given a compliment, I sometimes just don't know what to say.
_____ 27. If a couple near me in a theater or at a lecture were conversing rather loudly, I would ask them to be quiet or to take their conversation elsewhere.
_____ 28. Anyone attempting to push ahead of me in a line is in for a good battle.
_____ 29. I am quick to express an opinion.
_____ 30. There are times when I just can't say anything.

Source: Spencer A. Rathus, "A 30-Item Schedule for Assessing Assertive Behavior," _Behavior Therapy_ 4(1973): 398–406. © 1973 by Academic Press, reproduced by permission of the publisher.

Scoring: To score this scale, first change (reverse) the signs (+ or −) for your scores on items 1, 2, 4, 5, 9, 11, 12, 13, 14, 15, 16, 17, 19, 23, 24, 26, and 30. Now total the plus (+) items, total the minus (−) items, and subtract the minus total from the plus total to obtain your score. This score can range from −90 through 0 to +90. The higher the score (closer to +90), the more assertively you usually behave. The lower the score (closer to −90), the more nonassertive is your typical behavior. This particular scale does not measure aggressiveness.

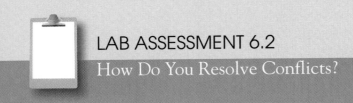

Directions: Circle the answer that best describes how you would react to each of the following situations.

1. If a salesperson refuses to give me a refund on a purchase because I've lost the sales slip,
   a. I say, "I'm sorry—I should have been more careful," and leave without the refund.
   b. I say, "You're the only store in town that handles this brand of merchandise. I demand a refund, or I'll never shop here again."
   c. I say, "Look, if I can't have a refund, can I exchange it for something else?"
2. If I had irritated a teacher by questioning his or her theoretical position and the teacher retaliated by giving me a D on an excellent paper,
   a. I wouldn't say anything; I would realize why it happened and be quieter in my next class.
   b. I would tell the teacher he or she was dead wrong and couldn't get away with being so unfair.
   c. I would try to talk to the teacher and see what could be done about it.
3. If I worked as a TV repairperson and my boss ordered me to double-charge customers, I would
   a. go along with the boss; it's the boss's business.
   b. tell the boss that he or she is a crook and that I won't go along with this dishonesty.
   c. tell the boss that he or she can overcharge on calls but I'm charging honestly on mine.
4. If I gave up my seat on the bus to an older woman with packages, but some teenager beat her to it,
   a. I would try to find the woman another seat.
   b. I would argue with the teenager until he or she moved.
   c. I would ignore it.
5. If I had been waiting in line at the supermarket for twenty minutes and then some woman rushed in front of me, saying, "Thank you—I'm in such a hurry!"
   a. I would smile and let her in.
   b. I would say, "Look, what do you think you're doing? Wait your turn!"
   c. I would let her in if she had a good reason for being in such a hurry.
6. If a friend was to meet me on a street corner at 7:00 p.m. one night and at 8:00 p.m. he still wasn't there, I would
   a. wait another thirty minutes.
   b. be furious at his thoughtlessness and leave.
   c. try to telephone him, thinking, "Boy, he'd better have a good excuse!"
7. If my wife (or husband) volunteered me for committee work with someone she (or he) knew I disliked, I would
   a. work on the committee.
   b. tell her (or him) that she (or he) had no business volunteering my time and then call and tell the committee chairperson the same.
   c. tell her (or him) that I want her (or him) to be more thoughtful in the future and then make a plausible excuse for her (or him) to give to the committee chairperson.
8. If my four-year-old son "refused" to obey an order I gave him, I would
   a. let him do what he wanted.
   b. say, "You do it—and you do it now!"
   c. say, "Maybe you'll want to do it later on."

Scoring: To score your responses for each item *except number 4*, give yourself 1 point for an *a* answer, 5 points for a *b* answer, and 3 points for a *c* answer. For item 4, give yourself 3 points for an *a*, 5 points for a *b*, and 1 point for a *c*. Add up your points. The total should fall between 8 and 40.

Your score should give you a hint regarding your usual manner of dealing with conflict. The closer you are to a score of 8, the more submissive (nonassertive) you are when involved in a conflict. The closer you are to a score of 40, the more aggressively you respond. A score near the midpoint (24) indicates you generally compromise as a means of dealing with conflict.

LAB ASSESSMENT 6.3
How Is Your Social Support?

Directions: To determine your social support, complete the following scale developed by Dwight Dean. For each statement, place one of the following letters in the blank space provided.

A = strongly agree
B = agree
C = uncertain
D = disagree
E = strongly disagree

_____ 1. Sometimes I feel all alone in the world.

_____ 2. I worry about the future facing today's children.

_____ 3. I don't get invited out by friends as often as I'd really like.

_____ 4. The end often justifies the means.

_____ 5. Most people today seldom feel lonely.

_____ 6. Sometimes I have the feeling other people are using me.

_____ 7. People's ideas change so much that I wonder if we'll ever have anything to depend on.

_____ 8. Real friends are as easy as ever to find.

_____ 9. It is frightening to be responsible for the development of a little child.

_____ 10. Everything is relative, and there just aren't any definite rules to live by.

_____ 11. One can always find friends, if one is friendly.

_____ 12. I often wonder what the meaning of life really is.

_____ 13. There is little or nothing I can do toward preventing a major "shooting" war.

_____ 14. The world in which we live is basically a friendly place.

_____ 15. There are so many decisions that have to be made today that sometimes I could just blow up.

_____ 16. The only thing one can be sure of today is that one can be sure of nothing.

_____ 17. There are few dependable ties between people anymore.

_____ 18. There is little chance for promotion on the job unless a person gets a break.

_____ 19. With so many religions abroad, one doesn't really know which to believe.

_____ 20. We're so regimented today that there's not much room for choice even in personal matters.

_____ 21. We are just cogs in the machinery of life.

_____ 22. People are just naturally friendly and helpful.

_____ 23. The future looks very dismal.

_____ 24. I don't get to visit friends as often as I'd like.

Scoring: This scale measures several factors of alienation, one of which is social isolation. High social isolation scores indicate low social support, and vice versa. The nine items making up the social isolation subscale and the scoring for those items follow:

Item	Scoring
1	A = 4, B = 3, C = 2, D = 1, E = 0
3	A = 4, B = 3, C = 2, D = 1, E = 0
5	A = 0, B = 1, C = 2, D = 3, E = 4
8	A = 0, B = 1, C = 2, D = 3, E = 4
11	A = 0, B = 1, C = 2, D = 3, E = 4
14	A = 0, B = 1, C = 2, D = 3, E = 4
17	A = 4, B = 3, C = 2, D = 1, E = 0
22	A = 0, B = 1, C = 2, D = 3, E = 4
24	A = 4, B = 3, C = 2, D = 1, E = 0

Your total score should range between 0 and 36. The higher your score, the more socially isolated you believe yourself to be. Therefore, the higher your score, the less effective you believe your social support system to be. Do you need to improve your relationship with significant others?

Source: Dwight Dean, "Alienation: Its Meaning and Measurement," *American Sociological Review* 26(1961): 753–58.

There's a story going around the sex education circuit that is used to introduce the topic of guilt about sexual behavior. It seems an elephant and an ant, in a moment of unbridled passion, spent the night making love. The next morning the ant learned that the elephant had a terminal disease and would soon die. Amazed and piqued, the ant said, "One night of passion and I spend the rest of my life digging a grave."

The ant viewed that situation as frustrating, unfair, and distressing. That needn't have been the case. The ant might have chosen to focus upon the enjoyable evening spent crawling all over the elephant's wrinkled skin (or however ants make love to elephants). Instead, the ant remembered the displeasing aspects of the situation. In short, that is what this chapter is about: perceiving life changes and other stressors as less distressing by attending to their positive aspects and de-emphasizing their negative ones.

The topics discussed here relate to your inner self—your **perceptions** of events and of your own self-worth. Among these are what to focus on (selective awareness), how to perceive stressors as more humorous than threatening (humor and stress), how to reduce an inner sense of hurriedness and hostility (Type A behavior pattern), ways to feel more confident about yourself (self-esteem), the value of feeling in control of events that affect your life (locus of control), reducing unrealistic fear (anxiety), and perceiving stressors as challenging and within your control and being committed to their resolution (hardiness).

perceptions
A person's cognitive interpretation of events.

Selective Awareness

On my office door, displayed prominently in large type for every passing soul to see, is the following newspaper account:

> Bob Weiland, 44, who lost his legs in Vietnam and propels himself with his hands and no wheelchair, completed the Marine Corps Marathon at about 10:15 p.m. Sunday, 79 hours 57 minutes after he started Thursday in Arlington.

I don't know about you, but I have a hard time feeling sorry for myself whenever I think of Bob Weiland. We are all free to choose what to think and on what to focus. We can think about Bob Weiland or we can bemoan not getting that grade we wanted. Too often, though, we don't exercise this control over our thoughts but allow them to ride the seas rudderless. To complicate matters, we have been taught to be critical rather than supportive—focusing on the bad rather than the good. If you doubt the validity of this observation, consider the following:

1. When people are complimented, they often feel embarrassed. A woman being told how nice her dress is might say, "Oh, it's really quite old." The translation might be "You don't have taste enough to recognize an old *schmatta* (rag)," when the woman is really flattered but too embarrassed (due to lack of experience in being complimented) to know how to react appropriately. Or consider this exchange: You may say, "Joe, that was a very nice thing you did." Joe answers, "Oh, it was nothing" (said with eyes looking down). Joe is really saying, "I'm too uncomfortable being told something nice. It doesn't happen very often. I'd know how to respond to criticism but have difficulty when I'm complimented."

2. When term papers are submitted to professors, too often they come back with comments directed only at improving the paper. Noticeably absent are notes underlining the good parts of the paper.

3. If you took two exams and received your grades back today, one a 43 percent and the other a 93 percent, which would you remember throughout the day—the one you passed or the one you failed?

Other examples of our inexperience in focusing on the positive can be offered, but I think the point is made. Now, what to do about it? The first step is to realize that in any situation there are both good and bad, positive and negative elements. Before I realized this, I couldn't bear to wait at airports for a plane. I defined that situation as a waste of my valuable time, unnecessary, and frustrating. Now I view the time I wait at airports as an opportunity to study people. I've learned a lot about parenting by observing a wide range of parenting styles in airport terminals. I've gotten ideas about how to coordinate my clothes by noticing well-dressed men at ticket counters. And I've become familiar with the types of literature people are interested in by noting their purchases at the gift shops located in most airports. What enjoyable and interesting places airports can be! Mind you, given the choice, I wouldn't opt for spending time at airports. The point is that I'm often not given a choice. If I want to travel by airplane (my initial choice), I must accept waiting in terminals. However, even though I may not be able to choose whether to wait at airports, I can choose how I perceive that situation. To put it physiologically, I can choose to raise my blood pressure, serum cholesterol, heart rate, and muscle tension, or I can choose not to alter these body processes. That choice is mine. Even if the situation is so bad that it couldn't possibly get any worse, I could choose to focus on the fact that things have to get better.

Some typically distressing situations are listed below. Being selectively aware of a positive aspect of each situation, write in the space provided your positive definition of that situation.

1. Waiting in a long line to purchase movie tickets _____

   _____

2. Being stuck in bumper-to-bumper traffic _____

   _____

3. Having to make a presentation before a group of people _____

   _____

4. Being rejected from something because you're too old _____

   _____

5. Having a relationship break up _____

   _____

Right now there are situations in your life that are causing you a great deal of stress. You may not like where you live, whom you're living with, or the work you're doing. You may not feel you have enough time to yourself or for leisure-time activities. You may not like the way you look. You may be in poor health. You may be alone. Some of these stressors you may be able to change; some you will not be able to change. You now know, however, that you can become selectively aware of their positive components while de-emphasizing (though not denying) their disturbing features. On a separate sheet of paper, why not list these stressors, and list the positive aspects of each on which you will choose to focus?

Why not go even further? Each time you do something that works out well, keep the memory of that with you. Tell others how proud of yourself you are. Pat yourself on the back. Take time just before bedtime (or some other convenient time of day) to recall all the good things about that day. Don't be like some of your friends who can't sleep because they still feel embarrassed about something they did that day or worried about something over which they have no control. In the words of a best seller of several years ago, "Be your own best friend." Revel in your good points and the glory of your day.

Stop to Smell the Roses

Life can be a celebration if you take the time to celebrate. It is the curse of the Great Somebody that we work long and hard to achieve some goal, bask in the glow of satisfaction only fleetingly, and proceed to work long and hard toward the next goal. I have been the adviser of many doctoral students. Many of these students have no idea that the four or five years of graduate school they endure will lead to a sense of accomplishment that will dissipate after only several months. For these students not to enjoy this graduate school experience, and to wonder at its conclusion where the time all went, is sad. From my perspective, and I suspect from theirs, graduate students who make the most of this experience but do not complete their degrees are far better off than those who get degrees but have not *experienced* the experience.

It is even sadder to see a person near the end of his or her life who achieved a lot but never enjoyed the achieving. In spite of acquiring money, property, fame, or doctoral degrees, he or she remains disheartened by missing out on what life is all about—living, experiencing, smelling the roses while trying not to get caught on the thorns.

What prevents us from being aware of life as we live it is often the routine of daily experience. When we experience something over and over again in the same manner, we become habituated to it. We are desensitized to that experience and interact with it out of habit, paying little attention to what we're doing. You and I do that very, very often. By way of example, I'll bet that when you travel to school or work, you take the same route each time. You probably chose this route because it was the fastest one. Other routes may be more scenic or interesting, but you chose quickness as your number-one priority. Other routes may bring you in contact with more cars and provide an opportunity to see more people, but you chose quickness as your number-one priority. Other routes may traverse rural, suburban, urban, and business areas, thereby allowing for more variety, but you chose quickness as your number-one priority.

Aside from missing out on scenery, other cars and people, and varied areas through which to travel, the sameness of whatever route we've chosen also desensitizes us to the experience. To create yet another barrier to experiencing the travel, we turn on our car radios. We travel to work or school and, before we know it, we're there. The time just flew. We lost that time and that experience by not being aware of it and not consciously smelling the roses en route. Think for a moment:

Do you experience the getting-there or only the having-gotten-there?

Have you ever consciously felt the *texture* of the steering wheel you hold so often?

Do you ever listen to the *sounds* of your car and of the neighborhoods through which you travel?

If you travel by public transportation, have you made an effort to talk with fellow passengers?

Have you gotten off the bus or train a stop before or after your usual one to walk through different streets?

There are other ways to experience life more fully, too. When I was in graduate school, I used to imagine that I was blind by shutting my eyes. This allowed me to concentrate upon my other senses; as a result, I smelled odors I hadn't smelled before and heard sounds to which I had previously been deaf. What's more, when I opened my eyes, I allowed myself to be bombarded with a psychedelic array of visual stimulation. For example, I would stare at the colors of the jackets of books in my bookcase. Have you ever done that? What a magnificent sight that can be! I also used to stare at my record album covers and the sizes, shapes, and colors of foods in my refrigerator. Again, the idea is to make yourself consciously aware of your experience, as you are going through it, by adopting less routine and habitual behavior.

Perspective and Selective Awareness

Whenever I think of the importance of perception in general, and selective awareness in particular, I recall one day several years ago that seemed to be heading downhill in a hurry. Before noon, I had received not only a telephone call notifying me that some consulting work I was attempting to organize wasn't coming together, but also a letter stating that a grant proposal I had submitted would not be funded; and a manuscript I had submitted was rejected. As you might imagine, I was down in the dumps. I was feeling very sorry for myself, forgetting all the consultations I had successfully completed, research studies I'd funded, and manuscripts I'd written and had published. Now I can say (the fog was too thick at the time) that I chose to be selectively aware of the defeats of that day rather than to focus upon past and anticipated future successes.

A proper perspective was soon achieved with just two phone calls. First, I received a call from a colleague at a university where I had previously taught. He told me about two former deans under whom we had worked. It seems that the married daughter of one of them awoke in the middle of the night and, not being able to sleep, arose from bed to get something in another room. Her husband, who was still sleeping when she arose, heard noises in the house, reached for his gun, and, thinking her a burglar, shot his wife in the head. As I write this, she is still in a coma. My heart went out to Harry when I heard about his daughter's ordeal (and, consequently, his).

The second story my colleague told me during that phone call described the recent accident another dean of ours had while pruning a tree. To prune the top of the tree, he extended a ladder and proceeded to climb it. When he found part of the tree out of his reach, he leaned and stretched toward that part, tipping the ladder, falling, and landing on a tree stump. Since he was still in the hospital, I called him to offer whatever feeble support I could. When I reached him, he described the accident, his severe injuries (to this day, he experiences pain daily), and the physical therapy he would need. But he said two things that I'll always remember. He said it took twenty minutes for the ambulance to arrive, during which time he was afraid to move, since he had landed on his back and feared a spinal injury. When he was placed on the stretcher, though, he wiggled his toes and fingers, and the knowledge that he was able to do that made him cry. The other thing he said was how great the hospital staff treated him, how competent the ambulance drivers were, and how lucky he was to be alive and able to move. I called him with the intention of cheering him up, and it turned out that he cheered me up. Warren was almost killed, fearful of paralysis, and in a great deal of pain as he spoke with me, but he chose to discuss how lucky he was!

After those telephone calls, my consulting, grant proposal, and manuscript did not seem very important. I had my health, a lovely family, and a job I really enjoyed. The rest of my day would, I decided, be appreciated. I would focus on the positive.

I'm reminded of the college student who wrote her parents describing the accident she had falling out of the sixth-floor window of her dormitory. She described how she was writing with her left hand, since her right side was paralyzed. She had met a hospital orderly, however, with whom she fell in love, and they had decided to elope and marry just as soon as she recovered. Although he wasn't very educated, was of a different race and religion, and was addicted to heroin, she wrote that he had promised to make a good husband. The letter continued in this way until the closing sentence, in which the daughter stated that everything she had written so far was untrue. There was no accident, no paralysis, and no hospital orderly to marry; however, she continued, "I did fail my chemistry course and wanted you to be able to view this in its proper perspective."

An Attitude of Gratitude

As previously mentioned, I conduct stress management workshops for parents and grandparents residing at the Ronald McDonald House in Washington, D.C. I've also conducted similar workshops for Ronald McDonald House parents in Atlanta,

Portland, Denver, and Houston. One of these workshops significantly impacted the way I view situations in my own life.

Parents residing at the Ronald McDonald House have children being treated at local hospitals for serious illnesses. Many have cancer or leukemia or are newborns with serious birth defects. Some have heart problems or other life-threatening illnesses. To stay at local hotels while their children are being treated would cost more than many of these families can afford. The Ronald McDonald House provides a residence for them. We like to refer to it as the "House That Love Built."

We begin these stress management workshops by sharing how we came to be at the Ronald McDonald House. I share my story and they share theirs. At one workshop, two mothers spoke of their children's illnesses. One had a teenager who was dying of cancer in a local hospital, and the other had a newborn who was not going to live very long. As these two mothers shared their stories, all I could think of was how lucky I was to have two children who were well. I couldn't imagine how anyone—myself?—could handle the stress that these mothers were describing. "This is as bad as it gets," I thought. It was about then that *both* mothers told us that this was their second child who was dying! I thought it was as bad as it could get; then it got worse in a hurry.

In spite of the situation in which they find themselves, during these workshops the parents develop an **attitude of gratitude.** They learn to be grateful for what they have, while not denying or ignoring the reality of their children's illnesses. In every situation, there is something about which to be grateful. The mother with the teenager learned to be grateful for all the years she had with her son, recognizing that the mother of the newborn would never have the same time with her child. The Ronald McDonald House parents learn to be thankful for the health of their other children, for the days in which their children are feeling well and can communicate effectively, for the expertise of the hospital staff, and for the support available to them (from other family members, church or synagogue congregants, and the Ronald McDonald House staff). Too often these families focus so intently on their children's life-threatening illnesses that they are blinded to positive factors in their lives. This may be understandable, but it isn't healthy and it isn't how it has to be.

These parents tell me that, because of the illness, they have conversations with their children at a very deep level which many of us will never experience with our children. They become grateful for these conversations. They learn on whom they can rely, and they become grateful for that. They often discover or develop a spiritual side of themselves that serves them during this troubling time and long afterward.

These factors for which the Ronald McDonald House parents learn to be thankful accompany their children's illnesses. The parents do not—cannot—lose sight of the horrendous situation with which their families are confronted, but they come to realize that there are other realities in their lives, positive ones that coexist with the reality on which they were solely focused. They learn to develop an "attitude of gratitude."

If the Ronald McDonald House parents can be grateful for aspects of their lives, the rest of us should have relatively little problem doing the same. Ever since that workshop, whenever I start feeling sorry for myself, I think of the Ronald McDonald House families, and it isn't long before I start feeling grateful for what I have and appreciative for what I do not have. If you can learn to appreciate the positive aspects of your life, perhaps you'll consider volunteering at a Ronald McDonald House, a hospice, or a hospital near you as a way of saying thank you.

attitude of gratitude
Focusing on things about which to be grateful.

Humor and Stress

Following is the definition of an optimist. A seventy-year-old man has an affair with a young, vivacious, curvaceous, twenty-year-old woman. Before too long, she finds out she's pregnant and irately calls her lover. "You old fool! You made me pregnant!" The elderly man answers, "Who's calling, please?"

Humor is used throughout this book. It captures your interest and thereby helps you to learn more about stress than you might otherwise. In addition, humor has been

A good hearty laugh can go a long way in relieving feelings of stress.

shown to be an effective means of coping with stress.[1-3] It can defuse stressful situations or feelings. Research investigations have verified this conclusion. For example, Phua, Tang, and Tham found that humor prevented negative life events from resulting in mood disturbances.[4] In a study of 334 undergraduates enrolled in introductory psychology classes, Labott and Martin also found that coping with humor acted as a buffer between negative life events and mood disturbances.[5]

The philosopher Friedrich Nietzsche recognized the value of humor when he stated that the "most acutely suffering animal on earth invented laughter."[6] Even the comedian Bill Cosby, whose son was murdered, advises that if you can laugh, you can survive any situation. Other famous and wise people have reminded us of the healing and beneficial effects of humor, including President Abraham Lincoln, Nazi concentration camp survivor Victor Frankl, comedian Charlie Chaplin, and author and magazine editor Norman Cousins. Although we realize the benefits of humor, it is ironic that as we get older, we laugh less. Fourteen-year-olds were found to laugh every four minutes, whereas American adults laugh only 15 times a day.[7] This is indeed unfortunate since the use of humor can help us convert a stressful situation into one with less unhealthy consequences.[8,9]

Humor can take several forms. It can use surprise, exaggeration, absurdity, incongruity (two or more incompatible ideas or feelings), word play (puns, double entendres), or the tragic twist (juxtaposition of the tragic and comic poles of a given phenomenon followed by reconciliation in a humorous synthesis).[10] Regardless of the type of humor, its effects on health have been studied for many years.[11-13] Summarizing a review of the effects of humor on health, Robinson states, "there has been much support for the emotionally therapeutic value of humor as an adaptive, coping behavior, as a catharsis for and relief of tension, as a defense against depression, as a sign of emotional maturity, and as a survival mechanism. . . . There is some evidence that humor is good for you."[14]

Humor results in both physiological and psychological changes. Laughter increases muscular activity, respiratory activity, oxygen exchange, heart rate, and the production of catecholamines and endorphins. These effects are soon followed by a relaxation state in which respiration, heart rate, blood pressure, and muscle tension rebound to below normal levels.[15] Psychological effects include the relief of anxiety, stress, and tension; an outlet for hostility and anger; an escape from reality; and a means of tolerating crises, tragedy, and chronic illnesses or disabilities.[16]

Humor and laughter have been shown to have health benefits for the elderly[17-19] and for other populations. In fact, because humor has been shown to improve the functioning of the immune system, increase tolerance of pain, and decrease the stress response,[20] it has been adopted as a therapy used in hospitals. Perhaps the most famous practitioner of humor in the hospital is Patch Adams, the subject of a major feature movie starring Robin Williams. Adams discovered the benefits of dressing like a clown as a form of therapy for his patients.[21] Laughter therapy has been used with many illnesses, including cancer.[22] Bennett and colleagues[23] found that mirthful laughter correlated with increased immune function in cancer patients. In particular, laughter increased cancer patients' Natural Killer (NK) cell activity, necessary to combat the cancer. Humor and laughter have also been found useful for patients who are receiving *palliative care*—care designed to make patients comfortable rather than cure them.[24] For example, terminally ill patients who receive hospice care are receiving palliative care. Lastly, humor has even been suggested as a means of overcoming posttraumatic stress disorder and of coping with terrorism.[25]

Humor also can be used inappropriately and can actually cause distress. Sands states this potential of humor well: "Anyone who has seen the hurt and puzzled expression on another's face in response to an ironic remark, or remembers how he or she may have felt as an object of a joke, has witnessed humor's power to cause distress."[26] Unfortunately, Sands continues, humor's effects are not always predictable. Consequently, it is recommended that humor be used carefully to help someone else cope with stress so as not to exacerbate the situation. However, once consideration is given to the potential negative effects of humor and they are judged to be minimal, don't hesitate to use this approach when you think it would be helpful. Regarding humor-coping for yourself, look for the humorous aspects of a stressful situation or a stress-producing person and you will be better able to manage the stress involved.

Type A behavior pattern
A cluster of behaviors associated with the development of coronary heart disease.

Type A Behavior Pattern

Far from humorous are people who always seem busy, are always rushing somewhere, and never seem to slow down. We usually envision these people as business executives with perspiration-stained armpits, cigarettes dangling from their lips, and shirtsleeves rolled up, working overtime at desks piled high with papers. However, others also fit into the hurry, rush syndrome. Unfortunately, this stereotype often fits ourselves or our loved ones as well. I say "unfortunately" because a large body of research relates this behavior to the early onset of coronary heart disease.

Before proceeding, complete Lab 7.1, which is based on a scale in *Type A Behavior and Your Heart* by Meyer Friedman and Ray Rosenman.

Type A behavior pattern is "a particular complex of personality traits, including excessive competitive drive, aggressiveness, impatience, and a harrying sense of time urgency," as well as a "free-floating but well-rationalized form of hostility, and almost always a deep-seated insecurity." This behavior pattern has been found to be associated with the development of coronary heart disease. But that's putting the cart before the horse. The manner in which this association was discovered is interesting in and of itself.

Two cardiologists called in an upholsterer to reupholster the seats in their waiting room. The upholsterer inquired about the type of practice these physicians had, since he noticed that only the front edges of the chair seats were worn out. These cardiologists later realized that people who came to them with heart disease seemed to be "on edge"; they literally sat on the edges of their seats as though preparing for some action.

A sense of time urgency is one component of the Type A behavior pattern.

Meyer Friedman and Ray Rosenman, the two cardiologists, defined and named the Type A behavior pattern. They later compared patients with coronary heart disease with healthy controls (people similar in all respects except they did not have coronary heart disease) and found a significantly greater degree of Type A behavior in the patients than in the controls. These retrospective studies[27,28] (comparisons *after* the development of the disease) were followed by prospective studies that monitored subjects without a history of coronary heart disease, tested them for the Type A behavior pattern, and then determined (after more than ten years) whether more Type A's developed coronary heart disease than Type B's.[29,30] Type B's possess an opposite behavior pattern. People possessing the **Type B behavior pattern** exhibit no free-floating hostility or sense of time urgency and aren't excessively competitive. As you might expect, significantly more Type A's than Type B's subsequently developed coronary heart disease.

Type A's tend to experience more job stress. Studies of nurses and teachers have verified this conclusion.[31] In addition, studies have found that Type A hospital employees were found to have significantly more health problems than did other hospital employees[32] and that young adults,[33] college teachers,[34] and nurses also suffer the effects of Type A behavior pattern.[35] Various reviews of the great body of research on the Type A behavior pattern and coronary heart disease have concluded that "individuals classified as Type A more frequently suffer from coronary disease and obstruction of the coronary vessels."[36] In addition, some researchers have found that Type A's who have a heart attack are more likely to have a second attack than Type B's who have a heart attack; they also have more severe heart attacks than Type B's.[37] However, for some as yet unexplained reason, Type A's are more likely to survive a heart attack than are Type B's.[38]

Type A behavior can be exhibited by females as well as by males, and it is just as unhealthy for women as it is for men. Type A women who were subjects in the Framingham Heart Study (where much of our knowledge about heart disease originates) were four times as likely to develop heart disease than their Type B counterparts.[39] In his more recent book, *Treating Type A Behavior and Your Heart*, Meyer Friedman reports that Type A business and professional workers were "found to be suffering from coronary heart disease approximately seven times more frequently than Type B women remaining in their homes as housewives."[40] More recent studies of women and Type A behavior have found a relationship between Type A and psychosomatic health,[41] and there is even evidence that Type A women give birth to Type A babies.[42]

However, as with most human behavior, Type A is more complex than simply a set of behaviors leading to a specific disease. Two excellent reviews of research on the Type A behavior pattern provide evidence of the problems associated with obtaining a definitive understanding of this concept.[43,44] For example, when Type A behavior is measured by an interview, different results may be obtained than when it is measured by a paper-and-pencil test.[45–47] In addition, several large studies have not found any relationship between Type A behavior pattern and mortality[48] or duration of stay in coronary care units.[49]

Part of the confusion and complexity associated with Type A appears to be related to the variables comprising it. For example, researchers have identified two components of Type A behavior that appear to operate in opposing directions.[50] One of these is termed Impatience/Irritability (II), the other Achievement Striving (AS). *Impatience/Irritability* is characterized by

Type B behavior pattern
Behavior pattern that is not excessively competitive, with no free-floating hostility and no sense of time urgency. Also develops coronary heart disease.

Hostility toward people, and even inanimate objects such as parking meters, is a characteristic of Type A behavior pattern.

impatience, time urgency, and irritability; *Achievement Striving* is characterized by job dedication, target setting, and hard-driving behavior. Only II is associated with physical health complaints,[51] depression,[52] job satisfaction,[53] and marital dissatisfaction.[54] It seems that AS has no relationship to these variables. Thus, researchers have suggested separating the *toxic* from the *nontoxic* components of Type A behavior to better understand its effects.[55]

Relative to the constellation of behaviors associated with Type A, it appears that hostility and anger may be the key. Barefoot, Dahlstrom, and Williams tested 255 medical school students on hostility and followed them over the next 25 years.[56] Independent of coronary risk factors such as age, smoking status, and family history of hypertension, hostility scores predicted incidence of coronary heart disease and all causes of mortality. Even a study of Type A drivers concluded that Type A behavior, with its accompanying hostility, resulted in a greater risk of traffic accidents occurring.[57] Furthermore, studies regarding anger have found that people who hold anger in are more prone to coronary heart disease than are those who express their anger or who at least discuss it .[58] As more studies are being conducted, a further clarification of the role of the Type A behavior pattern on health will develop. For now, at least, it seems prudent to attempt to modify Type A behavior.

What can you do about your Type A behavior? First, you must realize that Type A behavior, like all other behavior, is learned. From parents who rush us to clean up or get ready for bed, teachers who expect us to complete our work in the time allotted, and bosses who require us to get a lot done, Type A behavior finds reinforcements throughout our society. In fact, it was found that Type A fathers tend to produce Type A sons.[59] Behavior that is rewarded tends to be repeated. The key, then, is to reward Type B behavior while ignoring or punishing Type A behavior. For example, if you rush through a traffic light as it begins to turn red in an attempt to prevent delay, that behavior should be punished. You might decide to drive clear around the block for such a Type A demonstration. But when you make it through a week without doing business over lunch or you have a week in which you engage in some form of relaxation daily, buying yourself a new article of clothing, a tennis racket, or some other reward would be in order.

One way to begin a Type A behavior modification program is to set weekly, realistic, and attainable goals and to identify rewards to be applied when these goals are achieved. Similarly, list behaviors you wish to eliminate and punishments you are prepared to apply if these behaviors are not eliminated on schedule.

Friedman and Rosenman offer some additional suggestions for decreasing Type A behavior:

1. Recognize that life is always unfinished. It's unrealistic to believe you will finish everything needing to be done without something else presenting itself to be done.
2. Listen quietly to the conversation of other people, refraining from interrupting them or in any other way attempting to speed them up.
3. Concentrate on one thing at a time.
4. Don't interfere with others doing a job you think you can do faster.
5. When confronted with a task, ask yourself
   a. Will this matter have importance five years from now?
   b. Must I do this right now?
      Your answers will place tasks in proper perspective.
6. Before speaking ask yourself
   a. Do I really have anything important to say?
   b. Does anyone want to hear it?
   c. Is this the time to say it?
      If the answer to any of these is no, remain quiet.

Polyphasic behavior is doing two or more things at the same time. This often distracts from the attention each needs and deserves. It also is one component of the Type A behavior pattern.

7. Tell yourself daily that no activity ever failed because someone executed it too slowly, too well.

8. Refrain from making appointments or scheduling your activities when unnecessary. Try to maintain as flexible a schedule as possible.

9. Remember that your time is precious and must be protected. When possible, pay someone else to do bothersome chores and save your time.

10. Purposely frequent restaurants, theaters, and other such places where you know there will be some waiting required. Perceive such occasions as an opportunity to get to know your companion better or, if alone, as a chance to get some "downtime" away from the books, the phone, or people seeking your time.

11. Practice eliminating polyphasic behavior (doing two or more things at the same time) by reading books that demand your entire attention and patience. A several-volume novel that is complex would work well. (Proust's *The Remembrance of Things Past* has been recommended by Friedman and Rosenman.)

12. Plan relaxing breaks from activities you know will result in tension by nature of the time or effort required to do them. Plan these breaks to occur *prior* to the feelings of tension and pressure.

13. Engage in daily practice of a recognized relaxation technique.

14. Smile at as many people as you can so as to decrease free-floating hostility.

15. Thank people for nice things they've done.

16. Remind yourself daily that, no matter how many things you've acquired, unless they've improved your mind or spirit, they are relatively worthless.

17. Consider most of your opinions as only provisionally correct, while maintaining an open mind to new ideas.

18. Seek some "aloneness" regularly.

19. Consolidate your relationships with some friends and acquaintances to make them more intimate and rewarding.

20. Spend time periodically remembering your past and the well from which you sprang.*

*Source: Meyer Friedman and Ray H. Rosenman, *Treating Type A Behavior and Your Heart* (New York: Alfred A. Knopf, 1974), 260–71. Copyright © 1974 by Meyer Friedman. Reprinted by permission of Alfred A. Knopf, a Division of Random House, Inc.

Self-Esteem

Your **self-esteem**—how highly you regard yourself—affects how you behave. Self-esteem is explained shortly, but first complete Lab 7.2, checking whether the qualities described there are like or unlike yours. Then complete Lab 7.3 to assess how highly you regard your physical self—your physical self-esteem.

Why is self-esteem important? If you don't think well of yourself, you will not trust your opinions or your decisions, and you will be more apt to be influenced by others. Not "marching to the beat of your own drum" may result in your conforming to the behaviors of those with whom you frequently interact. As a matter of fact, poor self-esteem is related to drug abuse, irresponsible sexual behavior, and other "unhealthy" activities. People with high self-esteem engage in these activities to a significantly lesser extent.

We've already discussed assertiveness, success, and social support as components of stress management. Self-esteem is related to each of these. How can you assert yourself and demand your basic rights if you don't deem yourself worthy of these rights? If you hold yourself in low regard, how can you use nonverbal assertive behavior? To stand straight and steady, to speak clearly and fluently, to maintain eye contact, and to speak with assurance require a good degree of self-confidence.

Self-esteem is learned. How people react to us; what we come to believe are acceptable societal standards of beauty, competence, and intelligence; and how our performances are judged by parents, teachers, friends, and bosses affect how we feel about ourselves. It is common sense, then, to expect our successes to improve our self-esteem and our failures to diminish it.

Lastly, how can you expect to make friends and establish intimate relationships if you don't think enough of yourself to believe that others would want to be your friend or care about you? Since you now know of the buffering effect of social support, you can imagine how poor self-esteem, resulting in a poor social support network, would be related to the development of stress-related illness and disease.

The very essence of stress management requires confidence in yourself and in your decisions to control your life effectively.

Because self-esteem is so important, the means of improving it deserve your serious attention. There are no magic pills to take or laser beams with which you can be zapped to improve your sense of self-worth. It has developed over a long period of time, and it will take a while for you to change it. With time, attention, effort, and energy, you can enhance your sense of self or at least feel better about those parts of you that cannot be changed.

The first thing to do is to identify that part of yourself about which you want to feel better. If it's a part of your physical self, your scores (the 3's and 4's) on Lab 7.3 will direct you to specific body parts that need work. Perhaps an exercise program can improve that part, or you need to begin a weight-control program, pay more attention to how you dress, or use makeup more effectively. After this kind of introspection, one of my students decided to have electrolysis done to remove some hair above her lips. Another student began exercises to tighten the muscles in the buttocks. What can you do to improve a part of your physical self or to feel better about parts that cannot be improved?

To identify other components of your self-esteem that you might want to improve, look for your *lowest* subscale score in Lab 7.2. This is the part of yourself that you hold in lowest regard. Next, ask yourself what you can do to perform better at work or school, in your family role, or in social settings. Perhaps you need to spend more time with your family. Maybe you need to ask your boss if you can attend a training program being offered nearby. Asking the campus librarian to help you use the library better might do the trick. Seeking honest feedback from friends about your strengths and weaknesses could help, as well as being more open with them about your thoughts, feelings, passions, and frustrations.

Whatever you decide to do—
Do it now!
Stick with it!
You really can feel better about yourself.

Locus of Control

Before reading about locus of control, complete Lab 7.4, a scale measuring locus of control, which is the perception of the amount of personal control you believe you have over events that affect your life. People with an **external locus of control** believe they have little control of such events. People with an **internal locus of control** believe they have a good deal of control of these events.

Studies indicate that "externals" are less likely to take action to control their lives, since they believe such action to be fruitless. It was found, for example, that women who had an internal locus of control perceived themselves at greater risk of developing breast cancer and were, therefore, more likely to be screened than women with an external locus of control.[60] Also, since a person with an internal locus of control thinks something can be done to affect the situation, information is sought to be able to take appropriate action. Consequently, these people know more about their situation than do others.[61] Other studies found locus of control related to chronic fatigue syndrome,[62] sick leave from work,[63] and psychological and behavioral responses to a diagnosis of human papillomavirus.[64]

The concept of locus of control has been used to explain numerous behaviors over the years,[65,66] although it is becoming increasingly understood that you can feel in control of one part of your life (e.g., your social life) but not of another part (e.g., your academic life). If you had to guess which gambling games externals and internals prefer, what would you guess? If you guessed that externals prefer games of chance rather than skill, you were correct. Externals prefer roulette and bingo; internals prefer poker and blackjack.[67]

If you've learned anything so far from this book, I suspect it is that we are all in more control of our lives than we believe. But it is absurd to believe we are in total control of events that affect us. A colleague of mine, John Burt, coined the term **cocreator perception deficiency (CCPD)** to describe this important concept. He believes that we are all cocreators of our destiny; that some things we control, but others are beyond our control; and that too many people are deficient in this perception. According to Burt, too many people believe either that they are completely in control or that any significant control is beyond their reach, but neither is the case.

As with self-esteem, locus-of-control orientation develops over a long period of time and cannot be expected to change overnight. However, once the concept is understood, some miraculous possibilities present themselves. After a class on locus of control, one of the women came up to me and said, "You're right. I can become more in control of myself." She resolved right then and there never to smoke another cigarette (she smoked a pack a day). As she threw her half-smoked pack into the trash container on her way out, I knew she would successfully quit smoking. The last I heard, she hadn't smoked a cigarette since that day. Most of us, in contrast, need to take little steps to reacquire control of our lives and our actions. Certainly, we can exercise control over what we ingest, with whom we interact, how we spend our leisure time, and how we react to people.

One important point needs to be made explicit here: *Along with control comes responsibility.* Externals blame both their successes and their failures on things outside themselves. "Oh, I did such a good job because I work well under pressure." It's the pressure, not the person. "Oh, I didn't do too well because I didn't have enough time." It's the lack of time, not the person. Internals might say, "I did so well because of how I decided to adjust to the pressure and time constraints," or "I did poorly because I didn't work hard enough!" Internals accept responsibility for their successes and their failures.

I'm reminded of an activity in which I sometimes ask groups of people to participate. I form several teams, with team members standing at arm's length behind each other. The activity requires participants to raise their arms shoulder height, elbows straight, palms down, fingers together, and feet adjacent to one another. The first person on any team who either lowers the arms or bends the elbows disqualifies his or her entire team. The team that holds out longest is the winner. You've never seen a funnier sight! Initially, people believe the activity to be ridiculous but decide I'm such a nice fellow they'll humor me. Shortly, however, people try to convince members of other teams to drop their arms—"Your arms are *so* heavy. They hurt *so* badly. Why not drop

---

external locus of control
The perception that one has little control over events that affect one's life.

internal locus of control
The perception that one has control over events that affect one's life.

cocreator perception deficiency (CCPD)
The belief that one is either the victim of circumstances or the master of circumstances, each of which is erroneous.

them and relieve *all* that pain?" At the same time, they encourage their own team members to "hang in there." I've seen grown men and women endure such discomfort in this activity that, at first, I was shocked. However, discussions with the participants after this contest soon led me to believe that most of us understand and accept the responsibility accompanying freedom. Each participant was *free* to drop his or her arms at any time but instead endured physical pain because of a sense of responsibility to the rest of the team. Similarly, when we accept greater control of our lives, we also accept the consequences following the exercise of that control. We must be responsible for our behavior when we are free to choose how we behave.

Anxiety Management

Before we begin a discussion of anxiety, complete Lab 7.5. After you know how much anxiety you experience, we will explore ways to manage that anxiety.

What is this thing called anxiety? This is a difficult question to answer and one debated by experts. Charles Spielberger, the developer of the scale you completed in Lab 7.5, defines anxiety as a subjective feeling of tension, apprehension, nervousness, and worry accompanied by activation or arousal of the autonomic nervous system. For our purposes, we will define **anxiety** operationally as an unrealistic fear resulting in physiological arousal and accompanied by the behavioral signs of escape or avoidance. For you to be anxious, you must have each of the three components of our definition: You must feel fear; your heart rate, respiratory rate, blood pressure, and other physiological processes must be aroused; and you must seek to escape the stimulus making you anxious once it presents itself, or seek to avoid it in the first place. What's more, the fear you feel must be unrealistic. Those who fear heights, who find their hearts pounding when in a high place, and who immediately seek to come down are anxious. Those who fear crowds, adjust their lives to avoid crowds (have someone else shop for them, never attend a concert, and so forth), and perspire and feel faint when caught in a crowd are anxious.

Anxiety that does not diminish the quality of your life is probably not worth concern. For example, if you become anxious around snakes, avoiding the snake house when visiting the zoo or arranging never to see a snake again will probably not significantly decrease the satisfaction you derive from living. It's probably not worth the time or effort to eliminate your anxiety regarding snakes. However, if we substitute fear of flying in airplanes for fear of snakes, and add that your loved ones are scattered all over the world, your anxiety means you will not be able to see your loved ones as often as you'd like. In this instance, you'd better learn how to manage this anxiety.

Test Anxiety

One form of anxiety to which you might want to pay particular attention is test anxiety. Many students panic when they have to take tests. Before we discuss test anxiety in more detail, complete Lab 7.6.

Test anxiety has been conceptualized to consist of two major components: *worry* and *emotionality.* The worry component is "thoughts about the consequences of failure."[68] The emotional component refers to unpleasant feelings and physiological reactions brought on by tests. Worry items appear in *italics* in Lab 7.6. Score your responses again to obtain separate worry and emotionality scores. Scores above 4 on each component represent higher-than-average degrees of worry or emotionality regarding tests. If you scored high on this test anxiety scale, you might want to consult with your instructor or counselors at your campus health center.

Trait and State Anxiety

So far, we have been considering **state anxiety:** anxiety that is either temporary in nature or specific to a particular stimulus. However, a general sense of anxiety, **trait anxiety,** which is what the first anxiety scale measures, is a condition deserving serious attention. You should make a conscious effort to manage your trait anxiety if you scored high on this scale.

anxiety
An unrealistic fear that manifests itself in physiological arousal and behaviors to avoid or escape the anxiety-provoking stimulus.

state anxiety
Anxiety that is either temporary in nature or specific to a particular stimulus.

trait anxiety
A general sense of anxiety not specific to a particular stimulus.

Panic Disorder[69]

Another type of anxiety disorder is **panic disorder.** People with panic disorder have feelings of terror that strike suddenly and repeatedly with no warning. They can't predict when an attack will occur, and many of them develop intense anxiety between episodes, worrying when and where the next one will strike.

If you are having a panic attack, most likely your heart will pound and you may feel sweaty, weak, faint, or dizzy. Your hands may tingle or feel numb, and you might feel flushed or chilled. You may have nausea, chest pain or smothering sensations, a sense of unreality, or a sense of impending doom or loss of control. You may genuinely believe you're having a heart attack or losing your mind or on the verge of death. Panic attacks can occur at any time, even during sleep. An attack generally peaks within ten minutes, but some symptoms may last much longer.

Panic disorder affects about 2.4 million adult Americans[70] and is twice as common in women as in men.[71] It most often begins during late adolescence or early adulthood, and the risk of developing panic disorder appears to be inherited.[72] Not everyone who experiences panic attacks, however, will develop panic disorder. For example, many people have one attack but never have another.

For those who do have panic disorder, though, it's important to seek treatment. Untreated, the disorder can become very disabling. Some people's lives become so restricted that they avoid normal, everyday activities such as grocery shopping or driving. Some individuals become housebound or are able to confront a feared situation only if accompanied by a family member or some other trusted person.

Basically, people with panic disorder avoid any situation in which they would feel helpless if a panic attack were to occur. When people's lives become so restricted, as happens in about one-third of people with panic disorder,[73] the condition is called *agoraphobia*. Early treatment of panic disorder can often prevent agoraphobia.

Panic disorder is one of the most treatable of the anxiety disorders, responding in most cases to medications or to carefully targeted cognitive-behavioral therapy. Cognitive-behavioral therapy, also called exposure therapy, involves very slowly exposing patients to the fearful situation until they become desensitized to it. Breathing and relaxation techniques can help as well.

Social Phobia (Social Anxiety Disorder)[74]

Phobias aren't just extreme fears; they are irrational fears. You may be able to ski the world's tallest mountains with ease but feel panic going above the fifth floor of an office building. **Social phobia,** also called social anxiety disorder, involves overwhelming anxiety and excessive self-consciousness in everyday social situations. It is more than just being shy. People with social phobia have a persistent, intense, and chronic fear of being watched and judged by others and being embarrassed or humiliated by their own actions. Their fear may be so severe that it interferes with work or school and other ordinary activities. Although many people with social phobia recognize that their fear of being around people may be excessive or unreasonable, they are unable to overcome it. They often worry for days or weeks in advance of a dreaded situation.

Social phobia can be limited to only one type of situation—such as a fear of speaking in formal or informal situations, or eating, drinking, or writing in front of others—or, in its most severe form, it may be so broad that a person experiences symptoms almost anytime he or she is around other people. People may even develop social

Consider tests as opportunities to demonstrate how much you know about a topic. Viewed in this positive sense, exams will tend to be less anxiety-producing.

panic disorder
A condition in which feelings of terror arise from unrealistic fear, resulting in symptoms such as feeling numb, sweaty, weak, and faint.

social phobia
Overwhelming fear and excessive self-consciousness in everyday situations; a chronic fear of being watched by others and not performing well. Fear of public speaking is an example.

physique anxiety—fear of showing their body. To assess your social physique anxiety, complete Lab 7.7. Social phobia can be very debilitating. It may even keep people from going to work or school on some days. Many people with this illness have a hard time making and keeping friends.

Physical symptoms that often accompany the intense anxiety of social phobia include blushing, profuse sweating, trembling, nausea, and difficulty talking. If you suffer from social phobia, you may be painfully embarrassed by these symptoms and feel as though all eyes are focused on you. You may be afraid of being with people other than your family.

Social phobia affects about 5.3 million adult Americans.[75] Women and men are equally likely to develop it.[76] The disorder usually begins in childhood or early adolescence, and there is some evidence that genetic factors are involved.[77] Social phobia can be treated successfully with psychotherapy or medications. Relaxation and breathing exercises can also help reduce symptoms.

Specific Phobias[78]

A **specific phobia** is an intense fear of something that poses little or no actual danger. Some of the most common specific phobias are centered around closed-in places, heights, escalators, tunnels, highway driving, water, flying, dogs, and injuries involving blood. Such phobias aren't just extreme fears; they are irrational fears of particular things. Although adults with phobias realize that their fears are irrational, they often find that facing or even thinking about facing the feared object or situation brings on a panic attack or severe anxiety.

Specific phobias affect an estimated 6.3 million adult Americans[79] and are twice as common in women as in men.[80] The causes of specific phobias are not well understood, although there is some evidence that these phobias may run in families.[81] Specific phobias usually first appear during childhood or adolescence and tend to persist into adulthood.[82]

If the object of the fear is easy to avoid, people with specific phobias may not feel the need to seek treatment. Sometimes, though, they may make important career or personal decisions to avoid a phobic situation, and if this avoidance is carried to extreme lengths, it can be disabling. Specific phobias are highly treatable with carefully targeted psychotherapy. Relaxation and breathing exercises also can help reduce symptoms.

specific phobia
An intense fear of a specific situation that poses little or no actual danger. Fear of elevators is an example.

Coping Techniques

Unfortunately, too many people fail to cope successfully with dysfunctional anxiety and only make matters worse. You may do drugs, drink alcohol, or in some other manner alter your state of consciousness to avoid dealing with the anxiety-provoking stimulus. Obviously, these are only temporary solutions and are accompanied by unhealthy consequences. You not only keep your anxiety, but you now have a drug habit to boot. During that period of time when I was overstressed and vomiting on the sides of roads, I developed anxiety regarding speaking before large groups of people. I would decline invitations to run workshops or present speeches, would feel faint and perspire profusely when I did dare to accept such invitations, and was extremely fearful that I would either make a fool of myself or be laughed off the stage. Because my professional goals were thwarted by my anxiety, I decided I needed to do something quickly. I saw my physician, who, with the best of intent, advised me there was nothing to be fearful of and prescribed Valium (a tranquilizer) for those occasions when I could anticipate anxiety. Desperate, I had the prescription filled and a week or so later took two Valium prior to a television talk show on which I was interviewed for thirty minutes. After the show, I decided I would no longer rely upon external means to control my internal fears. I embarked upon a program to manage my anxiety, employing the following techniques.

Environmental Planning

As stated previously, sometimes it is appropriate to adjust your life and environment to avoid the anxiety-provoking stimulus. For individuals anxious in crowds, living in a small town will probably be preferable to living in a large city. For those fearful of airplane crashes, living in the flight pattern or too near an airport may not be the wisest of decisions.

I employed environmental planning with subsequent television and radio shows by arriving earlier than expected and being shown around the studio. In this way, the environment became somewhat familiar to me; therefore, I experienced it as less threatening. To this day, I arrive early for public speaking appearances.

Relabeling

Remembering the selective awareness concept, you can relabel any negative experience as a positive one. All that is required is to focus upon the positive aspects rather than the negative ones. If you have test anxiety, rather than considering the test as a possibility of failure, you could consider it an opportunity to find out or to show others how much you know. Rather than conceptualizing an airplane ride as risking your life, you can relabel it as an opportunity to ride on a sea of clouds or to see your hometown from a totally new and interesting perspective.

I relabeled public speaking appearances as opportunities to relate some ideas I thought to be valid and important, to help other people improve their lives, and to test the worth of my professional activities. Previously, I viewed these occasions as chances to be ridiculed, scorned, or rejected.

Self-Talk

This technique requires some objectivity. You must ask yourself what the real risk is in the anxiety-provoking situation. Usually, the real danger is not very significant, even if the worst result should occur, and the odds of that worst result occurring are usually meager. If you study well, the odds of failing a test, for example, are usually slim, and, if you do fail, so what? It's not good to fail tests, but you still will have your health. There will be other tests. Remember the story of my two former deans! If you're anxious about asking people out on dates, self-talk will help you realize of what you are really afraid: losing self-respect and feeling rejection. It will also help you understand that you probably won't be turned down for that date, but if you are, "there are plenty of fish in the sea." Even when your worst fears are realized, it's not really *that* bad.

I used self-talk to realize that people are generally polite. They won't boo or throw rotten tomatoes. If they thought me absurd, they'd probably fake listening so as not to appear rude. The worst that could realistically happen was that I wouldn't be asked back. That would mean I'd have more time for other activities. That's not all that bad.

Thought Stopping

As simple as it sounds, when you experience negative thoughts, you can shut them off. To employ thought stopping, you should learn deep muscle relaxation techniques. Then, whenever you have anxious thoughts you want to eliminate, tell yourself that you will not allow these thoughts to continue, and use the relaxation technique. The pleasant sensations of relaxation will reinforce the stopping of anxious thoughts, as well as prevent these thoughts from resulting in potentially harmful physiological consequences. An alternative to stopping to do deep muscle relaxation is to substitute a more realistic thought for the negative one. I began practicing meditation to better manage my anxiety and found it to be most helpful. Any of the other deep muscle relaxation techniques might serve just as well.

An alternative approach is to wear a rubber band around your wrist and snap it whenever you have a negative thought. This might be called the "ouch technique," but it works.

systematic desensitization
Either imagining or encountering an anxiety-provoking stimulus while practicing relaxation.

fear hierarchy
A list of small steps through an anxiety-provoking stimulus.

Systematic Desensitization

Developed by Joseph Wolpe, **systematic desensitization** involves imagining or experiencing an anxiety-provoking scene while practicing a response incompatible with anxiety (such as relaxation).[83] Widely used by psychotherapists, this technique was found to be nearly as effective when people used it by themselves.[84]

As part of this technique for managing anxiety, you must develop a **fear hierarchy.** The fear hierarchy is a sequence of small steps (at least ten) that leads up to the anxiety-provoking event. For example, if you fear flying in airplanes, your fear hierarchy could be as follows:

1. Deciding where to travel.
2. Telephoning the airport for a reservation.
3. Packing a suitcase for the trip.
4. Traveling to the airport.
5. Checking your luggage in at the airport.
6. Being assigned a seat at the gate.
7. Sitting in the waiting area prior to boarding.
8. Boarding the plane.
9. Being seated as the plane taxis down the runway.
10. Watching and feeling the plane leave the ground.
11. Flying above the clouds.

You can employ the desensitization procedure in a relatively safe environment by imagining yourself at an airport (**armchair desensitization**) or use it at an actual airport (***in vivo* desensitization**). The procedure (either armchair or *in vivo*) can be summarized as follows:

1. Learn deep muscle relaxation.
2. Develop a fear hierarchy: List a slightly feared stimulus, then a more fearsome one, and so on (include ten to twenty steps on the fear hierarchy).
3. Relax yourself and imagine the first item on the fear hierarchy for one to five seconds. Gradually increase the time to thirty seconds in subsequent sessions.
4. After imagining the stimulus for thirty seconds, immediately switch your focus to the feeling of relaxation for thirty seconds.
5. Move down the fear hierarchy similarly. If the stimulus provokes anxiety, shut out the scene and concentrate on the feeling of relaxation.
6. If you have difficulty moving from one point on the fear hierarchy to another, add some intermediate steps. For example, on the airplane flight fear hierarchy, you may have made too big a leap between step 8 (boarding the plane) and step 9 (the plane speeding down the runway). You may need three steps between those: (a) placing your coat in the rack above your seat, (b) sitting down and fastening your seat belt, and (c) listening to the engines start.

The ABCDE Technique

Psychologist Albert Ellis theorizes that anxiety is a function of irrational beliefs. Ellis argues that we believe the following:

1. We must be thoroughly competent, adequate, and achieving.
2. We must be loved or get approval from all others almost all the time.
3. If things don't go as we wish, it is horrible and catastrophic.[85]

Ellis continues, but I think the point is made. We become afraid to fail or do something different and develop unrealistic fears because of beliefs that, if we examined them, would prove to be irrational. Consequently, Ellis suggests we do just that—examine them. Ellis's method, the **ABCDE technique,** consists of examining irrational beliefs that make us anxious, changing those beliefs, and envisioning more positive consequences of our actions. The ABCDE technique involves the following steps:

A. Activating agent (identify the stressor).
B. Belief system (identify rational and irrational beliefs).
C. Consequences (mental, physical, and behavioral).

armchair desensitization
A form of systematic desensitization in which the stimulus is imagined.

***in vivo* desensitization**
A form of systematic desensitization in which the stimulus is actually encountered.

ABCDE technique
A method of coping with anxiety that consists of examining irrational beliefs.

D. Dispute irrational beliefs.

E. Effect (changed consequences).[86]

The self-talk technique described earlier in the chapter is helpful in changing old thoughts (irrational beliefs) into new thoughts. For example, the fear of speaking in front of the class might translate to "People will laugh at me and think I'm stupid." However, with self-talk, "I know many students who spoke in front of many classes and they survived," we might interpret speaking in front of the class as a challenge rather than a threat.

Furthermore, questions such as the following can help identify irrational beliefs:

1. What facts are there (if any) to support this belief?

2. Is it a rational or an irrational belief?

Why not complete the following Managing Anxiety Formula to apply the information you've learned in this section and to better control your anxiety?

Managing Anxiety Formula

1. I experience anxiety when _____

   _____

   _____

2. Self-talk that I could use to manage this anxiety includes

   a. _____

   b. _____

   c. _____

   d. _____

   e. _____

3. Environmental planning I could do to manage this anxiety includes

   a. _____

   b. _____

   c. _____

   d. _____

   e. _____

Getting Involved in Your Community

Too often, elderly residents of nursing homes feel abandoned and isolated from the rest of the community. This chapter provides you with the requisite knowledge to help elders use selective awareness to alleviate some of their stress. Volunteer with a local nursing home and teach the residents to focus on the positive, to be grateful for what they have (an "attitude of gratitude") rather than bemoan what they do not have.

You might even develop a comedy routine that elders would find funny—a few good jokes would probably do—and offer to "perform" at several local nursing homes. Because humor is an excellent stress management technique, you would be helping the elders be less stressful, even if it is for only a brief period of time.

Will you help the elders in your community, or will you ignore their needs? This is a choice only you can make.

4. If using desensitization to manage this anxiety, I would employ the following fear hierarchy:

   a. _____

   b. _____

   c. _____

   d. _____

   e. _____

   f. _____

   g. _____

   h. _____

   i. _____

   j. _____

5. How successful do you think the use of one or a combination of those coping techniques would be? _____ %

Hardiness

hardy

A state of mind and body that includes three factors: commitment, control, and challenge.

Some recent research has been directed at discovering what prevents stress from leading to illness for some people but not for others. Kobasa found three factors that differentiate the afflicted from the nonafflicted: *commitment, control,* and *challenge.*[87] Commitment is "the tendency to involve oneself in whatever one is doing, control involves the tendency to believe that and act as if one can influence the course of events, and challenge involves the related expectations that it is normal for life to change, and that changes will stimulate personal growth."[88] A key here seems to be viewing change as a challenge rather than a threat. People who have the "three C's" are termed **hardy** and seem to be able to withstand the onslaught of stressors. They don't become ill as often from stressors. A number of studies conducted since the hardiness concept was developed have verified the buffering effects of commitment, control, and challenge on one's health.[89–91] This has been true with various populations: Army Reserve forces,[92] student teachers,[93] senior-level employees of state government agencies,[94] Israeli Army recruits,[95] and dental surgery patients.[96] One study found hardiness was even more predictive of physical and psychological health than were anxiety, job stress, hassles, social support, or Type A behavior.[97]

In addition to the prevention of illness that hardiness appears to provide,[98,99] and its relationship to lower levels of blood pressure and triglycerides,[100] hardiness also affects nonmedical factors. For example, hardiness has been found to be related to less psychological distress,[101,102] increased happiness and adjustment,[103] and even marital happiness.[104]

That is not to say that all researchers agree that hardiness buffers against illness. As with many complex constructs, hardiness and its effects are sometimes elusive. For example, Funk concluded from his research that hardiness was not a separate entity at all but instead was really maladjustment.[105] Others have found that some but not all three of the hardiness factors have buffering effects.[106,107] In any case, the hardiness concept is being studied further. Attempts are being made to find out if people can actually be taught to become hardy, and if they can, whether they will then become less ill.

After repeatedly experiencing a stressor, such as public speaking, you generally become desensitized to the anxiety associated with that event.

summary

- Selective awareness is deciding on whether to focus on the good or on the bad in a situation or person. Focusing on the good is less stressful.

- Experiencing life as fully as possible requires conscious effort, since we become habituated to things that are repeated. Varying our experiences (such as taking different routes to school or work) can help in this process.

- Type A behavior pattern is a particular complex of personality traits, including excessive competitive drive, aggressiveness, impatience, a sense of time urgency, and a free-floating but well-rationalized form of hostility almost always accompanied by a deep-seated sense of insecurity. People exhibiting Type A behavior patterns are more prone to coronary heart disease than are Type B's. Type B's are less apt to contract heart disease and exhibit just the opposite behavior pattern from Type A's. Hostility and holding in anger seem to be the major variables associated with ill health resulting from Type A behavior.

- Self-esteem refers to how high a regard you hold for yourself. Individuals with low self-esteem experience stress from not thinking well of themselves, not trusting their own opinions, and acting nonassertively. Self-esteem is learned and can be changed.

- Locus of control is the perception of the amount of control you believe you have over events that affect your life. An external locus of control refers to a perception of very little control (control is outside yourself). An internal locus of control refers to a perception of a great deal of control.

- Anxiety is an unrealistic fear resulting in physiological arousal and accompanied by behavioral signs of escape or avoidance. State anxiety is either temporary in nature or specific to a particular stimulus. Trait anxiety is a generalized sense of anxiousness.

- Other types of anxiety include panic disorder, social phobia, and specific phobia. Panic disorder is a condition in which feelings of terror occur as a result of unrealistic fear. Social phobia is an overwhelming fear and self-consciousness. Specific phobia is an intense fear of a specific situation that poses little or no actual danger.

- Anxiety can be managed by environmental planning, relabeling, self-talk, thought stopping, or systematic desensitization.

- Albert Ellis developed the ABCDE technique for managing anxiety. It consists of examining irrational beliefs that make us anxious, changing those beliefs, and envisioning more positive consequences of our actions.

- Hardiness results from three factors: commitment, control, and challenge. Commitment is the tendency to involve oneself in what one is doing, control is the belief that one can influence the course of events, and challenge involves the expectation that change is both normal and will lead to personal growth. Studies have found hardiness associated with less illness, lower levels of blood pressure and triglycerides, less psychological distress, increased happiness and adjustment, and marital happiness.

notes

1. D. McFarlane, E. M. Duff, and E. Y. Bailey, "Coping with Occupational Stress in an Accident and Emergency Department," *Western Indian Medical Journal* 53(2004). 242–47.

2. S. Reed and P. R. Giacobbi, "The Stress and Coping Responses of Certified Graduate Athletic Training Students," *Journal of Athletic Training* 39(2004): 193–200.

3. P. Wooten, "Humor: An Antidote for Stress," *Holistic Nursing Practice* 10(1996): 49–56.

4. D. H. Phua, H. K. Tang, and K. Y. Tham, "Coping Responses of Emergency Physicians and Nurses to the 2003 Severe Acute Respiratory Syndrome Outbreak," *Academic Emergency Medicine* 12(2005): 322–28.

5. Susan M. Labott and Randall B. Martin, "The Stress-Moderating Effects of Weeping and Humor," *Journal of Human Stress* 13(1987): 159–64.

6. C. W. Metcalf and R. Felible, *Lighten Up: Survival Skills for People Under Pressure* (Reading, MA: Addison-Wesley, 1992).

7. D. S. Sobel and R. Ornstein, eds., *The Healthy Body and Healthy Mind Handbook* (New York: Patient Education Media, 1996).

8. J. R. Davidson, V. M. Payne, K. M. Connor, E. B. Foa, B. O. Rothbaum, M. A. Hertzberg, and R. H. Weisler, "Trauma, Resilience and Saliostasis: Effects of Treatment in Post-Traumatic Stress Disorder," *International Clinical Psychopharmacology* 20(2005): 43–48.

9. W. Christie and C. Moore, "The Impact of Humor on Patients with Cancer," *Clinical Journal of Oncological Nursing* 9(2005): 211–18.

10. Waleed Anthony Salameh, "Humor in Psychotherapy: Past Outlooks, Present Status, and Future Frontiers," in *Handbook of Humor Research,* ed. Paul E. Mcghee and Jeffrey H. Goldstein (New York: Springer-Verlag, 1983), 75–108.

11. G. J. Boyle and J. M. Joss-Reid, "Relationship of Humor to Health: A Psychometric Investigation," *British Journal of Health Psychology* 9(2004): 51–66.

12. A. D. Ong, C. S. Bergeman, and T. L. Bisconti, "The Role of Daily Positive Emotions During Conjugal Bereavement," *The Journals of Gerontology. Series B, Psychological Sciences and Social Sciences* 59(2004): P168–76.

13. M. McCaffery, N. Smith, and N. Oliver, "Is Laughter the Best Medicine?" *American Journal of Nursing* 98(1998): 12–14.

14. Vera M. Robinson, "Humor in Nursing," in *Behavioral Concepts and Nursing Intervention,* 2nd ed., ed. C. Carlson and B. Blackwell (Philadelphia: Lippincott, 1978).

15. AVMA Group Health and Life Insurance Trust, "Laugh Yourself Healthy: Studies Show Humor-Health Link," *Journal of the American Veterinary Medical Association* 226(2005): 1970–71.

16. Vera M. Robinson, "Humor and Health," *Handbook of Humor Research,* ed. Paul E. Mcghee and Jeffrey H. Goldstein (New York: Springer-Verlag, 1983), 111.

17. D. L. Mahony, W. J. Burroughs, and L. G. Lippman, "Perceived Attributes of Health-Promoting Laughter: A Cross-Generational Comparison," *Journal of Psychology* 136(2002): 171–81.

18. B. G. Celso, D. J. Ebener, and E. J. Burkhead, "Humor Coping, Health Status, and Life Satisfaction Among Older Adults Residing in Assisted Living Facilities," *Aging Mental Health* 7(2003): 438–445.

19. K. B. Colling, "Caregiver Interventions for Passive Behaviors in Dementia: Links to the NDB Model," *Aging and Mental Health* 8(2004): 117–25.

20. C. M. MacDonald, "A Chuckle a Day Keeps the Doctor Away: Therapeutic Humor and Laughter," *Journal of Psychosocial Nursing Mental Health Services* 42(2004): 18–25.

21. Patch Adams, "Humour and Love: The Origination of Clown Therapy," *Postgraduate Medical Journal* 78(2002): 447–48.

22. L. Erdman, "Laughter Therapy for Patients with Cancer," *Oncology Nursing Forum* 18(1991): 1359–63.

23. M. P. Bennett, J. M. Zeller, L. Rosenberg, and J. McCann, "The Effect of Mirthful Laughter on Stress and Natural Killer Cell Activity," *Alternative Therapeutic Health Medicine* 9(2003): 38–45.

24. R. A. Dean, "Humor and Laughter in Palliative Care," *Journal of Palliative Care* 13(1997): 34–39.

25. E. A. Pasquali, "Humor: An Antidote for Terrorism," *Journal of Holistic Nursing* 21(2003): 398–414.

26. Steven Sands, "The Use of Humor in Psychotherapy," *Psychoanalytic Review* 71(1984): 458.

27. Meyer Friedman and Ray H. Rosenman, "Association of Specific Overt Behavior Pattern with Blood and Cardiovascular Findings: Blood Clotting Time, Incidence of Arcus Senilis, and Clinical Coronary Artery Disease," *Journal of the American Medical Association* 169(1959): 1286–96.

28. Meyer Friedman, A. E. Brown, and Ray H. Rosenman, "Voice Analysis Test for Detection of Behavior Pattern: Responses of Normal Men and Coronary Patients," *Journal of the American Medical Association* 208(1969): 828–36.

29. Ray H. Rosenman, Meyer Friedman, and Reuban Strauss, "A Predictive Study of Coronary Heart Disease: The Western Collaborative Group Study," *Journal of the American Medical Association* 189(1964): 15–22.

30. Ray H. Rosenman, Richard Brand, and C. David Jenkins, "Coronary Heart Disease in the Western Collaborative Group Study: Final Follow-up Experience of 8 1/2 Years," *Journal of the American Medical Association* 223(1975): 872–77.

31. G. Lavanco, "Burnout Syndrome and Type-A Behavior in Nurses and Teachers in Sicily," *Psychological Reports* 81(1997): 523–28.

32. Muhammad Jamal and Vishwanath V. Baba, "Type-A Behavior, Components, and Outcomes: A Study of Canadian Employees," *International Journal of Stress Management* 10(2003): 39–50.

33. T. F. Garrity, J. M. Kotchen, H. E. McKean, D. Gurley, and M. McFadden, "The Association Between Type A Behavior and Change in Coronary Risk Factors Among Young Adults," *American Journal of Public Health* 80(1990): 1354–57.

34. Muhammad Jamal and Vishwanath V. Baba, "Type-A Behavior, Job Performance and Well-Being in College Teachers," *International Journal of Stress Management* 8(2001): 231–40.

35. Muhammad Jamal and Vishwanath V. Baba, "Type-A Behavior, Its Prevalence and Consequences Among Woman Nurses," *Human Relations* 44(1991): 1213–28.

36. Jack Sparacino, "The Type A Behavior Pattern: A Critical Assessment," *Journal of Human Stress* 5(1979): 37–51.

37. Ronald J. Burke, "Beliefs and Fears Underlying Type A Behavior: What Makes Sammy Run So Fast and Aggressively?" *Journal of Human Stress* 10(1984): 174–82.

38. David R. Ragland and Richard J. Brand, "Type A Behavior and Mortality from Coronary Heart Disease," *New England Journal of Medicine* 318(1988): 65–69.

39. Suzanne G. Haynes, M. Feinleib, and W. B. Kannel, "The Relationship of Psychosocial Factors to Coronary Heart Disease in the Framingham Study. III. Eight Year Incidence of Coronary Heart Disease," *American Journal of Epidemiology* 3(1980): 37–58.

40. Meyer Friedman and Diane Ulmer, *Treating Type A Behavior and Your Heart* (New York: Alfred A. Knopf, 1984), 84–85.

41. M. Jamal, "Relationship of Job Stress and Type-A Behavior to Employees' Job Satisfaction, Organizational Commitment, Psychosomatic Health Problems, and Turnover Motivation," *Human Relations* 43(1990): 727–38.

42. S. J. Parker and D. E. Barnett, "Maternal Type A Behavior During Pregnancy, Neonatal Crying, and Early Infant Temperament: Do Type A Women Have Type A Babies?" *Pediatrics* 89(1992): 474–79.

43. Karen A. Matthews, "Psychological Perspective on Type A Behavior Pattern," *Psychological Bulletin* 91(1982): 293–323.

44. Karen A. Matthews and Suzanne G. Haynes, "Reviews and Commentary: Type A Behavior Pattern and Coronary Disease Risk. Update and Critical Evaluation," *American Journal of Epidemiology* 123(1986): 923–60.

45. J. R. Anderson and I. Waldon, "Behavioral and Content Components of the Structured Interview Assessment of the Type A Behavior Pattern in Women," *Journal of Behavioral Medicine* 6(1983): 123–34.

46. Haynes, Feinleib, and Kannel, "The Relationship of Psychosocial Factors to Coronary Heart Disease," 37–58.

47. B. Kent Houston and C. R. Snyder, eds., *Type A Behavior Pattern: Research, Theory and Intervention* (New York: John Wiley & Sons, 1988).

48. R. B. Shekelle et al., "The MRFIT Behavior Pattern Study II. Type A Behavior and Incidence of Coronary Heart Disease," *American Journal of Epidemiology* 122(1985): 559–70.

49. R. B. Case et al., "Type A Behavior and Survival After Acute Myocardial Infarction," *New England Journal of Medicine* 312(1985): 737–41.

50. R. L. Helmreich, J. T. Spence, and R. S. Pred, "Making It Without Losing It: Type A, Achievement Motivation, and Scientific Attainment Revisited," *Personality and Social Psychology Bulletin* 14(1988): 495–504.

51. R. S. Pred, J. T. Spence, and R. L. Helmreich, "The Development of New Scales for the Jenkins Activity Survey Measure of the Type A Construct," *Social and Behavioral Sciences Documents* 16(1986), no. 2679.

52. S. D. Bluen, J. Barling, and W. Burns, "Predicting Sales Performance, Job Satisfaction, and Depression by Using the Achievement Strivings and Impatience-Irritability Dimensions of Type A Behavior," *Journal of Applied Psychology* 75(1990): 212–16.

53. Ibid.

54. J. Barling, S. D. Bluen, and V. Moss, "Dimensions of Type A Behavior and Marital Dissatisfaction," *Journal of Psychology* 124(1990): 311–19.

55. L. Wright, "The Type A Behavior Pattern and Coronary Artery Disease," *American Psychologist* 453(1988): 2–14.

56. J. C. Barefoot, W. G. Dahlstrom, and W. B. Williams, "Hostility, CHD Incidence, and Total Mortality: A 25-Year Follow-up Study of 255 Physicians," *Psychosomatic Medicine* 45(1983): 59–64.

57. H. Nabi, S. M. Consoli, J. F. Chastang, M. Chiron, S. Lafont, and E. Lagarde, "Type A Behavior Pattern, Risky Driving Behaviors, and Serious Road Traffic Accidents: A Prospective Study of the GAZEL Cohort," *American Journal of Epidemiology* 161(2005): 864–70.

58. Haynes, Feinleib, and Kannel, "The Relationship of Psychosocial Factors to Coronary Heart Disease," 37–58.

59. Marilyn Elias, "Type A's: Like Father, Like Son," *USA Today,* 7 August 1985, D1.

60. J. L. Rowe, G. H. Montgomery, P. R. Duberstein, and D. H. Bovbjerg, "Health Locus of Control and Perceived Risk for Breast Cancer in Healthy Women," *Behavioral Medicine* 31(2005): 33–40.

61. P. Winstead-Fry, C. G. Hernandez, G. M. Colgan, et al., "The Relationship of Rural Persons' Multidimensional Health Locus of Control to Knowledge of Cancer, Cancer Myths, and Cancer Danger Signs," *Cancer Nursing* 22(1999): 456–62.

62. E. M. van de Putte, R. H. Engelbert, W. Kuis, G. Sinnema, J. L. Kimpen, and C. S. Uiterwaal, "Chronic Fatigue Syndrome and Health Control in Adolescents and Parents," *Archives of Disease in Childhood* 90(2005): 1020–24.

63. A. Hansen, C. Edlund, and I. B. Branholm, "Significant Resources Needed for Return to Work After Sick Leave," *Work* 25(2005): 231–40.

64. J. A Kahn, G. B. Slap, D. I. Bernstein, L. M. Kollar, A. M. Tissot, P. A. Hillard, and S. L. Rosenthal. "Psychological, Behavioral, and Interpersonal Impact of Human Papillomavirus and Pap Test Results," *Journal of Women's Health* 14(2005): 650–59.

65. B. Strickland, "Internal-External Control Expectancies: From Contingency to Creativity," *American Psychologist* 44(1989): 1–12.

66. J. B. Rotter, "Internal Versus External Control of Reinforcement: A Case History of a Variable," *American Psychologist* 45(1990): 489–93.

67. D. Clarke, "Motivational Differences Between Slot Machine and Lottery Players," *Psychological Reports* 96(2005): 843–48.

68. R. M. Liebert and L. W. Morris, "Cognitive and Emotional Components of Test Anxiety: A Distinction and Some Initial Data," *Psychological Reports* 20(1967): 975–78.

69. National Institute of Mental Health, *Anxiety Disorders.* http://www.nimh.nih.gov/Publicat/anxiety.cfm

70. W. E. Narrow, D. S. Rae, and D. A. Regier, *NIMH Epidemiology Note: Prevalence of Anxiety Disorders. One-Year Prevalence Best Estimates Calculated from ECA and NCS Data. Population Estimates Based on U.S. Census Estimated Residential Population Age 18 to 54 on July 1, 1998,* unpublished. Available from http://www.nimh.nih.gov/nimhhome/index.cfm

71. L. N. Robins and D. A. Regier, eds., *Psychiatric Disorders in America: The Epidemiologic Catchment Area Study* (New York: Free Press, 1991).

72. The National Institute of Mental Health Genetics Workgroup, *Genetics and Mental Disorders,* NIH publication no. 98-4268 (Rockville, MD: National Institute of Mental Health, 1998).

73. Robins and Regier, *Psychiatric Disorders in America.*

74. National Institute of Mental Health, *Anxiety Disorders.*

75. Narrow, Rae, and Regier, *NIMH Epidemiology Note.*

76. K. H. Bourdon, J. H. Boyd, D. S. Rae, et al., "Gender Differences in Phobias: Results of the ECA Community Survey," *Journal of Anxiety Disorders* 2(1988): 227–41.

77. K. S. Kendler, E. E. Walters, K. R. Truett, et al., "A Twin-Family Study of Self-Report Symptoms of Panic-Phobia and Somatization," *Behavior Genetics* 25(1995): 499–515.

78. National Institute of Mental Health, *Anxiety Disorders.*

79. Narrow, Rae, and Regier, *NIMH Epidemiology Note.*

80. Bourdon, Boyd, Rae, et al., "Gender Differences in Phobias."

81. Kendler, Walters, Truett, et al., "A Twin-Family Study."

82. J. H. Boyd, D. S. Rae, J. W. Thompson, et al., "Phobia: Prevalence and Risk Factors," *Social Psychiatry and Psychiatric Epidemiology* 25(1990): 314–23.

83. Joseph Wolpe, *The Practice of Behavior Therapy,* 2nd ed. (New York: Pergamon, 1973).

84. Ronald B. Adler, *Confidence in Communication: A Guide to Assertive and Social Skills* (New York: Holt, Rinehart & Winston, 1977).

85. Albert Ellis and Robert Harper, *A New Guide to Rational Living* (Englewood Cliffs, NJ: PrenticeHall, 1979).

86. Albert Ellis and Catharine MacLaren, *Rational Emotive Behavior Therapy: A Therapist's Guide (Practical Therapist)* (Atascadero, CA: Impact Publishers, 2004).

87. Suzanne C. Kobasa, "Stressful Life Events, Personality, and Health: An Inquiry into Hardiness," *Journal of Personality and Social Psychology* 37(1979): 1–11.

88. Salvatore R. Maddi, "Personality as a Resource in Stress Resistance: The Hardy Type" (Paper presented in the symposium on "Personality Moderators of Stressful Life Events" at the annual meeting of the American Psychological Association, Montreal, September 1980).

89. Suzanne C. Kobasa et al., "Effectiveness of Hardiness, Exercise, and Social Support as Resources Against Illness," *Journal of Psychosomatic Research* 29(1985): 525–33.

90. Suzanne C. Kobasa, Salvatore R. Maddi, and Marc A. Zola, "Type A and Hardiness," *Journal of Behavioral Medicine* 6(1983): 41–51.

91. Suzanne C. Kobasa, Salvatore R. Maddi, and Mark C. Puccetti, "Personality and Exercise as Buffers in the Stress-Illness Relationship," *Journal of Behavioral Medicine* 5(1982): 391–404.

92. P. T. Bartone, "Hardiness Protects Against War-Related Stress in Army Reserve Forces," *Consulting Psychology Journal* 51(1999): 72–83.

93. W. C. Thomson and J. C. Wendt, "Contribution of Hardiness and School Climate to Alienation Experienced by Student Teachers," *Journal of Educational Research* 88(1995): 269–74.

94. M. C. Rush, W. A. Schoel, and S. M. Barnard, "Psychological Resiliency in the Public Sector: 'Hardiness' and Pressure for Change," *Journal of Vocational Behavior* 46(1995): 17–39.

95. V. Florian, M. Mikulincer, and O. Taubman, "Does Hardiness Contribute to Mental Health During a Stressful Real-Life Situation? The Roles of Appraisal and Coping," *Journal of Personality and Social Psychology* 68(1995): 687–95.

96. I. Solcava and J. Sykora, "Relation Between Psychological Hardiness and Physiological Response," *Homeostasis in Health and Disease* 36(1995): 30–34.

97. C. F. Sharpley, J. K. Dua, R. Reynolds, and A. Acosta, "The Direct and Relative Efficacy of Cognitive Hardiness, a Behavior Pattern: Coping Behavior and Social Support as Predictors of Stress and Ill-Health," *Scandinavian Journal of Behavior Therapy* 1(1999):15–29.

98. Jay G. Hull, Ronald R. Van-Treuren, and Suzanne Virnelli, "Hardiness and Health: A Critique and Alternative Approach," *Journal of Personality and Social Psychology* 53(1987): 518–30.

99. Meredith Duhamel, "Rising Above Stress: Staying Hardy," *Medical Selfcare,* January/February 1989, 26–29, 59.

100. John H. Howard, David A. Cunningham, and Peter A. Rechnitzer, "Personality (Hardiness) as a Moderator of Job Stress and Coronary Risk in Type A Individuals: A Longitudinal Study," *Journal of Behavioral Medicine* 9(1986): 229–44.

101. Kenneth M. Nowak, "Type A, Hardiness, and Psychological Distress," *Journal of Behavioral Medicine* 9(1986): 537–48.

102. Kenneth M. Nowak, "Coping Style, Cognitive Hardiness, and Health Status," *Journal of Behavioral Medicine* 12(1989): 145–58.

103. Kevin McNeil et al., "Measurement of Psychological Hardiness in Older Adults," *Canadian Journal on Aging* 5(1986): 43–48.

104. Julian Barling, "Interrole Conflict and Marital Functioning Amongst Employed Fathers," *Journal of Occupational Behaviour* 7(1986): 1–8.

105. Steven C. Funk and Kent B. Houston, "A Critical Analysis of the Hardiness Scale's Validity and Utility,"

Journal of Personality and Social Psychology 53(1987): 572–78.

106. Susan E. Pollock, "Human Response to Chronic Illness: Physiologic and Psychosocial Adaptation," *Nursing Research* 35(1986): 90–95.

107. Lori A. Schmied and Kathleen A. Lawler, "Hardiness, Type A Behavior, and the Stress-Illness Relation in Working Women," *Journal of Personality and Social Psychology* 51(1985): 1218–23.

internet resources

Use of Humor for Stress
www.jesthealth.com/artantistress.html
An article on humor as an antidote for stress, including how humor and laughter affect physiological changes in the body.

Stress Management Information
www.selfgrowth.com/stress.html
Links to sixty articles on managing stress, as well as to stress-related Web sites.

Stress Management for Patient and Physician
www.mentalhealth.com/mag1/p51-str.html
An article that lists ten practical techniques for reducing stress.

Stress, Aggression Bound Tightly Together
http://www.healthfinder.gov/news/newsstory.asp?docID=521490
The National Health Information Center of the U.S. Department of Health and Human Services describes the relationship between stress and anger and aggression.

How Worksite Stress and Self-Esteem Relate
www.wellnessnet.com/stress-self-esteem.htm
Summary of a research study on stress and self-esteem, including links to stress and self-esteem inventories.

Coping in Today's World

Are you easily angered? Do you know someone who is? Then pay attention because this hostile trait can result in cardiovascular disease and early death. Researchers from the University of Michigan measured hostility and anger in adults.[a] They interviewed these subjects and then analyzed their interaction style using the interpersonal hostility assessment technique, which emphasizes *how* participants respond rather than the content of their responses. Subjects were then asked to recall a time when they felt so angry they wanted to explode. As they did so, their systolic blood pressure, diastolic blood pressure, and heart rate were monitored. High Hostile subjects showed *greater* blood pressure responses to anger. In addition, the *duration* of time blood pressure was raised was longer in the High Hostile subjects. That translates into those with high hostility responding to a stressor, such as situation that elicits anger, with *higher blood pressure* for a *longer period of time* than those with low hostility. Because High Hostile subjects also respond more frequently with anger, not only is their blood pressure raised, and for a longer period of time, but this occurs more frequently with them. The result is that they are subject to developing cardiovascular heart disease and the potential of dying early from that disease.

[a]B. L. Frederickson, K. E. Maynard, M. J. Helms, T. L. Haney, I. C. Siegler, and J. C. Barefoot, "Hostility Predicts Magnitude and Duration of Blood Pressure Response to Anger," *Journal of Behavioral Medicine* 23(2000): 229–43.

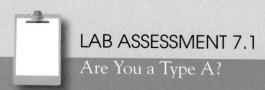

LAB ASSESSMENT 7.1
Are You a Type A?

Directions: Check whether the following statements are like you or unlike you.

Like Me	Unlike Me	
___	___	1. I explosively accentuate key words during ordinary speech.
___	___	2. I utter the last few words of a sentence more rapidly than the opening words.
___	___	3. I always move, walk, and eat rapidly.
___	___	4. I feel an impatience with the rate at which most events take place.
___	___	5. I hurry the speech of others by saying "Uh huh" or "Yes, yes," or by finishing their sentences for them.
___	___	6. I become enraged when a car ahead of me runs at a pace I consider too slow.
___	___	7. I find it anguishing to wait in line.
___	___	8. I find it intolerable to watch others perform tasks I know I can do faster.
___	___	9. I find myself hurrying my reading or attempting to obtain condensations or summaries of truly interesting and worthwhile literature.
___	___	10. I frequently strive to think about or do two or more things simultaneously.
___	___	11. I find it always difficult to refrain from talking about or bringing the theme of any conversation around to those subjects that especially interest me.
___	___	12. I always feel vaguely guilty when I relax or do nothing for several hours to several days.
___	___	13. I no longer observe the more important, interesting, or lovely objects I encounter.
___	___	14. I don't have any time to spare to become the things worth *being* because I am so preoccupied with getting the things worth *having*.
___	___	15. I attempt to schedule more and more in less and less time.
___	___	16. I am always rushed.
___	___	17. When meeting another aggressive, competitive person I feel a need to challenge that person.
___	___	18. In conversations, I frequently clench my fist, bang on the table, or pound one fist into the palm of another for emphasis.
___	___	19. I habitually clench my jaw, grind my teeth, or jerk back the corners of my mouth, exposing my teeth.
___	___	20. I believe that whatever success I enjoy is due in good part to my ability to get things done faster than others.
___	___	21. I find myself increasingly committed to translating and evaluating not only my own but also the activities of others in terms of "numbers."

If a majority of these statements describe you, you probably possess some degree of Type A behavior.

Source: Meyer Friedman and Ray H. Rosenman, *Type A Behavior and Your Heart* (New York: Alfred A. Knopf, 1974).

LAB ASSESSMENT 7.2

How Is Your Self-Esteem?

Directions: Check whether the following statements are like you or unlike you.

Like Me	Unlike Me	
_____	_____	1. I'm a lot of fun to be with.
_____	_____	2. I always do the right thing.
_____	_____	3. I get upset easily at home.
_____	_____	4. I'm proud of my schoolwork.
_____	_____	5. I never worry about anything.
_____	_____	6. I'm easy to like.
_____	_____	7. I like everyone I know.
_____	_____	8. There are many times I'd like to leave home.
_____	_____	9. I like to be called on in class.
_____	_____	10. No one pays much attention to me at home.
_____	_____	11. I'm pretty sure of myself.
_____	_____	12. I'm not doing as well at school as I'd like to.

You have just completed sample questions from a scale used to measure self-esteem that discloses in how much esteem you hold yourself (how highly you regard yourself, your sense of self-worth). Let's score these sample items and then discuss the implications of self-esteem for stress management. Place the number 1 to the left of items 1, 4, 6, 9, and 11 that you checked "like me." Place the number 1 to the left of items 2, 3, 5, 7, 8, 10, and 12 that you checked "unlike me."

Some people deliberately lie on these types of inventories because they think it's clever or because they are embarrassed to respond honestly to items that evidence their low regard for themselves. Other people do not provide accurate responses because they rush through the inventory without giving each item the attention and thought necessary. In any case, this inventory contains a *lie scale* to identify the inaccurate responders. A lie scale includes items that can only be answered one way if answered accurately. A look at the items making up the lie scale will quickly elucidate the point. Items 2, 5, and 7 can only be answered one way. No one always does the right thing, never worries, or likes everyone. Add up the points you scored on the lie scale by adding the 1's you placed alongside these three items. If you didn't score at least 2, the rest of your scores are suspect; they may not be valid. Eliminating the three lie-scale items, add up the remaining 1's for your total self-esteem score.

This general self-esteem score, however, doesn't provide the kind of information needed to improve your self-esteem and thereby decrease the stress you experience. You may feel good about one part of yourself (e.g., your physical appearance) but be embarrassed about another part (e.g., your intelligence). Your general self-esteem score, however, averages these scores, and you lose this important information. To respond to this concern, the measure consists of three subscales that are specific to various components of self-esteem. The subscales and the items included within them follow:

Social self	Items 1, 6, 11
Family self	Items 3, 8, 10
School/work self	Items 4, 9, 12

To determine in how much esteem you hold yourself in social settings and interactions, add up the 1's by those three items. Do likewise to see how much regard you hold for yourself in your family interactions and in school or work settings. The closer to 3 you score, the higher is your self-esteem for that particular subscale. Remember, however, that these scores are only a rough approximation; the entire *Coopersmith Inventory* would have to be taken and scored for an accurate reading.

LAB ASSESSMENT 7.3

How Is Your Physical Self-Esteem?

Directions: How do you feel about your physical self—your physical self-esteem? In the following blanks, place the number on the scale that best represents your view of each body part listed.

1 = very satisfied
2 = OK
3 = not very satisfied
4 = very dissatisfied

____ 1. hair

____ 2. face

____ 3. neck

____ 4. shoulders

____ 5. hips

____ 6. legs

____ 7. fingers

____ 8. abdomen

____ 9. nose

____ 10. ears

____ 11. buttocks

____ 12. hands

____ 13. chest

____ 14. eyes

____ 15. toes

____ 16. back

____ 17. mouth

____ 18. chin

____ 19. thighs

____ 20. arms

____ 21. knees

____ 22. genitals

____ 23. elbows

____ 24. calves

LAB ASSESSMENT 7.4

What Is Your Locus of Control?

Directions: For each numbered item, circle the answer that best describes your belief.

1. a. Grades are a function of the amount of work students do.
   b. Grades depend on the kindness of the instructor.
2. a. Promotions are earned by hard work.
   b. Promotions are a result of being in the right place at the right time.
3. a. Meeting someone to love is a matter of luck.
   b. Meeting someone to love depends on going out often so as to meet many people.
4. a. Living a long life is a function of heredity.
   b. Living a long life is a function of adopting healthy habits.
5. a. Being overweight is determined by the number of fat cells you were born with or developed early in life.
   b. Being overweight depends on what and how much food you eat.
6. a. People who exercise regularly set up their schedules to do so.
   b. Some people just don't have the time for regular exercise.
7. a. Winning at poker depends on betting correctly.
   b. Winning at poker is a matter of being lucky.
8. a. Staying married depends on working at the marriage.
   b. Marital breakup is a matter of being unlucky in choosing the wrong marriage partner.
9. a. Citizens can have some influence on their governments.
   b. There is nothing an individual can do to affect governmental function.
10. a. Being skilled at sports depends on being born well coordinated.
    b. Those skilled at sports work hard at learning those skills.
11. a. People with close friends are lucky to have met someone to be intimate with.
    b. Developing close friendships takes hard work.
12. a. Your future depends on whom you meet and on chance.
    b. Your future is up to you.
13. a. Most people are so sure of their opinions that their minds cannot be changed.
    b. A logical argument can convince most people.
14. a. People decide the direction of their lives.
    b. For the most part, we have little control of our futures.
15. a. People who don't like you just don't understand you.
    b. You can be liked by anyone you choose to like you.
16. a. You can make your life a happy one.
    b. Happiness is a matter of fate.
17. a. You evaluate feedback and make decisions based upon it.
    b. You tend to be easily influenced by others.
18. a. If voters studied nominees' records, they could elect honest politicians.
    b. Politics and politicians are corrupt by nature.
19. a. Parents, teachers, and bosses have a great deal to say about one's happiness and self-satisfaction.
    b. Whether you are happy depends on you.
20. a. Air pollution can be controlled if citizens would get angry about it.
    b. Air pollution is an inevitable result of technological progress.

Scoring: To determine your locus of control, give yourself one point for each of the following responses:

Item	Response	Item	Response
1	a	11	b
2	a	12	b
3	b	13	b
4	b	14	a
5	b	15	b
6	a	16	a
7	a	17	a
8	a	18	a
9	a	19	b
10	b	20	a

Scores above 10 indicate internality; scores below 11 indicate externality. Of course, there are degrees of each, and most people find themselves scoring near 10.

Directions: Following are a number of statements that people have used to describe themselves. Read each statement, and then circle the appropriate number to the right of the statement to indicate how you *generally* feel. There are no right or wrong answers. Do not spend too much time on any one statement, but give the answer that seems to describe how you generally feel.

	Not at All	Somewhat	Moderately So	Very Much So
1. I feel pleasant.	1	2	3	4
2. I feel nervous and restless.	1	2	3	4
3. I feel satisfied with myself.	1	2	3	4
4. I wish I could be as happy as others seem to be.	1	2	3	4
5. I worry too much over something that really doesn't matter.	1	2	3	4
6. I am happy.	1	2	3	4
7. I lack self-confidence.	1	2	3	4
8. I feel secure.	1	2	3	4
9. I am content.	1	2	3	4
10. `Some unimportant thought runs through my mind and bothers me.	1	2	3	4

Scoring: You have just completed a scale that measures the degree to which you are generally anxious. To score this scale, add the circled point values for items 2, 4, 5, 7, and 10. Reverse the point values for items 1, 3, 6, 8, and 9—that is, a circled 4 becomes 1 point, a circled 3 becomes 2 points, a circled 2 becomes 3 points, and a circled 1 becomes 4 points. Next, total these reversed scores and add that total to the total of the nonreversed items you previously obtained. The possible range of scores is between 10 and 40. The higher the score, the greater the anxiety.

Source: Modified and reproduced by special permission of the publisher, Mind Garden, Redwood City, CA 94061, from the *State-Trait Anxiety Inventory—Form Y* by Charles D. Spielberger, R. L. Gorsuch, R. Lushene, P. R. Vagg, and G. A. Jacobs. Copyright 1983 by Charles Spielberger. All rights reserved. Further reproduction is prohibited without the publisher's written consent. The complete *State-Trait Anxiety Inventory* and information about managing anxiety are available from Mind Garden, 1690 Woodside Road, #202, Redwood City, CA 94061, www.mindgarden.com.

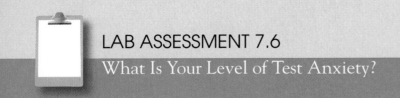

LAB ASSESSMENT 7.6

What Is Your Level of Test Anxiety?

Directions: Read each statement, and then circle the number under the column heading that best describes how you *generally* feel. There are no right or wrong answers. Do not spend too much time on any one statement, but give the answer that seems to describe how you generally feel. Add up the four numbers you have circled to get your score.

	Almost Never	Sometimes	Often	Almost Always
Thoughts of doing poorly interfere with my concentration on tests.	1	2	3	4
I feel very panicky when I take an important test.	1	2	3	4
I feel my heart beating very fast during important tests.	1	2	3	4
During tests I find myself thinking about the consequences of failing.	1	2	3	4

Scoring: To score this scale, add the numbers you circled. Test anxiety scores will range between 4 (very low) and 16 (very high).

Source: Modified and reproduced by special permission of the publisher, Mind Garden, Inc., 1690 Woodside Road, #202, Redwood City, CA 94061 USA, www.mindgarden.com, from the *State-Trait Anxiety Inventory* and *Test Anxiety Inventory* by C. D. Spielberger. Copyright 1980 by Charles D. Spielberger. All rights reserved. Further reproduction is prohibited without the publisher's written consent.

Directions: Stress does not only lead to physical illness and diseases. Psychological consequences can also result, such as anxiety associated with body image. This type of anxiety is called social physique anxiety. To determine your social physique anxiety, respond to the following statements using the scale below:

1 = not at all
2 = slightly
3 = moderately
4 = very
5 = extremely characteristic

1. I am comfortable with the appearance of my physique/figure. ____

2. I would never worry about wearing clothes that might make me look too thin or overweight. ____

3. I wish I wasn't so uptight about my physique/figure. ____

4. There are times when I am bothered by thoughts that other people are evaluating my weight or muscular development negatively. ____

5. When I look in the mirror I feel good about my physique/figure. ____

6. Unattractive features of my physique/figure make me nervous in certain social situations. ____

7. In the presence of others, I feel apprehensive about my physique/figure. ____

8. I am comfortable with how fit my body appears to others. ____

9. It would make me uncomfortable to know others were evaluating my physique/figure. ____

10. When it comes to displaying my physique/figure to others, I am a shy person. ____

11. I usually feel relaxed when it is obvious that others are looking at my physique/figure. ____

12. When in a bathing suit, I often feel nervous about the shape of my body. ____

Scoring: To score this scale, first reverse the values you assigned for items 1, 2, 5, 8, and 11. In other words, if you assigned a 1 for item 11, change that 1 to a 5, and if you assigned a 4 for item 2, change that to a 2. Next, add up the points assigned to all 12 items as they now appear. The average score (mean) for college students is 37.5 for females and approximately 30.1 for males. Scores higher than these means indicate the possibility that you experience social physique anxiety.

Social physique anxiety is the degree to which you are satisfied or dissatisfied with your body. As you might expect, social physique anxiety is related to self-esteem. If you feel good about your body, you will feel good about yourself, and vice versa. Social physique anxiety is also related to insecurity and depression. Experts on social physique anxiety state that "compared to people who are low on social physique anxiety, those who are highly anxious are likely to avoid situations in which their physique is under the scrutiny of others (e.g., swimming in public), become very distressed when their physiques are on display, avoid activities that accentuate their physiques (including aerobic activities that might be beneficial to them), suffer depression related to their bodies, and attempt to improve their physiques through a variety of means, some of which may be harmful (e.g., fasting, exercising in rubber suits)" (Hart, Leary, and Rejeski, 1989, p. 96.).

If you experience social physique anxiety, pay particular attention to the discussions of nutrition in Chapter 5, Anxiety in Chapter 7, and exercise in Chapter 13. Following the guidelines in these sections should help you improve your physique/figure and lower your level of social physique anxiety.

Source: Elizabeth A. Hart, Mark R. Leary, and W. Jack Rejeski, "The Measurement of Social Physique Anxiety," *Journal of Sport and Exercise Physiology* 11(1989): 94–104. Reprinted by permission.

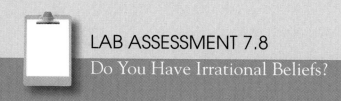

LAB ASSESSMENT 7.8

Do You Have Irrational Beliefs?

Directions: This is an inventory about the way you believe and feel about various things. Use the following scale to state how strongly you agree or disagree with each of the numbered statements:

DS: Disagree Strongly
DM: Disagree Moderately
  N: Neither Disagree nor Agree
AM: Agree Moderately
AS: Agree Strongly

Try to avoid the neutral "N" response as much as possible. Select this answer *only* if you really cannot decide whether you tend to agree or disagree with a statement.

_____ 1. It is important to me that others approve of me.

_____ 2. I hate to fail at anything.

_____ 3. There is a right way to do everything.

_____ 4. I like the respect of others, but I don't have to have it.

_____ 5. I avoid things I cannot do well.

_____ 6. There is no perfect solution to anything.

_____ 7. I want everyone to like me.

_____ 8. I don't mind competing in activities where others are better than me.

_____ 9. There is seldom an easy way out of life's difficulties.

_____ 10. I can like myself even when many others don't.

_____ 11. I like to succeed at something but don't feel I have to.

_____ 12. Some problems will always be with us.

_____ 13. If others dislike me, that's their problem, not mine.

_____ 14. It is highly important to me to be successful in everything I do.

_____ 15. Every problem has a correct solution.

_____ 16. I find it hard to go against what others think.

_____ 17. I enjoy activities for their own sake, no matter how good I am at them.

_____ 18. We live in a world of chance and probability.

_____ 19. Although I like approval, it is not a real need for me.

_____ 20. It bothers me when others are better than I am at something.

_____ 21. There is seldom an ideal solution to anything.

_____ 22. I often worry about how much people approve of and accept me.

_____ 23. It upsets me to make mistakes.

_____ 24. It is better to look for a practical solution than a perfect one.

_____ 25. I have considerable concern with what people are feeling about me.

_____ 26. I often become quite annoyed over little things.

_____ 27. I feel I must handle things in the right way.

_____ 28. It is annoying but not upsetting to be criticized.

_____ 29. I'm not afraid to do things that I cannot do well.

_____ 30. There is no such thing as an ideal set of circumstances.

Source: R. G. Jones. "A Factored Measure of Ellis' Irrational Belief System, with Personality and Maladjustment Correlates," *Dissertation Abstracts,* 69(1969): 6443.

Scoring: For items 1, 2, 3, 5, 7, 14, 15, 16, 20, 22, 23, 25, 26, and 27

DS: 1 point
DM: 2 points
N: 3 points
AM: 4 points
AS: 5 points

For items 4, 6, 8, 9, 10, 11, 12, 13, 17, 18, 19, 21, 24, 28, 29, and 30

DS: 5 points
DM: 4 points
N: 3 points
AM: 2 points
AS: 1 point

Add up the points for each of the three subscales described below.

You have just completed a scale to measure three different types of irrational beliefs.

1. *Approval of others:* The degree to which you believe you need to have the support of everyone you know or care about. Average score: Men = 27, Women = 30.

   Items: 1, 4, 7, 10, 13, 16, 19, 22, 25, 28

2. *Self-expectations:* The degree to which you believe that you must be successful, achieving, and thoroughly competent in every task you undertake, and the degree to which you judge your worthiness as a person on the basis of your successful accomplishments. Average score: Men = 29, Women = 30.

   Items: 2, 5, 8, 11, 14, 17, 20, 23, 26, 29

3. *Perfectionism:* The degree to which you believe that every problem has a "right" or perfect solution. And, the degree to which you cannot be satisfied until you find that perfect solution. Average score: Men = 29, Women = 28.

   Items: 3, 6, 9, 12, 15, 18, 21, 24, 27, 30

If you scored higher than the average, you believe these irrational beliefs to a greater extent than do most adults. Perhaps you want to step back and re-evaluate these beliefs.

One late afternoon on a sunny April day, I drove from Phoenix, Arizona, north toward Flagstaff and arrived at Oak Creek Canyon just as the sun was setting. The canyon walls, created over many centuries, surrounded a natural river that left me breathless. All I could think was, "The wonder of it all!" Later that evening, on the ride back to Phoenix, I was accompanied by what seemed like thousands of stars in a crystal clear sky. Any of you who have been to this part of the United States know that the stars appear so low in the night sky that they seem almost touchable. I could not drive too long—it seemed beyond my will—before I had to pull the car onto the shoulder of the roadway to get out and marvel at that sky with its twinkling ceiling.

It was impossible to be distressed that day. I was enraptured with these natural wonders and so intently focused upon them that the hassles and stressors I had experienced before I left Phoenix seemed inconsequential. Why sweat the small stuff in the face of the big stuff?

Too infrequently do we celebrate life's wonders with the attitude of gratitude that they deserve. Parents take their children for granted instead of marveling at their uniqueness and development. Students become desensitized to the beauty surrounding them on campus; to the quiet walks to the library; and to the opportunity to lie in the grass, reading Plato, Hemingway, or Poe. Professors forget to appreciate the cloistered environs in which they are honored by being allowed to devote their careers to labors of love. And creation itself often receives short shrift in a hurried society concerned with fast food, quick weight-loss diets, and electrodes that can stimulate muscular development without your even having to move. Quicker, faster, more, sooner, easier: We allow ourselves so little time to nourish the soul, to develop optimal spiritual health.

Spiritual Health

Spiritual health has been defined a number of ways. Some of these definitions recognize the existence of a supreme being, whereas others relate spirituality to one's relationships with others and one's place in this world. For example, one definition of **spiritual health** is adherence to doctrine as prescribed by a religion. The closer the adherence, the greater is the spiritual health. Another definition of spiritual health is the ability to discover and express your purpose in life; to learn how to experience love, joy, peace, and fulfillment; and to help yourself and others to achieve full potential.[1]

According to leading coronary health researcher and developer of the Lifestyle Heart Trial, Dr. Dean Ornish, a lack of emotional and spiritual health is the basic cause of heart disease, because the stress that develops as a result influences the development of negative health behaviors that place the individual at risk for heart disease. Dr. Ornish's program, therefore, includes activities designed to help individuals increase their connectedness with self, others, and a higher power.[2]

The Stress Reduction clinic of Jon Kabat-Zinn also recognizes the importance of spiritual health to stress reduction and general health. Using mindfulness meditation, clinic patients are taught to live in the moment, becoming acutely aware of feelings, thoughts, and sensations. The results are decreases in chronic pain,[3] anxiety, stress, and depression.[4]

It has been suggested, therefore, that "it may be useful to view techniques such as meditation, imagery, and group support within a broad framework as tools for enhancing the spiritual health components of self-awareness, connectedness with others, and meaning and purpose in life rather than looking at them narrowly as superficial stress reduction techniques that simply help people 'calm down' or escape from their problems."[5]

spiritual health
Adherence to religious doctrine; the ability to discover and express one's purpose in life; to experience love, joy, peace, and fullfillment; or to achieve and help others to achieve full potential.

Prayer can provide one with a sense of control over one's life.

Spiritual health may include answers to such questions as "Who am I?" "Why am I here?" and "Where am I headed?"—questions that confront you with the very fact of your existence and the meaning of your life. Answers to these questions may comfort you and alleviate stress with assurance that your life is headed in the direction you desire. Or your answers may disturb you. Perhaps you have not previously appreciated your relationship to humankind, to a supreme being, to nature, or to what has preceded you and what will remain when you no longer do. Should that occur, use that dissonance to make changes in your life so as to be more spiritual—take more walks in the woods, so to speak. Celebrate loved ones and natural wonders; find activities in which to make a contribution to your world and to the people who inhabit it; leave something of meaning behind; experience who you are and let others experience that as well. All of these changes will make you less distressed, more satisfied with your life, and more effective in your interactions with both your environment and the people about whom you care. We explore these and other issues related to spirituality and stress in detail in this chapter.

As you read about spirituality and spiritual health, you undoubtedly will see a connection between the "Getting Involved in Your Community" boxed material appearing at the end of each chapter and matters of the spirit. The inclusion of these boxes is one way of encouraging you to develop your spiritual side and be less "stressed out" as a result.

Religion and Spirituality

It seems clear that religious and spiritual involvement affects health.[6–9] Yet what is not so clear are the differences and similarities between religion and spirituality. **Spirituality** is "a person's orientation toward or experiences with the transcendent existential features of life (e.g., meaning, direction, purpose, connectedness), sometimes referred to as the search for the sacred in life."[10] **Religion** is an "external manifestation of spiritual experience," or an "organized social entity in which individuals share some basic beliefs and practices."[11] It is possible, therefore, to be spiritual but not be religious, or to be spiritual but antireligious. It is also possible to engage in a religious practice but to do so in a nonsecular, spiritual manner (e.g., using prayer to meditate rather than pray to a Supreme Being).

Spirituality and Health

Although both religion and spirituality have been associated with various health parameters (such as blood pressure[12]), researchers have also used religion and spirituality as interventions to improve health and alleviate stress. Some of these studies fit the traditional scientific mode, whereas others are more "exotic." In an interview pertaining to his and other researchers' studies on prayer and health, Larry Dossey describes a fascinating and controversial study he conducted.[13] A group of patients with the same illness was divided into two groups. Then a group of people who described themselves as religious believers prayed for one group of patients. Patients in neither group knew whether they were the objects of the believers' prayers, and those praying had no idea for whom they were praying. The patients who were prayed for improved their health to a greater extent than did

spirituality
A person's view of life's meaning, direction, purpose, and connectedness to other things, other people, and the past and future.

religion
An organized entity in which people have common beliefs and engage in common practices relevant to spiritual matters.

the other patients. This was a double-blind study, one of the most rigorous of research designs.

Dossey explains these findings in both spiritual and scientific terms:

> I've referred to these distant happenings as nonlocal events, because in essence they resemble the eerie, nonlocal events that physicists have demonstrated at the subatomic level between separate particles. These distant particles seem to behave as if they are united; if you change one, you change the other instantly and to the same degree. This is strongly analogous to distant, prayer-based healing, in which the separated individuals behave as if they are united. No one knows, however, if there is any real connection between the nonlocal behavior of subatomic particles and the nonlocal manifestations of intention and prayer.[14]

Dossey also points out that numerous studies have found that prayers of different religions seem to be equally effective. He lauds these findings for their validation of religious tolerance.

Many other, less controversial studies attest to the role of spirituality in health. For example, researchers have found spirituality or religion related to lower levels of psychological distress,[15,16] reduced risk of physical illness,[17] and lower mortality rates.[18] Researchers who have studied the relationship of spirituality and religion to health found them related to the adoption of healthy behaviors in general. Consequently, spiritual and religious people tend to be healthier. As one researcher stated, "a composite measure of spiritual health is more predictive of health-promoting behaviors, in general, than are isolated psychosocial variables (such as self-esteem, locus of control, connectedness, and sense of coherence)."[19] As regards stress in particular, spiritual health was found significantly related to assuming responsibility to manage one's stress.[20]

It is not only researchers who are aware of the relationship between spirituality and health. The public also is aware. A survey found that 63 percent of Americans wanted their doctors to discuss their spiritual or religious commitment with them, but only 10 percent of doctors did so.[21] Medical schools have changed as a result of the need for physicians to discuss spirituality and religion with their patients. In 1992, very few medical schools included spirituality in their curricula. In 2000, more than half did so.[22]

Patients have developed a *faith* in prayer to heal. In a study conducted by the Centers for Disease Control and Prevention of complementary and alternative medicine (CAM) use among American adults,[23] it was found that the most common form of CAM was praying. When respondents were asked about their practices during the past twelve-month period, 43 percent stated that they prayed specifically for their own health, 23 percent said that they had asked others to pray for their health, and 10 percent said that they had participated in a prayer group for their own health.

Businesses also are recognizing the role of spirituality in the health and satisfaction of their employees. Some companies hire chaplains who play a role similar to that of an Army chaplain. The rationale, according to the president of Marketplace Ministries, is that employees bring their spiritual issues to work with them and these issues affect their productivity.[24] In the huge Mall of America in Minneapolis, there is a 400-square-foot basement room that employees can use for a break from work. Among other things in that room are foot-washing stalls, shelves for shoes, prayer rugs, a compass to locate the direction east, and a poster displaying thirteen religions' interpretations of the Golden Rule.[25]

How Spirituality and Religion Affect Health

No one is certain about the exact mechanism that is working when spirituality affects a person's health status, but there are several theories.

Control Theory

Researchers have long known that when someone feels some degree of control over a stressor, that person's health will be less affected by the stressor than will the health of someone who perceives little or no control. There are two different approaches to increasing control: **Primary control** (similar to problem-focused coping) refers to attempts to change the situation. **Secondary control** refers to attempts to affect or control oneself. Secondary control can be more helpful in low-control situations.[26]

Religion and spirituality can function as either primary control or secondary control. **Intercessory prayer** (prayers for divine intervention) is a primary control activity. Reframing a situation so as to view it as the outcome of fate or of forces of nature is a secondary control activity. Other secondary control spiritual activities that lessen emotional reactions to stress include "meditation, contemplative prayer, rituals, or scripture readings."[27] One researcher even found prayer and devotional meditations more effective than progressive relaxation or no treatment in reducing anger and anxiety.[28]

Pargament[29,30] and his colleagues categorized religious approaches to increasing control as a coping mechanism:

Self-directing: Individual perceives him- or herself as responsible for the outcome, although God or nature has provided the resources the individual needs to be successful—the "God helps those who help themselves" approach.

Collaborative: Individual works with God or with forces of nature to control the situation.

Deferring: Entire situation is turned over to God or to forces of nature, with reliance on external forces to manage or cope with the situation.

Pleading: Individual begs God or forces of nature to intervene in the situation to resolve it.

Studies have found the self-directing and collaborative approaches associated with mental health and competence, and the deferring approach associated with lower levels of self-competence.[31] However, other researchers conclude that a collaborative or deferring approach may be healthier in situations in which the individual really does have little control (e.g., when about to have surgery).[32] In this instance, secondary control is facilitated by a deferring or collaborative approach.

Social Support Theory

Others conceptualize the value of spirituality and religion in more social terms. Participation in a church, synagogue, or other spiritual group often brings one in close contact, on a very personal level, with other people of similar mind. The sense of affiliation alone may help assuage feelings of anger and anxiety, thereby positively affecting one's health. In addition, church and synagogue affiliation or being a member of another type of spiritual group might bring into an individual's life people who can provide the various kinds of social support sometimes required to maintain health and well-being. They could provide emotional support during tough times or financial support when someone is laid off from work, or they could provide advice for overcoming temporary hardship. We know that social support is an effective means for managing stress and preventing ill effects from stressors.

primary control

Attempts to change a situation; similar to problem-focused coping.

secondary control

Attempts to control oneself or one's emotional reactions; similar to emotion-focused coping.

intercessory prayer

Prayers that seek divine intervention either to prevent an occurrence or to help overcome it.

The social support obtained through organized spiritual or religious groups can take on many different forms such as financial support, emotional support, or provision of advice when it is needed.

Therefore, it should be no surprise that religious and spiritual affiliations that provide social support can have profound effects on health.

Spirituality, Social Support, and Terrorism

Those directly involved, and those only peripherally involved, in the tragic events of September 11, 2001, can draw support through spiritual activities. We know that social support can take various forms, and much of this support can flow from organized spiritual activity such as attendance at religious services or from individual spiritual perspectives. For example, *emotional support* can be offered by fellow congregants or clergy. It is satisfying, as well as important for one's physical health, to have people with whom to share feelings about stressful events. For those not inclined to participate in religious activities, sharing feelings with friends and family can serve the same purpose. Counseling services can also supply emotional support in times of need.

Sometimes emotional support is not enough, and *financial support* is required. In the case of people who lost loved ones who were the family breadwinners, financial contributions made by churches, synagogues, and mosques can alleviate a significant amount of the stress they might otherwise experience. Again, friends and relatives can also provide financial support.

At other times, *informational support* is needed. Knowing where to go for help (e.g., social services) or what stress management techniques to use and how to use them can contribute to managing life crises. Such information is often available from clergy, teachers, family, friends, or governmental agencies.

Another type of social support that can be obtained through religious institutions or significant others is *advice support*. Sometimes being advised regarding what course of action to take can result in alleviating stress in confusing and traumatic times.

Lastly, the perception that life is meaningful, even when that meaning is elusive, can alleviate stress. Believing in an after-life, or in a connection with those who preceded you and those who will follow, can assuage feelings of haphazardness or of feeling victimized by traumatic events. As taught in the Book of Job and reiterated in Harold Kushner's book *When Bad Things Happen to Good People*, meaning can be found even in apparently unexplainable events. It is not easy finding and accepting that lesson, but others who care for you and for whom you care can be a source of inspiration during and following events such as those that occurred on September 11, 2001.

Placebo Theory

Some have argued that neither religious nor spiritual activities have any direct effect on health. Instead, they say, these health benefits are actually akin to what researchers find in other areas of study—namely, the placebo effect. When people believe something will help them, they often report that it actually does help them. It is for this reason that researchers try to conceal which research subjects are experiencing the treatment and which comprise the control group. Researchers even try to conceal this information, whenever possible, from those collecting the data as well. When both subjects and data collectors have no idea who the treatment subjects are and who the control subjects are, we call the studies **double-blind studies.** Although it is important to identify when the placebo effect is operating, it has been argued that whether it is operating or not is immaterial. As long as people either maintain health or improve it, what does it matter whether the improvement occurred because they believed a treatment would work or because the treatment actually worked? If religious and spiritual activities result in better health, for example, whether it is because of some metaphysical properties or a placebo effect may not matter to the individual at all.

Critics of this argument believe that effective treatments must be validated before time and resources are spent on replicating them. Therefore, if intercessory prayer improves health, we need to identify the particular reasons for this finding. Is it believing that prayer will work? Is it the particular nature of the prayer? Is it the result of some

double-blind studies
Research investigations in which neither the research subjects nor the data collectors are aware of who is in the control group and who is in the experimental group.

Forgiving others is good for your own health—physical and spiritual.

supernatural force? Once identified, the effective components can be applied in other treatments. With which view of the placebo effect do you most agree?

Forgiveness and Health

Take a moment and try to imagine someone who has done something so harmful to you that you cannot ever see yourself forgiving that person. Perhaps that person embarrassed you terribly, or fired you from a job you valued, or hurt a member of your family. You probably feel very angry when you think of this person, and that is perfectly natural. Being unforgiving is associated with feelings of anger. We also know, though, that anger can elicit a stress reaction with all of its physiological mechanisms. Ergo, being unforgiving is unhealthy. Imagine, then, when this unforgiving attitude is directed at a Supreme Being or God! Who might be expected to adopt such an attitude? People who have experienced a life tragedy (e.g., a child's death or chronic painful illness) may ascribe that to a Supreme Being or God and, as a result, not forgive the cause (God) until the condition is removed. Of course, the death of a loved one cannot be corrected; consequently, the unforgiving attitude may create chronic stress and associated ill health. That is exactly what researchers have found. For example, when college students were studied, difficulty in forgiving God was associated with anxiety and depression.[33] However, researchers also have found the reverse to be true as well: When people forgive God, they improve their health status.[34,35]

Extrapolating these findings to other relationships, researchers have found that forgiving others is associated with marital satisfaction,[36] effective families,[37] and improved mental health.[38] Furthermore, the ability to forgive oneself is also related to improved health status (e.g., higher self-esteem and less anxiety and depression).[39]

Therefore, forgiveness, a spiritual concept, has implications for your ability to manage stress and to maintain your health and well-being. It is for these reasons that I created the box entitled "Forgiving Others and Yourself."

Forgiving Others and Yourself

1. List three people whom you have had trouble forgiving:

   a. _____

   b. _____

   c. _____

2. Identify three negative effects this unforgiving attitude has on you:

   a. _____

   b. _____

   c. _____

3. Choose one or more of the three people you cited above and describe what you will do to forgive them, and the date by when you will do it:

   _____

   _____

   _____

Volunteerism as a Spiritual and Healthy Activity

Volunteering to help others is one spiritual activity that pays big dividends, not only to those receiving the volunteer service but also to the person performing it. As Ralph Waldo Emerson once said, "It is one of the most beautiful compensations of this life that no man can sincerely try to help another without helping himself." That certainly appears to be the case with volunteerism.

Several large-scale studies of college students' community service and service-learning activities have found numerous benefits for college students. Among these benefits are the development of a greater sense of civic responsibility (a commitment to serving the community), a higher level of academic achievement (academic self-concept, grades, degree aspirations, time devoted to academic endeavors), growth in life skills (leadership, interpersonal skills, self-confidence), increased commitment to helping others and to promoting racial understanding, and enhanced critical thinking and conflict resolution skills. In addition, benefits accrued to the colleges conducting the service activities and to the communities and agencies they served.[40,41] The good news is that college student volunteerism seems to be increasing. The elderly also are volunteering a great deal and benefiting from it. In a study in California, 31 percent of elders were found to volunteer,

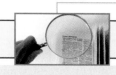

Mitzvah Day

In Rochester, New York, 150 Jewish teenagers participate in "Mitzvah Day," one day each year that synagogues devote to community service. The variety of activities in which they participate might give you some ideas how you can volunteer your time and benefit others while, at the same time, benefiting yourself. Here are some of the projects through which these teenagers provided service:[a]

1. Learned how to do CPR and then taught seven other people how to do it.
2. Taught a dozen people how to cook chicken soup, which was delivered to homebound individuals the following week.
3. Learned how to give manicures and hand massages so they could go to local nursing homes and provide these services to residents.
4. Learned how to dance to music from the Big Band era and then organized a Senior Ball at a nursing home during which the teenagers danced with the elders.
5. Learned how to act like a clown and perform magic tricks in preparation for putting on a show at a children's hospital.
6. Two young women cut two inches off of their hair and donated it to Locks of Love, an organization that makes wigs and provides them free of charge to children who experience hair loss from various medical treatments or illnesses or diseases.

What service can you volunteer?

What service will you volunteer?

Marian Wright Edelman, executive director of the Children's Defense Fund, once wrote that "service is the rent we pay for living. If you see a need, don't ask, 'Why doesn't somebody do something?' Ask, 'Why don't I do something?' . . . We are not all guilty but we are all equally responsible."[b]

[a] D. Seigel, "A Cold Day in Rochester," *Tikkun* 15(2000): 61.
[b] M. W. Edelman, *The Measure of Our Success* (Boston: Beacon Press, 1992).

When you volunteer to help others, you inevitably help yourself. Volunteering is associated with better health and less stress.

and those who did had lower mortality than nonvolunteers.[42] The researchers hypothesized that volunteering was associated with better physical functioning, healthier habits, and social support received from the staff of organizations through whom they volunteered and from the other volunteers. Volunteers have been found to have better health, be more sociable, possess more altruism, and be more interested in religion than nonvolunteers.[43] Adult volunteers report better perceived health,[44] and higher morale, self-esteem, and social integration.[45]

Historically volunteerism has been associated with religious organizations. However, there is also a long history of nonsecular volunteerism and community service in the United States and elsewhere. On many college campuses there is an office responsible for encouraging students, faculty, and staff to participate in community service. The "Getting Involved in Your Community" box at the conclusion of each chapter in this book will get you started volunteering. Remember, by doing so you are doing something good for yourself while doing something good for someone else. What more could you ask for?

Service-Learning: A Spiritual and Academic Activity

Service-learning involves students who provide service on or off campus using the knowledge or skills they learn in class. In this way, students have the opportunity to apply what they learn in the real world, and communities receive service they might not otherwise receive.

In each decade since 1990, the federal government has developed national health objectives intended to focus national attention and actions on improving the health of Americans. Several of these objectives for the year 2010 are directly and indirectly related to stress or other content presented in this book. Among the stress-related national health objectives are

- Increase the proportion of work sites employing fifty or more persons that provide programs to prevent or reduce employee stress.
- Increase the proportion of employees who participate in employer-sponsored health promotion activities.
- Reduce the suicide rate.
- Reduce the rate of suicide attempts by adolescents.
- Reduce the proportion of homeless adults who have serious mental illness.
- Reduce the relapse rates for persons with eating disorders including anorexia nervosa and bulimia nervosa.
- Increase the number of persons seen in primary health care who receive mental health screening and assessment.
- Increase the proportion of adults with mental disorders who receive treatment.
- Increase the number of states and territories, including the District of Columbia, with an operational mental health plan that addresses mental health crisis intervention, ongoing screening, and treatment services for elderly persons.
- Reduce the proportion of adults who engage in no leisure-time physical activity.
- Increase the proportion of adults and adolescents who engage regularly, preferably daily, in moderate physical activity for at least thirty minutes per day.
- Increase the proportion of adults and adolescents who engage in vigorous physical activity that promotes the development of cardiorespiratory fitness three or more days per week for twenty or more minutes per occasion.

Through service-learning, you can be supportive of these stress-related national health objectives. For example, you could conduct stress management workshops for others in your community. These workshops could be offered in community centers, in schools, or in housing projects. My students have conducted stress management workshops for cancer patients, nursing home residents and staff, volunteer firefighters, and many others.

Or you could organize fitness activities for younger students attending after-school programs, or for the elderly in your community. Participants will dissipate the built-up by-products of stress and have something on which to focus other than their stressors.

You can contribute to the achievement of these stress-related national health objectives in many ways. Service-learning is one way. Through service-learning, you can make your community, and the people in it, healthier. And by doing so, you will learn more about stress and stress management. Now, how can you beat that? Perhaps your instructor will work with you to organize a service-learning activity to derive those benefits.

Closing Thoughts on Spirituality, Health, and Managing Stress

Believing that your life is not an isolated event will be one of the developmental tasks of your later years. Many years ago, psychiatrist Erik Erikson said that the main challenge facing old people is to resolve what he termed the crisis between integrity and despair.[46] When this crisis is satisfactorily resolved, you feel connected to what came before you and to what will come after you. You believe that you contributed to the chain of life and that your life has had meaning and purpose. This is spiritual health. Some people find it through a religious belief, a belief in God and life in the hereafter as a reward for good deeds in this life. Others find it in a belief that all things are connected, that what affects me also affects you and all others. These people may feel strongly about protecting the environment, volunteering to serve others, and advocating for those less fortunate than themselves.

Getting Involved in Your Community

Many religious organization—synagogues, churches, mosques—conduct educational programs of varied kinds. You can offer to teach congregants to manage stress by using prayer on which to focus when meditating. Or you can organize youth members of the congregation to provide services to others in the community, similar to the Mitzvah Day activities described in the boxed material in this chapter.

If you are not active with a religious group or are nonreligious, you can still engage in community service of a spiritual nature. For example, you can organize a group of youth who frequent an after-school community center to offer services to the community. You can start a basketball league with all team registration fees, admission fees, and any other contributions people or area businesses are willing to make donated to a shelter for the homeless in your neighborhood or town.

When you offer service to your community, you can expect to feel your life is more meaningful and that you really matter and can make a difference. This might even be used as a definition of spiritual health. Volunteer. Be healthier and more fulfilled as a result. Be a person in your community who cares, and you will make a huge contribution in helping your neighbors live less stressful lives; and you, too, will be better able to manage stress in your own life.

This feeling of life having a purpose, of integrity rather than despair, can be invaluable during times of stress. It can help as an emotion-focused coping technique by allowing you to be more accepting of those things that are beyond your control, and it can provide something positive upon which to focus, thereby helping elicit a relaxation response.

Believing your life has a larger purpose can also serve as a problem-focused coping technique during stressful times. Possessing this level of spiritual health usually results in collaboration with other people in the pursuit of common goals. For some this will mean becoming a member of an organized religion—a church, synagogue, or mosque—and interacting with congregants with similar views. For others it will mean joining an organization that seeks to achieve the spiritual goals they find important. That could be joining the Sierra Club, or volunteering at a shelter for women who have experienced domestic violence, or delivering blankets to the homeless on cold winter nights. In either case, active participation in a religious group or in a non-secular one makes available people who can offer advice, financial support, or even shelter when that is needed during stressful times. These all serve as problem-focused coping interventions.

So, as we have seen, spiritual health not only is good for you physically and psychologically but is an important component of effective stress management. Having faith—be it in yourself, in God, or in other humans—goes a long way in helping us be soulful and happy. One author has described this another way. Gafni[47] speaks of "soul prints." Soul prints are people's unique stories, their reasons for being, their views of holy and holistic living, the unique patterns of their spirit. When people are not living their story, Gafni argues, they have **spiritual disease.** As might be expected, and as attested to by the research described earlier in this chapter, spiritual disease eventually results in physiological or psychological disease.

The lesson to be learned in all of this? Be true to yourself and to what you view as your purpose in life, contribute to enhancing the lives of others, and connect to what has come before and to what will come after. You will be healthier, happier, more fulfilled, and better able to manage stressful events. Now there's a formula for living!

spiritual disease
A condition in which people are not true to their spiritual selves and are living a "life story" that is inconsistent with their beliefs and values.

summary

- Spiritual health has been defined in a number of ways. Some definitions recognize the existence of a Supreme Being; others relate spirituality to one's relationships with others and to one's place in this world. One definition of spiritual health is adherence to doctrine as prescribed by a religion. Another definition of spiritual health is the ability to discover and express your purpose in life; to learn how to experience love, joy, peace, and fulfillment; and to help yourself and others to achieve full potential. Spiritual health may include answers to such questions as "Who am I?" "Why am I here?" and "Where am I headed?" Developing one's spiritual nature can help alleviate stress by feeling connected to others, by having purpose in life, and by being better able to view hassles and stressors with proper perspective.

- Spirituality is a person's orientation toward or experiences with the transcendent existential features of life such as meaning, direction, purpose, and connectedness.

- Spirituality is sometimes referred to as the search for the sacred life.

- Religion is an external manifestation of spiritual experience, or an organized social entity in which individuals share some basic beliefs and practices.

- It is possible to be spiritual without being religious, or to be spiritual but antireligious. It is also possible to engage in a religious practice but to do so in a nonsecular, spiritual manner, such as using prayer as the focus of meditation rather than as a means of praying to a Supreme Being.

- Spiritual health is related to a number of physiological conditions such as heart disease, anxiety, depression, and mortality.

- The means by which spiritual health affects other components of health has been explained by various theories: control theory, social support theory, and placebo theory. Religious approaches to increase control as a mechanism to cope include self-directing, collaboration, deferring, and pleading.

- Forgiveness is also associated with health and stress. The inability to forgive another person or a Supreme Being leads to anger, which in turn leads to ill health. For example, studies have shown an inability to forgive associated with anxiety and depression. The ability to forgive has been associated with marital satisfaction, effective families, improved mental health, and higher self-esteem.

- Volunteerism, a spiritual activity, is related to a variety of benefits for the person volunteering, the people and agencies receiving the service, and the college supporting student, faculty, and staff volunteers. Volunteerism has been associated with lower mortality, better physical functioning, healthier habits, and the availability of social support. Volunteers are more sociable, are more altruistic, are in better health, have higher morale, and possess higher self-esteem.

- Believing one is connected to the past and to the future, either through a religious belief or a belief in nature and the oneness of the world, is a developmental stage related to health and the ability to manage stress.

notes

1. Larry S. Chapman, "Developing a Useful Perspective on Spiritual Health: Well-Being, Spiritual Potential, and the Search for Meaning," *American Journal of Health Promotion,* Winter 1987, 31–39.

2. Dean Ornish, *Dr. Dean Ornish's Program for Reversing Heart Disease: The Only System Scientifically Proven to Reverse Heart Disease Without Drugs or Surgery* (New York: Ballantine Books, 1996).

3. Jon Kabat-Zinn et al., "Clinical Use of Mindfulness Meditation for the Self-Regulation of Chronic Pain," *Journal of Behavioral Medicine* 8(1985): 163–90.

4. Jon Kabat-Zinn et al., "Effectiveness of Meditation-Based Stress Reduction Program in the Treatment of Anxiety Disorders," *American Journal of Psychiatry* 149(1992): 936–43.

5. Steven R. Hawkes, Melisa L. Hull, Rebecca L. Thulman, and Paul M. Richins, "Review of Spiritual Health: Definition, Role, and Intervention Strategies in Health Promotion," *American Journal of Health Promotion* 9(1995): 371–78.

6. H. G. Koenig, *Is Religion Good for Your Health? The Effects of Religion on Physical and Mental Health* (New York: Haworth Pastoral Press, 1997).

7. D. Oman and D. Reed, "Religion and Mortality Among the Community-Dwelling Elderly," *American Journal of Public Health* 88(1998): 1469–75.

8. P. S. Richards and A. E. Bergin, *A Spiritual Strategy for Counseling and Psychotherapy* (Washington, DC: American Psychological Association, 1997).

9. E. L. Worthington, T. A. Kurusu, M. E. McCullough, and S. J. Sandage, "Empirical Research on Religion and Psychotherapeutic Processes and Outcomes: A 10-Year Review of Research Prospectus," *Psychological Bulletin* 119(1996): 448–87.

10. A. H. S. Harris, C. E. Thoresen, M. E. McCullough, and D. B. Larson, "Spirituality and Religiously Oriented Health Interventions," *Journal of Health Psychology* 4(1999): 413–33.

11. Ibid., 414.

12. K. A. Hixson, H. W. Gruchow, and D. W. Morgan, "The Relation Between Religiosity, Selected Health Behaviors, and Blood Pressure Among Adult Females," *Preventive Medicine* 27(1998): 545–52.

13. "An Interview with Larry Dossey," *Tikkun* 15(2000): 11–16.

14. Ibid., 12.

15. J. Gartner, "Religious Commitment, Mental Health, and Prosocial Behavior: A Review of the Empirical Literature," in *Religion and the Clinical Practice of Psychology,* ed. E. P. Shafranske (Washington, DC: American Psychological Association, 1996), 187–214.

16. J. S. Levin and P. L. Schiller, "Is There a Religious Factor in Health?" *Journal of Religion and Health* 26(1987): 9–36.

17. J. S. Levin and H. Vanderpool, "Is Religious Attendance Really Conducive to Better Health? Toward an Epidemiology of Religion," *Social Science and Medicine* 24(1987): 589–600.

18. W. J. Strawbridge, R. D. Cohen, S. J. Shema, and G. A. Kaplan, "Frequent Attendance at Religious Services and Mortality over 28 Years," *American Journal of Public Health* 87(1997): 957–61.

19. P. J. Waite, S. R. Hawks, and J. A. Gast, "The Correlation Between Spiritual Well-Being and Health Behaviors," *American Journal of Health Promotion* 13(1999): 159–62.

20. Ibid.

21. Lydia Strohl, "Faith: The Best Medicine," *The Washingtonian,* December 2000, 63–65, 138–40.

22. Ibid.

23. Patricia M. Barnes, Eve Powell-Griner, Kim McFann, and Richard L. Nahin, "Complementary and Alternative Medicine Use Among Adults: United States, 2002," *Advance Data,* 343(2004): 1.

24. Dixie L. Dennis and Brent G. Dennis, "Spirituality@ Work.Health," *American Journal of Health Education,* 34(2003): 297–301.

25. S. Scott, "A Great Deal for Mall Employees," *Lexington Herald-Leader,* 8 June 2002, E3.

26. E. Band and J. Weisz, "How to Feel Better When It Feels Bad: Children's Perspectives on Coping with Everyday Stress," *Developmental Psychology* 24(1988): 247–53.

27. K. I. Pargament, B. Cole, L. Vandecreek, T. Belavich, C. Brant, and L. Perez, "The Vigil: Religion and the Search for Control in the Hospital Waiting Room," *Journal of Health Psychology* 4(1999): 327–41.

28. C. Carlson, P. Bacaseta, and D. Simanton, "A Controlled Evaluation of Devotional Meditation and Progressive Relaxation," *Journal of Psychology and Theology* 16(1988): 362–68.

29. K. I. Pargament, D. S. Ensing, K. Falgout, H. Olsen, B. Reilly, K. Van Haitsma, and R. Warren, "God Helps Me: Religious Coping Efforts as Predictors of the Outcomes of Significant Negative Life Events," *American Journal of Community Psychology* 18(1990): 793–825.

30. K. I. Pargament, J. Kennel, W. Hathaway, N. Grevengoed, J. Newman, and W. Jones, "Religion and the Problem-Solving Process: Three Styles of Coping," *Journal of the Scientific Study of Religion* 27(1988): 90–104.

31. W. L. Hathaway and K. I. Pargament, "Intrinsic Religiousness, Religious Coping, and Psychological Competence: A Covariance Structure Analysis," *Journal for the Scientific Study of Religion* 29(1992): 423–41.

32. C. Bickel, J. W. Ciarrocchi, W. J. Sheers, B. K. Estadt, D. A. Powell, and K. I. Pargament, "Perceived Stress, Religious Coping Styles, and Depressive Affect," *Journal of Psychology and Christianity* 17(1998): 33–42.

33. J. Exline, A. M. Yali, and M. Lobel, "When God Disappoints: Difficulty Forgiving God and Its Role in Negative Emotion," *Journal of Health Psychology* 4(1999): 365–79.

34. J. N. Sells and T. D. Hargrove, "Forgiveness: A Review of the Theoretical and Empirical Literature," *Journal of Family Therapy* 20(1998): 21–36.

35. R. D. Enright and the Human Development Study Group, "Counseling Within the Forgiveness Triad: On Forgiving, Receiving Forgiveness, and Self-Forgiveness," *Counseling and Values* 40(1996): 107–26.

36. D. L. Fenell, "Characteristics of Long-Term First Marriages," *Journal of Mental Health Counseling* 15(1993): 446–60.

37. T. D. Hargrave and J. N. Sells, "The Development of a Forgiveness Scale," *Journal of Marital and Family Therapy* 23(1997): 41–62.

38. C. T. Coyle and R. D. Enright, "Forgiveness Intervention with Post-Abortion Men," *Journal of Consulting and Clinical Psychology* 65(1998): 1042–46.

39. P. A. Mauger, J. E. Perry, T. Freeman, D. C. Grove, A. G. McBride, and K. E. McKinney, "The Measurement of Forgiveness: Preliminary Research," *Journal of Psychology and Christianity* 11(1992): 170–80.

40. A. Melchior, *National Evaluation of Learn and Serve America School and Community-Based Programs* (Washington, DC: The Corporation for National Service, 1997).

41. A. W. Astin, L. J. Sax, and J. Avalos, "Long-Term Effects of Volunteerism During the Undergraduate Years," *Review of Higher Education* 22(1999): 187–202.

42. D. Oman, C. E. Thoresen, and K. McMahon, "Volunteerism and Mortality Among the Community-Dwelling Elderly," *Journal of Health Psychology* 4(1999): 301–16.

43. M. Ganguli, M. E. Lytle, M. D. Reynolds, and H. H. Dodge, "Random Versus Volunteer Selection for a Community-Based Study," *Journal of Gerontology* 53A(1998): M39–46.

44. F. W. Young and N. Glasgow, "Voluntary Social Participation and Health," *Research on Aging* 20(1998): 339–62.

45. E. Midlarsky and E. Kahana, "Predictors of Helping and Well-Being in Older Adults: A Cross-Sectional Survey Research Project," in *Altruism in Later Life* (Thousand Oaks, CA: Sage, 1994), 126–88.

46. E. Erikson, *Childhood and Society* (New York: Norton, 1963).

47. M. Gafni, "My Unique Pathology," *Tikkun* 15(2000): 8–9.

internet resources

About Religion and Spirituality
www.about.com/religion
Describes numerous religions' perspectives on spiritual issues.

Faith
www.faith.com
Provides a forum for exploring spirituality and religion without promoting any one religion or approach through articles, audio and video clips, and other resources.

Forgiving
www.forgiving.org
Provides research and resources about forgiveness in today's world, from everyday living to current events.

Spirituality and Health
www.spiritualityhealth.com
Contains links to many topics that relate spirituality to health. Also includes self-tests of spirituality-related variables.

Spirituality at Work
www.spiritualityatwork.com
Includes links to articles pertaining to spirituality. Also allows for online conversations with others interested in spirituality at work.

Coping in Today's World

Many African American churches have a "church nurse" or "health ministry." These church nurses perform several functions, including comforting the family of the deceased at funeral services. Church nurses can be seen distributing tissues and water to grieving family members at these funeral services. When a parishioner becomes too excited during services—becomes "overcome with the holy spirit"—the church nurse might be seen fanning this parishioner.

Today, though, these health ministries have been transformed so that, in addition to their previous responsibilities, they may organize health fairs, conduct health screenings (e.g., blood pressure and blood glucose), and visit ill or shut-in parishioners in their homes. The health ministry may also supervise a health library so interested parishioners may have written material to consult.

Furthermore, the health ministry may arrange for health experts to speak to the congregation on health issues that are differentially distributed among African Americans: hypertension, diabetes, HIV/AIDS, and obesity.

Health ministries in African American churches combine spirituality, religiosity, and health care for the betterment of their parishioners.

Directions: In today's modern world, with the stressors encountered and the challenges faced, experts argue that spirituality can help. How spiritual are you? To find out, complete the scale below. This is an inventory that measures how spiritual—not necessarily religious—you are. Indicate your response to each statement by circling the appropriate letters using the following scale:

SA = strongly agree
A = agree
AM = agree more than disagree
DM = disagree more than agree
D = disagree
SD = strongly disagree

There is no right or wrong answer. Please respond to what you think or how you feel at this point in time.

1. I have a general sense of belonging.	SA	A	AM	DM	D	SD
2. I am able to forgive people who have done wrong to me.	SA	A	AM	DM	D	SD
3. I have the ability to rise above or go beyond a physical or psychological condition.	SA	A	AM	DM	D	SD
4. I am concerned about destruction of the environment.	SA	A	AM	DM	D	SD
5. I have experienced moments of peace in a devastating event.	SA	A	AM	DM	D	SD
6. I feel a kinship to other people.	SA	A	AM	DM	D	SD
7. I feel a connection to all of life.	SA	A	AM	DM	D	SD
8. I rely on an inner strength in hard times.	SA	A	AM	DM	D	SD
9. I enjoy being of service to others.	SA	A	AM	DM	D	SD
10. I can go to a spiritual dimension within myself for guidance.	SA	A	AM	DM	D	SD
11. I have the ability to rise above or go beyond a body change or body loss.	SA	A	AM	DM	D	SD
12. I have a sense of harmony or inner peace.	SA	A	AM	DM	D	SD
13. I have the ability for self-healing.	SA	A	AM	DM	D	SD
14. I have an inner strength.	SA	A	AM	DM	D	SD
15. The boundaries of my universe extend beyond usual ideas of what space and time are thought to be.	SA	A	AM	DM	D	SD
16. I feel good about myself.	SA	A	AM	DM	D	SD
17. I have a sense of balance in my life.	SA	A	AM	DM	D	SD
18. There is fulfillment in my life.	SA	A	AM	DM	D	SD
19. I feel a responsibility to preserve the planet.	SA	A	AM	DM	D	SD
20. The meaning I have found for my life provides a sense of peace.	SA	A	AM	DM	D	SD
21. Even when I feel discouraged, I trust that life is good.	SA	A	AM	DM	D	SD
22. My life has meaning and purpose.	SA	A	AM	DM	D	SD
23. My innerness or an inner resource helps me deal with uncertainty in my life.	SA	A	AM	DM	D	SD
24. I have discovered my own strength in time of struggle.	SA	A	AM	DM	D	SD
25. Reconciling relationships is important to me.	SA	A	AM	DM	D	SD
26. I feel a part of the community in which I live.	SA	A	AM	DM	D	SD
27. My inner strength is related to a belief in a Higher Power or Supreme Being.	SA	A	AM	DM	D	SD
28. I have goals and aims for my life.	SA	A	AM	DM	D	SD

Scoring: Write alongside each statement, the points assigned for each response:

SD = 1, D = 2, DM = 3, AM = 4, A = 5, SA = 6

This scale also has several subscales. Add up the number of points for the responses you circled for each subscale's statements to obtain a score for that subscale.

Purpose and meaning in life (searching for events or relationships that provide a sense of worth, hope, or reason for living):
Statements: 18, 20, 22, 28

Innerness or inner resources (striving for wholeness, identity, and sense of empowerment):
Statements: 8, 10, 12, 14, 16, 17; 23; 24; 27

Unifying interconnectedness (feeling of relatedness or attachment to others and with the universe):
Statements: 1, 2, 4, 6, 7, 9, 19, 25, 26

Transcendence (ability to reach or go beyond the limits of usual experience):
Statements: 3, 5, 11, 13, 15, 21

If your total scale score is over 84, you tend to be a spiritual person. The higher your score, the more spiritual you are. To interpret your subscale scores, multiply the number of items in the subscale by 3. If your subscale score is above that number, you evidence that factor. The closer to the multiple of 3 times the number of total items in that subscale, the more you evidence that factor.

Source: J. W. Howden, *Spirituality Assessment Scale* (Corsicana, TX: Judy W. Howden, 1992).

General Applications
Relaxation Techniques

BEFORE YOU BEGIN PART 3, SOME INSTRUCTIONS ARE NECESSARY. Part 3 describes relaxation techniques: meditation, autogenic training, progressive relaxation, biofeedback, yoga, and others. A description of each technique, its historical development, how to do it, and its benefits are presented. Remember, these relaxation techniques are but one part of a comprehensive stress management program. Relaxation techniques relate to the level of emotional arousal on the stress model and serve as interventions between stress and illness and disease. Because you will learn how to do each technique, two additional comments need to be made.

Medical Caution

First, relaxation techniques result in changes in physiological processes. We've already seen that the relaxation response is a hypometabolic state of lowered blood pressure, heart rate, muscle tension, and serum cholesterol, with other physiological parameters being affected. Those of you using medication that is designed to affect, or, that incidentally affects, a physiological parameter might be affecting that parameter too much if you engage in relaxation techniques. For example, a person with high blood pressure who is taking medication to lower the blood pressure might lower it too much if relaxation training is added to the medication. It is because of these changes in physiological processes that people who are thinking of beginning relaxation training and are under medical care or taking medication are advised to get the permission of the medical specialist supervising their care *prior* to practicing relaxation skills. In particular, those with heart conditions, epilepsy, hypertension, diabetes, and psychological problems should obtain medical permission to begin relaxation training.

Relaxation Technique Trials

Second, the opportunity to try several different relaxation techniques is designed to help you find one that you prefer and will use regularly. To structure your evaluation of these techniques so you can decide which one is best for you, use the Lab Assessment rating scale that appears at the conclusion of each chapter. Unfortunately, there is no good research base to allow you to be diagnosed and a particular relaxation technique prescribed for you. Studies have been conducted to determine, for instance, whether people with certain personality characteristics benefit more from meditation than do people without those characteristics.* Those studies have not been able to differentiate in the manner intended; we still have no system to recommend particular relaxation techniques for particular people. Consequently, you will have to use trial and error to decide which relaxation technique you prefer. The rating scale should help, though.

To use the Lab Assessment rating scale, it is best to practice each technique for at least one week (the longer, the better). Your inner environment may change from day to day (e.g., you may eat different foods at different times of the day) and your outer environment is never constant (temperature, outside noises, and quality of the air vary), so a one-day trial of one relaxation technique compared with a one-day trial of another will not allow for a valid comparison. Also, practice the technique as recommended—correct posture, frequency, time of day, type of environment—and make your practice consistent with other suggestions. After a sufficient trial period, answer each of the questions in the Lab Assessment; then sum up the point values you gave each answer. The lower the total point value is, the more that relaxation technique fits you.

*Sheila A. Ramsey,"Perceptual Style as a Predictor of Successful Meditation Training" (Master's thesis, University of Maryland, 1981).

You may know that some meditators wear muslin robes, burn incense, shave their hair, and believe in the Far Eastern religions. You should also know that these things are *not required* in order to benefit from meditative practice. Although wine may be a part of a Catholic religious service, not all those who drink wine embrace Catholicism. Similarly, not all those who meditate need adopt a particular religion.

What Is Meditation?

Meditation is simply a mental exercise that affects body processes. Just as physical exercise has certain psychological benefits, meditation has certain physical benefits. The purpose of meditation is to gain control over your attention so that you can choose what to focus upon rather than being subject to the unpredictable ebb and flow of environmental circumstances.

Meditation has its tradition grounded in Eastern cultures (e.g., those of India and Tibet) but has been popularized for Western cultures. The major exporter of meditation to the Western world has been the Maharishi Mahesh Yogi. The Maharishi developed a large, worldwide, and highly effective organization to teach **transcendental meditation (TM)** to a population of people experiencing more and more stress and recognizing the need for more and more of an escape. The simplicity of this technique, coupled with the effectiveness of its marketing by TM organizations, quickly led to its popularity. In a short time, in spite of an initial fee of $125 (significantly higher now), large numbers of people learned and began regular practice of TM (10,000 persons were joining the program each month during the early 1970s in the United States).

The Maharishi's background is interesting in itself. Mahest Prasod Varma (his name at birth) was born in 1918 and earned a degree in physics in 1942 from Allahabad University in India. Before he began practicing his profession, however, he met and eventually studied under a religious leader, Swami Brahmananda Saraswati. Thirteen years of religious study later, he was assigned the task of finding a simple form of meditation that everyone could readily learn. It took two years of isolated life in a Himalayan cave to develop TM, which he later spread via mass communication, advertising, and the Students International Meditation Society.

Types of Meditation

Transcendental meditation is but one form of meditative practice. Chakra yoga, Rinzai Zen, Mudra yoga, Sufism, Zen meditation, and Soto Zen are examples of other meditative systems. In Soto Zen meditation, common external objects (e.g., flowers or a peaceful landscape) are focused upon. Tibetan Buddhists use a **mandala**— a geometrical figure with other geometric forms on it that has spiritual or philosophical importance—to meditate upon. Imagined sounds (thunder or a beating drum), termed **nadam**, and a silently repeated word termed **mantra**, have also been used. Rinzai Zen meditation uses **koans** (unanswerable, illogical riddles), Zazen focuses on subjective states of consciousness, Hindu meditation employs **pranayama** (prana means "life force" and refers to breathing), and Zen practitioners have been known to focus on **anapanasati** (counting breaths from one to ten repetitively).[1] There is also a revival of the centuries-old traditional Jewish meditation. This form of meditation does not require a belief in the traditional God or membership in

transcendental meditation (TM)
A relaxation technique involving the use of a Sanskrit word as the object of focus.

Meditation requires an object of focus. That can be a word—mantra, your breathing, or a geometric shape such as the mandala above.

mandala
A geometric figure used as the object of focus during meditation.

nadam
Imagined sounds used as the object of focus during meditation.

mantra
A word used as the object of focus during meditation.

koans
Unanswerable, illogical riddles used as the object of focus during meditation.

pranayama
A Hindu practice that involves breathing as the object of focus during meditation.

anapanasati
A Zen practice that involves counting breaths as the object of focus during meditation.

a synagogue. Instead it involves focusing on repetitive prayer, receiving the light of the divine with each breath, or chanting.[2]

Regardless of the type of meditation, however, one of two approaches is used: opening up of attention or focusing of attention. Opening up your attention requires a nonjudgmental attitude: You allow all external and internal stimuli to enter your awareness without trying to use these stimuli in any particular manner. As with a blotter (the inner self) and ink (the external and internal stimuli), everything is just absorbed. When the meditative method requires the focusing of attention, the object focused upon is something either repetitive (e.g., a word or phrase repeated in your mind) or something unchanging (e.g., a spot on the wall).

To understand the two basic methods of meditation, place an object in the center of your room. Try to get an object at least as high as your waist. Come on now. Your tendency will be to rush to get this chapter read rather than get the most out of it. Remember that people with the Type A behavior pattern, those most prone to coronary heart disease, rush through tasks rather than doing them well. Slow down. Get that object, and continue reading.

Now, look at that object for about five seconds. Most likely, you saw and focused upon the object while excluding the other stimuli in your field of vision. Behind the object (in your field of vision) might have been a wall, a window, a table, or maybe a poster. In spite of the presence of these other visual stimuli, you can put them in the background, ignore them, and focus your attention on one object. The object of focus is called the *figure*, and the objects in the background of your field of vision are called the *ground*. When you see and listen to a lecturer, you probably focus upon that person and his or her voice. You choose to place objects other than the lecturer in the background, as well as sounds other than the lecturer's voice. You may even be doing that now. As you read this book, you may be hearing your inner voice recite the words while placing in the background other sounds (the heating or cooling system, people and cars outside, birds chirping, or airplanes flying overhead).

Focusing-of-attention meditation is similar to focusing on the figure while excluding the ground. Opening-up-of-attention meditation blends the figure and ground together so they are one and the same.

One can meditate to the recurring sounds of the surf coming ashore or to pleasant sounds earlier recorded and replayed later on a tape recorder. Even though the surf may be preferable for most people, noisy and crowded beaches may necessitate the use of the tape recorder to drown out disturbing and distracting sounds. There are many innovative ways to create an environment conducive to relaxation.

Benefits of Meditation

Because it is so popular and can be learned quickly and easily,[3] meditation has been one of the most researched of the relaxation techniques. The research findings evidence the physiological and psychological effects of meditation. These findings follow. However, the shortcomings of generalizing results about relaxation techniques should be recognized. For example, even though we state findings about meditation, there are many different types of meditation. Findings with different types may differ. Sometimes the level of motivation of the research subjects can affect the results obtained. The experience of the meditators has also been found to affect results (those with at least six months' experience differ from novice meditators). In spite of these limitations, though, there are some things we can say about the effects of meditation.

Physiological Effects

The physiological effects of meditation were discovered by early research on Indian yogis and Zen masters. In 1946, Therese Brosse found that Indian yogis could

Meditation involves focusing on something that is repetitive—like this flame—or unchanging.

control their heart rates.[4] Another study of Indian yogis found that they could slow respiration (four to six breaths per minute), decrease by 70 percent their ability to conduct an electrical current (galvanic skin response), emit predominantly alpha brain waves, and slow their heart rate to twenty-four beats fewer than normal.[5] Other early studies of yogis and Zen meditators have reported similar results.[6,7]

More recent studies have verified these earlier findings of the physiological effects of meditation.[8] Allison compared the respiration rate of a subject meditating with that subject's respiration rate while watching television and while reading a book. Respiration rate decreased most while meditating (from twelve and one-half breaths per minute to seven).[9] The decrease in respiration rate as a result of meditation is a consistent finding across research studies.[10,11]

Several researchers have found a decrease in muscle tension associated with meditation. In one study by Arambula, et al. and another by Luskin, et al., the decrease in muscle tension in meditators was significantly greater than that experienced by a control group of nonmeditators.[12,13]

The decrease in heart rate found by early studies on Indian yogis has also been verified in more recent studies. When experienced (five years) and short-term (fourteen months) meditators were compared with novice (seven days) meditators and with people taught a different relaxation technique, it was found that the most significant decreases in heart rate occurred in the experienced and short-term meditators.[14] Even when meditators and nonmeditators were physiologically stimulated by viewing a film on laboratory accidents, the meditators' heart rates returned to normal sooner than the nonmeditators' heart rates.[15]

Galvanic skin response—the ability of skin to conduct an electrical current—differs between meditators and nonmeditators. The lower the conductance is, the less stress. These skin electrical conductance findings led researchers to conclude that meditators are better able to cope with stress and have more stable autonomic nervous systems.[16]

In summary then, meditation has been demonstrated to have positive effects on blood pressure and the prevention of hypertension,[17,18] treating pain,[19] lowering baseline cortisol,[20] and reducing alcohol consumption,[21] and several studies have found a decrease in the use of health services among meditators that, in turn, saves companies money on their health insurance premiums.[22–24]

Much of the research discussed so far was given impetus by the work of Robert Keith Wallace. Wallace was one of the first modern researchers to study the effects of meditation scientifically. In his initial study and in his subsequent work with Herbert Benson, Wallace showed that meditation resulted in decreased oxygen consumption, heart rate, and alpha brain-wave emissions. He also demonstrated that meditation increased skin resistance, decreased blood lactate (thought to be associated with lessened anxiety) and carbon dioxide production, and increased the peripheral blood flow to arms and legs.[25,26]

There is ample evidence, therefore, that meditation results in specific physiological changes that differ from those produced by other relaxation techniques (reading, watching television, sleeping). These changes are termed the **relaxation response (trophotropic response)** and are thought to have beneficial effects upon one's health.

Psychological Effects

At this point, you realize that the mind cannot be separated from the body. Consequently, you've probably guessed that the physiological effects of meditation have psychological implications. You are right. Numerous studies have found evidence that the psychological health of meditators is better than that of nonmeditators.

For example, meditators have been found to be less anxious.[27] Even more significant than this, however, is the finding that anxiety can be decreased by

relaxation response
The physiological state achieved when one is relaxed; also called the trophotropic response.

trophotropic response
The physiological state achieved when one is relaxed; also called the relaxation response.

teaching people to meditate. Schoolchildren decreased their test anxiety after eighteen weeks of meditation training.[28] Several other studies have shown that people's trait and state anxiety levels decreased after they practiced meditation for varying periods of time.[29,30]

In addition to its effect of decreasing anxiety, researchers have found that meditation is related to an internal locus of control, greater self-actualization, more positive feelings after encountering a stressor, improvement in sleep behavior, decreased cigarette smoking, headache relief, and a general state of positive mental health. In a comprehensive review of psychological effects of meditation, Shapiro and Giber cited studies that found meditation decreased drug abuse, reduced fears and phobias, showed potential for stress management, and was associated with positive subjective experiences.[31] Even eating disorders have been found positively affected by meditation. In a study of eighteen obese women taught meditation, binge eating decreased, anxiety decreased, and a sense of control increased.[32] Other researchers of eating disorders have found meditation similarly effective.[33]

I will now teach *you* how to meditate. In that way, you might be able to decrease your oxygen consumption and blood lactate level, change other physiological parameters, and be less anxious and more self-actualized. Are you ready?

How to Meditate

Meditation is best learned in a relatively quiet, comfortable environment. However, once you become experienced, you will be able to meditate almost anywhere. As I've already mentioned, I've meditated in the passenger seat of a moving automobile in Florida, on an airplane in flight to California, in my office at the University of Maryland, and under a tree on a golf course in the Bahamas. Of course, the quiet, serene setting of the golf course was the most preferred, but the others sufficed.

Once you have located a quiet place to learn meditation, find a comfortable chair. Because sleep is a different physiological state than meditation, you will not get the benefits of meditation if you fall asleep. To help prevent yourself from falling asleep, use a straight-backed chair. This type of chair encourages you to align your spine and requires only a minimum of muscular contraction to keep you erect (though not stiff). If you can find a chair that will support your upper back and head, all the better.

Be seated in this chair with your buttocks pushed against its back, feet slightly forward of your knees, and your hands resting either on the arms of the chair or in your lap.

Let your muscles relax as best you can. Don't try to relax. Trying is work, not relaxation. Just assume a passive attitude in which you focus upon your breathing. Allow whatever happens to happen. If you feel relaxed, fine; if not, accept that, too.

Next, close your eyes and repeat in your mind the word "one" every time you inhale and the word "two" every time you exhale. Do not consciously alter or control your breathing; breathe regularly. Continue to do this for twenty minutes. It is recommended that you meditate twice a day for approximately twenty minutes each time.

Although meditation was founded in Far Eastern cultures, it has significant health implications for Westerners.

Last, when you stop meditating, give your body a chance to become readjusted to normal routines. Open your eyes gradually, first focusing on one object in the room, then focusing upon several objects. Take several deep breaths. Then stretch while seated and, when you feel ready, stand and stretch. If you rush to leave the meditation session, you are apt to feel tired or to lose the sense of relaxation. Your blood pressure and heart rate are decreased while meditating, thus rising from the chair too quickly might make you dizzy and is not recommended.

Although you shouldn't experience any problems, if you feel uncomfortable or dizzy, or if you experience hallucinations or disturbing images, just open your eyes and stop meditating. These situations are rare but occasionally do occur. Here are several more recommendations:

1. Immediately upon rising and right before dinner tend to be good times to meditate. Do not meditate directly after a meal. After eating, the blood is pooled in the stomach area, participating in the digestive process. Since part of the relaxation response is an increased blood flow to the arms and legs, pooled blood in the abdomen is not conducive to relaxation. It is for this reason that you should meditate *before* breakfast and *before* dinner.

2. The object of meditation is to bring about a hypometabolic state. Because caffeine is a stimulant and is included in coffee, tea, cola, and some other soft drinks, and because you do not want to be stimulated but, rather, to relax, you should not ingest these substances before meditating. Likewise, you should avoid smoking cigarettes (which contain the stimulant nicotine) or using other stimulant drugs.

3. I'm often asked "What do I do with my head?" Well, do whatever you want to do with it. Some people prefer to keep it directly above the neck, others rest it against a high-backed chair, and still others let their chins drop onto their chests. If you choose the last position, you may experience some discomfort in your neck or shoulder muscles for several meditation sessions. This is because these muscles may not be flexible enough; for the same reason, some of you can't touch your toes without bending your knees. With stretching, these muscles will acquire greater flexibility and will not result in any discomfort when the head hangs forward.

4. Another question I'm often asked is "How do I know if twenty minutes are up?" The answer is so simple I'm usually embarrassed to give it: look at your watch. If twenty minutes are up, stop meditating; if not, continue. Although you don't want to interrupt your meditation every couple of minutes to look at your watch, once or twice when you think the time has expired will not affect your experience. An interesting observation I have noted is that, after a while, you acquire a built-in alarm and will know when twenty minutes have gone by.

5. Whatever you do, do not set an alarm clock to go off after twenty minutes. Your body will be in a hypometabolic state, and a loud sound may startle you too much. Similarly, disconnect the telephone or take the receiver off the hook so it doesn't ring. If the phone goes off, you'll go off.

6. You will not be able to focus on your breathing to the exclusion of other thoughts for very long. You will find yourself thinking of problems, anticipated experiences, and other sundry matters. This is normal. However, when you do realize you are thinking and not focusing on your breathing, gently—without feeling as though you've done something wrong—go back to repeating the word "one" on each inhalation and the word "two" on each exhalation.

7. I'm flabbergasted by people who decide to meditate for twenty minutes and then try to rush through it. They breathe quickly, fidget around a lot, and too often open their eyes to look at their watches in the hope that the twenty minutes have passed. During their meditations, they're planning their days and working out their problems. They'd be better off solving their problems

and meditating later. Once you commit yourself to time to meditate, relax and benefit from it. Twenty minutes are twenty minutes! You can't speed it up! Relax and enjoy it. Your problems will be there to greet you later. Don't worry, they're not going anywhere. You won't lose them. The only thing you'll do, perhaps, is to perceive them as less distressing after meditating than before.

Making Time for Meditation

Meditation can be quite pleasing and can help you better manage the stress in your life—but you have to *do* it. I have known men and women who have told me they see the benefits of meditating but can't get the time or the place to meditate. Either the kids are bothering them or their roommates are inconsiderate. They say they don't have the forty minutes a day to spare. I unsympathetically tell them that, if they don't have the time, they really need to meditate, and, if they can't find a quiet place in which to spend twenty minutes, they are the ones who need to meditate the most. The time is always available, although some of us choose to use our time for activities holding a higher priority for us. If you really value your health, you'll find the time to do healthy things. The place is available, too. As I've already said, I have left my wife, two children, and parents in my parents' apartment and sat in my car in the indoor parking garage, meditating. My health and well-being were that important to me. How important are your health and well-being to you?

If you want a more structured approach to meditation to help you get started, read *Insight Meditation*[34] by Sharon Salzberg and Joseph Goldstein. That book outlines a several-week program, taking the reader through various meditative exercises.

To assess the effects of meditation on you, complete Lab 9.1 at the end of this chapter.

Getting Involved in Your Community

Describing the benefits volunteers received from helping homeless people at the Lighthouse shelter, Walt Harrington wrote:

"I have decided this: . . . that people who volunteer at the Lighthouse are not better than people who don't. . . . No, the volunteers I met at the Lighthouse feel better about themselves not because they are better than anyone else, but because they are better than the people they used to be. They are more reflective and less self-obsessed. They are better in the way that a mother or father is better after having rocked a crying child to sleep in the middle of the night. The act may *feel* good to the mother or father, but it also is *good*—a beautifully pure moment when selfish and selfless are indistinguishable."[a]

Won't you experience this feeling? Teach a group of people in your community how to meditate so as to feel less "stressed out." Perhaps your student colleagues would like to learn this skill so they can use it before examinations. Perhaps patients of dentists in the community would like to learn how to relax by meditating prior to dental procedures. With some thought, you can identify people's lives that you can impact by teaching them how to meditate. If you choose to, you really can improve the health of your community.

[a]Walt W. Harrington; "Seeing the Light," *Washington Post Magazine,* 13 December 1993, 10–15, 22–25.

summary

- Meditation is a simple mental exercise designed to gain control over your attention so you can choose what to focus upon.

- Meditation involves focusing upon either something repetitive (such as a word repeated in your mind) or something unchanging (such as a spot on the wall).

- There are different types of meditation. Some types use external objects to focus upon, others employ a geometric figure called a mandala, and others use silently repeated words or sounds.

- Meditation has been used in the treatment of muscle tension, anxiety, drug abuse, and hypertension. It lowers blood pressure, heart and respiratory rates, and the skin's electrical conductance, and it increases the blood flow to the arms and legs.

- Meditation has been found to have several beneficial psychological effects. It can help alleviate anxiety and is related to an internal locus of control, greater self-actualization, improvement in sleep, decreased cigarette smoking, headache relief, and a general state of positive mental health.

- To learn to meditate, you need a quiet place. Sit in a straight-backed chair and in your mind repeat the word "one" when you inhale and the word "two" when you exhale with your eyes closed. These words should be repeated each time you breathe, and this should continue for twenty minutes.

- For meditation to be effective, you need to practice it regularly. It is recommended that you avoid consciously altering your breathing, forcing yourself to relax, or coming out of a meditative state too abruptly. Since digestion inhibits peripheral blood flow, it is best to meditate before eating in the morning and evening.

- Meditation's effectiveness is hindered by the administration of stimulants. Stimulants such as nicotine in cigarettes and caffeine in coffee, tea, and some soft drinks will interfere with the trophotropic (relaxation) response.

notes

1. Rolf Gates and Katrina Kenison, *Meditations from the Mat: Daily Reflections on the Path of Yoga* (Peterborough, Canada: Anchor Books, 2002).

2. N. Fink. "Jewish Meditation: An Emerging Spiritual Practice." *Tikkun* 13(1998): 60–61.

3. Steven E. Locke and Douglas Colligan, "Tapping Your Inner Resources: A New Science Links Your Mind to Your Health," *Shape* (May 1988): 112–14.

4. Therese Brosse, "A Psychophysiological Study of Yoga," *Main Currents in Modern Thought* 4(1946): 77–84.

5. B. K. Bagchi and M. A. Wengor, "Electrophysiological Correlates of Some Yogi Exercises," in *Electroencephalography, Clinical Neurophysiology and Epilepsy*, vol. 3 of the First International Congress of Neurological Sciences, ed. L. van Bagaert and J. Radermecker (London: Pergamon, 1959).

6. B. K. Anand, G. S. Chhina, and B. Singh, "Some Aspects of Electroencephalographic Studies in Yogis," *Electroencephalography and Clinical Neurophysiology* 13(1961): 452–56.

7. A. Kasamatsu and T. Hirai, "Studies of EEG's of Expert Zen Meditators," *Folia Psychiatrica Neurologica Japonica* 28(1966): 315.

8. R. P. Brown, and P. L. Gerbarg, "Sudarshan Kriya Yogic Breathing in the Treatment of Stress, Anxiety, and Depression: Part II—Clinical Applications and Guidelines," *Journal of Alternative and Complementary Medicine* 11(2005): 711–17.

9. J. Allison, "Respiratory Changes During Transcendental Meditation," *Lancet*, no. 7651(1970): 833–34.

10. W. E. Mehling, K. A. Hamel, M. Acree, N. Byl, and F. M. Hecht, "Randomized, Controlled Trial of Breath Therapy for Patients with Chronic Low-Back Pain," *Alternative Therapies in Health and Medicine* 11(2005): 44–52.

11. R. Vyas and N. Dikshit, "Effect of Meditation on Respiratory System, Cardiovascular System and Lipid Profile," *Indian Journal of Physiological Pharmacology* 46(2002): 487–91.

12. P. Arambula, E. Peper, M. Kawakami, and K. H. Gibney, "The Physiological Correlates of Kundalini Yoga Meditation: A Study of a Yoga Master," *Applied Psychophysiology and Biofeedback* 26(2001): 147–53.

13. F. M. Luskin, K. A. Newell, M. Griffith, M. Holmes, S. Telles, E. DiNucci, F. F. Marvasti, M. Hill, K. R. Pelletier, and W. L. Haskell, "A Review of Mind/Body Therapies in the Treatment of Musculoskeletal Disorders with Implications for the Elderly," *Alternative Therapies in Health and Medicine* 6(2000): 46–56.

14. N. R. Cauthen and C. A. Prymak, "Meditation Versus Relaxation: An Examination of the Physiological Effects of Relaxation Training and of Different Levels of Experience with Transcendental Meditation," *Journal of Consulting and Clinical Psychology* 45(1977): 496–97.

15. Daniel Goleman and Gary E. Schwartz, "Meditation as an Intervention in Stress Reactivity," *Journal of Consulting and Clinical Psychology* 44(1976): 456–66.

16. M. J. Ott, "Mindfulness Meditation: A Path of Transformation and Healing," *Journal of Psychosocial Nursing and Mental Health Services* 42(2004): 22–29.

17. K. Sothers and K. N. Anchor, "Prevention and Treatment of Essential Hypertension With Meditation-Relaxation Methods," *Medical Psychotherapy* 2(1989): 137–56.

18. R. Schneider, F. Staggers, C. Alexander, W. Sheppard, M. Rainforth, and C. King, "A Randomized Controlled Trial of Stress Reduction for the Treatment of Hypertension in Older African Americans," *Hypertension* 26(1995): 820–27.

19. J. Carrington, The *Book of Meditation* (Boston: Element, 1998).

20. C. MacLean et al., "Altered Responses of Cortisol, GH, TSH and Testosterone to Acute Stress After Four Months' Practice of Transcendental Meditation," *Annals of the New York Academy of Science* 746(1994): 381–84.

21. E. Taub, S. Steiner, E. Weingarten, and K. Walton, "Effectiveness of Broad Spectrum Approaches to Relapse Prevention in Severe Alcoholism: A Long-Term, Randomized, Controlled Trial of Transcendental Meditation, EMG, Biofeedback and Electronic Neurotherapy," *Alcohol Treatment Quarterly* 11(1994): 187–220.

22. R. E. Herron, S. L. Hillis, J. V. Mandarino, D. W. Orme-Johnson, and K. G. Walton, "The Impact of the Transcendental Meditation Program on Government Payments to Physicians in Quebec," *American Journal of Health Promotion* 10(1996): 208–16.

23. D. W. Orme-Johnson, "Medical Care Utilization and the Transcendental Meditation Program," *Psychosomatic Medicine* 49(1987): 493–507.

24. C. Alexander, G. Swanson, M. Rainforth, T. Carlisle, C. Todd, and R. Oates, "Effects of the Transcendental Meditation Program on Stress Reduction, Health, and Employee Development: A Prospective Study in Two Occupational Settings," *Anxiety, Stress, Coping* 6(1993): 245–62.

25. Robert Keith Wallace, "Physiological Effects of Transcendental Meditation," *Science* 167(1970): 1751–54.

26. Robert Keith Wallace and Herbert Benson, "The Physiology of Meditation," *Scientific American* 226(1972): 84–90.

27. Jon Kabat-Zinn et al., "Effectiveness of Meditation-Based Stress Reduction Program in the Treatment of Anxiety Disorders," *American Journal of Psychiatry* 149(1992): 936–43.

28. W. Linden, "Practicing of Meditation by School Children and Their Levels of Field Independence-Dependence, Test Anxiety, and Reading Achievement," *Journal of Consulting and Clinical Psychology* 41(1973): 139–43.

29. J. J. Miller, K. Fletcher, and J. Kabat-Zinn, "Three-Year Follow-Up and Clinical Implications of a Mindfulness Meditation-Based Stress Reduction Intervention in the Treatment of Anxiety Disorders," *General Hospital Psychiatry* 17(1995): 192–200.

30. J. B. Rubin, *Psychotherapy and Buddhism: Toward an Integration* (New York: Plenum Press, 1996).

31. D. H. Shapiro and D. Giber, "Meditation and Psychotherapeutic Effects," *Archives of General Psychiatry* 35(1978): 294–302.

32. J. L. Kristeller and C. B. Hallett, "An Exploratory Study of a Meditation-Based Intervention for Binge Eating Disorder," *Journal of Health Psychology* 4(July 1999): 357–63.

33. M. Epstein, *Thoughts Without a Thinker* (New York: HarperCollins, 1995).

34. Sharon Salzberg and Joseph Goldstein, *Insight Meditation: A Step-by-Step Course on How to Meditate* (Gilroy, CA: Sounds True, 2002).

internet resources

World Wide Online Meditation Center
www.meditationcenter.com/
Provides straightforward meditation instruction, including a variety of techniques, and includes sections on links and resources.

Holistic Online
http://1stholistic.com/Meditations/hol_meditation.htm
Discussions of how meditation works, the health-related benefits, and techniques.

Coping in Today's World

Recent evidence supports the view that meditation has profound effects on the brain and, consequently, awareness. Studying Buddhist monks who were long-term meditators, researchers found "electroencephalographic, high-amplitude gamma-based oscillations and phase synchrony during meditation."[a] The meaning of these changes in brain activation indicate that the brain can be trained with practice to be more coordinated, similar to training the body by physical activity. This is a change in understanding of the brain. Previously it was thought that connections in the brain were determined early in life and could not be altered. Now, brain researchers speak of *neuroplasticity*, the brain's ability to grow and develop and create new connections throughout one's life. And, mental training through meditation appears to be one way to develop this capacity.

[a]Lutz, A., Greischar, L.L., Rawlings, N.B., Ricard, M., and Davidson, R.J. "Long-Term Meditators Self-Induce High-Amplitude Gamma Synchrony During Mental Practice." *Proceedings of the National Academy of Sciences* 101 (2004): 16369–16373.

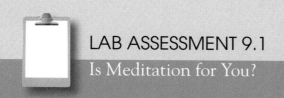

LAB ASSESSMENT 9.1

Is Meditation for You?

Directions: Practice meditation as suggested and regularly. After at least a one-week trial period, rate each statement, using the following scale.

1 = very true

2 = somewhat true

3 = not sure

4 = somewhat untrue

5 = very untrue

_____ 1. It felt good.

_____ 2. It was easy to fit into my schedule.

_____ 3. It made me feel relaxed.

_____ 4. I handled my daily chores better than I usually do.

_____ 5. It was an easy technique to learn.

_____ 6. I was able to close out my surroundings while practicing this technique.

_____ 7. I did not feel tired after practicing this relaxation technique.

_____ 8. My fingers and toes felt warmer directly after trying this relaxation technique.

_____ 9. Any stress symptoms I had (headache, tense muscles, anxiety) before doing this relaxation technique disappeared by the time I was done.

_____ 10. Each time I concluded this technique, my pulse rate was much lower than when I began.

Now sum up the values you responded with for a total score. Save this score and compare it with scores for other relaxation techniques you try. The lower the score is, the more appropriate a particular relaxation skill is for you.

You're at a magic show and, before you realize what you've done, you've volunteered to be hypnotized on stage. The hypnotist asks you to follow the pendulumlike movement of her chained watch as she slowly and softly mutters, "You're getting tired. Your eyelids are becoming heavy and are difficult to keep open. Your body feels weighted down—very full and heavy. You are relaxed, totally relaxed. You will now listen to my voice and obey its instructions." After several more sentences, you are willing to crow like a rooster, look at your watch on cue, or even stand up when a certain word is spoken. How is it that people can be made to do embarrassing things and be laughed at by other people? Whatever the reason, hypnosis can be a powerful tool if used appropriately. People who have had difficulty giving up cigarettes or other drugs, flying on airplanes, or losing weight have been helped by hypnosis.

An interesting aspect of hypnosis is that we can hypnotize ourselves. Autohypnosis is the basis of the relaxation technique to which this chapter is devoted—autogenic training.

What Is Autogenic Training?

Around 1900, Oskar Vogt (a brain physiologist) noted that some patients were able to place themselves in a hypnotic state. Vogt called this condition **autohypnosis.** These patients reported less fatigue, less tension, and fewer psychosomatic disorders (e. g., headaches) than other patients. German psychiatrist Johannes Schultz had used hypnosis with his patients. In 1932, he developed **autogenic training,** using the observations of Vogt as its basis.[1] Schultz had found that patients he hypnotized developed two physical sensations: general body warmth and heaviness in the limbs and torso. Schultz's autogenic training consisted of a series of exercises designed to bring about these two physical sensations and, thereby, an autohypnotic state. The generalized warmth was a function of the dilation of blood vessels, resulting in increased blood flow. The sensation of heaviness was caused by muscles relaxing. Because both vasodilation and muscle relaxation are components of the relaxation response, autogenic training exercises have been employed as a relaxation technique designed to help people better manage the stresses in their lives.

Schultz described autogenic training as a technique to treat neurotic patients and those with psychosomatic illness.[2] However, its use quickly expanded to healthy people who wanted to regulate their own psychological and physiological processes. Part of the reason that autogenic training became a well-known relaxation technique was its description in several sources by Schultz's student Wolfgang Luthe.[3–5] The details of how to do autogenic training as described by Schultz and Luthe appear in a later section of this chapter. For now, we will only mention the need for a passive attitude toward autogenic training exercises. Trying to relax gets in the way of relaxing. You just have to do the exercises and let what happens happen.

We should also note that, although autogenic training and meditation both lead to the relaxation response, they get there by different means. Meditation uses the mind to relax the body. Autogenic training uses the bodily sensations of heaviness and warmth to first relax the body and then expand this relaxed state to the mind by the use of imagery. This distinction will become more clear to you after the description of autogenic training exercises and your practice of them.

Those whom I have taught meditation and autogenic training report interesting and contradictory reactions. Some prefer meditation, because it requires very little learning, can be done almost anywhere, and allows the mind to be relatively

autohypnosis
Being able to place oneself in a hypnotic state.

autogenic training
A relaxation technique that involves imagining one's limbs to be heavy, warm, and tingling.

unoccupied. Meditation only requires the mind to focus upon something repetitive, such as a mantra, or something unchanging, such as a spot on the wall. Others find meditation boring and prefer autogenic training's switches of focus from one part of the body to another and its use of imagery to relax the mind. Whichever works for you is the relaxation technique you should employ. Use the rating scale in Lab 10.1 at the end of this chapter to help you evaluate the benefits you derive from your practice of autogenic training.

To summarize, autogenic training is a relaxation technique that uses exercises to bring about the sensations of body warmth and heaviness in the limbs and torso and then uses relaxing images to expand physical relaxation to the mind.

Benefits of Autogenic Training

Autogenic means "self-generating." That means you do the procedure to yourself. It also refers to the self-healing nature of autogenics. As you will now see, autogenic training has been shown to have physiological as well as psychological benefits. It is partially for this reason that autogenics is the relaxation method of choice in Europe.[6] Although there is some question as to whether any valid means are available for prescribing a particular relaxation technique for particular people, there is some indication that those who have an internal locus of control find autogenics more effective than do those with an external locus of control.[7]

Physiological Effects

The physiological effects of autogenic training are similar to those of other relaxation techniques that elicit the trophotropic response. Heart rate, respiratory rate, muscle tension, and serum-cholesterol level all decrease. Alpha brain waves and blood flow to the arms and legs increase. Autogenics has been used to improve the immune function in people with cancer[8] and to improve the quality of life of people with multiple sclerosis.[9] In addition, those suffering from headaches have experienced relief through autogenics.[10] Autogenics has also been effective in treating people of all ages who experience anxiety. These have included postwar Kosovo high school students,[11] patients undergoing coronary angioplasty,[12] and those wishing to employ self-help treatments for anxiety.[13] Autogenics has even been used to help people with drug abuse.[14]

Other studies have also documented the benefits of autogenics for a range of physiological and psychological conditions. Autogenics has been employed to help women alleviate menstrual discomfort.[15] When autogenic training was provided students with scoliosis, and their teachers were instructed in decreasing emotional distress in these students, fewer needed braces for their condition.[16] And, when researchers provided autogenic training for students experiencing dyspnea (painful breathing) they concluded that autogenics helped these students breath better.[17] The researchers conceptualized dyspnea as a symptom that provided patients with a way of expressing their reactions to perceived or anticipated stress. Thus, they suggested, stress reduction interventions (autogenic training) could prove extremely helpful in resolving this symptom.

Psychological Effects

In one dramatic demonstration of the psychological effects of autogenics, a subject was able to withstand for a minute and a half the pain of a third-degree burn brought about by a lighted cigarette placed on the back of the hand.[18] I don't suggest you attempt such a feat; still, it makes us marvel once again about the influence our minds exert over our bodies. In any case, autogenics can aid those with chronic illnesses that result in pain (e.g., arthritis) to tolerate that pain better.

In addition, autogenic training has been found to reduce anxiety and depression, decrease tiredness, and help people increase their resistance to stress.[19–21] For example, a woman who couldn't wear dentures without gagging was taught to control the gagging by learning autogenics.[22] Another woman who couldn't drive an automobile because of a previous accident and the associated anxiety was helped with autogenics.[23]

Autogenic meditation involves imagining a relaxing scene to calm the mind.

Even pregnant women were found to experience less pain and less anxiety during childbirth when employing autogenics.[24] Men having a problem with motion sickness also experienced less of a reaction after employing autogenics than did a control group of similar men.[25] And athletes have improved athletic performance by employing autogenic training to control anxiety associated with competition.[26]

How to Do Autogenic Training

Before describing autogenic training exercises, we should note that people with psychological problems who employ autogenics to alleviate these problems should do so in clinical situations with trained clinicians (e.g., a clinical psychologist or psychiatrist). When autogenics is used in this manner, it may take anywhere from two months to one year before a person becomes proficient.

Although the six initial stages of autogenic training and the second phase (autogenic meditation) are described below, the autogenic training practice that you will experience is a modified version of the standard procedures. Since the purpose of autogenics described here is relaxation rather than therapy, this modified version (easier to learn and found effective for teaching the relaxation response) will suffice.

Prerequisites

Schultz and Luthe cite several factors essential to successful autogenic training:[27]

1. High motivation and cooperation.

2. A reasonable degree of self-direction and self-control.

3. Maintenance of particular body posture conducive to success (see "Body Position," below).

4. Reduction of external stimuli to a minimum and mental focusing on the process to the exclusion of the external environment.

5. Concentrated attention on the bodily sensations.

Body Position

There are three basic positions for doing autogenics: one reclining and two seated. In the reclining position (see Figure 10.1), you lie on your back, feet slightly apart, toes pointing away from the body. Cushion any part of the body that feels uncomfortable. Use blankets or pillows for cushioning, but be careful not to misalign the body (e.g., by

Figure 10.1

The reclining position.

Figure 10.2

The first seated position.

Figure 10.3

The second seated position.

using pillows under the head that make the chin almost touch the chest). Your arms should lie alongside your body but not touch it, with a slight bend at the elbows and the palms facing upward.

The seated positions (see Figures 10.2 and 10.3) have two advantages: You can do them almost anywhere, and they are less apt to result in sleep. On the other hand, they don't allow as much total muscle relaxation as the reclining position. The best chair to use is a straight-backed one that will provide support for your head and align it with your torso. Your buttocks should be against the back of the chair, and the seat of the chair should be long enough to support your thighs. Your arms, hands, and fingers may relax on the arms of the chair or be supported in your lap.

The second seated position uses a stool or a low-backed chair, upon which you sit without support for your back. Sit at the forward part of the chair with your arms supported on your thighs, hands and fingers dangling loosely. The head hangs loosely, with the chin near the chest. Your feet should be placed at shoulder width, slightly forward of your knees.

Whichever position you choose, make sure your body is relaxed and that it is supported by as little muscular contraction as possible.

Six Initial Stages of Autogenic Training

Here are the six initial stages of autogenic training that precede the use of imagery:

1. Focus on sensations of heaviness throughout the arms and legs (beginning with the dominant arm or leg).
2. Focus on sensations of warmth throughout the arms and legs (beginning with the dominant arm or leg).
3. Focus on sensations of warmth and heaviness in the area of the heart.
4. Focus on breathing.
5. Focus on sensations of warmth in the abdomen.
6. Focus on sensations of coolness in the forehead.

These stages are sequential; you need to master the skills of each stage before practicing the next. Sample instructions for each of these stages appear below. Repeat each statement three times.

Stage 1: Heaviness
  My right arm is heavy . . .
  My left arm is heavy . . .
  Both of my arms are very heavy.
  My right leg is heavy . . .
  My left leg is heavy . . .
  Both of my legs are very heavy.
  My arms and legs are very heavy.

Stage 2: Warmth
  My right arm is warm . . .
  My left arm is warm . . .
  Both of my arms are very warm.
  My right leg is warm . . .
  My left leg is warm . . .
  Both of my legs are very warm.
  My arms and legs are very warm.

Stage 3: Heart
     My heartbeat is calm and regular. (Repeat four or five times.)

Stage 4: Respiration
     My breathing is calm and relaxed . . .
     It breathes me. (Repeat four or five times.)

Stage 5: Abdomen
     My abdomen is warm. (Repeat four or five times.)

Stage 6: Forehead
     My forehead is cool. (Repeat four or five times.)

With experience in autogenics, it should take you only a few minutes to feel heaviness and warmth in your limbs, a relaxed and calm heart and respiratory rate, warmth in your abdomen, and coolness in your forehead. Remember, though, that it usually takes several months or more of regular practice to get to that point. Regular practice means ten to forty minutes per day.[28] However, don't be too anxious to master autogenics, since trying too hard will interfere with learning the skills. Proceed at your own pace, moving to the next stage only after you have mastered the previous stage.

Imagery

Part of autogenic training employs images of relaxing scenes to translate body relaxation into mind relaxation. Some people visualize a sunny day spent on a sailboat on a quiet lake. Others find it relaxing to imagine birds flying gently through the air, the ocean surf reaching the shore, or a cozy, carpeted room warmed by a fire. You will use visualization later in this chapter as part of your practice of autogenic training. Rather than using a scene that *I* find relaxing (which may not be relaxing for you), identify an image you can use to relax yourself. The following questions will help you do that.

1. What is the temperature at the scene? _____

2. Who is there? _____

3. What colors are present in your scene? _____
   _____

4. What sounds are present in your scene? _____
   _____

5. What movement is occurring? _____
   _____

6. How are you feeling? _____
   _____

Sometimes called **autogenic meditation,** visualization of relaxing images begins by rotating your eyeballs inward and upward as if you are attempting to look at your own forehead. This procedure alone has been shown to result in increased alpha brain-wave activity.[29] The next step involves practicing visualizing one color in your whole field of vision—any color you choose. Next, visualize colors making pictures. When that is accomplished, practice visualizing one object against a dark background. This object should be seen clearly, be immobile, and be viewed for a long duration (practice sessions may run from forty to sixty minutes).

The next phase of autogenic meditation instructs you to visualize abstract ideas (such as freedom). This phase usually runs from two to six weeks. After this training period, you may then practice focusing upon feeling states while visualizing yourself in

autogenic meditation
Visualization of relaxing images used during autogenic training.

An Imagery Exercise

You are driving to the beach with your car window rolled down and no radio on in your car. The wind is blowing through your hair, and the sun is beating down on your thighs through the car window. You can see people walking with beach chairs and blankets, clad in bathing suits and carrying food in picnic baskets and coolers. You park your car, and, as you are walking to the beach, you hear the surf rolling onto the shore and can smell the salt in the air. You find a quiet spot of beach away from other people and spread your blanket out there. Being tired from the drive, you are relieved to allow your muscles to relax as you apply sunblock and lie on the blanket, with your feet extending beyond, onto the sand.

As you relax, you can taste the salt in the air. Droplets of ocean seem to fall on you as you hear the pounding of the surf and it ever-so-gently rolling back to sea. Everything seems light and yellow and tan and blue. The sun's bright yellow on the sand's relaxing tan contrasted with the ocean's vivid blue seems just the right combination of serenity. You decide to close your eyes and take in all the sensations through other senses.

The sun seems to move over your body. First your arms warm up from the intensity of the sun's rays. You can feel the heat pass through them, and the feeling is one of relaxation. Next your legs become caressed by the sun as they, too, become warm. The sun moves to warm your chest now and your whole chest area becomes heated and relaxed. But it doesn't stop there. The sun moves to your abdomen, bringing its relaxing warmth there. And, as though you've willed it, the sun next moves to your forehead, bringing warmth and relaxation there. Your whole body now feels warm and relaxed. Your muscles are relaxed, and your body feels as though it's sinking into the sand. Your body feels warm and heavy. Your body tingles from the sun's warmth.

You hear the sea gulls as you relax. They are flying over the ocean. They are free and light and peaceful. As they fly out to sea, they are carrying your problems and worries with them. You are relieved of your problems and worries and relaxed. You think of nothing but your body's heaviness and warmth and tingling sensation. You are totally relaxed.

You have relaxed all day like this, and now the sun is setting. As you feel the sun leaving, you slowly open your eyes, feeling wonderfully relaxed and content. You have no worries; you have no cares. You look at the sea gulls, which have left your problems and worries out at sea and you thank them. Feeling alert, you stand and stretch, feeling the still warm—yet cooling—sand between your toes, and you feel terrific. You feel so good that you know the car ride home will be pleasant. You welcome the time to be alone, in your car, at peace, without problems or cares. You fold your blanket and leave your piece of beach, taking with you your relaxation and contentment. You say goodbye to your beach as you walk from it, knowing you can return anytime you desire.

various situations. For example, you may focus upon your feelings as you imagine yourself floating on a cloud.

The next phase involves the visualization of other people, first neutral people (e.g., a storekeeper you know), then family or friends. It is hoped that such visualization will result in insight into relationships you have with these people. In particular, relationships with people with whom you are in conflict are thought to be improved by autogenic meditation insights.

Although you would do best to develop your own image of relaxation (different people find different things relaxing), an example of relaxing imagery appears in the "Imagery Exercise" box. In any relaxing imagery, there should be a very vivid scene. Use as many of your senses as you can to make the image as real as possible. You should smell the smells, hear the sounds, see the colors, feel the sensations, and even taste the tastes present. Images can be of clouds, valleys, a willow tree, a field of wildflowers, a cool forest, a log cabin, a clear stream, a sloping hill, or just about any other scene that would relax you. I have chosen a sunny beach as the image to use as an example. Remember, imagery has been shown to be extremely effective in eliciting either the stress or the relaxation response,[30,31] so use it to your advantage.

An Autogenic Training Experience

The six initial stages and the phases of autogenic meditation already described take a good deal of time to work through. A set of instructions follows that will take you through a modified autogenic training experience. Note that each of the six initial stages is presented at one sitting and that visualization is also a part of this exercise. For relaxation

Imagining a relaxing scene—for example, a beach, lake, or park—can be very calming on the mind, especially if the image is very vivid. What scene would relax you?

purposes, my students and others for whom I have conducted relaxation training report these instructions to be effective.

This exercise should be practiced at least once daily but preferably twice: once upon waking and once just before dinner. You can either memorize the phrases, ask someone to read them to you, or recite them into a tape recorder. In any case, these phrases should be presented calmly, softly, and with sufficient pause between them for you to be able to bring about the sensations to which each phrase refers.

Now, assuming that you are ready and haven't just eaten or ingested a stimulant, are located in a relatively quiet, comfortable environment, and have approximately thirty minutes for relaxation, position yourself in one of the three autogenic positions previously described. Repeat the following phrases:

I am calm.

It is quiet.

I am relaxed.

My right arm (if right-handed) is heavy. (Repeat four or five times.)

My right arm is warm. (Repeat four or five times.)

My right arm is tingly.

My right arm is heavy and warm.

My right arm is weighted down and feels warm.

My left arm is heavy. (Repeat four or five times.)

My left arm is warm. (Repeat four or five times.)

My left arm is tingly.

My left arm is heavy and warm.

My left arm is weighted down and warm.

Both my arms are heavy and warm. (Repeat four or five times.)

(Repeat the phrases above for the legs, beginning with the dominant leg.)

My heart is beating calmly.

I am relaxed.

My heart is calm and relaxed. (Repeat four or five times.)

My breathing is regular.

My breathing is calm.

My breathing is calm and relaxed. (Repeat four or five times.)

It breathes me. (Repeat four or five times.)

My abdomen is warm. (Repeat four or five times.)

I feel warmth throughout my abdomen. (Repeat four or five times.)

My forehead is cool. (Repeat four or five times.)

I am calm.

I am relaxed.

I am quiet.

Now think of a relaxing scene.

(Refer to the scene you identified earlier in this chapter as relaxing for you.)

Imagine yourself there.

See this scene clearly.

Experience it.

Be one with it.

Hear the sounds.

See the colors.

This scene relaxes you.

You are calm.

You are quiet.

You are at peace.

Your mind is quiet.

Your whole body is quiet, heavy, warm, and relaxed.

Your thoughts are of your quiet, heavy, warm body and of your scene.

Tell yourself you feel quiet, you feel relaxed, you feel calm.

Now prepare to leave your scene.

Count backward from five.

With each number, you will be more alert.

With each number, you will be closer to opening your eyes.

Five.

You are leaving your scene.

You wave goodbye.

Four.

You are back in this room.

You are seated (or reclined).

You know where you are.

Three.

Prepare to open your eyes.

Think of what you will see when you open your eyes.

Two.

Open your eyes.

Focus upon one object in the room.

At a conference I attended a while ago, a seventy-one-year-old woman who was a participant in the Foster Grandparent Program rose to describe her volunteer experience. She was a "cuddler" for "crack babies" at Johns Hopkins University Hospital. I will never forget the smile on her face as she described how the babies stopped crying and calmed down when she held them. The audience was moved to applause.

You, too, can have an impact on the well-being of those in your community. For example, you might offer to teach autogenic training to teenage, unmarried mothers at a local high school. These women experience a great deal of stress as a result of being a student while caring for a child. The respite that autogenics could offer them would be most welcomed. Or you might teach autogenics to a support group of working mothers, a group that also experiences a great deal of stress.

Will you give some of your time and stress-related knowledge to make the lives of your community neighbors better?

Take a deep breath.

One.

Focus on objects about the room.

Take several deep breaths.

When you feel ready, stretch your arms and legs.

Now stand and stretch.

Take several more deep breaths.

Now proceed with your regular activities, knowing that you are refreshed and revitalized.

To assess the effects of autogenics for you complete Lab 10.1.

summary

- Autogenic training is a relaxation technique that consists of a series of exercises designed to bring about body warmth and heaviness in the limbs and torso. In addition, relaxing images are employed to expand physical relaxation to the mind.

- Autogenic training results in the trophotropic (relaxation) response. *Autogenic* means "self-generating" and refers to the fact that the response is self-induced.

- Autogenics has been used in the treatment of Raynaud's disease, migraine headaches, insomnia, hypertension, bronchial asthma, constipation, writer's cramp, indigestion, ulcers, hemorrhoids, tuberculosis, diabetes, and lower back pain.

- Prerequisites for doing autogenics include high motivation, a measure of self-direction, maintenance of the recommended body position, blocking out the external environment, focusing inward, and giving up ego boundaries.

- Autogenic training can be done while you are lying down or in a seated position. Cushion parts of your body that feel uncomfortable, and let your body relax.

- The six initial stages of autogenic training involve focusing on heaviness in the limbs, warmth in the limbs, heaviness and warmth in the area of the heart, regular breathing, sensations of warmth in the abdomen, and sensations of coolness in the forehead.

- Sometimes called autogenic meditation, visualization of relaxing images begins by rotating the eyeballs inward and upward. The next step involves choosing one color to visualize and then numerous colors. Next follows visualization of abstract images and then of people.

notes

1. Daniel A. Girdano and George S. Everly, Jr., *Controlling Stress and Tension: A Holistic Approach* (Englewood Cliffs, NJ: Prentice-Hall, 1986), 175.

2. Johannes Schultz, *Das Autogene Training* (Stuttgart: Georg-Thieme Verlag, 1953).

3. Wolfgang Luthe, ed., *Autogenic Therapy*, 6 vols. (New York: Grune and Stratton, 1969).

4. Wolfgang Luthe, "Method, Research and Application of Autogenic Training," *American Journal of Clinical Hypnosis* 5(1962): 17–23.

5. Johannes Schultz and Wolfgang Luthe, *Autogenic Training: A Psychophysiologic Approach to Psychotherapy* (New York: Grune and Stratton, 1959).

6. Phillip L. Rice, *Stress and Health* (Monterey, CA: Brooks/Cole, 1999), 329.

7. P. M. Lehrer, "Varieties of Relaxation Methods and Their Unique Effects," *International Journal of Stress Management* 3(1996): 1–15.

8. M. Hidderley and M. Holt, "A Pilot Randomized Trial Assessing the Effects of Autogenic Training in Early Stage Cancer Patients in Relation to Psychological Status and Immune System Responses," *European Journal of Oncology Nursing: The Official Journal of European Oncology Nursing Society* 8(2004): 61–65.

9. G. Sutherland, M. B. Andersen, and T. Morris, "Relaxation and Health-Related Quality of Life in Multiple Sclerosis: The Example of Autogenic Training," *Journal of Behavioral Medicine* 28(2005): 249–56.

10. E. E. Labbe "Treatment of Childhood Migraine with Autogenic Training and Skin Temperature Biofeedback: A Component Analysis," *Headache* 35(1995): 10–13.

11. J. S. Gordon, J. K. Staples, A. Blyta, and M. Bytyqi, "Treatment of Posttraumatic Stress Disorder in Postwar Kosovo High School Students Using Mind-Body Skills Groups: A Pilot Study," *Journal of Traumatic Stress* 17(2004): 143–47.

12. N. Kanji, A. R. White, and E. Ernst, "Autogenic Training Reduces Anxiety After Coronary Angioplasty: A Randomized Clinical Trial," *American Heart Journal* 147(2004): E10.

13. A. F. Jorm, H. Christensen, K. M. Griffiths, R. A. Parslow, B. Rodgers, and K. A. Blewitt, "Effectiveness of Complementary and Self-Help Treatments for Anxiety Disorders," *Medical Journal of Australia* 181(2004): S29–46.

14. G. Potter, "Intensive Therapy: Utilizing Hypnosis in the Treatment of Substance Abuse Disorders," *American Journal of Clinical Hypnosis* 47(2004): 21–28.

15. E. B. Blanchard and M. Kim, "The Effect of the Definition of Menstrually-Related Headache on the Response to Biofeedback Treatment," *Applied Psychophysiology and Biofeedback* 30(2005): 53–63.

16. S. Matsunaga, K. Hayashi, T. Naruo, S. Nozoe, and S. Komiya, "Psychologic Management of Brace Therapy for Patients with Idiopathic Scoliosis," *Spine* 30(2005): 547–50.

17. R. D. Anbar, "Stressors Associated with Dyspnea in Childhood: Patients' Insights and a Case Report," *American Journal of Clinical Hypnosis* 47(2004): 93–101.

18. B. Gorton, "Autogenic Training," *American Journal of Clinical Hypnosis* 2(1959): 31–41.

19. Shoshana Shapiro and Paul M. Lehrer, "Psychophysiological Effects of Autogenic Training and Progressive Relaxation," *Biofeedback and Self-Regulation* 5(1980): 249–55.

20. Malcomb Carruthers, "Autogenic Training," *Journal of Psychosomatic Research* 23(1979): 437–40.

21. Martha Davis, Matthew McKay, and Elizabeth Robbins Eshelman, *The Relaxation and Stress Reduction Workbook* (Richmond, CA: New Harbinger Publications, 1980), 82.

22. Jack A. Gerschman et al., "Hypnosis in the Control of Gagging," *Australian Journal of Clinical and Experimental Hypnosis* 9(1981): 53–59.

23. Jon D. Boller and Raymond P. Flom, "Behavioral Treatment of Persistent Posttraumatic Startle Response," *Journal of Behavior Therapy and Experimental Psychiatry* 12(1981): 321–24.

24. Tansella Zimmerman, "Preparation Courses for Childbirth in Primipara: A Comparison," *Journal of Psychosomatic Research* 23(1979): 227–33.

25. Patricia S. Cowing, "Reducing Motion Sickness: A Comparison of Autogenic-Feedback Training and an Alternative Cognitive Task," *Aviation, Space, and Environmental Medicine* 53(1982): 449–53.

26. Eric W. Krenz and Keith P. Henschen, "The Effects of Modified Autogenic Training on Stress in Athletic Performance," in *Human Stress: Current Selected Research*, vol. 1, ed. James H. Humphrey (New York: AMS Press, 1986), 199–205.

27. Kenneth Pelletier, *Mind as Healer—Mind as Slayer: A Holistic Approach to Preventing Stress Disorders* (New York: Bantam Doubleday Dell, 1984).

28. Davis, McKay, and Eshelman, *Relaxation and Stress Reduction Workbook,* 88.

29. J. Kamiya, "Conscious Control of Brain Waves," *Psychology Today* 1(1978): 57–60.

30. T. S. Newmark and D. F. Bogacki, "The Use of Relaxation, Hypnosis, and Imagery in Sport Psychiatry," *Clinics in Sports Medicine* 24(2005): 973–77.

31. G. Elkins, M. H. Rajab, and J. Marcus, "Complementary and Alternative Medicine Use by Psychiatric Inpatients," *Psychological Reports* 96(2005): 163–66.

internet resources

Guided Imagery
www.guidedimageryinc.com
Stress and the benefits of imagery are examined. Includes information about how to
obtain guided imagery audiotapes.

Stress Management Training Program
www.stresscontrol.com/ProMaterials/ProMaterials.php
A program designed to facilitate education and training in relaxation and
stress management.

Coping in Today's World

Reporter Sally Stich[a] visited a Laughter Club in Orville, Ohio, and found the class weak from giggling. The Laughter Club is the brainchild of Dr. Stephen Wilson, a psychologist from Columbus, Ohio. With the goal of helping people improve their physical and mental health, Wilson and colleagues developed the World Laughter Tour. Having studied with Madan Kataria, the Indian physician credited with starting laughter clubs in Bombay, Wilson based his Tour on Kataria's clubs. By 2002, there were more than three hundred laughter clubs in the United States. As one advocate of laughter to relieve stress stated, "Mirthful laughter is like taking an internal jog." What he meant was that laughter uses up the stress by-products: (e.g., muscle tension and elevated blood pressure). Laughter also increases effectiveness of the immunological system and its ability to combat infection and similar threats. It has been reported that the average child laughs four hundred times per day; whereas the average adult laughs or smiles just fifteen times per day.[b] Therefore, the laughter clubs. They are devoted to helping adults laugh more often and, thereby, acquire laughter's stress relieving effects. So, learn a new joke today and share it with others.

Source: [a] Stich, S. "Together, They Laugh Stress Away." *Parade Magazine,* April 21, 2002, 22.
[b] Ibid.

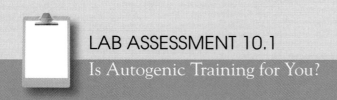

LAB ASSESSMENT 10.1

Is Autogenic Training for You?

Directions: Practice autogenic training as suggested and regularly. After at least a one-week trial period, rate each statement, using the following scale.

1 = very true

2 = somewhat true

3 = not sure

4 = somewhat untrue

5 = very untrue

_____ 1. It felt good.

_____ 2. It was easy to fit into my schedule.

_____ 3. It made me feel relaxed.

_____ 4. I handled my daily chores better than I usually do.

_____ 5. It was an easy technique to learn.

_____ 6. I was able to close out my surroundings while practicing this technique.

_____ 7. I did not feel tired after practicing this relaxation technique.

_____ 8. My fingers and toes felt warmer directly after trying this relaxation technique.

_____ 9. Any stress symptoms I had (headache, tense muscles, anxiety) before doing this relaxation technique disappeared by the time I was done.

_____ 10. Each time I concluded this technique, my pulse rate was much lower than when I began.

Now sum up the values you responded with for a total score. Save this score and compare it with scores for other relaxation techniques you try. The lower the score is, the more appropriate a particular relaxation skill is for you.

I'll never forget my first lesson in downhill skiing. Having been selected the most valuable player on my college basketball team and having found success at some local tennis tournaments, I considered myself an accomplished athlete. An accomplished skier I was not and never became, and, as I prepare to relate the story of my skiing lesson, I'm reminded of the poem by A. E. Housman, from the collection entitled *A Shropshire Lad,* in which he talks "To an Athlete Dying Young":

> Runners whom renown outran
> And the name died before the man.

The area where I learned to ski (rather, attempted to learn to ski) had three slopes: beginner, intermediate, and advanced. My first lesson, this first day ever on a pair of skis, consisted of one hour of falling, learning how to rise (no easy task in snow with long, thin objects protruding fore and aft from my feet), and snowplowing. Believing my entry on the Olympic team as a downhill slalom racer assured after this lesson, I immediately attacked the intermediate course. With ineffective snowplowing to avoid some skiers and a loud "Watch out!" that worked even better to avoid a crash with most of the others, I managed to get to the bottom of the slope without even getting snow on my ski outfit (consisting of my Army long johns, tennis socks, jeans, and an old sweatshirt). As I waited for the lift to return me to the top so I could break the downhill speed record, I was awed by the grace and ease with which the more accomplished skiers appeared to be floating downhill. Effortlessly, it seemed, they moved left, then right, then tucked, then stopped smoothly at the bottom.

I never learned to ski well. In fact, the very next (and last) time I was silly enough to find myself at the top of a series of ski slopes and recklessly let my fragile body begin sliding downward, I found that my snowplowing was good enough to get me about one-third down a zigzagging slope, though I wound up a little farther and farther behind each successive curve. The one-third point was where I attempted to save my body from the oncoming woods by turning to the left, only to learn that it was too late and my skills were too few. Using my brains as the only way out, I sat down and skidded just short of a threatening blue spruce. Recalling something about wisdom being the better part of valor, I removed my skis, smacked the snow off my derrière, and marched downhill to spend the rest of the day in what was for me a more natural habitat—the fireplace-warmed lodge.

Bracing

I relate this embarrassing story because what I really want to discuss is the grace and effortlessness I observed in the good skiers. The reason they appeared this way is that they were using proper *form.* Some of you have probably had lessons in tennis, golf, or another sport, during which you were taught the proper form. Proper form means moving the body to accomplish the task most effectively—with the least amount of energy. Proper form allows you to be effective and efficient. What has always been interesting to me is that too much muscular contraction can often interfere with using proper form. The approach of Tim Gallwey in teaching tennis is to prevent the mind from scaring the body into tensing so much that proper form is impossible.[1] For example, Gallwey instructs players to try to read the writing on the ball as it comes toward them rather than worry about having to hit a backhand return.

Doing things effectively and efficiently is important for our daily routines as well. Too often, we use too much muscular contraction, with the consequences being backache, headache, pains in the neck or shoulders, and other illnesses. Unnecessary

Progressive relaxation involves tensing and relaxing muscle throughout the body and paying attention to the sensations of muscle tension and muscle relaxation.

muscular contraction occurs when your shoulders are raised, your hands are holding something too tightly, your forearm muscles are tensed, or your abdominal muscles are sort of squeezing you in. These are all signs of bracing: the muscles contracted, the body ready for some action it seldom takes. As McGuigan states, "The person who falls victim to stressors reflexively reacts to them, often emotionally. If such muscular reactions are prolonged, as they often are, they can eventually lead to the malfunction of some system of the body. Such chronic overtension may lead to a variety of psychosomatic (somatoform) and psychiatric disorders."[2]

The next time you drive an automobile, notice how tightly you grasp the steering wheel. With the power steering of most modern cars, the steering wheel need only be held gently. To do otherwise is to brace.

The next time you take notes during a lecture, notice how tightly you hold the pen or pencil. If you hold too tightly or press down too hard, you are bracing.

The next time you visit a dentist, notice how you cling to the arms of the chair. The chair will probably not move, so your grip on it is unnecessary. You are bracing.

On numerous occasions, we use muscular contraction inefficiently, and the result is poor health. However, we can learn to use our muscles in a more healthy manner through a relaxation technique called progressive relaxation.

What Is Progressive Relaxation?

Progressive relaxation is a technique used to induce nerve-muscle relaxation. Developed by Edmund Jacobson and described in his book *Progressive Relaxation*, this technique was originally designed for hospital patients who appeared tense.[3] Jacobson, a physician, observed that tense patients, as evidenced by such small muscle movement as frowning or wrinkling the forehead, did not recuperate quickly or well. Seeking to intervene in this residual muscle tension syndrome, Jacobson taught his patients a series of exercises that first required them to contract a muscle group, then relax it, moving (or progressing) from one muscle group to another. The purpose of first contracting the muscle is to teach people to recognize more readily what muscle tension feels like.[4] At first glance this appears unnecessary, but remember our discussion of bracing. The purpose of the relaxation phase is to become familiar enough with this sensation so that it can be voluntarily induced. The idea, then, is to sense more readily when we are muscularly tense and, on those occasions, to be able to relax those muscles. "One who has acquired the ability to momentarily relax in the face of a stressor creates the opportunity to rationally select the most appropriate mode of responding. That is, rather than reflexively reacting, one can pause and consider the nature of the threat, weigh the consequences of various possible reactions, and then engage in the most effective one."[5]

Sometimes termed **neuromuscular relaxation** (because the nerves control muscular contraction) or **Jacobsonian relaxation** (named after its developer), progressive relaxation starts with one muscle group, adds another when the first is relaxed, and progresses through the body until total body relaxation occurs. It starts with the distal muscle groups (the feet and legs) and moves to the proximal muscle groups (the head and trunk) afterward.[6] Like autogenic training, progressive relaxation relaxes the mind by first relaxing the body. However, unlike autogenic training and meditation, progressive relaxation does not produce a hypnotic state.[7] Like the other relaxation techniques presented in this book, progressive relaxation should be practiced regularly, and you should expect to become more proficient as you gain experience with the technique.

Benefits of Progressive Relaxation

This relaxation technique has proven effective in helping people relax and does not require any special equipment. Although it takes several years of practice as originally described by Jacobson, benefits can result in several weeks of three daily practice sessions of just five minutes each.[8] Some researchers caution that other relaxation techniques, such as meditation and autogenics, will produce more immediate effects.[9] Nevertheless, progressive relaxation has been shown to have both physiological and psychological benefits.

Physiological Effects

In describing Jacobson's research on the effects of progressive relaxation, Brown states that learned relaxation of skeletal muscles can be generalized to smooth muscles, causing relaxation of the gastrointestinal and cardiovascular systems.[10] Other researchers have found progressive relaxation effective in treating headaches,[11] backaches,[12] side effects of cancer,[13] insomnia,[14] pain,[15] and high blood pressure (although meditation is even more effective).[16] It appears that conditions resulting from bracing or ineffective muscular tension can be alleviated,[17] or at least their symptoms diminished, with regular practice of progressive relaxation—even writer's cramp.[18]

Psychological Effects

Progressive relaxation has been demonstrated to have wide-ranging effects upon psychological well-being, as well as upon behavioral change. For example, college students with poor self-concepts improved their perceptions of themselves through training in progressive relaxation.[19] Further, both depression[20] and anxiety[21,22] were lessened in people trained in progressive relaxation. Even insomniacs were helped to sleep by using this relaxation technique.[23] Alcoholism,[24] drug abuse,[25] and even batting slumps[26] were aided by regular practice of progressive relaxation. When baseball players were taught progressive relaxation, they were better able to perform (bat) under stress than their teammates who did not practice relaxation techniques. They had higher batting averages. This should not be surprising, since we know that stress (up at the plate or before an audience) can interfere with performance. In the stress management classes I teach, several students have been performers (a singer and a violinist come to mind) who reported performing better when using stress management techniques.

It should be noted that virtually every form of relaxation has the potential of eliciting anxiety; when the mind relaxes, anxious thoughts may creep in or rise to the surface.[27] However, progressive relaxation, though no exception to this rule, is less likely than other relaxation techniques to generate anxiety.[28] It is, therefore, recommended when anxiety is of particular concern to the person seeking relaxation.

How to Do Progressive Relaxation

As with the other relaxation techniques, learning progressive relaxation necessitates several prerequisites, as well as learning the appropriate body position for performing the exercises.

Cues Identifying Tension

First of all, it is helpful to recognize that you are tense. You may have aches in your shoulders, back, neck, or head. Your body may feel stiff. You may sense that you are generally holding yourself too tightly or rigidly. You may have difficulty sitting comfortably, or your hands may tremble.

As you become more experienced with regular practice of progressive relaxation, you will more readily recognize these signs of tension and be better prepared to relax

Muscle tension can often be easily seen. Obviously, this drill instructor is not having a calm discussion with this sailor. His muscle tension is visible in his facial expression and body language.

them away. In addition, regular practice will help prevent these signs of tension from occurring in the first place.

Look for these signs of tension and use them as cues to doing progressive relaxation. A good idea is to check for these cues just prior to meals so you can relax them away before eating. As we've discussed earlier, food in your stomach results in the blood flow increasing to that area of your body. This makes it more difficult to bring about relaxation, since the relaxation response includes increasing the blood flow to the arms and legs.

Prerequisites

When learning progressive relaxation, seek a relatively quiet, distraction-free environment. That means any telephones must be removed from the room or the receiver removed from the cradle and muffled with a towel. The lights should be dimmed and the threat of cats, dogs, kids, or roommates disturbing you eliminated. If, after making adjustments in your environment, the noise is still impeding your learning, you might try headphones or cotton in your ears to block out the noise. Make sure you remove or loosen any tight clothing or jewelry and that the room is warm. It is difficult to relax in a cold environment, because the blood doesn't readily travel to cold extremities. Removing your shoes is also advisable.

Last, approach the exercises knowing that any discomfort can quickly be eliminated by just stopping the exercise. Learning is designed to proceed slowly, so don't expect to be proficient at progressive relaxation after only a few sessions. Don't contract a muscle that is strained, pained, or cramped. There's always another day. There have actually been reports of musculoskeletal injuries when subjects tensed their muscles too much during progressive relaxation.[29] Lastly, if you have high blood pressure, try a different relaxation technique since contractions can raise systolic blood pressure.

Body Position

To do progressive relaxation, stretch out on the floor (see Figure 11.1). The idea is to have your body supported by the floor rather than by your muscles. Lying on your back, let your arms and legs go. You can rest your hands on your abdomen or at your sides, and your legs and feet will most likely rotate outward. Just relax. You can support your neck with a pillow (small enough to fit behind your neck between your shoulders and where your head is resting on the floor); you may also find that a pillow placed under your knees feels comfortable. If not, rearrange your body so that you are comfortable. After you have more experience with progressive relaxation, you will be able to relax particular muscle groups when seated or even when standing in line (for example, those muscles in the neck). However, it is best to learn these exercises while reclined.

Figure 11.1

Reclining position for progressive relaxation exercise.

After you become proficient, you can eliminate the contraction phase and focus totally on relaxation. It may take several weeks or months of regular practice, though, to develop the "muscle sense" that the contraction phase teaches. Because this phase teaches you to recognize muscle tension, it is important not to rush to eliminate it. But, as you will soon find out, it is the relaxation phase that is most pleasant and has the most health-related benefits. If you are having difficulty with progressive relaxation, you can even work with a partner.[30]

Exercises

Stress management experts have developed several variations of muscle relaxation exercises. For example, Forman and Myers suggest contracting a muscle group by pushing against an immovable object.[31] They recommend pushing down with the fingertips on a desktop, for instance. Their reasoning is that this resistance technique requires more muscular contractions, which, in turn, increases the ability to recognize the difference between the contracted and relaxed states. Smith, in contrast, recommends eleven isometric squeeze exercises: hand squeeze, arm squeeze, arm and side squeeze, back squeeze, shoulder squeeze, back and neck squeeze, face squeeze, front of neck squeeze, stomach and chest squeeze, leg squeeze, and foot squeeze.[32] (After all those squeezes, you're probably entitled to squeeze someone you love.) Smith argues that, too often, students of progressive relaxation are taught to stretch the muscles too quickly during the contraction phase. He believes isometric contractions will be experienced as more pleasurable, thereby being more effective in teaching relaxation.

The exercises that follow are simple enough to learn yet powerful enough to be used for the control of stress and tension. Try them several times a day for at least a week. Then complete the rating scale in Lab 11.1 to evaluate progressive relaxation's benefits to you, compared with the other relaxation techniques you have tried.

The following instructions, which were developed by Jenny Steinmetz, can be read to you, memorized, or recited into a tape recorder. Follow each instruction carefully and completely. Don't skip any part of the body (unless injured) and don't skip any exercises. Also, make sure that you spend twice as much time relaxing a muscle as you do tensing that muscle. We begin with the hips, thighs, and calves.

Relaxation of the hips, thighs, and calves (four or five minutes)

Let go of all tensions and relax.

Now flex your buttocks and thighs.

Flex your thighs by pressing down your heels as hard as you can.

Relax and notice the difference.

Straighten your knees and flex your thigh muscles again.

Hold the tension.

Relax your hips and thighs . . .

Allow the relaxation to proceed on its own.

Press your feet and toes downward, away from your face, so that your calf muscles become tense.

Study that tension.

Relax your feet and calves.

This time, bend your feet toward your face so that you feel tension along your shins.

Bring your toes right up.

Relax again . . . keep relaxing for awhile . . .

Now let yourself relax further all over . . .

Relax your feet, ankles, calves and shins, knees, thighs, buttocks, and hips . . .

Feel the heaviness of your lower body as you relax still further.

Now spread the relaxation to your stomach, waist, and lower back.

Let go more and more deeply . . .

Make sure no tension has crept into your throat.

Relax your neck and your jaws and all your facial muscles.

Keep relaxing your whole body like that for a while . . .

Let yourself relax.

Now you can become twice as relaxed as you are merely by taking in a really deep breath and slowly exhaling, with your eyes closed, so that you become less aware of objects and movements around you, and thus prevent any surface tensions from developing.

Breathe in deeply and feel yourself becoming heavier.

Take in a long, deep breath and exhale very slowly . . .

Feel how heavy and relaxed you have become.

In a state of perfect relaxation, you should feel unwilling to move a single muscle in your body.

Think about the effort that would be required to raise your right arm.

As you think about that, see if you can notice any tensions that might have crept into your shoulders and arm.

Now you decide not to lift the arm, but to continue relaxing . . .

Observe the relief and the disappearance of the tension.

Just carry on, relaxing like that . . . continue relaxing . . .

When you wish to get up, count backwards from four to one.

You should now feel fine and refreshed, wide-awake and calm.

Relaxation of the chest, stomach, and lower back (four or five minutes)

Relax your entire body to the best of your ability.

Feel that comfortable heaviness that accompanies relaxation.

Breathe easily and freely in and out . . .

Notice how the relaxation increases as you exhale . . .

As you breathe out, just feel that relaxation.

Now breathe right in and fill your lungs.

Inhale deeply and hold your breath.

Study the tension.

Now exhale, let the walls of your chest grow loose, and push the air out automatically.

Continue relaxing, and breathe freely and gently . . .

Feel the relaxation, and enjoy it.

With the rest of your body as relaxed as possible, fill your lungs again.

Breathe in deeply, and hold it again.

Now breathe out, and appreciate the relief, just breathe normally . . .

Continue relaxing your chest, and let the relaxation spread to your back, shoulders, neck, and arms . . .

Merely let go, and enjoy the relaxation.

Now let's pay attention to your abdominal muscles, your stomach area.

Tighten your stomach muscles; make your abdomen hard.

Notice the tension.

And relax, let the muscles loosen, and notice the contrast.

Once more, press and tighten your stomach muscles.

Hold the tension and study it.

And relax; notice the general well-being that comes with relaxing your stomach.

Now draw your stomach in.

Pull the muscles right in and feel the tension this way.

Now relax again . . . let your stomach out . . .

Continue breathing normally and easily, and feel the gentle massaging action all over your chest and stomach.

Now pull your stomach in again, and hold the tension.

Once more pull in, and feel the tension.

Now relax your stomach fully . . .

Let the tension dissolve as the relaxation grows deeper.

Each time you breathe out, notice the rhythmic relaxation both in your lungs and in your stomach . . .

Notice how your chest and your stomach relax more and more . . .

Let go of all contractions anywhere in your body.

Now direct your attention to your lower back.

Arch up your back, make your lower back quite hollow, and feel the tension along your spine.

Now settle down comfortably again, relaxing the lower back.

Just arch your back up, and feel the tension as you do so.

Keep the rest of your body as relaxed as possible.

Localize the tension throughout your lower back area.

Relax once more, relaxing further and further . . .

Relax your lower back, relax your upper back, spread the relaxation to your stomach, chest, shoulders, arms, and facial area . . .

These parts relax further and further and further and even deeper.

Relaxation of the face, neck, shoulders, and upper back (four or five minutes)

Let all your muscles go loose and heavy.

Just settle back quietly and comfortably.

Wrinkle up your forehead now, wrinkle it tighter.

And now stop wrinkling up your forehead.

Relax and smooth it out . . .

Picture the entire forehead and scalp becoming smoother, as the relaxation increases.

Now frown and crease your brows, and study the tension.

Let go of the tension again . . .

Smooth out the forehead once more.

Now close your eyes.

Keep your eyes closed, gently, comfortably, and notice the relaxation.

Now clench your jaws, push your teeth together.

Study the tension throughout the jaws.

Relax your jaws now . . .

Let your lips part slightly . . .

Appreciate the relaxation.

Now press your tongue hard against the roof of your mouth.

Look for the tension.

All right, let your tongue return to a comfortable and relaxed position.

Now purse your lips; press your lips together tighter and tighter.

Relax the lips . . .

Notice the contrast between tension and relaxation . . .

Feel the relaxation all over your face, all over your forehead, and scalp, eyes, jaws, lips, tongue, and throat . . .

The relaxation progresses further and further.

Now attend to your neck muscles.

Press your head back as far as it can go, and feel the tension in the neck.

Roll it to the right, and feel the tension shift . . .

Now roll it to the left.

Straighten your head, and bring it forward.

Press your chin against your chest.

Let your head return to a comfortable position, and study the relaxation . . .

Let the relaxation develop.

Shrug your shoulders right up.

Hold the tension.

Drop your shoulders and feel the relaxation . . .

Neck and shoulders relaxed.

Shrug your shoulders again, and move them around.

Bring your shoulders up and forward and back.

Feel the tension in your shoulders and in your upper back.

Drop your shoulders once more and relax . . .

Let the relaxation spread deep into the shoulders right into your back muscles.

Relax your neck and throat, and your jaws and other facial areas, as the pure relaxation takes over and grows deeper . . . deeper . . . even deeper.

Relaxation of the arms (four or five minutes)

Settle back as comfortably as you can and let yourself relax to the best of your ability.

Now, as you relax, clench your right fist.

Clench it tighter and tighter, and study the tension as you do so.

Keep it clenched, and feel the tension in your right fist, hand, and forearm.

Now relax . . .

Let the fingers of your right hand become loose . . .

Observe the contrast in your feelings.

Now, let yourself go and allow yourself to become more relaxed all over.

Once more, clench your right fist really tight.

Hold it, and notice the tension again.

Now, let go, relax, let your fingers straighten out . . .

Notice the difference once more.

Now repeat that with your left fist.

Clench your left fist while the rest of your body relaxes.

Clench that fist tighter, and feel the tension.

And now relax . . . again, enjoy the contrast.

Repeat that once more, clench the left fist, tight and tense.

Now do the opposite of tension—relax and feel the difference . . .

Continue relaxing like that for awhile.

Clench both fists tighter and tighter, both fists tense, forearms tense.

Study the sensations . . . and relax . . .

Straighten out your fingers and feel that relaxation . . .

Continue relaxing your hands and forearms more and more.

Now bend your elbows, and tense your biceps.

Tense them harder, and study the tension feeling.

All right, straighten out your arms . . .

Let them relax, and feel the difference again . . .

Let the relaxation develop.

Once more, tense your biceps.

Hold the tension, and observe it carefully.

Straighten the arms, and relax . . .

Relax to the best of your ability . . .

Each time pay close attention to your feelings when you tense up and when you relax.

Now straighten your arms; straighten them so that you feel the most tension in the triceps muscles along the back of your arms.

Stretch your arms, and feel the tension.

And now relax . . .

Get your arms back into a comfortable position . . .

Let the relaxation proceed on its own . . .

The arms should feel comfortably heavy as you allow them to relax.

Straighten the arms once more so that you feel the tension in the triceps muscles.

Feel that tension . . . and relax.

Now let's concentrate on pure relaxation in the arms without any tension . . .

Get your arms comfortable and let them relax further and further . . .

Continue relaxing your arms even further . . .

Even when your arms seem fully relaxed, allow yourself to go that extra bit further . . .

Allow yourself to achieve deeper and deeper levels of relaxation.*

*Source: Jenny Steinmetz, *Managing Stress Before It Manages You* (Palo Alto, CA: Bull Publishing Co. 1980), 20–27.

Other Short Exercises

There may be occasions when you choose not to devote as much time to relaxation as the exercises just presented require. In those instances, you can still practice a modified, simplified, and quick version of progressive relaxation. For example, you may be working at your desk and notice that your shoulder muscles are tense. To relax them, you can tense them further—raising your shoulders as high as you can get them—and then let them relax. Focus on the sensations of your relaxed shoulder muscles, paying particular attention to any warm and tingly sensations.

Another quick exercise you can do involves your abdominal muscles. Make these muscles tense by keeping your abdominal area flat but tight. Notice how you breathe

with these muscles tensed—with the expansion of your chest muscles alone. Be aware of the sensations of breathing this way. Now relax your abdominal muscles and let your abdominal area stick out. Breathe by the expansion and contraction of your abdominal area rather than your chest. To help breathe this way, place the palm of your hand on your abdomen. Let your hand rise and fall as your abdomen rises when you inhale and falls when you exhale. Notice how relaxed you feel breathing in this manner.

You can improvise your own quick, modified version of progressive relaxation by identifying any particular muscle group that feels tense and then tensing it further. Next, relax that muscle group and focus upon the feelings of relaxation. After approximately five minutes of such an exercise, you can begin to feel less tense and more relaxed—and better able to proceed with the rest of your day. You might even do such exercises on schedule each day, considering that five minutes as a "vacation period" in which you leave your daily cares to travel to a more relaxed state.

To assess the effects of progressive relaxation on you, complete Lab 11.1.

summary

- People often use more muscular contraction than necessary. This can lead to backache, headache, and pains in the shoulders and neck.

- Muscular tension that prepares the body for action that is never taken is termed bracing. Raising your shoulders throughout the day is an example of bracing.

- Progressive relaxation is a technique used to induce nerve-muscle relaxation. It involves contraction of a muscle group and then relaxation of it, progressing from one muscle group to another throughout the body.

- The contraction phase of progressive relaxation is designed to help people better recognize when they are bracing. The relaxation phase is designed to help people recognize and bring on a relaxed state when they choose.

- Progressive relaxation has been used to treat tension headaches, migraine headaches, backaches, and other conditions. It has also been used to treat psychological conditions, such as poor self-concept, depression, anxiety, and insomnia.

- When learning progressive relaxation, seek a distraction-free environment and lie on your back. Proceed slowly and carefully, stopping if you experience muscle cramping or pain.

- It may take several weeks or months of regular practice of progressive relaxation before you develop the "muscle sense" that the contracting phase teaches, but the relaxation will benefit you much sooner.

notes

1. W. Timothy Gallwey, *The Inner Game of Tennis* (New York: Random House, 1997).

2. F. J. McGuigan, "Stress Management Through Progressive Relaxation," *International Journal of Stress Management* 1(1994): 205–14.

3. Edmund Jacobson, *Progressive Relaxation* (Chicago: University of Chicago Press, 1938).

4. James H. Humphrey, *Childhood Stress in Contemporary Society* (New York: The Haworth Press, 2004), 132–33.

5. McGuigan, "Stress Management," 205–14.

6. Daniel S. Girdano, George S. Everly, and Dorothy E. Dusek, *Controlling Stress and Tension* (Boston: Allyn and Bacon, 2001), 224.

7. Edmund Jacobson, *You Must Relax* (New York: McGraw-Hill Book Co., 1970).

8. M. Matsumoto and J. C. Smith, "Progressive Muscle Relaxation, Breathing Exercises, and ABC Relaxation Theory," *Journal of Clinical Psychology* 57(2001): 1551–57.

9. P. M. Lehrer, "Varieties of Relaxation Methods and Their Unique Effects," *International Journal of Stress Management* 3(1996): 1–15.

10. Barbara B. Brown, *Stress and the Art of Biofeedback* (New York: Harper & Row, 1977), 45.

11. T. Devineni and E. B. Blanchard, "A Randomized Controlled Trial of an Internet-Based Treatment for Chronic Headache," *Behaviour Research and Therapy* 43(2005): 277–92.

12. R. W. Ostelo, M. W. van Tulder, J. W. Vlaeyen, S. J. Linton, S. J Morley, and W. J. Assendelft, "Behavioural Treatment for Chronic Low-Back Pain," *Cochrane Database of Systematic Reviews* 1(2005): CD002014.

13. H. J. Yoo, S. H. Ahn, S. B. Kim, W. K. Kim, and O. S. Han, "Efficacy of Progressive Muscle Relaxation Training and Guided Imagery in Reducing Chemotherapy Side Effects in Patients with Breast Cancer and in Improving Their Quality of Life," *Supportive Care in Cancer* 13(2005): 826–33.

14. W. F. Waters, M. J. Hurry, P. G. Binks, C. E. Carney, L. E. Lajos, K. H. Fuller, B. Betz, J. Johnson, T. Anderson, and J. M. Tucci, "Behavioral and Hypnotic Treatments for Insomnia Subtypes," *Behavioral Sleep Medicine* 1(2003): 81–101.

15. C. L. Baird and L. Sands, "A Pilot Study of the Effectiveness of Guided Imagery with Progressive Muscle Relaxation to Reduce Chronic Pain and Mobility Difficulties of Osteoarthritis," *Pain Management Nursing* 5(2004): 97–104.

16. R. H. Schneider, C. N. Alexander, F. Staggers, D. W. Orme-Johnson, M. Rainforth, J. W. Salerno, W. Sheppard, A. Castillo-Richmond, V. A. Barnes, and S. I. Nidich, "A Randomized Controlled Trial of Stress Reduction in African Americans Treated for Hypertension for Over One Year," *American Journal of Hypertension* 18(2005): 88–98.

17. Girdano, Everly, and Dusek, *Controlling Stress and Tension,* 222.

18. Daniel A. Girdano and George S. Everly, *Controlling Stress and Tension: A Holistic Approach* (Englewood Cliffs, NJ: Prentice-Hall, 1986), 145.

19. Maureen Dion, "A Study of the Effects of Progressive Relaxation Training on Changes in Self Concepts in Low Self-Concept College Students," *Dissertation Abstracts International* 37(1977): 4860.

20. L. A. Pawlow, P. M. O'Neil, and R. J. Malcolm, "Night Eating Syndrome: Effects of Brief Relaxation Training on Stress, Mood, Hunger, and Eating Patterns," *International Journal of Obesity and Related Metabolic Disorders* 27(2003): 970–78.

21. D. H. Powell, "Behavioral Treatment of Debilitating Test Anxiety Among Medical Students," *Journal of Clinical Psychology* 60(2004): 853–65.

22. Y. L. Cheung, A. Molassiotis, and A. M. Chang, "The Effect of Progressive Muscle Relaxation Training on Anxiety and Quality of Life After Stoma Surgery in Colorectal Cancer Patients," *Psychooncology* 12(2003): 254–66.

23. K. Morgan, S. Dixon, N. Mathers, J. Thompson, and M. Tomeny, "Psychological Treatment for Insomnia in the Regulation of Long-Term Hypnotic Drug Use," *Health Technology Assessment* 8(2004): iii–iv, 1–68.

24. A. P. Greeff and W. S. Conradie, "Use of Progressive Relaxation Training for Chronic Alcoholics with Insomnia," *Psychological Reports* 82(1998): 407–12.

25. Brown, *Stress and the Art of Biofeedback,* 89.

26. Kenneth J. Kukla, "The Effects of Progressive Relaxation Training upon Athletic Performance During Stress," *Dissertation Abstracts International* 37(1977): 6392.

27. E. J. Heide and T. D. Borkovec, "Relaxation-Induced Anxiety: Mechanisms and Theoretical Implications," *Behaviour Research and Therapy* 22(1984): 1–12.

28. P. M. Lehrer and R. L. Woolfolk, "Are Stress Reduction Techniques Interchangeable, or Do They Have Specific Effect?: A Review of the Comparative Empirical Literature," in *Principles and Practice of Stress Management,* ed. R. L. Woolfolk and P. M. Lehrer (New York: Guilford, 1984).

29. Lehrer, "Varieties of Relaxation Methods," 1–15.

30. John D. Curtis Richard A. Detert, Jay Schindler, and Kip Zirkel, *Teaching Stress Management and Relaxation Skills: An Instructor's Guide* (La Crosse, WI: Coulee Press, 1985), 167.

31. Jeffrey W. Forman and Dave Myers, *The Personal Stress Reduction Program* (Englewood Cliffs, NJ: Prentice-Hall, 1987), 72.

32. Jonathan C. Smith, *Relaxation Dynamics: Nine World Approaches to Self-Relaxation* (Champaign, IL: Research Press, 1985), 65.

internet resources

Stress Management and Relaxation Web sites
www.siu.edu/departments/bushea/stress.html
Links to stress management sites.

Stress Less
www.stressless.com
Offers a wide selection of stress reduction products and programs for use in coping with the effects of excess stress.

Progressive Muscle Relaxation
ourworld.compuserve.com/homepages/har/les1.htm
Step-by-step lesson in progressive muscle relaxation.

Stress Education Center
www.dstress.com/guided.htm
This Web site guides the reader through a relaxation exercise and also includes information about how to obtain additional resources (tapes and books) for coping with stress.

Coping in Today's World

Complementary and alternative medicine (CAM) continues to be of interest to the American public, and is now accessed with greater frequency than ever before. Among CAM therapies are several that employ relaxation techniques to improve health. To protect the American public from spending their money on ineffective CAM therapies, or employing CAM therapies rather than proven traditional medical interventions when these traditional interventions are more effective, the federal government established the National Center for Complementary and Alternative Medicine (NCCAM). NCCAM, a unit of the National Institutes of Health, funds research to test the safety and effectiveness of CAM therapies. A brief summary of research findings pertaining to select CAM therapies is presented here. Interested readers should consult the NCAAM Web site for more detail (http://nccam.nih.gov).

- Acupuncture has been found to be effective in the short-term alleviation of chronic low back pain and to help relieve pain in the knee from osteoarthritis.

- Massage therapy can help people feel better if accompanied by physical therapy and instruction regarding proper posture. Massage therapy has also been shown to have beneficial effects on the immunological system, such as reducing levels of substance P (a protein associated with pain).

- Mind/body therapies, such as meditation, have been shown to "improve postsurgical outcomes and reduce mortality rates from coronary heart disease by using techniques to reduce anger, hostility and stress," and have been shown to be "effective in treating incontinence, chronic low-back pain, headaches, insomnia, and nausea, vomiting, pain and functional problems caused by chemotherapy."[a]

- Using magnetic resonance imagery (MRI), meditation has been found to increase left brain activity, which is associated with positive emotional feelings. It also activates parts of the brain that enhance attention and control of the nervous system.

- Biofeedback has been shown to be effective in treating more than a hundred medical conditions, among which are migraine headache, arthritis, and fibromyalgia. This benefit is achieved by patients learning to control their heart rates, muscle tension, rate and pattern of breathing, blood pressure, and skin temperature.

- Cognitive behavioral therapy—a form of psychotherapy in which patients explore the meaning they attach to their surroundings and events in their lives and the influence that meaning has on their behavior—helps relieve stress. Consequently, cognitive behavior therapy is effective as an adjunct treatment for coronary heart disease and chronic pain.

[a]Payne, J. W. "What Really Works? Forget Hearsay. Here's How Science Sizes up Some Therapies." *Washington Post,* July 12, 2005, HE01.

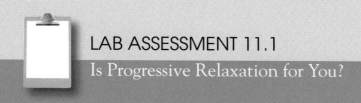

LAB ASSESSMENT 11.1

Is Progressive Relaxation for You?

Directions: Practice progressive relaxation as suggested and regularly. After at least a one-week trial period, rate each statement, using the following scale.

1 = very true

2 = somewhat true

3 = not sure

4 = somewhat untrue

5 = very untrue

_____ 1. It felt good.

_____ 2. It was easy to fit into my schedule.

_____ 3. It made me feel relaxed.

_____ 4. I handled my daily chores better than I usually do.

_____ 5. It was an easy technique to learn.

_____ 6. I was able to close out my surroundings while practicing this technique.

_____ 7. I did not feel tired after practicing this relaxation technique.

_____ 8. My fingers and toes felt warmer directly after trying this relaxation technique.

_____ 9. Any stress symptoms I had (headache, tense muscles, anxiety) before doing this relaxation technique disappeared by the time I was done.

_____ 10. Each time I concluded this technique, my pulse rate was much lower than when I began.

Now sum up the values you responded with for a total score. Save this score and compare it with scores for other relaxation techniques you try. The lower the score is, the more appropriate a particular relaxation skill is for you.

My friend and colleague, Dr. Jack Osman, goes around the country offering his lecture, "Fat Is Where It's At." A good speaker, creative, and well informed, Jack is always looking for new ways to have his audience appreciate that the charts listing how much you should weigh for your sex and height (and sometimes body build) are invalid. We were sitting in my office one day when Jack described his latest motivational device, soon to be tested on an unsuspecting audience. "I'm going to purchase old bathroom scales from junkyards. They'll probably cost a dollar apiece. Then I'll get a sledgehammer. The first thing I'm going to do after I'm introduced to the audience is use that sledgehammer to whack the hell out of a scale. I'll hit that sucker until it begs for mercy."

Being the gentleman that he is (really), Jack cares about those he educates. He wants them to know that weight charts consider not body fat but, rather, total weight. A well-developed weight lifter, for instance, may weigh more than the weight chart advises but not be "overfat."

Your body's weight can be conveyed to you by a scale, or your degree of fat can be determined by a skin caliper. In a sense, then, the scale and caliper are "biofeedback instruments."

Biofeedback

Biofeedback has been defined as "the use of instrumentation to mirror psychophysiological processes of which the individual is not normally aware and which may be brought under voluntary control."[1] That's just a fancy way of saying biofeedback is receiving information about what is occurring in your body at a particular time and then helping you to control that occurrence. A biofeedback instrument is just a tool used to obtain the measure about the part of your body in which you are interested. Consequently, a basal body thermometer is a biofeedback instrument—albeit slow and not as accurate as more sophisticated equipment—since it gives you information about a parameter of the body (its core temperature).

To better understand the concept of biofeedback and biofeedback instrumentation, tape a basal body thermometer to your middle finger, making sure the sensitive bulb of the thermometer is against the skin of your finger. In a short period of time (five minutes), the thermometer will stabilize at a reading, indicating the temperature at the surface of that finger. Record that temperature here:

_____ °F

Your task now is to increase the temperature at the surface of that finger by increasing the peripheral blood flow. As you should recall, either meditation or autogenic training will result in more blood flow to the arms and legs (and fingers and toes). Therefore, use either of these relaxation techniques for ten or fifteen minutes to accomplish your task and then record the temperature of the surface of your finger here:

_____ °F

Biofeedback, however, is also a process. It has been determined, and more than adequately validated, that, once people are fed back information about their body processes, they can be taught to control these processes. Biofeedback has been defined as

> a process in which a person learns to reliably influence physiological responses of two kinds: either responses which are not ordinarily under voluntary control or responses which ordinarily are easily regulated but for which regulation has broken down due to trauma or disease.[2]

biofeedback
The use of instrumentation to measure psychophysiological processes and a means of reporting that measurement back to the person being monitored.

209

Biofeedback really involves three phases:

1. *Measuring* the physiological parameter (The sensitive mercury in the bulb of the thermometer senses temperature.)

2. *Converting* this measurement to some understandable form (The mercury in the thermometer rises in a tube calibrated by degrees Fahrenheit, allowing the temperature of the finger to be determined visually.)

3. *Feeding back* this information to the person who is learning to control his or her body processes

Before this system could be developed, however, researchers had to demonstrate that body processes previously believed to be involuntary could, in fact, be brought under voluntary control. The early research in biofeedback was directed toward demonstrating this fact. It was shown, for instance, that subjects could change their heart rate,[3–5] the electrical conductance of their skin (galvanic skin response),[6–8] the dilation of their blood vessels,[9] and the brain waves they emitted.[10,11] Numerous other physiological parameters can also be controlled by biofeedback training: muscle tension, blood pressure, penile erection, and secretion of hydrochloric acid in the stomach, to name a few. Although it still has not been determined *how* people control their physiology, that they can is no longer questioned.

Benefits of Biofeedback

Biofeedback has many benefits, not the least of which is the demonstration (objectively and physiologically) that we have much greater control of ourselves than most of us realize. If we can demonstrate through measurable means that we can control blood pressure and brain waves, shouldn't we be able to control cigarette smoking and exercise behavior? If we can increase or decrease heart rate or the amount of stomach acid we secrete, how difficult could it be to conquer stage fright or an alcohol problem? Biofeedback demonstrates to us that our behavior, as well as our physiology, is pretty much our own doing. That being the case, we must accept responsibility for our behavioral choices.

In addition, biofeedback has specific physiological and psychological benefits. These benefits are presented next.

Physiological Effects

As we shall soon see, biofeedback has been used to improve the physical health of many people. However, an interesting point is made by Elmer Green and his associates:

> In actuality, there is no such thing as training in brain wave control, there is training only in the elicitation of certain subjective states. . . . What are detected and manipulated (in some as yet unknown way) are subjective feelings, focus of attention, and thought processes.[12]

Once again, the relationship between mind and body is demonstrated. Changes in subjective states result in changes in physiology during biofeedback practice.

In any case, **electromyographic (EMG) biofeedback** alone, which focuses upon muscle tension, has been effective in treating the following conditions:

electromyographic (EMG) biofeedback
Biofeedback that measures muscle contraction.

asthma	ulcers
hypertension	muscle spasms
bruxism	nerve-muscle injuries (stroke, paralysis)
hyperkinesia	spasmodic torticollis
spasticity	tinnitus
cerebral palsy	migraine headache
dystonias	tension headache
dysphonia	colitis

thermal biofeedback
Biofeedback that measures temperature.

Thermal (temperature) **biofeedback** has been successful in treating Raynaud's disease (a condition resulting in too little blood flowing into the fingers), migraine headaches, and hypertension.[13]

Even scoliosis—an S-shaped curvature of the spine—is being remedied through biofeedback. To correct this curvature of the spine, many patients wear a body brace, which may be uncomfortable and psychologically disturbing. Because this condition occurs most often in adolescent girls, a body brace can be particularly bothersome during this developmental period. Neal Miller and Barry Dworkin developed an alternative to the typical body brace.[14] This harness is made of a nylon fiber, which makes it lightweight and less cumbersome than other braces. Its supports run both vertically and horizontally. A sensor determines when the wearer is not standing straight, and a tone then sounds. Such innovative uses of biofeedback are the wave of the future.

However, researchers have found contradictory results regarding some of these benefits and uses of biofeedback. For example, whereas Kaushik et al.,[15] Powers and Andrasik,[16] Biondi,[17] Blanchard,[18] and Collet[19] found that biofeedback helped subjects in their studies reduce the pain of headaches, graines.[18] Chapman,[20] Callon,[21] and Lacroix[22] found it to be ineffective. When Szekely studied the use of biofeedback to treat headaches resulting from menstrual pain, she did not find it to be an effective treatment.[23]

More recent research has found some interesting physiological benefits of bio-feedback. For example, biofeedback was helpful in patients with palmar hyperhidrosis (a fancy name for sweating of the palms),[24] incontinence,[25] constipation,[26] leg muscle weakness,[27] asthma,[28] migraine headache,[29] jaw tapping,[30] temperomandibular disorder (TMJ),[31] epilepsy,[32] diabetes,[33] and attention deficit disorder.[34] Biofeedback has even been successfully employed in children with attention deficit/hyperactivity disorder (ADHD) to calm them down.

Psychological Effects

Biofeedback has been used to help people improve their psychological health and make changes in their health-related behavior. Phobias, anxiety, stage fright, insomnia, alcoholism, drug abuse, depression, and hyperactivity in children have been successfully treated with biofeedback. Tension headaches, sexual dysfunction, substance abuse, and even stuttering have responded to biofeedback as well.[35–39]

Summarizing the research pertaining to biofeedback's effectiveness and usefulness, Rice perhaps best describes the current state of the art by posing and then answering three questions:

> The first is whether biofeedback can be used to teach a person how to alter a specific internal process. The answer seems to be an unqualified yes. The second question is whether biofeedback is useful for treating a variety of stress and health problems. The answer seems to be a qualified maybe. The third question is whether the positive outcomes are a result of some unique property of biofeedback not present in other procedures. The answer is mostly no. In fact, the more biofeedback is studied, the more it appears to share common elements with both relaxation and cognitive stress management procedures.[40]

Yet biofeedback has recently been shown to be effective in treating anxiety and burn-out,[41] enhancing health locus of control,[42] regulation of mental state,[43] psychogenic cough,[44] phobia,[45] and various affective disorders.[46]

How to Relax Using Biofeedback

Biofeedback equipment is not designed to be used during the routine stressful moments we all experience daily. Rather, it is a training device. Biofeedback is used to train people to gain greater control of their physiological processes. You can't walk around all day long attached to some biofeedback apparatus or "hook up" whenever you are stressed. The equipment is used to teach you the sensations of relaxation and its physiological correlates: decreased muscle tension, heart rate, respiratory rate, blood pressure, and so forth. The hope is that, once you are able to control more of your physiological responses to stressors, you will not react to stress dysfunctionally.

Biofeedback instrumentation comes in various forms and measures various physiological parameters. Included is (a) a galvanic skin response (electrical conductivity) instrument with accompanying kit. To make biofeedback training more interesting, and to encourage the bodily changes desired, different displays are offered. Two of theses displays are depicted in (b) and (c).

(a)

(b)

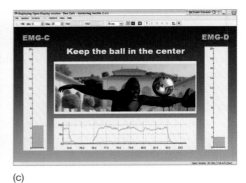

(c)

Since you cannot remain connected to biofeedback equipment forever, another relaxation technique is usually taught to you and used in conjunction with biofeedback for purposes of stress management. Autogenic training, meditation, and progressive relaxation have all been employed in this manner. In one respect, the biofeedback equipment just objectively verifies that the other relaxation technique has been learned. It also, of course, may facilitate such learning by serving as a reinforcer and quickly identifying what is and what is not working.

An example of how I used biofeedback with one of my students will illustrate this last point. After teaching several different types of relaxation techniques to my students and providing them with sufficient time for practice of these techniques, I found one of my students frustrated. It seems he felt that none of the techniques helped him to relax. He said he really didn't remember relaxing much during his fifty-odd years of life. When we worked with the biofeedback equipment, however, it was a different story. With electromyographic biofeedback, this student was able to demonstrate a remarkably low frontalis (forehead) muscle tension. Since the frontalis muscle is believed to be a mirror to general body relaxation, I was glad to see this student finally achieve a deep state of relaxation. Afterward, we spoke, and he told me that, for some reason, whenever he imagined a tunnel with black walls with purple blotches on them, the equipment reported he was at a very low level of muscular tension. He never saw that tunnel before, nor could he associate it with any symbolic meaning. However, the vision of it relaxed him. The biofeedback training, then, served this student well, because it helped him to identify an image that he could recall whenever he chose to, enabling him to relax.

How to Arrange for Biofeedback Training

In spite of the limited availability of biofeedback equipment, its high cost, and the frequent need to also learn another relaxation technique, you can still do biofeedback training if you're cagey enough. Seek out the psychology, counseling, health education, or a similar department on a college campus, and you'll often find biofeedback equipment. Next, make yourself available to faculty and graduate students who need subjects for their biofeedback research. Perhaps there's even a course that employs biofeedback as a component. If so, enroll in it.

In addition to universities, many hospitals have biofeedback equipment. Perhaps you can qualify for third-party payment (health insurance) for biofeedback training. Perhaps the hospital personnel are also conducting biofeedback research and need subjects.

Diaphragmatic Breathing

When you are distressed, your breathing becomes rapid and shallow, and it stems from your chest. There are several different ways that people breathe. When you expand the upper third of the chest, you are doing *upper costal breathing* (named after the intercostal muscles that connect the ribs). Most people breathe by expanding the middle third of their chest (approximately at the sixth rib down). This is known as *thoracic breathing* or *middle costal breathing*. However, the more relaxing and healthier form of breathing is to expand the belly. This is called **diaphragmatic breathing,**[47] because you expand the diaphragm when you breathe this way. Sometimes we make a deep sigh to relieve stress by inhaling a large amount of air and exhaling it slowly. This we call *very deep breathing,* and it is quite effective as an immediate response to stress.

diaphragmatic breathing
Deep breathing that expands the belly rather than just the chest.

To help people practice breathing diaphragmatically, Krucoff and Krucoff recommend the following:[48]

1. Lie on your back and place a book on your belly. Make the book rise with your breathing.

2. Sit with your right hand on your abdomen and your left hand on your chest and make your right hand rise as you breath.

3. Use a second hand on a clock and inhale for five seconds and exhale for five seconds.

4. Repeat a mantra and breathe in synchrony as you say it in your mind. Zen master Thich Nhat Hahn suggests repeating, "Breathing in I calm myself, breathing out I smile."

Let's practice diaphragmatic breathing. Lie on your back, with the palms of your hands placed on your lower stomach area. As you breathe, expand your chest area while keeping your stomach flat. Become aware that this is thoracic breathing and learn to recognize it as such. Next, expand your abdomen so that your stomach rises and falls with each breath while your chest size remains relatively constant (it will expand some). Recognize this type of breathing as diaphragmatic breathing. Practice it at various times of the day (when seated doing school work, for instance). Diaphragmatic breathing is basic to all forms of relaxation. It is difficult being relaxed if you are breathing thoracically. In addition, diaphragmatic breathing may be helpful in treating migraine, Raynaud's disease, hypertension, asthma, and anxiety.[49]

Many other breathing exercises can help you relax. Consistent with what we discussed earlier about relaxation techniques, these breathing exercises require you to focus on something other than events that have the potential to elicit a stress response. In this case, you focus on your breathing. When doing the two exercises described next, be sure *not* to try to control the rate of your breathing. Instead, regulate the *phases* of your breathing: inhalation and exhalation. Inhale deeply and slowly, and exhale completely and slowly.

- *Color breathing:* While seated comfortably, imagine the ground below you is filled with an energizing red color. Slowly inhale and visualize drawing in this red

King Kong wasn't concerned with holding in his abdomen and showing a "six pack." Doesn't he look relaxed as he breathes diaphragmatically?

color through your feet, legs, and upward throughout your body. Then slowly exhale the red color out of your body, imagining the space around you turning completely red. Try this exercise with other colors as well. Some colors may be more relaxing for you than others.

- *Nasal switching:* Whether or not you realize it, you typically breathe through one nostril at a time, switching nostrils periodically. Paying attention to which nostril you are using and practicing switching from one nostril to the other will help you focus away from stressors you encounter. Breathe through one nostril for a series of breaths, and then focus on breathing through the other nostril for the same amount of breaths.

Body Scanning

body scanning
A relaxation technique that searches for relaxed body parts and transports that sensation to less relaxed areas.

Even when you are tense, there is some part of your body that feels relaxed. **Body scanning**[50] requires you to search for that part and, identifying it, spread that sensation to the more tense parts of yourself. For example, if you pay attention to your bodily sensations, you may find that your calf muscles feel particularly relaxed. You would then focus upon the feelings in your calf muscles, becoming aware of the sensations experienced there. Then you would attempt to transfer these sensations to other parts of your body that are more tense—for example, your shoulder muscles. The relaxed sensation can be imagined to be a warm ball that travels to various bodily locations, warming and relaxing them.

Massage and Acupressure

reflexology
A massage technique that massages a "reflex zone" in the foot in which damage to body parts is thought to be manifested.

Many cultures developed forms of massage. Traditional Chinese and Indian medical care have over the centuries viewed massage as an important component of treatment. In the eighteenth century, Per Hendrik Ling developed what we today know as Swedish massage. In the past twenty to thirty years, Swedish massage has been embraced by therapists for physiological, psychological, and spiritual health.

Several techniques that originally derived from European massage have been developed in recent years. One of these is **reflexology.** In reflexology, areas of the foot are believed to correspond to organs or structures of the body. Damage to these body parts is manifested in a "reflex zone" of the foot.[51] Treatment then consists of massaging this zone.

Another technique associated with massage is **aromatherapy.** In aromatherapy, oils derived from plants are mixed with massage oil. This lubricant has a pleasing smell and, some claim, has medicinal qualities such as the ability to heal wounds, fight infection, assist in circulation of blood, and aid in digestion. Proponents of aromatherapy state that the beneficial effects are a result of the pharmacological properties of the plant material being absorbed into the bloodstream through the skin and by the breathing in of the aromas.[52]

Massage has a way of relaxing the muscles of a tense body. Various forms of massage exist, but acupressure massage (**shiatsu**)—pressing down on points of the body where knots or bands of muscle tension frequently occur—appears to be one of the more popular forms. Although any object can be used to employ pressure, most often the hands are used for massaging. To use acupressure correctly, you should obtain a chart of acupressure points.

Massage, as opposed to acupressure, involves warming a massage lotion (such as vitamin E or body lotion) and employing one of several techniques: caressing, gliding, or kneading. Never press directly on the vertebrae, just on their sides, and never apply hard pressure on the neck or lower back region.

The different techniques used during massage include[53]

1. *Effleurage*—gentle stroking along the length of a muscle.
2. *Petrissage*—gentle pressure applied across the width of a muscle.
3. *Friction*—vigorous pressure by circular motions of the thumb or fingertips.
4. *Kneading*—squeezing across the width of a muscle.
5. *Hacking*—light slaps or karate chops.

Massage has been shown to improve health in various ways. For example, it has been used to reduce anxiety[54] and stress;[55] to help children with ADHD calm down;[56] to treat bulimic adolescents;[57] and to facilitate growth, reduce pain, increase alertness, diminish depression, and enhance immune function.[58] An interesting study was conducted in which elders were taught to massage infants at a nursery school. After just one day, the elders themselves had less anxiety, less depression, and lower stress hormone (catecholamine) levels.[59]

aromatherapy
The use of plant material added to massage oil thought to have pharmacological qualities that improve health.

massage
A relaxation technique that involves manipulating points in the body that are muscularly tense.

shiatsu
Acupressure massage.

Yoga can relax the mind and the body, especially when one focuses on the position being sought. In that way, concentration is on the yoga position rather than on the stressors of the day.

Yoga and Stretching

yoga
A set of Hindu relaxation techniques.

Yoga[60] comes from a root word that has many meanings: to bind, join, attach, and yoke; to direct and concentrate one's attention; or communion with God.[61] Actually, yoga should more accurately be called "yogas" since there are so many types: Prana Yoga, Brahma Yoga, Kriya Yoga, Kundalini Yoga, Raja Yoga, Tantra Yoga, and the most widely known in the Western world, Hatha Yoga (involving stretching exercises). It is no wonder, therefore, that yoga is proposed to serve many different functions: from cleansing the body, to activating the nervous system, to improving one's intelligence or sex life. The stretching involved in yoga can be quite relaxing, and the prescribed yoga positions (called **asanas**) encourage this benefit. However, be careful not to stretch in a way that is uncomfortable—remember, you're trying to relax—or in a way in which you will injure yourself. Although space here does not allow a complete description of the yogic stretching positions, there are many other sources you can consult if you wish to learn more about Hatha Yoga.[62,63]

asanas
Body positions used during the practice of yoga.

Yoga has been found to have many beneficial effects. Illustrative of these are studies that have found yoga increases spatial memory,[64] improves body awareness,[65] decreases resting heart rate,[66] and enhances physical relaxation.[67]

Repetitive Prayer

Cardiologist Herbert Benson, author of *The Relaxation Response*[68] and other books[69,70] and stress researcher, wondered if prayer—in particular, repetitive prayer—would have the same relaxation-inducing effect as meditation. Benson's initial interest in prayer stemmed from his frustration with people giving up meditation. He thought that if they meditated on prayer, they might be more apt to stay with their relaxation program. Benson did find that repetitive prayer—such as "Hail Mary, full of grace" for Catholics, "Shalom" for Jews, and "Our Father who art in heaven"—did evoke the relaxation response.[71] Benson called this finding the "faith factor." Interestingly, a small group of runners and walkers took off (no pun intended) on Benson's idea and jogged or walked in cadence with the prayer they repeated. They called this exercise "aerobic prayers." If prayer or religion is an important part of your life, perhaps you might want to try to relax by repeating a prayer or a phrase from a prayer with which you are familiar.

Repetitive prayer can be relaxing as it focuses attention away from stressors.

Quieting Reflex (QR)
A six-step relaxation technique that results in relaxation in seconds.

Quieting Reflex

Psychologist Charles Stroebel developed a relaxation technique designed to elicit relaxation quickly. Stroebel says that, with practice, the **Quieting Reflex (QR)**[72] can relax you in merely six seconds. In fact, Elizabeth Stroebel, Charles' wife, tested a variation of the Quieting Reflex—the Kiddie QR—with young children and found it effective in helping them relax as well.[73] To practice the QR,

1. Think about something that makes you afraid or anxious.
2. Smile inside. This breaks up the anxious facial muscle tension.
3. Tell yourself, "I can keep a calm body in an alert mind."
4. Inhale a quiet, easy breath.

5. Let your jaw go loose as you exhale; keep your upper and lower teeth slightly apart.

6. Imagine heaviness and warmth moving throughout your body—from head to toes.

As difficult as it may be to imagine, these six steps can be done in merely six seconds—that is, with practice.

Instant Calming Sequence

Author and developer of the Health and Fitness Excellence program, Robert Cooper, teaches a relaxation technique that he says takes just seconds to elicit the relaxation response. The **Instant Calming Sequence (ICS)**[74] is based on Cooper's belief that the most effective way to manage stressful situations is to recognize the first signs of stress and immediately begin to respond. ICS's five steps are:

Step 1: *Uninterrupted Breathing.* In the face of the stressor, keep breathing smoothly, deeply, and evenly.

Step 2: *Positive Face.* Flash a slight smile as soon as you recognize you are being stressed.

Step 3: *Balanced Posture.* Keep your chest high, head up, neck long, chin in, and in other ways balanced. Imagine being lifted from a hook at the top of your head.

Step 4: *Wave of Relaxation.* Send a "wave of relaxation" to those parts of your body that appear tense.

Step 5: *Mental Control.* Acknowledge the reality of the situation. Cooper suggests saying, "What's happening is real, and I'm finding the best possible solution right now."

Mindfulness

Mindfulness is focusing your attention on the present moment. It is paying attention to each moment, living in the here-and-now. Instead of the *what-ifs* and *if-onlys,* the focus is on the *what-is.* Its opposite, mindlessness, is going through life ignoring the present moment because of attention directed toward the goal rather than the experience. Mindlessness occurs when you drive to school or work and describe yourself as being on automatic pilot. All of a sudden, you are at your destination without having really experienced the trip. How sad it is that some people reach the end of their lives without ever having truly experienced the trip along the way.

Mindfulness dates all the way back to Eastern and Western traditions of religion, philosophy, and psychology. It recognizes existentialist philosophy, such as that of Albert Camus, which argues that *who we are* is more important than *what we do.* When patients have been taught to have this focus, mindfulness has been found effective in treating chronic pain,[75] psoriasis,[76] and anxiety disorders.[77] Because stress is often caused by a preoccupation with the past (guilt, shame, regret) or with the future (fear of upcoming events), mindfulness is an excellent way to help manage stress.

Mindfulness can be developed in a number of ways. One is to focus on your breathing, called mindful breathing.[78] In this way, the mind is quieted and attention is drawn to the here-and-now. Another way to develop mindfulness is presented in Table 12.1. More mindfulness exercises appear in the book *Moment by Moment.*[79]

Music and Relaxation

Sound can have a relaxing effect with the result of other physiological and psychological benefits. Imagine closing your eyes and listening to the surf roll up to a beach, or birds chirping in the woods, or the wind rustling through the leaves. We call that

Instant Calming Sequence (ICS)
A relaxation technique that elicits relaxation quickly in a five-step approach.

mindfulness
Focusing attention on the present moment to relax.

Music can be relaxing if it is not too loud or too fast in tempo.

Relaxing at Your Computer?

Some computer software manufacturers have developed CD-ROMs to help us relax. For example, *Take Five: Relaxation at Your Fingertips* is a CD-ROM developed for a Macintosh computer by Voyager Company. It offers four programs for relaxation: Visual Vacation, the Mind's Eye, Music of the Spheres, and Stretch Yourself. Included are forty-two photos of tranquil scenes: beaches, mountains, lakes, and the like.

Is this new development—computer relaxation—a relaxation aid or an oxymoron? I wonder if we need to spend more time in front of our computers and, if we do, can we possibly relax doing so? Excuse me while I get up from this computer on which I am now typing this book. I need to relax and there's no way I'm going to do it sitting here!

"white noise" since it can wipe out more disturbing sounds. White noise is often used in conjunction with the practice of a relaxation technique as a way of drowning out distracting sounds.

Another form of sound that can be relaxing is soothing music. My guess is that you probably already use music as a means of relaxation. However, remember that music can stimulate as well as relax, depending on the type of music and the level of the sound and beat. When the music listened to is soothing, it can reduce blood pressure,[80] diminish feelings of depression,[81] improve self-esteem,[82] and even enhance spirituality.[83] An interesting study even found that when music was played in a neonatal intensive care unit, premature infants had increased oxygen saturation levels, increased weight, and shorter hospital stays.[84] Obviously, music has the potential to produce many beneficial effects, not the least of which is to facilitate relaxation.

Table 12.1
THE MINDFULNESS PROCESS

1. What is my purpose in this moment?

   (Doing your daily mindfulness practice, use focusing on your breath as your purpose. Other purposes you can use include such activities as completing a report, talking to a patient/client, or reading a bedtime story to your child.) What am I here for? Returning to your purpose in the moment offers a focus for your practice.

2. When your mind wanders, stop and observe: in this moment, where is my awareness or attention?

   What am I thinking? (about the past or future, planning, worrying)

   What am I feeling? (pleasant, unpleasant, neutral)

   What am I sensing? (seeing, hearing, tasting, smelling, touching)

   What am I experiencing in my body? (tension, breath, tightness)

   Simply note thinking, feeling, sensing, or whatever you are experiencing in your body.

3. Bring your awareness/attention back to the moment and your purpose by breathing in and breathing out. Do not attempt to change your breathing, but merely observe and experience the in-and-out of your breath and return to your purpose in the moment.

4. Repeat these steps as necessary to bring yourself back to the moment.

   A good way to apply this process is to practice it daily and use breathing as the focal point (purpose) for the mindfulness process. Finding a quiet place and consistent time helps develop this process, which slowly can be applied to all activities, experiences, and interactions.

Source: Eric P. Trunnell and Jerry F. Braza, "Mindfulness in the Workplace," *Journal of Health Education* 26(1995): 288.

Tai Chi requires slow, balanced movements and focused breathing. The result is a relaxed state.

Tai Chi

Tai Chi is an exercise and relaxation technique that originated in China about 300 years ago. It was conceived as a form of martial arts using the Taoist philosophy of Yin and Yang (opposite forces) and breathing techniques.[85] Tai Chi uses slow, smooth, dancelike movements along with meditation and control of breathing. The person engaging in Tai Chi tries to integrate the mind and body through respiration, and mental and visual concentration, thereby eliciting a relaxation response.[86]

Five basic principles guide the practice of Tai Chi:[87]

1. *Relaxation*—the conservation of energy by using just the required amount to perform the movements

2. *Separating Yin and Yang*—employing opposing forces such as speed and stillness, force versus relaxation

3. *Turning the Waist*—development of a flexible waist

4. *Keeping an Erect Back*—to maintain balance and relaxation, the body must remain perpendicular to the ground

5. *Total Body Movement*—rather than moving limb by limb, the body moves as one, all the time consistent with the preceding four principles

There have not been a lot of empirical studies of the effects of Tai Chi. However, to engage in Tai Chi requires a great deal of focus and, as we have stated elsewhere in this book, such a focus takes one's mind away from stressors, daily hassles, and worries. As a result, it is no surprise that practitioners report that Tai Chi elicits a relaxation response. If you are interested in pursuing Tai Chi, a first stop might be one of the many books written for beginners.[88–90]

Tai Chi
An exercise and relaxation technique developed in China that involves focused, slow, rhythmic movement.

Having a pet has been shown to help manage stress. Even just petting a dog has been found to lower blood pressure—for the owner and the dog.

Pets and Stress

Many stress management techniques have one thing in common: a focus on something that will take a person's mind off daily worries and stressors. Often that focus is on a word or object, such as with meditation. Sometimes it is on internal feelings, such as with autogenics and progressive relaxation. At other times it is on an activity, such as with Tai Chi or yoga. Similarly, focusing on pets can alleviate stress, for several reasons. Pets allow us to focus on their care and away from our own concerns. They provide social support in the form of companionship, and they can provide entertainment.

Numerous research studies support the beneficial health effects and, in particular, stress-related benefits of pets.[91] For example, women were asked to perform a stress task in the laboratory and then, two weeks later, at home. While at home, the women were divided into three groups. Each group performed the task under different conditions. One group performed it with a friend present, one with a dog present, and the third with neither present. The group with a dog showed less physiological reactivity than did the other two groups.[92,93] In a similar experiment, women were given mental arithmetic and cold pressor stress tests. Pet owners among the women had lower heart rates and lower blood pressure levels even before the stress tests. During the test, the lowest physiological reactivity and the quickest recovery time occurred among pet owners. Furthermore, their reactivity and recovery time were less when the pet was present.[94]

It is not only women who benefit from pets. It is well known that petting a dog, for instance, lowers the blood pressure of both the pet owner and the dog.[95] Elderly people who own pets make fewer visits to physicians and feel less alone.[96] One study found that elders who were not pet owners deteriorated more quickly in their ability to perform daily tasks than did pet owners.[97] When hospitalized, elderly pet owners stayed in the hospital an average of eight days, and elderly individuals who were not pet owners stayed in the hospital for thirteen days.

In an interesting study,[98] researchers wanted to determine the effect of dogs in decreasing physiological arousal and behavioral distress among children experiencing a routine physical examination. Children three to six years of age were given two physical exams—one without a dog present, the other with a dog. The children's blood pressure and heart rates were lower when the dog was present. In addition, the children with the dog present manifested less behavioral distress.

Getting Involved in Your Community

Just think of all of the people in your community who are "stressed out." There are people with various life-threatening illnesses, people living in conditions of poverty, and people whose loneliness is almost too much for them to bear. Sometimes these people band together to form groups from which they derive support. As such, there are groups of people living with cancer who call themselves cancer survivors, there are groups of single parents who seek advice and emotional support from other single parents, and there are counseling groups organized into group therapy sessions to support the growth and development of its members. Knowing your community (either off-campus or on-campus), you can probably identify individuals and/or groups that experience a significant amount of stress.

Wouldn't it be wonderful if you could somehow help these individuals or group members feel just a little bit better, a little less "stressed out"? Well, you can. You may not be able to alleviate the condition about which they experience stress, but you certainly can help them find moments of respite in spite of the turmoil of their daily existence. Now that you have studied various relaxation techniques, you can volunteer to teach members of your community how to relax. Then, when they feel particularly stressful, they can take a few moments to imagine themselves in a different place in a different time—through the use of imagery, for instance.

In fact, one might argue that to have this knowledge and to merely stand by, observing the stressful situations in which your neighbors find themselves without sharing this knowledge is downright negligent. It certainly is uncaring. We are all busy, but some of us can make a difference—albeit a small one—in other people's lives, and if we can, we probably owe it to our community to take the time and energy to do so.

Pets have been used to help people cope with particular conditions. For example, when pets were used with patients with spinal cord injuries, the patients experienced less stress and an increase in their self-esteem, and they were better able to express their feelings.[99] Pet therapy also has been used successfully with people experiencing posttraumatic stress disorder.[100]

Organizations that study and support pet ownership cite research showing that pets can[101]

- Reduce blood pressure and levels of stress hormones.
- Improve chances of survival after a life-threatening illness.
- Reduce health care costs by preventing illness and promoting recovery.
- Provide companionship and improve social interaction.
- Promote social responses from withdrawn people.
- Reduce aggressive behavior by those prone to violence.
- Enrich the lives of older people and those who are lonely and depressed.

The Mayo Clinic reports that living and caring for a pet[102]

- *Helps people recover from heart attacks.* Researchers have found that people who own dogs are more likely than those who are not dog owners to be alive one year after a heart attack.

- *Protect the heart and blood vessels.* Pet owners tend to have lower heart rates and lower blood pressure levels. Furthermore, pet owners physiologically react less to stressful events and recover from them faster than do people who are not pet owners.

- *Helps manage blood pressure.* Blood pressure levels decrease when a person owns a pet, even if the person is taking medication for hypertension.
- *Improves mood and well-being.* Elderly pet owners are less likely to experience depression, are better able to tolerate living alone, and are more active than elders who do not have a pet. People with AIDS who own a pet report feeling less depressed. Pets also reduce loneliness among nursing home residents.

It is for these reasons that clinical psychologists and stress management experts often prescribe interacting with a pet as a way of coping with life's stressors. Recognizing the value of pets, hospitals have developed pet programs with dogs trained to behave in acceptable ways in that setting. Nursing homes have adopted pet programs for elders, as have organizations that treat people with various disabilities.

If you are experiencing undue stress, perhaps you might consider having a pet as a means to help you cope with that stress. Pets can be obtained from your local ASPCA and many other outlets in your community. If you think this is a good idea but are not inclined to have a dog or a cat, perhaps tropical fish would to the trick?

summary

- Biofeedback is the use of instrumentation to receive information about occurrences within the body. People fed back such information can learn to control these body processes.
- Biofeedback involves three phases: measuring the physiological parameter, converting this measurement to some understandable form, and feeding back this information to the person learning to control his or her body processes.
- Biofeedback has been used to help people control their heart rates, skin's electrical conductance, blood vessels' dilation, and brain waves. Biofeedback has also been used to control muscle tension, blood pressure, penile erection, and secretion of hydrochloric acid.
- Electromyographic biofeedback has been used to treat asthma, hypertension, ulcers, muscle spasms, migraine and tension headaches, colitis, cerebral palsy, and other conditions.
- Thermal biofeedback has been used to treat Raynaud's disease, migraine headaches, and hypertension.
- When used for relaxation purposes, biofeedback is often employed in conjunction with another relaxation technique. Oftentimes, autogenics or meditation is used during biofeedback training.
- There are many types of relaxation techniques other than meditation, autogenic training, progressive relaxation, and the use of biofeedback instrumentation. Among these are diaphragmatic breathing, body scanning, massage and acupressure, yoga and stretching, repetitive prayer, Quieting Reflex, the Instant Calming Sequence, mindfulness, music, Tai Chi, and pet ownership.

notes

1. George D. Fuller, *Biofeedback: Methods and Procedures in Clinical Practice* (San Francisco: Biofeedback Press, 1977), 3.
2. Edward B. Blanchard and Leonard H. Epstein, *A Biofeedback Primer* (Reading, MA: Addison-Wesley, 1978), 2.
3. D. W. Shearn, "Operant Conditioning of Heart Rate," *Science* 137(1962): 530–31.
4. T. W. Frazier, "Avoidance Conditioning of Heart Rate in Humans," *Psychophysiology* 3(1966): 188–202.
5. Neal E. Miller, "Learning of Visceral and Glandular Response," *Science* 163(1969): 434–45.
6. H. D. Kimmell and F. A. Hill, "Operant Conditioning of the GSR," *Psychological Reports* 7(1960): 555–62.
7. H. D. Kimmel, "Instrumental Conditioning of Autonomically Mediated Behavior," *Psychological Bulletin* 67(1967): 337–45.
8. W. A. Greene, "Operant Conditioning of the GSR Using Partial Reinforcement," *Psychological Reports* 19(1976): 571–78.

9. L. V. DiCara and Neal E. Miller, "Instrumental Learning of Vasomotor Responses by Rats: Learning to Respond Differentially in the Two Ears," *Science* 159(1968): 1485.

10. Joseph Kamiya, "Conscious Control of Brain Waves," *Psychology Today* 1(1968): 57–60.

11. Barbara B. Brown, "Recognition Aspects of Consciousness Through Association with EEG Alpha Activity Represented by a Light Signal," *Psychophysiology* 6(1970): 442–52.

12. Elmer E. Green, A. M. Green, and E. D. Walters, "Voluntary Control of Internal States: Psychological and Physiological," *Journal of Transpersonal Psychology* 2(1970): 1–26.

13. G. D. Rose and J. G. Carlson, "The Behavioral Treatment of Raynaud's Disease: A Review," *Biofeedback and Self-Regulation* 12(1987): 257–72.

14. Neal E. Miller, "RX: Biofeedback," *Psychology Today*, February 1985, 54–59.

15. R. Kaushik, R. M. Kaushik, S. K. Mahajan, and V. Rajesh, "Biofeedback Assisted Diaphragmatic Breathing and Systematic Relaxation Versus Propranolol in Long Term Prophylaxis of Migraine," *Complementary Therapies in Medicine* 13(2005): 165–74.

16. S. W. Powers and F. Andrasik, "Biobehavioral Treatment, Disability, and Psychological Effects of Pediatric Headache," *Pediatric Annals* 34(2005): 461–65.

17. D. M. Biondi, "Physical Treatments for Headache: A Structured Review," *Headache* 45(2005): 738–46.

18. Edward B. Blanchard et al., "Two, Three, and Four Year Follow-Up on the Self-Regulatory Treatment of Chronic Headache," *Journal of Consulting and Clinical Psychology* 55(1987): 257–59.

19. L. Collet, "MMPI and Headache: A Special Focus on Differential Diagnosis, Prediction of Treatment Outcome and Patient: Treatment Matching," *Pain* 29(1987): 267–68.

20. Stanley L. Chapman, "A Review and Clinical Perspective on the Use of EMG and Thermal Biofeedback for Chronic Headaches," *Pain* 27(1986): 1–43.

21. Eleanor W. Callon et al., "The Effect of Muscle Contraction Headache Chronicity on Frontal EMG," *Headache* 26(1986): 356–59.

22. J. Michael Lacroix et al., "Physiological Changes After Biofeedback and Relaxation Training for Multiple-Pain Tension-Headache Patients," *Perceptual and Motor Skills* 63(1986): 139–53.

23. Barbara Szekely, "Nonpharmacological Treatment of Menstrual Headache: Relaxation-Biofeedback Behavior Therapy and Person-Centered Insight Therapy," *Headache* 26(1986): 86–92.

24. M. Hashmonai, D. Kopelman, and A. Assalia, "The Treatment of Primary Palmar Hyperhidrosis: A Review," *Surgery Today* 30(2000): 211–18.

25. T. I. Klausner, "The Best Kept Secret: Pelvic Floor Muscle Therapy for Urinary Incontinence," *Advance for Nurse Practitioners* 13(2005): 43–46, 48.

26. H. J. Mason, E. Serrano-Ikkos, and M. A. Kamm, "Psychological State and Quality of Life in Patients Having Behavioral Treatment (Biofeedback) for Intractable Constipation," *American Journal of Gastroenterology* 97(2002): 3154–59.

27. T. A. Buhr, D. B. Chaffin, and B. J. Martin, "EMG Biofeedback as a Tool for Simulating the Effects of Specific Leg Muscle Weakness on a Lifting Task," *Journal of Occupational Rehabilitation* 9(1999): 247–66.

28. C. L. Kern-Buell, A. V. McGrady, P. B. Conran, and L. A. Nelson, "Asthma Severity, Psychophysiological Indicators of Arousal, and Immune Function in Asthma Patients Undergoing Biofeedback-Assisted Relaxation," *Applied Psychophysiology and Biofeedback* 25(2000): 79–91.

29. M. Siniatchkin, A. Hierundar, P. Kropp, R. Kuhnert, W. Gerber, and U. Stephani, "Self-Regulation of Slow Cortical Potentials in Children with Migraine: An Exploratory Study," *Applied Psychophysiology and Biofeedback* 25(2000): 13–32.

30. H. Suenaga, R. Yamashita, Y. Yamabe, T. Torisu, T. Yoshimatsu, and H. Fujii, "Regulation of Human Jaw Tapping Force with Visual Biofeedback," *Journal of Oral Rehabilitation* 27(2000): 355–60.

31. K. D. Mishra, R. J. Gatchel, and M. A. Gardea, "The Relative Efficacy of Three Cognitive-Behavioral Treatment Approaches to Temporomandibular Disorders," *Journal of Behavioral Medicine* 23(2000): 293–309.

32. R. D. Sheth, C. E. Stafstrom, and D. Hsu, "Nonpharmacological Treatment Options for Epilepsy," *Seminars in Pediatric Neurology* 12(2005): 106–13.

33. R. A. McGinnis, A. McGrady, S. A. Cox, and K. A. Grower-Dowling, "Biofeedback-Assisted Relaxation in Type 2 Diabetes," *Diabetes Care* 28(2005): 2145–49.

34. V. J. Monastra, S. Lynn, M. Linden, J. F. Lubar, J. Gruzelier, and T. J. LaVaque, "Electroencephalographic Biofeedback in the Treatment of Attention-Deficit/Hyperactivity Disorder," *Applied Psychophysiology and Biofeedback* 30(2005): 95–114.

35. W. C. Scott, D. Kaiser, S. Othmer, and S. I. Sideroff, "Effects of an EEG Biofeedback Protocol on a Mixed Substance Abusing Population," *American Journal of Drug and Alcohol Abuse* 31(2005): 455–69.

36. G. Dorey, M. J. Speakman, R. C. Feneley, A. Swinkels, and C. D. Dunn, "Pelvic Floor Exercises for Erectile Dysfunction," *BJU International* 96(2005): 595–97.

37. J. T. Seo, J. H. Choe, W. S. Lee, and K. H. Kim, "Efficacy of Functional Electrical Stimulation-Biofeedback with Sexual Cognitive-Behavioral Therapy as Treatment of Vaginismus," *Urology* 66(2005): 77–81.

38. B. Guitar, "Reduction of Stuttering Frequency Using Analogue Electromyographic Feedback," *Journal of Speech and Hearing Research* 18(1975): 672–85.

39. Edward B. Blanchard et al., "Three Studies of the Psychologic Changes in Chronic Headache Patients Associated with Biofeedback and Relaxation Therapies," *Psychosomatic Medicine* 48(1986): 73–83.

40. Phillip L. Rice, *Stress and Health: Principles and Practice for Coping and Wellness* (Monterey, CA: Brooks/Cole, 1987), 313.

41. H. C. Ossebaard, "Stress Reduction by Technology? An Experimental Study into the Effects of Brainmachines on Burnout and State Anxiety," *Applied Psychophysiology and Biofeedback* 25(2000): 93–101.

42. W. W. Chen, "Enhancement of Health Locus of Control Through Biofeedback," *Perceptual Motor Skills* 80(1995): 466.

43. B. Blumenstein, I. Breslav, M. Bar-Eli, G. Tenenbaum, and Y. Weinstein, "Regulation of Mental States and Biofeedback Techniques: Effects on Breathing Pattern," *Biofeedback Self-Regulation* 20(1995): 155–67.

44. B. Reigel et al., "Psychogenic Cough Treated with Biofeedback and Psychotherapy: A Review and Case Report," *American Journal of Physical Medicine and Rehabilitation* 74(1995): 155–58.

45. E. Somer, "Biofeedback-Aided Hypnotherapy for Intractable Phobic Anxiety," *American Journal of Clinical Hypnosis* 37(1995): 54–64.

46. J. P. Rosenfeld, G. Cha, T. Blair, and I. H. Gotlib, "Operant (Biofeedback) Control of Left-Right Frontal Alpha Power Differences: Potential Neurotherapy for Affective Disorders," *Biofeedback Self-Regulation* 20(1995): 241–58.

47. Jeffrey W. Forman and Dave Myers, *The Personal Stress Reduction Program* (Englewood Cliffs, NJ: Prentice-Hall, 1987), 31–36.

48. Carol Krucoff and Mitchell Krucoff, *Healing Moves: How to Cure, Relieve, and Prevent Common Ailments with Exercise* (New York: Harmony Books, 2000).

49. Roger Poppen, *Behavioral Relaxation Training and Assessment* (New York: Pergamon Press, 1988), 66.

50. John D. Curtis and Richard A. Detert, *How to Relax: A Holistic Approach to Stress Management* (Palo Alto, CA: Mayfield, 1981), 80–81.

51. Andrew Vickers and Catherine Zollman, "ABC of Complementary Medicine: Massage Therapies," *British Medical Journal* 319(1999): 1254–57.

52. Ibid.

53. Ibid.

54. Karen R. Shulman and Gwen E. Jones, "The Effectiveness of Massage Therapy Intervention on Reducing Anxiety in the Workplace," *Journal of Applied Behavioral Science* 32(1996): 160–73.

55. Steven H. Cady and Gwen E. Jones, "Massage Therapy as a Workplace Intervention for Reduction of Stress," *Perceptual and Motor Skills* 84(1997): 157–58.

56. Tiffany Field, Olga Quintino, and Maria Hernandez-Reif, "Adolescents with Attention Deficit Hyperactivity Disorder Benefit from Massage Therapy," *Adolescence* 33(1998): 103–8.

57. Tiffany Field, Saul Schanberg, and Cynthia Kuhn, "Bulimic Adolescents Benefit from Massage Therapy," *Adolescence* 33(1998): 555–63.

58. Tiffany M. Field, "Massage Therapy Effects," *American Psychologist* 53(1998): 1270–81.

59. Tiffany Field, Maria Hernandez-Reif, and Olga Quintino, "Elder Retired Volunteers Benefit from Giving Massage Therapy to Infants," *Journal of Applied Gerontology* 17(1998): 229–39.

60. Maxine Tobias and Mary Stewart, *Stretch and Relax: A Day by Day Workout and Relaxation Program* (Tucson, AZ: The Body Press, 1975).

61. Jonathan C. Smith, *Relaxation Dynamics: Nine World Approaches to Self-Relaxation* (Champaign, IL: Research Press, 1985), 83.

62. Georg Feuerstein, Larry Payne, and Lilias Folan, *Yoga for Dummies* (Foster City, CA: IDG Books Worldwide, 1999).

63. Alan Finger and Al Bingham, *Yoga Zone Introduction to Yoga: A Beginner's Guide to Health, Fitness, and Relaxation* (Three Rivers, CA: Three Rivers Press, 2000).

64. K. V. Naveen, R. Nagarathna, and H. R. Nagendra, "Yoga Breathing Through a Particular Nostril Increases Spatial Memory Scores Without Lateralized Effects," *Psychological Reports* 81(1997): 555–61.

65. N. Jhansi Rani and P. V. Krishna Rao, "Body Awareness and Yoga Training," *Perceptual and Motor Skills* 79(1994): 1103–6.

66. S. Telles, S. Narendran, and P. Raghuraj, "Comparison of Changes in Autonomic and Respiratory Parameters of Girls After Yoga and Games at a Community Home," *Perceptual Motor Sports* 84(1997): 251–57.

67. Amy D. Khasky and Jonathan C. Smith, "Stress, Relaxation States, and Creativity," *Perceptual and Motor Skills* 88(April 1999): 409–16.

68. Herbert Benson and Miriam Z. Klipper, *The Relaxation Response* (New York: William Morrow, 2000).

69. Herbert Benson and William Proctor, *Beyond the Relaxation Response* (East Rutherford, NJ: Berkley Publishing Group, 1985).

70. Herbert Benson and Marg Stark, *Timeless Healing: The Power and Biology of Belief* (New York: Simon & Schuster, 1996).

71. Stephen Kiesling and T. George Harris, "The Prayer War," *Psychology Today,* October 1989, 65–66.

72. Charles F. Stroebel, *QR: The Quieting Reflex* (New York: Berkley Books, 1983).

73. Sandy Rovner, "Learning Ways to Beat Stress," *Washington Post Health,* 22 September 1987, 16.

74. Bobbie Hasslebring, "Health and Fitness According to Robert Cooper," *Medical Selfcare,* September/October 1989, 52–56, 69–70.

75. J. Kabat-Zinn et al., "Four-Year Follow-Up of a Meditation-Based Program for the Self-Regulation of Chronic Pain: Treatment Outcomes and Compliance," *The Clinical Journal of Pain* 2(1987): 159–73.

76. J. D. Bernhard, J. Kristeller, and J. Kabat-Zinn, "Effectiveness of Relaxation and Visualization Techniques as an Adjunct to Phototherapy and Photochemotherapy of Psoriasis," *Journal of the American Academy of Dermatology* 19(1988): 573–74.

77. J. Kabat-Zinn et al., "Effectiveness of a Meditation-Based Stress Reduction Program in the Treatment of Anxiety Disorders," *American Journal of Psychiatry* 149(1992): 936–43.

78. Eric P. Trunnell and Jerry F. Braza, "Mindfulness in the Workplace," *Journal of Health Education* 26(1995): 285–91.

79. Jerry F. Braza, *Moment by Moment* (Salt Lake City: Healing Resources, 1993).

80. T. Hatta and M. Nakamura, "Can Antistress Music Tapes Reduce Mental Stress?" *Stress Medicine* 7(1991): 181–84.

81. Nancy Aaron Jones and Tiffany Field, "Massage and Music Therapies Attenuate Frontal EEG Asymmetry in Depressed Adolescents," *Adolescence* 34(1999): 529–34.

82. Suzanne B. Hanser and Larry W. Thompson, "Effects of a Music Therapy Strategy on Depressed Older Adults," *Journal of Gerontology* 49(1994): 265–69.

83. Michael J. Lowis and Jenny Hughes, "A Comparison of the Effects of Sacred and Secular Music on Elderly People," *Journal of Psychology* 131(1997): 45–55.

84. Charles Marwick, "Music Hath Charms for Care of Preemies," *Journal of the American Medical Association* 283(2000): 468.

85. Erica S. Sandlund and Torsten Norlander, "The Effects of Tai Chi Chuan Relaxation and Exercise on Stress Responses and Well-Being: An Overview of Research," *International Journal of Stress Management* 7(2000): 139–49.

86. T. Dunn, "The Practice and Spirit of T'ai Chi Chuan," *Yoga Journal* (1987): 62–68.

87. Sandlund and Norlander, "The Effects of Tai Chi Chuan," 140–41.

88. Nigel Sutton, *Applied Tai Chi Chuan* (Tokyo: Charles E. Tuttle, 1998).

89. Stewart McFarlane and Mew Hong Tan, *Complete Book of T'ai Chi* (London: DK Publishing, 1997).

90. Martin Lee, Emily Lee, Melinda Lee, Joyce Lee, and T. C. Master, *The Healing Art of Tai Chi: Becoming One with Nature* (New York: Sterling Publications, 1996).

91. Stephen D. Shappell, "Health Benefits of Pets," *HealthCenterOnline,* 2004, http:www.healthcenteronline.com/Health_Benefits _of_Pets.html

92. Karen Allen, Jim Blascovich, Joe Tomaka, and Robert M. Kelsey, "Presence of Human Friend and Pet Dogs as Moderators of Autonomic Responses to Stress in Women," *Journal of Personality and Social Psychology* 61(1991): 582–89.

93. K. Allen, B. E. Shykoff and J. L. Izzo, Jr., "Pet Ownership, but Not ACE Inhibitor Therapy, Blunts Home Blood Pressure Responses to Mental Stress," *Hypertension* 38(2001): 15–20.

94. Karen Allen, Jim Blascovich, and Wendy B. Mendes, "Cardiovascular Reactivity and the Presence of Pets, Friends, and Spouses: The Truth About Cats and Dogs," *Psychosomatic Medicine* 64(2002): 727–39.

95. Christine R. McLaughlin, "Furry Friends Can Aid Your Health," *Discovery Health Channel,* 2004, http:www.health.discovery.com/centers/aging/ powerofpets/powerofpets_print.html

96. J. M. Siegel, "Stressful Life Events and Use of Physician Services Among the Elderly: The Moderating Role of Pet Ownership," *Journal of Personality and Social Psychology* 58(1990): 1081–86.

97. Parminder Raina, D. Waltner-Toews, B. Bonnett, C. Woodward, and T. J. Abernathy, "Influence of Companion Animals on the Physical and Psychological Health of Older People: An Analysis of a One-Year Longitudinal Study," *American Geriatric Society* 47(1999): 323–29.

98. S. L. Nagengast, M. M. Baun, M Megel, and J. M. Leibowitz, "The Effects of the Presence of a Companion Animal on Physiological Arousal and Behavioral Distress in Children During a Physical Examination," *Journal of Pediatric Nursing* 12(1997): 323–30.

99. C. M. Counsell, J. Abram, and M. Gilbert, "Animal Assisted Therapy and the Individual with Spinal Cord Injury," *SCI Nursing* 14(1997): 52–55.

100. E. L. Altschuler, "Pet-Facilitated Therapy for Posttraumatic Stress Disorder," *Annals of Clinical Psychiatry* 11(1999): 29–30.

101. Dafoni Carlisle, "A Pet for Life," *Pets & Health,* 2004, http://www.hda-online.org.uk/hdt/0802/pets.html

102. Mayo Foundation for Medical Education and Research, *The Health Benefits of Caring for a Pet,* 2006, http://www.mayoclinic.com

internet resources

Holistic-Online
www.holistic-online.com/stress/stress_home.htm
Addresses general information about stress and coping strategies. Examines the numerous relaxation techniques in brief, including massage, meditation, acupuncture, biofeedback, yoga, and reiki.

The Biofeedback Webzine
www.webideas.com/biofeedback
News, meetings, and research, including a searchable database for biofeedback-related topics.

American Yoga Association
www.americanyogaassociation.org
A description of yoga, its history, descriptions of books and tapes, as well as an online yoga lesson.

YogaJournal Magazine
www.yogajournal.com
A magazine about the practice and philosophy of yoga.

Stress Management and Relaxation Central
www.futurehealth.org/stresscn.htm
Provides information and tools for managing stress, including relaxation and hypnosis tapes and books, articles and biofeedback instruments, and computer products.

They seemingly come at us from every angle, from every direction, from all areas of our lives, regardless of our age. I am speaking of *stressors*. If it isn't the cell phone ringing, the e-mail messages, or the PDAs designed so we can always "be in touch," it is the surveillance cameras recording our every move on the street or when driving past traffic lights. Some workers, such as telephone operators, have their work performance constantly monitored and their lunch hour timed to the minute. Depending on our past experiences, there may be databases that include our fingerprints, face recognition, DNA, or retina images.

Add to this volatile stressor mix the fact that road rage seems to be increasing; people and politicians appear to have lost any semblance of civility; and our cherished athletes too often "lose it" and, in fits of anger, violently attack one another.

And then, there are *boomerang kids* or *adultolescents*. These are adult children who move back home with their parents to save money or delay their financial and/or emotional independence. That creates what has been termed the *sandwich generation*. These are adults who are sandwiched between caring for their adult children while also caring for their own aged parents. This sense of responsibility to loved ones both younger and older can be extremely stressful. Where do those who have reluctantly joined the sandwich generation find the time to care for themselves or to maintain positive relationships with their own partners?

Even school children are not immune to modern-day stressors. Large numbers feel pressured to do well in school. In the United States, approximately 30 percent of fifteen-year-olds and 23 percent of thirteen-year-olds feel very pressured by their schoolwork, and approximately one-third of fifteen-year-old students feel their teachers expect too much of them.[a]

There are physical strains as well. School children lug heavy backpacks, while adults sit hunched over computers and work desks at angles that only exacerbate the typical stressors and strains associated with aging.

Given these modern-day stressors, the need to engage in effective relaxation techniques—regularly—is vital. The specific technique chosen is unimportant, as long as it results in a relaxation response. My friend Paul has tanks of tropical fish. He has red ones, green ones, yellow ones—of all sizes and shapes. When Paul comes home from work, he sits by those fish tanks and watches the fish swim back and forth, up and down. He watches those fish so intently that he is almost in the tank swimming with them. When he is that interested in what the fish are doing, he cannot be thinking of the stressors and hassles he experienced that day. This is an effective relaxation technique for Paul. It matters little if this technique appears in professional journals or not. It works for Paul, and, therefore, he ought to continue employing this technique of managing his stress. What ways of managing stress work for you? That is, how can you elicit a relaxation response? Of course, there are many methods of relaxation described in this book. Still, there are others that are also effective. Seek these out and make them a part of your daily stress management routine.

[a]Smith, D. "Stressed at School." *Washington Post,* September 9, 2000, A14.

LAB ASSESSMENT 12.1

How Do You Cause Stress, and What Will You Do About It?

When I conduct stress management workshops or teach stress management classes, the participants already know what causes them stress. Instead, they want to learn how to manage that stress and how to prevent stress from making them ill. One assumption is that stress comes at them from others: The professor expects too much work in too short a period of time; the parent expects chores to be done immediately; the boss demands the work be done as the boss prescribes and in the time frame the boss expects. It seems that everyone is "emitting" stress with the exception of the participant. Seldom is thought given as to how participants cause others stress. This Lab is devoted to that consideration. If we all caused others less stress, there would be less need to use relaxation techniques to manage stress. That is not to say that relaxation techniques would no longer be useful, just that the urgency to use them would diminish. With that result, relaxation techniques would be employed in a more relaxed fashion and might be expected to be more effective.

List three people about whom you care. One should be a family member, one a friend, and the other anyone else you wish to list.

1. Family member: _____

2. Friend: _____

3. Anyone else: _____

For each person listed, cite three ways in which you cause that person stress:

1. Family member:
   a. _____
   b. _____
   c. _____

2. Friend:
   a. _____
   b. _____
   c. _____

3. Anyone else:
   a. _____
   b. _____
   c. _____

Now, list three ways in which you can cause that person less stress:

1. Family member:
   a. _____
   b. _____
   c. _____

2. Friend:
   a. _____
   b. _____
   c. _____

3. Anyone else:
   a. _____
   b. _____
   c. _____

Choose one way you can cause less stress for each person listed. Commit yourself to doing that by writing a contract and having someone sign it as a witness. Then, at some specified date, report back to the witness regarding what you did and how it worked out. If we each caused others less stress, wouldn't this be a better world?

LAB ASSESSMENT 12.2

Pets: Stress Busters in Spite of It All?

My son's dog has a degenerative condition that will diminish the quality of, and shorten, the dog's life. As you might imagine, my son is quite stressed out about that. That led me to wonder if pets cause more stress than the stress-busting benefits ascribed to them. What do you think? If you have or have had a pet, answer the questions below with that pet in mind. If you have never had a pet, you probably know someone who has. In that case, answer the questions relative to that person and his or her pet.

What are the stressful aspects of having a pet?

1. _____
2. _____
3. _____
4. _____
5. _____

What are the stress-related beneficial aspects of having a pet?

1. _____
2. _____
3. _____
4. _____
5. _____

Do the beneficial aspects outweigh the stressful aspects? Why did you answer as you did?

_____
_____
_____

If you had it to do all over again, would you, or the person who you are thinking about, have another pet? Why do you think that is so?

_____
_____
_____

What can you conclude about pets and stress?

_____
_____
_____

part 4

General Applications

Physiological Arousal and Behavior Change Interventions

My father was admitted to the hospital on a sunny day in September, just days before his sixty-ninth birthday. He had experienced a few small strokes and several minor heart attacks that resulted in his being scheduled for coronary bypass surgery the next morning. My mother, brothers, and I left him at about 8 p.m., promising to return before the time of his surgery—8 a.m. When we arrived the next day, bright and early at 7:00 a.m., my father was not behaving as usual. It did not take long before we realized he had suffered a stroke in the middle of the night. Obviously, surgery was postponed with the intent of having my father recover sufficiently to be a candidate for the bypass.

It took three weeks in the hospital before the surgeons determined surgery could be performed. I will never forget the presurgery conference, at which all the things that could go wrong, given that my father was a high-risk patient, were discussed. Yet the surgery went well. Dad was alert afterward and we were all optimistic. Unfortunately, that mood lasted only a few short days before my father suffered another, more serious stroke that left him uncommunicative and unable to care for himself. We did not even know if he understood us. My father's death provided a relief from his prolonged ordeal and was neither unexpected nor unwelcomed when it occurred a couple of weeks later.

The stress I experienced from the time of my father's admission to the hospital through his strokes and subsequent death was greater than I had ever known. All my stress management strategies were called into action. Of those coping techniques, I found exercise particularly effective.

When emotions build up, we seek physical outlets. It feels good to "let it all out" so we slam doors, punch walls, and scream loudly, throwing our whole bodies into it. Now that you are familiar with the stress response and recognize that the body has been physically prepared to do something physical (fight-or-flight), you can appreciate the value of using your body in some active way.

In attempting to do this, some people behave in unacceptable or dysfunctional ways. I have a friend who punched a wall, only to find it surprisingly softer than his knuckles. The repair of his swollen hand occurred several weeks prior to the repair of the hole in the wall. Other people beat up their spouses or children when distressed or wind up fighting with anyone in sight. However, there are socially acceptable ways of using the stress products in a manner that will make you feel better without violating anyone else's rights.

Let me tell you about Dick. Dick and I played tennis together, and Dick never won. Our talents were not dissimilar, but Dick seemed invariably to hit the ball harder than necessary and, consequently, could not control it as I did. One day I suggested to him that he hit easier but try to control the ball better. You know, it's not how hard you hit it but where it goes. Dick's response taught me an important lesson. He said that the ball represented his boss, his wife, or anyone else he was upset with at the moment. No way was he going to hit that "sucker" easier! I was concerned about winning; Dick was concerned about his health. I was frustrated when I hit a poor shot; as long as Dick got "good wood" on that ball, he was satisfied. Dick used physical exercise to alleviate stressful feelings and the buildup of stress products.

That is what this chapter is about—how to use exercise to manage stress. In particular, exercise is presented as a means of *using* the stress products—increased heart and respiratory rates, blood fats, muscle tension, and so forth—so they are not able to affect your health negatively. In addition, exercise can redirect your attention from stressors to the exercise.

One way to use the body's preparedness for doing something physical is to beat up on something soft. A punching bag would do, as would a pillow or mattress.

Exercise and Health

Aerobic and Anaerobic Exercise

There are two basic types of exercise, aerobic and anaerobic. **Aerobic exercises** are of relatively long duration, use large muscle groups, and do not require more oxygen than you can take in. **Anaerobic exercises** are of short duration, done "all out," and for which oxygen inhaled is insufficient for the intensity of the activity. Aerobic exercises include jogging, bicycling, long-distance swimming, walking, and rope jumping. Anaerobic exercises include sprinting and short swimming races. Aerobic exercise is the kind that builds up cardiovascular endurance; however, both aerobic and anaerobic exercises are effective for managing stress and using stress products. Either form of exercise helps you use your body physically—which is what the fight-or-flight response prepares you for—as well as focuses your attention away from stressors you would otherwise be thinking about.

Physical Health

When people speak of health, most often they are referring to physical health. Physical health is the status of your body and its parts. Aerobic exercise does the following:

1. Improves the functioning of the lungs and circulatory system so that transportation of food and oxygen to cells is facilitated.

2. Provides the lungs with greater elasticity to breathe in more air by expanding more.

3. Delays the degenerative changes of aging.

4. Increases the production of red blood cells in the bone marrow, resulting in a greater ability to transport oxygen to the parts of the body where it is needed.

5. Helps to maintain normal blood pressure in normotensives and lower blood pressure in hypertensives.

6. Results in a quicker recovery time from strenuous activity.

7. Strengthens the heart muscle the way other muscles are strengthened—by exercising it.

8. Results in a lower pulse rate, indicating that the heart is working more efficiently.

Physical exercise can help manage stress by using built-up stress by-products.

9. Burns calories, thereby helping to prevent hypertension, heart disease, diabetes, and other conditions related to excess body fat.

10. Accelerates the speed and efficiency with which food is absorbed.

11. Tones muscle to improve strength and create a more visually appealing physique.

12. Increases endurance.

13. Improves posture.

14. Decreases low-density lipoproteins (associated with heart disease) and serum cholesterol.

15. Raises high-density lipoproteins (protective against heart disease).

Most of us know that regular exercise can improve our physical fitness, but many of us do not know what that term actually means. **Physical fitness,** the ability to do one's work and have energy remaining for recreational activities, is comprised of several components:[1]

physical fitness
Ability to do one's work and have energy remaining for recreational activities. Consists of muscular strength, muscular endurance, cardiorespiratory endurance, flexibility, body composition, and agility.

1. *Muscular strength:* the absolute maximum force that a muscle can generate, the most that can be lifted in one lift.

2. *Muscular endurance:* the ability to do continuous muscular work, the amount of work that can be done over time.

3. *Cardiorespiratory endurance:* the ability of the circulatory system (heart, lungs, and blood vessels) to supply oxygen to the muscles and remove waste products of muscular contraction.

4. *Flexibility:* the ability to move the joints of the body through their fullest range of motion.

5. *Body composition:* the proportion of lean body mass (bones and muscles) to the percentage of body fat.

6. *Agility:* the ability to move with quickness, speed, and balance.

Physical fitness, however, does not develop from just any physical activity. Certain activities are better than others. Figure 13.1 depicts the benefits of several sports and exercises, and Table 13.1 gives the energy required by various activities (the amount of calories used). Your attention is directed not only to the total physical fitness rating for

Figure 13.1

Physical fitness scorecard for selected sports and exercise.

A rating of 21 indicates maximum benefit. Ratings were made on the basis of regular (minimum of four times per week), vigorous (duration of thirty minutes to one hour per session) participation in each activity.

	Jogging	Bicycling	Swimming	Skating (ice or roller)	Handball/Squash	Skiing—cross country	Skiing—downhill	Basketball	Tennis	Calisthenics	Walking	Golf*	Softball	Bowling
Physical Fitness														
Cardiorespiratory endurance (stamina)	21	19	21	18	19	19	16	19	16	10	13	8	6	5
Muscular endurance	20	18	20	17	18	19	18	17	16	13	14	8	8	5
Muscular strength	17	16	14	15	15	15	15	15	14	16	11	9	7	5
Flexibility	9	9	15	13	16	14	14	13	14	19	7	8	9	7
Balance	17	18	12	20	17	16	21	16	16	15	8	8	7	6
General Well-being														
Weight control	21	20	15	17	19	17	15	19	16	12	13	6	7	5
Muscle definition	14	15	14	14	11	12	14	13	13	18	11	6	5	5
Digestion	13	12	13	11	13	12	9	10	12	11	11	7	8	7
Sleep	16	15	16	15	12	15	12	12	11	12	14	6	7	6
Total	148	142	140	140	140	139	134	134	128	126	102	66	64	51

*Ratings for golf are based on the fact that many Americans use a golf cart and/or caddy. If you walk the links, the physical fitness value moves up appreciably.

each of these sports, but to the individual fitness component scores. If you have a particular need, certain sports will be better than others. For example, if you need to lose weight, you'd be advised to jog (it gives you a score of 21). If you want to develop cardiovascular fitness, you need to expend approximately 300 calories per exercise session, three times a week, or approximately 1,000 calories per week. Therefore, the activities using more calories per hour are better for you. But if flexibility is your concern, you'd be better off doing calisthenics or playing handball or squash (they give you scores of 19 and 16, respectively).

If you exercise, you will be more sensitive to your body. For example, you will more readily recognize muscle tension. Further, an exercised body will improve your physical self-esteem. In these ways, exercise will help you to be less stressed. In addition, exercising will allow you to focus on something other than your daily problems, as well as use the products of stress such as increased blood glucose, heart rate, and muscle tension.

Table 13.1
ENERGY EXPENDITURE CHART BY A 150-POUND PERSON IN VARIOUS ACTIVITIES

	Energy Costs Cals/Hour*
A. Sedentary Activities	
Lying down or sleeping	90
Sitting quietly	84
Sitting and writing, card playing, etc.	114
B. Moderate Activities	**(150–350)**
Bicycling (5 mph)	174
Canoeing (2.5 mph)	174
Dancing (Ballroom)	210
Golf (twosome, carrying clubs)	324
Horseback riding (sitting to trot)	246
Light housework, cleaning, etc.	246
Swimming (crawl, 20 yd per min)	288
Tennis (recreational doubles)	312
Volleyball (recreational)	264
Walking (2 mph)	198
C. Vigorous Activities	**More than 350**
Aerobic dancing	546
Basketball (recreational)	450
Bicycling (13 mph)	612
Circuit weight training	756
Cross-country skiing	690
Football (touch, vigorous)	498
Ice skating (9 mph)	384
Racquetball	588
Roller skating (9 mph)	384
Jogging (10-min mile, 6 mph)	654
Scrubbing floors	440
Swimming (crawl, 45 yd per min)	522
Tennis (recreational singles)	450

Source: President's Council on Physical Fitness and Sports, *Exercise and Weight Control* (Washington, DC: President's Council on Physical Fitness and Sports, 2005). http://www.fitness.gov/activelife/exerciseweight.html

Psychological Health

The benefits of exercise for psychological health include the following:

1. Having more self-esteem due to feeling fit and feeling good about your body.

2. Being more positively perceived by others, since a more attractive physical appearance leads other people to consider you more poised, sensitive, kind, sincere, and more socially and occupationally successful.[2]

3. Feeling more alert and able.

4. Being a better worker, since healthy men and women miss fewer days of work, have less illness, are involved in fewer accidents, and have a better attitude toward work.[3]

5. Decreasing feelings of depression[4] and anxiety.[5]

6. Being better able to manage stress, with a resulting decrease in stress-related behaviors.[6,7]

In addition to all of these benefits, exercise can be fun. That is reason enough to engage in it.

It should be pointed out that exercise can also result in unhealthy outcomes, if performed incorrectly. For example, exercise done in a rubberized sweat suit has the potential to dehydrate you and may even precipitate heat stroke or a heart attack. Exercising while wearing inappropriate clothing (e.g., dressing too warm in the summer and too lightly in the winter) can also lead to physical consequences. In addition, your attitude when exercising is important. For example, if you associate your self-esteem with winning a sports event (such as a tennis match or basketball game) and instead you lose, you may feel less adequate and less confident. Furthermore, should you be injured while exercising, you might develop a sense of vulnerability that far exceeds reality. In all of these examples, exercise resulted in negative outcomes. And yet, it was not the exercise that was the culprit, rather it was the exerciser who did not approach the activity in an appropriate manner. As stated frequently in this book, you are in control of many aspects of your life, and that includes the manner in which you approach exercise. It is in your power to make it a positive experience or organize it so it has unhealthy consequences.

One reason for the psychological benefits of exercise is the release of chemical substances by the body during exercise. One of these types of substances is a brain neurotransmitters called **endorphins.** Endorphins act as opiates might act—that is, they decrease pain and produce feelings of well-being. The much discussed and researched "runners' high"—a feeling of peace and euphoria reported by long-distance runners—is suspected of being a result of endorphin secretions by the brain. Evidence for endorphins' effects can be found in studies that use naloxone—a substance that blocks the effects of opiates—to interfere with these euphoric feelings. One such study[8] had runners do two hard 6-mile runs on different days. One day they were administered naloxone, and the other day they were administered a placebo—a pill that looked like naloxone but had no effect on body processes. After taking the placebo, runners reported euphoria. After taking naloxone, no such feelings were reported by the runners.

Endorphins are not the only chemicals the body secretes during exercise. Dopamine is also produced. Dopamine is thought to be an antidepressant as well as an activator of erotic and sexual feelings. In addition, when you are about to exercise, the hormones epinephrine and norepinephrine are released. There substances prepare your body for the physical activity that will soon follow. Levels of these hormones remain elevated until you cease exercising. At that point, signals from the parasympathetic nervous system stop epinephrine and norepinephrine secretions, and a calming sensation occurs. Physically fit people return to their usual resting state sooner than individuals who are less fit. Those who are extremely well conditioned rebound below their resting heart rate and catecholamine levels. This *parasympathetic rebound* is one of the reasons why exercise is so helpful as a stress management tool. There is plenty of evidence of a physiological basis for the psychological and stress-reducing benefits of exercise.

endorphins
Brain neurotransmitters that decrease pain and produce feelings of well-being.

Can Physical Fitness and Exercise Make You Smarter?

Several research findings indicate that physical fitness and exercise can increase cognitive functioning. The evidence for this conclusion is severalfold: Moderate- to high-intensity exercise has been shown to result in large increases of cerebral blood flow, supplying glucose and oxygen to enhance brain functioning.[9,10] Exercise results in increases of norepinephrine,[11] serotonin,[12] and endorphins.[13] Research in mice has shown that increases in norepinephrine are associated with increase in memory. It is suspected that exercise may

Being Paid to Exercise

More than a few companies are realizing the tremendous benefits exercise can have for their employees and, more important to them, on their bottom line. As a result, companies are paying employees to work out. Quaker Oats found that, by paying employees up to $600 a year, they could save $2.8 million a year. The Providence General Medical Center in Everett, Washington, which paid employees between $250 and $325, saved almost $2.2 million a year.

When employees exercise regularly, they are sick less frequently; therefore, their days being absent from work decrease, they use their health insurance less frequently, resulting in a decrease in the company's health insurance premiums, and they are more alert, which translates into better decisions and greater productivity.

Source: Carol Krucoff, "Cash for Working Out: Exercise Pays Off at Companies with Financial Incentive Programs," *Washington Post,* 4 November 1997, 24.

lead to changes in the brain itself or in the brain environment, leading to enhanced cognitive functioning.[14] When Anthony reviewed the psychological aspects of exercises, he concluded that a high correlation exists between exercise and intellectual and memory capabilities.[15] In a meta-analysis of studies pertaining to exercise and cognitive functioning, Etnier and colleagues[16] concluded that "exercise that is administered as a chronic treatment to produce fitness gains, or exercise that has been adopted by an individual for a sufficiently long period of time to produce fitness gains, may be a useful intervention for enhancing cognitive abilities."

So, if you want to get smart, exercise![17]

The Healthy Way to Exercise

Have you ever seen someone jogging on a hot summer day wearing a rubberized sweat suit? Any time you overdress for exercise you are endangering your health. Your body needs to cool itself, and the evaporation of perspiration is its primary method. If you interfere with this cooling process, you can overtax your heart or court heatstroke or heat exhaustion. The result could even be death.

Sounds ridiculous, doesn't it? You think you're doing something *for* your health and instead you're doing something *against* it. People don't flirt with rubberized sweat suits because they want to see how far they can tempt the gods. They are probably just trying to lose a little more weight and think the more they perspire, the more weight they will lose. They don't know that the fluid lost through perspiration will be replenished by drinking water and by urinating less. They don't know of the dangers they are inviting. The problem is a lack of knowledge.

This section will describe how to exercise in a healthy manner. Among the topics discussed will be what to do before exercise, which exercises are appropriate, how fatigued you should get, and competition. In addition, a sample

It is necessary to replenish fluid loss during and after exercise.

exercise program will be offered. All of this is designed to aid you in making exercise an effective stress management technique.

Figure 13.2

Physical Activity Readiness
Questionnaire - PAR-Q
(revised 2002)

PAR-Q & YOU

(A Questionnaire for People Aged 15 to 69)

Regular physical activity is fun and healthy, and increasingly more people are starting to become more active every day. Being more active is very safe for most people. However, some people should check with their doctor before they start becoming much more physically active.

If you are planning to become much more physically active than you are now, start by answering the seven questions in the box below. If you are between the ages of 15 and 69, the PAR-Q will tell you if you should check with your doctor before you start. If you are over 69 years of age, and you are not used to being very active, check with your doctor.

Common sense is your best guide when you answer these questions. Please read the questions carefully and answer each one honestly: check YES or NO.

YES	NO	
☐	☐	1. Has your doctor ever said that you have a heart condition <u>and</u> that you should only do physical activity recommended by a doctor?
☐	☐	2. Do you feel pain in your chest when you do physical activity?
☐	☐	3. In the past month, have you had chest pain when you were not doing physical activity?
☐	☐	4. Do you lose your balance because of dizziness or do you ever lose consciousness?
☐	☐	5. Do you have a bone or joint problem (for example, back, knee or hip) that could be made worse by a change in your physical activity?
☐	☐	6. Is your doctor currently prescribing drugs (for example, water pills) for your blood pressure or heart condition?
☐	☐	7. Do you know of <u>any other reason</u> why you should not do physical activity?

If you answered

YES to one or more questions

Talk with your doctor by phone or in person BEFORE you start becoming much more physically active or BEFORE you have a fitness appraisal. Tell your doctor about the PAR-Q and which questions you answered YES.

- You may be able to do any activity you want — as long as you start slowly and build up gradually. Or, you may need to restrict your activities to those which are safe for you. Talk with your doctor about the kinds of activities you wish to participate in and follow his/her advice.
- Find out which community programs are safe and helpful for you.

NO to all questions

If you answered NO honestly to <u>all</u> PAR-Q questions, you can be reasonably sure that you can:
- start becoming much more physically active – begin slowly and build up gradually. This is the safest and easiest way to go.
- take part in a fitness appraisal – this is an excellent way to determine your basic fitness so that you can plan the best way for you to live actively. It is also highly recommended that you have your blood pressure evaluated. If your reading is over 144/94, talk with your doctor before you start becoming much more physically active.

→ **DELAY BECOMING MUCH MORE ACTIVE:**
- if you are not feeling well because of a temporary illness such as a cold or a fever – wait until you feel better; or
- if you are or may be pregnant – talk to your doctor before you start becoming more active.

PLEASE NOTE: If your health changes so that you then answer YES to any of the above questions, tell your fitness or health professional. Ask whether you should change your physical activity plan.

<u>Informed Use of the PAR-Q</u>: The Canadian Society for Exercise Physiology, Health Canada, and their agents assume no liability for persons who undertake physical activity, and if in doubt after completing this questionnaire, consult your doctor prior to physical activity.

No changes permitted. You are encouraged to photocopy the PAR-Q but only if you use the entire form.

Source: Physical Activity Readiness Questionnaire (PAR-Q) © 2002. Reprinted with permission from the Canadian Society for Exercise Physiology. http:www.csep.ca/forms.asp.

One way to decide whether you are ready to exercise is to answer the questions on the American College of Sports Medicine's (ACSM's) *Physical Activity Readiness Questionnaire (PAR-Q)*.[18] The PAR-Q is presented in Figure 13.2. If you answer "yes" to one or more questions in Figure 13.2, call your personal physician or health care provider before increasing your physical activity. On the basis of personal characteristics and medical history, the ASCM classifies people's readiness for exercise, as well as the intensity of exercise in which they ought to engage. Those individuals who are apparently healthy, who are not aware of any condition or symptom that would affect exercising, can safely engage in exercise of moderate intensity without a medical examination or exercise test. The ACSM recommends that anyone not in the apparently healthy category obtain an exercise test, medical examination, medical supervision while exercising, or a combination of all three.[19] The ACSM, the leading organizational authority on exercise and sports, also offers guidelines for when it is necessary for someone embarking on an exercise program to undergo medical screening.

Principles of Exercise

Intensity, Frequency, and Duration

You need not be a marathoner to derive the benefits of physical activity. In fact, research summarized in the Surgeon General's report on physical activity and health[20] concludes that moderate physical activity for thirty to forty-five minutes per day provides numerous health benefits. By "moderate exercise" is meant such activities as gardening, brisk walking, bicycling, and working around the house. It should be obvious to you after having already read the first half of this book that, for stress management, exercise of any kind can be effective. Physical activity requires a focus of attention on the activity itself; thus, you cannot be thinking about your stressors and hassles. This is a form of selective awareness.

Of course, more strenuous exercise can result in even greater benefits. For strenuous exercise to have a beneficial cardiovascular effect, it should be done with the heart rate raised to 60 to 80 percent of its maximum. To indirectly determine your maximal heart rate, subtract your age in years from 220. Take 60 to 80 percent of that number, and that is how fast your heart should be beating during strenuous exercise. For example, if you are thirty, your maximal heart rate is 190 beats per minute. You should, therefore, exercise so that your heart is beating between 60 and 80 percent of 190 (114 to 152 beats per minute). This is called your **target heart rate range** and should be at the 60 percent level when beginning an exercise program and gradually increase to the 80 percent level as your physical fitness improves. A good rule to follow is to take your pulse—every five minutes if you are just beginning to exercise and every fifteen minutes if you are more experienced—during exercise to determine if you are not working hard enough or if you are working too hard. The pulse rate should be taken for six seconds and multiplied by 10 to get its one-minute rate (see Chapter 1 for instructions on how to do this).

For a training effect to occur, you should exercise twenty to thirty minutes three or four days each week. Because cardiorespiratory endurance decreases after forty-eight hours, you should make sure to exercise at least every other day. You might want to schedule your exercise as you do other events in your life. In this way,

target heart rate range
The maximal heart rate while exercising.

Everyone can benefit from exercise and alleviate stress by doing so, even in spite of barriers such as lack of time, low level of fitness, and physical challenges.

TABLE 13.2   FITNESS CLASSIFICATION FOR 1-MILE WALK TEST

Fitness Category	Age (Years)			
	13–19	20–29	30–39	40+
	Men			
Very poor	>17:30	>18:00	>19:00	>21:30
Poor	16:01–17:30	16:31–18:00	17:31–19:00	18:31–21:30
Average	14:01–16:00	14:31–16:30	15:31–17:30	16:01–18:30
Good	12:30–14:00	14:31–16:30	16:31–17:30	14:00–16:00
Excellent	<12:30	<13:00	<13:30	<14:00
	Women			
Very poor	>18:01	>18:31	>19:31	>20:01
Poor	16:31–18:00	17:01–18:30	18:01–19:30	19:31–20:00
Average	14:31–16:30	15:01–17:00	16:01–18:00	18:00–19:00
Good	13:31–14:30	13:31–15:00	14:01–16:00	14:31–17:59
Excellent	<13:00	<13:30	<14:00	<14:30

you might view it as a commitment and be more apt to do the exercise, rather than assuming you'll exercise when you have the time and finding yourself continually postponing it.

Assessing Your Cardiorespiratory Fitness

Many exercise programs focus on cardiorespiratory endurance. The publicity surrounding the benefits of exercise for the nation's leading killer (heart disease) is probably responsible for the emphasis on improving the functioning of the heart, circulatory system, and lungs. If you were to concentrate on only one component of fitness, this would be the best one to choose. Exercises that overload the oxygen transport system (aerobic exercise) lead to an increase in cardiorespiratory endurance and often an increase in strength for selected large muscle groups.[21]

One way to assess your cardiorespiratory fitness is to take the *Rockport Fitness Walking Test.* After a five- to ten-minute warm-up that includes stretching and slow walking, walk one mile (on an oval track is fine) as quickly as possible. Record your starting and finishing time, and then compute the time it took to walk the mile. Table 13.2 provides an interpretation of your cardiorespiratory fitness.

Starting an Exercise Program

Assuming you have determined you're a candidate for exercise, how do you begin? *Slowly!* If you have been sedentary, a good way to start is by walking. Walking can be quite enjoyable when you notice the surroundings—the foliage, the sounds, the buildings, the people, the sky, the colors. If you walk briskly, it can also be good exercise. After years of trying, I finally convinced my father to get off the bus one stop sooner on the way home from work and walk the rest of the way. He told me he never felt better. His body felt limber, he had a sense of accomplishment, and he felt less stressed.

Swimming and bicycle riding are other good ways to begin exercise programs if done moderately. If your body's like mine, you probably don't qualify to play the role

1. Reduce the proportion of adults who engage in no leisure-time physical activity.
2. Increase the proportion of adults who engage in regular, preferably daily, moderate physical activity for at least 30 minutes per day.
3. Increase the proportion of adults who engage in vigorous physical activity that promotes the development and maintenance of cardiorespiratory fitness 3 or more days per week for 20 or more minutes per occasion.
4. Increase the proportion of adults who perform physical activities that enhance and maintain muscular strength and endurance.
5. Increase the proportion of adults who perform physical activities that enhance and maintain flexibility.
6. Increase the proportion of adolescents who engage in moderate physical activity for at least 30 minutes on 5 or more of the previous 7 days.
7. Increase the proportion of adolescents who engage in vigorous physical activity that promotes cardiorespiratory fitness 3 or more days per week for 20 or more minutes per occasion.
8. Increase the proportion of adolescents who view television 2 or fewer hours on a school day.
9. Increase the proportion of worksites offering employer-sponsored physical activity and fitness programs.
10. Increase the proportion of trips made by adults by walking.
11. Increase the proportion of trips made by children and adolescents by walking.
12. Increase the proportion of trips made by adults by bicycling.
13. Increase the proportion of trips made by children and adolescents by bicycling.

of Tarzan anyhow, so take it easy. Since your body is supported by water when swimming and by the seat when biking, if you begin slowly, these are excellent beginning activities. Swimming and biking can also be done more strenuously when you get in better shape.

How to Exercise

You should remember several points when exercising. First, keep in mind that exercise *trains,* too much exercise *strains.* I never cease being amazed at friends of mine who jog long distances but are always complaining about a knee that hurts, an Achilles tendon that is tender, or the presence of shinsplints. They approach running as a religion rather than as exercise for leisure and health. Do you exercise at a pace and with a frequency that makes it healthy and fun rather than harmful? Have a fun run, not strain and pain.

Do's and Don'ts
Warm-Up and Cool-Down
Research has indicated that beginning exercise too abruptly can cause cardiac rhythm problems.[22] Since these problems have the potential to result in heart attacks (even in an otherwise healthy heart), a ten- or fifteen-minute warm-up is recommended before any strenuous exercise. The warm-up will also help to stretch the muscles and will decrease the chance of muscle strains during the exercise itself.

After exercising vigorously, there is the possibility of too much blood pooling in the veins. This can lead to fainting. Though this possibility is somewhat remote, you should take a five- or ten-minute cool-down period after strenuous exercise. The cool-down will also help rid the muscles of lactate—a waste product of exercise—which in turn will decrease residual soreness in the muscles. Walking and stretching exercises serve as a good cool-down.

Clothing
Light-colored clothing that reflects the sun's rays is cooler in the summer, and dark clothes are warmer in the winter. When the weather is very cold, it's better to wear several layers of light clothing than one or two heavy layers. The extra layers help trap heat, and it's easy to shed one of them if you become too warm.

You should wear something on your head when it's cold, or when it's hot and sunny. Wool watch caps or ski caps are recommended for winter wear, and some form of tennis or sailor's hat that provides shade and can be soaked in water is good for summer.

If you dress properly, you can exercise in almost any weather, but it's advisable not to exercise outdoors when it's extremely hot and humid. On such days, plan to exercise early in the morning or in the evening.

Fluids
Drink plenty of water before and after exercising. The American College of Sports Medicine recommends drinking 14 to 22 oz. of water two hours before exercise, 6 to 12 oz. during exercise, and after exercise 16 to 24 oz. for every pound of body weight lost.[23]

Equipment
Use appropriate equipment. Poor-fitting sneakers or a tennis racket with too large a grip can lead to injury and more stress rather than less.

Know Your Body
Become aware of how your body usually feels so you can recognize when it doesn't feel right. The following may be signs of overtraining and may indicate you should cut down on your exercise:

1. Unusual soreness in muscles and joints.
2. Unusual heaviness in arms and legs.

3. Inability to relax.
4. Persistent tiredness.
5. Unusual loss of appetite.
6. Unusual loss of weight.
7. Constipation or diarrhea.
8. Repeated injury.

Competition and Enjoyment

When I first started long-distance running, I was very competitive. Each time I went out, I tried to beat my best personal record. My wristwatch was as important a piece of equipment as my running shorts and shoes. Pretty soon I stopped enjoying running. It became a thing I had to do. Running became discouraging, because there was a day I ran so well that subsequent runs could never be as fast. I started developing aches in my legs and stiffness in my knees.

It was at that point that I decided to make a change. From that day on, I have never worn a wristwatch while jogging and have never had anyone else time me. I run at a pace that affords me a training effect and is comfortable. If someone attempts to pass me or if I am about to pass someone else, I'll try to carry on a brief conversation: "Nice day for a run, isn't it? How far are you going? Do you like those running shoes?" I now pay attention to the color of the trees (what a great time of year autumn is for running), hear the sound of my running shoes crunching the snow (what a great time of year winter is for running), notice the budding of flowers (what a great time of year spring is for running), and actually enjoy the feel of the sun on my body (what a great time of year summer is for running). Get the picture? For me, jogging has now become an enjoyable and stress-reducing technique rather than a pain and a stressor.

Competition, either with others or just with ourselves, often changes a recreational activity into one that does not recreate. Now, competition can be positive. It often takes competition for us to realize our potential. For example, you'll never know how good your return of service is in tennis unless your opponent hits a good serve for you to return. Too often, though, competition means we are comparing ourselves with others or with an idealized self. When we come off second best (or even worse), we often do not enjoy the activity, or we develop a diminished sense of self-worth, or both. Further, we plug our satisfaction into an end result rather than enjoying the experience regardless of the outcome. All of this can add to stress reactivity rather than help to manage stress.

If you can use competition in a healthy manner to actualize your potential, more power to you. Continue what you're doing. However, if you're like my friend Don, who one day—after missing a return of serve—flung his tennis racket over a fence and several trees into a creek and then had the nerve to ask if I would help him get it before it floated too far downstream, you'd be advised to approach sports and exercise differently. Realize you're not a professional athlete and that sports and exercise should be fun. Do your best, try hard, but enjoy the effort in spite of how it turns out. Use sports and exercise to manage stress, not create it.

Choosing an Exercise Program

There are many different types of exercise programs. In this section, several exercise possibilities are described and addresses provided where you can get information about others. Also consult the sources listed in the "Notes" section at the chapter's conclusion for still more information about options for exercise.

Swimming

It may surprise you to know that as long ago as January 1980 there were almost 2 million in-ground swimming pools in the United States and another 2 million above the ground. Obviously, swimming is a viable exercise for many of us. Swimming can provide benefits similar to other exercises but has one decided advantage: it diminishes the chances of athletic injury: When you are submerged up to the neck, the water supports 90 percent of your weight.[24] Therefore, your feet and legs need only support 10 percent of your body weight and will not be injured as easily as during weight-bearing exercises (e.g., basketball).

Many people use lap swimming to keep fit and to manage stress. Others do not have access to pools large enough to swim laps but can still use the water to obtain adequate exercise. These people can participate in aqua dynamics. **Aqua dynamics** is a program of structured exercises conducted in limited water areas involving standing water drills (e.g., alternate toe touching, side-straddle hopping, toe bouncing, and jogging in place); poolside standing drills (such as stretching out the arms, pressing the back flat against the wall, and raising the knees to the chest); gutter-holding drills (such as knees to chest; hop-twisting; front, back, and side flutter kicking; bobbing; and treading water). If you have your own pool and feel it is too small for lap swimming, you might want to write to the President's Council on Physical Fitness and Sports, Washington, DC 20201, for the *Aqua Dynamics* booklet. Other good sources are articles entitled "The W.E.T. Workout" by Jane Katz[25] and "Cool Water Workout" by Mindy McCurdy.[26]

aqua dynamics
A program consisting of structured exercises conducted in limited water areas.

Rope Jumping

Rope jumping is another excellent exercise. When I was thirteen, my friend Steven and I both fell head over heels in love with twelve-year-old, blonde, adorable, vivacious Jill. I'm talking about the heart-pounding, palm-perspiring, any-spare-time-spent-with-her love. Steven and I would do anything for Jill. We even spent hours playing *Who Stole the Cookie from the Cookie Jar?* while our friends played baseball or basketball. That was the summer I learned to jump rope, the whole time made frantic by the thought that this was a "sissy" activity. If my other friends had seen me, I would have died.

Well, I'm no longer crippled by that thought because I have since learned that the gender you were born with need not stop you from engaging in an enjoyable activity. I have also learned that rope jumping is an excellent way to develop cardiorespiratory endurance, strength, agility, coordination, and a sense of wellness. Fortunately, many other people have learned a similar lesson, and rope jumping has become very popular. Here are some pointers for jumping rope:

1. Determine the best length for your rope by standing on the center of the rope. The handles should then reach to each armpit.
2. When jumping, keep your upper arms close to your body, with your elbows almost touching your sides. Have your forearms out at right angles, and turn the rope by making small circles with your hands and wrists. Keep your feet, ankles, and knees together.
3. Relax. Don't tense up. Enjoy yourself.
4. Keep your body erect, with your head and eyes up.
5. Start slowly.
6. Land on the balls of your feet, bending your knees slightly.
7. Maintain a steady rhythm.
8. Jump just one or two inches from the floor.
9. Try jumping to music. Maintain the rhythm of the music.
10. When you get good, improvise. Create new stunts. Have fun.

The American Heart Association recommends rope jumping stunts. If interested, write to receive a brochure describing these stunts.

Bicycling

Biking can take place on the road or in your room. Either road or stationary biking can use the built-up stress products and help you develop physical fitness if done regularly and at the proper intensity. To bike on the road, you need a bicycle with gears; they vary greatly in cost. A good multiple-speed bike will cost well over $400. If you shop around or buy a secondhand bicycle, you can probably get a good ten-speed for half the cost of a new one. You will also need a helmet (approximately $50), gloves with padded palms (about $20), and pant clips or special clothing. Of course, many people bike with less sophisticated equipment and still get the benefits of the exercise.

Another alternative is to bike and never go anywhere; this is especially appealing on a snowy day. For this you need a stationary bicycle. While riding a stationary bicycle, you need to pay attention to adjusting it correctly. In particular, you should make sure the handlebars and the seat are where they should be. The seat needs to be adjusted so that your knee is just slightly bent when the pedal is in its lowest position. The handlebars need to be set so you are relaxed and leaning slightly forward.

Walking

Walking is an excellent lead-in to other, more vigorous physical fitness activities, but usually it is not a sufficient stimulus for young people to raise their heart rates high enough for a training effect.[27] However, for the deconditioned, overweight, or elderly person who is beginning an exercise program, walking is recommended, or, for younger people, if they increase the pace sufficiently to reach their target heart rate. If you take up walking, use the following rule to gauge your readiness to progress to other, more vigorous forms of fitness activities: once you can walk three miles in forty-five minutes, you are ready.

Of course, we are referring to natural-gait walking. Race walking or speed walking is another story altogether. These forms of exercise are excellent means of using the built-up stress by-products, as well as means to develop an increased level of physical fitness. In race walking, the lead foot must be on the ground when your trailing leg pushes off, and you must keep your knee straight as your body passes over that leg. What is surprising to many people is that a race walker burns more calories than does a jogger. For example, whereas a jogger at a twelve-minute-a-mile pace will burn off 480 calories per hour, a race walker at the same pace will burn off 530 calories per hour.[28] To perform race walking correctly, remember the following guidelines:

1. Keep your back straight and walk tall.
2. Point your feet straight and plant them at a forty-degree angle to the ground.
3. As you pull forward with one leg, push straight back with the other leg until the toe of that leg is off the ground.
4. Stretch your hips forward rather than from side to side.

If you are interested in learning more about walking or have decided to participate in this activity, there are a couple of organizations you may want to contact. The Walkablock Club of America, walk@walkablock.com, (925) 373-4816, and the Rockport Walking Institute, P.O. Box 480, Marlboro, MA 01752, can provide advice and encouragement for your walking program.

Jogging

Running is such a good form of exercise because it requires a minimum of equipment (the only expense is a good pair of running shoes), it can be done almost anywhere, anytime, and it does not require a special skill.

In most sports, we are taught to run for speed and power. In running for fitness, the objectives are different and so is the form. Here are some suggestions (see Figure 13.3) to help you develop a comfortable, economical running style:

1. Run in an upright position, avoiding excessive forward lean. Keep your back as straight as you comfortably can and keep your head up. Don't look at your feet.

Walking is an excellent activity to begin an exercise program, especially if you have not engaged in physical activity regularly. Some walkers increase the intensity of walking by carrying dumbbells. Walking can also provide social support when the walk is shared with others.

Jogging is an excellent activity to combine the physical benefits of exercise with the psychological benefits of relaxation. Running in a pleasing environment, enjoying the sounds of nature, and focusing on one's bodily sensations can also be a meaningful spiritual experience.

2. Carry your arms slightly away from the body, with elbows bent so that forearms are roughly parallel to the ground. Occasionally, shake and relax your arms to prevent tightness in your shoulders.

3. Land on the heel of the foot and rock forward to drive off the ball of the foot. If this proves difficult, try a more flat-footed style. Running only on the balls of your feet will tire you quickly and make your legs sore.

4. Keep your stride relatively short. Don't force your pace by reaching for extra distance.

5. Breathe deeply, with your mouth open.

The American Podiatry Association recommends the following running program:[29]

1–6 weeks

Warm up with walking and stretching movement.

Jog 55 yards; walk 55 yards (four times).

Jog 110 yards; walk 110 yards (four times).

Jog 55 yards; walk 55 yards (four times).

Pace: 110 yards in about forty-five seconds.

6–12 weeks

Increase jogging and reduce walking.

Pace: 110 yards in thirty to thirty-seven seconds.

12–24 weeks

Jog a nine-minute mile. (However, since you need to work out aerobically for twenty to thirty minutes to gain cardiorespiratory endurance, you should add other exercise as well.)

30+ weeks

The second workout each week, add variety—continuous jogging or running and walking alternately at a slow, varying pace for distances up to 2 miles.

Aerobic Dance

One of the best fitness activities is dance. Just look at the bodies of dancers! They are remarkably muscularly developed, incredibly supple, and ready to meet the demands strenuous exercise places on their hearts, circulatory systems, and respiratory systems.

A different form of dance is aerobic dance. Aerobic dance combines calisthenics and a variety of dance movements, all done to music. Aerobic dance, a term coined by Jacki Sorenson in 1979,[30] involves choreographed routines that include walking, jumping, hopping, bouncing, kicking, and various arm movements designed to develop cardiorespiratory endurance, flexibility, and muscular strength and endurance. What's more, it's fun. Dancing to music is an enjoyable activity for many people who would not otherwise exercise. And because aerobic dance is often done in groups, the social contact makes it even more enjoyable. Its potential for using up stress by-products, as well as its potential for developing a social support network, makes aerobic dance an excellent fitness activity for stress management.

To maximize the fitness benefits of aerobic dance, you should maintain the dancing for approximately thirty-five to forty-five minutes and work out three or four times a week. In addition, you should check periodically to see if you are maintaining your target heart rate. Many communities offer aerobic dance classes (some may be

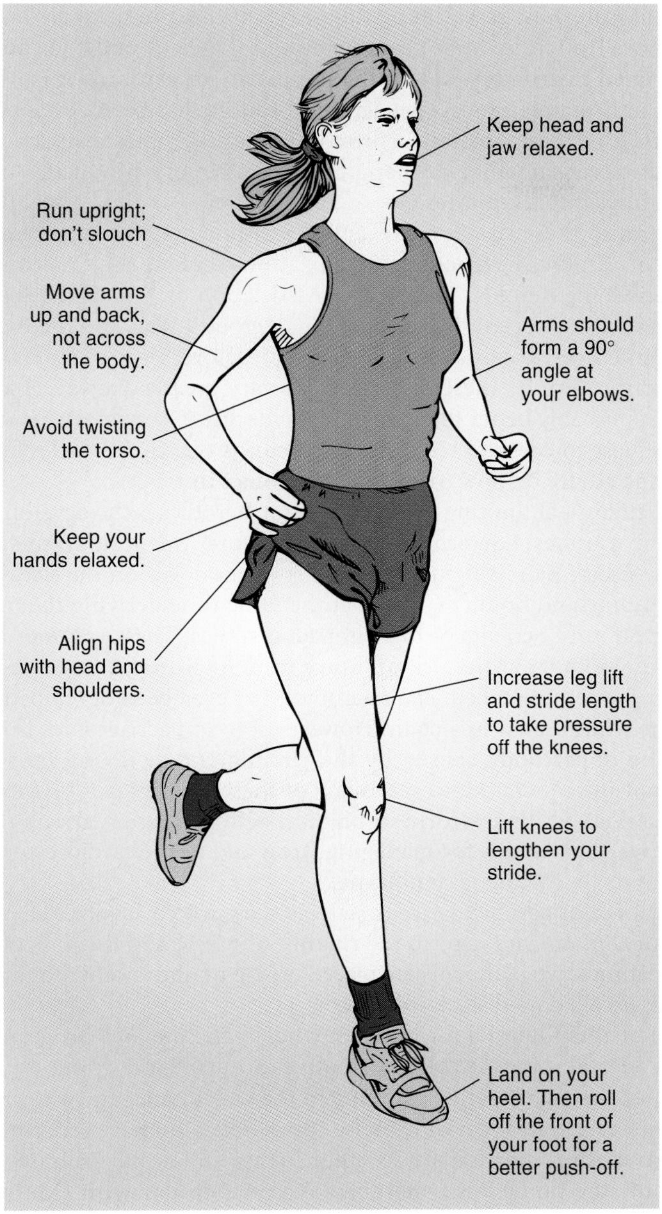

Figure 13.3

Running correctly.

Keep head and jaw relaxed.

Run upright; don't slouch

Move arms up and back, not across the body.

Avoid twisting the torso.

Keep your hands relaxed.

Align hips with head and shoulders.

Arms should form a 90° angle at your elbows.

Increase leg lift and stride length to take pressure off the knees.

Lift knees to lengthen your stride.

Land on your heel. Then roll off the front of your foot for a better push-off.

called Dancercize or Jazzercise) through YM/YWCAs, colleges, and local schools, and even on morning television programs, so maintaining a regular dance regimen should not be difficult. The only equipment you will need is a good pair of aerobic dance shoes with good shock absorbency, stability, and outer sole flexibility and clothes to work out in. One caution: Don't dance on a concrete floor, since the constant pounding could result in shinsplints. A wooden floor is preferred.

Low-Impact Aerobic Dance

Several factors associated with aerobic dance have led some experts to question the manner in which it is usually conducted. A study by the American Aerobics Association found 80 percent of its teachers and students were getting injured during workouts, and another questionnaire administered to aerobics instructors found 55 percent reported significant injuries.[31] Among the causes of these injuries are bad floors (too hard), bad shoes (too little shock absorbency and stability), and bad routines offered by poorly trained instructors.[32] With the popularity of aerobics, it is not surprising what is done in its name. Even a "pet aerobics" routine has been developed for pudgy dogs and cats. It is, therefore, no surprise that many aerobics instructors are poorly trained and teach routines that are inappropriate and injury-producing, using surfaces that result in high-impact injuries.

To respond to these concerns, several developments have occurred. One is the certification of aerobics instructors. Organizations such as the American College of Sports Medicine, the Aerobics and Fitness Association of America, the International Dance and Exercise Association, Ken Cooper's Aerobics Way, and the Aerobic Center have all instituted certification for aerobics instructors. Unfortunately, the requirements for certification by these organizations vary greatly. However, some form of certification is probably better than none. If you decide to participate in aerobic dance, you would be wise to check to see if the instructor is certified. Articles have also been written offering advice on how to choose an aerobics instructor.[33]

Another attempt at limiting the injuries from aerobics is the development of *low-impact* aerobic routines. Low-impact aerobics features one foot on the ground at all times and the use of light weights. The idea is to cut down on the stress to the body caused by jumping and bouncing while at the same time deriving the muscle toning and cardiorespiratory benefits of high-impact aerobics. These routines have become more and more popular as the risk of injury from high-impact aerobics has become better known. Something called "chair aerobics" has even been developed.[34] It involves routines done while seated in a chair. However, low-impact aerobics is not risk-free. Injuries to the upper body caused by the circling and swinging movements with weights are not infrequent. However, many of these injuries can be treated at home and are not serious. With any form of physical activity there is always the chance of injury. However, the benefits for managing stress and to the cardiorespiratory system and the rest of the body can be significant.

Another form of aerobic dance is *step aerobics,* which involves stepping up and down on a small platform (step) to the rhythm of music and the directions of an instructor. Sometimes two platforms are placed on top of one another for a more intense workout. This is called *double-step aerobics.*

To decrease the potential for injury further, *water aerobics* programs have been developed. Water aerobics involves listening to music and doing exercises to the directions of an instructor while standing in the water. Since the water supports the body, this is an excellent form of exercise for people who have structural problems or lack the strength to participate in other forms of aerobic exercise. In addition, the water cools the body. Water aerobics is very popular with elderly people for these reasons.

Stretching

Stretching is an excellent stress reduction technique. In fact, a form of stretching is used during Hatha Yoga exercises. A word of caution: never stretch a muscle that has not been warmed up. To do so courts injury, since the muscle may tear or strain. Also, don't bounce or strain into the stretch. A gradual stretching motion feels best and *is* best for preventing injury.

Weight Training

Weight training has become more and more popular. People are beginning to realize that aerobic fitness is only one piece of the physical fitness equation. Muscular strength and endurance are also important. Weight training also has benefits for managing stress. Not only can weight training use built-up stress by-products, but the increased self-confidence and self-esteem from feeling that your body is attractive can help you manage stressors more effectively. If you are interested in pursuing a weight-training program, a good start might be to enroll in a weight-training course at your college or one offered through a YMCA, Jewish community center, or local recreation center. Reading about the proper way to weight train can also help you prevent injury.[35]

Exercise and the Elderly

Exercise is not only for the young. People of all ages can benefit from it. Just ask my eighty-nine-year-old mother! Among the benefits of exercise for the elderly is the slowing of declines in aerobic capacity, in cardiovascular fitness, in flexibility, and in muscle mass that inevitably occur with aging.[36] In addition, exercise decreases blood pressure, produces favorable changes in blood lipids, helps prevent osteoporosis, improves glucose tolerance, increases bone density thereby decreasing the chances of a bone break, and helps maintain strength, endurance, and flexibility in the arms and legs. These physiological benefits foster continued independence in performing activities of daily living (such as dressing, bathing, and shopping). Even older adults who are not interested in pursuing sports often find it easier to carry groceries, climb stairs, or play with children if they maintain muscular strength.[37] In addition, it will be easier for them to maintain balance, thereby lessening their susceptibility to falling.

Furthermore, regular exercise can enhance wellness and social health when engaged in with other people. It can also contribute to spiritual health when it occurs outdoors and when attention is paid to nature and the surroundings. And, of course, exercise uses the built-up by-products of stress. Consequently, the negative consequences of stress can be reduced if seniors engage in physical activity on a regular basis.

Seniors are advised to participate in moderately intense physical activity thirty minutes a day at least three to five times a week. Climbing stairs, walking, doing yard work, gardening, cycling, and doing heavy housework all qualify. Yet the majority of Americans do not exercise regularly. One of the U.S. government's Healthy People 2010 objectives is to increase the percentage of Americans exercising regularly to 30 percent by the year 2010.[38]

People of all ages can benefit from regular exercise, physically and psychologically.

Where to Get More Information

If you want more detailed information about a particular sport or physical fitness activity, you can contact the following organizations.

Aerobics and Fitness Association of America

> 15250 Ventura Boulevard
> Suite 200
> Sherman Oaks, CA 91403
> 800-446-2322
> 818-905-0040 (For callers outside North America)
> Contact AFAA @afaa.com
> www.afaa.com

The Aerobics and Fitness Association of America (AFAA) is an international membership organization committed to promoting, teaching, and researching safe and proper ways of achieving fitness through aerobic exercise. The association has a national certification program and training curriculum for aerobic exercise instructors and personal trainers. In addition, AFFA's nonprofit foundation sponsors fitness-related benefits. The group is supported by workshops, membership dues, and the sale of subscriptions to its journal.

American Alliance for Health, Physical Education, Recreation and Dance

1900 Association Drive
Reston, VA 20191
800-213-7193 (Voice—Toll-free)
703-476-3400 (Voice)
www.aahperd.org

The American Alliance for Health, Physical Education, Recreation and Dance (AAHPERD) was founded in 1885 as a voluntary professional organization made up of six national and six regional associations, with fifty-four state and territorial affiliates. AAHPERD functions primarily through the national associations. Special programs have been developed in the following areas: health, fitness, and leisure for older Americans; career education; and activity programs for the handicapped. The Information and Research Utilization Center (IRUC) disseminates information about current resources for individuals with physical disabilities. AAHPERD is also the sponsor of Jump Rope for Heart, an exercise program that encourages youths and adults to be physically active to maintain a healthy cardiovascular system. The project also promotes school physical education programs and raises funds for research and education programs of the American Heart Association.

American College of Sports Medicine

401 W. Michigan Street
Indianapolis, IN 46202
317-637-9200 (Voice)
317-634-7817 (Fax)
publicinfo@acsm.org
www.acsm.org

The American College of Sports Medicine (ACSM) is a nonprofit, multidisciplinary professional membership organization. ASCM is dedicated to generating and disseminating knowledge concerning the motivation, responses, adaptations, and health aspects of persons engaged in sports and exercise. ACSM sponsors an annual meeting, a team physicians conference, and a variety of workshops and lecture tours; provides continuing medical education; and certifies program directors, exercise specialists, exercise test technologists, health/fitness directors, instructors, and aerobic exercise leaders. ASCM also sponsors a new investigator award, a visiting scholar award, honor awards, and citations. There are twelve regional chapters.

American Council on Exercise®

4851 Paramount Drive
San Diego, CA 92123
858-279-8227
800-825-3636 (Voice—Toll-free)
858-279-8064 (Fax)
www.acefitness.org

The mission of the American Council on Exercise® (ACE) is to promote active, healthy lifestyles and their positive effects on the mind, body, and spirit. ACE's goal is to enable all segments of society to enjoy the benefits of physical activity and protect the public against unsafe and ineffective fitness products and instruction.

Aquatic Exercise Association

> 3439 Technology Drive
> Suite 6
> North Venice, FL 34275
> 888-AEA-WAVE (Voice—Toll-free)
> 941-486-8600 (Voice)
> 941-486-8820 (Fax)
> info@aeawave.com
> aeawave.com

The Aquatic Exercise Association (AEA) is a nonprofit organization committed to increasing the healthy life span for individuals through education and participation in safe and effective aquatic exercise programs. The AEA Research Committee is dedicated to reviewing and reporting on all findings in aquatic fitness. The committee provides many services including research references, resources, bibliographies, and case study planning for all aspects of research. The AEA is recognized internationally and has certified instructors in over thirty-five countries.

American Association for Active Lifestyles and Fitness

> 1900 Association Drive
> Reston, VA 20191
> 800-213-7193 (Voice—Toll-free)
> 703-476-3430 (Voice)
> aaalf@aahperd.org
> www.aahperd.org/aaalf/template.cfm

The goal of AAALF, its eleven councils, and one society is to promote active lifestyles and fitness for all populations through support of research, development of leaders, and dissemination of current information.

Disabled Sports USA

> 451 Hungerford Drive
> Suite 100
> Rockville, MD 20850
> 301-217-0960 (Voice)
> 301-217-0968 (Fax)
> dsusa@dsusa.org
> www.dsusa.org

Disabled Sports USA (DS/USA), formerly the National Handicapped Sports and Recreation Association, was started by a group of Vietnam veterans in 1967 to serve those injured in the war. DS/USA provides year-round sports and recreational activities for persons of all ages with orthopedic, spinal cord, neuromuscular, and visual impairments. DS/USA's national office provides technical assistance to its local chapters and other recreation programs so they can better serve the disabled population in their communities. The organization has a nationwide network of eighty-eight community-based chapters in seventy-nine cities. Since 1972, DS/USA has held the annual National Handicapped Ski Championships and Winter Festival, the largest winter sports event for physically disabled people in the United States.

National Association for Health and Fitness: The Network of State and Governor's Councils

> c/o New York State Physical Activity Coalition
> 65 Niagara Square, Room 607
> Buffalo, NY 14202
> 716-583-0521 (Voice)
> 716-851-4309 (Fax)
> NAHF@hotmail.com
> www.physicalfitness.org

The National Association for Health and Fitness is a not-for-profit organization that exists to improve the quality of life for individuals in the United States through the promotion of physical fitness, sports, and healthy lifestyles and by fostering and supporting Governor's Councils on Physical Fitness and Sports in every state and U.S. territory. Currently, twenty-nine states and one U.S. territory have active councils that promote physical fitness for persons of all ages and abilities.

National Strength and Conditioning Association

> 1885 Bob Johnson Drive
> Colorado Springs, CO 80906
> 719-632-6722 (Voice)
> 719-632-6367 (Fax)
> nsca@nsca-lift.org
> www.nsca-lift.org

A nonprofit organization, the National Strength and Conditioning Association (NSCA) is a worldwide authority on strength and conditioning for improved physical performance. NSCA creates and disseminates related information and resources to the general public.

President's Council on Physical Fitness and Sports

> 200 Independence Avenue, SW
> Room 738-H
> Washington, DC 20201
> 202-690-9000 (Voice)
> 202-690-5211 (Fax)
> PCPFS@OSOPHS-DHHS.GOV
> http://www.fitness.gov

The President's Council on Physical Fitness and Sports serves as an advisory body to the president and secretary of health and human services on matters involving physical activity, fitness, and sports that enhance and improve health. It encourages regular participation in sports and physical activities for people of all ages and abilities. The council coordinates several national programs that encourage improved physical fitness, including the President's Challenge, the Presidential Sports Awards, and, in May, National Physical Fitness and Sports Month. The council works with its partners in education, business, and government to develop and promote quality programs for individuals, institutions, and organizations.

Wheelchair Sports, USA

> 1668 320th Way
> Earlham, IA 50072
> 515-833-2450 (Voice)
> 515-833-2450 (Fax)
> WSUSA@aol.com
> www.wsusa.org

Wheelchair Sports, USA (WSUSA), organizes and governs wheelchair sports in the United States. Its activities are directed by the National Wheelchair Athletic Committee, which maintains rules on wheelchair athletics, records rule changes, maintains records, selects sites for national championship meets, sanctions meets, and promotes wheelchair sports. The organization believes in the positive psychological aspects of a rehabilitation program of competitive sports, and hopes that the media attention gained from sponsoring meets will serve to educate the public. WSUSA offers activities in the following: archery, athletics, shooting, swimming, table tennis, weight lifting, and fencing. WSUSA also has two team sports: quad rugby and basketball. Membership is available for a fee.

Women's Sports Foundation®

Eisenhower Park
East Meadow, NY 11554
800-227-3988 (Voice—Toll-free)
516-542-4700 (Voice)
516-542-4716 (Fax)
wosport@AOL.com
www.womenssportsfoundation.org

The Women's Sports Foundation® is a national nonprofit, educational, member-based organization dedicated to promoting the lifelong participation of all girls and women in sports and fitness. Established in 1974 by Billie Jean King, its founder; Donna de Varona, a founding member and its first president; and many other champion female athletes, the foundation seeks to create an educated public that encourages females' participation and supports gender equality in sports. The foundation provides educational services, opportunity, advocacy, and recognition programs.

Exercise—Keeping It Going

Among other benefits, physical fitness has been shown to decrease the risk of coronary heart disease by 62 percent,[39] decrease the risk of breast cancer in women by 14 percent,[40] and decrease the risk of stroke by one-third.[41] Exercise can also help you manage stress by using the products of stress: muscle tension, serum cholesterol, and increased heart and respiratory rate.

This chapter has provided you with the information you need to begin an exercise program. You can do it. You can exercise regularly and improve your physical and psychological health. You can use those stress products before they result in illness or disease. You are in control of your exercise behavior, and you can exercise (no pun intended) that control.

Getting Involved in Your Community

So now you know that exercise is a terrific way of managing stress. So what? Well, you certainly can use this knowledge and the skills developed in this chapter to feel less "stressed out." However, you can also use this knowledge and these skills to help others within your community better manage the stress they experience. One way to do this is by volunteering to coach a youth sports team, such as Little League baseball, a community center youth soccer or basketball team, or a children's swim club. Encouraging youngsters to become involved in exercise can help them also feel less stressed.

You might also consider volunteering with your community's chapter of the Special Olympics, an organization that provides athletic training and competition for people of all ages with disabilities. Think of what a difference you can make in the lives of these people—your community neighbors—by providing them with the opportunity to focus selectively on the joy of athletic competition rather than on their disability.

If you are particularly interested in older people, you can volunteer to conduct exercise programs for elders at the local YMCA, Jewish community center, senior citizen community center, or other places where elders gather. One caution, however: Make sure you check out the duration, intensity, and frequency of the program you are planning with an expert in exercise physiology and gerontology. You want to help the program participants, not put them in danger.

summary

- Aerobic exercise is of relatively long duration, uses large muscle groups, builds cardiovascular fitness, and does not require more oxygen than you can take in. Anaerobic exercise is of short duration and high intensity and requires more oxygen than you can take in.

- Exercise improves the functioning of the lungs and circulatory system, delays the degenerative changes of aging, increases the blood's ability to transport oxygen to body parts, strengthens the heart muscle, burns calories, and lowers serum cholesterol.

- Physical fitness consists of several components: muscular strength, muscular endurance, cardiorespiratory endurance, flexibility, body composition, and agility.

- The psychological benefits of exercise include improving self-esteem, being perceived more positively by others, feeling more alert, having a better attitude toward work, decreasing feelings of depression and anxiety, and being better able to manage stress.

- Endorphins are released by the brain during exercise and produce a euphoric, relaxed state.

- The American College of Sports Medicine has developed recommendations regarding the need for testing prior to commencing an exercise program. ACSM guidelines state that if you are apparently healthy—no signs or symptoms of cardiorespiratory disease—then you can start a moderate exercise program without the need for exercise testing or a medical examination. If signs or symptoms have occurred, you are advised to obtain a medical examination or be supervised during exercise, depending on the degree of the symptoms.

- The intensity, frequency, and duration of exercise are important considerations if cardiorespiratory endurance is the goal.

- When exercising, do warm-up and cool-down routines, wear clothing appropriate to the weather, drink plenty of fluids, use properly fitted equipment, and recognize when your body is telling you you're overdoing it.

- An exercise program can consist of a number of activities such as swimming, rope jumping, bicycling, walking, jogging, aerobic dance, low-impact aerobic dance, step aerobics, water aerobics, stretching, and weight training.

- There are many organizations from which you can obtain more information about specific physical fitness activities or a particular sport.

notes

1. Jerrold S. Greenberg, George B. Dintiman, and Barbee Myers Oakes, *Physical Fitness and Wellness,* 3rd ed. (Champaign, IL: Human Kinetics, 2004), 6.

2. Jane E. Brody, "Effects of Beauty Found to Run Surprisingly Deep," *New York Times,* 1 September 1981, C1–C3.

3. President's Council on Physical Fitness and Sports, *Building a Healthier Company* (Washington, DC: President's Council on Physical Fitness and Sports, n.d.).

4. W. J. Strawbridge, S. Deleger, R. E. Roberst, and G. A. Kaplan, "Physical Activity Reduces the Risk of Subsequent Depression for Older Adults," *American Journal of Epidemiology* 156(2002): 328–34.

5. Rod Buckworth and Janet Dishman, *Exercise Psychology* (Champaign, IL: Human Kinetics, 2000).

6. William J. Stone, *Adult Fitness Programs: Planning, Designing, Managing, and Improving Fitness Programs* (Glenview, IL: Scott, Foresman and Company, 1987), 34–35.

7. S. Haugland, B. Wold, and T. Torsheim, "Relieving the Pressure? The Role of Physical Activity in the Relationship Between School-Related Stress and Adolescent Health Complaints," *Research Quarterly for Exercise and Sport* 74(2003): 127–35.

8. Kevin Cobb, "Managing Your Mileage—Are You Feeling Groovy or Burning Out?" *American Health,* October 1989, 78–84.

9. L. G. Jorgensen, M. Perko, B. Hanel, T. V. Schroeder, and N. H. Secher, "Middle Cerebral Arterial Flow Velocity and Blood Flow During Exercise and Muscle Ischemia in Humans," *Journal of Applied Physiology* 72(1992): 1123–32.

10. J. B. Mitchell, M. G. Flynn, A. H. Goldfarb, V. Ben-Ezra, and T. L. Copmann, "The Effects of Training on the Norepinephrine Response at Rest and During Exercise in 5° and 20° C Environments," *Journal of Sports Medicine and Physical Fitness* 30(1990): 235–40.

11. N. Miyai, M. Arita, I. Morioka, S. Takeda, and K. Miyashita, "Ambulatory Blood Pressure, Sympathetic Activity, and

Left Ventricular Structure and Function in Middle-Aged Normotensive Men with Exaggerated Blood Pressure Response to Exercise," *Medical Science Monitor* 11(2005): CR478–484.

12. H. Marin and M. A. Menza, "The Management of Fatigue in Depressed Patients," *Essential Psychopharmacology* 6(2005): 185–92.

13. R. E. Dustmann, R. Emmerson, and D. Shearer, "Physical Activity, Age, and Cognitive-Neuropsychological Function," *Journal of Aging and Physical Activity* 2(1994): 143–81.

14. J. Anthony, "Psychological Aspects of Exercise," *Clinics in Sports Medicine* 10(1991): 171–80.

15. Ibid.

16. J. L. Etnier, W. Salazar, D. M. Landers, S. J. Pertruzello, M. Han, and P. Nowell, "The Influence of Physical Fitness and Exercise upon Cognitive Functioning: A Meta-Analysis," *Journal of Sport and Exercise Psychology* 19(1997): 249–77.

17. C. W. Cotman and C. Engesser, "Exercise Enhances and Protects Brain Function," *Exercise and Sports Sciences Reviews*, 30(2002): 75–79.

18. American College of Sports Medicine, "AHA/ACSM Joint Statement: Recommendations for Cardiovascular Screening, Staffing, and Emergency Policies at Health Fitness Facilities," *Medicine and Science in Sports and Exercise* 30(1998): 1–19.

19. Ibid.

20. U.S. Public Health Service, *Physical Activity and Health: A Report of the Surgeon General* (Washington, DC: U.S. Department of Health and Human Services, 1996).

21. Greenberg, Dintiman, and Oakes, *Physical Fitness and Wellness.*

22. S. Pasupathy, K. M. Naseem, and S. Homer-Vanniasinkam, "Effects of Warm-Up on Exercise Capacity, Platelet Activation and Platelet-Leucocyte Aggregation in Patients with Claudication," *British Journal of Surgery* 92(2005): 50–55.

23. American College of Sports Medicine, "Nutrition and Athletic Performance," *Medicine and Science in Sports and Exercise* 32 (2000): 2130–45.

24. President's Council on Physical Fitness and Sports, *Aqua Dynamics* (Washington, DC: President's Council on Physical Fitness and Sports, 1981), 1.

25. Jane Katz, "The W.E.T. Workout: A Swimmer's Guide to Water Exercise Techniques," *Shape*, June 1986, 82–88+.

26. Mindy McCurdy, "Cool Water Workout," *Shape*, August 1990, 64–73.

27. Frank D. Rosato, *Fitness and Wellness: The Physical Connection* (St. Paul: West, 1986), 253.

28. Stephen Kiesling, "Loosen Your Hips: Walkshaping," *American Health,* October 1986, 62–67.

29. American Podiatry Association, *Jogging Advice from Your Podiatrist* (Washington, DC: American Podiatry Association, n.d.).

30. Jacki Sorenson, *Aerobic Dancing* (New York: Rawson, Wade, 1979).

31. Jean Rosenbaum, "Aerobics Without Injury," *Medical Self-Care*, Fall 1984, 30–33.

32. Beth Schwinn, "Burned in Pursuit of the Burn," *Washington Post, Health*, 14 August 1986, 12.

33. Shelley White-Corey, "Five-Star Instructors—Choosing a Fitness Instructor," *American Fitness,* January/February 1996.

   http://www.findarticles.com/p/articles/mi_m0675/is_n1_v14/ai_17793077#continue

34. Tim Green, "My Favorite Routine: Chair Aerobics," *Shape*, June 1986, 150–53.

35. American College of Sports Medicine, "ACSM Position Stand on the Recommended Quantity and Quality of Exercise for Developing and Maintaining Cardiorespiratory and Muscular Fitness and Flexibility in Healthy Adults," *Medicine and Science in Sports and Exercise* 30(1998): 975–91.

36. Greenberg, Dintiman, and Oakes, *Physical Fitness and Wellness.*

37. "Strength Training Among Adults Aged > (65 Years—United States, 2001," *Morbidity and Mortality Weekly Report* 53(2004): 25–28.

38. U.S. Department of Health and Human Services, *Healthy People 2010: Understanding and Improving Health*, rev. ed. (Washington, DC: U.S. Government Printing Office, 2001).

39. S. Yu, J. W. G. Yarnell, P. M. Sweetnam, and L. Murray, "What Level of Physical Activity Protects Against Premature Cardiovascular Death? The Caerphilly Study," *Heart* 89(2003): 502–6.

40. Anne McTiernan, Charles Kooperberg, Emily White, Sara Wilcox, Ralph Coates, Lucile L. Adams-Campbell, Nancy Woods, and Judith Ockene, "Recreational Physical Activity and the Risk of Breast Cancer in Postmenopausal Women: The Women's Health Initiative Study," *Journal of the American Medical Association* 290(2003): l33l–36.

41. Sudhir Kurl, Jan A. Laukkanen, Rainer Rauramaa, Timo A. Lakka, Juhani Sivenius, and Jukka T. Salonen, "Cardiorespiratory Fitness and the Risk of Stroke in Men," *Archives of Internal Medicine* 163(2003): 1682–88.

internet resources

Exercise as a Stress Management Modality
www.imt.net/~randolfi/ExerciseStress.html
A description of how physical activity can function as a therapeutic modality. Includes recommendations on the use of physical activity to promote emotional health.

Heart Information Network
www.heartinfo.org
Provides guidelines about heart conditions, diet, and more.

Mayo Clinic
www.mayoclinic.com
Tips for making fitness a lifelong commitment.

Coping in Today's World

Fitness activities can have a significant effect on physical health, mental and emotional health, and spiritual health. Witness Rabbi Hirscel Jaffe. Rabbi Jaffe used marathon running as a means of fighting the cancer he experienced. When he recovered, he decided to share his good fortune and began helping others overcome diversity.

Rabbi Jaffe began counseling cancer patients, became a co-editor of *Gates of Healing* (a book distributed to hospital patients), wrote a highly acclaimed book called *Why Me, Why Anyone?,* and developed a videotape entitled *Hanging on to Hope*. In 1988, he received the American Cancer Society's Award of Courage from President Ronald Reagan.

With his physical self healed, Rabbi Jaffe decided he needed to express his spirituality. He visited American hostages in Iran in 1980, and in 1992 he led a unity march in Newburgh, New York to protest the appearance of the Ku Klux Klan in his town. More than three thousand people participated in that march.

Those who knew him best called him the "running Rabbi"— both for his marathon participation and his tireless efforts on behalf of others. Rabbi Jaffe demonstrates how physical activity can improve physical, mental, and emotional health and provide expression of one's spirituality. What better way of coping with stress can one devise?

LAB ASSESSMENT 13.1
Can You Overcome Roadblocks to Exercise?

All of us know we should be exercising. It is good for our bodies and our minds, and it is one of the most effective stress management strategies. Yet, too many Americans live sedentary lives—not because they don't want to exercise or don't believe the claims regarding the benefits of exercise. Rather, there are barriers/roadblocks to their exercising that are so strong, and for which they do not have effective strategies to overcome, that these roadblocks interfere with them doing what they know they should do. This Lab is designed to help you identify and plan to overcome roadblocks that interfere with you engaging in regular exercise and, thereby, be better at managing the stress you experience.

Directions: Two examples of commonly experienced roadblocks to exercising appear here, with strategies to bypass these roadblocks. List the roadblocks specific to you and the strategies you can use to bypass those roadblocks.

Roadblock	Strategy
You may have a lot to do with little time to get it done. Term papers are due, midterm or final exams are approaching, you are invited to a party, you are expected to attend a dinner celebrating your sister's birthday, your team is scheduled for an intramural game, and your professor is holding a study session.	When lumped together, responsibilities often appear overwhelming. In this case, use the *divide and conquer* strategy. Buy a large calendar and schedule the activities of the semester by writing on the calendar when you will perform them. Do not forget to include nonacademic activities as well as those related to school. You will soon realize you have plenty of time. You simply need to be organized. That realization will go a long way in relieving unnecessary stress.
Exercise just isn't fun anymore, and you no longer look forward to your workout sessions. Even if you do get into the workout, you are not motivated to put forth much effort.	You may be experiencing some of the emotional and physical effects of overtraining or exercising too often. To renew your interest, try one or more of the following: • Change aerobic activities every other day as a cross-training technique. If you are jogging daily, substitute cycling or lap swimming two or three times weekly. • Change the time you exercise. Try early mornings, noon, or just before bedtime to see if your mood improves. • Vary the level of difficulty (intensity) of your workouts. Work out hard and easy on alternate days. • Exercise with friends and make it a social occasion as well as a workout.

Roadblock	Strategy
1. _____	1. _____
2. _____	2. _____

Now you need to actually implement that strategy so you are more likely to engage in regular exercise and, as a result, better manage the stress you experience.

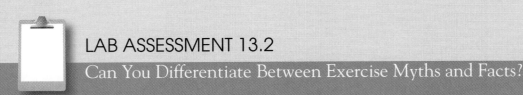

LAB ASSESSMENT 13.2

Can You Differentiate Between Exercise Myths and Facts?

For each of the statements below, place an F in the space provided if you think the statement is a FACT, and an M if you think the statement is a MYTH.

_____ 1. The most important component of overall health is physical health.

_____ 2. Being physically fit makes you healthier, but you probably won't feel any different about yourself.

_____ 3. The more you exercise, the more benefits you will achieve.

_____ 4. "No pain, no gain" means that you must train until it hurts to reap the benefits.

_____ 5. You are more likely to stick with an exercise program if you maintain the same exercise program each workout.

_____ 6. Stretching activities are excellent warm-ups for an exercise program.

_____ 7. Weight training decreases flexibility.

_____ 8. Exercise is stressful because of the toll it takes physically.

All of the statements above are **myth**s. An explanation follows:

1. Health consists of more than just physical health. It includes social, emotional, mental, and spiritual health as well. Who is to say which component of health is more important than another for any individual?

2. If you become physically fit, you will feel better about yourself and your self-esteem will improve. You will develop more confidence, feel less depressed, and experience a sense of more control in your life. The benefits of exercise go well beyond the healthy changes that occur within your body.

3. Too little exercise and the benefits are limited. On the other hand, too much exercise can place you at risk of overuse injuries. Sprains, strains, and fatigue can result when exercising too intensely or too frequently. Instead, there is an optimal level of exercise that will provide the benefits sought while minimizing the risk of injury or illness.

4. Exercise should be difficult, but it should not hurt. If you experience anything other than discomfort, you are exercising too intensely or too often. Cut back before you become injured.

5. Many people find their motivation tends to decrease when engaging in the same exercise routine weeks or months. Cross-training is a way to put the pizzazz back in your workout. Switching activities once or twice a week may provide the variety you need to stay motivated over the long haul.

6. You should never stretch cold muscles. That can subject you to risk of injury or muscle soreness. Instead, begin an exercise session with a routine that involves large muscle groups, such as walking or jogging, for at least five minutes or until perspiring. After that, you can stretch to complete the warm-up.

7. When you perform weight training exercises correctly through the full range of motion, flexibility actually improves.

8. Exercise is an excellent way of managing stress. It uses up the body's stress by-products—muscle tension, increased heart rate and blood pressure, serum cholesterol—that have prepared the body to do something physical, fight-or-flight.

Why can't I stop smoking? Why did I drink too much at the party last Saturday night? Why can't I learn to relax? How many times do we say we wish we had or had not done something? Some of the activities or actions that we *take* or *fail to take* are stressful to us. For example, we say to ourselves we are going to go out and meet new people, but somehow we never get around to doing it; we are going to change our diet but do not stick to the new diet. We worry about our inability to change our behavior. We feel less in control of ourselves. Consequently, our self-esteem may decline. In sum, we may experience a fight-or-flight response when we cannot behave as we would like to. The focus of this chapter is to present a number of behaviors that are stressful to us, either because we want to give them up and cannot or because we want to adopt them but have been unable to. It also describes methods that will help us make changes in these behaviors. With greater control of our behaviors, we will be better at managing our stress.

Health and Lifestyle Behaviors

We will look at two types of behaviors: health behaviors and lifestyle behaviors. Health behaviors are considered a subclass of lifestyle behaviors and are differentiated for emphasis. **Health behaviors** are defined as activities undertaken by people who believe themselves to be healthy for the purpose of preventing disease or detecting it in an asymptomatic stage.[1,2] Examples of health behaviors are limiting sugar and salt in your diet, avoiding smoking cigarettes, using a seat belt, engaging in physical exercise, limiting your use of alcoholic beverages, and practicing relaxation techniques. **Lifestyle behaviors** encompass the whole host of activities in which people engage. Examples of lifestyle behaviors include everyday activities such as doing chores, going to school or work, and enjoying leisure times. Examples of other, less common lifestyle behaviors are asking someone for assistance, writing a letter to a friend, listening intently to a speaker, and meeting new people.

health behavior

Activities that are taken by people who believe themselves to be healthy and that are designed to maintain health, a subclass of lifestyle behaviors.

lifestyle behaviors

All of the activities in which people engage.

Health-Behavior Assessment

Before you can go about changing your health-related behaviors, you should first identify which behaviors need changing. Lab Assessment 14.1, at the end of this chapter, will help you assess how well you are doing at staying healthy and identify areas that need improvement. Lab 14.1 is adopted from the *National College Health Assessment* and the Office of Disease Prevention and Health Promotion of the Public Health Service, U.S. Department of Health and Human Services.

Selected Lifestyle Behaviors

Lab Assessment 14.2 presents a list of lifestyle activities that some people find stressful. The purpose of Lab 14.2 is to help you identify lifestyle behaviors that you would like to adopt. Feel free to choose other lifestyle activities that are not on this selected list that you would like to adopt. It is important to identify these behaviors, because your inability to engage in these activities worries you and causes you distress.

Later in this chapter, we present techniques that you can use to change your behavior, thereby eliminating stress in your life. However, before we look at strategies to change lifestyle and health behaviors, there are a few more sets of factors that need to be considered. The first is barriers to action.

This chapter was written by Robert Feldman, PhD, of the Department of Public and Community Health, University of Maryland, College Park, Maryland.

Barriers to Action

Good intentions are abundant. Yes, I plan to contact you. Yes, I plan to stop smoking, lose weight, save money, or get involved. But somehow I never have the time. It is too hot to jog today. I will start running tomorrow. I am embarrassed to speak in front of a group of people. I will do it another time. I really want to develop hobbies, but I have so many other obligations. Excuses, excuses.

It would be more fruitful to consider these "excuses" **barriers**—that is, barriers that we perceive as preventing us from engaging in a number of activities. To the person whose spouse brings home a high-calorie dessert, the lack of family support is a barrier to maintaining weight. A series of rainy days is a barrier to the novice jogger. A heavy work or school schedule is a barrier to getting involved in worthwhile causes. The lack of availability of low-salt foods is a barrier to reducing one's intake of salt. In other words, to help you understand ways to change health and lifestyle behaviors, it is useful to identify the barriers in the way of adopting the behavior you want to adopt. Lab Assessment 14.3[3] lists a number of possible factors—barriers—that may have kept *you* from engaging in these activities.

barriers
Reasons given or situations that interfere with someone engaging in behaviors that he or she wishes to engage in.

Locus of Control

Another aspect of health and lifestyle behavior change concerns the issue of personal control. Although **locus of control** can be a generalized perception of the control you have over events that affect your life, it can also be specific to parts of your life. For example, you may believe you can control your social life and events that affect it—for example, going out and meeting people—but you may believe that your health is a matter of chance or luck: "It's whom you're born to, not what you do." The locus of control for health is the focus of this section.

Some people feel that it's their physician's responsibility to keep them well: "That's what I'm paying her for." However, a growing number of people feel that they actually do have control over their health and other life outcomes: "Yes, I can prevent illness from stress." "Yes, I can maintain a desired weight."

Now it is your turn to find out whether you feel you have control over your health—that is, your health locus of control. Complete Lab Assessment 14.4. Lab 14.4 is adapted from the *Multidimensional Health Locus-of-Control Scales.*[4] It measures three subscales of locus of control:

locus of control
The perception of the amount of control one has over events that affect one's life.

1. Internal health (**I**): This subscale measures whether you feel that you have personal control over your health.
2. Powerful others health (**P**): This subscale measures whether you feel that powerful individuals (e.g., physicians) control your health.
3. Chance health (**C**): This subscale measures whether you feel that your health is due to luck, fate, or chance.

You should now have completed four Lab Assessments. These assessments should assist you in determining the following:

1. What health behaviors you need to change to reduce your risk of illness and injury.
2. Which lifestyle changes you are *distressed* about and would like to change.
3. What barriers are preventing you from carrying out these changes in health and lifestyle activities.
4. Your perceptions of control over your health.

Now we are ready to examine ways of making changes in your health and lifestyle behaviors.

Methods for Decreasing Stressful Behaviors

One day I decided that I wanted to lose weight. This time I was going to do it! I was determined to keep to a strict diet and lose weight. I started on Monday morning. I began by writing a *contract*—a set of rules that I agreed to follow during my dieting.

I have known myself to finish off a dessert while deeply involved in a book, unaware of what or how much I was eating. Now, I separated the two activities and gained control over my eating habits. No more eating while doing something else. I discussed these plans with my partner, who agreed to give me encouragement and approval for adhering to my diet.

I also used a smaller plate. The smaller portions filled up the plate, and I did not feel that I was depriving myself. In addition, I increased the portions of the lower-calorie foods, such as salads and vegetables, and decreased the portions of the higher-calorie foods, such as meats and certain starches. If I snacked during the day, it was a piece of low-calorie fruit. If I was able to successfully follow the rules that I set down in my contract, I would reward myself by purchasing a CD at the end of the week.

The preceding account describes a diet plan that includes a number of psychological and behavioral techniques that can be used to change and modify health and lifestyle behaviors. In this section, we will examine some frequently used methods of decreasing stressful behaviors:

1. Self-monitoring
2. Tailoring
3. Material reinforcement
4. Social reinforcement
5. Social support
6. Self-contracting
7. Contracting with a significant other
8. Shaping
9. Reminders
10. Self-help groups
11. Professional help

Some of these techniques overlap and have procedures in common. However, they are listed separately in order to give emphasis to different aspects of the techniques.

Self-Monitoring

One aspect common to many of these methods involves the monitoring of behavior. **Self-monitoring** is a process of observing and recording your own behavior.[5] Suppose you are a person who tends to be late to meetings and appointments. You have good intentions, but somehow you are not able to make it on time. You may not realize how often you are late or how late you are to appointments and meetings. Self-monitoring is a method to increase your awareness of your behavior. Every time you have an appointment or a meeting, note whether you arrived on time. If you are late, note how many minutes (or hours?!) you were late. This will help you avoid being late by making you aware of just how much of a problem this behavior is. In addition, self-monitoring will provide a benchmark to compare your behavior at the point at which you began your behavioral change program with the change you have actually made. In this manner, your progress becomes, in itself, reinforcing.

self-monitoring
The process of observing and recording behavior.

Tailoring

Programs that are adapted to the specific routines, lifestyles, abilities, and unique circumstances of an individual are said to be tailored to that individual.[6,7] Let's say you find yourself under a lot of pressure and are having difficulty relaxing. You decide that you will begin a relaxation program. Someone suggests that you awake a half hour earlier and do your relaxation exercises in the morning. You awake the following Monday a half hour earlier and do your relaxation exercises. You feel tired Monday evening but continue on Tuesday, Wednesday, and Thursday mornings. You feel tired on these evenings as well and oversleep on Friday morning. The following week you oversleep on Thursday and Friday mornings and feel discouraged. What you need is **tailoring.**

Since you are not a "morning person," it would make sense to do your relaxation exercises after school or work. The program should be adapted to your particular schedule. It should be tailored to your unique characteristics and circumstances. Programs that are tailored to the specific characteristics of a person tend to be more effective. For example, if Sunday evening is a quiet time in your weekly schedule, then that would be a good time to call those people whom you have been meaning to call.

Before you initiate a behavior change program, examine your schedule and lifestyle. When is the best time to do your chores? What time must you leave in order to be on time for your appointments and meetings? When should you exercise? When is the best time to engage in relaxation?

If you consistently brush your teeth twice a day (e.g., early morning and late at night), relaxation techniques could be practiced at that time. In other words, relaxation techniques would be *paired* with teeth-brushing behavior. If you do not consistently brush your teeth twice a day, then relaxation techniques could be embedded into another part of your schedule (e.g., after work or before dinner). Tailoring offers you a way to maximize your success in a behavior change program by allowing you to fit the change into your particular circumstances.

Material Reinforcement

An important component in programs to increase healthy behavior is reinforcement, or reward.[8,9] If you remember, I stayed with my diet all week and therefore rewarded myself with a CD. The CD is, of course, **material reinforcement.** You could reward yourself (self-reward) or you could be rewarded by another. If I refrain from smoking for a week, I could buy myself a book or magazine. Or I could be in a smoking-cessation program in which I receive five dollars a week for not smoking. Other examples of material reinforcement include bonuses, commissions, clothes, tickets for a show or concert, antiques, or any other items of value. Both material and social reinforcement increase the probability of the behavior being repeated. A point to note: What is reinforcing for Jack may not be reinforcing for Jill. If a person does not like to attend folk concerts, then tickets to a folk concert are *not* a reinforcer. A reinforcer is something of value to a particular individual. Money is a powerful and useful reinforcer, because it can be exchanged for a countless number of objects that are rewarding and valued.

Social Reinforcement

Reinforcement may also take the form of social reinforcement. Another person (a friend, roommate, spouse, or coworker) can be a source of encouragement and can assist you in overcoming various hurdles. Also, this person can be a source of social reinforcement. The significant other can tell you that you are doing a good job and give you praise. Acknowledgment, praise, a pat on the back, and even a smile are forms of **social reinforcement.** Research supports the observation that social reinforcement increases the frequency of the behavior that it follows.[10]

Imagine you are trying to stop smoking. You go a full day without smoking and your roommate says, "That's great." That statement from your roommate is an example of social reinforcement. Or suppose you are at work and you take on a new assignment. The assignment turns out well, and your boss pats you on the back. You feel good about the completed assignment and take on another new assignment. In

---

tailoring
Making a behavior change program specific to the life of the individual.

material reinforcement
Rewarding a behavior with a tangible object.

social reinforcement
Rewarding a behavior with social approval by someone else.

our interactions with other people, we sometimes tell others they are doing a good job. These forms of social reinforcement are useful methods of encouraging people to continue what they are doing.

However, a word of caution should be added. What you are doing is for yourself. Therefore, do not expect a pat on the back every time you do a good job or a good deed. Your own sense of satisfaction may be all you need to continue the behavior. If you engage in regular practice of a relaxation technique, for instance, the sensation obtained and the knowledge that you are doing something that is healthy may be enough to encourage you to continue this behavior.

Social Support

A concept related to social reinforcement is social support. Social support, as noted earlier in this book, can reduce stress directly. It also can reduce stress indirectly. If you are having a difficult time trying to stay on a diet, emotional support from a trusted friend can relieve some of your stress by providing expressions of empathy, love, trust, and caring[11] to improve your coping ability and reduce stress. Informational support, another type of social support, can also help. For example, advice, suggestions, and information on how to stay on a diet can improve coping ability and relieve stress.

Self-Contracting

Once you have established a base rate for a particular behavior (e.g., I am late two out of three times), then you can create a set of rules for changing that behavior and set up a contract.[12,13] A contract takes the form of an "if-then" rule. For example, *if* I am on time to a meeting, *then* I will watch TV tonight. "Being on time to a meeting" is the behavior of interest, and "watching TV tonight" is the reward or consequence of the behavior. In addition, if I am *not* on time to a meeting today, then I will *not* watch TV tonight. I did not exhibit the desired behavior; therefore, I did not reap the reward. **Self-contracting** means that you administer your own rewards. As part of this procedure, then, you must list things that you would consider rewarding. Obviously, different things are rewarding for different people.

self-contracting
Making a contract with oneself to change a behavior.

Contracting with a Significant Other

Contracting with another person may be even more successful than self-contracting. Mahoney and Thoresen suggest five principles for contracts:

1. The contract should be fair.
2. The terms of the contract should be very clear.
3. The contract should be generally positive.
4. Procedures should be systematic and consistent.
5. At least one other person should participate.[14]

Contracts have the value of involving people in the planning of their lifestyle changes. When you actually write down which behaviors will be tied to which rewards or consequences, you will be less likely to forget about it. In addition, contracting with significant others makes the contract a *public* commitment. A **significant other** may be a spouse, a partner, a roommate, a friend, or a relative. The significant other does not necessarily have to live under the same roof. A significant other is a person who has meaning to you, in whom you can confide, and to whom you can be made accountable.

significant other
Another person who is important to an individual.

For example, you decide that you want to initiate an exercise program. You plan to jog vigorously for twenty minutes at a time, three times a week: Monday, Wednesday, and Friday. If you successfully carry out this exercise program, you will buy yourself a DVD on Saturday. You write up a contract specifying what activity (jogging for twenty

There are many ways to develop a network of social support on a college campus. You can join a campus group or organize study time with your classmates.

cold turkey
Stopping a behavior all at once.

shaping
Changing a behavior a little bit at a time.

reminder system
A means of reminding oneself to perform a particular behavior.

minutes), how frequently (three times a week: Monday, Wednesday, and Friday), and what reward (a DVD) you will receive if you successfully complete the activity. Because you are contracting with a significant other, you show your spouse or close friend your contract. You discuss the contract with your significant other, actually sign the contract in his or her presence (making a public behavioral commitment), and may have the significant other sign the contract (a witness) as well. In general, contracting has been found to be a useful technique in a variety of health and lifestyle situations.[15]

Shaping

It is difficult to go **cold turkey**—stopping the undesired behavior all at once. Therefore, programs have been established to "shape" desired behaviors. **Shaping** is the process of introducing components of a program sequentially as the individual learns and performs prior steps in the sequence.[16] The steps are graded in order of difficulty. For example, if you want to reduce your caloric intake by 1,000 calories a day, you may begin by reducing your dinner by 250 calories. Once you have successfully completed this part of the program, you may then reduce your lunch by 250 calories a day. If you want to start an exercise program, you can begin by exercising once a week for twenty minutes. Once you are able to carry out this task, you could increase your program to twice a week for thirty minutes, then three times a week for thirty minutes. Shaping has been widely used in a variety of behavioral programs.

Reminders

If you intended to save money this pay period but forgot, why not place a note on each payday on your kitchen calendar? Set up a **reminder system.** Then place a check mark on the calendar *after* you put money into your savings each pay period. A calendar that you look at each day is an ideal place to put reminder messages: Write Joe on Friday; exercise on Monday at 4:30 p.m.; call Mom on Saturday. In some cases, you could ask a significant other to remind you (as long as it does not lead to arguments or antagonisms).

Self-Help Groups

Many people with alcoholism problems have found successful solutions to their problems with self-help groups such as Alcoholics Anonymous. Other self-help groups include Gamblers Anonymous, Weight Watchers, Overeaters Anonymous, self-help drug programs, self-help psychiatric groups, self-help divorce groups, and self-help groups for battered and abused spouses and children. The self-help movement has generated numerous groups to assist people with common problems. You may be able to locate a self-help group where you live that deals with your particular concern.

Professional Help

If a self-help group is not available, then professional help is an alternative. Physicians, nurses, psychiatrists, psychologists, therapists, social workers, counselors, and health educators are available in almost every community and can assist you in health and lifestyle behavior changes.

Application of Behavior Change Techniques

To better understand the variety of techniques used to modify the stressful behaviors described in this chapter and to integrate the material presented, an illustrative example follows.

Example: Exercise

Exercise can be considered a health behavior and a lifestyle behavior. We have included it among the health behaviors because of its importance to health in such areas as cardiovascular health and weight control.

Let's say that you completed the health-behavior questionnaire (Lab 14.1), and exercise/fitness was one of the behaviors you were distressed about not engaging in regularly. You decide to change that behavior. You turn to the barriers-to-action questionnaire (Lab 14.3). The greatest barriers to exercise are time, inconvenience, and fatigue. Now you are ready to turn to the "Methods" section to decrease stressful behaviors. The first thing that you need to know is how often you exercise. If you do not exercise at all, then you already know the answer. If you exercise occasionally, then you need to *self-monitor* your exercise behavior. Observe and record the duration, frequency, and intensity of your exercise.

The next step is to write a *contract*. For example, you can state, "I will vigorously jog twenty minutes from 6:00–6:20 p.m. on Monday, Wednesday, and Friday." The contract can be either a *self-contract* or a *contract with a significant other*. Contracts with significant others are more effective because they make you accountable to another person. Therefore, let's assume that you show the contract to your spouse, partner, roommate, or close friend.

To overcome the three barriers of time, inconvenience, and fatigue, you need to *tailor* your exercise schedule to your unique circumstances. Three twenty-minute periods a week is only one hour a week. Given your time constraints, can you spare one hour a week? After or before work, you can set aside time to engage in your thrice-weekly exercise activity.

To increase the probability that you will succeed in your exercise program, *social* or *material reinforcement* should follow your exercise. Your spouse, partner, roommate, or close friend could tell you how well you are doing, and, at the end of the week, you could treat yourself to a CD, book, movie, or other reward.

If you have difficulty initiating and maintaining a thrice-weekly exercise schedule, then *shaping* might help. Start with one day a week. Once that has been successfully maintained, increase your exercise to twice a week. After that has been established, initiate a thrice-weekly program.

Decreasing Stressful Behaviors: A Guide

To assist you in making changes in your behaviors, use this guide, which is based on the material in this chapter.

1. Behavior I would like to change: _____
   _____

2. What barriers are preventing me from making these changes?
   _____
   _____

3. Techniques to decrease stressful behaviors
   a. Self-monitoring: How often do I do this behavior? _____
   b. Contract: If I do this behavior _____
      then I will receive this reward _____
   c. Significant other: Who will be witness to this contract?
      _____
   d. Tailoring: When is the best time to do this behavior? _____
      _____
      Where is the best place to do this behavior? _____
   e. Social reinforcement: Who will reward me?
      _____
      How will that person socially reward me?
      _____
   f. Material reinforcement: What type of material rewards?
      _____
   g. Shaping: I will change my behavior in steps. List the steps:
      (1) _____
      (2) _____
      (3) _____
      (4) _____
   h. Reminders: What aids can I use to remind me to do this behavior (e.g., calendar)?
      _____
   i. Self-help groups: What self-help groups are available for my particular concern?
      _____
   j. Professional help: Do I need professional help with my problem? If so, where is it
      available? _____
      _____

To maintain the program over time, use *reminders*. A note on your calendar, by your bed, on your dresser, or even taped to the bathroom mirror could be used to remind you that today is exercise day. You could also use another person to remind you that today is exercise day. If all else fails, you might ask *self-help* and *professional help groups* for assistance.

This example includes all the methods of decreasing stressful behaviors: self-monitoring, self-contracting, contracting with a significant other, tailoring, social reinforcement, material reinforcement, shaping, reminders, self-help groups, and professional groups.

Behavior Change Theories and Stress

Theories can help *explain* behavior or help in *changing* behavior. These two purposes of theory are interrelated: If we can explain why a behavior is adopted or not adopted, we can intervene and control or change that behavior. There are many theories you can employ to take charge of your stress-related behavior. A good source to consult if you want to learn about these theories of health behavior is *Health Behavior and Health Education*, edited by Karen Glanz and her colleagues (see note 2 at the end of this chapter). Several theories are presented here as examples of how behavior change theories can be helpful in coping with stress.

Stages of Change Theory

James Prochaska and his colleagues theorize that people are at different points in motivation, or readiness, to change a behavior.[17] The five stages of their stages of change theory differentiate one's readiness to change:

- *Precontemplation.* One is unaware of the problem or the need to change. Consequently, no action to change is even contemplated. For example, if you don't know the benefits of relaxation techniques, you are not likely to be thinking about engaging in them.

- *Contemplation.* One is thinking about changing a behavior but has not taken any action to do so. For example, you know that exercise is a good way to manage stress and are thinking about starting an exercise program, but not soon.

- *Decision/determination.* One actually starts planning to change the behavior. For example, you start researching stress management programs offered in your area and write to obtain their fees and schedules.

- *Action.* One implements a stress management program. For example, you start jogging every other day, and meditate daily.

- *Maintenance.* One continues the changed behavior over time. For example, you exercise at a health club throughout the year, and you continue to engage in a relaxation technique each day.

Recognizing the stage of change at which you are located will help you strategize to take charge of your stress-related behavior. If you are at the precontemplation level, you might need to begin by reading about the benefits of managing stress to motivate you to move toward engaging in stress management activities regularly. If you are at the contemplation stage, you might realize that you value stress management techniques and know that you need to start planning to engage in those activities. Perhaps the first step is to speak with someone who is knowledgeable about stress management, such as your instructor. If you are ready for the action stage, you will need to make concrete plans to exercise regularly, engage in a relaxation technique daily, change your perception of events (see the discussion on developing an attitude of gratitude in Chapter 7), and try other stress management techniques. Write down the steps you will take and the dates by which you will take them. Again, your instructor might be a good resource to help you develop your plan. If you are at the action stage, keep a journal to monitor changes in your pulse rate, days in which you experience perceived stress, days in which you exercise and engage in a relaxation technique, and other stress-related variables. In that way, you will be reinforcing the continuation of your healthy coping behavior. Lastly, if you have been coping with stress effectively and are at the maintenance stage of change, you could schedule your exercise and relaxation times—for example, in your date book—or place reminders to engage in these and other stress-related activities on your refrigerator.

Self-Efficacy Theory

Self-efficacy is the amount of confidence an individual has about performing a particular task or activity. The greater your confidence that you can carry out an activity, including overcoming any barriers, the greater is the likelihood that you will actually perform that activity. According to Albert Bandura,[18] the more confident an individual is in his or her ability to stop smoking, the greater is the probability that that person will actually quit. Self-efficacy is important because it influences how much effort you will put into performing a task and the level of your performance. According to self-efficacy theory, people's beliefs about their capabilities are a better predictor of their accomplishments than are their actual knowledge, skills, or past accomplishments.

Because self-efficacy is so important, the question arises as to how one can increase one's confidence or self-efficacy in performing healthy behaviors. Bandura describes four ways to increase self-efficacy:

1. *Performance attainment.* Nothing succeeds like success. The most effective method of improving self-efficacy is successfully carrying out an activity. If you were able to exercise, even for a short time yesterday, then you will have more confidence that you can exercise today. If you do well on your first exam, then you will have greater confidence (self-efficacy) that you will do well on your next one. Recall from our description of shaping that breaking a complex behavior into small steps makes change possible.

2. *Vicarious experience.* All of us are influenced by observing other people. If we see someone similar to ourselves overcome an alcohol problem, we are more likely to believe (i.e., have greater confidence) that we too can overcome a similar problem. Being exposed to successful models who are similar to us and accomplish goals or overcome obstacles similar to ours is a very powerful tool for increasing self-efficacy.

3. *Verbal persuasion.* This approach is commonly used to encourage individuals to make changes in their health practices. People are assured that they have the ability to make changes in their own lives. "You can do it!" Though limited in its ability to produce long-lasting changes, verbal persuasion can bolster a person's confidence.

4. *Physiological state.* We receive information from our physiological state when determining our level of stress. If you feel very anxious (e.g., you have sweaty palms) about a situation, you are not likely to feel confident about doing well in that situation. If you are perspiring heavily and shaking before an audition, you are not likely to feel confident about doing well at the audition. By learning to relax, you can reduce stress and increase your self-efficacy.

The Theory of Reasoned Action and the Theory of Planned Behavior

These two theories shed light on what motivates individuals to engage in particular behaviors. The theory of reasoned action is concerned with the relationship among attitudes, norms, intentions, and behavior. It was formulated by Martin Fishbein[19] to increase understanding of why individuals' actions (behaviors) differ from their beliefs (attitudes): "I think that smoking is bad, yet I smoke." "I think that it is smart to exercise, yet I can't seem to get into an exercise program."

According to the theory of reasoned action, the best predictors of our behaviors are not our attitudes but our behavioral intentions. *Behavioral intention* is the perceived likelihood of performing a behavior. If you want to predict or understand whether Danielle will stop smoking, you need to ask Danielle not whether she thinks that smoking is disgusting but whether she will stop smoking on a specific date (such as within the next thirty days). You need to ask her what is the likelihood that she will stop smoking by, for example, May 11. Behavioral intentions are strong predictors of actions. The greater Danielle's commitment to carrying out a behavior is, the greater is the likelihood that she will carry it out.

According to the theory of reasoned action, two factors influence our behavioral intentions. One of them is our *attitude toward the behavior,* not our attitude toward a specific objective. What is important, for example, is not whether I think that eating five fruits and vegetables a day is desirable, but whether I think that *my* eating five fruits and vegetable a day is desirable. If we want to make changes in our behaviors and reduce stressful situations, we need to understand our own attitudes toward engaging in specific behaviors. How do I feel about *my* smoking, *my* alcohol use, or *my* sexual activities?

The other factor that, according to the theory of reasoned action, influences behavioral intentions is *subjective norms*. A subjective norm is our perception of whether most of the people who are important to us approve or disapprove of our behavior. Do most of the people who are important to me think that I should join an exercise program in the next thirty days? It is far easier to make a change in my behavior if most of the people who are important to me support that action.

Fishbein's theory assumes that individuals have control over their actions: If they intend to engage in an activity, they will be able to carry out that activity. However, situations may arise in which people do not have a large degree of control. For example, environmental factors such as lack of money or availability may prevent a person from eating five fruits and vegetables a day. Recognizing such limitations, Icek Ajzen formulated the theory of planned behavior.[20,21] To Fishbein's theory, Ajzen added a factor that he called *perceived behavioral control,* an individual's perception of whether he or she has control over a particular situation. This perception influences both a person's behavioral intention to engage in a behavior and his or her actual behavior. According to the theory of planned behavior, to make a healthy behavioral change it is important not only to intend to make the change but also to perceive that you have control over the situation.

Theories of behavior change can help you take charge of your stress-related behaviors. Now it is up to you to do so. The information in this chapter can help you be less distressed over behaviors you wish to change but have not been able to eliminate. Try these methods. Modify them to fit your circumstances, and continue your search for better health and a satisfying lifestyle.

summary

- By decreasing stressful behaviors and increasing healthy behaviors, you can better manage the stress in your life.

- To decrease stressful behaviors, it is useful to identify the barriers that prevent changing these behaviors. Once the barriers are identified, strategies can be developed to eliminate or reduce them.

- Perceptions of control over your health influence whether you engage in healthy behaviors. If you perceive you have control over your health, you are more apt to engage in healthy behaviors than if you believe your health is a function of luck, chance, fate, or powerful others.

- Self-monitoring is observing and recording your behavior. Self-monitoring health and lifestyle behaviors can increase your awareness of your behavior, which is the first step in decreasing stressful behaviors.

- Tailoring a health-behavior program offers a way to maximize your success by allowing you to fit the program into your particular circumstances.

- The use of material and social reinforcement, or rewards, increases the likelihood that healthy behaviors will be repeated.

- Self-contracting and contracting with a significant other formalizes a commitment to engage in a particular behavior. Contracts have proven to be an effective means of decreasing stressful behaviors.

- Shaping a behavior is the gradual introduction of various components of a program. This technique is particularly helpful when a person has difficulty carrying out a total program—for example, a weight control or exercise program. A reminder system can also be helpful.

- Self-help groups have been formed to offer emotional support and information to individuals with similar health and lifestyle problems. Professional help has also been found valuable in assisting people to decrease their stressful behavior.

- There are several behavior change theories that can be used to explain and change health behavior. Among these are stages of change theory, self-efficacy theory, theory of reasoned action, and theory of planned behavior.

- The stages of change theory postulates people are at different points in motivation to change. These points—stages of readiness to change—are precontemplation, contemplation, decision/determination, action, and maintenance.

- Self-efficacy theory states that the more confident people are that they can perform a behavior, termed their *self-efficacy,* the more likely they are to perform that behavior.

- The theory of reasoned action recognizes that behavior is a result of attitudes, norms, and intentions. Behavioral intent, the perceived likelihood of performing the behavior, has been shown to be the best predictor of the behavior actually being performed.

- The theory of planned behavior adds the construct *perceived behavioral control* to the theory of reasoned action. People's perceptions of whether they have control over situations influences their intent to engage in a particular behavior.

notes

1. Stanislav V. Kasl and Sidney Cobb, "Health Behavior, Illness Behavior, and Sick-Role Behavior," *Archives of Environmental Health* 12(1966): 246–66.

2. Karen Glanz, Barbara K. Rimer, and Frances Marcus Lewis (eds.), *Health Behavior and Health Education* (San Francisco: Jossey-Bass, 2002).

3. Melody P. Noland and Robert H. L. Feldman, "An Empirical Investigation of Exercise Behavior in Adult Women," *Health Education* 16(1985): 29–33.

4. Kenneth A. Wallston, Barbara S. Wallston, and Robert DeVillis, "Development of the Multidimensional Health Locus of Control (MHLC) Scales," *Health Education Monographs* 6(1978): 160–70.

5. Jodi S. Holtrop and Amy Slonim, "Sticking to It: A Multifactor Cancer Risk-Reduction Program for Low-Income Clients," *Journal of Health Education* 31(2000): 122–27.

6. Jerrold S. Greenberg, George B. Dintiman, and Barbee Myers Oakes, *Physical Fitness and Wellness,* 3rd ed. (Champaign, IL: Human Kinetics, 2004).

7. Judith K. Ockene et al., "Relapse and Maintenance Issues for Smoking Cessation," *Health Psychology* 19(2000): 17–31.

8. Robert H. L. Feldman, "The Assessment and Enhancement of Health Compliance in the Workplace," in *Occupational Health Promotion: Health Behavior in the Workplace,* ed. George S. Everly and Robert H. L. Feldman (New York: John Wiley & Sons, 1985), 33–46.

9. Kerry S. Courneya, Paul A. Estabrooks, and Claudio R. Nigg, "A Simple Reinforcement Strategy for Increasing Attendance at a Fitness Facility," *Health Education and Health Behavior* 2(1997): 708–15.

10. Rena R. Wing and Robert W. Jeffery, "Benefits of Recruiting Participants with Friends and Increasing Social Support for Weight Loss and Maintenance," *Journal of Consulting and Clinical Psychology* 67(1999): 132–38.

11. Teresa E. Seeman, Tina M. Lusignolo, Marilyn Albert, and Lisa Beckman, "Social Relationships, Social Support, and Patterns of Cognitive Aging in Healthy, High-Functioning Older Adults: MacArthur Studies of Successful Aging," *Health Psychology* 20(2001): 243–255.

12. C. Feingold and L. J. Perlich, "Teaching Critical Thinking Through a Health-Contract," *Nurse Education* 24(1999): 42–44.

13. Vicki S. Coon, Jeffrey C. Valentine, and Harris M. Cooper, "Interventions to Increase Physical Activity Among Aging Adults," *Annals of Behavioral Medicine* 24(2002): 190–200.

14. M. J. Mahoney and C. E. Thoresen, *Self-Control: Power to the Person* (Monterey, CA: Brooks/Cole, 1974).

15. F. L. Greenway, G. A. Bray, and R. L. Marlin, "Methods to Maximize Retention in Weight Loss Studies," *Obesity Research* 7(1999): 593–96.

16. Shiriki K. Kumanyika, "Maintenance of Dietary Behavior Change," *Health Psychology* 19(2000): 42–56.

17. James Prochaska, C. C. DiClemente, and J. D. Norcross, "In Search of How People Change, Applications to Addictive Behaviors," *American Psychologist* 47(1992): 1102–14.

18. Albert Bandura, *Self-Efficacy: The Exercise of Control* (New York: W. H. Freeman, 1997).

19. Icek Ajzen and Martin Fishbein, *Understanding Attitudes and Predicting Social Behavior* (Englewood Cliffs, NJ: Prentice-Hall, 1980).

20. Icek Ajzen, "The Theory of Planned Behavior," *Organizational Behavior and Human Decision Process* 50(1991): 179–211.

21. Derek W. Johnston, Marie Johnston, Beth Pollard, Ann-Louise Kinmonth, and David Mant, "Motivation Is Not Enough: Prediction of Risk Behavior Following Diagnosis of Coronary Heart Disease from the Theory of Planned Behavior," *Health Psychology* 23(2004): 533–538.

internet resources

Stress Management
www.pp.okstate.edu/ehs/links/stress.htm
Online library of stress management links.

Stress Cure
www.stresscure.com
Contains a Health Resource Network for general stress information as well as strategies for coping with stress.

The American Institute of Stress
www.stress.org
The AIS is a nonprofit organization that is committed to helping advance knowledge of the role of stress in health and disease. It is a clearinghouse for information on all stress-related subjects.

Coping in Today's World

To take charge of your behavior in today's potentially stressful world, you can use the Health Belief Model as a guide, which states that people will change their health behavior if

- They believe they are *susceptible* to an illness or disease.
- They believe the consequences of contracting that illness or disease can be serious or *severe.*
- They perceive the health behavior has *benefits* and can be effective in preventing that illness or disease.
- They perceive themselves capable of *overcoming barriers* to performing the health behavior.
- They perceive themselves capable of performing the health behavior that will prevent contracting the illness or disease (this is termed *self-efficacy*).
- They develop *cues to action,* encouraging them to perform the health behavior.

Let's use regularly engaging in a relaxation technique—meditation—as an example:

- If you believe you are *susceptible* to serious (*severity*) illnesses such as coronary heart disease or hypertension if you do not regularly meditate, you will be more apt to meditate.
- If you believe that meditation can be effective (has the *benefit*) to prevent developing these severe illnesses to which you are susceptible, you will be more apt to meditate.
- If you believe that you can remove *barriers* to meditating (such as having a busy schedule that makes it difficult to find the time to meditate) and can, therefore, meditate regularly (you feel *self-efficacious*), you will be more apt to meditate.
- If you are willing to provide *cues to action* that encourage meditating (e.g., placing reminders to meditate on your bathroom mirror or writing it in your schedule book), you will be more apt to meditate.

Choose a stress-related health behavior you wish to adopt, and apply the Health Belief Model to enhance the chances you will be successful adopting that behavior.

LAB ASSESSMENT 14.1
Are Your Behaviors Healthy?

This is not a pass-fail test. The purpose of the questionnaire is simply to tell you how well you are doing at staying healthy. Some of the behaviors covered in the test may not apply to persons with certain chronic diseases or disabilities. Such persons may require special instructions from their physician or other health professional.

Directions: The questionnaire has six sections: safety; alcohol, tobacco, and other drugs; sexual behavior; eating habits; exercise/fitness; and stress control. Complete one section at a time by circling the number corresponding to the answer that best describes your behavior. Then add the numbers you have circled to determine your score for that section. Write the score on the line provided at the end of each section. The highest score you can get for each section is 100.

Safety

Within the **last school year,** how often did you:

(Please mark the appropriate column for each row)

	N/A didn't do this within the last 12 months	Never	Rarely	Sometimes	Most of the time	Always
	5	1	2	3	4	5
Wear a seatbelt when you rode in a car?	○	○	○	○	○	○
Wear a helmet when you rode a bicycle?	○	○	○	○	○	○
Wear a helmet when you rode a motorcycle?	○	○	○	○	○	○
Wear a helmet when you were inline skating?	○	○	○	○	○	○

total _____

Multiply total by 5: Safety score _____

Alcohol, Tobacco, and Other Drugs

Within the **last 30 days,** on how many days did you use:

(Please mark the appropriate column for each row)

	Never used	Have used, but not in last 30 days	1-2 days	3-5 days	6-9 days	10-19 days	20-29 days	All 30 days
	11	10	9	8	7	6	5	4
Cigarettes	○	○	○	○	○	○	○	○
Cigars	○	○	○	○	○	○	○	○
Smokeless tobacco	○	○	○	○	○	○	○	○
Alcohol (beer, wine, liquor)	○	○	○	○	○	○	○	○
Marijuana (pot, hash, hash oil)	○	○	○	○	○	○	○	○
Cocaine (crack, rock, freebase)	○	○	○	○	○	○	○	○
Amphetamines (diet pills, speed, meth, crank)	○	○	○	○	○	○	○	○
Rohypnol (roofies), GHB, or Liquid X (intentional use)	○	○	○	○	○	○	○	○
Other drugs	○	○	○	○	○	○	○	○

Alcohol, Tobacco, and Drugs score _____

Sexual Behavior

Within the **last 30 days,** if you are sexually active and unmarried, how often did you or your partner(s) use a condom during:

(Please mark the appropriate column for each row)

	Never did this sexual activity	Have not done this during last 30 days	Never	Rarely	Sometimes	Mostly	Always
	10	10	2	4	6	8	10
Oral sex?	○	○	○	○	○	○	○
Vaginal intercourse?	○	○	○	○	○	○	○
Anal intercourse?	○	○	○	○	○	○	○

total _____

Multiply total by 3: Sexual Behavior score _____

Continued

Eating Habits

How many servings of fruits and vegetables do you usually have **per day** (1 serving = 1 medium piece of fruit, 1/2 cup chopped, cooked, or canned fruits/vegetables, 3/4 cup fruit/vegetable juice, small bowl of salad greens, or 1/2 cup dried fruit)?

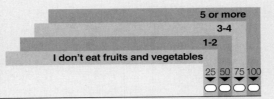

5 or more
3-4
1-2
I don't eat fruits and vegetables

25 50 75 100

Eating Habits score _____

Exercise/Fitness

On how many of the **past 7 days** did you:

(Please mark the appropriate column for each row)

	0 days	1 day	2 days	3 days	4 days	5 days	6 days	7 days
	3	4	5	6	7	8	9	10
Participate in vigorous exercise for at least 20 minutes or moderate exercise for at least 30 minutes?	◯	◯	◯	◯	◯	◯	◯	◯
Do exercises to strengthen or tone your muscles, such as push-ups, sit-ups, or weightlifting?	◯	◯	◯	◯	◯	◯	◯	◯
Get enough sleep so that you felt rested when you woke up in the morning?	◯	◯	◯	◯	◯	◯	◯	◯

total _____

Multiply total by 3: Exercise/Fitness score _____

Stress Control

(Please mark the appropriate column for each row)

	Never	Rarely	Sometimes	Often	Always
		1	2	3	4
I have a job or do other work that I enjoy.		◯	◯	◯	◯
I find it easy to relax and express my feelings freely.		◯	◯	◯	◯
I recognize early, and prepare for, events or situations likely to be stressful for me.		◯	◯	◯	◯
I have close friends, relatives, or others whom I can talk to about personal matters and call on for help when needed.		◯	◯	◯	◯
I participate in group activities (such as community organizations) or hobbies that I enjoy.		◯	◯	◯	◯

Multiply total by 5: Stress Control score _____

Scoring: There is no total score for this questionnaire. Consider each section separately. You are trying to identify aspects of your health behavior that you can improve in order to be healthier and to reduce the risk of illness. Let's see what your scores reveal.

Scores of 80–100

Excellent! Your answers show that you are aware of the importance of this area to your health. More important, you are putting your knowledge to work by practicing good health habits. As long as you continue to do so, this area should not pose a serious health risk. It's likely that you are setting an example for your family and friends to follow. Since you got a very high score on this part of the questionnaire, you may want to consider other areas where your scores indicate room for improvement.

Scores of 60–79

Your health practices in this area are good, but there is room for improvement. Look again at the items you answered with "sometimes" or "almost never." What changes can you make to improve your score? Even a small change can often help you achieve better health.

Scores of 40–59

Your health may be at risk. Would you like more information about the risks you are facing and the reasons why it is important for you to change these behaviors? Perhaps you need help in deciding how to make the changes you desire. In either case, help is available.

Scores of 0–39

You may be taking serious and unnecessary risks with your health. Perhaps you are not aware of the risks and what to do about them. You can easily get the information and help you need to improve.

LAB ASSESSMENT 14.2

Are Your Lifestyle Behaviors Healthy?

Directions: Use the scale below to describe how often you engage in the behaviors listed.

2 = almost always
1 = sometimes
0 = almost never

_____ 1. I go out and meet new people.

_____ 2. I am able to ask for help from others.

_____ 3. I listen intently to other people.

_____ 4. I am able to communicate with others.

_____ 5. I avoid needless arguments.

_____ 6. I am able to say I am sorry.

_____ 7. I spend time with friends.

_____ 8. I am punctual in writing friends.

_____ 9. I play a musical instrument.

_____ 10. I participate in artistic activities.

_____ 11. I participate in sports.

_____ 12. I travel to different places.

_____ 13. I am involved with hobbies.

_____ 14. I do volunteer work for worthwhile causes.

_____ 15. I am not afraid to try something new.

_____ 16. I enjoy talking in front of groups of people.

_____ 17. I am on time for meetings and appointments.

_____ 18. I do my work/studying on time.

_____ 19. I punctually do my day-to-day chores.

_____ 20. I am able to save money.

Once you have completed this questionnaire, examine the items for which you chose 0. From those items, choose two lifestyle behaviors that may cause you stress and that you would like to change. Use the strategies presented in this chapter to help you make that change.

LAB ASSESSMENT 14.3

What Are Your Barriers to Behaving Healthfully?

Directions: Below are listed a number of possible factors—barriers—that may have kept *you* from engaging in certain health and lifestyle behaviors. Choose one health or lifestyle behavior you would like to change and, for each item on the questionnaire, circle a number from 1 to 7 that represents the degree to which that factor is a barrier to your adopting this behavior.

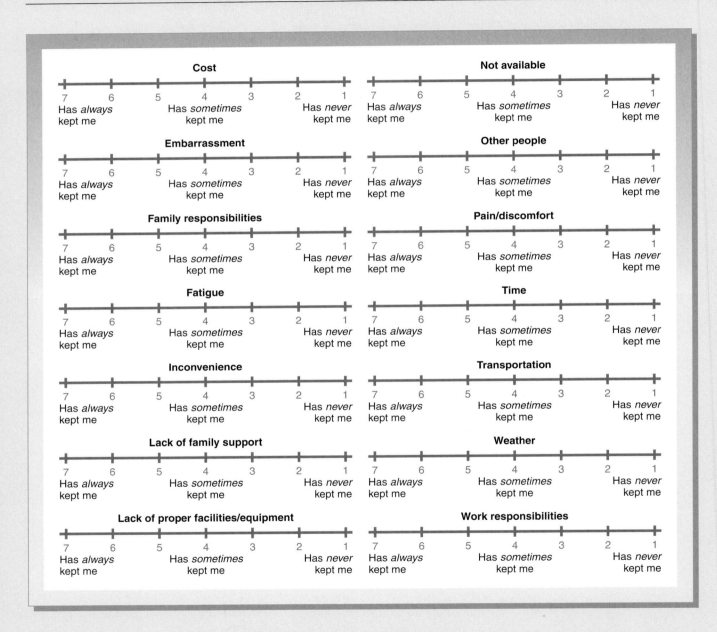

You now have information concerning some barriers and obstacles that have impeded your adopting certain health and lifestyle behaviors. The items for which you circled 7, 6, or 5 are major obstacles to performing the particular behavior that you are interested in changing. Use this information when we examine methods of changing behaviors that are stressful to you.

LAB ASSESSMENT 14.4

How Much Control Do You Have?

This assessment measures three subscales of locus of control:

1. Internal health (**I**): This subscale measures whether you feel that you have personal control over your health.

2. Powerful others health (**P**): This subscale measures whether you feel that powerful individuals (e.g., physicians) control your health.

3. Chance health (**C**): This subscale measures whether you feel that your health is due to luck, fate, or chance.

Directions: Use the scale below to designate in how much agreement you are with each statement.

5 = strongly agree

4 = agree

3 = neither agree nor disagree

2 = disagree

1 = strongly disagree

Internal Health Locus of Control

_____ 1. If I get sick, it is my own behavior that determines how soon I get well.

_____ 2. I am in control of my health.

_____ 3. When I get sick, I am to blame.

_____ 4. The main thing that affects my health is what I, myself, do.

_____ 5. If I take care of myself, I can avoid illness.

_____ 6. If I take the right actions, I can stay healthy.

Powerful Others Health Locus of Control

_____ 1. Having regular contact with my physician is the best way for me to avoid illness.

_____ 2. Whenever I don't feel well, I should consult a medically trained professional.

_____ 3. My family has a lot to do with my becoming sick or staying healthy.

_____ 4. Health professionals control my health.

_____ 5. When I recover from an illness, it's usually because other people (e.g., doctors, nurses, family, and friends) have been taking good care of me.

_____ 6. Regarding my health, I can do only what my doctor tells me to do.

Chance Health Locus of Control

_____ 1. No matter what I do, if I am going to get sick, I will get sick.

_____ 2. Most things that affect my health happen to me by accident.

_____ 3. Luck plays a big part in determining how soon I will recover from an illness.

_____ 4. My good health is largely a matter of good fortune.

_____ 5. No matter what I do, I'm likely to get sick.

_____ 6. If it's meant to be, I will stay healthy.

Scoring: To obtain your score for a subscale, add the numbers you chose in that subscale.

1. A score of 23–30 on any subscale means you have a strong inclination to that particular dimension. For example, a high **C** score indicates you hold strong beliefs that your health is a matter of chance.

2. A score of 15–22 means you are moderate on that particular dimension. For example, a moderate **P** score indicates you have moderate belief that your health is due to powerful others.

3. A score of 6–14 means you are low on that particular dimension. For example, a low **I** score means that you generally do not believe that you personally control your health.

If you scored _high_ on the internal health locus-of-control scale and low or moderate on the powerful others and chance scales, you are a person who feels that your health is basically under your control. If you scored _moderately_ on internal health locus of control, you are a person who feels that sometimes your health is under your control and sometimes it is not. For the moderately internal individual, the scores on the powerful others and chance scales determine the relative weight of these other two dimensions.

If you scored _low_ on the internal health locus-of-control scale, you are a person who feels that you do not have control over your own health. Your scores on the powerful others and chance scales determine the relative influence of these other two dimensions. If you scored relatively high on the powerful others scale and moderate to low on the other two scales, you are a person who feels that powerful others (e.g., physicians) control your health. If you scored relatively high on the chance scale and moderate to low on the other two scales, you are a person who feels that chance, fate, or luck determines your health status.

You should have gained insight into your perceptions of control over your health. We neither have complete control nor lack of complete control over life outcomes. As we learn how to gain greater control over aspects of our environment, we will be able to make changes in stressful behaviors.

What do you know, Jew boy?" That's what my son heard from a classmate on the school bus in junior high school. After we notified the school—hate crimes and discriminatory acts were especially targeted that school year—and had a discussion with that student's parents, we were assured that comment would not be made again. Still, there was no way to assure my son that he would not be the object of other acts of prejudice—for example, when he wanted to rush a fraternity or when he went after a job he desired.

My son cannot be visually identified as Jewish (although his last name does the job pretty well—Greenberg has never been mistaken as Irish), so he might escape prejudice he would otherwise experience. Imagine the potential for prejudice and discrimination when someone is physically, and therefore visually, identifiable as a minority—African American, Native American, Asian American, or Hispanic, for example. I recently returned from a trip to Japan, where I was easily recognized as "different" from the typical Japanese. I experienced, for the first time, what many minorities experience every day.

This chapter considers the relationship between diversity and stress. We consider such factors as health, poverty, education, and family structure as they relate to race and ethnicity, cultural background, gender, age, and disabilities. We begin with the realization that membership in a minority group often comes with a cost. It is frequently associated with poorer health, lower education, lower socioeconomic status, higher unemployment, and an atypical family structure. Of course, many people of color, elderly, and people with disabilities excel—but often against tremendous odds. Certainly, they are the exceptions, but they are also sources of hope, especially to young people who come from similar backgrounds and circumstances and are motivated to make themselves successful. There is no denying the burden associated with being considered a minority in the United States, but that those of you who are minorities are not inevitably heading toward a disadvantaged future. Although you may unjustly be swimming upstream, there are role models who have swum ahead of you and who are now on the banks of the river, enjoying the rewards of their effort.

"Minority" Defined

Let's get specific about what is meant by the term *minority*. The necessity of this task becomes clear when we realize that women are often grouped into this category, although they make up the majority of U.S. citizens. Furthermore, when other minority populations are grouped together, they constitute a significant segment of our society today and, it is expected, will constitute an even greater percentage of the population in years to come. For example, the Census Bureau reported that in 2000 the U.S. population was distributed as follows:

White 75.1%	**Hispanic 12.5%**
African American 12.3%	**Native American 0.9%**
Asian American 3.6%	

Here are the projections for the year 2050:

White 52.5%	**Hispanic 22.5%**
African American 14.4%	**Native American 0.9%**
Asian American 9.7%	

You can see how the population is projected to change. In fact, by the year 2010 it is expected that Hispanics will far outdistance African Americans as the largest minority group in the United States. Other changes will occur as well. The population will increase by 52 percent by 2050 to a whopping 392 million. Eighty million of these U.S. citizens will be older than sixty-five. That is approximately 20 percent of the population (as compared with 12.5 percent today). And there will be an additional 26 million children under eighteen years of age by the year 2050, comprising 23 percent of the population.

Webster's New World College Dictionary defines *minority* as "a racial, religious, or ethnic, or political group smaller than and differing from the larger, controlling group in the community, nation, etc."[1] That definition leads to the need to define *race* and *ethnicity*.[2] **Race** distinguishes people by a variety of variables such as physical traits (e. g., hair, eyes, skin color), blood types, genetic patterns, and inherited characteristics unique to a population. The three primary racial divisions are Caucasoid, Negroid, and Mongoloid. **Ethnicity** refers to a group having a common heritage as distinguished by customs, characteristics, language, and a common history. Hispanic is an example of an ethnic group.

Now that seems to be fairly straightforward; however, it is anything but. For example, Hispanic is a term of convenience used by the government to classify people. The reason for this classification is to be able to serve specific needs of specific populations. So, for example, if data indicate a specific health problem among that ethnic group, early intervention is possible. The problem is that these ethnic terms are often too encompassing. Relative to the Hispanic population in the United States, there is quite a difference in culture, education, health status, and so on, between those originally from Peru, for example, and those from Mexico, or those from El Salvador and those from Bolivia. The same can be said of the Asian American population. Asian Americans from Japan differ from Asian Americans from China, or Korea, or Vietnam.

That having been said, the problem I faced in writing this chapter can be better understood, and the limitations better appreciated. The data presented in this chapter comply with governmental categories for the sake of convenience; they are the only kinds of data available. When the data can be made more specific, they are presented that way.

For the purposes of this chapter, minority populations include African Americans, Hispanics, Asian Americans, Native Americans, the elderly, and people with disabilities. You might argue that a particular population has been omitted (e.g., children) or that one included should be deleted, but someone had to make a judgment as to what was feasible for this chapter, given its space limitations and focus. In this case, that someone was me. Still, if you are interested in learning more about these minority populations or others, you can consult the works cited in the "Notes" section at the end of this chapter.

Positive Aspects of Minority Status

In this section, a discussion of the health status of minorities is presented. As you will learn, in general, minorities experience poorer health, greater poverty, poorer education, and a range of unique problems. That can be depressing and, if you are a member of a minority group, disturbing. But not to be lost in this chapter on diversity are the major contributions of minority groups to the health and well-being of all of us.

If we were to look at the Asian American community, for example, we could point to acupuncture's adoption by the medical establishment as a mainstream practice and the contribution that has made to the health of Americans of many different ethnic, racial, cultural, and religious backgrounds. Or we could point to the introduction of herbal medicines, or use of such relaxation techniques as meditation, or many other contributions that have enhanced American life. The respect for authority, the value for education, self-discipline, adoption of modesty, and the sense of responsibility toward the elderly are examples of other contributions made by Asian Americans to their own community and models of behavior for other Americans.

race

A group of people with similar physical traits, blood types, genetic patterns, and inherited characteristics.

ethnicity

A group of people having a common heritage such as common customs, characteristics, language, and history.

Native Americans have helped us understand the concept of holism that has sprung into the holistic movement. Harmony and health have long been concepts embraced by Native Americans.[3] They helped the rest of us recognize that all things are physical, spiritual, emotional, and social, and that to remain healthy, there needs to be harmony (balance) among them. Furthermore, this sense of harmony translates into a belief in the oneness with all things—that is, harmony with others and with the universe. The concern for the environment, a traditional focus of Native Americans, can be seen as stemming from this worldview.

Culture can have significant effects on families. Asian American families, for example, are noted for close family ties and value of educational achievement.

Latinos have demonstrated to the rest of us the value of social and family support. Although this sometimes turns into a deficit (e.g., when medical care is not sought early enough and, instead, family members' advice is relied on), Latino families often feel responsible for one another, make themselves available to one another, and protect one another from potentially harmful elements (such as homelessness). And the family to which they feel connected is an extended one (aunts, uncles, cousins, etc.). It would not be unusual, for example, to find a Hispanic family, without much room in their home for their own family, housing immigrant family members new to the United States. In addition, the spiritual aspects of health, the importance of which recent empirical studies support, has always been at the forefront in the Latino community. The church is a central part of daily life and a resource during stressful times.

Similar to Latinos, for African Americans, the church plays a major function in the community. African Americans often participate in the activities of the church by serving on various committees and contributing to community service efforts. These kinds of institutions and the activities they organize and the support they provide contribute a great deal toward managing stress. Churches provide emotional support and often provide resources as well (e.g., financial assistance). These institutions, their congregants, and their activities provide a model that the rest of the population would be wise to emulate. The value placed on enjoying one's life through activities such as sports, the arts, and social interactions is another contribution that African Americans make to our society. It has been stated repeatedly in this book that stress management requires a comprehensive approach. That point is so important that the word *comprehensive* appears in the title. Certainly, African Americans appreciate this point and model its value for the rest of us.

An Introduction to the Descriptions of Problems Faced by Minorities

One of the reviewers of this chapter suggested it is too negative—that is, too many disturbing statistics are presented and problems are emphasized. If that is the case, I offer no apology. It angers me that minorities in the greatest country in the world suffer disproportionately from poor health, poverty, low educational levels, infant mortality, crime and violence, and so forth. I present the data that follow without sugarcoating the reality of what they mean. And that meaning is that minorities in the United States of America, and probably elsewhere in the world, are disadvantaged in significant ways that result in a great deal of stress.

Stressors Challenging Minorities

Minorities experience stressors that create unique challenges for them and that affect their health. In fact, minorities report higher levels of stress than white adults. In one study, the Commonwealth Fund conducted a survey and found 36 percent of minorities reported high levels of stress, whereas only 26 percent of white adults reported such high levels of stress.[4] The stressors found particularly higher for minorities than for white adults concerned money (25 percent versus 17 percent), fear of crime or violence (18 percent versus 8 percent), their spouse or partner (11 percent versus 6 percent), and mistreatment of a family member for race or cultural reasons (5 percent versus less than 0.5 percent). Furthermore, minorities were more likely to have been physically assaulted than Caucasians sometime within the past five years (12 percent versus 9 percent).

Racism

Among the most significant of these stressors is racism. Racial prejudice rests on the belief that one's own race is superior to another's race. Among the myriad effects of racism are anger, stroke, heart attack, and a number of other diseases associated with high blood pressure, as well as cancer.[5]

Culture Conflicts

When someone leaves one culture and enters another, there is a need to "fit in." The immigrant seeks to learn the new cultural standards of behavior and the new reward system in order to be successful in the new environment. Complicating this difficult transition is the realization that some of the new culture's standards are at odds with the norms and values of the native culture. When that is the case, what should be the adaptation strategy? Ignore the new culture's standards and norms, and remain faithful to the the familiar traditional standards and norms? By way of example, some Asian cultures value obedience and respect and teach these traits to their children. However, when Asians emigrate to the United States—a culture that values independence, assertiveness, and competitiveness—the traits they were taught to value are not those that will facilitate their becoming fully acculturated and successful. They are caught in a clash of cultures.

Culture clashes can occur in a number of different ways. Irujo presented some examples of common culture clashes that occur in the United States:[6]

> Not looking another person in the eye is a recognition of that person's authority for African-Americans, while whites interpret this as shiftiness and unreliability.
> Differences in gaze behavior may cause some misunderstandings. Latinos interpret a direct gaze as having sexual connotations, and a steady stare with raised eyebrows as anger.
> Africans, Arabs, and Hispanic Americans touch a great deal in interpersonal relationships, whereas in Britain, Japan, and the United States there is very little touching. Touching in certain circumstances causes embarrassment and discomfort.

Culture clash was evident in a poll of Latinos conducted by the *Washington Post* in collaboration with the Henry J. Kaiser Foundation and Harvard University.[7] More than 2,000 Latinos, and a comparable number of non-Hispanic whites and African Americans who were used for comparison purposes, were interviewed regarding their views and lifestyles. Nearly 90 percent stated they believed it was important to maintain their native culture, and almost 60 percent said they had little or nothing in common with Anglos or African Americans. Most also believed that discrimination directed toward Latinos was a significant problem. Imagine trying to succeed in a culture you perceive in this way.

Acculturation Stressors

As has been shown, entering a new culture often requires a great deal of adaptation, which often results in stress and ill health. That may explain the higher blood pressure, mental illness, and higher rates of attempted suicide among immigrants when compared with the population in their country of origin.[8] One of these adaptations relates to language. Language barriers can interfere with obtaining employment, or result in menial jobs with low salaries. This is in spite of many immigrants having been highly educated and respected professionals in their original countries.[9] The resulting low self-esteem is only one of the effects of this situation. Another is the need to work long hours to support a family, necessitating being away from the family and the supervision and upbringing of children. For example, although Asian Americans are thought to be one of the most economically successful minority groups in America, they receive less income per education than white workers, requiring them to work longer hours for the same rewards.[10] Like a chain reaction, when the parents are away from home working long hours, the children may suffer the consequences.

Children usually acculturate faster than their parents. Their original culture is not as ingrained, and children tend to be more malleable in general. When children become "Americanized" and their parents adjust more slowly, clashes often occur within families. For example, children may want to be more independent than their original culture allowed, or they may want to wear clothing that reveals more of the body than their country of origin found acceptable, or they may not want to speak their native language at home, preferring to speak English. However, their parents may feel quite differently and remain steadfast in requiring their children to behave in a manner consistent with their traditional cultural standards and values. Both children and parents may feel the effects of this stress.

Other Acculturation Stressors

In addition to language, employment, and family cultural clashes, minorities often live in inner cities, where they may experience a particular type of prejudice For example, police may disproportionately target minorities in traffic stops—in spite of the fact that such profiling is unconstitutional—or inquire about their presence in "upscale" neighborhoods.

hate crimes
Crimes against people based on their race, ethnicity, sexual orientation, or religion.

In addition, crime and violence are more prevalent in the inner cities and are therefore encountered disproportionately by minorities. A subset of crime is crimes against people on the basis of their race, ethnicity, sexual orientation, or religion. These are called **hate crimes.** Unfortunately, hate crimes are additional stressors with which minorities must cope. In 2003, 53 percent of hate crimes were racially motivated: 66 percent against African Americans, 21 percent against whites, 6 percent against Asian Americans, 2 percent against American Indians, and 2 percent against others.[11]

These stressors that challenge minorities have the potential to have an effect physiologically and psychologically, as do all stressors. We next explore the health-related implications of stress for minority individuals and minority communities.

Health Status

One of the most dramatic differences between minority populations and European Americans (whites) is health. Imagine how stressful it is to realize that a tremendous disparity exists in health status between minorities and the general population, especially if you are a member of a minority group. As stated in a government report identifying national health objectives designed to be achieved by the year 2000:

The economically disadvantaged—low income, poorly educated, nonprofessional—and women seem to be at higher risk for both psychosocial and psychophysiologic stress reactions, with the unemployed and the part-time

Exercise is an effective strategy to maintain health and decrease health disparities.

employed, minorities . . . at higher risk for psychophysiologic distress.[12] In fact, when the national health objectives were developed for the year 2010, one of the two over-arching goals was to "eliminate health disparities."[13]

It is clear that racism can have negative health effects, and to surmise that so do sexism, ageism, and prejudice and discrimination by socioeconomic status and physical abilities is not unreasonable. In this chapter, we look at several indices of health as they are related to minorities.

National Health Objectives and Diversity

Whereas health objectives for the nation have been developed each decade since 1990, the year 2010 objectives took a different path than in the past. For the first time, the nation committed itself to the elimination of health disparities. Recognizing the gap in health status between those who are advantaged and those who are not is nothing new. The federal government has had a goal of closing that gap in previous editions of the nation's health objectives. However, the government is committed to eliminating that gap altogether by 2010.

Evidence of the need for such a lofty goal was presented by the U.S. Department of Health and Human Services in its publication *Healthy People 2010:*[14]

Gender
- Men have a life expectancy that is six years less than women's.
- Men have a higher death rate for each of the ten leading causes of death.
- Women are at a greater risk of Alzheimer's disease than men, and are twice as likely to be affected by depression.

Race and Ethnicity
- The infant mortality rate among African Americans is more than double that of whites.
- Heart disease rates are more than 40 percent higher for African Americans than for whites.
- The death rate for all cancers is 30 percent higher for African Americans than for whites.
- The prostate cancer rate for African Americans is more than double the rate for whites.
- African American women have a higher death rate from breast cancer than white women.
- The death rate from HIV/AIDS of African Americans is more than seven times that of whites.
- Hispanics are twice as likely as non-Hispanic whites to die of diabetes.
- Although only approximately 11 percent of the population, Hispanics account for 20 percent of new cases of tuberculosis.
- Hispanics have higher rates of high blood pressure and obesity than do non-Hispanic whites.
- Native Americans and Alaska Natives have an infant mortality rate almost twice that of whites.
- Native Americans and Alaska Natives have disproportionately high death rates from unintentional injuries and suicide.
- American women of Vietnamese origin experience cervical cancer at nearly five times the rate of white women.
- Asian/Pacific Islander Americans have higher rates of new cases of hepatitis than whites.

Disability

- People with disabilities have higher rates of anxiety, pain, sleeplessness, and days of depression than others.
- People with disabilities have fewer days of vitality.
- People with disabilities have lower rates of physical activity and higher rates of obesity.

Sexual Orientation

- Gay and lesbian Americans have higher rates of HIV/AIDS and other sexually transmitted infections.
- Gay and lesbian Americans have higher rates of substance abuse, depression, and suicide.
- Lesbians have higher rates of smoking, overweight, alcohol abuse, and stress than heterosexual women.

Whether we can achieve the goal of eliminating these health disparities may be questionable. Still, that we recognize them and are not willing to accept them is laudable.

Although infant mortality rates have declined in recent years in the United States, proportionately more African American infants than white infants die.

Infant Mortality

The disparity in health status is no more evident than in the rates of infant mortality. In 2000, the **infant mortality** rate in the United States was 6.9 deaths per 1,000 live births. When broken down, the rate for whites was 5.7, whereas for African Americans it was 13.5.[15] The reasons for this difference are varied. For example, African American pregnant women on average obtain prenatal care later, are more likely to live in poverty, and are generally less educated than their white counterparts. Asian American mothers had the lowest infant mortality rate (4.9 per 1,000 live births). Other groups' infant mortality rates are shown in Table 15.1.

The reasons for these statistics are varied. In addition to those already stated, cost and access to health care are significant contributors to late prenatal care and, as a result, to a high infant mortality rate. Minorities are disproportionately represented among those lacking health insurance. Because most private health insurance is obtained through one's employer, and minorities have a higher unemployment rate than does the general population, it is not surprising that minorities have low health insurance rates. Individuals without health insurance—pregnant women as well as others—tend to postpone health care until a problem presents itself.

Also, there is often a lack of health care facilities within easy access of minority populations. I established a community-campus health partnership with a city near my university and serve as vice chair of that partnership. Ninety-seven percent of that

infant mortality
Death of infants before one year of age.

All Mothers	6.9 per 1,000 Live Births
White	5.7
African American	13.5
Native American or Alaskan Native	8.3
Asian/Pacific Islander American	4.9
Hispanic Origin	5.6

Table 15.1
INFANT MORTALITY RATES

Source: National Center for Health Statistics, *Health, United States, 2003* (Hyattsville, MD: National Center for Health Statistics, 2003), 149.

city's population of five thousand is African American. The city has only one health care provider, a dentist. To obtain health care, residents must travel out of the city. This is just one example of the barriers that minority groups in communities across the United States encounter in their attempt to obtain health care.

Life Expectancy

life expectancy
The number of years a person is expected to live when born.

Life expectancy is the number of years a person is expected to live when born. Life expectancy at birth in the United States in 2000 was 76.9 years. A baby born in 2000 is expected to live 76.9 years. However, for white males, life expectancy in 2000 was 6.6 years longer than for African American males (74.8 compared with 68.2). And life expectancy for white females was 5.1 years longer than for African American females (80.0 compared with 74.9). However, the gap is getting narrower. Whereas overall life expectancy increased by 1.5 years between 1990 and 2000, the increase for white males was 2.1 years, compared with African American males' increase of 3.7 years. The increase for white females was 0.6 years; for African American females it was 1.3 years.[16]

Years of Potential Life Lost

years of potential life lost
The number of years between when a person is expected to live and the age of death; a measure of premature death.

Years of potential life lost is a measure of premature death. When we look at the causes of premature death among various minority populations, differences emerge. For the general population, heart disease, cancer, and stroke are the leading causes of death, and unintentional injuries and lung disease rank fourth and fifth. This varies, though, for different minorities (see Table 15.2). For example, AIDS is the seventh

Table 15.2 LEADING CAUSES OF DEATH

	Rank				
Cause of Death	White	African American	Native American	Asian/Pacific Islander	Hispanic
Diseases of the heart	1	1	1	2	1
Stroke	3	3	5	3	4
Cancers	2	2	2	1	2
Lung disease	4	8	7	5	8
Pneumonia and influenza	6	10	9	6	9
Liver disease	9	—	6	—	6
Diabetes mellitus	7	5	4	7	5
Kidney disease	9	9	10	9	—
HIV infection (AIDS)	—	7	—	—	—
Unintentional injuries	5	4	3	4	3
Suicide	10	—	8	8	—
Homicide	—	6	—	—	7
Perinatal diseases	—	10	—	10	10
Alzheimer's disease	8	—	—	—	10

Source: National Center for Health Statistics. *Health, United States, 2003* (Hyattsville, Md: National Center for Health Statistics, 2003), 145.

leading cause of death among African American males, but it does not rank in the top ten among Native American males. And there are significant differences between males and females.

High Blood Pressure

Essential hypertension is characterized by high blood pressure of unknown origin. It is estimated that 90 percent of high blood pressure can be classified as essential, yet high blood pressure does not affect all people to the same degree or in the same manner. Essential hypertension occurs in 24 percent of white males, but it is found in 35 percent of African American males. It occurs in 19 percent of white females, but it occurs in 34 percent of African American females.[17] As a result, proportionately more African Americans die of heart disease (199 per 100,000 population) than do white Americans (133 per 100,000 population). When broken down by gender and ethnicity, diseases of the heart result in almost twice as many years of potential life lost for African American men than for white men, and almost three times as many years of potential life lost for African American women than for white women. Consequently, one of the national health objectives established by the U.S. Department of Health and Human Services is to encourage at least 95 percent of African American hypertensive men aged eighteen through thirty-four to take action to control their blood pressure. When last evaluated, only 50 percent of these men were doing something to control their blood pressure.[18]

It is interesting to note that Hispanics have a lower rate of coronary heart disease than do whites, both men and women. Furthermore, although heart disease is the leading cause of death for Asian/Pacific Islander Americans, Asian Americans are at a lower risk of dying from coronary heart disease than are other minority groups or whites.

The mechanism for African Americans' being at increased risk of developing hypertension has been studied, and some interesting findings have emerged. Several researchers have found that when African Americans are exposed to stress in the laboratory—for example, by experiencing extreme cold, playing an electronic video game, riding an exercise bicycle, or performing mathematical functions—they react with greater increases in blood pressure than do whites.[19–21] Other research indicates that African Americans may produce fewer endorphins than whites when stressed.[22] This combination may explain the disparity in prevalence of high blood pressure.

Acquired Immune Deficiency Syndrome (AIDS)

As of December 31, 2004, there were 944,306 persons with **AIDS** reported to the Federal Centers for Disease Control and Prevention.[23] Of these, 756,399 were adult or adolescent males, 178,463 were adult or adolescent females, and 9,443 were children. However, as with other indices of health, rates of HIV (**human immunodeficiency virus**) infection vary greatly in subgroups of the population. For example, whereas African Americans make up approximately 13 percent of the population, they comprised 50 percent of the reported AIDS cases in 2004. Among children reported with HIV infection in 2002, 64 percent were African American. In the United States in 2004, 11,978 African Americans died of AIDS.[24] The AIDS death rate for African Americans is ten times that for whites. Even more alarming, the AIDS death rate for African American women is approximately thirteen times that of white women. Among women with AIDS, 64 percent are African American. Sandra Quinn[25] researched AIDS in the African American community and concluded that it is a result of several factors: intravenous drug use or sexual partners who are I.V. drug users, poverty, low educational levels, a lack of perception that they are at risk for HIV infection, and unemployment.

There is also variation in the HIV death rate by gender. The death rate from AIDS in 2000 for American males aged twenty-five to thirty-four was 19.8 per 100,000 population,

AIDS
Acquired immune deficiency syndrome.

human immunodeficiency virus
The virus that causes acquired immune deficiency syndrome (AIDS).

and it was 4.2 for females. The death rate from HIV infection was 3.8 for Hispanic males and 2.9 for Hispanic females. And the HIV death rate was 35.1 for African American males and 13.2 for African American females.

Cancer

Several cancers are more prevalent among particular groups of Americans than others. For example, Native Americans and Alaskan Natives contract cancers of the gallbladder, kidney, stomach, and cervix at high rates but have lower rates of cancers of the breast, uterus, ovaries, prostate, lung, colon, rectum, and urinary bladder, as well as lower rates of leukemia and skin cancer.[26] In addition, African American men's death rate from trachea, bronchus, and lung cancer is greater than that of white men (70.8 and 49.4 per 100,000 population, respectively), although African American women and white women have comparable rates (27.2 and 27.4 per 100,000, respectively).[27] In general, African American men experience more cancers than do white men, but African American and white women's cancer rates do not differ greatly.

Mental Health

One mental health issue that varies by subpopulation is suicide. The suicide rate differs dramatically by ethnicity, race, and culture. For example, in 2000, the suicide rate for males aged fifteen to twenty-four was 26.2 for Native Americans, 19.5 for Hispanics, 17.9 for Caucasians, 14.2 for African Americans, and 9.1 for Asian Americans.[28]

Homicide also varies by ethnicity, gender and cultural background. The death rate from homicide in 1998 for African American men and women was significantly higher than for other groups; the death rate was higher for men than for women; and it decreased as people reached their later forties.

Part of the problem with homicides and unintentional injuries is the number of firearms in American homes. It is estimated by the U.S. Bureau of Alcohol, Tobacco, and Firearms that 200 million firearms exist in the United States and that approximately 50 percent of all households contain a firearm. In 2002, almost 38,000 deaths occurred by firearm accidents, in addition to firearm deaths by homicide and suicide.[29] Making matters even worse, in any one month approximately 25 percent of high school students carry a gun to school; 14.5 percent of African American male students and 8.2 percent of Hispanic male students reported they had taken a gun to school within the past month.[30] Even junior high school students are taking guns to school in alarming numbers.[31] Imagine how stressful it can be to attend a school in which a gun might go off at any time!

Poverty and Educational Level

Because poverty and low educational level are related, we discuss these stressful conditions together. Both are associated with poorer health. Across all ethnic and cultural groups, the higher the educational level, the better the health status is. Because higher educational level is associated with higher income, poverty is also a cause of poor health: the lower the socioeconomic level, the poorer the health status. Table 15.3 shows the number and percentage of people and families in the United States below the poverty level as of 2000. Notice the disparity in the poverty level among whites and the minority groups.

Surely, poverty is caused by many factors. Still, racism, ageism, and other "isms" can be included in that mix. For example, it is generally agreed that women workers, compared with male workers, earn less, receive fewer fringe benefits, and acquire less prestige at work. Women also have fewer opportunities for on-the-job training, their turnover rate tends to be higher, and their working conditions tend to be

Table 15.3

PERSONS AND FAMILIES BELOW
THE POVERTY LEVEL, 2002

	Percentage Below Poverty Level	Number Below Poverty Level
All Persons		
All races	12.1	34,570,000
White	10.2	23,466,000
African American	24.1	8,602,000
Hispanic	21.8	8,555,000
Asian	10.1	1,161,000
Children Under 18		
All races	16.7	12,133,000
White	13.8	7,549,000
African American	32.3	3,645,000
Hispanic	28.6	3,782,000
Asian or Pacific Islander	11.7	315,000

Source: U.S. Census Bureau, *Statistical Abstracts of the United States: 2004–2005* (Washington, DC: U.S. Census Bureau, 2004) p. 453.

poorer.[32] Furthermore, poverty in old age is more prevalent among women than among men.

The stressful effects of being African American described by Dowd and Bengston remain true to this day: "Being old in an industrialized society is burden enough; being old *and* a member of a minority group is seen by many as constituting double jeopardy."[33]

Imagine the stress felt by a person with a physical disability seeking employment only to discover that he or she is unable to find work because of the disabling condition, or a sixty-year-old worker laid off due to a downturn in the economy who finds other companies unwilling to hire and train a person whom they perceive to be near retirement, or a young woman who cannot find a job because of employers' notions that she might soon become pregnant, thereby requiring time away from the job. Even though all of these actions are discriminatory, abhorrent, and illegal, many employers ignore the law and express their prejudices through their hiring practices. This behavior has implication for stress, health, and quality of life.

Family Life

In this section we consider two important factors related to stress: homelessness and family structure.

Homelessness

I will never forget the time I was asked to organize a presentation on homelessness at a national conference in Chicago. The presentation was in the Gold Room of a fancy downtown hotel. It was called the Gold Room because of the gold trim on the walls and moldings and the gold chandeliers hanging from the ceiling. To describe this room as opulent is an understatement. The irony of discussing homelessness in the Gold Room was, to say the least, an embarrassment.

Getting exact figures on homelessness is difficult. However, according to some estimates, on any given night between 444,000 and 842,000 people in the United

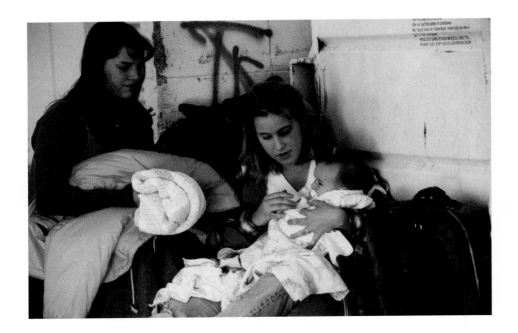

Every night, large numbers of Americans experience the stress of homelessness, and many of the homeless are families that include children.

States are homeless, and up to 3.5 million experience homelessness sometime during the year.[34] What is even more disturbing is that rather than decreasing, homelessness is actually increasing.[35] A U.S. Conference of Mayors survey[36] of homelessness in thirty cities found that families with children under eighteen years of age accounted for 40 percent of the urban homeless, and 4 percent of the urban homeless are unaccompanied minors. Single men comprised 40 percent of the urban homeless and single women 14 percent. The number of homeless families increased dramatically throughout the 1990s. Families with children are the fastest-growing segment of the homeless population.[37] Families with children constitute 40 percent of the homeless.[38] Families, single mothers, and children make up the largest group of homeless people in rural areas.[39]

The homeless population in urban areas is comprised of 50 percent African Americans, 35 percent Caucasians, 12 percent Hispanics, 2 percent Native Americans, and 1 percent Asian Americans.[40] In rural areas, the homeless consist of Caucasians more than other racial or ethnic groups.[41]

Homelessness results from many factors. Predominant among them are domestic violence and lack of employment or minimum-wage jobs. Fifty percent of homeless parents left their residence because of domestic violence, and 46 percent of cities surveyed identified domestic violence as a primary cause of homelessness.[42] Furthermore, when people are employed in minimum-wage jobs, they cannot afford housing. In fact, a minimum-wage worker would have to work 87 hours a week to afford a two-bedroom apartment at 30 percent of his or her income. Interestingly, 20 percent of the homeless are employed. Obviously, these workers are not earning enough to avoid homelessness.[43]

Family Structure

For many reasons, there are differences in the stress experienced by minority families. For example, higher socioeconomic status affords some families the option of day care, time away from parental responsibilities, a lack of stress about money for food and shelter, and less concern about the ability to afford adequate health care. Consequently, they report fewer divorces and a higher percentage of two-parent families. In contrast, people living at poverty levels—we have already shown that minorities are disproportionately represented in this population—experience the stress of trying to afford the very basics, much less anything beyond that. These families, perhaps as a result of the increased stress they encounter, are statistically different. For example, in 2000, 63 percent of African American children were living with either one parent or no parent, 36 percent of Hispanic children were living with either one or no parent, and 27 percent of white children came from one- or no-parent families. Furthermore, in 2003, African American adults were found more likely to be single (42 percent of African American men and 37 percent of African American women were never married). For Hispanic adults the percentages of the never married were 36 percent for males and 25 percent for females. The comparable figures for whites were 26 percent for men and 18 percent for women.[44]

This discussion should not be interpreted to mean that minorities are the only families headed by one parent. In 2000, only 33 percent of households with children under the age of eighteen consisted of a married couple and their children.

The importance of family structure becomes evident when we consider child health. Research over the past decade clearly shows that marital dissolution and child-bearing outside of marriage often have long-term negative effects on children. Children who grow up with two parents do better in many ways than children who grow up with only one. For example, children from one-parent homes have lower intellectual test scores and are more likely to drop out of school. Girls from such families are more prone to become single mothers in their teens, and boys from such families are more prone to engage in antisocial behavior. These differences are seen in children from many social classes and ethnic groups.[45]

The *National Study of the Changing Workforce*[46] found that 26 percent of employees felt emotionally drained by their work, 36 percent felt *used up* at the end of the work day, and 28 percent did not have enough energy to do things with their families. If these families reported such a high level of stress feelings, imagine the stress experienced by minority families: families with only one parent present, families living in poverty, families with lower levels of education and job training, and families who are discriminated against only too regularly.

Age and Physical Disability

Elders and individuals with physical disabilities fare no better when it comes to stereotyping and stress.

Elders

In many other countries—Japan is a good example—elderly citizens are revered for their experience and knowledge. Unfortunately, in the United States, when people become old, they are expected to retire, to step aside and let younger people contribute to society's evolution. However, retirees need not be inactive. Many take part-time jobs and have sufficient time to do the things they were not able to do when working full-time. Still, ageism can make a person feel useless or worse—a burden. That must be a very stressful feeling!

The federal government has established health objectives specifically for older adults. One of the goals of these objectives is to increase the productive years of elders and their years of quality life. Another objective seeks to increase years of healthy life. At the time this objective was written for the year 2010, years of healthy life were sixty-two for the general population.

People with Disabilities

Too often we do not appreciate something until we have lost it. Recently, while playing basketball, a friend struck me in my eye with his thumb. I had never experienced such pain in my life! It turned out that the scratch on the cornea and the cut on the white of my eye were the least of my worries. The blow had so traumatized the eye muscles that I had double vision. The ophthalmologist guessed that

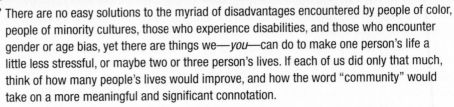

time would heal the muscles and restore my vision to normal. I only half believed him. Luckily, he was right and I was wrong. Four months later, I was able to reach for something, confident I would grab it rather than its phantom image. During those four months, though, the double vision led to headaches, dizziness, and nausea. Now I *really* appreciate my eyesight and the complexity of lining up two eyes to see one image.

People with disabling conditions experience the hardship I experienced (usually to a much greater degree), but their condition is not temporary. How cruel it is to add to their burden by subjecting them to discriminatory attitudes and practices that create even greater stress than they would normally experience, yet that is what too often occurs. Again, although it is against the law to discriminate because of physical disability, too many employers still do. Although access to buildings and accommodations to allow for greater mobility have been created, too many barriers still exist. And, in spite of such heroic accomplishments as completing a marathon in a wheelchair or running across the country on an artificial leg, too much disrespect for persons with disabilities still exists. Recognizing the necessity of responding to the needs of people with disabilities, the federal government established health objectives specifically for this population. Among these national health objectives are to reduce by 43 percent the number of days of depression, and by 34 percent the number of days of anxiety, experienced by adults with activity limitations.[47]

The effects of gender bias, age discrimination, and prejudice against people with disabilities can be devastating for people who wish only to be treated equally and fairly—that is, to be given an equal opportunity to experience the American dream. However, more women live in poverty than do men, as do more of the female elderly and more of the female physically disabled. We have already explored the relationship between poverty and poor health. One might argue that treating our compatriots in this biased manner not only has negative consequences for them but also diminishes us. Anyone who has ever helped people in need knows the feeling experienced by doing the helping. When we behave in a discriminatory fashion, we deprive ourselves of the opportunity to have this feeling and are thereby less happy, proud, and self-respectful than we might be.

summary

- Cultural diversity is related to stress and, in turn, to health and well-being.

- Although approximately three-quarters of the U.S. population is white, it is projected that by the year 2050 just over 52 percent will be white. Estimates are that, by 2050, 23 percent of Americans will be Hispanic, 14 percent will be African American, and 10 percent will be Asian American.

- Diversity is related to such health indices as infant mortality, life expectancy, years of potential life lost, hypertension, AIDS, cancer, and mental health.

- The infant mortality rate for the general population is 6.9 deaths per 1,000 live births. However, it is 13.5 for African Americans. For whites, the infant mortality rate is 5.7, for Hispanics it is 5.6, for Native Americans it is 8.3, and for Asian Americans it is 4.9.

- Life expectancy at birth for the general population is 76.9 years. However, for white males, life expectancy is 9 years longer than for African American males (74.8 compared with 68.2). And life expectancy for white females is 5.1 years longer than for African American females (80.0 compared with 74.9).

- The major causes of death vary somewhat by ethnicity and race, cultural background, and gender. For example, AIDS is the ninth leading cause of death among African Americans, but it is not included in the top ten causes of death for whites, Native Americans, Asian Americans, or Hispanics.

- High blood pressure and acquired immune deficiency syndrome (AIDS) affect African Americans to a greater extent than they affect other subgroups of the population. African Americans have a disproportionate incidence of high blood pressure and comprise 50 percent of the AIDS cases.

- The suicide rate for Native American male youths aged fifteen to twenty-four (26.2 deaths per 100,000) is nearly 1.5 that of white male youths, about 2 times the rate for African Americans, 1.5 times the rate for Hispanic males, and 2.5 times the rate for Asian American males.

- Poverty is also associated with poor health. Although 12 percent of the general population lives in poverty, 22 percent of African Americans, 21 percent of Hispanics, and 11 percent of Asian/Pacific Islanders live in poverty. By contrast, only 9 percent of white Americans live in poverty.

- Rather than decreasing, homelessness is actually increasing. On any given night, some estimates are that between 444,000 and 842,000 people in the United States are homeless and up to 3.5 million experience homelessness sometime during the year. The number of homeless families has increased dramatically. Families with children are the fastest-growing segment of the homeless population. Families with children under eighteen years of age account for 40 percent of the urban homeless, and 4 percent of the urban homeless are unaccompanied children.

- Nearly 63 percent of African American children live with one parent only, 36 percent of Hispanic children live with only one parent, and 27 percent of white children come from one-parent families. Furthermore, African American adults are more likely to be single (40 percent of African American men and 38 percent of African American women are unmarried). The comparable figures for whites are 25 percent for men and 18 percent for women.

notes

1. *Webster's New World College Dictionary,* 4th ed. (New York: Macmillan, 1999).

2. Ibid.

3. Raymond Nakamura, *Health in America: A Multicultural Prespective* (Dubuque, IA: Kendall Hunt, 2003).

4. The Commonwealth Fund, *A Comparative Survey of Minority Health* (New York: The Commonwealth Fund). www.cmwf.org:80/minhlth.html.

5. H. Landrine and E. Klonoff, *African American Acculturation: Deconstructing Race and Reviving Culture* (Thousand Oaks, CA: Sage, 1996).

6. Suzzane Irujo, "An Introduction to Intercultural Differences and Similarities in Nonverbal Communication," in *Toward Multiculturalism,* ed. J. Wurzel (Yarmouth, ME: Intercultural Press, 1988), 142–50.

7. Amy Goldstein and Roberto Suro, "A Journey of Stages: Assimilation's Pull Is Still Strong, but Its Pace Varies," *Washington Post,* 16 January 2000, A1.

8. C. Helman, *Culture, Health and Illness* (Bristol, England: John Wright, 1986).

9. J. Okamura and A. Agbayani, "Filipino Americans," in *Handbook of Social Services for Asians and Pacific Islanders,* ed. Noreen Mokuau (New York: Greenwood Press, 1991), 97–115.

10. Franklin Ng (ed.), *Asian American Issues Relating to Labor, Economics, and Socioeconomic Status (Asians*

in America: The Peoples of East, Southeast, and South Asia in American Life and Culture) (Berlin, Germany: Garland Publishing, 1998).

11. Federal Bureau of Investigation. *Hate Crime Statistics, 2003* (Washington, DC: U.S. Department of Justice, 2004).

12. U.S. Public Health Service, *Healthy People 2000: National Health Promotion and Disease Objectives* (Washington, DC: U.S. Department of Health and Human Services, September 1992), 215.

13. U.S. Public Health Service, *Healthy People: The Surgeon General's Report on Health Promotion and Disease Prevention* (Washington, DC: U.S. Government Printing Office, 1999).

14. Office of Disease Prevention and Health Promotion, *Healthy People 2010* (Washington, DC: U.S. Department of Health and Human Services, 2000).

15. National Center for Health Statistics, *Health, United States, 2003* (Hyattsville, MD: National Center for Health Statistics, 2003), 121.

16. Ibid., 133.

17. Office of Disease Prevention and Health Promotion, *Healthy People 2010.*

18. Ibid.

19. N. B. Anderson, "Racial Differences in Stress-Induced Cardiovascular Reactivity and Hypertension: Current Status and Substantive Issues," *Psychological Bulletin* 105(1989): 89–105.

20. K. C. Light and A. Sherman, "Race, Borderline Hypertension, and Hemodynamic Responses to Behavioral Stress Before and After Beta-Andrenergic Blockade," *Health Psychology* 8(1989): 577–95.

21. N. B. Anderson et al., "Race, Parental History of Hypertension, and Patterns of Cardiovascular Reactivity in Women," *Psychophysiology* 26(1989): 39–47.

22. M. McNeilly and A. Zeichner, "Neuropeptide and Cardiovascular Response to Intravenous Catheterization in Normotensive and Hypertensive Blacks and Whites," *Health Psychology* 8(1989): 487–501.

23. Centers for Disease Control and Prevention, *HIV/AIDS Surveillance Report, 2004.* Volume 16. Atlanta, GA: US Department of Health and Human Services, Centers for Disease Control and Prevention; 2005.

24. Ibid.

25. S. C. Quinn, "Perspective: AIDS and the African American Woman: The Triple Burden of Race, Class, and Gender," *Health Education Quarterly* 20(1993): 305–20.

26. American Cancer Society, *Facts and Figures, 2006* (Atlanta: American Cancer Society, 2006).

27. Office of Disease Prevention and Health Promotion, *Healthy People 2010.*

28. National Center for Health Statistics, *Health, United States, 2003,* 187–89.

29. U.S. Census Bureau, *Statistical Abstract of the United States, 2005* (Washington, DC: U.S. Government Printing Office, 2005).

30. "Youth Risk Behavior Surveillance—United States, 1999," *Mortality and Morbidity Weekly Report 49* (2000): 1–96.

31. D. W. Webster, P. S. Gainer, and H. R. Champion, "Weapon Carrying Among Inner-City Junior High School Students: Defensive Behavior vs. Aggressive Delinquency," *American Journal of Public Health* 83(1993): 1604–8.

32. B. J. Logue, "Women at Risk: Predictors of Financial Stress for Retired Women Workers," *Gerontologist* 31(1991): 657–65.

33. J. J. Dowd and V. L. Bengston, "Aging in Minority Populations: An Examination of the Double Jeopardy Hypothesis," in *Aging, the Individual, and Society: Readings in Social Gerontology,* ed. J. S. Quadango (New York: St. Martin's Press, 1984).

34. National Coalition for Homelessness, "How Many People Experience Homelessness?" *NCH Fact Sheet,* 2(2002): 2.

35. National Coalition for Homelessness, "Who Is Homeless?" *NCH Fact Sheet,* 3(2005): 1.

36. National Law Center for Homelessness and Poverty, "Poverty in America: Overview," 25 July 2002. http://www.nlchp.org/FA_HAPIA/

37. National Coalition for Homelessness, "Who Is Homeless?" 2.

38. U.S. Conference of Mayors, *17th Annual Conference Survey of Hunger, Homelessness Documents Increasein Current Demands,* 17 December 2001. http://www.usmayors.org/uscm/ us_mayor_newspaper/documents/ 12_17_01/hunger_homelessness.asp

39. Yvonee Vissing, *Out of Sight, Out of Mind: Homeless Children and Families in Small Town America* (Lexington: University Press of Kentucky, 1996).

40. U.S. Conference of Mayors, 17th Annual Conference Survey.

41. National Coalition for Homelessness. "Who Is Homeless?"

42. National Coalition for Homelessness, "Who Is Homeless?" 3.

43. National Law Center for Homelessness and Poverty, "Poverty in America."

44. U.S. Census Bureau, *Statistical Abstract of the United States, 2004–2005* (Washington, DC: U.S. Government Printing Office, 2004), 48.

45. National Institute of Mental Health, "Family Process and Social Networks," in *Basic Behavioral Science Research for Mental Health* (Washington, DC:

National Institute of Mental Health, updated 1 June 1999). http://www.nimh.nih.gov/publicat/baschap6.cfm

46. J. T. Bond, E. Galinsky, and J. E. Swanberg, *The 1997 National Study of the Changing Workforce* (New York: Families and Work Institute, 1998).

47. Office of Disease Prevention and Health Promotion, *Healthy People 2010.*

internet resources

Psychological Stress and Cancer
www.oncolink.upenn.edu/coping/index.cfm
Includes Web links and resources to contact for additional information when coping with cancer.

The Wellness Community
www.wellness-community.org
Description of the services provided by The Wellness Community, a nonprofit organization whose mission is to help reduce stress for people with cancer and their families through free programs that offer emotional support and education. Includes a list of facilities by state.

HIV and Depression
www.psycom.net/depression.central.hiv.html
A central clearinghouse for information on all types of depressive disorders and on the most effective treatments for individuals suffering from depression related to HIV status.

Office of Minority Health Resource Center
http://www.omhrc.gov
Provides statistics and resources regarding minorities.

As we discussed in this chapter, there is wide variation in the health of subgroups of Americans. We call these variations *health disparities*. Here is some additional information on that topic:

- Mortality from stroke is 80 percent higher in African Americans than whites.

- The mortality rate for hypertension is three times higher in African Americans than whites.

- The mortality rate for all cancers is higher among African Americans than all other racial or ethnic groups. The incidence of cervical and liver cancer in Asian Americans is five times higher than it is for other racial and ethnic groups.

- African Americans and Hispanics make up 55 percent of all AIDS cases, yet they comprise merely 25 percent of the American population. Seventy-seven percent of AIDS cases among females occur in African American and Hispanic women. Fifty-seven percent of pediatric AIDS cases occur in African American babies and 24 percent in Hispanic babies.

- African Americans and Native Americans are two times more likely to die from diabetes than whites, and Hispanics are two times more likely to experience diabetes-associated renal failure than whites.

- Immunization rates are lowest among minorities, children from low-income families, and children from less-educated families.

- African American and Hispanic HIV patients are less likely than white HIV patients to receive experimental medications.

Approximately 10 percent of African American HIV patients and 11 percent of Hispanic HIV patients participated in a clinical trial of HIV medication, compared with 18 percent of white HIV patients.

- Women of color who perceive they are the target of racism or gender discrimination have been found to experience more stress, depression, psychological distress, hypertension, higher blood pressure, and decreased satisfaction with medical care received.

Several reasons are proposed to explain why health disparities exist. Among these are racism and discrimination, disproportionate poverty and low education levels among certain minorities, inadequate health insurance, lack of minority medical care providers (in particular, physicians), communication barriers, and bias among physicians and nurses.

Sources: K.G. Keppel, J.N. Pearcy, and D.K. Wagener, "Trends in Racial and Ethnic-Specific Rates for the Health Status Indicators: United States, 1990–98," *Healthy People 2000 Statistical Notes, no. 23* (Hyattsville, MD: National Center for Health Statistics, 2002).

"Communication/Cultural Barriers May Affect Receipt of Cardiovascular Procedures Among Hispanics." *Research Activities* 261(2002): 3–4.

C. Connolly, "Report Says Minorities Get Lower-Quality Health Care," *Washington Post,* 21 March 2002, A2.

K. L. Walters and J. M. Simoni, "Reconceptualizing Native Women's Health: An 'Indigent' Stress-Coping Model," *American Journal of Public Health* 92(2002): 520–24.

K. Glanz, R. T. Coyne, V. Y. Chollette, and V. W. Pinn, "Cancer-Related Health Disparities in Women," *American Journal of Public Health* 93(2003): 292–98.

W. E. Cunningham, K. C. Heslin, et al. "Participation in Research and Access to Experimental Treatments for HIV-Infected Patients," *Research Activities* 261(2002): 5.

LAB ASSESSMENT 15.1

How Has Prejudice Affected Your Level of Stress?

Almost everyone has experienced prejudice. Some of us have been the victims of bias because of our skin color, others because of our sex, some because of our religion, and others because of our physical appearance. Maybe we have a disability that has resulted in us being the brunt of prejudice, or perhaps we have been disadvantaged because of our athletic ability or intellectual capacity. When we experience prejudiced behavior, our stress levels rise. Recalling the stress model presented in Chapter 4, the biased actions become the life situation that is perceived as distressing. In turn, we experience emotional arousal (e.g., anger), which leads to physiological arousal (e.g., increased muscle tension). The consequences could be the development of a psychosomatic illness or any of the other potential consequences described in Chapter 3.

Describe an instance when you experienced prejudice against you.

_____

_____

_____

_____

How did you react? What did you do?

_____

_____

_____

_____

What were the consequences you experienced? Think of physical, psychological, and social consequences.

_____

_____

_____

_____

Describe how you could have reacted in a more appropriate or healthier way.

_____

_____

_____

_____

The next time you experience prejudicial behavior, think of this exercise and try to react in a way that is healthier for you. You cannot control the other person, but you can always control your reaction to the behavior of that other person. As you have learned throughout this book, no one forces you to perceive life situations as distressing. Instead, you could laugh at the stupidity of the biased person, or pray for him or her. Even if that does not change that person, it will prevent you from getting ill over it.

LAB ASSESSMENT 15.2

What Biases Do You Possess?

Although we may profess we are unbiased, and we would prefer to be so, all of us have our prejudices. Some of us feel uncomfortable with people who are different from us. As a result, we hang around those who are more like we are. If you doubt the truth of this statement, think of who eats lunch together in a school cafeteria. Do the popular kids sit together? Do different ethnic groups congregate together? Or, which socioeconomic groups socialize with one another, or join the same organizations? It is when this discomfort hurtfully excludes others that it becomes especially problematic.

When have you acted in a prejudicial way?

_____
_____
_____
_____

How do you feel now about having acted that way?

_____
_____
_____
_____

How would you prefer to act if a similar situation presents itself in the future?

_____
_____
_____
_____

If you see someone else behaving in a biased fashion, would you do something about that? If not, why not? If you would do something, what would that be?

_____
_____
_____
_____

If we admit to our own biases, we will be more likely to recognize them when they crop up and prevent them from resulting in a prejudiced behavior toward someone else. In that case, we will have prevented both the other person and ourselves from experiencing a stressful response.

part 5

Specific Applications

It was over dinner in a seafood restaurant with fishnets and lobster cages on the walls that my father-in-law was bemoaning his choice of professions. Witnessed by a stuffed marlin looking at us from across the room, he was expressing his envy of his physician friends who "made $300,000 a year, worked three days a week, and played golf the rest of the time." I was surprised to hear him speak this way because he always seemed to me to be excited about his law practice and proud that he was a second-generation attorney in business with his son. "If I had to do it all over again, I'd be a physician," he said as his eyes wandered upward and his mind visualized how delightful that kind of life would have been. When he lowered his eyes, they fell upon me and the inevitable question fell from his lips. "What would you be if you had to do it all over again?" Well, that was ten years ago and today Ralph is retired. He still looks back, wondering how life might have been. In spite of the ten-year interval, though, my answer to his question remains the same. "I'd do just what I am doing now." Upon some study I learned that my answer is not uncommon among my fellow college professors. It seems that "professoring" is consistently reported to be a satisfying profession by its practitioners. Being a professor is accompanied by certain traits associated with low-stress occupations. This chapter will discuss these characteristics in particular and occupational stress in general.

By the way, what would you do if you could start all over?

Occupational Stress Cycle

Before proceeding, answer the questions in Lab 16.1 (at the end of this chapter) to get a better handle on occupational stress. If you are presently employed, answer these questions as they relate to your job. If you are not now working but have worked, answer these questions as they relate to your last job. If you have never worked, write me immediately to let me know your secret. In the meantime, answer these questions as you think they relate to a loved one who is presently working.

Now, before you get to Lab 16.1, I need to make one point. When I talk with groups of people about occupational stress, inevitably a woman raises her hand to say she's never worked and therefore can't answer these questions. Upon further investigation, we find she worked very hard but never received an outright salary. She was a mother, laundered, cleaned, arranged car pools, and counseled. If you are a woman or a man and work at home, answer these questions for that occupation.

Figure 16.1 depicts the relationship between the scores on Lab 16.1 and the incidence of disease when 1,540 workers were studied.[1] The expectation that a large amount of stress would be associated with a greater incidence of disease was supported. However, a small amount of stress was also associated with a greater incidence of disease. In other words, there was an optimal amount of stress (not too little and not too much) that was found to be healthiest. Several hypotheses can be offered to explain this finding. However, the one I think most plausible is that low scores on this instrument mean these respondents felt underutilized and unneeded. They felt little responsibility and believed their jobs were not very important. They could easily be replaced. Believing this created a great deal of stress rather than a little, but this type of stress was not measured by the scale. Further support for this interpretation can be found later in this chapter.

What Is Occupational Stress?

Occupational stress is an extremely difficult construct to define. Obviously, it is stress on the job, but stress on the job occurs in a person. Here is where we run into problems because any worker brings to the job a level of predisposition to be

occupational stress
The combination of sources of stress at work, individual characteristics, and extraorganizational stressors.

Figure 16.1

Percentage distribution of stress scores.

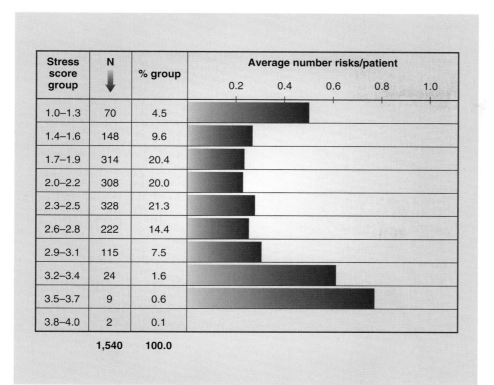

Stress score group	N ↓	% group	Average number risks/patient
1.0–1.3	70	4.5	
1.4–1.6	148	9.6	
1.7–1.9	314	20.4	
2.0–2.2	308	20.0	
2.3–2.5	328	21.3	
2.6–2.8	222	14.4	
2.9–3.1	115	7.5	
3.2–3.4	24	1.6	
3.5–3.7	9	0.6	
3.8–4.0	2	0.1	
	1,540	**100.0**	

stressed. One way to depict the complexity of occupational stress is shown in Figure 16.2.

We shall soon consider some of the sources of work stress in detail. For now, note that several sources of occupational stress exist. Some of these stressors are intrinsic to the job. Some are related to the employee's role within the organization, some to career development, some to relationships at work, and some to the structure and climate of the organization.

Interacting with these work stressors are the individual's characteristics. These are brought to the workplace rather than being a function of it, but they are important ingredients in occupational stress, nevertheless. These characteristics include the worker's levels of anxiety and neuroticism, tolerance of ambiguity, and Type A behavior pattern.

Added to this brew are the sources of stress that come from outside the workplace and outside the worker. These extraorganizational sources of stress stem from family problems, life crises, financial matters, and environmental factors. Mix it all up and out come symptoms of occupational health problems that may develop into full-blown disease.

This model of occupational stress, as complex as it appears, is simplified by limiting the examples of stress at work, individual characteristics, and extra-organizational sources of stress. Many others could be included. Further, the interaction of these three factors is depicted as evenly weighted. In actuality, different workplaces have different levels of intrinsic job stressors and career development stressors. Different workers have different levels of anxiety and tolerances of ambiguity, and different workers experience different amounts of family and financial problems. To assume that all of these ingredients can be quantified is naive.

Another way of looking at occupational stress utilizes the Occupational Stress Evaluation Grid.[2] Although developed in 1977, the grid is still a good way to understand occupational stress and stressors. This grid, presented in Table 16.1, recognizes that occupational stressors occur in different contexts—sociocultural,

Time pressure at work can make us so tense we can become ill.

Figure 16.2 Occupational stress model.

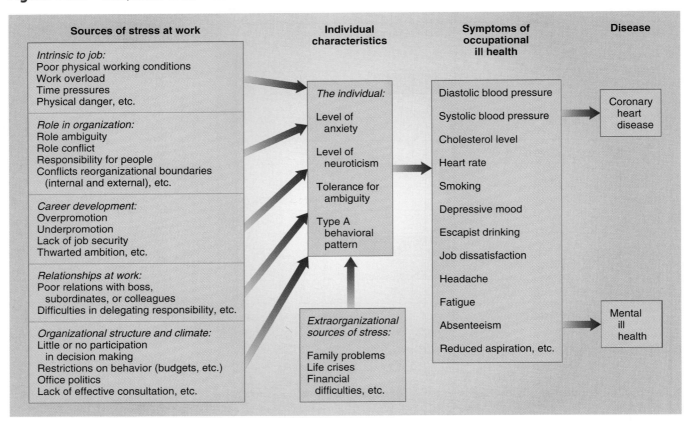

organizational, work setting, interpersonal, psychological, biological, and physical/environmental. The grid identifies formal and informal means of intervening for each of these levels of stressors. Like the model of occupational stress presented in Figure 16.2, the Occupational Stress Evaluation Grid recognizes occupational stress to be a more complex construct than merely inclusive of some sources of stress at work.

Why Is Occupational Stress of Concern?

One reason occupational stress receives so much attention is that businesses are genuinely beginning to care about employee welfare. You don't buy that? Well, how about this? Work stress is costing businesses billions of dollars. Sounds more plausible, doesn't it?

It was estimated in 1992 by the International Labor Organization that stress on the job cost businesses over $200 billion per year.[3] Imagine what the cost is now. These costs include salaries for sick days, costs of hospitalization and outpatient care, and costs related to decreased productivity. Other stress-related factors are catching the eyes of business leaders. For example, health-benefit costs to employers have increased dramatically.

Employees trained over a long period of time, at great cost, may break down when stressed on the job. They may make poor decisions, miss days of work, begin abusing alcohol and other drugs, or die and have to be replaced by other workers who need training. All of this is costly.

In the 2004 Unscheduled Absence Survey, absences attributed to stress tripled between 1995 (6 percent) and 2004 (11 percent).[4,5] In addition, absenteeism attributed to "entitlement mentality" (workers call in sick but are not) increased from 9 percent to 10 percent. Between 1995 and 1996 alone, there was a 100 percent increase in

Table 16.1 OCCUPATIONAL STRESS EVALUATION GRID

Context	Stressors	Interventions	
		Formal	**Informal**
Sociocultural	Racism, sexism Ecological shifts Economic downturns Political changes Military crises	Elections Lobbying/political action Political changes Trade associations	Grass roots organizing Petitions Demonstrations Migration Spouse employment
Organizational	Hiring policies Plant closings Layoffs, relocation Automation, market shifts, retraining Organizational priorities	Corporate decision Reorganization New management model Management consultant (in-service/retraining)	Social activities Contests, incentives Manager involvement and ties with workers Continuing education Moonlighting
Work setting	Task (time, speed, autonomy, creativity) Supervision Coworkers Ergonomics Participation in decision making	Supervisor meetings Health/safety meetings Union grievance Employee involvement Quality circles Job redesign In-service training	Slow down/speed up Redefine tasks Support of other workers Sabotage, theft Quit, change jobs
Interpersonal	Divorce, separation, marital discord Conflict, family/friend Death, illness in family Intergenerational conflict Legal/financial difficulties Early parenthood	Legal/financial services Leave of absence Counseling, psychotherapy Insurance plans Family therapy Loans/credit unions Day care	Seek social support/advice Seek legal/financial assistance Self-help groups Vacation/sick days Child care
Psychological	Neurosis, mental illness Disturbance of affect, cognition, or behavior Ineffective coping skills Poor self-image Poor communication Addictive behavior	Employee assistance (referral/in house) Counseling, psychotherapy Medication Supervisory training Stress management workshop	Seek support from friends, family, church Self-help groups/books Self-medication Recreation, leisure Sexual activity "Mental health" days
Biological	Disease, disability Sleep, appetite disturbance Chemical dependency Biochemical imbalance Pregnancy	Preplacement screening Counseling Medical treatment Health education Employee assistance Maternity leave	Change sleep/wake habits Bag lunch Self-medication Cosmetics Diets, exercise Consult physician
Physical/environmental	Poor air, climate Noise exposure Toxic substance exposure Poor lighting Radiation exposure Poor equipment design Bad architecture	Protective clothing/equipment Climate control Health/safety committee Interior decoration Muzak Union grievance	Own equipment, decoration Walkman, radio Consult personal physician Letters of complaint

Source: M. J. Smith et al., "A Review of NIOSH Psychological Stress Research—1977," *NIOSH Proceedings of Occupational Stress Conference* (Cincinnati: National Institute of Occupational Health and Safety, March 1978), 27–28.

absences due to mental health reasons.[6] In 2004, more than 62 percent of the time when workers called in "sick," they were not sick.

Stress is being encountered at ever-increasing rates. In 1983, 55 percent of people reported experiencing stress on a weekly basis.[7] By 1992, one in three reported experiencing great stress daily or several times a week, up 20 percent from ten years earlier.[8] Later still, in 1996, almost 75 percent reported experiencing great stress on a daily basis.[9] Of the stress Americans experience, one study found 82 percent complained that work was their biggest source of stress.[10] Thirty-five percent of American workers also reported their jobs negatively affected their physical or emotional well-being.[11] Recognizing occupational stress to be more than just an American phenomenon, the World Health Organization considered it to be "the twentieth century disease" indicating it was prevalent in almost every occupation around the world and had become a "global epidemic."[12]

To make matters worse, American workers take fewer vacation days than do workers in other developed countries, and Americans average 8.1 vacation days after a year on the job and 10.2 days after three years.[13] By contrast, Australians average five weeks of vacation a year, four of those weeks guaranteed by law. The United States is the only industrialized nation with no minimum paid-leave law. Europeans get four or five weeks of paid vacation each year, by law. Japanese workers are guaranteed two weeks of vacation by law, Chinese workers three weeks. Researchers argue that the high value placed on hard work and productivity in the United States and a strong work ethic have led to this unfortunate vacation-time disparity.[14]

Not the least of the factors giving rise to the tremendous increase in occupational stress is the development of technological advances. Although many Americans enjoy the fact that they are never out of reach—given their cell phones and car phones, fax machines, laptop and handheld computers, e-mail addresses, and beepers and pagers—being "always on call" can be quite stressful in itself. The extent of this problem is evident in the results of a Gallup poll that found that, on average, workers receive 190 messages a day, by telephone, e-mail, voicemail, interoffice mail, regular mail, fax, Post-it notes, phone message slips, pager, overnight courier, and cell phone.[15]

The effects of occupational stress have attracted the attention of businesses. Some companies offer **flextime,** allowing workers to consider their lifestyles and non-work-related priorities when scheduling their hours of work. Flextime arrangements are attractive to many job seekers. More than 80 percent of young men between the ages of twenty and thirty-nine said that having a work schedule that allows them to spend time with their families is more important than doing challenging work or earning a high salary.[16]

More and more companies offer child care programs to alleviate stress associated with leaving children during work. Chase Manhattan Bank is one of these. Workers for the bank can receive up to twenty days of free care per child each year. A cost analysis found this program saved Chase Manhattan $825,000 in 1996.[17] Parents did not miss work because of the need to care for a child, did not worry about the child's welfare during the workday and could therefore concentrate on work-related tasks, and did not become ill because of stress about the welfare of the child.

Some companies are even opening their own elementary schools for workers' children. Hewlett-Packard in Santa Rosa, California, and Target in Minneapolis are examples of such enterprises. Most of these schools are a collaboration between the local school system—which supplies teachers, curricula, and instructional materials—and the company, which usually owns the land, builds the school, maintains the school, and pays the utilities. American Bankers Insurance Group opened a company school in Miami in 1987. It costs the company $140,000 annually to operate it, yet it saves the company $475,000 per year because it decreases employee absenteeism and turnover. Job turnover among parents whose children attend the school is 6 percent, versus a 13.3 percent rate for the company as a whole.[18]

Still other perks are being offered to help workers experience less stress. Some companies offer free chair massages at workers' desks, job sharing to relieve workload burdens, or telecommuting one or more days a week to diminish the effects of rush-hour traffic on workers. A unique approach has been adopted by Texas Instruments in Dallas. TI offers concierge service for its workers. An employee can call the concierge to set up a birthday party for a child, for example. The employee pays the cost

flextime
Scheduling work at irregular times to meet one's lifestyle.

of the party, but Texas Instruments pays for the concierge service. Approximately 1,500 employees used the service during the first two months it was made available.[19] Concierge programs are now being offered by many other large businesses.

J.C. Penney's Plano, Texas, employees can pick up a chef-prepared take-home meal as they leave work. Other companies offer employees discounts on home computer equipment or elder care programs for workers' parents or grandparents. Twenty-two of the largest corporations in America—including IBM, Lucent Technologies, Xerox, AT&T, Hewlett-Packard, Deloitte and Touche, Price Waterhouse, and ExxonMobil— formed an alliance to offer quality child and elder care for their employees.[20]

Another reason businesses have become interested in their employees' health is that they may be held liable for a worker's ill health resulting from occupational stress. The worker compensation laws of more and more states are making workers injured from stress on the job eligible for compensation. Furthermore, there has been a tremendous rise in employee compensation lawsuits claiming occupational stress as the cause of workers' emotional and physical disabilities.

Since 1987, however, there has been a drop every year in the number of these claims—the result of tighter controls at the state level rather than changes in the workplace. In Oregon, for example, a change in the law allows stress claims to be filed only if injuries were a direct consequence of work (rates decreased from 4.9 per 1,000 claims in 1987 to 2.2 per 1,000 claims in 1990), and in California, the law now requires 50 percent of the disability to be directly related to work rather than only 10 percent, as was the case previously. Still, it is obvious that responding to stress is not only ethical but is good business.

High-Stress Jobs

Researcher Robert Karasek and colleagues studied job stress and found the most stressful jobs are those that allow for very little decision making yet place a high psychological demand on the worker. Examples of psychological demands are having to work quickly and having a huge workload. The most stressful and least stressful jobs were

Most Stressful	Least Stressful
Electrical assembler	Architect
Forger	Dentist
Cashier	Forester
Electrical laborer	Therapist
Cook	Tool maker

Is the occupation you're training for one that expects a lot of you but does not allow you to make enough decisions about how you'll function on the job? If so, perhaps you want to reconsider whether you want to experience the stress and strain that job might entail.

Source: Robert A. Karasek et al., "Job Characteristics in Relation to the Prevalence of Myocardial Infarction in the U.S. Health Examination Survey (HES) and the Health and Nutrition Examination Survey (HANES)," *American Journal of Public Health* 78(1988): 910–18.

Workers Are All Stressed Out

A study in Europe found that work stress was so prevalent as to be a major problem. When the European Foundation for the Improvement of Living and Working Conditions conducted its Second European Survey they found that one in four workers felt stressed by work, one in five felt fatigue, and one in eight suffered from headaches.

The survey also found that work stress is experienced somewhat differently in different countries. For example, about 50 percent of Dutch workers reported a high work pace. In England, about 67 percent of workers reported that stress was the most serious problem in their working lives. Furthermore, British doctors and nurses believed stress was increasing and 20 percent had considered suicide. English teachers also experience a great deal of stress. More than half of them have considered leaving the teaching profession. Swedish teachers feel similarly. In fact, 75 percent of Swedish teachers considered the psychological demands of their jobs extremely high.

The lesson to be learned by the Second European Survey is that work stress is a problem throughout the world, one that needs immediate attention and alleviation if the health and well-being of our workforce is to be protected.

Source: "More than One Worker in Four Feels Stressed by Work," *Euro Review on Research in Health and Safety at Work,* 1997, 6–7.

Gender and Occupational Stress

Researchers have begun to identify sources of stress particularly experienced by women: career blocks, sexual harassment, male-dominated organizational structures and climates, performance pressure, gender stereotyping, isolation, and lack of role models.[21] One study of managers found that females tended to experience stressors emotionally.[22] Their stress was due to pressure to meet expectations to be responsible for people both inside and outside the home. By contrast, males tended to focus on themselves and regard other things as beyond their control.

Female workers take on more of the household work, and the accompanying stress, than do male workers.[23] In a study of Canadian workers, approximately 21 percent of women workers but only 8 percent of men workers spent 30 hours or more doing housework.[24] Many married and employed women with substantial household responsibilities intentionally limit their career aspirations and purposefully reduce their involvement in work, in comparison with their male counterparts.[25] The occupational stress that male workers experience has been found to be related to their concerns about the power structure within the organization that employs them. Female workers, in contrast, experience occupational stress when there is a conflict between job requirements and family responsibilities.[26]

Stress management experts recommend that work organizations develop a culture that members perceive to be supportive of their efforts to balance their career and family lives.[27] Many companies are trying to do so. Those that are recognized for these efforts—a recent article listed the top ten healthiest companies for women.[28]—are well positioned to recruit and retain top-notch workers of both genders.

Disease and Occupational Stress

The link between occupational stress and disease is a difficult one to prove since this relationship is complicated by the workers' characteristics and stressors outside of the workplace. There is, however, evidence that supports the conclusion that occupational

Two Alternative Occupational Stress Models

One way of conceptualizing work stress is the *job strain* model described in this chapter. The job strain model conceives of stress as the result of high job demands and low job control. You can imagine how frustrating, and stressful, it would be to be expected to be highly productive, while at the same time not being able to decide how to do that. In a sense, the manner in which you are evaluated (meeting the high job demands) depends on factors beyond your control. How unfair that must feel!

Another way of conceptualizing work stress is the *effort-reward imbalance* model. The effort-reward imbalance model conceives of work stress as a function of too great a work effort required to do the job accompanied by low reward for a job well done. This model considers such effort as high workload on one end of the equation and such rewards as salary, esteem, and occupational status on the other. According to the effort-reward imbalance model, "demanding tasks under insecure conditions, lack of promotion, and low wages compared to qualifications may in the long run threaten workers' health and well-being."[a]

Perhaps occupational stress is a combination of the factors included in each of these models. High work demand, low job control, and lack of accompanying reward are all probably factors that contribute to work stress.

[a]"Chronic Load Is Dangerous for Health and Well-Being," *Euro Review on Research in Health and Safety at Work,* 1997, 13.

stress is related to illness and disease. This evidence falls into two categories: evidence of the physiological effects of occupational stress and evidence of disease states associated with occupational stress.

Physiological Effects

Several studies have shown that physiological arousal accompanies occupational stress. For example, several investigators have found the work environment associated with hypertension,[29,30] serum cholesterol,[31] increase in left ventricular mass,[32] high concentrations of catecholamines,[33] high plasma fibrinogen concentrations,[34,35] and associated behavioral risk factors such as tobacco use[36] and ingestion of alcohol.[37]

An interesting finding is that the amount of work does not seem as critical to health as the control the worker has over the work rate or related work processes. For example, workers in jobs with higher workload and pacing demands, and very little control of these demands, have increased rates of coronary heart disease and higher blood pressure than workers in jobs not so characterized.[38,39]

Disease States

Many studies have implicated occupational stress in the development of illness and disease. Given the increase in blood pressure, serum cholesterol, catecholamines, and plasma fibrinogen, it should be no surprise to learn that occupational stress is related to coronary heart disease.[40,41] And it is related to death from heart disease.[42] It is also associated with obesity,[43] probably because people eat as a way of relieving stress at work. Those workers experiencing occupational stress report low levels of job satisfaction and more psychosomatic symptoms,[44,45] as well as feelings of anger and alienation.[46,47]

When a job demands too much work in too little time, stress can develop

In addition to coronary heart disease, work stress has been related to hypertension, diabetes, and peptic ulcers.[48] Occupational stress may, in fact, lead to any of the stress-related diseases discussed in Chapter 3. The impact of work stress can be so devastating that at least one researcher found higher rates of heart attacks on "back-to-work" Mondays than on any other day of the week, and the fewest heart attacks on Fridays (TGIF).[49] Why ruin the weekend?

Psychological Effects

Occupational stress also has consequences for psychological health. Some occupational stressors can result in low self-confidence, increased job tension, and lower job satisfaction.[50] A summary of ninety-six studies of the psychological effects of occupational stress found that absenteeism and poor job performance are related to stress on the job.[51]

Occupational Stressors

Workers report more occupational stress when work objectives are unclear, when they have conflicting demands placed upon them, when they have too little or too much to do, when they have little input into decisions that affect them, and when they are responsible for other workers' professional development.

Lack of Participation

One of the factors of the workplace and of the organization's modus operandi that is related to stress is the degree of participation. Workers' perceptions of the degree of their participation in the decision-making process, the degree to which they are consulted on issues affecting the organization, and their involvement in establishing rules of behavior at work have proven to be related to job satisfaction, job-related feelings of threat, and feelings of self-esteem.[52,53] Researchers also have found that nonparticipation is related to overall poor physical health, escapist drinking, depression, dissatisfaction with life, low motivation to work, intention to leave the job, and absenteeism.[54] Figure 16.3 depicts the effects of high participation on the job. Low participation can be expected to have the opposite effect.

Role Problems

A clear sense of your role in an organization and a sense that you can "play the part" are important in keeping stress at a minimum. A variety of role-related problems may arise for workers who lack these feelings.

Role Overload

When job demands are so great that the worker feels an inability to cope, stress will develop. You can imagine the feeling of having too much to do in too little time.

Role Insufficiency

When workers lack the training, education, skills, or experience to accomplish the job, they feel stressed. A poor fit between workers' talents and the organization's expectations creates disharmony and dissatisfaction.[55]

Role Ambiguity

When aspects of the job and workplace are unclear, frustration and stress are likely to develop. Workers should know the criteria for career advancement, the priorities of the organization, and generally what is expected of them.

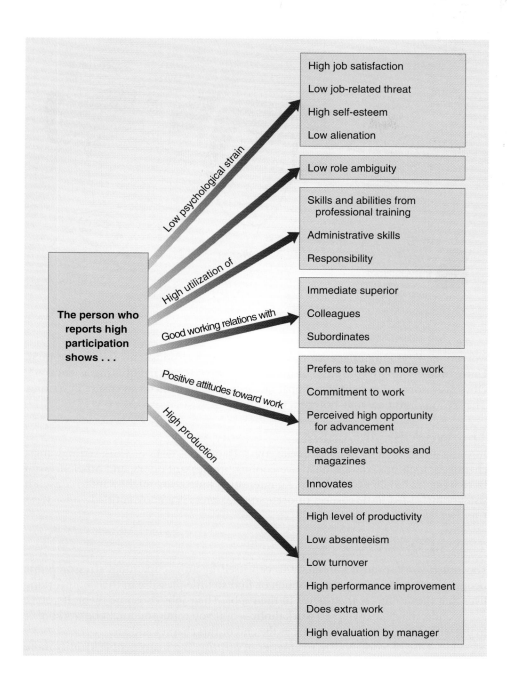

The person who reports high participation shows . . .

Low psychological strain →
- High job satisfaction
- Low job-related threat
- High self-esteem
- Low alienation

→
- Low role ambiguity

High utilization of →
- Skills and abilities from professional training
- Administrative skills
- Responsibility

Good working relations with →
- Immediate superior
- Colleagues
- Subordinates

Positive attitudes toward work →
- Prefers to take on more work
- Commitment to work
- Perceived high opportunity for advancement
- Reads relevant books and magazines
- Innovates

High production →
- High level of productivity
- Low absenteeism
- Low turnover
- High performance improvement
- Does extra work
- High evaluation by manager

Role Conflict

Sometimes workers get caught in a bind. Two supervisors each expect something different. The worker may be faced with conflicting demands (see Figure 16.4). This is the "damned if you do, damned if you don't" dilemma. Such a situation is a factor in occupational stress.

Job Dissatisfaction

The factors that are typically thought related to dissatisfaction on the job are salary and conditions of the workplace (e.g., noise, poor lighting, poor ventilation, crowding, etc.). However, even if workers were paid well and worked in hygienic conditions, they might still be dissatisfied. A class of work-related factors, called **motivational factors**, can affect job satisfaction. These factors include the degree of stimulating tasks involved, the amount of recognition for jobs done well, relationships with fellow

motivational factors
Variables associated with job satisfaction; includes working on stimulating tasks, being recognized for work well done, and positive relationships with work colleagues.

Figure 16.4

Role conflict: which demands to meet?

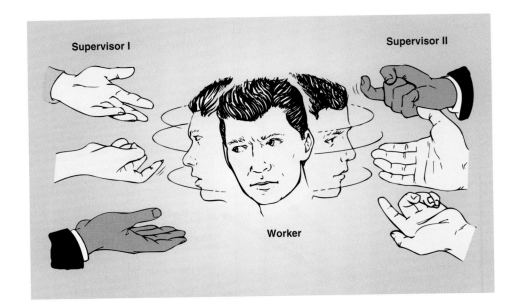

Supervisor I

Supervisor II

Worker

workers, and the amount of encouragement to take on responsibility (see Figure 16.5). Unfortunately, many unions ignore these factors when negotiating a contract. Obviously, some of these motivational factors would be difficult to ensure in writing. They're important enough, however, to try for.

The Work Environment

In some places of work, hazards create stress. Dangerous tasks or work settings, toxic chemicals, high noise levels, dust, overcooling, unpleasant odors, and other stressful factors can lead to illness or disease. An interesting source you might want to consult if you are interested in this aspect of occupational stress is a book entitled *Office Work Can Be Dangerous to Your Health.*[56]

The Workaholic

Too much work, even if you enjoy it, can itself be an occupational stressor. Some people either enjoy their work so much or find so little pleasure in their nonworking lives that they immerse themselves in their jobs. Their jobs consume them. If you've ever wondered whether you're a **workaholic**—or if you think you might be working or living with one—complete Lab 16.2 at the end of this chapter and see.

One cause of workaholism is a matter of *identity.* Too many people identify more with their roles as workers than with their roles as individual persons. Are you a person who happens to be a student, or are you a student who happens to be a person? The answer to this question determines your priorities and how you allocate your time. The self-worth of some workers is a function of what they produce. Some professors may judge their self-worth by how many articles they publish or by how many awards they receive. Do you judge yourself by your grades or by the number of credits you have accumulated? Or do you consider what kind of a friend you are or how much you contribute to your family and community? A strong personal identity offers the best way to prevent workaholism and other occupational stressors from negatively impacting on your life.

Workaholics can be of several different kinds. Naughton dichotomizes workaholics on the basis of career commitment and obsession-compulsion.[57] He hypothesizes that *job-involved workaholics* (high work commitment, low obsession-compulsion) perform well in demanding jobs, have high job satisfaction, and have little interest in nonjob activities. *Compulsive workaholics* (high work commitment, high obsession-compulsion) are impatient and not creative and therefore do not perform well on the

workaholic
Immersing oneself excessively in work at the expense of nonwork activities.

Figure 16.5

Human needs and their job-related satisfiers.

Self-realization needs	Job-related satisfiers
Reaching your potential Independence Creativity Self-expression	Involvement in planning your work Freedom to make decisions affecting work Creative work to perform Opportunities for growth and development

Esteem needs	Job-related satisfiers
Responsibility Self-respect Recognition Sense of accomplishment	Status symbols Merit awards Challenging work Sharing in decisions Opportunity for advancement

Social needs	Job-related satisfiers
Companionship Acceptance Love and affection Group membership	Opportunities for interaction with others Team spirit Friendly coworkers

Safety needs	Job-related satisfiers
Security for self and possessions Avoidance of risks Avoidance of harm Avoidance of pain	Safe working conditions Seniority Fringe benefits Proper supervision Sound company policies, programs, and practices

Physical needs	Job-related satisfiers
Food Clothing Shelter Comfort Self-preservation	Pleasant working conditions Adequate wage or salary Rest periods Labor-saving devices Efficient work methods

job. *Nonworkaholics* (low work commitment, low obsession-compulsion) spend an excessive amount of time on nonwork activities and are, as a result, unsuccessful on the job.

Scott, Moore, and Miceli[58] categorize workaholics in a somewhat different way. The *compulsive-dependent workaholic* is so focused on work that high levels of anxiety, stress, and physical and psychological consequences develop. The *perfectionist workaholic* can tolerate nothing less than perfection and, as a result, experiences high stress and low job satisfaction as well as physical and psychological consequences. The *achievement-oriented workaholic* does not obsess about work but strives to achieve; the result is high job and life satisfaction, low stress, and good health.

Spence and Robbins[59] propose a workaholic triad: *work involvement, drivenness,* and *work enjoyment. Workaholics* have high work involvement and are driven, but they score low on work enjoyment. *Work enthusiasts* score high on work involvement and work enjoyment but low on driveness. Work enthusiasts exhibit a healthier, more satisfying work style.

In a review of the literature on workaholism, McMillan and colleagues hypothesized that it is an addiction to work and is similar to other addictions.[60] These researchers concluded that workaholism is related to stress, Type A behavior pattern, and moderately related to obsessive-compulsiveness.

Workaholism has serious consequences. It undermines family functioning.[61] Adult children of workaholics experience more depression, anxiety, external locus of control, and obsessive-compulsiveness than do children of nonworkaholics.[62,63] According to the Academy of Matrimonial Lawyers, workaholism is one of the top four causes of divorce.[64] Another study found workaholism has a major effect on marital cohesion.[65]

To combat workaholism, try these tips:

1. Focus on the work you most love doing, and try to find ways to stop doing, delegate, or minimize the parts of your work you dislike.

2. Ask yourself, "What work would I do for free?" Then try to evolve your work in that direction.

3. Use your time; don't let it use you. Decide how much time you want to spend working; then limit your work time accordingly. For example, you might arrange to stop working at 5:30 p.m. by making a commitment to go running with a friend every workday at 5:45. Arrangements like these help workaholics return to feeling more refreshed—and more productive.

4. Build friendships at work. Arrange to spend quality time with coworkers.

5. Schedule open time into your work life. If, for instance, you now schedule work-related appointments every thirty minutes, try to evolve toward scheduling them every forty-five minutes instead.

6. Learn to say no to new demands on your time. If this is difficult, say that you'd like some time to think about it; then say no later.

7. Decorate your workplace to create an environment that pleases you. You deserve it.

8. Try to stay in touch with the positive aspects of your work: the pleasure of doing work that fulfills you, the freedom, the opportunity to be of service to others, or other aspects of your work you find rewarding.

9. Heavy involvement in work usually entitles you to have a good deal to say about the way you work. How might you change or restructure your work to make it feel more fulfilling?

In addition to these suggestions, remember that the workaholic enjoys work and therefore might not notice the harm it is doing. Family members often suffer more than the workaholic. Time is taken away from them and family responsibilities accrue to them because of the workaholic's work style. To intervene between workaholism and poor family health, time should be scheduled for family activities that will get the workaholic away from the telephone, the computer, and job commitments. Hiking and backpacking are useful for this purpose.

Burnout

burnout
An adverse stress reaction to work with psychological, psychophysiological, and behavioral components.

Too much work or frequent frustration at work can lead to a syndrome of physical and emotional exhaustion. This syndrome is called **burnout.** Burnout is "an adverse work stress reaction with psychological, psychophysiological, and behavioral components. Moreover, burnout appears to be a major factor in low worker morale, high absenteeism and job turnover rates, physical illness and distress, increased alcohol and drug use, marital and family conflict, and various psychological problems."[66] The symptoms of burnout include the following:

1. *Diminished sense of humor:* inability to laugh at daily, on-the-job situations.

2. *Skipping rest and food breaks:* continually having no time for coffee or lunch breaks to restore stamina.

3. *Increased overtime and no vacation:* indispensable to the organization; reluctant to say *no* to working on scheduled off-days.

4. *Increased physical complaints:* fatigue, irritability, muscle tension, stomach upset, and susceptibility to illness.

5. *Social withdrawal:* pulling away from coworkers, peers, family members.

6. *Changed job performance:* increased absenteeism, tardiness, use of sick leave, and decreased efficiency or productivity.

7. *Self-medication:* increased use of alcohol, tranquilizers, and other mood-altering drugs.

8. *Internal changes:* emotional exhaustion, loss of self-esteem, depression, frustration, and a "trapped" feeling.

Complete Lab 16.3 at the end of this chapter to determine if you are experiencing burnout.

Burnout is particularly prevalent among professionals who work with people: correctional officers, police officers, teachers, social workers, mental health counselors, nurses.[67,68] In addition to the symptoms listed, burnout may manifest itself in absenteeism, a negative attitude toward other people, callousness, emotional exhaustion, low morale, poor job performance, high turnover, accidents at work, and poor relationships.[69]

A different way of looking at how burnout develops involves a progressive five-stage approach:

Stage one (the honeymoon). At this stage, the worker is usually satisfied with the job and the tasks involved and remains enthusiastic toward the work. However, as this stage continues, the tasks become unenjoyable and the worker loses energy.

Stage two (fuel shortage). At this stage, fatigue sets in, and the worker may respond by abusing drugs. Difficulty sleeping is another symptom of this stage.

Stage three (chronic symptoms). At this stage, overwork leads to physical effects that include constant exhaustion and susceptibility to disease and psychological effects that include acute anger and feelings of depression.

Stage four (crisis). At this stage, actual illness can develop that results in the worker not being able to attend to the job. Relationships at home may

We each need time alone. A chance to get away and relax can be rejuvenating. When did you last sit and do nothing?

Women in the workplace experience some unique stressors. For example, they do not make as much money as men do, and they are more likely to be subjected to sexual harassment.

also be affected due to a sense of pessimism, self-doubt, or obsession with problems.

Stage five (hitting the wall). At this stage, the physical and psychological problems can become severe enough to cause illness that is life threatening. The worker now has so many problems at work that his or her career is actually threatened.

What can one do about burnout? An expert in this field suggests the following:

1. *"What do I work for?"* List all things—material and abstract—that you get out of your job. Identify your motivations, the value and meaning of your job.

2. *"I really want to do that."* List all activities you like and rank them in order of importance. Then note the last time you engaged in each.

3. *Create a support group.* Friends or coworkers meet on a regular basis.

4. *Start a physical self-care program.* Include exercise, nutrition, and elimination of destructive habits such as smoking.

5. *Start a psychological self-care program.* Include training in relaxation, negotiation, time management, and assertiveness.

6. *Do something silly every day.* Roller skate, play tiddlywinks, blow bubbles, or make a funny face. Relax, smile, and avoid taking yourself too seriously.[70]

Have you had it with school? With work? Are you near burnout? If so, will you do something about it? You're in control of yourself and your feelings. You can exercise this control. You don't have to suffer from burnout if you choose not to.

Women and Work Outside the Home

Although the work women do inside the home may be as important as (or more important than) the work they do outside, this section focuses on outside work.

Before proceeding, it may be interesting to see how much you know about women's economic roles. Decide which of the following statements are true and which are false:

1. Women get paid the same amount of money as men when they do the same job.

2. Women get paid the same amount of money as men when they have a comparable educational level.

3. Men are sexually harassed on the job about as often as are women.

4. Traditionally female occupations have become inundated with many males.

5. Women in racial, ethnic, and other minority groups have salaries comparable to those of minority men.

If you answered that all five statements are false, you get an honorary membership in the Burbank Friends of Truth Museum. If you answered that all are true, you get a stuffed male chauvinist pig for Christmas or Chanukah.

Statistics clearly demonstrate women are disadvantaged in the world of work, minority women particularly so. They make less money than their male counterparts, even when they perform similar jobs and have similar educational backgrounds. As though that weren't enough of an insult, women are subjected to sexual harassment and sexual discrimination at work to a much greater extent than are men.

Although a large number of women are working outside the home (56 percent),[71] they are still predominantly employed in traditional women's roles. Secretaries, receptionists, nurses, bookkeepers, nursing aides, and elementary school teachers are occupations still made up of more than 80 percent women.[72]

Just as stressful is the fact that women earn less than men in almost all job categories and at all ages. This discrepancy holds up even in comparisons of men and women with the same levels of education. In 2003, the median earnings of female executives, administrators, and managers were $36,861 whereas they were $53,044 for male executives. For professionals, the median earnings of females were $31,791, of male professionals $50,966. Even in the traditional female service occupations category, females earned less than males ($11,883 compared to $16,752).[73] In the year 2006, the U.S. Bureau of Labor reported women earned 80.6 cents on the dollar compared with men.

In some categories in 2000, women actually earned more than male counterparts. For example, female chief executives' annual salaries averaged $275,000, compared to $253,100 for male chief executives, and female physicians and female occupational therapists earned more than their male counterparts.[74]

Many women who reach the upper echelons of business careers do not receive the recognition they deserve. They bump into a "glass ceiling" and can rise no higher in the company, even as men with comparable or less talent continue to advance. For example, although the percentage of women on *Fortune* 500 company boards of directors has risen consistently (from 8.3 percent in 1993 to 10.6 percent in 1997), of the 6,081 total number of board members in 1997, 5,438 were men and only 643 were women.[75]

Also alarming, though unfortunately not surprising, is the penalty minority workers pay. Minority men earn less money than do white men, and minority women earn less than do white women. These differences involve significant amounts of money.

Last, women who work outside the home must also work inside the home. When children are involved, the stress associated with working can be magnified, yet more and more women with young children are entering the labor force. In 2004, 68 percent of married women with children younger than eighteen were in the labor force, as were approximately 75 percent of married women with children between the ages of six and seventeen. Fifty-nine percent of married women with children under six years of age were employed outside the home in 2004.

Frustration is also growing among working women over the division of labor in the home. A study conducted by the U.S. Department of Labor found that wives working outside the home do less housework than wives who work inside the home, but they still do the majority of the housework.[76] Some husbands help with housework,

Stress and Sexual Health

Researchers from the Harvard School of Public Health's Center for Communication,[a] in conjunction with the editors of *Ladies' Home Journal,* conducted a study of stress and women. They found that 21 percent of very anxious women have had vaginitis, whereas only 2 percent of "calm" women have experienced that infection. Further, only 21 percent of "calm" women suffer from premenstrual syndrome, whereas 41 percent of very anxious women do. What caused this stress? Well, the most frequently cited stressor was "problems at work" (32 percent), next was "fights with their man" (26 percent), and next was "clashes with their children" (25 percent).

[a]Editors of the *Ladies' Home Journal* and the Harvard School of Public Health's Center for Communication, "Your Body, Your Health," *Ladies' Home Journal,* February 1988, 91–93, 134–36.

The Family and Medical Leave Act

To help employees cope with the stress resulting from major family crises, in 1993 the U.S. Congress passed the Family and Medical Leave Act, and it was signed into law by President Clinton. The Family and Medical Leave Act requires companies to

1. Allow employees as much as twelve weeks of unpaid leave during any twelve-month period for the birth of a child, to care for a spouse or parent who becomes seriously ill, or to care for themselves if their own health condition prevents them from performing job responsibilities.

2. Allow employees who choose to take a leave to return to their former jobs or to an equivalent position upon their return to work.

3. Keep providing workers with health care benefits although workers on leave do not have to be paid. However, if workers do not return when their leave expires, the business can recapture from the former worker the health care premiums they paid during the leave.

To be eligible,

1. Employees must work for a business that has fifty or more workers.

2. Employees must have worked for the business for at least one year and for at least 1,250 hours (25 hours a week).

3. Employees can be required to provide documentation of the reason for their leave. Up to three medical opinions on the need for the leave can be requested by the employer.

---

but not to the extent that many wives would like to see.[77] Women argue that they are being abused and treated unfairly by their spouses. Score another point for the stress response.

Sexual Harassment at Work

Sexual harassment at work has typically meant sexual advances made by someone of power or authority who threatens firing, lack of promotion, or some other sanction if sexual activity is declined. A sexual advance at work that is politely made and that carries no threat of sanction is not sexual harassment, although some offended workers interpret such advances as harassment. The problem area in sexual harassment is a sexual advance from someone of a higher job status to someone of a lower job status. The person of lower job status may feel pressured to say yes, even though no job sanction has been made explicit.

Sexual advances are not the only criterion for sexual harassment. If jokes and sexual innuendos so permeate the workplace that workers feel uncomfortable, are unable to perform well, and thus suffer in their careers, that work environment itself qualifies as sexual harassment. Furthermore, even if the company is unaware that such harassment is occurring, the Supreme Court ruled in *Meritor Savings Bank v. Vinson* in 1986, and again in 1998, that the company is still legally liable for the results of such harassment. It is for this reason that organizations have instituted educational programs to notify supervisors that sexual harassment in the workplace will not be tolerated.

Some researchers believe that the effort to expose sexual harassment has been hampered by the mistaken view that sexual advances are motivated by sexual desire, which should be private, not by discrimination, which should be public.[78] Still, a telephone poll conducted by Louis Harris and Associates found 31 percent of female workers and 7 percent of male workers experienced sexual harassment, although 62 percent took no action. Of the female workers harassed, all of them were harassed by a man. Of the male harassment victims, 59 percent were harassed by a woman and 41 percent by another man.[79]

The Equal Employment Opportunity Commission describes three different forms of sexual harassment:

> Unwelcome sexual advances, requests for sexual favors, and other verbal and physical conduct of a sexual nature constitute sexual harassment when (1) submission to such conduct is made either explicitly or implicitly a term or condition of an individual's employment; (2) submission to, or rejection of, such conduct by an individual is used as the basis for employment decisions affecting such individual; or (3) such conduct has the purpose or effect of substantially interfering with an individual's work performance or creating an intimidating, hostile, or offensive working environment.[80]

Sexual harassment occurs in the form of unwelcome touching, grabbing or groping, whistling at someone, lewd comments, foul or obscene language, or asking about one's sex life or experiences. Repeated requests for dates, sexually oriented or explicit remarks, and the display of sexually explicit posters or calendars also constitute sexual harassment.

Awareness of what constitutes sexual harassment and of what can be done about it is very important. In fact, after the Clarence Thomas Supreme Court confirmation hearings, at which Anita Hill accused Thomas of sexual harassment, the Equal Employment Opportunity Commission reported that formal complaints of sexual harassment against corporate employers jumped to 1,244, compared with 728 during the same period of time the previous year.[81] Even junior and senior high school students report sexual harassment. A study conducted by the American Association of University Women[82] of sexual harassment experienced by students in grades eight through eleven found 81 percent of students (85 percent of girls and 76 percent of boys) had encountered sexual harassment.

Sexual harassment also occurs in the military, sometimes with startling results. Are you surprised to learn that more men than women are sexually harassed while serving their country, although more women than men report harassment to persons in authority? In a study of 14,498 men and women on active duty in the Army conducted in 1997, nearly twice as many men as women said they had been sexually harassed sometime during the previous year.[83] This is not what we are striving to achieve when we speak of gender equality! These figures may be a little misleading, though. Women comprise 14 percent of the Army's 480,000 soldiers (67,200 women and 412,800 men). Even though 22 percent of the Army's women soldiers and only 7 percent of the Army's men soldiers reported being sexually harassed, because of the disparity in total numbers, more men (28,900) than women (14,800) were harassed. Regardless of gender, these numbers are alarming.

The effects of sexual harassment are varied. Women who have been forced to have sexual intercourse or other sexual experiences as children, for example, are nearly twice as likely to be unhappy in their lives, more than twice as likely to say that sex is not pleasurable, and more likely to experience sexual dysfunction.[84] There may be *physical consequences* such as headaches, sleep disturbance, stomach upset, nightmares, phobias, and substance abuse. There may be *emotional consequences* such as anxiety, anger, fear, insecurity, embarrassment, powerlessness, and guilt. There may be *self-perception consequences* such as a negative self-concept and lower self-esteem, a feeling of lack of control, and hopelessness. There may be *social, interpersonal, and sexual consequences* such as withdrawal, fear of new people, lack of trust, and sexual dysfunction. And there may be *career consequences* such as a change in work or study habits, unfavorable performance evaluation, drop in academic or work performance due to stress, absenteeism, and a change in career goals.[85]

Remedies have been developed to be used by those who have been sexually harassed. Grievance procedures in many businesses and colleges have been established to deal with complaints. Educational campaigns are being conducted at work and school sites. And women's groups counsel the sexually harassed about their legal options. Do you know your campus's procedures for charges of sexual harassment?

Working in the Home

The bank was a typical one: leather upholstered chairs, wooden gates with swinging doors, red carpet, caged-in tellers, and cheap replicas of attractive paintings on the walls. It didn't look like a studio setting, yet a TV camera hanging conspicuously in the corner of the room recorded all the exciting goings-on. I was there with my wife, seeking approval of a mortgage well beyond our means but just this side of our aspirations. The bank manager, who, to her credit, sized up the situation quickly, was asking all the usual embarrassing questions—"How much did you make last year? Can you prove it? To whom do you owe money? Is your car paid for?"

Well, the trouble was just beginning. It soon came time for my wife to answer the same questions. The first one did it—"Do you work?" How innocent those three little words sounded. Nevertheless, I knew what to expect as I leaned back in my chair in an unconscious nonverbal expression that said, "I don't want any part of this one!"

"I most certainly do," was my wife's answer.

"How much do you earn?"

"I don't earn anything. I work at home."

"Oh, you're just a housewife."

"No, I'm not *just* a housewife."

"Sorry, I didn't mean any offense."

Sorry or not, the damage was done. Had I bothered to, I'm sure I could have objectively verified what I knew to be my wife's biomedical condition—elevated blood pressure, increased heart rate, rapid and shallow breathing, and tense muscles. By now you recognize the stress response.

One of the stressors women experience is the denigration of their home-making role. My wife's term—domestic engineer—is an accurate one. Full-time homemaking is difficult, is tiring, and requires a great deal of skill, time, effort, creativity, and

When men and women work full time outside of the home, women still do more than an equal share of work inside the home.

commitment. Although there is nothing that makes women more suited than men for this role, tradition has made full-time homemaking a job done predominantly by women. In recent years, more attention has been paid to men who occupy this role, and their designation—househusband—is as demeaning as the female version—housewife. Men and women who work as full-time homemakers are certainly not married to the house, and their priorities aren't there, either. Rather, their homemaking role is designed to make themselves and those with whom they live feel comfortable. They organize car pools, umpire baseball games, place Band-Aids on wounds that heal better for their loving care, and do other varied and meaningful tasks such as watching over the family's health and nutrition.

That some people, men and women, downplay the significance and value of homemaking is unfortunate. Certainly this role is not one that everyone would choose, but it is a role that many women and some men occupy by choice and perform exceptionally well. It is an extremely important role that can be divided by members of the family or performed by one person.

The stressors associated with domestic engineering are similar to other occupational stressors: too much to do in too little time (role overload), not being specifically trained for many of the tasks (role insufficiency), having to answer to too many different family members' demands (role conflict), and not being clear about all that is expected (role ambiguity). When the denigration of the role is added to these stressors, the load may become too much to bear, and illness and disease may occur.

Women with children face another stressor—the empty-nest syndrome. One day, after years of mothering, the last child moves out. Some women feel their value is diminished at this point because they feel less needed than before. Even for women who see the empty nest as offering an opportunity to do things that they didn't have time to do before, obstacles present themselves. Some employers view empty-nester applicants as lacking in experience. Career counselors, however, have been helping women market themselves as well-trained and abundantly experienced in organizational skills, time management, interpersonal relationships, problem solving, and purchasing. How many employers would not want to hire an applicant who has demonstrated an ability to handle tiresome, difficult chores requiring a great deal of skill, time, effort, creativity, and commitment? These are the traits that I used several paragraphs earlier to describe homemaking.

Interventions

More and more businesses are offering health promotion programs with stress management as a primary component. One of the national health objectives to be achieved by the year 2010 is to have at least 60 percent of work sites employing fifty or more people provide programs to reduce employee stress. In 1992, 37 percent provided employee stress programs.[86]

Using our stress model, we know we can intervene between occupational stress and its negative consequences by changing life situations, our perceptions or cognitive appraisal of those situations, or our emotional reactions, or by doing something physical to use up the stress by-products. This section will describe how to specifically apply these interventions.

Life-Situation Interventions

If you dislike your job and it is causing you either to feel ill or to behave in ways that are detrimental to your career or your home life, you can always quit that job. Short of that, you can ask for a change in job responsibilities, or you can request a less stressful job within the same organization. If you are experiencing burnout, learn to organize your time better and to say no when asked to take on additional responsibilities. In addition, some stress-reducing rules might help:

1. Don't take work home.
2. Take a full hour for lunch.

3. Do not discuss business over lunch.

4. Discuss your feelings about occupational stress with whomever is close by whenever those feelings develop.

Perception Interventions

Recognizing that your perceptions of your occupational stress are as important as the actual events precipitating that stress, you will need to intervene in these perceptions. These suggestions should help:

1. *Look for the humor in your stressors at work.* A resourceful teacher, frustrated by inane memos from the principal with which she was repeatedly and unmercifully bombarded, kept a file of these memos and eventually wrote a very humorous and successful book based upon them. The principal may not have found humor in this teacher's survival technique, but the teacher sure did; besides, she had tenure.

2. *Try to see things for what they really are.* Here's an example, but keep this between us. Publishers are notorious for requesting manuscripts from authors by certain *firm* deadline dates. Unfortunately, too often these manuscripts sit on an editor's desk before being processed. Through some bitter experiences, I have learned that publishers' *deadlines* are really not deadlines. Rather, they are dates *close* to when they would like to receive a manuscript and, knowing that many authors will be late with their submissions, these editors have selected dates with a margin for delay. I have learned to allow myself more time to get a job done when I have been able to perceive that I really have more time to complete that work than I first thought. You can use that strategy as well. Perhaps you, too, have "deadlines" that really aren't deadlines.

3. *Distinguish between need and desire.* For example, "I *must* get this task completed" might be more truthfully stated as "I *wish* I could get this task completed."

4. *Separate your self-worth from the task.* If you fail at a task, it does not mean you are a failure.

5. *Identify situations and employ the appropriate style of coping.* Lazarus and Folkman differentiated between **problem-focused coping** and **emotion-focused coping**.[87] Problem-focused coping is the use of activities specific to getting the task accomplished, whereas emotion-focused coping is the use of activities to feel better about the task. If you employed problem-focused coping for a task that was beyond your accomplishment (e.g., turning in a 200-page treatise on the migratory habits of aardvarks for tomorrow's class), you would only frustrate yourself and become distressed. Given such an impossible task, you would do better to joke about it, discuss your feelings with a friend, or leave a real aardvark in your professor's mailbox with a note instructing him or her to observe this creature's migratory habits and get back to you. Conversely, if a task can be accomplished but you dillydally by joking and partying with friends, you are employing emotion-focused coping when you should have engaged in activities to get the task done (problem-focused coping). Perceiving what is called for in a particular situation will allow you to better determine which method of coping is most appropriate.

Emotional Arousal Interventions

Relaxation techniques, if done regularly, can help prevent occupational stress from making you ill, creating disharmony in your relationships at work or at home, or leading to your abuse of alcohol or other drugs, as well as prevent the other harmful consequences of occupational stress. I have had participants in my classes and workshops tell me they have found out-of-the-way places at work where they meditate during part of their lunch hour or during breaks in the workday. Others have had to leave the

problem-focused coping
The use of activities specific to getting a task done.

emotion-focused coping
The use of activities to feel better about the task.

work site but have found nearby parks or golf courses, where they, too, practice a relaxation technique. Still others have been able to get their companies to establish one area as the relaxation area—usually an infrequently used lounge or work area. You can use a relaxation technique to intervene at this level if you choose to. Be ingenious, be assertive, be committed to caring for you.

Physiological Arousal Interventions

Exercise is an excellent way to use up the stress products created by occupational stress. Recognizing this, many businesses have built gymnasiums or outside exercise areas (for example, running tracks or par courses). If you have these facilities at work, use them. If not, you can join an exercise club (if you need the company of others) or exercise on your own.

Managing Occupational Stress

In conclusion, occupational stress may be difficult to define and measure because of the personal stressors people bring to their jobs and their varying personality characteristics, but we all know when we are experiencing it. Fortunately, we can manage occupational stress by using the stress model to set up roadblocks between occupational stress and illness and disease. We can change jobs (life-situation intervention), perceive the stressors associated with our jobs as challenges rather than burdens to bear (perception intervention), practice relaxation techniques regularly (emotional arousal intervention), and exercise regularly to use up the accumulated products of stress (physiological arousal intervention). But whether we do anything is our own choice. "Grinning and bearing it" won't help; neither will always complaining about jobs or bosses. Help is available, and a reading of this book is a good start.

Getting Involved in Your Community

I conduct lunchtime seminars for various businesses as a representative of the Ronald McDonald House. The intent is to offer a free, yet valued, service for which the participants will be so grateful that they will contribute to the Ronald McDonald House during charity fund-raising campaigns and at other times during the year. Well, sometimes I am unavailable at the time when the business requests a seminar. On those occasions, I ask a student to conduct the seminar for me. I am delighted to report that these students have done an excellent job. After all, they do not want to embarrass themselves, so they learn the material extremely well and prepare an educational and interesting presentation. What a wonderful opportunity they have. Not only do they provide a service to a community organization, but at the same time they learn more about stress, and they add a line on their résumés that will make them more marketable when they graduate. If there ever was a win-win situation, this is it.

You do not have to wait to be invited to conduct a stress management seminar for a community business establishment. You can initiate such requests by letting businesses know of your availability and willingness to run a stress management seminar for them. You can do this by sending out letters to various businesses, by arranging for meetings with directors of health promotion or human resources staff, or by developing a one-page flyer announcing the availability of stress management lunchtime seminars. In this way, you will be contributing to your community's health while deriving many benefits for yourself.

summary

- Too little occupational stress is almost as unhealthy as too much. There is an optimal level of occupational stress that is desirable.

- Occupational stress consists of a mix of work site stressors, the individual's characteristics, and extraorganizational stressors. These stressors can lead to symptoms of occupational ill health or to actual disease.

- Businesses have become interested in occupational stress because it costs them money to ignore it due to employees' ill health, poor decision making, and absenteeism. In addition, stress management programs are used to attract prospective employees whom the company is recruiting.

- Workers report more occupational stress when work objectives are unclear, when conflicting demands are placed upon them, when they have too little or too much to do, when they have little input in decisions that affect them, and when they are responsible for other workers' development.

- Role problems that can result in occupational stress include role overload, role insufficiency, role ambiguity, and role conflict.

- Workaholics spend much of their time working, often eat while working, prefer work to play, and can and do work anytime and anywhere. They are intense and energetic and have difficulty sleeping and taking vacations.

- Burnout is a syndrome of physical and emotional exhaustion; it is an adverse work stress reaction with psychological, psychophysiological, and behavioral components. Symptoms include diminished sense of humor, skipping rest and food breaks, increased overtime and no vacations, increased physical complaints, social withdrawal, diminishing job performance, self-medication, and psychological changes such as depression or a "trapped" feeling.

- More and more women are working outside the home. Given that many of these women have more than their share of responsibilities in the home, and that many have young children, that they experience the effects of occupational stress should be no surprise.

- Part of the stress experienced by women who work outside the home relates to the fact that, at each educational level and for comparable jobs, women earn less than men. In addition, women are still predominantly employed in traditional women's roles (nurse, dental hygienist, cashier, secretary, waitress, and child care worker).

- Sexual harassment at work involves sexual advances made by someone of power or authority who threatens firing, lack of promotion, or some other sanction if sexual activity is declined. In addition, creating an uncomfortable or unproductive work environment by repeatedly telling jokes of a sexual nature or by any other means is also legally defined as sexual harassment. Both men and women suffer from sexual harassment, although women are more likely to be its victims.

- The stress associated with domestic engineering (homemaking) can be similar to the stress resulting from other jobs. Such components of occupational stress as role overload, role conflict, role insufficiency, and role ambiguity may be present in the homemaking situation, just as they can be associated with many jobs outside the home.

- Life situation, perception, and emotional and physiological arousal interventions can be effective in managing sex-role stress.

- Researchers have identified sources of stress particularly experienced by women: career blocks, sexual harassment, male-dominated organizational structures and climates, performance pressure, gender stereotyping, isolation, and lack of role models. Female workers take on more of the household work, and the accompanying stress, than do male workers. Many married and employed women with substantial household responsibilities intentionally limit their career aspirations and purposefully reduce their involvement in work in comparison with their male counterparts.

notes

1. Clinton G. Weiman, "A Study of the Occupational Stressor and the Incidence of Disease/Risk," *NIOSH Proceeding: Reducing Occupational Stress* (Cincinnati: National Institute for Occupational Safety and Health, April 1978), 55.

2. Jefferson A. Singer, Michael S. Neale, and Gary E. Schwartz, "The Nuts and Bolts of Assessing Occupational Stress: A Collaborative Effort with Labor," in *Stress Management in Work Settings,* ed. Lawrence R. Murphy and Theodore F. Schoenborn (Washington, DC: National Institute for Occupational Safety and Health, 1987), 3–29.

3. F. Swoboda, "Employers Recognizing What Stress Costs Them, U.N. Report Suggests," *Washington Post,* 28 March 1992, H2.

4. Elizabeth Chang, "Absence-Minded," *Washington Post,* 9 April 2000, 9.

5. CCH Inc., *2004 CCH Unscheduled Absence Survey* (Riverside, CA: CCH Inc., 2004).

6. "The Dream Is Danger, Roper Starch Worldwide Inc. Report," *Wall Street Journal,* 29 November 1994, B1.

7. E. R. Greenberg and C. Canzoneri, *Organizational Staffing and Disability Claims* (New York: American Management Association Report, 1996).

8. "1992 Baxter Survey of American Health Habits," in *How Employers Are Saving Through Wellness and Fitness Programs,* ed. B. Kerber. (Wall Township, NJ: American Business Publishing, 1994), p. 32.

9. Greenberg and Canzoneri, *Organizational Staffing and Disability Claims.*

10. Marlin Company, *Attitudes in the American Workplace VII* (North Haven, CT: Marlin Company, 2001).

11. Ibid.

12. National Safety Council Report, *Stress Management* (Boston: Jones & Bartlett, 1995).

13. Joe Robinson, "Ahh, Free at La—Oops! Time's Up," *Washington Post,* 27 July 2003, B1, B3.

14. Michael Peterson and John F. Wilson, "Work Stress in America," *International Journal of Stress Management* 11(2004): 911–13.

15. Kirstin Downey Grimsley, "Message Overload Taking Toll on Workers," *Washington Post,* 5 May 1998, C13.

16. Kirstin Downey Grimsley, "Family a Priority for Young Workers," *Washington Post,* 3 May 2000, E1, E2.

17. Kirstin Downey Grimsley, "A Little Baby Powder on the Bottom Line," *Washington Post,* 17 July 1998, F1, F-5.

18. Kirstin Downey Grimsley, "At Work-Site Schools, Kids Learn While Parents Earn," *Washington Post,* 8 September 1998, A1, A8.

19. Diana Kunde, "When the Massage Is the Message," *Washington Post,* 24 May 1998, H6.

20. Kirstin Downey Grimsley, "Companies See Results After 6 Years of Unusual Alliance on Work-Life Issues," *Washington Post,* 23 November 1997, H1.

21. M. J. Davidson and C. L. Cooper, *Shattering the Glass Ceiling: The Woman Manager* (London: Paul Chapman, 1992).

22. Yoshi Iwasaki, Kelly J. MacKay, and Janice Ristock, "Gender-Based Analysis of Stress Among Professional Managers: An Exploratory Qualitative Study," *International Journal of Stress Management* 11(2004): 56–79

23. M. J. Davidson and S. Fielden, "Stress and the Working Woman," in ed. *Handbook of Gender and Work,* G. N. Powell (Thousand Oaks, CA: Sage, 1999), 413–426.

24. Statistics Canada, *2001 Census* (Ottawa, 2001).

25. S. D. Friedman and J. H. Greenhaus, *Allies or Enemys? How Choices About Work and Family Affect the Quality of Men's and Women's Lives* (New York: Oxford University Press, 2000).

26. Peter R. Vagg, Charles D. Spielberger, and Carol F. Wasala, "Effects of Organizational Level and Gender on Stress in the Workplace," *International Journal of Stress Management* 9(2002): 243–261.

27. Michael P. O'Driscoll, Steven Poelmans, Paul E. Spector, Thomas Kalliath, Tammy D. Allen, Cary L. Cooper, and Juan I. Sanchez, "Family-Responsive Interventions Perceived Organizational and Supervisor Support, Work-Family Conflict, and Psychological Strain," *International Journal of Stress Management* 10(2003): 326–344.

28. Lambeth Hochwald, "The Top 10 Healthiest Companies for Women," *Health,* July/August 2003,148–155, 202.

29. A. Steptoe, "Impact of Job and Marital Strain on Ambulatory Blood Pressure," *American Journal of Hypertension* 18(2005): 1138.

30. H. Riese, L. J. Van Doornen, I. L. Houtman, and E. J. De Geus, "Job Strain in Relation to Ambulatory Blood Pressure, Heart Rate, and Heart Rate Variability Among Female Nurses," *Scandinavian Journal of Work, Environment & Health* 30(2004): 477–85.

31. Y. Kobayashi, T. Hirose, Y. Tada, A. Tsutsumi, and N. Kawakami, "Relationship Between Two Job Stress Models and Coronary Risk Factors Among Japanese Part-Time Female Employees of a Retail Company," *Journal of Occupational Health* 47(2005): 201–10.

32. P. L. Schnall et al., "The Relationship Between Job Strain, Workplace Diastolic Blood Pressure, and Left Ventricular Mass Index," *Journal of the American Medical Association* 263(1990): 1929–35.

33. A. B. Harenstam and T. P. G. Theorell, "Work Conditions and Urinary Excretion of Catecholamines—A Study of Prison Staff in Sweden," *Scandinavian Journal of Work and Environmental Health* 14(1988): 257–64.

34. E. Brunner, G. Davey Smith, M. Marmot, R. Canner, M. Bekinska, and J. O'Brien, "Childhood Social Circumstances and Psychosocial and Behavioural Factors as Determinants of Plasma Fibrinogen," *Lancet* 347(1996): 1008–13.

35. Janet Schecter, Lawrence W. Green, Lise Olsen, Karen Kruse, and Margaret Cargo, "Application of Karasek's Demand/Control Model in a Canadian Occupational Setting Including Shift Workers During a Period of Reorganization and Downsizing," *American Journal of Health Promotion* 11(1997): 394–99.

36. S. Cohen, J. E. Schwartz, E. J. Bromet, and D. K. Parkinson, "Mental Health, Stress, and Poor Behaviours in Two Community Samples," *Preventive Medicine* 20(1991): 306–15.

37. Jenny Head, Stephen A. Stansfeld, and Johannes Siegrist. "The Psychosocial Work Environment and Alcohol

Dependence: A. Prospective Study," *Occupational and Environmental Medicine* 61(2004): 219–24.

38. R. A. Karasek, J. Schwartz, and T. Theorell, *Job Characteristics, Occupation, and Coronary Heart Disease,* final report on contract no. R-01-0H00906 (Cincinnati: National Institute for Occupational Safety and Health, 1982).

39. Robert A. Karasek et al., "Job Characteristics in Relation to the Prevalence of Myocardial Infarction in the U.S. Health Examination Survey (HES) and the Health and Nutrition Examination Survey (HANES)," *American Journal of Public Health* 78(1988): 910–18.

40. S. V. Kasl, "The Influence of the Work Environment on Cardiovascular Health: A Historical, Conceptual, and Methodological Perspective," *Journal of Occupational Health Psychology* 1(1996): 42–56.

41. Akizumi Tsutsumi, Tores Theorell, Johan Hallqvist, Christina Reuterwall, and Ulf de Faire, "Association Between Job Characteristics and Plasma Fibrinogen in a Normal Working Population: A Cross Sectional Analysis in Referents of the SHEEP Study," *Journal of Epidemiology and Community Health* 53(1999): 348–54.

42. Jeffrey V. Johnson, Walter Stewart, Ellen M. Hall, Peeter Fredlund, and Tores Theorell, "Long-Term Psychosocial Work Environment and Cardiovascular Mortality Among Swedish Men," *American Journal of Public Health* 86(1996): 324–31.

43. Isabelle Niedhammer, Marcel Goldberg, Annette Leclerc, Simone David, Isabelle Bugel, and Marie-France Landre, "Psychosocial Work Environment and Cardiovascular Risk Factors in an Occupational Cohort in France," *Journal of Epidemiology and Community Health* 52(1998): 93–100.

44. R. J. Burke, "Work and Non-Work Stressors and Well-Being Among Police Officers: The Role of Coping," *Anxiety, Stress and Coping* 14(1998): 1–18.

45. M. P. Leiter, "Coping Patterns as Predictors of Burnout: The Function of Control and Escapist Coping Patterns," *Journal of Organizational Behavior* 12(1991): 123–44.

46. R. J. Burke and D. L. Nelson, "Mergers and Acquisitions, Downsizing, and Privitization: A North American Perspective," in *The New Organizational Reality,* ed. M. K. Gowing, J. D. Kraft, and J. C. Quick (Washington, DC: American Psychological Association, 1998), 21–54.

47. R. J. Burke and M. P. Leiter, "Contemporary Organizational Realities and Professional Efficacy: Downsizing, Reorganization, and Transition," in *Coping, Health and Organizations,* ed. P. Deue, M. P. Leiter, and T. Cox (London: Taylor & Francis, 2000), 237–56.

48. E. E. Agardh, A. Ahlbom, T. Andersson, S. Efendic, V. Grill, J. Hallqvist, A. Norman, and C. G. Ostenson, "Work Stress and Low Sense of Coherence Is Associated with Type 2 Diabetes in Middle-Aged Swedish Women," *Diabetes Care* 26(2003): 719–24.

49. S. Rabkin and F. Matthewson, "Chronobiology of Cardiac Sudden Death in Men," *Journal of the American Medical Association* 244(1980): 1357–58.

50. F. G. Benavidesa, J. Benacha, A. V. Diez-Rouxb, and C. Romana, "How Do Types of Employment Relate to Health Indicators? Findings from the Second European Survey on Working Conditions," *Journal of Epidemiology and Community Health* 54(2000): 494–501.

51. D. C. Mohren, G. M. Swaen, I. Kant, C. P. van Schayck, and J. M. Galama, "Fatigue and Job Stress as Predictors for Sickness Absence During Common Infections," *International Journal of Behavioral Medicine* 12(2005): 11–20.

52. J. R. P. French and R. D. Caplan, "Psychosocial Factors in Coronary Heart Disease," *Industrial Medicine* 39(1970): 383–97.

53. V. A. Beehr and J. E. Newman, "Job Stress, Employee Health, and Organizational Effectiveness: A Facet Analysis, Model, and Literature Review," *Personnel Psychology* 31(1978): 665–99.

54. B. L. Margolis, W. H. Kroes, and R. P. Quinn, "Job Stress: An Unlisted Occupational Hazard," *Journal of Occupational Medicine* 16(1974): 654–61.

55. Samuel H. Osipow and Arnold R. Spokane, "Occupational Environment Scales" (unpublished scales, University of Maryland, 1980).

56. Jeanne Stellman and Mary Sue Henifen, *Office Work Can Be Dangerous to Your Health* (New York: Pantheon, 1983).

57. T. J. Naughton, "A Conceptual View of Workaholism and Implications for Career Counseling and Research," *The Career Development Quarterly* 14(1987): 180–87.

58. K. S. Scott, K. S. Moore, and M. P. Miceli, "An Exploration of the Meaning and Consequences of Workaholism," *Human Relations* 50(1997): 287–314.

59. J. T. Spence and A. S. Robbins, "Workaholism: Definition, Measurement, and Preliminary Results," *Journal of Personality Assessment* 58(1992): 160–78.

60. Lynley H. W. McMillan, Michael P. O'Driscoll, Nigel V. Marsh, and Elizabeth C. Brady, "Understanding Workaholism: Data Synthesis, Theoretical Critique, and Future Design Strategies," *International Journal of Stress Management* 8(2001): 69–91.

61. B. E. Robinson and P. Post, "Risk of Addiction to Work and Family Functioning," *Psychological Reports* 81(1997): 91–95.

62. B. E. Robinson and L. Kelley, "Adult Children of Workaholics: Self-Concept, Locus of Control, Anxiety, and Depression," *The American Journal of Family Therapy* 26(1998): 223–38.

63. S. Navarette, "An Empirical Study of Adult Children of Workaholics: Psychological Functioning and Intergenerational Transmission," (doctoral diss., California Graduate Institute, 1998.)

64. B. E. Robinson, *Chained to the Desk: A Guidebook for Workaholics, Their Partners and Children, and the Clinicians Who Treat Them* (New York: New York University Press, 1998).

65. Bryan F. Robinson, Claudia Flowers, and Jane Carroll, "Work Stress and Marriage: Examining the Relationship Between Workaholism and Marital Cohesion," *International Journal of Stress Management* 8(2001): 165–75.

66. John W. Jones, "A Measure of Staff Burnout Among Health Professionals" (paper presented at the annual meeting of the American Psychological Association, Montreal, September 1980).

67. C. Maslach and W. B. Schaufeli, "Historical and Conceptual Development of Burnout," in *Professional Burnout: Recent Developments in Theory and Research,* ed. W. B. Schaufeli, C. Maslach, and T. Marck (Washington. DC: Taylor & Francis, 1993), 1–16.

68. Wilmar B. Schaufeli and Maria C. W. Peeters, "Job Stress and Burnout Among Correctional Officers: A Literature Review," *International Journal of Stress Management* 7(2000): 19–48.

69. Marcia Kessler, "Preventing Burnout: Taking the Stress out of the Job," *The Journal of Volunteer Administration* 9(1991): 15–20.

70. Pamela K. S. Patrick, *Health Care Worker Burnout: What It Is, What to Do About It* (Chicago: Blue Cross Association, Inquiry Books, 1981), 87–111.

71. U.S. Census Bureau, *Statistical Abstract of the United States, 2005* (Washington, DC: U.S. Government Printing Office, 2005), 372.

72. Ibid., 391.

73. Ibid., 412.

74. Matthew Barakat, "Women Narrow the Salary Gap," *Washington Post,* 4 July 2000, E3.

75. "In the Company of (Few) Women," *Washington Post,* 20 November 1997, D1.

76. U.S. Department of Labor, Bureau of Labor Statistics, "Time-Use Survey—First Results Announced by BLS," News, 14 September 2004, http://www.bls.gov/tus

77. Eleanor Grant, "The Housework Gap," *Psychology Today,* January 1988, 8.

78. V. Schultz, "Reconceptualizing Sexual Harassment," *Yale Law Journal* 107(1998): 1683.

79. "Statistics on Sexual Harassment," Capstone Communications, 1999, http:/www.capstn.com/stats.htm

80. Diane Roberts, "Sexual Harassment in the Workplace: Considerations, Concerns, and Challenges," *SIECUS Report* 28(2000): 8–11.

81. Dana Priest, "Hill-Thomas Legacy May Be Challenges to Old Workplace Patterns," *Washington Post,* 12 March 1992, A8.

82. Anne L. Bryant, "Hostile Hallways: The AAUW Survey on Sexual Harassment in America's Schools," *Journal of School Health* 63(1993): 355–57.

83. Richard Morin, "Who's Sexually Harassing America's Fighting Men?" *Washington Post,* 16 November 1997, C5.

84. R. T. Michael, J. H. Gagnon, E. O. Laumann, and G. Kolata, *Sex in America* (New York: Little, Brown and Company, 1994).

85. M. A. Paludi and R. B. Barickman, "In Their Own Voices: Responses from Individuals Who Have Experienced Sexual Harassment and Supportive Techniques for Dealing with Victims of Sexual Harassment," in *Academic and Workplace Sexual Harassment: A Resource Manual* (Albany: State University of New York Press, 1991), 29–30.

86. Office of Disease Prevention and Health Promotion, *Healthy People 2010* (Washington, DC: Department of Health and Human Services, 2000).

87. Richard S. Lazarus and Susan Folkman, *Stress, Appraisal, and Coping* (New York: Springer, 1984).

internet resources

Job Stress Network
www.workhealth.org
Information about and related to job strain and work stress, by the Center for Social Epidemiology, a private nonprofit foundation whose purpose is to promote public awareness of the role of environmental and occupational stress in the etiology of cardiovascular disease.

18 Ways to Survive Your Company's Reorganization, Takeover, Downsizing,
or Other Major Change
www.stresscure.com/jobstress/reorg.html
*An article that offers practical suggestions for coping with the stresses related to major
changes in the workplace.*

NIOSH/Stress at Work
www.cdc.gov/niosh/stresswk.html
*Developed by the National Institute for Occupational Safety and Health, this site provides
information about current NIOSH activities in the area of work, stress, and
health and provides access to resources to help prevent stressful working
conditions.*

American Institute of Stress
http://www.stressorg/job.htm
*Facts and figures about job stress and reference to current information about occupational
stress.*

Coping in Today's World

Did you know that American workers spend more time working than workers in other developed countries? According to a Harris Interactive poll reported in the *Washington Post,* in 2005, American workers gave back 421 million vacation days.[a] That is, they did not use 421 million days to which they were entitled to use as vacation days. That amounted to an average of three days for each worker. Nearly one-third of workers, in spite of reporting they felt rejuvenated after a vacation, did not use all of the vacation days to which they were entitled. The average length of vacation time spent away from home decreased from more than a week in 1980, to 5.4 nights in 1985, and 4 nights in 2003. There are many reasons for this situation. Some workers get paid for unused vacation days. Other workers are too disorganized to schedule vacations in advance, as is often required. And, still others believe they are too busy at work to get away. To make matters worse, of those who do get away, 16 percent check e-mail or voicemail while on vacation.

American workers are quite different in this regard than workers in other countries. For example, in France, workers are provided 39 days of vacation time per year. Nearly half of French workers take three to four weeks of vacation each year. Canadian workers receive an average of 20 vacation days annually, although they, too, give back an average of three vacation days each year.

And, not only do workers not take all of the vacation days to which they are entitled, they do not even take time off each day to which they are entitled. Fifty percent of Americans do things other than just eating lunch during their lunch hour. Then again, *lunch hour* is a misnomer. On average, Americans spend just 38 minutes for lunch.[b] In fact, 14 percent of workers do not take any time for lunch.

Any wonder why so many people experience occupational stress? Will you allow yourself to be so susceptible? Or will you take charge of your life and balance work with leisure and relaxation?

[a]Joyce, A. "At the Breaking Point, Passing up Vacation." *Washington Post,* May 22, 2005a, F6.

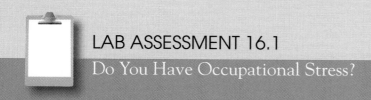

LAB ASSESSMENT 16.1

Do You Have Occupational Stress?

Directions: For each question below, place the number that represents your answer in the space provided.

1 = never

2 = seldom

3 = sometimes

4 = frequently

5 = nearly all the time

_____ 1. How often do you feel that you have too little authority to carry out your responsibilities?

_____ 2. How often do you feel unclear about just what the scope and responsibilities of your job are?

_____ 3. How often do you not know what opportunities for advancement or promotion exist for you?

_____ 4. How often do you feel that you have too heavy a workload, one that you could not possibly finish during an ordinary workday?

_____ 5. How often do you think that you will not be able to satisfy the conflicting demands of various people around you?

_____ 6. How often do you feel that you are not fully qualified to handle your job?

_____ 7. How often do you not know what your superior thinks of you, how he or she evaluates your performance?

_____ 8. How often do you find yourself unable to get information needed to carry out your job?

_____ 9. How often do you worry about decisions that affect the lives of people you know?

_____ 10. How often do you feel that you may not be liked and accepted by people at work?

_____ 11. How often do you feel unable to influence your immediate supervisor's decisions and actions that affect you?

_____ 12. How often do you not know just what the people you work with expect of you?

_____ 13. How often do you think that the amount of work you have to do may interfere with how well it is done?

_____ 14. How often do you feel that you have to do things on the job that are against your better judgment?

_____ 15. How often do you feel that your job interferes with your family life?

Scoring: To score this occupational stress scale, add up your answers and divide by 15. The higher your score is, the greater is your occupational stress.

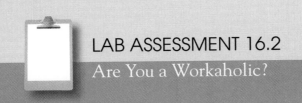

LAB ASSESSMENT 16.2

Are You a Workaholic?

Directions: Check "Yes" or "No" for each question as it applies to you.

Yes   No

____ ____ 1. *Do you get up early, no matter how late you go to bed?*

As one management consultant confessed, "I'd get home and work until [about] 2 a.m., and then get up at 5 a.m. and think, 'Gee, aren't I terrific!' "

____ ____ 2. *If you are eating lunch alone, do you read or work while you eat?*

Robert Moses, New York's long-time Parks Commissioner, reportedly considered lunches a bore and a bother because he couldn't bear to interrupt work. He used a large table as a desk so lunch could be served right there.

____ ____ 3. *Do you make daily lists of things to do?*

Ever-present appointment books and cluttered calendars are a hallmark of workaholics. Indeed, their main way of wasting time, admits Dr. Elizabeth Whelan, a Harvard University epidemiologist, may be looking for lost lists!

____ ____ 4. *Do you find it difficult to "do nothing"?*

It was claimed that David Mahoney, the hardworking chairman of Norton Simon Inc., abandoned transcendental meditation because he found it impossible to sit still for twenty minutes.

____ ____ 5. *Are you energetic and competitive?*

President Johnson once asked Doris Kearns, then a White House Fellow, if she were energetic. Kearns replied, "I hear you need only five hours of sleep, but I need only four, so it stands to reason that I've got even more energy than you."

____ ____ 6. *Do you work on weekends and holidays?*

In *Working,* author Studs Terkel related that the president of a Chicago radio station confessed that he regularly works in his home on weekends. But, he added, "When I do this on holidays, like Christmas, New Year's, and Thanksgiving, I have to sneak a bit so the family doesn't know what I'm doing."

____ ____ 7. *Can you work anytime and anywhere?*

Two associates at Cravath, Swaine and Moore, one of Manhattan's most prestigious law firms, were said to have bet about who could bill the most hours in a day. One worked around the clock, billed twenty-four, and felt assured of victory. His competitor, however, having flown to California in the course of the day and worked on the plane, was able to bill twenty-seven.

____ ____ 8. *Do you find vacations "hard to take"?*

George Lois, the art director who heads Lois Pitts Gershon, an advertising agency, had to think awhile when I asked him when he had taken his last vacation. Finally, he recalled when it was: 1964—almost fourteen years before!

____ ____ 9. *Do you dread retirement?*

After retiring from the ad agency where she had created such classic slogans as Clairol's "Does she . . . or doesn't she?" Shirley Polykoff started her own advertising agency. As president of Shirley Polykoff Advertising in New York she still—some six years later—has no plans to slow up or step down. She says, "I'm doing more now than I've ever done. I don't know how you retire if you're still healthy and exuberant about living. They'll have to carry me out in a box!"

____ ____ 10. *Do you really enjoy your work?*

As Joyce Carol Oates, the novelist, once told the *New York Times,* "I am not conscious of working especially hard, or of 'working' at all. . . . Writing and teaching have always been, for me, so richly rewarding that I do not think of them as work in the usual sense of the word."

If you answer "Yes" to eight or more questions, you may be a workaholic. Refer back to the section "The Workaholic" for tips to combat workaholism.

Source: Reprinted from Marilyn Machlowitz. *Workaholics: Living with Them* (Reading, MA: Addison-Wesley, 1980), 17–20.

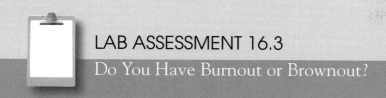

LAB ASSESSMENT 16.3

Do You Have Burnout or Brownout?

Directions: Determine whether you are suffering from burnout, or if you are only partway there (brownout). Complete the brownout inventory below and find out. For each statement, write a *T* if that statement is true for you or an *F* if it isn't.

_____ 1. Is your efficiency at work declining?

_____ 2. Have you lost some of your initiative at work?

_____ 3. Have you lost interest in your work?

_____ 4. Does work stress get to you more than it used to?

_____ 5. Do you feel fatigued or run down?

_____ 6. Do you get headaches?

_____ 7. Do you get stomachaches?

_____ 8. Have you lost weight recently?

_____ 9. Do you have trouble sleeping?

_____ 10. Do you experience shortness of breath?

_____ 11. Do you have frequently changing or depressing moods?

_____ 12. Are you easy to anger?

_____ 13. Do you get frustrated easily?

_____ 14. Are you more suspicious than you used to be?

_____ 15. Do you feel more helpless than you used to?

_____ 16. Are you using too many mood-altering drugs (e.g., tranquilizers or alcohol)?

_____ 17. Are you becoming more inflexible?

_____ 18. Are you becoming more critical of your own and others' competencies?

_____ 19. Are you working more but feeling that you're getting less done?

_____ 20. Have you lost some of your sense of humor?

If you answered *true* for more than half the statements, you may be experiencing brownout. If you answered *true* for fifteen or more of these statements, you may be burning out (or already burnt out). Recognize, however, that you can remedy this situation by employing the stress management suggestions described in this chapter.

Jack's best friend put a gun to his own head and pulled the trigger. Aside from feeling a deep sense of loss, Jack was angry and disappointed. "I was his best friend. Why didn't he talk with me about this? Why did he have to kill himself?" It seemed that much of Jack's day was preoccupied by such questions. His schoolwork and his job outside of school were both affected.

Kim was a student from Taiwan who was sent, at great expense to her family, to the United States to attend college. With the difficulty she had with studying in a second language and the pressure she felt to succeed in school (her parents sacrificed to send her to school in the United States), she was just keeping her head above water. She barely passed several courses and had to take incompletes in others. Her concern and frustration about her schoolwork overflowed into her social life. She found herself being angry and argumentative with friends and devoting so much time to her studies that she soon had no friends. Alone and lonely in a foreign country, not doing well in school, Kim was experiencing a great deal of stress.

Bill was a mail carrier who was attending college at night to prepare for another career when he retired from the postal service. He was having problems with his marriage, his job, and his schooling. There never seemed enough time for any of these. His wife and daughter complained that with being at work and school he was seldom home, and, when he was, he was always doing schoolwork. His supervisor at the post office claimed he always seemed tired and grouchy, and this was affecting his job performance. His professors told Bill that he was not turning in his work on time, nor was it of sufficient quality to pass his courses. When Bill finally left his family (his domestic problems became more and more serious), he brooded so much that he had less time, instead of more, to concentrate on the other aspects of his life.

These are but a few of the students enrolled in my stress management classes during *one semester*. They came to me to discuss these problems and to get guidance regarding how to manage them. Too often the life of the college student is depicted as "rah-rah," fraternity row, and football games. These are carefree and fun years for many students. For many others, though, college is just another life change to which they must adapt. They may be young and experiencing the growing and developing pains of youth; they may be older students with too many other responsibilities to enjoy their schooling; or they may experience unique situations during the time they are supposed to be concentrating on their studies. In any case, college is very stressful for a large number of students.

There is plenty of evidence that chronic stress is often a companion of college students. As they observed college students, researchers Towbes and Cohen[1] concluded that college students are particularly prone to chronic stress as a result of their experiencing and having to manage developmental transitions. To make matters worse, the stress experienced by college students can interfere with the learning processes (acquisition, manipulation, and consolidation of knowledge) necessary for academic success.[2] Having difficulties academically then feeds back into the stress loop as a life-situation stressor to create even more stress. Other stress researchers have noted students' concerns such as finances,[3] living arrangements,[4] safety,[5] and their weight[6] to be significant stressors. On my own campus, a survey of the top health issues found stress to be second only to fitness and exercise. What do you think students on your campus would rate as the top-three health issues? I'll bet stress is one of them.

The Younger College Student

College students have a lot of stressors in their lives, only one of which relates to their schoolwork.

The younger college student—one who enters college from high school or shortly thereafter—experiences stressors such as the dramatic lifestyle change from high school to college, grades, course overload, managing finances, making friends, love and sex stressors, shyness, jealousy, and breakups.

Lifestyle Change

The more life changes you experience, the more stress you will feel and the more likely it is that illness and disease will result. Just imagine all the life changes associated with attending college for the first time!

You attend high school while living at home, under the supervision of your parents, and usually without the need to work. There is plenty of time to meet friends after school, to do homework, and to relax. After all, the laundry is done by someone else, the meals are prepared by someone else, and the car may even be filled with gas by someone else. Food somehow, miraculously, appears in the refrigerator and cupboards, and the dust on the furniture and floors periodically vanishes.

Although many high school students do take on household responsibilities and do have jobs, generally the high school years are comfortable ones. When college begins, however, a dramatic change takes place. Time must be set aside for shopping, cooking, cleaning, doing the laundry, and myriad other routine chores. For the first time in many students' lives, they must assume responsibilities they never had to assume before. Further, no one keeps asking if they've done their homework. They must remember to fit this in between all their other activities.

However, in addition to all of these, other changes are dictated by college life. Usually it requires finding an apartment or choosing a dormitory in which to live. A whole new network of same-sex and opposite-sex friends must be established. Schoolwork seems excessive, and it seems that not enough time is available to accomplish it. The fear of flunking permeates the air.

Although college is fraught with stress, many students believe the reward at the end makes it all worthwhile. What do you believe?

As though all of this weren't enough, the younger college student is confronted with several important tasks during that time of his or her life:

1. Achieving emotional independence from family.
2. Choosing and preparing for a career.
3. Preparing for emotional commitment and family life.
4. Developing an ethical system.[7]

Managing these transitional changes requires college students to develop new roles and modify old ones, and that can result in a great deal of stress. One observer of college students and the stressors they experience noted that "the popular notion of university students enjoying a relaxed and stress-free lifestyle is likely to be wide of the mark."[8]

Considering all these changes and the effects of stress on the immunological system, it is no small wonder that influenza epidemics and bouts of mononucleosis are frequent visitors to college campuses. Of course, the close living quarters exacerbate this situation. We also should not be surprised to learn that suicide is the second leading cause of death on college campuses (accidents being number one).

Grades

The old story of the college professor who tossed the term papers down the stairs and graded those landing on the top three steps an A, those on the next three steps a B, and so on emphasizes the confusion about grading. Grades—students have to get them and professors have to give them. Unfortunately, both groups seem to gear too much of their behavior toward them. Students see their goal as getting good grades instead of learning as much as they can. Professors see their goal as accurately differentiating between an A student and a B student rather than teaching as much as they can. As with all such generalizations, there are numerous exceptions. However, I think anyone associated with a college campus will agree that too much emphasis is placed upon grades.

Students may even link their self-worth with their grades—for example, "Boy am I dumb. I flunked English." Instead, they'd be better off saying, "Boy I guess I didn't study long enough or well enough. I'll have to remember that for the next test."

Let's not kid ourselves, though. Grades are very important. They are important to students who want to go to graduate school or whose prospective employers consider them prior to hiring. They are also important to the university that wants its graduates considered competent and well educated. The university will use grades to weed out those who will not reflect well upon it. However, I have seen students so preoccupied by grades that they have let their physical health deteriorate. They give up exercise, don't have enough time to prepare balanced meals, or pull "all-nighters" so frequently that they walk around with bags under their eyes. I have seen other students so grade-conscious that they don't have a social life—they're always studying.

Course Overload

Related to the issue of grades is **course overload.** Course overload is having too many courses or courses that are too difficult to do well during any one semester. In today's goal-oriented, rush–rush society, the more you accomplish in the shortest period of time, the better. The result is people rushing through their lives and experiencing very little. They achieve a lot of goals but don't enjoy the trip to those goals.

Course overload results in a similar predicament. If I had a dollar for every student who, upon graduation, told me "I wish I had taken more courses I enjoyed" or "I wish I had devoted more time to my studies" or "I wish I had taken fewer courses each semester and learned more in the ones I did enroll in," I'd be wealthy today. Hoping to graduate in the shortest time possible, too many students overload themselves and suffer physically, psychologically, socially, and educationally for it. They may get physically ill, their

course overload
Having too many courses or courses too difficult to complete well during one semester.

The life of the typical college student may be quite hectic. For this reason, it is very important that students make time for relaxation; that is, relaxation in a healthy way such as regularly employing a relaxation technique, exercising, and using the social support of family and friends.

emotions may be ready to explode, they may not have time for friends, and, while taking more courses, they actually learn less. In this case, more is less.

Finances

Some of the most significant stressors that college students experience relate to money. To begin with, paying for college is a challenge for many students and their families. In 2003–2004, the average cost of tuition and fees at four-year private colleges was $19,710 a year. At four-year public colleges it was $4,694; at two-year public colleges, $1,905. Depending on the type of college, room and board cost from $337 to $368 more than in the previous year.[9] During the 1990s, when adjusted for inflation, tuition and fees at four-year public colleges and universities increased 49 percent; at four-year private institutions they increased 32 percent.[10] That increase occurred while median family income rose a mere 4 percent.

Given these figures, it is no surprise that many students graduate with a good deal of debt. In 1999–2000, 64 percent of students graduated with student-loan debt; the average loan debt doubled over an eight-year period to $16,928.[11] The number of seniors who graduated with more than $20,000 in debt increased from 5 percent in 1992–1993 to 33 percent in 1999–2000. Eighty-four percent of African American and 66 percent of Hispanic college students graduate with debt.

The loan industry suggests that monthly student-loan payments should not exceed 8 percent of monthly income before taxes. However, 39 percent of all student borrowers graduate with debt requiring payments higher than this amount. This loan debt affects minority students more than others. Fifty-five percent of African American student borrowers and 58 percent of Hispanic student borrowers graduated with debt requiring payments greater than 8 percent of their pretax monthly income.

Of course, that is not the only debt college students incur. The Department of Education's National Postsecondary Student Aid Study reported that in 1999–2000, 41 percent of graduating seniors carried a credit card balance and the average balance was $3,176. How to use a credit card appropriately is one of the tasks college students seem to have difficulty learning. And that is not the only financial skill that gets college students into financial hot water and thereby causes them stress. In a study of more than 1,000 college students from 27 universities in 19 states,[12] it was found that 92 percent knew how to balance a checkbook but only 62 percent actually did it. Furthermore, 32 percent had credit card debt, and 16 percent were in debt for more than $5,000. Developing a budget and adhering to it would help these students a great deal. Yet only 38 percent prepared a monthly budget, and only 28 percent of those that did so stuck to it.

Friendship

Giving up or changing old friendships and developing new ones is often a stressful activity associated with college life. Will people like me? Will I find someone with similar interests? How about boyfriends and girlfriends? Will people want to date me? All of these questions and many others are of concern during this phase of life. Old friends were accompanied by old routines—you knew just how much you could tell whom. Since friendship is a function of the degree of self-disclosure friends are willing to share, new friends require a period of testing to see just how much self-disclosure feels comfortable with this new person. To demonstrate this point, complete Lab 17.1 (at the end of this chapter) on friendship and "acquaintanceship."

Love

With old friends and family back home, many students fill the void with new love relationships. These relationships themselves, however, may create new stresses. Any new relationship requires a new set of rules and standards. How often do we see each other? How often do we telephone? Where should we go on dates? Who should pay? With whose friends should we hang out?

In addition, some love relationships involve two people who are different types of lovers. To understand this point better, complete Lab 17.2 at the end of this chapter. If you are now involved in a love relationship, perhaps you'll want your lover to complete Lab 17.2 as well.

Erotic love (eros) is a passionate, all-enveloping love. The heart races, a fluttering appears in the stomach, and there's a shortness of breath when erotic lovers meet. **Ludic love (ludus)** is a playful, flirtatious love. It involves no long-term commitment and is basically for amusement. Ludic love is usually played with several partners at once. **Storgic love (storge)** is a calm, companionate love. Storgic lovers are quietly affectionate and have goals of marriage and children for the relationship. **Manic love (mania)** is a combination of erotic and ludic love. A manic lover's needs for affection are insatiable. He or she is often racked with highs of irrational joy, lows of anxiety and depression, and bouts of extreme jealousy. Manic attachments seldom develop into lasting love.

Imagine that a ludic lover is in a love relationship with a storgic lover. One is playing games with no intention of a lasting or exclusive relationship, and the other is thinking marriage and children. Love relationships on college campuses may be stressful because of misunderstandings regarding the types of love involved.

What is your love style? If you are presently in a love relationship, is your love style compatible with your lover? Recognizing that love styles may change during different stages of your life, when do you think you will adopt a different love style from the one you have now? Do you look forward to this transition, or not? Why? As with other aspects of your life, you are in control of the types of relationships that you enter, and you can choose compatible ones or ones that can result in stress. Why not ask someone with whom you might have an initial romantic interest to complete Lab 17.2 and see if you are compatible before you become too committed?

There are online "love tests" now-a-days that match people on a variety of characteristics and personality traits. Some of the variables they measure are adventurousness,

erotic love (eros)
A passionate, all-enveloping type of love recognized by the heart racing and other signs of excitement.

ludic love (ludus)
A playful, flirtatious type of love involving no long commitment.

storgic love (storge)
A calm, companionate type of love conceiving of a long commitment.

manic love (mania)
A combination of passionate love (eros) and flirtatious playing love characterized by jealousy and irrational joy that usually does not result in a long commitment.

communication style, relationship role, temperament, romanticism, importance of wealth, and need for independence. During one month in 2003, approximately 37 million people used online matching services such as Match.com, Americansingles.com, and Date.com.[13] Online personal ads generated $302 million in 2002, up from $72 million in 2001. It seems that a lot of people are looking for love and are willing to pay for it.

Sex

One of the assignments in my undergraduate stress management class is for students to keep a journal of stressors they encounter. Invariably, several female students describe the pressure they are receiving—from their female friends as well as their boyfriends—to engage in sexual intercourse. It's the talk of the dorm or sorority house. Although no male student has ever described a similar stressor, I'm convinced that the pressure to be sexually active is at least as great for male students as it is for female students. Why else would young males feel compelled to exaggerate their sexual experiences or describe an enjoyable, relaxing evening as a Roman orgy? I believe that males are just less apt to admit that they feel stressed by pressure to be sexually active.

To compound this stressor, the older public looks at college students as a promiscuous, pill-popping, irresponsible group of rascals and tolerates them only because they are young and soon will learn better. At age nineteen, however, many females have never experienced sexual intercourse, yet even college students tend to exaggerate the sexual experience of their compatriots.

To determine just how much you really know about sexuality and about the sexual behavior of your peers, and how any misconceptions affect the degree of stress you experience, answer the following true-false questions:

_____ 1. By the time they graduate from college, all students have masturbated.

_____ 2. Almost all college students have experienced sexual intercourse several times.

_____ 3. Masturbation is a habit of the young and is eliminated as one becomes an adult.

_____ 4. Any sexual behavior between consenting adults done in private is legal.

_____ 5. As long as "safe sex" is practiced, both pregnancy and sexually transmitted diseases can be prevented.

_____ 6. Masturbation can result in either physical illness or psychological harm.

_____ 7. Sexual fantasies are wishes you have for participation in sex.

_____ 8. Oral-genital sex is abnormal and perverse.

All of the previous statements are false. Let's look more closely at them one at a time.

1. Most researchers have found that approximately 90 percent of men and 60 percent of women have masturbated at some time. Stated another way, approximately 10 percent of men and 40 percent of women have *not* had masturbatory experience. In a landmark study of sex in America, Laumann and his colleagues found that both males and females masturbate, although 85 percent of men as opposed to 45 percent of women masturbated in the year prior to the study.[14]

2. Fifty-one percent of males and 47 percent of females who are fifteen to nineteen year old have never had sexual intercourse. Twelve percent of males and 13 percent of females who are twenty to twenty-four year old have never had sexual intercourse. Even 5 percent of males and 3 percent of females who are twenty-four to twenty-nine years old have never had sexual intercourse.[15] Obviously, not everyone is doing "it," and when they are, it isn't with everyone on campus.

3. Masturbation is engaged in throughout one's life. Whether it's because one's sexual partner is unavailable, pregnant, or ill, or just for the pleasure of it, masturbation is practiced by adults at all ages.

4. There are sodomy laws in some states that specifically outlaw certain sexual behaviors, even if those engaging in these behaviors consent to them and perform them in private. Oral-genital sex, anal sexual intercourse, and homosexual activities are usually the sex acts prohibited. However, coitus between unmarried people is also against the law in some states.

5. We shall discuss sexually transmitted diseases, and AIDS in particular, shortly. For now, you should know that there is no such thing as safe sex. Anytime coitus occurs, for instance, there is the chance of a pregnancy resulting (there is no *100 percent* effective means of birth control) and the possibility of contracting one of several sexually transmitted diseases. However, there are ways to engage in "safer" sex—that is, decreasing the chances of conception or of disease occurring—for example, using a condom.

6. Experts agree that the only danger of masturbation is the psychological harm resulting from guilt, shame, or embarrassment one associates with it. If people were to learn how prevalent masturbation is, how it doesn't interfere with normal relationships or the ability to later be sexually functional, and that it usually continues throughout one's life (albeit at a lesser frequency), masturbation might not be associated with guilt and other negative feelings and thereby not create any harm at all.

7. Because you fantasize about something doesn't necessarily mean you would actually like to experience that fantasy. For example, when you become angry with a professor, you might dream about slashing the tires on his or her car. However, most of us would not do that even if we knew we wouldn't get caught (at least I hope my students reading this agree). Likewise, sexual thoughts and fantasies may or may not be events we would like to experience. We shouldn't feel guilty or embarrassed about our sexual thoughts; that can only do us harm. However, we should be held accountable for our sexual *behavior*.

8. Many men and women have engaged in oral sex. In a national survey conducted by Michael and his colleagues, they found that 77 percent of men and 68 percent of women reported having given oral sex *to* a partner, and 79 percent of men and 73 percent of women had received oral sex *from* a partner.[16] Whether one chooses to view oral-genital sex as perverse depends on one's values. However, given its frequency, it certainly cannot be considered abnormal.

Does the information regarding sexual myths surprise you? If so, don't worry. You are probably in good company, with significant numbers of your classmates also believing many of the same myths about the sexual behavior of college students. Given the misconceptions you have regarding how sexually active you "would be" if you were "normal," the pressure for you to engage in sex can be intense. This pressure comes from outside yourself and from within. The pressure might lead to stress that interferes with your health, grades, and interpersonal relationships. Hopefully, a more realistic perception of the sexual behavior of your classmates will help you see yourself as not unusual in your own sexual behavior and thereby help you to better deal with the pressure to be sexually active, whether you are sexually experienced or inexperienced. (Remember, in either case you are in the company of a large number of other college students.)

HIV/AIDS

There is a good deal of concern both on and off college campuses regarding the spread of sexually transmitted infections—in particular, **acquired immune deficiency syndrome (AIDS).** This section describes the causes, treatments, and means of prevention of AIDS, with the hope that knowledge will aid in alleviating undue stress regarding your sexual behavior and will help you prevent AIDS from developing in the first place.

acquired immune deficiency syndrome (AIDS)
A condition transmitted through sexual contact and the sharing of intravenous needles that leads to the mixing of blood or semen, in which the immune system becomes progressively ineffective.

Acquired immune deficiency syndrome is caused by a virus called the **human immunodeficiency virus (HIV).** AIDS results in an ineffectiveness of the immunological system so that its victims develop opportunistic infections that eventually lead to death. The Centers for Disease Control reports that, by 2003, 524,060 Americans died of AIDS. In 2003, there were 43,171 new cases of AIDS.[17]

There is no known cure for AIDS, although there are some drugs that can slow the course of the disease and prolong the life of the AIDS victim. The most effective of these drugs is azidothymidine (AZT) used in combination with other drugs such as protease inhibitors (called combination therapy or "drug cocktail").

HIV is transmitted through bodily fluids such as blood and semen. High-risk groups are homosexuals, intravenous drug users, and infants born to women with the virus in their bloodstream. However, public health officials would rather direct attention to high-risk *behaviors* than to high-risk *groups,* since membership in the group is immaterial—it's what you *do* that can give you AIDS, not what group you belong to. If you share needles with others (as I.V. drug users are prone to do), if you engage in oral or genital sex without using a condom or in anal sex even if you do use a condom, or if you have multiple sex partners, you are more likely to contract AIDS than if you don't engage in these high-risk behaviors. In spite of some widespread misconceptions, AIDS is not transmitted casually. It cannot be contracted by touching a person with AIDS, sharing eating utensils, swimming in the same swimming pool, being in the same classroom, being stung by a mosquito, or kissing.[18] You also cannot acquire AIDS by giving blood; since 1985, the blood supply has been screened so that contracting AIDS through a blood transfusion is only a remote possibility. AIDS is classified as a *sexually* transmitted infection, even though it can be transmitted in nonsexual ways (e.g., when a health care worker accidentally comes in contact with HIV-infected blood).

To alleviate some distress you may have regarding AIDS, engage in behaviors that can make you less prone to contracting it. There are several things you can do to protect yourself. The best approach in terms of prevention is to abstain from sex: oral sex, coitus, and anal sex. If you decide that alternative is not acceptable to you, the next best approach is to maintain a monogamous sexual relationship with someone you know to be AIDS-free. The problem here, though, is determining that someone is AIDS-free. The test for AIDS actually tests for the presence of antibodies that you develop after coming in contact with HIV. Since the test may not identify the presence of these antibodies for up to six or eight months after exposure, even if someone has a negative AIDS test today, if that person had sex with someone else within the past eight months, he or she may still possess the virus. What the experts say is really true: When you sleep with someone, you are sleeping with that person's previous sexual partners and those previous partners' sexual partners. In any case, if you engage in sex, always use a condom made of latex rather than animal skin (such as lambskin), since the animal skin condom may be too porous to prevent the virus from penetrating.

Unfortunately, too many college students do not use condoms, or do not use them often enough, even though they engage in sexual behaviors that put them at risk of contracting HIV infection. In a study[19] of the sexual behavior of U.S. male youths aged fifteen to nineteen, it was found that two-thirds reported using a condom at last intercourse. Although this is an increase from previous years, still one-third did not use a condom. In another study of sexually active women, condom use was at a minimum: 24 percent of eighteen- to nineteen-year-olds used a condom as their method of birth control, 15 percent of twenty- to twenty-four-year-olds, and 14 percent of twenty-five- to twenty-nine-year-olds.[20] Of course many of these women who did not use a condom used some other method of contraception. However, they did not get the benefit and protection from HIV and other sexually transmitted infections that a condom can provide. In addition, there is an alarming number of sexually active young women who do not use any method of contraception. Piccinino and Mosher reported that 7 percent of fifteen- to nineteen-year-olds, 6 percent of twenty- to twenty-four-year-olds, and 5 percent of twenty-five to twenty-nine-year-olds did not use any contraceptive method even though they were sexually active during the prior three months.[21]

Approximately 15 percent of AIDS cases have occurred in people between the ages of twenty and twenty-nine,[22] and experts believe that many of the cases discovered in people in their twenties were actually contracted when they were in their teens and college-age years. A study of HIV infection on college campuses found 5 of every 1,000 students infected.[23] In the population at large, AIDS is now the tenth leading cause of death among U.S. men and women between the ages of fifteen and twenty-four, and the fifth leading cause of death among those twenty-five to forty-four.[24]

Other Sexually Transmitted Infections

It should be noted that AIDS is only one of several **sexually transmitted infections (STIs)** that are threats to health. Syphilis, gonorrhea, chlamydia, genital warts, herpes genitalis, and pelvic inflammatory disease are others that also need to be paid attention to. Many of the same preventive measures we've discussed regarding AIDS are also effective against the other STIs.

This little bit of knowledge should help you take greater control of preventing AIDS and other sexually transmitted diseases. This is one instance when an internal locus of control can actually save your life! Use this information, and AIDS will be less of a stressor for you.

Date Rape

As if the threat of contracting a sexually transmitted infection such as AIDS is not stressful enough, imagine the feelings evoked when sex is forced upon someone. That is precisely what is happening on college campuses. It is most often the male forcing sex on his female date: "She said NO but I knew she really wanted it. It just took a little coercion." Well, that is RAPE! Anytime sex is forced on someone else, that is legally defined as rape. **Acquaintance rape,** forcible sex between people who know one another (such as dates), occurs most frequently among college students, particularly freshmen, than any other age group. One in four women report being victims of rape; 84 percent of their assailants were dating partners or acquaintances. One in four college men have admitted to using sexual aggression with women. Victims of date rape may feel ashamed, guilty, betrayed, and frightened. The psychological effects can be devastating and last for a long time. Date rape is a serious matter and needs to be prevented.

Interestingly, experts recognize that rape is more about violence and control than it is about sex. Rapists may want to act out violently against the person being raped because of some past experiences. The rapist may believe that a history of rejection or feeling inferior can, for the moment, be forgotten through this violent behavior. Alternatively, the rapist may wish to demonstrate control over someone else in the most intimate part of that person's life.

Not to be lost in this discussion is the role that sex plays in our society. Look at ads in magazines and on television, and you will note that sex is used to sell even the most remote of products. Pay attention in movies, and you will undoubtedly see sex portrayed in one way or another. The Internet makes pornographic images and films readily available. The behavior portrayed in these films is anything but sensitive, romantic, or respectful. It is shameful when people use these actions as models for what they think will be exciting sex. That can lead to forceful sex, which is rape.

Below you will read some suggestions for protecting yourself from being forced to engage in sexual activity or from forcing another to do so. As you read these helpful

2010 National Health Objectives Related to Sexually Transmitted Infections

1. Reduce the proportion of adolescents and young adults with Chlamydia trachomatis infections.
2. Reduce gonorrhea.
3. Eliminate sustained domestic transmission of primary and secondary syphilis.
4. Reduce the proportion of adults with genital herpes.
5. Reduce the proportion of persons with human papillomavirus (HPV) infection.
6. Reduce the proportion of females who have ever required treatment for pelvic inflammatory disease (PID).
7. Reduce the proportion of childless families with fertility problems who have had a sexually transmitted disease or who have required treatment for pelvic inflammatory disease.
8. Reduce HIV infections in adolescent and young adult females aged 13 to 24 that are associated with heterosexual contact.
9. Reduce congenital syphilis.
10. Increase the proportion of adolescents who abstain from sexual intercourse or use condoms if currently sexually active.
11. Increase the number of positive messages related to responsible sexual behavior during weekday and nightly prime-time television programming.

sexually transmitted infections (STIs)
Diseases such as syphilis, gonorrhea, chlamydia, and genital warts that are transmitted through sexual activity.

acquaintance rape
Forcible sexual intercourse between people who know each other.

suggestions, keep in mind that it is not your responsibility to prevent yourself from being raped. It doesn't matter what you wear, how you act, or the setting in which you are in. None of this excuses rape—none of it!

The American College Health Association recommends the following to prevent acquaintance rape:

Think: Think about how you respond to social pressures and ask yourself
- What role does sex play in my life?
- What role do I want it to play?
- How does alcohol affect my sexual decision making?
- How do I learn someone's desires and limits?
- How do I express my own?

Challenge the myths and stereotypes: Challenge your friends who belittle rape or don't understand it, who accept definitions of sex and gender roles that include forcing someone to have sex or getting him or her too drunk to say no. Talk with friends and give one another the opportunity to be assertive, respectful, honest, and caring.

Communicate effectively: Saying *no* or *yes* may be difficult, but it's important. Acting sorry or unsure sends mixed messages. The other person can't really know how you feel without hearing it from you.

Trust your instincts: Even if you can't explain why, you have the right to trust your feelings and have them respected. Tell your partner what you want—or don't want—and stick with your decision.

Listen . . . carefully to what the other person is saying. Are you getting mixed messages? Do you understand him or her? If not—ask.

Ask . . . rather than assume. Let you and your partner talk about what would be most enjoyable together.

Remember . . . effective and assertive communication may not always work. Sometimes people simply don't listen. However—NO ONE DESERVES TO BE RAPED![25]

In addition, avoid excessive use of alcohol or other drugs that may cloud your ability to make decisions in your best interest. The American College Health Association reminds us that consenting sex requires sober, verbal communication without intimidation or threats. Many states have laws acknowledging that someone who is drunk is not capable of consenting to sex.

Several colleges have developed guidelines to help limit date rape. Perhaps the most controversial of these was produced at Antioch College. At Antioch, students are required to verbally request permission to proceed sexually. They must ask if they can kiss their partner, then if they can touch their partner, then if they can sleep with their partner, and so on. Permission must be explicit. Proceeding without verbal permission can place a student at risk of being accused of date rape. The intent is to prevent miscommunication—that is, a student believing that *no* really means "yes." Some opponents of this policy describe it at best as silly, and at worse as interfering with students' private relationships. What do you think of Antioch's policy on date rape? Would you like to see it adopted at your school?

Shyness

Because entering college is a new experience, and the people and surroundings are new, it is not surprising to find many students feeling and acting shy. **Shyness** can be a significant stressor for some college students, but it is one, as we shall see later, that can be effectively responded to.

> To be shy is to be afraid of people, especially people who for some reason are emotionally threatening: strangers because of their novelty or uncertainty, authorities

shyness
To be afraid of people and being worried of what strangers and powerful others think of oneself.

who wield power, members of the opposite sex who represent potential intimate encounters.

Shyness can be a mental handicap as crippling as the most severe of physical handicaps, and its consequences can be devastating.

Shyness makes it difficult to meet new people, make friends, or enjoy potentially good experiences.

It prevents you from speaking up for your rights and expressing your own opinions and values.

Shyness limits positive evaluations by others of your personal strengths.

It encourages self-consciousness and an excessive preoccupation with your own reactions.

Shyness makes it hard to think clearly and communicate effectively.

Negative feelings like depression, anxiety, and loneliness typically accompany shyness.[26]

College students may experience stress due to their shyness with professors, club leaders, or people whom they would like to date. This shyness is uncomfortable and, as cited above, may have severe consequences.

Jealousy

College students need to make new friends—both same-sex and opposite-sex ones. Making new friends is ego-threatening ("What if they don't want to be friends with me?"), requires a risk, takes time, and takes a good deal of energy. After all of that, friendship becomes comfortable. We know with whom we can go places, in whom we can confide, and from whom we can receive love. It is understandable, then, that we should value these friendships greatly and become protective and defensive when they are threatened. Even if the threat is only a perceived one—not a real one—jealousy may result.

Jealousy is the fear of losing our property, whether that be our lover, friend, status, or power. It has two basic components: (1) a feeling of battered pride and (2) a feeling that our property rights have been violated.[27] We respond to jealousy by either protecting our egos—for example, arguing with our friends or trying to get even—or trying to improve the relationship. Obviously, the second way is preferable.

Jealousy is a stressor some college students experience. It becomes stressful whether we are jealous ourselves or our friends or lovers are the jealous ones.

jealousy
Fear of losing one's property, such as a lover, friend, status, or power.

Breakups

Jealousy sometimes becomes so stressful that it results in a breakup of the relationship. Sometimes relationships break up because the partners are too dissimilar (one may be interested in sports and the other in the theater) or because they have different expectations of the relationship (one may be a ludic lover and the other a storgic lover). Younger college students are at a stage of life in which they are experimenting with different kinds of relationships, so it is not surprising that many of these relationships do not become permanent. Younger college students usually experience several breakups of relationships during the college years, and these breakups can be quite stressful.

Students experiencing the most distress from a breakup are those who have highly invested in the relationship in terms of time and commitment, whose partners break up with them (being left by the other), whose partner has an interest in other relationships and has more alternatives to pursue that interest, and who are fearful of abandonment in the first place.[28] Since most relationship breakups are nonmutual,[29] and we have already seen that having control of a potentially stressful situation can alleviate some of the stress, it is understandable that many relationships result in distress on the part of the person left.

Breakups can be very stressful, especially for the person not wanting to end the relationship.

The Older College Student

Many college students are not in their early twenties. More and more, college student populations include a large percentage of older students. These older students have been in the armed services, have developed careers, have raised families, or were engaged in some other activities that led them to postpone their college educations. Those other responsibilities well managed or completed, they are now entering college. More than 40 percent of American college students—undergraduate and graduate— are over age twenty-five, and 37 percent of undergraduates are over twenty-five years of age.[30] In my home state of Maryland, the college student population is expected to increase dramatically during the early 2000s. The response will be large class sizes and more distance learning using the Internet.[31] This is a trend occurring throughout the United States. These students experience stressors similar to those experienced by younger college students: grades, course overload, jealousy, and breakups. However, they also experience some stressors that are unique to them. We shall briefly discuss three of these: mixing career and school, handling family and school responsibilities concurrently, and doubting their abilities to do well in college.

Career and School

The year was 1964, and I was teaching in a high school in New York City. The students were from Harlem and had problems that were foreign to me. Still, I was very concerned with responding to their needs and, within the limits that existed, helping them to improve the quality of their lives. In other words, I was committed to my job. As the last period of the school day ended, however, I had to rush to the subway to take a thirty-minute train ride to C.C.N.Y., where I was taking twelve credits toward my master's degree. My classes were over at about 9:30 p.m., which is when I rushed to the subway to take a one-hour train ride back to my apartment in Brooklyn.

This situation is not unique. Now that I teach on a college campus, I see many students experiencing what I experienced. I recall one student, for example, whose job required her to be in Europe Thursday through Sunday—she was an airline flight attendant—but she was taking several college courses on Monday and

Tuesday. Others have had careers that they were committed to—students of mine who were social workers, accountants, and police officers come to mind—but were enrolled in college, too. The need to do well with a career may cause stress, and the need to do well at school may also cause stress. Even though each of these stressors may be manageable alone, when they coexist there may be an overload. The result may be illness or disease.

Family and School

Not only are many older college students working, but many have family responsibilities as well. A number of students have discussed with me the problem of what to do with after-work time. Should they work on their term paper? Study for an exam? Read next week's chapter? Or should they play with their kids or spend time with their spouses? Will the in-laws understand if they don't visit because they're doing schoolwork?

It takes a very understanding spouse to provide psychological support for a student who has family and work responsibilities, too. It is tiring and often frustrating to have so much to do in a day. It is stressful and may be unhealthy as well. A spouse who can provide those extra few minutes with the kids that the student-parent can't, who can take on more than his or her share of the household chores, and who can provide a shoulder to lean on and an ear to listen, can go a long way in intervening between stress and illness for the older college student.

Not to be forgotten in this discussion is the financial investment necessary to attend college. Older students who must support a family must decide if the investment in education is worthwhile. There will be a payoff down the road—either in increased income or in improved lifestyle that a more enjoyable or less demanding job may afford. Often, however, a financial sacrifice is required by the student and his or her family while the schooling takes place. This sacrifice is easier to bear if the whole family believes it worthwhile and is willing to put off immediate pleasures to achieve long-range goals. If the older student continually has to justify the expense of college, or if the family's sacrifice is periodically brought up to make him or her feel guilty, the stress associated with college will be greater than otherwise.

Self-Doubt

Some colleges are recognizing that returning college students—those who dropped out years ago—and older, first-time college students have all sorts of doubts about their ability to be successful in their studies. Consequently, they are offering counseling programs for these students. These self-doubts are understandable, since our society too often perceives learning as a young person's activity. How can I compete with young, bright people? How can I do well when I'm also working full-time? How can I pass my courses when I need to devote time to my family? How will I be able to spend as much time at the library as students who live on campus? I don't have someone to study with or professors to consult with frequently, as does the student living on campus. I've forgotten how to study; I haven't taken an exam in ages. These are some of the stressful concerns of the older college student.

The Minority College Student

Minority college students face stressors that are similar to those faced by other college students. However, in addition they can experience other stressors that are specific to their minority status. One obvious stressor is racism. In a study of the effects of racism on the health of African American college students, Armstead and her colleagues stated that "exposure to racist stimuli significantly increases the blood pressure of normotensive Black college students. . . . Racism that occurs in American society may pose a serious health hazard to its Black citizens."[32]

Racism can also have devastating effects on students' grades. A study conducted at the University of Maryland[33] found Hispanic students' grades were lower when they

Terrorism and College Students' Stress

Just like everyone else, college students are affected by current events, and the events of September 11, 2001, were no exception. In a study of students at Michigan State University, Nancy Lange found that students felt significantly or somewhat more positive about

- Their country (71 percent).
- Their interest in discussions about world issues (66 percent).
- Their level of closeness to their family (63 percent).
- The role and responsibilities of citizenship (56 percent).
- The quality of relationships with friends (53 percent).

Students also reported feeling significantly or somewhat more positive about

- Their level of personal safety (48 percent).
- How the news media cover such events (46 percent).
- Their level of concentration on their academic work (45 percent).
- Traveling to other countries (44 percent).
- Studying abroad (39 percent).

The areas not changed after 9/11 were

- Their choice of academic major (69 percent).
- Their career plan (68 percent).
- Having a diverse friendship group (67 percent).
- Their ability to manage their emotions and thoughts (63 percent).
- Participating in community service (62 percent).
- Participating in discussions on diversity and multiculturalism (62 percent).

Source: Nancy Lange, "How Did September 11th Affect Students?" *About Campus* 7(2002): 21–24. This material is used by permission of John Wiley & Sons, Inc.

experienced racism. It should be noted, though, that Hispanic students who took advantage of campus minority services were able to handle the racism better and, as a result, their grades were higher than those of other Hispanic students. If you experience racism, consult with your instructor regarding services available on your campus.

Language can also be a stressor affecting minority students. Imagine having to take classes in a language with which you are not comfortable. I continue to be amazed and in awe of my foreign-born students who do just that. Asian Americans and Hispanic Americans may be from several different countries, and English may be their second language. Fortunately, many colleges provide support services to help these students succeed in their studies. These services often include help in editing of term papers, proctoring of untimed exams, and assistance in using the campus libraries.

Another stressor experienced by minority college students relates to the manner in which college classes are conducted. For example, some classes rely on debate and confrontation to discuss controversial issues. Certain cultural groups' values of politeness and respect for others may be at odds with the type of classroom climate fostered by some college instructors. Furthermore, when accommodations in the classroom are recognized as needed to adjust to the different learning styles of minority students, too often the interpretation results in broad generalizations about the intellectual ability of these students. Rather than the accommodations being considered a flexible approach by the instructor, minority student deficits requiring remediation is the stereotypical conclusion drawn.

In addition, the pressure to perform well academically from well-meaning family members may be very stressful for some minority students. This pressure may stem from a cultural value placed on education, or it may relate to the student being the first one in his or her family to go to college. In either case, the family is invested in the student's success in college.

These are not the only stressful situations encountered by minority college students. Some of these students attended a high school in which they were the majority. Now having minority status requires an adjustment that can be stressful.[34] Other students may not have appropriate role models at their colleges with whom to consult and from whom to receive guidance and encouragement. There is still an underrepresentation of minority faculty and university administrators on college campuses.

In spite of these unique stressors that minority college students can and often do experience, many do exceptionally well in their studies. If you are a minority on your campus, use the resources available to you to be one of the successful ones. Consult with your instructor for assistance, speak with someone at the counseling center or the campus health center, or seek the help of any campus organizations designed to assist minority students.

Interventions

Interventions can diminish the stress of college for both younger and older students. These interventions can be at the levels of life situation, perception, emotional arousal, or physiological arousal.

Life-Situation Interventions

Students entering college are bombarded with numerous life changes. To prevent adding to these needed adjustments, other aspects of life should be made as routine as possible. More life changes mean more stress; thus, entering college is not the time to take on added job responsibilities, to have a baby, or to break up old relationships. I've long suspected that the large number of college dropouts is more a function of stress than of grades. When we consider that most students enter college, move out of their homes, leave old friends, make new friends, accept new responsibilities, and live in a new town, it is not surprising that all of these life changes are stressful to them. Recognizing this situation, at least two suggestions seem sensible: (1) that high schools teach stress management and (2) that colleges offer stress management workshops during orientation sessions for entering students. More and more of this is occurring, but still not enough. High school graduates are not only entering college; some are entering the military, some are taking full-time jobs, and some are raising families. In spite of what they do when they leave high school, their lives change dramatically and swiftly. They should be helped to deal with this change by managing the stress accompanying it. And they should be taught how to manage their finances during this time of greater independence. This, too, should be a part of orientation programs for students entering college.

Another life-situation intervention responds to the need to make new friends. The more people you meet, the more likely you are to find a new friend. Joining clubs, participating in intramurals, going to parties and dances, and working with other students to improve campus life are all good ways to meet people. Remember, however, that the idea is to improve your health—psychological and physical—so don't engage in unhealthy or dysfunctional activities just to be part of a group. I've had several students talk with me about their problem with abusing alcohol because

Alcohol is sometimes thought of as the answer to all problems. After the alcohol wears off, however, the stressful problems remain or are sometimes made even worse by attempting to cope by drinking.

"all" their friends spend their time drinking at an off-campus hangout. When we looked more closely at the situation, we found that not "all" the friends drank and that friendships could be maintained with those who did drink without having to get drunk oneself. Once students realized that it was they, not their friends, who were responsible for their drinking, they were better able to control it.

To respond to stressors associated with shyness and self-doubt, try some of the following suggestions. These suggestions come from one of the country's authorities on shyness and the director of the Stanford University Shyness Clinic.[35]

1. Recognize your strengths and weaknesses and set your goals accordingly.

2. Decide what you value, what you believe in, what you realistically would like your life to be like. Take inventory of your library of stored scripts and bring them up-to-date, in line with the psychological space you are in now, so they will serve you where you are headed.

3. Determine what your roots are. By examining your past, seek out the lines of continuity and the decisions that have brought you to your present place. Try to understand and forgive those who have hurt you and not helped when they could have. Forgive yourself for mistakes, sins, failures, and past embarrassments. Permanently bury all negative self-remembrances after you have sifted out any constructive value they may provide. The bad past lives on in your memory only as long as you let it be a tenant. Prepare an eviction notice immediately. Give the room to memories of your past successes, however minor.

4. Guilt and shame have limited personal value in shaping your behavior toward positive goals. Don't allow yourself to indulge in them.

5. Look for the causes of your behavior in physical, social, economic, and political aspects of your current situation and not in personality defects in you.

6. Remind yourself that there are alternative views to every event. "Reality" is never more than shared agreements among people to call it the same way rather than as each one separately sees it. This enables you to be more tolerant in your interpretation of others' intentions and more generous in dismissing what might appear to be rejections or putdowns of you.

7. Never say bad things about yourself; especially, never attribute to yourself irreversible negative traits such as "stupid," "ugly," "uncreative," "a failure," "incorrigible."

8. Don't allow others to criticize you as a person; it is your specific actions that are open for evaluation and available for improvement—accept such constructive feedback graciously if it will help you.

9. Remember that sometimes failure and disappointment are blessings in disguise, telling you the goals were not right for you, the effort was not worth it, and a bigger letdown later on may be avoided.

10. Do not tolerate people, jobs, and situations that make you feel inadequate. If you can't change them or yourself enough to make you feel more worthwhile, walk on out, or pass them by. Life is too short to waste time on downers.

11. Give yourself the time to relax, to meditate, to listen to yourself, to enjoy hobbies and activities you can do alone. In this way, you can get in touch with yourself.

12. Practice being a social animal. Enjoy feeling the energy that other people transmit, the unique qualities and range of variability of our brothers and sisters. Imagine what their fears and insecurities might be and how you could help them. Decide what you need from them and what you have to give. Then, let them know that you are ready and open to sharing.

13. Stop being so overprotective about your ego; it is tougher and more resilient than you imagine. It bruises but never breaks. Better it should get hurt occasionally from an emotional commitment that didn't work out as planned than get numbed from the emotional insulation of playing it too cool.

14. Develop long-range goals in life, with highly specific short-range subgoals. Develop realistic means to achieve these subgoals. Evaluate your progress regularly and be the first to pat yourself on the back or whisper a word of praise in your ear. You don't have to worry about being unduly modest if no one else hears you boasting.

15. You are not an object to which bad things just happen, a passive nonentity hoping, like a garden slug, to avoid being stepped on. You are the culmination of millions of years of evolution of our species, of your parents' dreams, of God's image. You are a unique individual who, as an active actor in life's drama, can make things happen. You can change the direction of your entire life anytime you choose to do so. With confidence in yourself, obstacles turn into challenges and challenges into accomplishments. Shyness then recedes, because, instead of always preparing for and worrying about how you will live your life, you forget yourself as you become absorbed in the living of it.

For jealousy-related stress, Walster and Walster recommend three steps.[36] The first step involves finding out exactly what is making you jealous. Key questions to ask are "What was going on just before you started feeling jealous?" and "What are you afraid of?" As we discussed earlier, you're probably afraid of losing something (e.g., love, self-esteem, property, status, or power). The second step asks you to put your jealous feeling in proper perspective. Is it really so awful that your friend is interested in someone else? Aren't you interested in other people as well? Is your jealousy irrational? What's the difference between *having* to have this person love you and *wishing* this person loved you? Is it really true that you couldn't stand to lose this person's love? Or is it that you'd *like* not to?

Lastly, you can negotiate a "contract" with the other person. This contract should help you be less jealous but must not be too restrictive on the other person. To expect your friend to lunch only with you might be unfair. To expect your friend to lunch with you on Tuesdays and Thursdays, on the other hand, might ensure you're spending time together while allowing each of you the freedom to spend time with other people.

Other life-situation interventions follow:

1. Limit the courses in which you enroll to a number you can handle without overloading yourself.

2. Improve your communication with a romantic lover so both of you have the same expectations for, and understanding of, the relationship.

3. The best way to manage a breakup is to seek out new relationships. Get involved with other people—and not only romantically.

4. To coordinate family and school responsibilities, schedule each of these. Working out specific times for schoolwork with your family will ensure you're getting your work done and your family is not being disappointed you're not with them. Working out specific times to be with your family will ensure that you do not overlook their needs.

When intervening at the life-situation level, don't forget some obvious resources. You can consult with your professor, seek assistance from personnel at the campus health center, speak with your adviser, or get help from the community health department. These and other resources have proven valuable to many of my students, and I believe they will for you as well. Help is all around you if you look and ask for it.

Perception Interventions

As we've stated many times in this book, as important as external events are in relation to stress, so is your perception of those events. The following are some ways to perceive the stressors of college life as less distressing:

1. To perceive shyness and jealousy as less threatening, questions such as "What am I really afraid of? How probable is it that this thing I fear will happen? How bad is it if it does happen?" will help you view the shyness or jealousy more realistically.

2. Use selective awareness to focus upon the positive aspects of college. The opportunity to learn new things, meet new people, prepare for a future you are looking forward to, and find out how capable you really are should occupy your thoughts, rather than how difficult or time-consuming it is or how much time it requires away from your family and your job.

3. Smell the roses along the way—literally and figuratively. I love the look and smell of my campus. Whether it be winter or summer, spring or fall, the trees, bushes, buildings, and grounds have a pleasing nature. I sometimes walk off the path to hear the crunch of snow under my feet, and I've been known to walk right up to a flowering crab apple tree to smell its fragrance. Maybe your campus isn't as pretty as mine, or maybe it's prettier. In any case, there are things about your campus that, if you paid attention to them, would make the time you spend there more pleasant.

4. When looking at all of your responsibilities, you might feel overloaded. However, if you were to write a schedule for them, you would probably recognize that you do have enough time for it all. Only when viewed collectively do they appear overwhelming.

Emotional Arousal Interventions

As with other stressors, college-related ones can be managed at the emotional level by regular practice of relaxation techniques. When I mention this to groups of people who have so little time (e.g., students who work full-time and also have family responsibilities), I'm frequently told that there just aren't forty minutes a day for relaxation. I tell them that if they don't have the time then they, in particular, need the regular relaxation. The paradox is that those without the time probably need the practice more than those who can fit it in. At this point in your reading, you should

Getting Involved in Your Community

Academic concerns certainly can cause many college students a great deal of stress. After all, in college you are preparing for your future. However, students also experience stress unrelated to their coursework. That is one reason many campuses have a health center.

Of course, campus health centers concern themselves with flu and measles outbreaks and other illnesses and diseases. But they also offer services related to the mental health of the college community. At the health center on my campus, counseling services are available to students who are feeling "stressed out" about their relationships with other students, their girlfriends or boyfriends, or their parents. I have referred more than one student to that health center who was wrestling with feelings associated with the death of a close friend or relative. And, unfortunately, a college, like any other community, has its share of violence and crime, so we also have a rape crisis hotline and sexuality counseling program.

Interestingly, many of these services are offered by students themselves. These are volunteers who go through a fairly extensive training program so as to offer effective service. These peer education and peer counseling programs are highly regarded by our campus community, and they provide an invaluable service.

Does your campus have a health center? Does that health center offer similar programs? If so, perhaps you might consider volunteering to participate in a peer education or counseling program. If such a program does not presently exist on your campus, perhaps you can organize one.

recognize that we all have the time; we just choose to use it for something else. You can rearrange how you use your time so you can practice a relaxation technique regularly. It's up to you!

Physiological Arousal Interventions

Regular exercise will use the stress products you build up. The body is prepared to do something physical, and exercise will afford it a healthy way to make use of this preparation.

College students are more fortunate than others relative to physiological arousal intervention, since they usually have access to exercise facilities and equipment. They can join intramural teams, participate in recreational sports hours (these usually occur during the noon hour or late afternoon or evening), or do exercise alone (e.g., jog around campus or shoot baskets).

College life can be made less stressful with attention paid to managing college-related stressors. You're probably tired of reading this, *but* whether it's stressful or not is really up to you.

summary

- College life can be quite stressful because it requires adapting to a dramatic life change. College life involves assuming greater responsibility for one's life, managing finances, making new friends, studying a great deal, and learning about a new environment.

- Specific stressors experienced by college students include striving for good grades, coping with a greater amount of schoolwork, making friends, managing pressure to be sexually active, preventing date rape, being shy, becoming jealous, and breaking up with a dating partner.

- The typical college student today is older than the college student of past years. Many college students are over twenty-five years of age.

- Older college students experience stressors unique to their situations. They must juggle career, school, and family responsibilities.

- Older college students often doubt their abilities to return to school, to achieve academically, and to interact well with classmates who may be much younger.

- Colleges and high schools need to offer stress management educational experiences to their students to help them manage the degree of change that occurs upon graduating from high school and entering college.

- To manage jealousy-related stress, determine what makes you jealous, put your jealous feelings in proper perspective, or negotiate a contract with the other person.

- Minority college students can face unique stressors. Among these are racism, language barriers, classrooms conducted in ways that are at odds with cultural values, pressure to succeed in school, minority status in school for the first time, and the lack of role models from whom to seek guidance and encouragement.

notes

1. L. C. Towbes and L. H. Cohen, "Chronic Stress in the Lives of College Students: Scale Development and Prospective Prediction of Distress," *Journal of Youth and Adolescence* 25(1996): 199–217.

2. S. Fisher, *Stress in Academic Life* (Buckingham, England: Open University Press, 1994).

3. P. McCarthy and R. Humphrey, "Debt: The Reality of Student Life," *Higher Education Quarterly* 49(1995): 78–86.

4. R. Humphrey and P. McCarthy, "High Debt and Poor Housing: A Taxing Life for Contemporary Students," *Youth and Policy* 56(1997): 55–64.

5. Robin Humphrey et al., "Stress and the Contemporary Student," *Higher Education Quarterly* 52(1998): 221–42.

6. Ibid.

7. A. Chickering and R. Havighurst, "The Life Cycle," in *The Modern American College,* ed. A. Chickering et al. (San Francisco: Jossey-Bass, 1998).

8. Humphrey et al., "Stress and the Contemporary Student."

9. College Board, "2003–2004 College Costs," *CollegeBoard.com for Students,* 2004, http://www.collegeboard.com

10. Kenneth B. Redd, "Why Do Students Borrow So Much? Recent National Trends in Student Loan Debt," *ERIC Digest,* 2001, http://www.ericfacility.net/ericdigests/ed451759.html

11. Tracey King and Ellynne Bannon, *The Burden of Borrowing: A Report on the Rising Rates of Student Loan Debt.* The State PIRG's Higher Education Project, 2002, http://www.pirg.org/highered

12. "Student Finances, by the Numbers," *Chronicle of Higher Education,* 49(2002): 13.

13. Ariana Eunjung Cha, "ISO Romance? Online Matchmakers Put Love to the Test," *Washington Post,* 4 May 2003, A1, A14–A15.

14. Edward O. Laumann, John H. Gagnon, Robert T. Michaels, and Stuart Michaels, *The Social Organization of Sexuality: Sexual Practices in the United States* (Chicago: University of Chicago Press, 1994).

15. National Center for Health Statistics, "Sexual Behavior and Selected Health Measures: Men and Women 15–44 Years of Age, United States, 2002," *Advance Data* 32(2005): 21–22, 25.

16. Robert T. Michael, John H. Gagnon, Edward O. Laumann, and G. Kolata, *Sex in America: A Definitive Survey* (New York: Warner Books, 1995).

17. Centers for Disease Control and Prevention, *HIV/AIDS Surveillance Report,* 2003, 12, 2005.

18. C. Everett Koop, *Understanding AIDS: A Message from the Surgeon General* (Washington, DC: Department of Health and Human Services, 1988).

19. Freya L. Sonenstein, Leighton Ku, Laura Duberstein Lindberg, Charles F. Turner, and Joseph H. Pleck, "Changes in Sexual Behavior and Condom Use Among Teenage Males: 1988 to 1995," *American Journal of Public Health* 88(1998): 956–59.

20. Akinrinola Bankole, Jacqueline E. Darroch, and Susheela Singh, "Determinants of Trends in Condom Use in the United States, 1988–1995," *Family Planning Perspectives* 31(1999): 264–71.

21. Linda J. Piccinino and William D. Mosher, "Trends in Contraceptive Use in the United States: 1982–1995," *Family Planning Perspectives* 30(1998): 4–10, 46.

22. National Center for Health Statistics, *Health, United States,* 2004 (Hyattsville, MD: National Center for Health Statistics, 2004): 208.

23. M. Winship, *CDC Seroprevalence Study,* unpublished raw data.

24. National Center for Health Statistics, *Health, United States, 2003* (Hyattsville, MD: National Center for Health Statistics, 2003).

25. American College Health Association, *Acquaintance Rape* (Baltimore: American College Health Association, 1992).

26. Philip G. Zimbardo, *Shyness: What It Is and What to Do About It* (Reading, MA: Addison-Wesley, 1990), 12, 158–60.

27. Elaine Walster and G. William Walster, *A New Look at Love* (Reading, MA: Addison-Wesley, 1978), 87.

28. Susan Sprecher, Diane Felmlee, Sandra Metts, Beverley Fehr, and Debra Vanni, "Factors Associated with Distress Following the Breakup of a Close Relationship," *Journal of Social and Personal Relationships* 15(1998): 791–809.

29. Susan Sprecher, "Two Sides of the Breakup of Dating Relationship," *Personal Relationships* 1(1994): 199–222.

30. Eric L. Wee, "More College Students Live, Then Learn," *Washington Post,* 5 March 1996, A1, A7.

31. Amy Argetsinger, "Colleges Brace for the Baby Boom," *Washington Post,* 8 July 2000, B5.

32. Cheryl A. Armstead et al., "Relationship of Racial Stressors to Blood Pressure Responses and Anger Expression in Black College Students," *Health Psychology* 8(1989): 554.

33. Martha R. Carkcl, "Grades and Racism Linked in Report," *The Diamondback,* 11 October 1993, 1, 7.

34. Laura L. B. Border and Nancy Van Note Chism, "Teaching for Diversity," *New Directions for Teaching and Learning* 49(1992): 12.

35. Zimbardo, *Shyness,* 158–60.

36. Walster and Walster, *A New Look at Love,* 91–93.

internet resources

CampusBlues.com
http://www.campusblues.com/stress.asp
Discussion of college students and stress along with warning signs and ways to manage stress; suggests humor as a way to manage stress.

Managing Stress: A Guide for College Students
http://www.uhs.uga.edu/stress/
Produced by the University of Georgia University Health Center, this site places a discussion of stress within a wellness lifestyle view.

Help Now: Stress Management
http://ub-counseling.buffalo.edu/stressmanagement.shtml
Managed by the University of Buffalo, this site discusses what stress is, its symptoms, causes of stress, and what to do about it.

Managing Stress
http://www.utexas.edu/student/cmhc/booklets/stress/stress.html
The Counseling & Mental Health Center at the University of Texas at Austin presents signs of stress that include feelings, thoughts, behaviors, and physical signs.

Lisa is so busy she has no time to work on the term paper that is due next week. Since the grade on that paper makes up a significant percent of the grade in that course, Lisa decides to pay a friend to write the term paper for her.

In Juan's stress management course, students are assigned to groups. Each group is expected to develop an outline and conduct a workshop for people, off campus, in need of learning stress management skills. In past semesters, groups have helped cancer patients cope better with their disease, taught elementary school children to manage conflict with classmates less confrontationally, and shown nursing home residents how to communicate more effectively with staff and family members to experience less stressful relationships. However, Juan is studying in preparation to take the MCATs for entrance to medical school. How he does on that exam will determine whether he gets accepted to a medical school and, therefore, whether he can achieve his goal of becoming a physician. So, Juan decides to study for the exam rather than attend planning meetings scheduled by his group or participating in the development of the group's workshop outline. At the end of the semester, Juan asks the group to put his name on their project paper even though he hardly contributed to it. The professor will never know, he argues.

Tonya and Latricia are good friends. Both recognize that Latricia learns more easily and is a more conscientious student. So when it comes to taking the midterm exam in the course for which they are both enrolled, Tonya, relying on their friendship, expects Latricia will let her copy off of her answer sheet.

The situations described above all include ethical violations by college students. They involve taking credit for a paper or group project to which the student made little if any contribution, or relying on cheating on an exam. Ethical behavior, while always important, has recently been highlighted by corporate scandals such as the collapse of large businesses like Enron and WorldCom—which resulted from unethical behavior by corporate executives that involved financial lies and "cooking the books." However, the rest of us too often do not realize that some of our common behaviors are also unethical. Forty-four percent of Americans lie about their work history when applying for a job, 25 percent have downloaded music illegally, 30 percent own pirated software, and 75 percent of high school and college students admit to some form of cheating.[a] Furthermore, 79 percent of workers say they would steal from their employers, 17 percent lie on their tax returns, and 3 percent of scientists admit to unethical scientific conduct such as fabricating data.

Imagine the stress associated with behaving unethically. First there is the energy required to engage in the unethical act and then to hide it from others. Then there are the potential consequences if the unethical behavior is uncovered. Many universities and colleges have Honor Codes, and violations can result in suspension, expulsion, and/or notations on violators' permanent records. Embarrassment before one's family and friends is another stressful consequence that can be expected. And, even if one is not caught, the loss of trust and respect among those who do know about the act (e.g., friends and classmates) can be quite stressful. As with other stressors, the best place to set up a roadblock is at the life situation level of our stress model. In other words, do not act unethically in the first place and none of the potential stress reactions will occur.

[a]"Lies, Damn Lies, and Statistics." *Wired* March 24, 2004: 60–61.

LAB ASSESSMENT 17.1

How Intimate Are Your Friendships?

Directions: Think of a casual acquaintance and one of your closest friends. First circle the number of the following statements that you discuss with your friends in private conversation. Next, list the same set of statements you would discuss with a casual acquaintance.

1. Whether or not I have ever gone to a church other than my own (2.85)
2. The number of children I want to have after I am married (5.91)
3. How frequently I like to engage in sexual activity (10.02)
4. Whether I would rather live in an apartment or a house after getting married (3.09)
5. What birth control methods I would use in marriage (9.31)
6. What I do to attract a member of the opposite sex whom I like (8.54)
7. How often I usually go on dates (5.28)
8. Times that I have lied to my girlfriend or boyfriend (8.56)
9. My feelings about discussing sex with my friends (7.00)
10. How I might feel (or actually felt) if I saw my father hit my mother (9.50)
11. The degree of independence and freedom from family rules that I have (had) while living at home (5.39)
12. How often my family gets together (2.89)
13. Who my favorite relatives (aunts, uncles, and so on) are and why (5.83)
14. How I feel about getting old (6.36)
15. The parts of my body I am most ashamed for anyone to see (8.88)
16. My feelings about lending money (4.75)
17. My most pressing need for money right now (outstanding debts, some major purchases that are needed or desired) (6.88)
18. How much I spend for my clothes (7.17)
19. Laws that I would like to see put in effect (3.08)
20. Whether or not I have ever cried as an adult when I was sad (8.94)
21. How angry I get when people hurry me (5.33)
22. What animals make me nervous (3.44)
23. What it takes to hurt my feelings deeply (9.37)
24. What I am most afraid of (8.25)
25. How I really feel about the people I work for or with (7.29)
26. The kinds of things I do that I don't want people to watch (8.85)

The amount of disclosure is shown by the number of statements circled for each person. Intimacy of disclosure is found by adding up the numbers in parentheses for the circled statements, divided by the total number of statements circled. For instance, if you have circled statements 1, 4, 12, 19, and 22 for an acquaintance, 5 indicates the amount you would disclose, and 3.07 (2.85 + 3.09 + 2.89 + 3.08 + 3.44 = 15.35 ÷ 5) would be the intimacy of disclosure figure—not very much in this case.

As you can see by the results of the friendship and acquaintanceship questionnaire you just completed, self-disclosure is a vital ingredient in friendship. Without self-disclosure of a significant degree, your relationship stops at the acquaintance level. Although acquaintances may help alleviate loneliness, they don't provide the social support that friends do, which we have learned can act as a buffer for our stress.

Source: D. A. Taylor and I. Altman, "Intimacy-Scaled Stimuli for Use in Research on Interpersonal Exchange," *Naval Medical Research Institute Technical Report No. 9,* MF 022, 01.03–1002, May 1966.

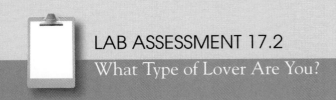

LAB ASSESSMENT 17.2

What Type of Lover Are You?

Directions: To find out what type of lover you are, answer each question as it applies to your boyfriends, girlfriends, lovers, or spouse.

A = almost always

U = usually

R = rarely

N = never (or almost never)

_____ 1. You have a clearly defined image of your desired partner.

_____ 2. You felt a strong emotional reaction to him or her on the first encounter.

_____ 3. You are preoccupied with thoughts about him or her.

_____ 4. You are eager to see him or her every day.

_____ 5. You discuss future plans and a wide range of interests and experiences.

_____ 6. Tactile, sensual contact is important to the relationship.

_____ 7. Sexual intimacy was achieved early in the relationship.

_____ 8. You feel that success in love is more important than success in other areas of your life.

_____ 9. You want to be in love or have love as security.

_____ 10. You try to force him or her to show more feeling and commitment.

_____ 11. You declared your love first.

_____ 12. You are willing to suffer neglect and abuse from him or her.

_____ 13. You deliberately restrain frequency of contact with him or her.

_____ 14. You restrict discussion and display of your feelings with him or her.

_____ 15. If a breakup is coming, you feel it is better to drop the other person before being dropped.

_____ 16. You play the field and have several persons who could love you.

_____ 17. You are more interested in pleasure than in emotional attachment.

_____ 18. You feel the need to love someone you have grown accustomed to.

_____ 19. You believe that the test of time is the only sure way to find real love.

_____ 20. You don't believe that true love happens suddenly or dramatically.

Some researchers have identified four basic types of love: erotic, ludic, storgic, and manic. If you answered A or U to 1–8, you are probably an erotic lover. If you answered A or U to 3–4 and 8–12, your love style tends to be manic. If you answered A or U to 13–17 and R or N to the other questions, you are probably a ludic lover. If you answered A or U to 17–20, together with R or N for the other statements, your love style tends to be storgic. Refer back to the section on love for descriptions of these types of lovers.

Source: John Alan Lee, *The Colours of Love* (Toronto: New Press, 1973).

I'll never forget the voice breaking with emotion, the tears being held back, as he eulogized his forty-two-year-old brother after his brother's premature death:

> My brother need not be idealized or enlarged in death beyond what he was in life. To be remembered simply as a good and decent man who saw wrong and tried to right it, who saw suffering and tried to heal it, who saw war and tried to stop it. Those of us who loved him and who take him to his rest today, pray that what he was to us, what he wished for others, may come to pass for all the world. As he said many times in many parts of this nation, to those he touched and who sought to touch him: Some men see things as they are. I dream things that never were and say, why not?

These words were spoken in New York City's St. Patrick's Cathedral in early June of 1968 as the nation stopped to mourn with Edward Kennedy the death of his brother Robert. As I listened to the eulogy and participated in the funeral, albeit from afar, I could not help thinking of *my* two brothers, Stephen and Mark. Stephen, the businessman bent on making a million dollars, and Mark, the musician and artist, are as different from me as they are from each other. And yet, we are family. We grew up sharing one bedroom, fought with each other regularly, and shared the sorrows and joys accompanying twenty-some years of life under one roof.

This chapter is about such bonds—family bonds—and how the changes in family life can be stressful. It describes ways to intervene between family stress and illness and disease.

The Family

A family is a set of intimate and personal relationships. These relationships may be legal (as in marriage) or extralegal (as in communal family groups). We speak of *a family of friends,* fraternity *brothers,* sorority *sisters,* and kissing *cousins,* using family-related terms to communicate the intimacy of these relationships. Our discussion, however, will be limited in this section to the **nuclear family**—a married couple and their children—and the **extended family**—relatives other than spouses and children.

nuclear family
A married couple and their children.

extended family
Relatives other than spouses and children.

Needs Satisfied by the Family

One of the functions of a family is to govern societal control of reproduction and child rearing. Although there are some marriage partners who do not have children—by choice or anatomical condition—for those who do have them, the societal expectation is that these children will be raised within a family structure. This family may take many forms, and, although some single women choose to conceive children, the social expectation is still that a child will be born to a married couple.

The family may also provide economic support. Food, clothing, and shelter are provided by family members who assist one another in their various tasks and functions. For example, one family member might cook the food that another family member earns money to buy, or both marriage partners may take jobs outside the home to earn money to eat out. While children are growing up, they are supported by the more self-sufficient family members (parents, older siblings, or other relatives), and their physiological, safety, and security needs are provided for.

Lastly, the family may provide for many emotional needs. It can provide love, eliminate feelings of isolation, foster a sense of belonging, and teach you that others are concerned about and care for you. In a family you can really be yourself—even

In addition to dealing with important things, the effective family has fun together.

your worst self—and usually still feel you belong to the group. Your family may not like your behavior or your decisions, but you'll still be welcome for Thanksgiving dinner, so to speak. Families can also serve you well in times of crisis. As we noted earlier in this book, having people with whom you can discuss your problems (social support) can help prevent you from becoming ill from those problems.

These words describing the needs families can meet convey the role of the family only in an academic, intellectual sense. For many people, family life serves a real emotional need as well. They have been made to feel secure and loved and have developed a sense of belonging from their families. I'm reminded of a story I recently read in the newspaper of an automobile accident in which a family of five was involved. The car crash killed the father, mother, and two young children, but the two-year-old daughter, who wore a seat belt, survived. As I read the story, my heart went out to this child, and I felt her loss. By that, I do not mean I was concerned about who would care for her, feed her, or shelter her. Rather, I was feeling her *irreplaceable* loss—the loss of her blood relatives, whose connection with her could never be totally compensated. There's something about the family bond that makes it unique.

Now, having said all of that, we need to recognize that not all families function as described. Some parents are abusive, some family members are separated from each other, and some people are so impoverished (financially, emotionally, or morally) that the last thing on their minds is helping to satisfy family needs. There are single-parent families, blended families, and dysfunctional families. And there are families whose members just don't know any better or who are so busy providing some of the needs (e.g., economic support) that other needs go unmet (e.g., love). However, when the family is effective, it can be such a major influence that nothing can compare with its effect on your total existence and future.

The Effective Family

What makes a family effective? One observer of families, author Jane Howard, found the following characteristics expressed in effective families:

1. *They have a chief;* that is, there is someone around whom other family members cluster.

2. *They have a switchboard operator;* that is, there is someone who keeps track of what all the others are up to.

3. *They are much to all their members but everything to none;* that is, family members are encouraged to be involved with and have some of their needs met by people outside of the family.

4. *They are hospitable;* that is, they recognize that hosts need guests as much as guests need hosts, and they maintain a surrounding of honorary family members. These "guests" become additional support systems for family members.

5. *They deal squarely with direness;* that is, when trouble comes—and in family life occasional trouble is unavoidable—it is dealt with quickly and openly and is not allowed to threaten family bonds.

6. *They prize their rituals;* that is, they observe holidays together, grieve at funerals together, and in other ways encourage a sense of continuity and connectedness.

7. *They are affectionate;* that is, family members hug, kiss, and gingerly shake hands. They are quick to demonstrate love and caring for one another.

8. *They have a sense of place;* that is, there is a house, a town, or some other place to which they feel connected. Even families who have moved often can feel connected to the place in which they presently find themselves.

9. *They connect with posterity;* that is, family members feel as though something came before them and something will continue when they die to which they are linked.

10. *They honor their elders;* that is, grandparents and other elderly relatives are respected and cared for. Their experience and wisdom—and they, themselves—are valued.[1]

We may be tempted to judge our families against the characteristics of effective families and assign blame whenever we come up short. We would be better advised, however, to *analyze* our families as objectively as possible and identify areas for and means of improvement. Assigning blame serves no purpose and may actually interfere with any improvements you attempt to make.

Also recognize that some of us come from families that may be beyond repair. If a parent has been either physically abusive or incestuous, and this has occurred over a number of years, the child may never be forgiving. In this situation, the total family may not be able to be reunited, although there are cases in which counseling has helped even these kinds of families forgive—not forget—and function at a higher level. Still, if the total family cannot be made whole, selected family members can work on improving and maintaining their relationship. For example, brothers and sisters, some of whom may have also been victims of parental abuse, can remain close the rest of their lives. Here is still another situation in which selective awareness can be helpful. Although child abuse is not something any of us would wish to experience, the closeness developed between siblings who have been abused can be intense. Focusing on the understanding and empathy of a brother or sister can go a long way in helping to cope with the stress resulting from this situation.

The Changing Family

The predominant family style in America is the breadwinning father, homemaking mother, and resident children. Right? Wrong! Check out these surprising statistics about family life in 2004 America:

- Almost 118 million U.S. adults (52 percent of the adult population) were married and living with a spouse.

- Among twenty-five- to twenty-nine-year-olds, 49 percent (over 9 million people) had never been married, 67 percent of African Americans in that age group had never been married.

- Almost 10 percent of adults (22 million) were currently divorced.

- 32 percent of all children under eighteen lived with a single parent.

- Of children living with a single parent, 84 percent lived with their mothers, 42 percent of whom had never married.

- Approximately 1.5 million children under eighteen lived in the household of their grandparents with neither parent present.[2,3]

Fewer than half (46 percent) of married-couple households have children under eighteen years of age living at home.[4] However, children older than eighteen years of age also move back in with their parent(s) or never move out. Those who move out and return—because of divorce, economic hardship, or myriad other reasons—are sometimes referred to as **boomerang children.** Fourteen percent of family households had these children eighteen or older living at home. Of family households with children under eighteen, 27 percent were maintained by single parents;

boomerang children
Children who leave home to live elsewhere but subsequently return to live with the parents.

Covenant Marriages

In 1997, Louisiana passed a law requiring couples applying for marriage licenses to choose one of two types of marital contracts. The Standard Marital Contract allows married partners to divorce after living separately for six months, or immediately if one spouse is guilty of adultery, has been sentenced to prison, or dies. The Covenant Marital Contract allows the couple to divorce only after they have lived apart for two years or after one spouse commits adultery, is sentenced to prison for a felony, abandons the home for at least a year, or physically or sexually abuses the spouse or child, and the couple must participate in premarital counseling from either a member of the clergy or a counselor. In other words, with a Covenant Marital Contract, the couple waive their right to a no-fault (easily obtained) divorce. The intent is to require couples deciding to marry to consider their commitment and to make sure they are making the right decision, then, when problems in the marriage surface, as they do in most marriages, to encourage couples to work through these problems rather than take the easy route to divorce. However, opponents argue that marriages that are in trouble only create distress for the couple and negatively influence children.

If you were about to become married, which contract would you choose?

Marriage can be quite joyful, with couples sharing happy occasions. At the same time, marriage can be stressful as two people who lived apart now must accommodate one another.

cohabitation
Romantically involved couples living together although not married.

there were almost 10 million mother-child family groups and 2 million father-child family groups. Furthermore, in the mother-child single-parent family groups, 42 percent of the mothers had never been married.[5] The types of households are depicted in Figure 18.1.

Marriage

Many aspects of marriage have remained unchanged for centuries, and many others have changed radically. June marriages are still the most popular, more adults still get married rather than remain single, marriage is still a legal entity requiring a marriage license and a marriage ceremony (either civil or religious), and more women still take their husband's last name than do not.

On the other hand, marriage has changed considerably over the years. People of the same sex may be legally married in some states. In 2004, 58.5 percent of the adult population were married and living with their spouses. Yet, a large number of adults have never married. Among people twenty to twenty-four years old, 86 percent of males have never married and 75.4 percent of females have never married.[6]

Marriage can be quite joyful, but even in the best of marriages it can also be quite stressful. Are *you* ready for marriage? Complete Lab 18.1 at the end of this chapter to help you decide.

Cohabitation

More and more people choose to live with someone with whom they are romantically involved but to whom they are not married. Between 1970 and 1976, the number of people living together with someone of the opposite sex without marrying doubled to 1.3 million people. Until around 1970, **cohabitation** was illegal in all 50 states.[7]

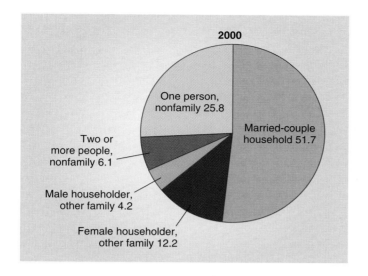

Figure 18.1

Households by Type, 2000

Source: U.S. Census Bureau, Census 2000 Summary File 1; 1990 Census of Population, *Summary Population and Housing Characteristics, United States* (1990 CPH-1-1).

By 2000 it was reported that there were 3 million Americans cohabiting with someone of the opposite sex[8] and another 1.5 million same-sex cohabiting partners.[9] People between the ages of twenty and twenty-four are most likely to be currently cohabiting, with ages twenty-five to twenty-nine next most likely.[10]

A survey[11] of women aged twenty-five to thirty-nine discovered that 30 percent cohabited before they married and 34 percent cohabited at some time in their lives. Of all first cohabitations by women aged fifteen to forty-four, slightly more than half resulted in marriage, about one-third dissolved without marriage, and 10 percent were ongoing at the time of the survey.

Cohabitation is prevalent on college campuses but is not exclusive to young adults. Many elderly people who are widowed are living together because of the financial benefits—their two separate Social Security checks may be larger than one check when remarried—or because they feel no need to formalize their union. The separated and divorced are also choosing to cohabit more than in the past. Figure 18.2 depicts the growth in the number of cohabiting couples since 1960.

Divorce

Table 18.1 shows the divorce rate from 1950 through 2003. As can be seen, the divorce rate rose consistently from 1958 to about 1981; it has been dropping ever since. As of 2000, 10 percent of Americans eighteen years of age and older were divorced. That amounted to

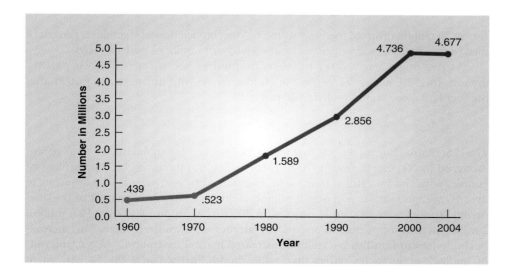

Figure 18.2

Number of Cohabiting, Unmarried, Adult Couples of the Opposite Sex, by Year, United States

U.S. Census Bureau. "Opposite Sex Unmarried Partner Households, by Labor Force Status of Both Partners, and Race and Hispanic Origin: 2004." *America's Families and Living Arrangements, 2004.* Washington, DC: U.S. Census Bureau, 2006. Available at http://www.census.gov/population/socdemo/hhfam/cps2004/tabUC1-all.csv

Table 18.1
DIVORCES AND DIVORCE RATES:
UNITED STATES, 1950 TO 2003

Year	Divorces	Rate per Population
2003	NA	3.8
2002	NA	4.0
2001	NA	4.0
2000	NA	4.1
1999	NA	4.2
1998	NA	4.3
1997	1,163,000	4.3
1996	1,150,000	4.3
1995	1,169,000	4.4
1994	1,191,000	4.6
1992	1,215,000	4.8
1991	1,187,000	4.7
1985	1,190,000	5.0
1981	1,213,000	5.3
1975	1,036,000	4.8
1970	708,000	3.5
1965	479,000	2.5
1960	393,000	2.2
1958	368,000	2.1
1955	377,000	2.3
1950	385,000	2.6

Sources: National Center for Health Statistics, "Annual Summary of Births, Marriages, Divorces, and Deaths: United States, 1992," *Monthly Vital Statistics Report* 41(28 September 1993), 4–5; "National Center for Health Statistics, Births, Marriages, Divorces, and Deaths for 1995," *Monthly Vital Statistics Report* 44 (24 July 1996) 1; National Center for Health Statistics, "Births, Marriages, Divorces, and Deaths for 1996," *Monthly Vital Statistics Report* 45 (17 July 1997), 1; U.S. Census Bureau, Statistical Abstract of the United States, 1999.; National Center for Health Statistics, "Births, Marriages, Divorces, and Deaths: Provisional Data for 2003," *National Vital Statistics Report* 52 (10 June 2004), 1.

almost 20 million divorced men and women. When broken down by gender, 9 percent of men (over 8 million) and 11 percent of women (over 11 million) were divorced.

As you might guess, large numbers of children are affected by their parents' divorce. In 1970, merely 12 percent of children lived with one parent. By 2000, that number had more than doubled to 26 percent.[12]

Single-Parent Families

The U.S. Census Bureau reports that the number of families maintained by one parent increased by 80 percent from 1970 to 1980. By 2000, approximately 23 percent of all families with children still at home were maintained by one parent. That amounts to over 16 million families and over 9 million children. Seventy-six percent of the one-parent families were headed by women in 2000. That amounts to over 12.6 million families. In addition, 4 million one-parent families were headed by men. This increase in **single-parent families** is a result of increased marital separation, divorce, and out-of-wedlock pregnancies rather than widowhood. Further, in 2000, 52 percent of

single-parent families

Families in which the father or the mother is absent because of divorce, marital separation, out-of-wedlock pregnancy, or death.

Family Insight

To learn things about your family about which even you are unaware, try this activity: draw a picture of your family participating in some activity. Do this now on a separate piece of paper.

The next time you are with a group of people—perhaps in class—ask several people to look at your drawing and, on its back, write one sentence describing their perceptions of either the family in general or any member in particular. You will be surprised how people who may not know you or any other members of your family very well can be so accurate in their perceptions of your family. I'll give you some examples now of how this works, but, since these examples may influence what you draw, don't read on until your drawing is complete.

In one group that I asked to do this activity, a woman drew a picture of herself at the ironing board, with her husband on his back on the rug with their baby held up in his extended arms. Several written comments noted that it seemed she did the housework while her husband relaxed and had fun. She said, "Yes, you know, that's true. I'm going to speak to him about helping out."

Another group included a man who drew himself, his wife, and his son in some activity, with his daughter doing something else at some distance from the other three. Several comments suggested that the daughter seemed left out of family activities. The man thought about this for a while and agreed. He said he was going to make a conscious effort to include his daughter in family activities from then on.

When you have other people comment on your drawing, do not reject any comments without giving them thought. Perhaps you were not consciously aware of some aspects of your family dynamics but subconsciously attuned to them so that they were included in your drawing. Of course, those commenting on your drawings will probably not be psychoanalysts, but my experience is that their comments will be insightful. What's more, their comments will help you to begin improving your family's effectiveness and making your family life less stressful.

African American families with children at home, 32 percent of Hispanic families with children at home, and 19 percent of white families with children at home were maintained by one parent.[13]

Gay and Lesbian Families

Should gay and lesbian couples be allowed to adopt children? Some people argue that children raised in a gay or lesbian household are especially likely to adopt a homosexual lifestyle. They strongly lament the lack of male and female gender role models during children's developmental years. They warn that homosexuality is sinful, and they believe that children should not be allowed to be brought up in sinful homes.

Other people argue that there is no reason to believe, or evidence to indicate, that children raised by gays and lesbians are more likely than other children to become homosexuals themselves. Furthermore, they continue, gay and lesbian households can be as ethical, spiritual, or religious as any other household, for sexual orientation does not preclude a moral setting in which children can be raised.

One way in which gays and lesbians are reacting to this societal debate is by conceiving children through artificial insemination or other means. In that way, they need not seek the approval of adoption agencies to establish a family with children. Both gay couples and lesbian couples are parenting such children.

Although most single-parent families are headed by women, men also can be, and often are, effective single parents.

The right to raise children is not the only family-related stressor with which gays and lesbians must cope. Gay and lesbian marriage is another one. Several states have sanctioned marriage between homosexual couples. The first state supreme courts to rule bans on gay and lesbian marriages unconstitutional were those of Hawaii (1993) and Alaska (1998). However, the legislatures of both states later amended their state constitutions to outlaw gay marriage. Elsewhere, alarmed by the thought of state-sanctioned gay marriages, opponents were successful in convincing thirty-seven states to adopt laws prohibiting legalized same-sex marriages.[14] Then in 2003 the Massachusetts Supreme Judicial Court ruled that "the right to marry means little if it does not include the right to marry the person of one's choice."[15] By a 4-to-3 vote, that court approved gay marriage. Since then, many gay couples have been married.

When the public was polled about gay marriage, most respondents were opposed to it.[16] Sixty-one percent stated that they were opposed to their state passing a law permitting same-sex marriage. Yet 50 percent opposed amending the United States Constitution to prohibit states from allowing these marriages, and 51 percent favored civil unions among same-sex couples. Civil unions would not be sanctioned marriages but would provide gay couples inheritance, insurance, pension, and other rights enjoyed by heterosexual couples.

It can be quite stressful for gays and lesbians, and their children, to be perceived as living an immoral, sinful life. Like other forms of bias, being singled out in this way can lead to stress reactivity, which in turn can result in negative consequences such as illness and disease.

Issue: Is Family Life Worse Than It Used to Be?

A Gallup poll prepared for the White House Conference on Families found 45 percent of Americans think family life has gotten worse. Of the 1,592 adults polled, 18 percent said they personally knew of a child-abuse situation, and 18 percent also knew of husband or wife abuse cases. Lastly, 25 percent reported that alcohol-related problems had adversely affected their family lives.

Others believed that, although it has certainly changed, family life has not worsened. Citing more equal sex roles and chores of family members, the greater opportunity for women to work outside the home, the increased availability of quality child-care services, and the positive effect of divorce upon children when the historical alternative has been to grow up with two parents constantly bickering, some people actually perceive the family to have evolved into a more effective unit.

Do you believe the family unit has worsened, or do you believe it has become more responsive to its members' needs? Why did you answer as you did?

Family Stressors

Although the family may not be dying—as some sociologists argue—it certainly is in transition. All the changes in family life previously cited need to be adapted to and are therefore stressful. Some of these stressors are discussed in this section.

The Dual-Career Family

More women who are married and have young children are working outside the home than ever before. Not only does a woman who works outside the home experience stress about juggling all of her responsibilities, but she is also bothered over what she is missing. As one mother who worked out of economic necessity put it: "Having to deal with a babysitter is very painful. All I can see is another woman holding, loving, and caring for my new baby. I am actually paying her to do all the things I wish I could be doing."[17] And it is not only women who experience these feelings. Men who work outside the home and therefore have less contact with their children than they would wish may also have feelings similar to those expressed by the woman quoted above.

Both working parents must also adapt to a lifestyle in which they share housework and child-rearing responsibilities. Certainly, working women still assume more than their fair share of these responsibilities, and that imbalance can be stressful. Still, spouses of working women take on more of these chores, and working women take on fewer of these chores, than in households in which only men work outside the home.

Finally, in this equation, the child also must adapt to parents not being around as much. The child must cope with a babysitter or day care staff and learn to be more self-sufficient at an earlier age.

dual-career family
A family in which both spouses work outside the home with careers of their own.

All of this is not to say that women or men should not or need not work outside the home. People who are trained for a career and not pursuing it may experience more stress than that associated with combining parenting, homemaking, and a career. If they feel more stress, the chances are that so will their spouses and children. However, that **dual-career families** are potentially stressful should not be denied.

Children

A friend once warned me that children are geometric, rather than arithmetic, stressors. What he meant was that a couple who has a child has added stressors equivalent to two extra adults; a couple with one child who has another multiplies their stress by some number other than 1 or 2; and a couple with two children . . . Anyone who has ever read any of Erma Bombeck's newspaper columns or books knows what my friend meant. Children are wonderful, but they certainly are stressful. This is understandable, since stress involves adjusting to change. Although all of us are changing, children are changing more rapidly, repeatedly, and dramatically than mature adults. Children's bodies are changing, their minds developing, and their social skills and life-space expanding. To expect such change not to be stressful is unrealistic.

Further, when children change, so does the family. Oftentimes, children are able to assume more responsibilities, take on more jobs, become more self-sufficient, and hold more firm opinions than when they were younger. These changes affect other members of the family. For example, when children become old enough to drive the family car, the parents no longer need to make themselves available for car pools. However, they must take on other stressors: "Will Johnny and the car both get home in one piece tonight?" This leads us to those notorious teenage years.

Even when women work full time outside of the home, they still take on more than half of the work necessary at home.

Parents who see their children approaching "teenagehood" sometimes find their knees knocking together, their hearts racing, and their headaches visiting more frequently. Teenagers may get involved with drugs, sex, vandalism, shoplifting, automobile accidents, or truancy; they may be impossible to discipline, talk with, or get to see very often; or they may have problems with their teachers, their friends, or their bosses. Or they may be companions, helpers, and interesting to talk with; they may be brilliant, committed to causes, and willing to persevere to achieve goals; and they may be individuals of whom we are very, very proud. Lest we forget, these years are stressful for teenagers as well. A sobering piece of evidence of this is the number of attempted suicides by teenagers.

Other years of growing up may be stressful for parents and children, too. The parent-child relationship has been described as three-phased: bonding, detachment, and reunion.[18] During the *bonding* years, the child learns love, approval, and acceptance from the family. During the *detachment* years, the child learns independence and relies less on the family. The *reunion* years occur after the child is independent and is secure enough to rebond with the family. Bonding is a preteen phase, detachment a teen phase, and reunion a post teen phase. Each phase has its own stressors and its own joys.

Family Planning

A discussion of stress and children must include a discussion of planning for how many children to have. Two topics pertaining to this consideration are discussed in this section: contraception and abortion and their relationship to family stress.

When couples decide to control conception to limit the number of children they have, they must decide upon a method. There is no perfect method of birth control. Each has its advantages and disadvantages, and all should be studied before one is chosen. This choice, however, may generate disagreement between the sexual partners and cause distress. Who should be responsible for birth control, the man or the woman? How much inconvenience or interruption are they willing to tolerate in sexual activity? What religious proscriptions should they adhere to? How much risk—both in terms of their health and in terms of the chances of a pregnancy—are they willing to accept?

Once the decision about birth control is made, there is still the possibility of pregnancy. No method except abstinence is 100 percent effective. If unwanted pregnancy does occur, what then? Another child? An **abortion**? These decisions, too, can be very stressful and more complicated than at first thought. To demonstrate the complexity

abortion
The termination of a pregnancy.

Helping Children Cope with Violence

The following is a list of online resources for families to help children manage the stress associated with violence and terrorism in the world today.

Afterschool Alliance

http://www.afterschoolalliance.org
This site provides links to many resource for helping youth deal with tragedy and terrorism, increase their cultural tolerance, and interpret media messages.

American Academy of Pediatrics

http://www.aap.org/advocacy/releases/disastercomm.htm
This site offers advice on communicating with children and adolescents after a disaster.

KidsHealth

http://www.kidshealth.org/index.html
It has an online section dedicated to the aftermath of the September 11 attack.

National Education Association

http://www.nea.org/nr/nr020819.html
NEA's Web page includes *Helping Families and Children Cope with This National Tragedy.*

National Parent Teacher Association

http://www.pta.org/parentinivolvement/helpchild/respectdiff/resources/talking.asp
The National PTA offers a resource online entitled *Helping Children Cope with Tragedy.*
For more Web sites, visit the Online Learning Center at www.mhhe.com/greenberg10e.

and stress associated with abortion, complete Lab 18.2 at the end of this chapter. You might want to discuss and compare your responses with those of your classmates. If you do, you'll find that there are no easy answers to this complex, and stressful, situation. That is precisely why our society is still debating this issue.

Adoption

Some families experience the stress associated with the inability to conceive their own children. For these families, adoption is an alternative, although the adoption process itself can be a stressor.

Types of Adoptions

There are two basic types of adoption.[19] **Closed adoptions** are confidential; there is no contact between the birth parents and the adoptive parents. The identities of the birth parents and adoptive parents are kept secret from one another. In **open adoptions** there is contact between the birth and adoptive parents. In fact, the birth parents may even select the adoptive parents. This contact can occur regularly or intermittently throughout the child's upbringing.

Although there have been some highly publicized cases of birth parents seeking to reverse them, adoptions are legally binding and irreversible after a short, limited period of time. Birth parents sign "relinquishment papers" after the baby is born and, unless both birth parents did not sign these papers, the courts refuse to reverse adoptions.

closed adoption
Adoptions in which there is no contact between the birth parents and the adoptive parents.

open adoption
Adoptions where there is contact between the birth parents and the adoptive parents.

Adoptions are arranged in three ways: agency adoption, independent adoption, and adoption by relatives.[20] **Agency adoptions** occur when the parents relinquish their baby to an adoption agency. These agencies are licensed by the government and may provide a number of services. They provide counseling, handle legal matters, make the hospital arrangements for the birth, select adoptive parents, and refer the mother to agencies if financial assistance is needed. Usually, although not always, adoptions arranged through agencies are closed adoptions. Adoption agencies can be located through most religious organizations or by writing the National Council for Adoption at 1930 17th Street, NW, Washington, DC 20009 or by telephoning them at (202) 328-1200. They will even accept collect calls from pregnant women. Their Web address is www.ncfa-USA.org.

In **independent adoptions,** the birth parents select the adoptive parents and relinquish the baby into their care. Independent adoptions are often arranged through a physician or lawyer and, in some states, by independent adoption centers. Independent adoptions are usually open adoptions and, although not legal in all states, they are supervised by a lawyer who usually represents both sides. However, it is recommended that the birth parents and the adoptive parents have separate legal representation to protect either from being exploited. Often, the adoptive parents agree to pay the medical costs associated with the pregnancy and may even agree to provide living expenses during that time. At the birth of the baby, the adoptive parents sign a "take into care" form that allows them to take the baby to their home while the state investigates their ability to raise the baby. This investigation usually takes six to eight weeks. At any time while this investigation is occurring, either set of parents can change their minds. At the end of the investigation, the birth parents sign "relinquishment papers." Independent adoption can be facilitated by the Independent Adoption Center at 319 Taylor Boulevard, Suite 100, Pleasant Hills, CA 94523. The Independent Adoption Center's telephone number is (800) 877-6736, and their Web address is www.adoptionhelp.org.

Adoption by relative is used when the birth parents want the child to stay in the family. Even so, these adoptions require the approval of the courts. As in other adoptions, the relatives will have to be investigated by the state to determine their ability to provide care for the child. Once the adoption is approved, the birth parents have no more rights pertaining to the child than they would have in any other form of adoption.

Readiness to Adopt

Although adopting a child may sound like a good idea, it is a decision that is usually associated with a great deal of stress and therefore requires thoughtful consideration. So does the decision to give a child up for adoption. Planned Parenthood of America suggests that anyone considering giving a child up for adoption ask these questions:[21]

1. Can you accept your child living with someone else?
2. Will going through pregnancy and delivery change your mind?
3. Are you willing to get good prenatal care?
4. Are you choosing adoption because abortion scares you?
5. Will the child's father approve of adoption?
6. Is anyone pressuring you to choose adoption?
7. Are you confident your child will be treated well?
8. Can you not be jealous of the adoptive parents?
9. Do you care what other people will think?
10. Do you respect women who place their children for adoption?

Someone contemplating placing a child for adoption may want to discuss these questions with their partner, clergy, a professional counselor, or a trusted relative or friend.

Foster Care and Adoption

For parents who are not ready to decide between placing a child for adoption and parenting, many cities and counties provide temporary residences for their children. This arrangement is termed **foster care.** To arrange for this option, the birth parents must sign a legal foster care agreement that allows another family to care for the child. Often, foster care agreements specify how often visits between the child and birth parents will be allowed, the duration of stay with the foster care family, the amount of money the birth parents will have to provide the foster care parents for caring for their child, and the agreed-upon number and frequency of visits to a professional counselor (usually a social worker). Although foster care arrangements and regulations vary from state to state, if the foster care agreement is violated, the birth parents can lose the child permanently.

Foster care is also provided for children who are taken from their birth parents for abuse, neglect, or other behavior that precludes them from being able to raise their children and places their children at risk. Children placed in foster care permanently are eligible for adoption and, in fact, that is the goal of state agencies that supervise foster care arrangements.

The foster care system includes about 500,000 children, of which 100,000 are eligible for adoption. Thankfully, more and more of these children are being adopted. In the United States in 1995, 20,000 children in the foster care system were adopted. That number increased to 28,000 in 1996 and to 31,000 in 1997. In 1997, the U.S. Congress passed the Adoption and Safe Families Act designed to speed up adoption of children in the foster care system. That legislation provided bonuses of $4,000 to states for every child in the child protective system they arranged to be adopted. For particularly hard cases—such as older children or those with disabilities—states were provided $6,000 for each adoption. To further the goal of arranging for adoptions of children in foster care, in July 2002, President Bush announced the first federal adoption Web site, www.AdoptUSKids.org, which features photographs and profiles of children who are available for adoption, as well as a database of prospective adoptive parents who have been approved by a state government. The Web site features 6,500 children from 46 states. President Bush stated that 130,000 children in the foster care system were waiting to be adopted.[22]

Adoption of children from other countries has been increasing.

foster care
An arrangement in which temporary care for a child is provided by someone other than the birth parents.

Finding the Birth Parent

As adults, many adopted children seek to identify their birth parents. This search is fraught with stress related to the search itself and to the reactions of both the adoptive parents and the birth parents. There is a good deal of disagreement as to whether and how this process should be facilitated. Some experts believe that contacting the birth parents might make them feel guilty about the adoption years earlier, or that they might reject the adopted child—now an adult—and the child might develop unhealthy reactions to that rejection.

Before World War II, it was common practice for adoption records to be open. However, after the war, the combination of an increase in out-of-wedlock pregnancies and a conservative mood in the country resulted in adoption going "into the closet." Adoption records became sealed so secrecy could be maintained. Since then, only two states, Alaska and Tennessee, have passed legislation to open these records, although at the time of this writing the Tennessee law was being challenged in the courts and therefore had not yet been implemented.

Residents of the state of Oregon decided this issue for themselves.[23] In November 1998, Oregon voters approved a ballot initiative requiring the state to unseal confidential birth records. Upon request, adoptees would be given all the information about their past—this in spite of the wishes of their birth parents. As you can imagine, this precipitated an outcry from opponents and supporters alike. The American Civil Liberties Union opposed the initiative, arguing it was an invasion of the privacy earlier promised to birth parents who placed their children for adoption. Supporters argued that the question was, "Who should have more rights? A parent who gives up a child or the child who was adopted?" Clearly they came down on the side of the child. It is expected that the Oregon situation will encourage supporters of unsealed adoption records in other states and that, as a result, similar initiatives will appear on ballots across the country.

Mobility

There was a time when the members of an extended family all lived in the same town and visited frequently. When I was growing up, a "family circle" met one Sunday a month. All the aunts, uncles, cousins, and Grandma Mary and Grandpa Barney gathered to talk, play cards, play ball, argue, and eat. We would sometimes pile into the back of my grandfather's pickup truck, sit on empty wooden milk crates, and be off for a day at the beach. We all felt close to one another and were caught up in one another's lives. I knew whom my cousin Marcia was dating, and she knew what sports I liked.

How times have changed! My children were born in Buffalo and now live in the Washington, DC, area. We have no relatives living in either of these places. We make a point of renewing family ties once a year at a Passover seder rather than once a month, as when I was young. My children rarely play with their cousins and don't know much about their relatives' lives. Their grandmother doesn't come over every Friday night for dinner, as mine did. She lives 300 miles away. When they had a babysitter, it wasn't their cousin Larry from next door, as it was for me. Their babysitter was a nonrelative from a list of sitters we maintained ("supported" might be a more accurate term).

What's more, families pick up and move so often nowadays that even close friends who might serve as surrogate extended family are left elsewhere. New friendships need to be developed, and it takes time for these new relationships to become meaningful.

In addition to the lack of involvement with extended family, mobility has led to other stressors. When you move, you need to find new physicians, dentists, gas stations, shopping malls, libraries, and so forth. Many of your surroundings and habits change—and we know by now that change can be stressful.

Violence: A Family Matter

It is unfortunate that families, or for that matter anyone, cannot feel safe, yet that is the situation in many communities around the country. Street crime is on everyone's mind as our prisons expand in population and number, without any noticeable effect in limiting the crime and violence to which we are all subjected. This situation has resulted in additional stress in our already stressful lives and particularly in additional stress for families. As the accompanying box clearly shows, even our children are not immune to the devastating effects of violence. In any one year, almost 5,000 children under twenty years of age are killed by firearms alone, and over 112,000 children under eighteen years of age are arrested for violent crimes. Every two hours a child is murdered!

Child Abuse

As if that weren't enough, domestic violence—violence among family members and violence occurring in the home—has also exploded. As early as 1994, the U.S. secretary of health and human services, described domestic violence as a crisis, a plague, a sickness, an epidemic, and terrorism in the home.[24] From 1990 to 1996, there was an 18 percent increase in child abuse and neglect cases reported to state child protective services. In 2002, 896,000 children were found to be victims of child abuse or neglect.[25] The causes of child abuse and neglect are a result of drug abuse by family members, poverty and economic stress, and a lack of parenting skills.[26]

One reason children are the victims of violence may be the number of guns and firearms in U.S. homes and the improper care of those guns. In a study[27] of inner-city

Waiting in traffic after a stressful day at work could add to violence at home.

first and second graders, 25 percent of African American students and 40 percent of white students stated that someone in their homes owned a gun. More alarming, 75 to 80 percent (depending on ethnicity and gender) knew where the gun was kept. Although guns are kept for protection, one study found they were eighteen times more likely to be used to kill a household member than to kill an intruder.[28]

Domestic Abuse

The Bureau of Justice Statistics of the U.S. Department of Justice maintains statistics on violence by intimates.[29] Intimates are defined as spouses, ex-spouses, boyfriends, and girlfriends. Intimate violence primarily affects women. Of violent crimes experienced by women, 20 percent are by intimates, whereas only 3 percent of violent crimes experienced by men are by intimates. In 2000, just under 1,700 murders were attributed to intimates, and 74 percent of these murders had a female

Every Day in America: The Violent Lives of America's Children

6 children and youths under 20 commit suicide

11 children and youths under 20 are homicide victims

12 children and youths under 20 die from firearms

36 children and youths under 20 die from accidents

237 children are arrested for violent crimes

420 children are arrested for drug abuse

2,658 public school children are corporally punished

5,388 children are arrested

Source: Children's Defense Fund, *The State of America's Children Yearbook: 1999* (Washington, DC: Children's Defense Fund, 1999).

victim. Although violence by intimates has been decreasing, that is small consolation. In 2001, women experienced 588,490 rapes, sexual assaults, robberies, aggravated assaults, and simple assaults at the hands of an intimate. Men were victims of 103,220 violent crimes committed by an intimate. Women aged sixteen to twenty-four experienced the highest per-capita rates of intimate violence, and slightly more than half of female victims of intimate violence lived in households with children under the age of twelve. The Federal Bureau of Investigation[30] maintains similar statistics but defines "family violence" to include spouses, common-law spouses, parents, siblings, children, grandparents, grandchildren, in-laws, stepchildren, and other family members. Under that broader definition, 27 percent of victims of violent offenses were related to their offenders. In addition to reporting that 71 percent of these victims were women, the FBI also reports that 74 percent of family violence victims were white.

Unfortunately, too many of these crimes go unreported. Only about half the incidents of violence by intimates are reported to the police. The most common reasons given by victims for not contacting the police were that they considered the incident a private or personal matter, they feared retaliation, or they believed the police would not be able to do anything about the incident. The irony is that 38 percent of couples in a violent relationship separate or divorce within two years anyhow.[31]

As you might suspect, the perpetrators of intimate violence are not the most valued members of society. In fact, of those in jail, 78 percent of abusers have a prior criminal record, although not necessarily for intimate violence. Forty percent of jail inmates convicted of a violent crime against an intimate had a criminal justice status at the time of the crime; about 20 percent were on probation, 9 percent were under a restraining order, and just under 10 percent were on parole, pretrial release, or other status. They also have a history of drug and alcohol abuse. More than half the inmates serving time for violence against an intimate were using drugs or alcohol or both at the time of the incident. Battering men typically have low self-esteem, traditional sex role expectations, jealousy, a need to control, abusive family backgrounds, and a need to blame others.[32]

In addition to physical abuse, domestic violence can take other forms. The National Resource Center on Domestic Violence includes sexual abuse (forcing a partner to engage in unwanted sexual behaviors), emotional abuse (name calling, put downs, threatening, and stalking), and property/economic abuse (stealing or destroying property).[33]

There are things we can all do to help prevent family violence. Here are a few suggestions.

- Ask your local schools or school board to include dating violence in the curriculum.
- Call your local media and remind them to acknowledge Domestic Violence Awareness Month (October).
- Ask local businesses to display the telephone number of the National Domestic Violence Hotline (1-800-799-SAFE).
- Ask local clergy to offer sermons on domestic violence.

Financial Stressors

Another category of stressors experienced by many families relates to finances. Some families live in poverty and, as we have seen, that often results in poor physical and psychological health, low education, poor housing arrangements, being susceptible to acts of violence, and a range of other negative consequences. Even attempts to encourage people out of poverty by requiring them to work have not been as successful as hoped. For example, in the mid-1990s, the welfare laws were changed to set a limit on the amount of years someone could receive benefits without being employed. Touting the value of these new regulations, the government cited the number of former welfare recipients who became employed. What was left unsaid, however, was the number of Americans employed in minimum-wage or close to minimum-wage jobs who could not afford health insurance or health care for themselves or their children, did not have enough money from their salaries for decent housing accommodations, and generally could not support their families as they would like. Imagine how stressful being in this situation can be!

Even middle-class Americans encounter significant financial stressors. Too often people overspend and wind up with debt from which they have a hard time escaping. This is not unusual for college students who may be using a credit card independently for the first time. Given the high interest rates charged by many credit card companies, getting out from under credit card debt can be very difficult. But it is not only college students who overspend. Some middle-class Americans want to drive a nice, new car, or live in the best of neighborhoods, or wear the flashiest of clothes. Wanting these things creates no problem. It is purchasing them that does. Living within one's means is a developmental task that people need to learn, but too often it is learned at great financial and emotional cost. As is discussed in the "Interventions" section later in this chapter, budgeting goes a long way to help prevent or resolve financial problems.

Almost all families, but especially those that did not plan well, have financial concerns regarding the raising of children. The cost of raising a child through age seventeen ranges from $337,690 for a relatively high-income family to $169,920 for a low-income family.[34] These costs include housing, child

Save your money if you intend to have children. They cost a great deal to raise, and that can be quite stressful.

care, health care, clothing, transportation, food, and miscellaneous expenses. And that is for *one* child! Add other children and the costs obviously increase. Furthermore, these costs do not include expenses for children beyond the age of seventeen, when they may be attending college or graduate or professional school, getting married with costs associated with a wedding, or needing financial assistance as they begin their careers at relatively low-paying jobs.

Prosperous families also experience financial stress. Although not as stressful in the same way as having to deal with poverty, *any* change in financial condition may be accompanied by stress. Maybe Aunt Abigail died and left a large sum of cash to Mom or Dad. Maybe a killing was made in the stock market or some other investment. You now need to protect that money to minimize tax payments. This means tax shelters, real estate deals, money market funds, or other financial wizardry. The fear of losing the new wealth raises its head, and you must direct attention, time, and energy at preventing such a loss. In addition, you may go out and buy a new car, move into a bigger house in a better neighborhood, buy more fashionable clothing, or arrange for vacations to faraway places instead of visiting relatives nearby. While these may be lifestyle adaptations you feel good and are excited about, they are adjustments and changes, nevertheless. That means they are stressors with the potential to result in illness or disease.

Other Stressors

There are many other stressors for which space dictates only a mention. Disagreements between parents regarding how to discipline children can be stressful. What to do with elderly parents—place them in a nursing home or have them live with you—creates stress for many families. Other families find their sexual lives stressful—for example, how often they should have sexual intercourse, who should initiate it, or which sexual

Figure 18.3 Family stress model.

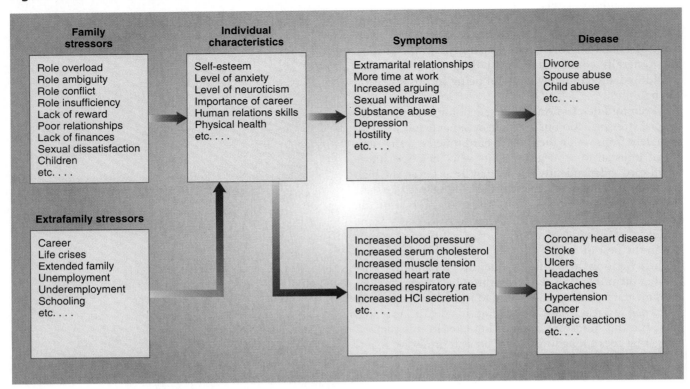

activities they should engage in. Some parents are raising children alone or are in the midst of a divorce. Some parents, usually fathers, may be living apart from their children. I'm sure you can add to this list. Since family life is dynamic, it is always changing—and therefore stressful.

A Model of Family Stress

To intervene in family stress, it is necessary to have a clear understanding of the situation. I have developed a model of family stress (see Figure 18.3) to help with this task. People who have applied the model have found it useful to help appreciate the components and manifestations of stress in families they know.

This model demonstrates that stressors are occurring within the family but are screened through individuals who differ on a number of important variables. It also demonstrates how these individual family members are affected by stressors that occur outside the context of the family but that, nonetheless, affect how family stressors are perceived and reacted to. The result of the interaction of family stressors and extrafamily stressors upon differing family members may be signs and symptoms of family stress or full-blown family disease. Once this complex of family stress is understood, the interventions described in this chapter can be better tailored to meet each family's needs.

Interventions

Family stress can be prevented from resulting in illness and disease through employing life-situation interventions, perception interventions, emotional arousal interventions, and physiological arousal interventions.

Families both create stress and serve as social support networks to help us manage stress better.

Life-Situation Interventions

Lack of time is a major stressor in dual-career families. It prevents some chores from being done, takes time away from other family members, and creates stress when you hurry to complete as much as possible in the little time available. To manage this stress, you can seek the help of other family members or friends. For example, they can do some shopping for you or pick up the kids from soccer practice. You might also hire someone to do some of the less important chores, such as cleaning the house or doing the laundry, to free you to do the more important ones. Your first priority after work hours, whether you are male or female, should be your family. To maximize your time with the family, you can plan vacations for work holidays and weekends—vacations that will get you all away from friends and chores so you can focus more upon each other. Fishing trips and hiking excursions provide a relaxing setting and an opportunity for conversing with each other. Trips to fancy hotels, where the kids attend a day camp and the parents golf all day, are not conducive to sharing meaningful family time together.

Marriage is said to be hard work. Maintaining all family relationships can be substituted for the word *marriage* in the previous sentence. Successful marriage partners share a commitment to their mates as demonstrated by the following traits from a study of married couples that asked about the qualities that made their marriages successful:[35]

1. Honesty
2. Love
3. Trust
4. Communication
5. Respect
6. Commitment

Perhaps all of us need to spend time and energy developing similar feelings for our families. To do so, though, requires a commitment to organize our lives so as to be together, sharing meaningful activities and developing a positive family history. The suggestions in this chapter should help.

For most of the family stressors described in this chapter, improving the communication between members of the family would be helpful. One of the most important

Parenting requires scheduling time to spend with the children.

prerequisites of communication, and one that is so obvious it is almost forgotten, is that you need to set aside time to communicate. Family members are usually involved in so many activities that they almost never have time to sit and talk and get to know one another. The kids are out playing, have practice for some team they are on, or are doing schoolwork. The parents are busy with their careers, sports, or friends. To make sure that time will be available for other family members, some families actually schedule it in. Other families set up weekly gripe sessions for any member to complain about anything bothering him or her. A while ago, I realized that I wasn't spending enough time with my son and, in particular, understanding what he was doing in school. I rearranged my time so we could spend fifteen minutes together after dinner on Tuesdays and Thursdays (a time convenient to both of us). During that time, he showed me all of his schoolwork and pointed out how far he had gone in his textbooks. At other times, either my son or my daughter would sit on my lap and we would have a "conversation"—our key word for a discussion of our feelings. We would discuss what makes us happy, sad, frightened, angry, or any other emotion one of us suggested. Far from being the perfect parent, I cite these examples of our family life because they worked for us. Maybe they will work for you and your family.

Regarding stress associated with divorce, the best advice is to get involved with people. Also, work at maintaining your sense of self-worth. One author presents some advice to the divorced parent who does not have custody of the children:[36]

Avoid	Aim At
Arguing directly against whatever the other parent has been saying	Listening to what your child has to say and taking a friendly interest
Trying to pull the other parent down in your child's estimation	Answering questions in a way that expands conversation—that is, without laying down the law
Trying to persuade your child that your view of everything is the right one	Noticing any problems, where you might be able to help
Reacting defensively at any hint of criticism from child or other parent	Being around on a dependable, reliable basis
Preaching any particular religious, moral, or social doctrines that you know are contradictory to the home views	Showing that you have your own standards and that, even if these are different from those at home, at least you are consistent
Trying to solve your problems through your child	Enjoying time together, rather than treating it as an opportunity to impress or persuade

This advice will help the formation of a more positive relationship with the children and the ex-spouse and thereby decrease the stress experienced as a result of the divorce.

Regarding stress about family planning, you might want to talk with a counselor—for example, one at Planned Parenthood—to better understand your options. One of the best sources of information about family planning, which identifies the methods available, their effectiveness, and their advantages and disadvantages, is a book entitled *Contraceptive Technology,* written by Robert Hatcher and published by the Irvington Publishers (551 Fifth Avenue, New York, NY 10017). You might want to write for that book. If you have moral, ethical, or religious concerns about birth control, consult with your clergy. In addition to all of these steps, remember to involve your partner. To be less distressed over these decisions, you need to work together, relying on each other to help sort out all the issues involved.

Regarding the stress of living long distances from members of your extended family, you can plan vacations to visit them rather than going other places. You can also telephone them regularly. Regular phone calls will allow some time for small talk—important in getting to know each other—since less time between calls will mean there are fewer major issues to discuss. Another means of maintaining your connection with your extended family—less expensive than visiting or telephoning—is exchanging letters with them. Notice I said *letters*, not cards. Birthday or anniversary cards won't serve the same purpose, nor will e-mail messages. Your relatives should know that you are making a special effort to communicate with them; then they will understand how important keeping in touch is to you and will be more apt to write back. Letters will better convey this need than will cards or e-mail.

Financial Stress Interventions

Financial stress can be devastating. It can undermine relationships between family members as they act out their frustrations on each other. Serious health consequences may result if medical care is postponed until it is absolutely necessary. Financial stress also may have negative psychological and emotional effects on family members' self-esteem and sense of control over their lives, and it may foster the development of anger and alienation. For these reasons financial stress interventions are highlighted in this chapter.

Perhaps the most valuable intervention is the formulation of a budget that guides financial considerations. Budgets can help prevent debt that, if unpaid, can result in bad credit and, sometimes, legal action. The budget can let you control your finances rather than let your finances control you. The correct way to establish a budget is to review how you spent money last year. For example, you could review canceled checks, bank records, and credit card records. Also, review income for the year. If you are not able to obtain records for the past year, or are not motivated to go back that far, do so for the previous two months. Then,

- Identify income you expect to acquire for each month in the present year.
- Identify anticipated expenses for each month.
- Try to set aside some money each month for savings, depending on the amount of income above expenses and your goals (savings are important to meet unforeseen emergencies or expenses).
- If you owe money, try to pay off some of your debt each month.

The percentage of your income that you spend in each category is an individual decision. The less you make, the greater is the percentage of income that you will have to spend on basic needs (e.g., shelter and food). However, as a general rule, you should spend between 20 to 35 percent on housing, 15 to 30 percent on food, 3 to 10 percent on clothing, 6 to 20 percent on transportation, 2 to 6 percent on entertainment, and 5 to 9 percent for savings.[37] If you find it difficult to stick to your budget, you can set up a system by which you place the money budgeted for each category in separate envelopes as you receive income. Of course, you can borrow from one envelope (category) for another, but if that happens too often, the budget will be destroyed.

Several other strategies should help:

- Control spending. Leave your checkbook and credits cards at home when not needed
- Pay bills on time thereby avoiding interest charges (credit card interest rates are quite high).
- Review the budget periodically to make sure it is still appropriate.
- If eligible, enroll your children in state health insurance programs (states, with federal assistance, offer a Children's Health Insurance Program for low-income families).

- If you have too much debt, contact the Consumer Credit Counseling Service for help (1-800-777-7526).
- When making purchases, avoid the extended warranties (fewer than 20 percent of products covered by extended warranties are ever brought in for repair).[38]
- Compare gasoline prices at different gas stations rather than purchasing gas at the most convenient station.
- Shop around for the least expensive automobile and homeowner's or rental insurance.
- Consult organizational evaluations of products before purchasing them (e.g., Consumers Union).
- Only purchase telephone services that are necessary, and purchase your telephone rather than lease it.
- Make long-distance telephone calls during evening or weekend hours when they are less expensive.
- Use generic drugs rather than brand-name drugs when generics are available.

Perception Interventions

Many perception interventions are applicable to family stress. For example, you can use selective awareness to perceive the changes in your family life as exciting, interesting, and challenging, and remind yourself that in the long run you will all be closer for having experienced these changes together. Viewed in this way, family transitions will be less stressful.

You can also "smell the roses"—that is, enjoy your family life as fully as possible. Sometimes, while I was reading, my daughter would climb onto my lap. My first inclination was to figure out a way to get her off without having her feel rejected so I could continue reading undisturbed, and she would grow up with one less psychological scar. Most of the time, however, I put down what I was reading and tried to appreciate Keri on my lap. I stopped to recognize that, in all too few more years, lap-sitting with her Dad would be a thing of the past—my loss more than hers, I'm sure. With that realization, I wanted to soak up as much lap-sitting and appreciation from lap-sitting as I could get. The interesting thing, though, is that, with this attitude of "smelling the roses," *each* new phase of our relationship will be experienced fully. It may be lap-sitting today and boyfriend problems tomorrow. Because one phase is over, I need not be distressed over its loss if I experienced it to its fullest, since the next phase offers new wonders. Children will cause less stress if we wonder at them—if we watch them grow and marvel at their uniqueness.

Understanding of the Type A behavior pattern can be used to manage family stress. One characteristic of Type A people is that they are concerned with quantity more than with quality. They try to do many things, allowing the quality of each to suffer, rather than doing fewer things well. Generalizing this characteristic and relating it to stress caused by too little time to spend with family members, spend the limited time you have qualitatively. Talk with each other rather than watch television together. Go out for dinner rather than to a movie, where you can't converse. With elderly family members, try to get them to talk about the past and perhaps video-record or tape-record those discussions so they won't be lost to future generations. The elderly, you will find, have so many interesting stories and have experienced a world so different from ours that honoring their past in

Families that spend time together can better manage stressors as they are encountered.

this manner will not only alleviate some of their stress—they will feel as though they have something worthwhile to offer—but will help us connect to the past from which we sprang. It will give us roots and help us to see that our lives are not just fleeting moments but, rather, a link in the chain of humankind.

It has been found that wives do about thirty-one hours of housework per week and their husbands do about sixteen hours of housework per week.[39] For working wives, the situation is somewhat improved: They do only 70 percent of the housework compared with 83 percent for homemakers.[40] One might argue that a fifty-fifty split of the housework between husbands and wives who work outside the home full-time would be the only fair arrangement. However, some experts on family relations suggest that some women may have difficulty sharing home and parenting duties because of the fear of losing their identities as women and mothers.[41] If you or someone you know is experiencing these concerns, discuss the quality-of-time versus quantity-of-time issue with them to better help them perceive the need to be willing to share routine household and parenting responsibilities. Only if they realize they are not superwomen and cannot do everything themselves will women who work outside the home free up time to improve their family relationships and decrease the potential for family stress. Men, too, need to perceive their limitations and delegate responsibilities to other family members when they are overburdened. However, as the data indicate, this need, at least at home, is not as much of a concern for men as it is for women.

Lastly, your perceptions of the control you can exercise over events that affect your life—your locus of control—influence how you respond to family stressors. If you work to develop internality, you will believe you can do something to experience less stress from your family life. You will, therefore, try some of the suggestions appearing in this chapter and even seek others. One of the best ways to develop internality is to try controlling some events and analyzing how that attempt fared. Was it successful? If so, why? If not, why not? Experience in actually exercising control over aspects of your life will reinforce your notion that such control is possible. Try some of the suggestions given in this section. Choose one that you think has the best chance of being successful and then move on to some others. You will find that you really can do something to manage family stress better.

Getting Involved in Your Community

Given the number of single-parent families and the number of dual-career families with very young children, there is a need to arrange for the health and safety of those children. There are several ways in which you can contribute to this task:

1. You might participate in an after-school recreational program at a local community center. These centers often need coaches, referees and umpires, and recreation leaders.

2. You might consider developing, or at least advocating, that others in the community develop a hotline accessible to children who find themselves alone after school (latchkey children) and needing the assistance of an adult.

3. You might offer to do some of the chores that an especially stressful family does not have the time to perform. For example, you might offer to do grocery shopping, yard work, tutoring of the children, or even transporting an elder to a doctor's office.

It takes only the motivation to help, and the ingenuity to figure out how, to improve the level of stress experienced by families in your community.

Emotional Arousal Interventions

Family stress can be less unhealthy if you regularly practice some relaxation techniques. Any of the techniques described in this book will do. With family stress as your particular concern here, you might want to engage in relaxation as a family. Perhaps you can schedule a "relaxation time" when everyone in the family meditates. Maybe you can all take a Yoga class together. Regular practice of relaxation will help you cope better with normal family transitions as well as with unusual and unanticipated family stressors.

Physiological Arousal Interventions

Like other stressors, family stressors increase serum cholesterol, heart rate, and blood pressure and change other body processes. Exercise can use these stress products in a healthy manner and prevent them from making you ill. Why not exercise as a family? You could bike, swim, play tennis, or even jog as a family.

summary

- A family is a unique set of intimate relationships.

- The nuclear family is a married couple and their children. The extended family includes relatives other than spouses and their children.

- The family satisfies several needs. These include the social control of reproduction and child rearing, economic support, security and safety needs, and the emotional needs of love and a sense of belonging.

- The effective family has a leader and someone who keeps track of what others are doing. It encourages members to be involved with people outside the family, is hospitable, deals squarely with dire events, prizes its rituals, is affectionate, provides a sense of place, allows for a connection for posterity, and honors its elders.

- The family has changed in recent years. People are marrying later and more people are choosing to remain single. More people are cohabiting rather than marrying, and a large number of divorces are occurring, with more than 1 million children involved each year.

- Family stressors include financial concerns, dual-career marriages, increased mobility, child rearing, contraception decisions, separation from extended families, and violence.

- Family stress is a complex of family stressors, individual family members' characteristics, and extrafamily stressors. These can lead to symptoms of family stress or to stress-related illness.

- Effective communication and conflict resolution skills can help manage family stress.

- Adoption occurs in several formats. There are closed adoptions that are confidential, and open adoptions in which there is contact between the birth parents and the adoptive parents. There are agency adoptions, independent adoptions, and adoptions by relatives.

- Foster care is provided for children who are taken from their birth parents because of abuse, neglect, or other behavior that precludes them from being able to care for their children.

notes

1. Jane Howard, *Families* (New York: Simon & Schuster, 1978), 350.
2. U.S. Census Bureau, "America's Families and Living Arrangements, 2004," *Current Population Reports*, 2001.
3. U.S. Census Bureau. *Statistical Abstracts of the United States: 2006.* Washington, DC: U.S. Government Printing Office, 2005.
4. U.S. Census Bureau, "Married-Couple and Unmarried-Partner Households, 2000," *Census 2000 Special Reports*, 2003, 10.

5. U.S. Census Bureau, "Household and Family Characteristics, March 1998 (Update)," *Current Population Reports,* 1998.

6. U.S. Census Bureau, *Statistical Abstract of the United States, 2006* (Washington, DC: U.S. Government Printing Office, 2005).

7. Jerold S. Greenberg, Clint E. Bruess, and Debra W. Haffner, *Exploring the Dimensions of Human Sexuality* (Boston: Jones & Bartlett, 2004).

8. U.S. Census Bureau, "America's Families and Living Arrangements, 2000."

9. M. Miller and D. Solot, *Organization for Unmarried People Condemns Cohabitation Report,* 8 February 1999.

10. U.S. Census Bureau, *Statistical Abstract of the United States, 2004–2005* (Washington, DC: U.S. Government Printing Office, 2005).

11. J. Aloma et al., "Fertility, Family Planning and Women's Health: New Data from the 1995 Survey of Family Growth, *Vital Health Statistics* 23(1997).

12. U.S. Census Bureau, "America's Families and Living Arrangements, 2000," 7.

13. U.S. Census Bureau, *Statistical Abstract of the United States,* 2002, 51.

14. Charles Lane, "States' Recognition of Same-Sex Unions May Be Tested," *Washington Post,* 19 November 2003, A8.

15. David Von Drehl, "Gay Marriage Is a Right, Massachusetts Court Rules," *Washington Post,* 19 November 2003, Al.

16. Annenberg Public Policy Center, "American Public Remains Opposed to Same-Sex Marriages as They Begin in Massachusetts, Annenberg Data Show," *National Annenherg Election Survey,* http://www.annnenbergpublicpolicycenter.org

17. Janet DiVittorio Morgan, "I Work Because I Have to," in *The Mothers' Book: Shared Experiences,* ed. Ronnie Friedland and Carol Kort (Boston: Houghton Mifflin, 1981), 96.

18. Jean Rosenbaum and Veryl Rosenbaum, *Living with Teenagers* (New York: Stein & Day, 1980).

19. Cheryl A. Kolander, Danny J. Ballard, and Cynthia K. Chandler, *Contemporary Women's Health,* 2nd ed. (New York: McGraw-Hill, 2005).

20. Planned Parenthood of America, www.plannedparenthood.org

21. Ibid.

22. Mike Allen, "With Adoption Push, Bush Adopts a Clinton Tactic," *Washington Post,* 24 July 2002, A2.

23. Rene Sanchez, "Oregon Ignites Revolution in Adoption," *Washington Post,* 26 November 1998, A1.

24. Don Colburn, "When Violence Begins at Home," *Washington Post Health,* 15 March 1994, 7.

25. National Clearinghouse on Child Abuse and Neglect Information, *Child Maltreatment 2002: Summary of Key Findings,* http://www.nccanch.acf.hhs.gov

26. Center on Child Abuse Prevention Research, *Current Trends in Child Abuse Reporting and Fatalities: The Results of the 1997 Annual 50 State Survey* (Chicago: National Committee to Prevent Child Abuse, 1998).

27. Susan K. Telljohann and James H. Price, "A Preliminary Investigation of Inner City Primary Grade Students' Perceptions of Guns," *Journal of Health Education* 25(1994): 41–46.

28. Colburn, "When Violence Begins at Home," 7.

29. Callie Marie Rennison, "Intimate Partner Violence, 1993-2001," *Bureau of Justice Statistics: Crime Data Brief,* February 2003.

30. Federal Bureau of Investigation, "Crime in the United States," *Uniform Crime Reports,* 2002.

31. N. S. Jacobson, J. M. Gottman, E. Gortner, S. Burns, and J. W. Shortt, "Psychological Factors in the Longitudinal Course of Battering: When Do the Couples Split Up? When Does the Abuse Decrease?" *Violence and Victims* 11(1996): 71–88.

32. Greenberg, Bruess, and Haffner, *Exploring the Dimensions of Human Sexuality,* 648–649.

33. *Help End Domestic Violence,* National Resource Center on Domestic Violence, n.d.

34. U.S. Department of Agriculture, *Expenditures on Children by Families, 2001 Annual Report* (Washington, DC: U.S. Department of Agriculture, 2002).

35. Sheri Stritof and Bob Stritof, "Marriage Qualities Survey Results," *Your Guide to Marriage,* June 2005, http://marriage.about.com/od/keysforsuccess/a/qualresults.htm

36. Peter Rowlands, *Saturday Parent* (New York: Continuum, 1980), 24.

37. Consumer Action, *Budgeting and Planning: Building a Better Future,* www.consumeraction.org/Library/English/Money_Mgt/MM-I-01_EN/MM-I-01_EN.html

38. Consumers Union. *Holiday Shopping and Credit Tips,* www.consumersunion.org/finance/holiday2wc1198.html

39. University of Michigan, "U.S. Husbands Are Doing More Housework While Wives Are Doing Less," *News and Information Services,* 12 March 2002

40. Eleanor Grant, "The Housework Gap," *Psychology Today* 22(1988): 8.

41. Holly Hall, "A Woman's Place . . ." *Psychology Today* 22(1988): 28–29.

internet resources

Working Women and Stress
http://www.amwa-doc.org/index.cfm?objectid=2A0DF9EA-D567-0B25-
5B22B1120AEAD3FE
*An article that describes the stressors experienced by women who work outside the
home, the effects of that stress on their health, and strategies to prevent those
negative effects.*

Infertility and Stress Management
www.ivf.com/stress.html
Contains practical suggestions for identifying and managing stress.

Coping in Today's World

Want to maintain a healthy life? Get married! At least that is what data from the Centers for Disease Control and Prevention indicate. CDC researchers studied more than 127,000 Americans ages eighteen and older and found that, regardless of the sub-group (age, sex, race, culture, education, or income), married adults were healthier than other adults.[a] For example, *fair or poor health* was highest among widows (19.6 percent) and lowest among married adults (10.5 percent). Next to widows in prevalence of fair or poor health were divorced or separated adults (16.7 percent), then cohabiting adults (14.0 percent), and never-married adults (12.5 percent). Married adults were also less likely to experience health-related limitations in their activities than any other marital status group (never married, widowed, divorced or separated, or cohabitating).

Two theories suggest reasons for these data: The *marriage protection theory* states that married people have more advantages in terms of economic resources, social and psychological support, and support for healthy lifestyles. The *marital selection theory* states that healthier people get married and stay married. In any case, the importance of family to health, not marriage alone, is undisputed.

[a]Schoenborn, C.A. "Marital Status and Health: United States, 1999–2002." *Advance Data from the Vital and Health Statistics* 351(2004): 1.

LAB ASSESSMENT 18.1

Are You Ready for Marriage?

Directions: The following questions are designed to assist you in clarifying your readiness for marriage. Although there are no absolutely "right" or "wrong" answers, these questions can help identify some issues for you to focus on as you think about marriage. Check the appropriate blank for each of the following questions.

Yes   No

_____   _____   1. Even though you may accept advice from other people (parents, instructors, friends), do you make important decisions on your own?

_____   _____   2. Do you have a good working knowledge of the physiology of human sexuality, and do you understand the emotional and interpersonal factors that are involved in sexual adjustment?

_____   _____   3. Have you had the experience of contributing to or sharing in the financial support of yourself and at least one other person?

_____   _____   4. Have you and someone with whom you have had an intimate relationship ever worked through disagreements to a definite conclusion that was acceptable to both of you?

_____   _____   5. Are you usually free of jealousy?

_____   _____   6. Have you thought carefully about the goals you will strive for in marriage?

_____   _____   7. Do you find yourself able to give up gracefully something you wanted very much?

_____   _____   8. Can you postpone something you want for the sake of later enjoyment?

_____   _____   9. Do you generally feel embarrassed or uneasy about giving or receiving affection?

_____   _____   10. Are your feelings easily hurt by criticism?

_____   _____   11. In an argument, do you lose your temper easily?

_____   _____   12. Do you frequently feel like rebelling against responsibilities (work, family, school, and so on)?

_____   _____   13. Are you often sarcastic toward others?

_____   _____   14. Do you find yourself strongly emphasizing the more glamorous aspects of marriage, such as its social components?

_____   _____   15. Are you often homesick when you are away from your family?

Scoring and interpretation: In questions 1–8, the more yes responses you have, the readier you are for marriage. In questions 9–15, the more no responses you have, the readier you are for marriage. Each question can help you identify areas that need some attention before you enter into marriage.

- Questions 1, 3, 4, 6, 7, and 8 explore *behaviors* that will affect the success of your marriage.

- Question 2 concerns *knowledge* that will affect the success of your marriage. Knowledge about human sexuality is an important prerequisite to sexual adjustment in marriage.

- Questions 5, 9, 10, 11, 12, 13, 14, and 15 enable you to estimate your *emotional readiness* for marriage. Question 5, for example, explores jealousy, an emotion that has been shown to be destructive to marital stability. If you are a jealous person in general, it may be important for you to seek professional guidance in dealing with issues such as trust and self-esteem before you contemplate marriage.

Source: Questions adapted from L. A. Kirkendall and W. J. Adams, *The Students' Guide to Marriage and Family Life Literature,* 8th ed. (Dubuque, IA: Wm. C. Brown Communications, 1980), 157.

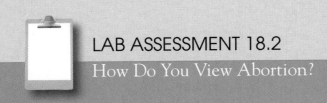

LAB ASSESSMENT 18.2

How Do You View Abortion?

Directions: Depending on your viewpoint, check "Yes" or "No" for each question.

	Yes	No
1. Should abortions ever be allowed?	____	____
2. If yes, under which circumstances?	____	____
a. If conception is a result of rape	____	____
b. If the pregnancy will be an economic hardship	____	____
c. If the pregnancy is harmful to the woman's mental health	____	____
d. If the pregnancy is unwanted	____	____
e. If the pregnancy is dangerous to the woman's physical health	____	____
f. If the pregnancy is a result of not using contraception	____	____
g. If the pregnancy is a result of the failure of contraception that was used	____	____
h. If the woman is unmarried	____	____
i. If the woman is a teenager	____	____
j. If the woman is over forty	____	____
3. Should government funds be used for abortions for women who can't afford them?	____	____
4. Should the father's signature be required before an abortion can be performed?	____	____
5. Should the father be held financially responsible for paying for half of the cost for the abortion?	____	____

Interpretation: There are no right or wrong answers to these questions. Instead, they offer a way for you to organize your thoughts about this very controversial societal issue. If you answered no for question 1, you are convinced that under no circumstances should abortions ever occur. If you answered yes to question 1, you then need to clarify when you believe abortion is an acceptable option. Question 2 helps you do that. Questions 3–5 inquire about the involvement of others—the government and the father.

Discuss your answers with your family and your classmates to get their perspectives on abortion and all that it involves. An intelligent person listens to other points of view and gathers information before making decisions. Abortion-related decisions are no exception.

Like most people, I always took my parents for granted. They would always be here, and they would be relatively stress free. While I was growing up, they seemed invincible; they were always right, they were always able to raise and support a family, and they always seemed to know who would make the best president. How wrong I was! As I approached adulthood and my children looked up to me as I had looked up to my parents, I came to realize that they did the best they could but were certainly not invincible.

As though to drive this point home with a hammer, my father died in 1985. As we hugged and cried together in his hospital room, his vulnerability came through. He was, after all, human, with human fears, insecurities, and foibles. My mother survives and makes the best of a bad situation. She organized a new life for herself with new activities and a new cohort of friends. This type of change is stressful and fraught with the consequences of stress.

In retrospect, I can see the stressors that my parents endured together and the stressors that my mother endures now. However, these are not unique to my family. Old age is a time of life replete with changes. Retirement, failing health, the death of friends and relatives, financial insecurity—all create the need for adjustment; all may be stressful and pose a threat to our health and happiness.

On the other hand, old age has been described as a "state of mind." You are old when you allow yourself to feel old. This can occur at age thirty for some and at age sixty-five for others, or it may never arrive for those who remain "young at heart." Recall our discussion of selective awareness. You can focus on the stressful parts of old age, or you can focus on the pleasing aspects. You can bemoan the inability to play tennis as you once could, or you can be grateful to still be able to play doubles. You can feel sorry for yourself because of a forced retirement, or you can welcome the availability of time to spend with your grandchildren. The focus is up to each and every one of us. It is our choice what we will pay most attention to.

My mother remains thankful for the years spent with Dad, and we often laugh at how he would become the life of the party with a crowd around him as he told one of the hundreds of jokes he committed to memory. Certainly, we cry during particular moments, but generally we go on with our lives because there is no other choice if we want to be happy and healthy.

This chapter is concerned with showing how one can recognize and manage the stress associated with the later years. We will see that certain stressors can be anticipated and their consequences minimized, while other stressors—those less predictable—can be perceived in ways to decrease their potential for harm. Finally, we will recognize that the later years can be just as rewarding as the earlier years if we insist they be that way and if we apply the stress management skills presented in this book and, in particular, in this chapter.

The Elderly: A Description

In 1900, the number of people in the United States over sixty-five years of age was slightly over 3 million, or 3.9 percent of the population. By 1990, there were over 31 million U.S. citizens over sixty-five, or 12.4 percent of the population. As of 2002, there were 35.6 million people over sixty-five, or 12.3 percent of the population.[1] In fact, in 2002, there were 4.6 million people eighty-five years and older. The elderly are the fastest-growing segment of the population in the United States. A conservative estimate by the U.S. government is that there will be 71.5 million U.S. citizens over the age of sixty-five by 2010, and 70.3 million by 2030.[2]

Test of Knowledge About the Elderly

How much do you know about the elderly? To find out, decide which statements are true and which are false:

1. The majority of elders live in nursing homes.
2. Elderly people in the United States live far away from their children.
3. Elderly people have little contact with their grown children.
4. Loneliness is a problem for the elderly.
5. The elderly are not very interested in sex.
6. The focus of the elderly on the past is unhealthy.
7. Elders are treated with respect by others.

All of these statements are misconceptions.

Contrary to popular belief, less than 5 percent of the elderly live in nursing homes, and only 18 percent of those eighty-five years of age or older live in nursing homes.[3] In fact, in spite of our mobile society, two-thirds of noninstitutionalized elders live within thirty minutes of a son or daughter or have weekly visits from their children. When frequent visits are not possible, their children telephone; 76 percent of elderly people speak by telephone with their children weekly.[4] Furthermore, 73 percent of noninstitutionalized male elders and 41 percent of female elders are married and live with their spouses.[5] For these and other reasons, loneliness is a problem for only a minority of elders.

The perception that sex is of no interest to elders is just dead wrong. In a study of more than 100 men and women aged 80 to 102 who were living in retirement homes, there was more sex than you might imagine. The most common form of sex was touching (82 percent of men and 64 percent of women), followed by masturbation (72 percent of men and 40 percent of women), and then sexual intercourse (63 percent of men and 30 percent of women).[6] And these were people over eighty! Vaginal lubrication and penile erection may arrive later and leave sooner, but study after study finds the elderly still sexually active. Masters and Johnson reported studying a sexually active ninety-four-year-old man.

Finally, it is true that the elderly often reminisce, but this is not unhealthy. As we shall soon see, one of the needs of the later years is to see ourselves as part of humankind—as being attached to a past and a future. Reminiscing helps with this task.

Unfortunately, not all is rosy for our elderly citizens. As opposed to treating older people with the respect many have deserved over years of work, family support, and civic responsibility, not only do we ignore them and treat them as bothersome and with disrespect, but we sometimes actually cause them harm. Hard as it may be to believe, just over half a million elders are physically harmed or neglected each year.[7]

Adjustment in the Later Years

Several theories of adult development attempt to explain stress in the elderly. A discussion of these theories follows.

Erik Erikson: Life Crises

Erik Erikson described life as consisting of eight stages during which crises are encountered. The crisis of late adulthood is acquiring a sense of integrity and fending off a sense of despair. Erikson saw this stage of life as one in which the successful person has some fairly clear understanding of identity, is aware of both successes and failures, and is willing to affirm the lifestyle he or she has lived. Death would, therefore, not seem the ultimate end of life. A person who is unsuccessful with this crisis is likely to be overcome by despair because the time left is so short, death approaches too rapidly, and there is no time to try another route to integrity. Disgust may be used to hide this despair; the person then becomes bitter, depressed, and paranoid.[8]

Robert Havighurst: Developmental Tasks

Robert Havighurst viewed life as a series of **developmental tasks** that we must master before moving on to the next stage of development.[9] Havighurst defined a developmental task as one that "arises at or about a certain period of the life of the individual, successful achievement of which leads to happiness and success with later tasks, while failure leads to unhappiness in the individual, disapproval by the society, and difficulty with later tasks."[10] Havighurst's final stage, later adulthood, begins at age fifty-five. This stage, like the earlier stages, is characterized by new experiences and new situations to deal with. Havighurst considers that old age is still developmental. The six developmental tasks of the elderly as outlined by Havighurst follow:

1. Adjusting to decreased physical strength and health.
2. Adjusting to retirement and reduced income.
3. Adjusting to death of spouse.
4. Establishing an explicit affiliation with one's age group.
5. Meeting social and civic obligations.
6. Establishing satisfactory physical living arrangements.[11]

As a major stressor involves adapting to change, one can readily see the implications of stress for old age according to Havighurst's theory.

developmental tasks
A series of life tasks that need to be achieved at various stages of life in order for the next stage of life to be happy and successful.

Positive Change

Lest we forget the good changes (eustress) accompanying old age, let's cite some here. For many of the elderly, their grandchildren become a source of joy. The relationship between grandparents and grandchildren is unique. Free of the responsibility for disciplining the children, grandparents can just play with them and help them learn and have fun. Those grandparents with daily caregiving responsibilities for their grandchildren also may experience the joy associated with helping a loved one grow and develop into a young adult.

In many societies, old age has another benefit. The elderly are viewed as the wisest in the society and consulted and honored for their wisdom. Unfortunately, in our society this is more often the exception than the rule. However, some companies and governmental agencies do value the knowledge and experience of their elderly workers and have even been known to ask the advice of some retirees.

Old age also often presents us with free time to pursue interests earlier postponed. For example, Grandma Moses didn't paint until she was quite old. We often hear that people have retired and moved to where they always wanted to live or are doing something (maybe traveling) they always longed to do but never did.

I think you get the picture: Some stressors of old age are adaptations that have good results, but they are stressors, nevertheless.

Exercise and the Elderly

A section of U.S. Surgeon General's report on *Physical Activity and Health* concerns exercise and the elderly.[12] Exercise is an excellent way to manage stress in all age groups, with the added benefits of achieving and maintaining health. Without good health, the elderly experience a significant stressor with which they must cope. Here is a summary of the key points made in the Surgeon General's report:

- Older adults, both male and female, can benefit from regular physical activity.
- Physical activity need not be strenuous to yield health benefits.

As with younger persons, elders need regular exercise to maintain their health and to help manage stress.

- Older adults can obtain significant health benefits with a moderate amount of physical activity, preferably daily. A moderate amount of activity can be obtained in longer sessions of moderately intense activities (such as walking) or in shorter sessions of more vigorous activities (such as fast walking or stairwalking).
- Additional health benefits can be gained through greater amounts of physical activity, by increasing the duration, intensity, or frequency. Because risk of injury increases at high levels of physical activity, care should be taken not to engage in excessive amounts of activity.
- Previously sedentary older adults who begin physical activity programs should start with short intervals of moderate physical activity (5–10 minutes) and gradually build up to the desired amount.
- Older adults should consult with a physician before beginning a new physical activity program.
- In addition to cardiorespiratory endurance (aerobic) activity, older adults can benefit from muscle-strengthening activities. Stronger muscles help reduce the risk of falling and improve the ability to perform the routine tasks of daily life.
- The loss of strength and stamina attributed to aging is in part caused by reduced physical activity.
- Inactivity increases with age. By age seventy-five, about one in three men and one in two women engage in no physical activity.
- Among adults aged sixty-five years and older, walking and gardening or yard work are, by far, the most popular physical activities.
- Social support from family and friends has been consistently and positively related to regular physical activity.

Regular exercise by the elderly has the following positive effects:

- Helps maintain the ability to live independently and reduces the risk of falling and fracturing bones.
- Reduces the risk of dying from coronary heart disease and of developing high blood pressure, colon cancer, and diabetes.
- Can help reduce blood pressure in some people with hypertension.
- Helps people with chronic, disabling conditions improve their stamina and muscle strength.
- Reduces symptoms of anxiety and depression, and fosters improvements in mood and feelings of well-being.
- Helps maintain healthy bones, muscles, and joints.
- Helps control joint swelling and pain associated with arthritis.

For more information you can contact:

The President's Council on Physical Fitness and Sports
200 Independence Avenue, SW
Room 738-H
Washington, DC 20201

Retirement

Retiring from work is one of the most significant events of one's life. How successfully this event is adjusted to has a major effect on the satisfaction and rewards of later life. When we recognize that retirement has far-reaching implications, we can see its importance. What will retirees think of their self-worth when no longer "productive" at work? Will they miss fellow workers themselves or the idea of people with whom to interact? Can they replace the stimulation of learning new skills? Will they miss the sense of being needed that work provided?

Retirement affects not only retirees but their families as well. Will the retirement benefits be so meager as to force the spouse to make sacrifices along with the retiree? Will more frequent visits be made to family members who live out of town?

Because a growing number of elderly people are choosing not to retire and because our Social Security system is being taxed by the large increase in the elderly population, the government is encouraging later retirements. When one heard Buckminster Fuller or René Dubos or some other elderly person of tremendous wisdom and ability, one could not help but be supportive of later retirements. In 1978, Congress extended the mandatory retirement age from sixty-five to seventy and removed the age limit completely for federal employees. President Ronald Reagan was seventy-three years old when elected for his second term of office, demonstrating that chronological age is not as important as mental and physiological age. Many people will choose to work their whole lives, whereas others will choose to retire to another job or from work completely. This choice allows people to exercise greater control over their lives than when retirement was mandatory at age sixty-five.

Retirement, whether it's viewed as a positive or negative experience, requires adjustment. Our work is such an important part of our lives for such a long time that

Retirement is whatever you make of it. Trying a new game, hobby, or activity can keep an elderly mind active.

Two Views of Retirement

It's Boring

"They gave me a gold watch—a beautiful thing—six month's pay, a new car, and a fabulous pension," Baird explained. "We spent three months traveling, playing golf, fishing, and getting lazy. At first, I thought it was great. You know, for years you look forward to the freedom, the leisure time, the no hassles. But, let me tell you, friend, it gets old. After six months I was bored stiff, and my wife, she was getting fed up, too. You know, she had her friends and her activities and didn't need me underfoot. Then, I found this job, and it's great. I love it! New people; people from all over and I am able to make their stay a little more pleasant. Don't ever retire friend; if you got a job, stick with it. Retirement is for the birds. Unless you're a lazy bird."

It's Great

"I don't feel any great loss at all. No, no. I taught math and science for thirty-one years, and, if I hadn't taken time out to raise two daughters, I would have made it forty. I loved every minute of it, but now it is time to take a rest. After all that time I have earned it, don't you think? Why would I want to go on teaching? I have my retirement, my insurance, and my health. Now I just want to enjoy it."

self-worth becomes tied to it. When retirement occurs, we may lack other ways to affirm our self-worth and status. Retired workers may see themselves as neither needed nor contributing to some useful endeavor.

In addition, retirement often means an adjustment to a leisure-oriented way of life. No longer required to wake up early, to be at work at a particular time, to limit when and how long lunch will be, and to save leisure-time activities for evenings and weekends, retired people encounter a whole new lifestyle to which they must adjust. For those not used to having leisure—for example, workaholics—this adjustment is a major one. They may lack leisure skills such as conversing well with others, various sports skills, or simply the ability to enjoy themselves at an activity that is not specifically "productive."

To further complicate retirement, many retirees must adjust to decreased financial resources. With more leisure time and less money available to spend on leisure activities, many retirees feel frustrated.

Also, retirees must sometimes put up with the negative attitudes of others (workers) who may consider them outsiders. For example, one researcher found that health professionals are significantly more negative in their attitudes toward treatment of older people than they are toward treatment of younger people. **Ageism,** like sexism and racism, is a negative social reality with which the elderly are faced.

Mixed into this brew of necessary adjustments during retirement are aloneness—not necessarily "loneliness" but, rather, living alone after the death of a spouse—and health problems. Those with degenerative diseases, such as diabetes, arthritis, and arteriosclerosis, may find these conditions worsening as they get older, and more restrictions may be placed on their activity during their retirement years.

The test of your knowledge about the elderly presented earlier showed that many of the problems named were experienced by a minority of the elderly. Although they are in the minority, significant numbers of the aged do experience stressors to which they must adapt upon retirement. Some adapt better than others. When retirees were

ageism
Prejudice based on a person's age.

studied by the National Institute of Mental Health (NIMH), four patterns of adjustment were found that are still relevant today.[13]

1. *Maintenance:* the pattern of people who try to satisfy the same needs after retirement as before retirement in the same kind of way. They continue work in one way or another; for example, they take part-time jobs.

2. *Withdrawal:* the pattern of people who consider retirement as a time to relax. They give up many of their former activities and adopt new ones; for example, they take up golf.

3. *Changed activities:* the pattern of people who attempt to satisfy the same needs as before retirement, but by different means; for example, they volunteer to work as aides in hospitals or for charitable organizations.

4. *Changed needs:* the pattern of people who attempt to satisfy a different set of needs than before retirement. They view retirement as a time of relaxation but may continue many of their previous activities. In addition, they may adopt a few new activities.

All in all, NIMH found that over half of the retirees studied felt positively toward their retirement, yet a large number had negative feelings.

Caregiving

In spite of large numbers of the elderly being able to care for themselves, there is a significant population of older people in the United States who do need taking care of. As a person gets older, the care he or she needs tends to increase. Almost 39 percent of those sixty-five and older experience limitation of activity caused by a chronic condition. Whereas only 29 percent of those between sixty-five and seventy-four experience a limitation of activity, 47 percent of those seventy-five to eight-four do.[14] Among the young elderly, sixty-five- to seventy-four-year-olds, 5 percent experience three to five limitations, 13 percent of seventy-five- to eighty-four-year-olds experience three to five limitations, and 36 percent of those eighty-five and older experience as many as three to five limitations of activity.[15] Although these data indicate that limitations of activity are not unusual among the elderly, they occur with far less frequency than is generally believed. A Census Bureau study reported that 52 percent of Americans aged sixty-five and older had some type of physical or mental disability. However, excluding

Caring for an elderly relative can be very rewarding, and yet quite stressful.

mental impairments, only 20 percent of households age sixty-two and older report having someone with at least one physical limitation. These limitations included mobility (12 percent of households), seeing (7 percent), hearing (7 percent), or performing any of the basic activities of daily living such as bathing, dressing, eating, and others (12 percent). Even more remarkable, only 40 percent of households headed by a person age eighty-five or older reported having any significant personal physical problem. Perhaps that perspective is what enabled them to live so long.[16]

What are the limitations elders encounter? One study[17] found 14 percent of sixty-five- to seventy-nine-year-olds had difficulty seeing words in a newspaper, 22 percent had difficulty lifting and carrying 10 pounds, and 27 percent had difficulty climbing stairs or walking a quarter mile or three city blocks. Although these numbers increased with age, still only 29 percent of those eighty and older had difficulty seeing words in a newspaper, 43 percent had difficulty lifting and carrying 10 pounds, 45 percent had difficulty climbing stairs, and 50 percent had difficulty walking a quarter mile or three city blocks. When comparing these levels of limitations of activity with the previous decade, the researchers concluded that for all age groups there were significant declines in limitations.

Functional limitations also need not be permanent. In fact, a portion of elders improve in functional status each year.[18] In a study conducted in 1997, 56 percent of elders did not change in functional status, 37 percent deteriorated, and 7 percent actually improved.[19] **Caregivers** of the elderly may experience a great deal of stress from the feeling of being captive to the needs of the elderly person for whom they are caring and because of the changes necessitated in their daily family lives. In 2004 the National Alliance for Caregiving reported that 61 percent of caregivers for the elderly were women, the average age of the caregiver was forty-six, and 17 percent of these caregivers rated their own health as fair or poor.[20] To complicate matters further, 64 percent of these caregivers were employed full- or part-time, 41 percent were also caring for children under the age of eighteen, and 30 percent were caring for more than one elder.[21]

You can imagine the stress associated with the caregiver role, and the resulting ill effects. One study found that caregivers who were experiencing strain associated with their caregiving role had mortality risks 63 percent higher than noncaregivers.[22] Among the signs of caregiver stress were the following:[23]

- *Denial* about the ill person's condition.
- *Anger* that no cure exists and that others don't understand enough about the condition.
- *Social withdrawal* from friends and activities that used to be pleasurable.
- *Anxiety* about what the next day will bring.
- *Depression* that breaks one's spirit.
- *Exhaustion* making it difficult to get through the day.
- *Sleeplessness* caused by constant concerns.
- *Irritability* leading to negative responses to others.
- *Lack of concentration* leading to diminished performance of necessary tasks.
- *Health problems* that are either emotional or physical.

Caregivers cope with stress in various ways. Praying is the most common strategy; 73 percent prayed as a means to manage the stress of caregiving. Sixty-one percent talked with friends or relatives, 44 percent read about caregiving, 41 percent exercised, and 33 percent went on the Internet for information. Only 27 percent sought counseling from a mental health professional or a member of the clergy, and only 12 percent took medication to deal with the stress associated with caregiving.[24]

Both male and female children of aging parents make changes at work to accommodate caregiving responsibilities. Both have modified their schedules (men, 54 percent; women, 56 percent). Both have come in late and/or left early (men, 78 percent; women, 84 percent), and both have altered their work-related travel (men, 38 percent; women, 27 percent).[25]

caregivers
People who provide care for children, elders, or the disabled.

We will all die. The important question is, How will we live?

Recognizing this cost, some businesses offer support services for their employees. For example, Southern Bell publishes a manual listing services in the community that can help workers who are caring for elderly relatives; Stride Rite Corporation added an adult care component to the company's existing child care center; and Potomac Electric Power Company gives workers unpaid leaves to care for both elders and children. In addition to these societal adjustments recognizing the needs of caregivers, educational programs have been developed to help them be more effective and better able to cope with the stress they experience.

Death and Dying

Before beginning this section, complete Lab 19.1 at the end of this chapter to assess your attitudes toward death. If you discuss the results of Lab 19.1 with others, you will find that attitudes toward death vary greatly. No one is right, and no one is wrong. Different attitudes coexist.

You probably scored somewhere in the middle ranges on Lab 19.1. Although death is not something you look forward to, it also is not something you go around thinking about and being depressed over each day. If you scored at either end of the scale (below 217 or above 243), you should discuss your feelings with someone whose opinion you respect and in whom you have confidence. In some instances, counseling from a professional might be warranted—in particular, if you are dysfunctionally depressed or overly enthusiastic about death. Your instructor might be a good person to begin with, and he or she might be able to recommend someone who would meet your needs. Death is a stressor for many people, and if it is for you, you are not unusual. Intervention is recommended when thoughts of death interfere with living fully.

Death

One of the stressors for everyone, and for the aged in particular, is death. We try to postpone it, and to some extent we can—by exercising, watching our diet and our weight, and managing our stress, and by not smoking—but a major influence on the age at which we die is our heredity. Born to parents who lived long, our chances of living long are greatly increased. A reporter once asked a 103-year-old man the question

Kubler-Ross' Stages of Dying and Stress

With more advanced medical technology than ever before, physicians are able to diagnose terminal illnesses to a greater extent. Consequently, it is becoming increasingly common for people with cancer, for example, to become aware of their impending death months, and sometimes years, prior. How can we help these loved ones to manage the stress they experience from such a prognosis?

The work of thanatologist (an expert on death and dying) Elisabeth Kubler-Ross is often used as a guide in recognizing the stages through which dying people progress. If you can anticipate what dying loved ones will experience, you will be better equipped to help them through these stages, alleviating some stress along the way. Dr. Kubler-Ross identified five stages that dying people usually experience: *denial* of impending death; *anger* at having to die; *bargaining* (e.g., "If I could have one more month I'd spend it doing only good."); *depression;* and, finally, *acceptance* of death.

At the denial stage, you can help by assisting the dying person to accept the prognosis of death by arranging for a second opinion to verify the medical condition. In addition, it is helpful to acknowledge the value of denial as a protective device. Saying something like "It must be difficult to accept that you're going to die" may help.

During the anger stage, you should acknowledge the person's feelings with statements such as, "I can understand how angry you feel. I would feel that way too if I were in your situation." In addition, recognize that the anger is not directed at you and, therefore, do not respond angrily or in disbelief that you are spoken to in that way.

The bargaining stage is more complex. For many people, bargaining is obviously dysfunctional. Regardless of what they propose as the bargain, they will inevitably die as prognosticated. For these people, it is helpful to assist the loved one to accept that no bargain can delay his or her imminent death. In these instances, it might help to say something like, "I, too, wish that I could give one month of my life so you could live that much longer, but unfortunately neither of us can make such a deal." However, those with a strong belief in a higher power—a god—might be comforted by bargaining with this Supreme Being and comforted by believing this god will answer his or her prayers. In this instance, you could assist by praying with the loved one or by helping to transport him or her to church, synagogue, or mosque.

Depression is a stage that is quite understandable. After all, wouldn't you be depressed if you thought you were dying soon? As with anger, loved ones should be encouraged to express feelings of depression, and these feelings should be accepted by family and friends. Loved ones' feelings of depression should be acknowledged by a statement such as, "What a heavy burden you must bear. I can understand you're feeling depressed. I'm sure I would be too. Do you want to talk about it?"

Acceptance is the last stage of dying as described by Kubler-Ross. It is the goal of the terminally ill, although not all dying people reach this stage. For those who do, you can help them alleviate some stress by assisting in their organizing of their affairs so they feel everything is in order. Their will should be updated, health and life insurance policies handy, living wills or durable powers of attorney should be available, a list of bank accounts prepared, and funeral or burial arrangements made.

People move through these stages at different rates and may move back and forth between stages, or not go through them at all. However, these stages are helpful for identifying what dying loved ones are experiencing, and communicating with them differently based on the stage of dying in which they find themselves. Paying attention to Kubler-Ross' stages of dying can go a long way to help you assist dying loved ones to alleviate some—though, obviously, not all—of the stress they experience.

Source: Elisabeth Kubler-Ross, *On Death and Dying* (New York: Simon and Schuster, 1970).

"If you had your life to live over again, would you do anything differently?" "Well," the old man said thoughtfully, "if I knew I was going to live to be 103, I sure would have taken better care of myself."

To learn more about what death means to you and how it influences your life, complete Lab 19.2 at the end of this chapter.

Dying

Just as the thought of death is a stressor for the aged, so is dying. Some people may fear not death itself but the dying process—for example, the pain and indignity. The significance of dying as a stressor is best understood when it is recognized that most people who die in the United States have chronic degenerative diseases, which usually result in a prolonged period of dying. In 2000, 2.4 million Americans died. Fifty percent of these deaths occurred in a hospital. One-quarter occurred in a nursing home, and another 25 percent occurred at home or elsewhere.[26]

One of the organizations making it easier for people to die more comfortably and where they choose is hospice. In medieval times, the term *hospice* was used to describe a shelter for weary and sick travelers. In 1967, Dr. Cicely Saunders established St. Christopher's Hospice in a suburb of London as a place to provide humane and compassionate care for dying people.[27] Today, hospices are free-standing agencies, or parts of hospitals, or provide visiting care in people's own homes or in nursing homes. In 1999, 29 percent of all Americans who died received hospice services. In 2002, 58 percent of hospice patients died at home, 22 percent died in a nursing facility, 9 percent died in a hospital, 5 percent died in a hospice unit, and 7 percent died in other settings.[28] When asked where they prefer to die, the great majority of people report they would prefer to die at home; most say they do not want to die in a hospital or nursing home.

Grief

Part of life as an aged person is the death of loved ones. Be they spouses, children, brothers, sisters, or friends, the death of these loved ones results in **grief** for their loss. The grieving process long ago was described as a three-stage phenomenon (see Table 19.1). The first stage involves shock and disbelief regarding the death and is

grief
The sad feelings associated with the death of a loved one.

Timetable	Manifestations
Stage 1: Begins immediately after death, usually lasts one to three days	Shock Disbelief, denial Numbness Weeping Wailing Agitation
Stage 2: Peaks between two and four weeks after death, begins to subside after three months, usually lasts up to one year	Painful longing Preoccupation Memories Mental images of the deceased Sense of the deceased being present Sadness Tearfulness Insomnia Anorexia Loss of interest Irritability Restlessness
Stage 3: Usually occurs within a year after death	Resolution Decreasing episodes of sadness Ability to recall the past with pleasure Resumption of ordinary activities

Table 19.1
STAGES OF ORDINARY GRIEF

Source: Robert B. White and Leroy T. Gathman, "The Syndrome of Ordinary Grief," *American Family Physician* 8(1973): 98. 1973 American Academy of Family Physicians, Kansas City, Missouri. Reprinted with permission.

accompanied by crying and a great deal of distress. The second stage is characterized by a painful longing for and preoccupation with the deceased. There is a loss of appetite, crying, and difficulty in sleeping. The last stage of grief brings with it diminishing sadness and a resumption of normal activities.

Numerous studies have investigated the relationship between grief and the subsequent illness and death of those bereaved. Elderly spousal caregivers with a history of chronic illness themselves, who are experiencing caregiving related stress, have a 63 percent higher mortality rate than their noncaregiving peers.[29] Other researchers have also uncovered a relationship between death from heart disease and elder care.[30] The phrase *broken heart* acquired a new and more fatal meaning. A more recent study found several factors associated with this increased death rate among those bereaved. Helsing and his colleagues found that widows and widowers living alone had higher mortality rates.[31] Helsing concluded that his findings add "further support for the hypothesis that a social support network is effective in ameliorating the effects of a stressful life event such as bereavement."[32] Other researchers support this conclusion.[33] Lastly, a finding has been made that explains the physiological mechanism behind the susceptibility of the bereaved—a finding that at this point should not surprise you. Schleifer and his associates found a suppression of lymphocyte stimulation—meaning a decrease in the effectiveness of the immunological system—among grieving men.[34] No wonder grief and bereavement, and the stress associated with them, can make people ill or kill them.

It should be noted that we grieve for losses other than death. When you graduate from college, you might grieve for the lifestyle with which you have become accustomed. When you have a breakup in a romantic relationship, you might grieve for the person you "lost." As we are reminded by the Hospice Foundation of America, we never have to like a loss, but we have to learn to accept and cope with it.[35]

Interventions

Stressors of the later years of life need not result in illness or disease. Interventions can occur at the life-situation level, the perception level, the emotional arousal level, or the physiological arousal level of the stress model described in Chapter 4.

Life-Situation Interventions

There are many people nowadays who decide to work until they die. They will not voluntarily retire, and if they are forced to retire, they take another full-time or part-time job. They do this to continue to feel needed and productive, thereby maintaining their sense of self-worth. Others will retire but, rather than consider themselves useless, will use their retirement to do all those exciting and interesting things they were unable to do earlier. They become active in helping others, in periodically using their experience to act as consultants, or in serving their families more directly than they had time to do before their retirement.

If loneliness or aloneness is a problem, the elderly can arrange to spend time with their compatriots. They could move to Florida or other areas of the country where there are large populations of elderly citizens. They could move into living facilities that cater to the elderly, or while living at home they could visit places where the elderly congregate. My grandmother—at eighty-five-year-old, matriarch of the family—regularly spent her Saturdays with her sister at a shopping mall in Brooklyn, window-shopping and conversing with other people her own age. It seemed that this shopping mall was a "hangout"—not for teenagers but for the elderly.

The later years of life can be as active, as enjoyable, and as unstressful as any other phase of life. It is up to the individual to look for the brighter side of each day.

The elderly are in the last stages of their lives, so their need to see their lives as having some meaning is important. Time spent with children and grandchildren will help the aged see themselves as connected to life—a connection that will continue after their death. This connection need not be with people; it might be with organizations. For example, the dean of my college retired. He has been very important to the growth of the college and is proud of its national reputation. The college will be a monument, so to speak, to Marv Eyler's talents and efforts and will connect him to life long after he is dead. In fact, I wouldn't be surprised to see the name of the building in which our offices are housed named after him.

All of us could adopt interventions at the life-situation level in our earlier years that will serve us well when we become aged. If you have not yet adopted life-situation interventions, try the following exercise. For each decade of your life, list one major goal.

Decade	Goal
0–10	
11–20	
21–30	
31–40	
41–50	
51–60	
61–70	
71–80	
80+	

Now rank these goals in order of importance. Next, cross out the goals already achieved. If you were to die ten years from now, which goals would not have been accomplished? Of these unaccomplished goals, how many are in the top four of importance?[36]

Can you reestablish your goals so that the important ones are achieved earlier in life? If so, you might relieve the stress associated with unaccomplished goals and the feeling that life is running out. Recognizing that, for all of us, regardless of age, death can occur momentarily, we can see that to have at least accomplished our important goals is stress reducing.

You can also prevent stress by arranging your affairs so as to feel organized in the eventuality of death:

1. You should have a will that identifies what should be done with your belongings and estate.

2. There should be funeral and burial instructions (who should officiate, where you want to be buried, how your body should be disposed of, who the pallbearers ought to be).

3. You should leave the names, addresses, and telephone numbers of people to contact (friends, relatives, clergy, banker, attorney, stockbroker, and insurance agent).

4. There should be a record of bank accounts and their numbers, and who is authorized access to those accounts.

5. You should leave a record of the location and contents of any safety deposit boxes.

6. There should be a record of all credit card numbers and billing addresses.

7. Other records that should be left are certificates of deposit, outstanding loans, retirement accounts, profit-sharing plans, past income tax returns, and insurance policy information.

A good reference regarding getting things in order in case of death is entitled "Putting Your House in Order" and is available from the Continental Association of Funeral and Memorial Societies, 2001 S Street, NW, Washington, DC 20009.

Figure 19.1

Sample donor card.

UNIFORM DONOR CARD

OF_____
Print or type name of donor

In the hope that I may help others, I hereby make this anatomical gift, if medically acceptable, to take effect upon my death. The words and marks below indicate my desires.

I give: (a) _____ any needed organs or parts
        (b) _____ only the following organs or parts

_____
Specify the organ(s) or part(s)

for the purposes of transplantation, therapy, medical research or education;
        (c) _____ my body for anatomical study if needed.

Limitations or
special wishes, if any: _____

- -

Signed by the donor and the following two witnesses in the presence of each other:

_____   _____
Signature of Donor   Date of Birth of Donor

_____   _____
Date Signed   City & State

_____   _____
Witness   Witness

This is a legal document under the Uniform Anatomical Gift Act or similar laws.

For further imformation consult your physician or

KF Kidney Foundation of Iowa
3615 Douglas Avenue
Des Moines, Iowa 50310

living will
Instructions regarding the type of medical care wanted in the case of being incapacitated with a terminal disease or being in a vegetative state.

You can also prevent stress by developing a **living will.** In this way, you can be assured that your desires regarding medical intervention and the prolonging of your life when all hope for life as we know it is gone, will be stated. Perhaps you want to donate parts of your body to be used after your death by someone needing them. Figure 19.1 presents a sample donor card that you can carry with you at all times. Then, when you die, your organs can be used to save or enhance the life of someone else. In this manner, you will be assured that your life will have some beneficial purpose, regardless of what else you might do.

In addition to these life-situation interventions, behaviors adopted throughout your life will affect the stress, illness, and disease you experience in your later years. You should be concerned about the following:

1. Eating nutritionally balanced meals.
2. Smoking cigarettes.
3. Abusing or misusing alcohol and other drugs.
4. Managing stress.
5. Having significant others in your life to act as a support system.
6. Having a positive outlook on life.
7. Having periodic medical examinations.
8. Living in an urban, suburban, or rural environment (urban dwellers die at younger ages).
9. Being wealthy or poor (both extremes can be stressful).
10. Maintaining a clean and safe physical environment at home.
11. Spending your days in useful, meaningful activity.
12. Maintaining appropriate body weight.
13. Enjoying leisure time.
14. Exercising regularly.

Florida Living Will

Instructions	
Print the date	
Print your name	
Please initial each that applies	

Declaration made this _____ day of _____, _____ .
                          (day)   *(month)*   *(year)*

I, _____ , willfully and voluntarily make known my desire that my dying not be artificially prolonged under the circumstances set forth below, and I do hereby declare that:

If at any time I am incapacitated and
      _____ I have a terminal condition, or
      _____ I have an end-stage condition, or
      _____ I am in a persistent vegetative state

and if my attending or treating physician and another consulting physician have determined that there is no reasonable medical probability of my recovery from such condition, I direct that life-prolonging procedures be withheld or withdrawn when the application of such procedures would serve only to prolong artificially the process of dying, and that I be permitted to die naturally with only the administration or the performance of any medical procedure deemed necessary to provide me with comfort care or to alleviate pain.

It is my intention that this declaration be honored by my family and physician as the final expression of my legal right to refuse medical or surgical treatment and to accept the consequences for such refusal.

In the event that I have been determined to be unable to provide express and informed consent regarding the withholding, withdrawal, or continuation of life-prolonging procedures, I wish to designate, as my surrogate to carry out the provisions of the declarations:

Print the name, home address and telephone number of your surrogate

Name: _____

Address: _____

_____ Zip Code: _____

Phone: _____

© 2000
Partnership for
Caring, Inc.

All of these are within your control, at least to some degree, which means the quality of your later adult years is a function of what you do prior to those years.

Perception Interventions

Retirement is a good life situation to use when discussing perception interventions. Imagine two people who retire. One considers retirement a signal of dropping out of life, being unproductive, and having a diminished self-worth. The other views retirement as a reward for years of hard work, as an opportunity to do things time

A living will (continued).

```
┌──────────────────────────────────────────────────────────────────────────┐
│                                                                            │
│  ┌───────────────┐   ┌────────────────────────────────────────────────┐   │
│  │               │   │        Florida Living Will—Page 2 of 2          │   │
│  │               │   └────────────────────────────────────────────────┘   │
│  │               │                                                          │
│  │               │    I wish to designate the following person as my alter-│
│  │               │    nate surrogate to carry out the provisions of this   │
│  │               │    declaration should my surrogate be unwilling or      │
│  │  Print name,  │    unable to act on my behalf:                          │
│  │  home address │                                                         │
│  │      and      │    Name: _____       │
│  │   telephone   │                                                         │
│  │   number of   │    Address: _____       │
│  │      your     │                                                         │
│  │   alternate   │    _____ Zip Code: _____     │
│  │   surrogate   │                                                         │
│  │               │    Phone: _____       │
│  │               │                                                         │
│  │  Add personal │    Additional instructions (optional):                 │
│  │  instructions │                                                         │
│  │    (if any)   │                                                         │
│  │               │                                                         │
│  │               │                                                         │
│  │               │                                                         │
│  │               │                                                         │
│  │               │    I understand the full import of this declaration,    │
│  │               │    and I am emotionally and mentally competent to make  │
│  │               │    this declaration.                                    │
│  │               │                                                         │
│  │   Sign the    │    Signed: _____       │
│  │   document    │                                                         │
│  │               │    Witness 1:                                           │
│  │  Witnessing   │                                                         │
│  │  Procedure    │        Signed: _____       │
│  │               │                                                         │
│  │      Two      │        Address: _____       │
│  │   witnesses   │                                                         │
│  │  must sign and│    Witness 2:                                           │
│  │  print their  │                                                         │
│  │   addresses   │        Signed: _____       │
│  │               │                                                         │
│  │               │        Address: _____       │
│  │               │                                                         │
│  │  © 2000       │   ┌────────────────────────────────────────────┐ 6/00 │
│  │  Partnership  │   │  Courtesy of Partnership for Caring, Inc.    │      │
│  │  for Caring,  │   │  1035 30th Street, NW Washington, DC 20007    │      │
│  │  Inc.         │   │  800-989-9455                                 │      │
│  └───────────────┘   └────────────────────────────────────────────┘      │
│                                                                            │
└──────────────────────────────────────────────────────────────────────────┘
```

Reprinted by permission of *Partnership for Caring*, 1620 Eye Street, NW, Washington, DC 20006; (800) 989-9455.

did not permit earlier, or as a chance to help others or spend time helping family members enjoy their lives more. They face the same event but have different perceptions of it.

We can spend our time complaining about aches and pains or be grateful for the degree of mobility and intellectual ability we still have. We can dwell on how fast the years went and on how few remain, or we can consider the remaining years as more than some others have had. We can perceive our aloneness as loneliness or as an opportunity to get to know ourselves better. We can bemoan the little time our families spend with us or be appreciative for the love and time they do give us.

Fun certainly is not limited to the young. Getting together with elderly people can help both the elder and the young person feel less stressed.

In short, we can dwell on the negative aspects of old age or on its positive ones. The choice is ours. Focusing on the negatives will only make them more negative. For example, complaining to our families about the little time they spend with us will make them enjoy that time less. They might then spend even less time with us. Focusing upon death might so concern us that we don't live out our remaining years to the fullest. Paying too much attention to aches and pains might make them more bothersome. If we could focus on something or someone else, perhaps we'd forget about our aches and pains for a while.

An example of how negative thoughts can make us ill or, on the other hand, positive thoughts can insulate us from stress is that of caregiving. Researchers asking the question "Why do some caregivers maintain high levels of care with little stress, while others all but crumble under the strain?" hypothesize that perception is important to the answer. They believe that people who perceive caring for a loved one in terms of fulfillment rather than sacrifice don't feel burdened but instead feel privileged.[37] With this rationale, the Elderly Support Project has developed a program to help caregivers identify and increase the positive aspects of caregiving they get from those for whom they provide care—affection, companionship, and cooperation. Once again, self-awareness comes to the rescue!

Like the life-situation interventions, perception interventions are up to us. We have the ability to intervene in the stress of old age by perceiving the good associated with those years. The choice is ours.

Emotional Arousal Interventions

Relaxation techniques can be used as emotional arousal interventions. These certainly are appropriate for the elderly. In addition to these interventions, many elderly people use prayer to focus outside themselves and achieve emotional peace. The repetitious nature of some prayers makes them even more particularly suited to emotional arousal intervention.

Another intervention used by the elderly is similar to one used by a younger friend of mine. He has tanks and tanks of tropical fish and spends an endless amount of time watching these fish swim back and forth. He is "into" his fish and "out of" his problems. As he watches them swim, he forgets his business problems. He relaxes. Many of the elderly do the same, except that the rest of us become their fish. Watching from their windows, they see us going to work, returning from work, arguing with the kids, playing, and doing various other life activities. Unfortunately, too many people view the elderly who engage in this emotional arousal intervention as "nosy." However, they are able to prevent emotional arousal by watching us "fish" in our tanks of life and focusing away from the negative aspects of old age. We'd be better advised to help them clean their windows so they can see better than to complain about their nosiness.

Physiological Arousal Interventions

The elderly, like everyone else, can profit from regular exercise. Sometimes, because of particular disabilities or health concerns, the exercise has to be adapted to the individual, but exercise itself need not be eliminated. Recognizing this, some elderly people will play doubles in tennis or handball rather than singles. Some will run a marathon a little slower than when they were younger, but they will complete the 26-mile course just the same. Some will swim fewer miles than when they were imitating Johnny Weissmuller, but they will swim each day just the same. Using the products of stress—the increased muscle tension, serum cholesterol, and blood pressure—is as important for the elderly as for the rest of us, and the psychological benefits of exercise are not exclusive to the young. Even if your whole life has been inactive, you can still begin regular exercise when you are older. However, consult a physician prior to beginning a program. A walking program is a good way to begin if you have been inactive most of your life.

The choice is yours. If you are elderly, you can manage your stress by intervening at various levels of the stress model presented in this book. If you are younger, you can prepare yourself now with numerous intervention strategies to diminish the harmful effects of stress during your later years.

Getting Involved in Your Community

The elders in your community have earned respect and dignity, yet too many experience ageism and neglect. Understandably, this causes them a great deal of stress. This need not be the case, and you can contribute in this regard in several ways:

1. Volunteer at a senior citizens' center. You can offer a skill to the seniors, such as conducting a photography class, an arts and crafts group, or a painting class.

2. Volunteer at a local nursing home. You can establish a relationship with one or a couple of elders and periodically visit with them. Or you can develop a phone pal relationship in which you periodically telephone to converse with an elder.

3. Participate in the Meals on Wheels program, which delivers food to elders who cannot get out on their own to buy food.

4. Organize retired people in your community so they can continue to offer their professional services. For example, my father-in-law retired as an attorney but regularly volunteered at his local senior citizens' center, offering legal advice to elders who could not afford their own lawyers. Retired physicians, nurses, and other health professionals organized a group called Volunteers in Medicine in Hilton Head, South Carolina, that offers health services free of charge to poor people living on the island. This has been so successful that it has become a national model that is being replicated in communities across the United States. Perhaps you can help your community make arrangements to adopt a local chapter.

There are many things you can do to make the lives of your elderly neighbors less stressful. Will you do something for them now, or are you too busy?

Someone told me of a person who came home one evening holding the steering wheel of the family car, hair and clothes disheveled and speckled with glass from the windshield, and smelling of engine oil, and who with a faint, halfhearted smile said to the waiting spouse, "Well, at least you won't have to waste your Fridays at the car wash any longer."

If only we could adopt that attitude toward the future and the stressors it will bring. Alvin Toffler wrote of the nature of the future in his classic book *Future Shock*.[1] Toffler described the rapid and pervasive changes that we will, and do, experience. As we have learned, such changes have the potential to elicit a stress response—that is, they're stressors.

The knowledge of today often becomes the misinformation of tomorrow. For example, most of us were taught and believed that parallel lines never meet, yet today physicists say that they do meet somewhere in infinity. We learned that eggs and liver were good for us and that we should eat them frequently, yet some cardiologists now believe that they contain so much cholesterol that we should limit how much of them we eat. Knowledge is expanding exponentially; new knowledge often replaces old "knowledge." This situation creates confusion—what do we believe? It creates frustration, one example of which is the oft-heard lament "Everything seems to cause cancer." It creates stress—how do we manage in a world that has so much scientific knowledge and technology that a few individuals could destroy it by pushing several buttons? Well, at least we wouldn't have to waste Fridays at the car wash.

In *The Third Wave,* Toffler continued describing a changing society, focusing upon the influence of science and technology on our daily lives.[2] I recalled Toffler's description of the effects that new forms of communication and computers would have upon us (e.g., we can now shop, bank, and work from the desktop computer terminals in our homes) when I read of an experiment that took place during a football game. The Racine Gladiators were playing the Columbus Metros in a semipro football game way back in July of 1980. The cable TV system televising the game allowed subscribers to communicate through it instantaneously by punching buttons on a hand-held control unit in their homes, and that is exactly what more than 5,000 viewers did. Prior to each play, the viewers voted on the next play they wanted their hometown Metros to run, out of a choice of five different plays. In ten seconds the responses were tallied and flashed on a screen at the stadium—unseen by the players—and the vote was relayed to the quarterback. The Metros lost the game 10–7 but their coach said he probably couldn't have called the plays any better. "The times they are a-changing."

If we are going to survive and flourish in a rapidly changing society, we had better learn how to manage the inevitable stress. We must adjust our life situations to eliminate unnecessary stressors and to find comfort in rewarding, routine, and stable relationships and activities. We need to strengthen our families, do meaningful and enjoyable work, and organize our leisure time to be fun and recreating (which is where the word *recreation* came from). Furthermore, we need to perceive those distressing life situations that we cannot change as less threatening and disturbing. This includes viewing ourselves as worthwhile beings, believing we can control many events and consequences in our lives, and considering life's tests as challenges and growth experiences rather than as plagues to be shunned, avoided, and forgotten.

Added to these recommendations must be the regular practice of relaxation and exercise. Relaxation skills provide a "reservoir of relaxation" from which we can draw when our lives become particularly stressful. These skills will also serve to intervene between life situations that we perceive to be distressing and subsequent illnesses and diseases by diminishing the physiological arousal caused by stressors.

In the hope that this book enhances your ability to manage the stress in your life, I leave you with the following thought. This Persian proverb has meant much to me, and my hope is that it will also have significance for you. It is short, so you can easily commit it to memory:

I murmured because I had no shoes,
Until I met a man who had no feet.

notes

1. Alvin Toffler, *Future Shock* (New York: Random House, 1970).

2. Alvin Toffler, *The Third Wave* (New York: William Morrow & Co., 1980).

Stress Information Resources

Information on stress and stress management is available from the publications and organizations described in this appendix. Compiled for the general public and for health professionals who provide information to the public, it is divided into two sections. The first describes organizations and the second describes publications. The publications, all free or low-cost materials written for the lay public, concern general adult and childhood stress. Order publications directly from the sources indicated. Prices include postage and handling and are subject to change.

ORGANIZATIONS

Emotions Anonymous (EA), P.O. Box 4245, St. Paul, MN 55104, (651) 647-9712, www.emotionsanonymous.org. Supports local peer support groups open to anyone seeking help for their emotional or living problems. Publishes a magazine, literature on emotional illness, and guidelines for conducting local groups. There are currently about 600 EA groups in the United States, and contact information on local groups is available from the national office.

National Institute of Mental Health (NIMH), 6001 Executive Boulevard, Rm. 8184, MSC 9663, Bethesda, MD 20892, (301) 443-4513, www.nimh.him.gov. Provides informative publications about stress and stress management, as well as other aspects of mental health. NIMH is the primary source of mental health information in the federal government. Publications are targeted at the lay public as well as to health professionals.

National Mental Health Association (NMHA), 2001 N. Beauregard Street, Alexandria, VA 22311, (703)-684-7722, www.nmha.org. Works to improve public understanding of mental health and mental illness and to assist the mentally ill and their families. A total of 850 state and local chapters provide information services to individuals and community groups, emotional support for families, and assistance to school systems and local governments. Contact information for state and local chapters and a publications catalog are available from the national office.

PUBLICATIONS

A Real Illness: Post-Traumatic Stress Disorder (PTSD). Describes post-traumatic stress disorder and discusses when it starts, how long it lasts, how prevalent it is, what a person experiencing PTSD can do to help him or herself, and what professional help is available. Copy free from the National Institute of Mental Health, NIMH Inquires, 6001 Executive Boulevard, Rm. 8184, MSC 9663, Bethesda, MD 20892, (301) 443-4513.
http://www.nimh.nih.gov/publist/004675.cfm

Anxiety Disorders. Discusses panic disorder, obsessive-compulsive disorder, post-traumatic stress disorder, social phobia (social anxiety disorder), specific phobias, generalized anxiety disorder, the role of research in improving the understanding and treatment of anxiety disorder, treatment of anxiety disorders, and how to get help for anxiety disorders strategies to make treatment more effective. Copy free from the National Institute of Mental Health, NIMH Inquires, 6001 Executive Boulevard, Rm. 8184, MSC 9663, Bethesda, MD 20892,
(301) 443-4513. http://www.nimh.nih.gov/anxiety/anxiety.cfm

Anxiety Disorders in Children and Adolescents. Describes anxiety disorders and discusses the signs of anxiety disorder, its prevalence, who is at risk, what help is available, and what parents can do to help their children and adolescents. Copy free from the United States Department of Health and Human Services' Substance Abuse and Mental Health Services Administration, P.O. Box 42490, Washington, DC 20015, (866) 889-3627. http://www.mentalhealth.samhsa.gov/

Coping with the Death of a Parent. Discusses emotional responses an adult child may feel or experience after the death of a parent. Also included are ways to remember your parent and where to obtain grief support if needed. (Stock # English D16832, Spanish D17533). Copies available free from AARP, 601 E Street, NW, Washington, DC 20049, (800) 424-3410.

Depression. Discusses what a depressive disorder is, types of depression, symptoms of depression and mania, causes of depression, diagnostic evaluation and treatment, psychotherapies, how to help yourself if you are depressed, and where to get help and further information. National Institute of Mental Health, NIMH Inquires, 6001 Executive Boulevard, Rm. 8184, MSC 9663, Bethesda, MD 20892, (301) 443-4513.
http://www.nimh.nih.gov/publicat/depression.cfm

Facts About Post-Traumatic Stress Disorder. Discusses symptoms of PTSD, its prevalence, when it first occurs, what treatments are available, whether other illnesses tend to accompany PTSD, who is most likely to acquire PTSD, and what scientists are learning from research on PTSD. Copy free from the National Institute of Mental Health, NIMH Inquires, 6001 Executive Boulevard, Rm. 8184, MSC 9663, Bethesda, MD 20892, (301) 443-4513.
http://www.nimh.nih.gov/anxiety/ptsdfacts.cfm

How to Get Unstressed: The Bare Facts. 14 pages. Defines stress; describes how it affects the body. Discusses the difference between good and bad stress and suggests techniques for coping with stress. For sale by the Wisconsin Clearinghouse, University of Wisconsin Hospitals and Clinics, 1954 East Washington Ave., Madison, WI 53704, (608) 263-2797. $1; bulk discounts available.

Plain Talk About the Art of Relaxation. 2 pages. Defines relaxation, explains some causes of stress, and suggests ways to relax. Single copy free from the Public Inquiries Section, Science Communication Branch, National Institute of Mental Health, Parklawn Bldg., Room 15C-17, 5600 Fishers Lane, Rockville, MD 20857, (301) 443-4513.

Plain Talk About Dealing with the Angry Child. 2 pages. Discusses ways parents can help a child cope with feelings of anger and aggression. Also available in Spanish: *Charla franca: como tratar al nino enojado.* Single copy free from the Consumer Information Center, Dept. M, Pueblo, CO 81009.

Plain Talk About Handling Stress. 2 pages. Defines stress, explaining how our bodies react to stress and how to handle it. Also available in Spanish: *Charla franca: sobre la tension.* Single copy free from the Public Inquiries Section, Science Communication Branch, National Institute of Mental Health, Parklawn Bldg., Room 15C-17, 5600 Fishers Lane, Rockville, MD 20857, (301) 443-4513.

The Road to Resilience. Helps readers become resilient by describing resiliency, citing factors that affect people dealing with hardship, strategies for building resilience, and ten ways to specifically develop resiliency. Copies available free from the American Psychological Association, 750 First Street, NE, Washington, DC 20002-4242. (800) 964-2000.

Stress. 96 pages. Presents articles by experts, in lay language, on many aspects of this topic, including stress in childhood, adolescence, and aging; stress at home and on the job; and ways to relax. Contact your local Blue Cross/Blue Shield Association.

Stress and Your Health. 4 pages. Defines stress, explains the different types, and suggests ways to avoid physical and mental problems associated with stress. Lists other sources of information. Single copy free with stamped, self-addressed envelope from the Metropolitan Life Insurance Company, Health and Safety Education Division, One Madison Ave., New York, NY 10012, (212) 578-2211.

Talk to Someone Who Can Help. Cites ways to find help for one's problems. Discussed in particular are how therapy works, whether therapy is covered by health insurance, and how one chooses a therapist. Copies available free from the American Psychological Association, 750 First Street, NE, Washington, DC 20002-4242, (800) 964-2000.

Understanding the Grief Process. Gives basic information about grief and the many ways we grieve the loss of a loved one. While directed towards the person who has experienced a major loss, it contains information helpful to family members and friends wanting to be of assistance. (Stock # English D16832, Spanish D17533). Copies available free from AARP, 601 E Street, NW, Washington, DC 20049, (800) 424-3410.

Warning Signs. A brochure to help youth avoid violent situations and stop violence before it happens. Covered are reasons for violence, dealing with anger, and controlling your own risk for violent behavior. Copies available free from the American Psychological Association, 750 First Street, NE, Washington, DC 20002-4242, (800) 964-2000.

What Everyone Should Know About Stress. 15 pages. Focuses on change as one of the main causes of stress; also discusses anxiety and depression. Suggests ways to cope with and relieve these conditions, as well as where to find outside help. For sale by Channing L. Bete Company, 200-State Rd., South Deerfield, MA 01373, (413) 665-7611, (800) 628-7733. $.69, minimum order of 25; bulk discounts available.

When a Parent Loses a Spouse. Provides useful information to adult children whose parent has lost a spouse. Items covered include the impact of a spouse's death, ways adult children assist their parents, and where to get other help. (Stock # English D16832, Spanish D17533). Copies available free from AARP, 601 E Street, NW, Washington, DC 20049, (800) 424-3410.

A

A,B,C Lists: a time management technique in which tasks are prioritized. (p. 108)

ABCDE Technique: a method of coping with anxiety that consists of examining irrational beliefs. (p. 135)

Abortion: the termination of a pregnancy. (p. 364)

Acquaintance Rape: forcible sexual intercourse between people who know each other. (p. 339)

Acquired Immune Deficiency Syndrome (AIDS): a condition transmitted through sexual contact and the sharing of intravenous needles that leads to the mixing of blood or semen, in which the immune system becomes progressively ineffective. (p. 337)

Active Listening: paraphrasing the speaker's words and feelings; also called reflective listening. (p. 104)

Adoption by Relative: adoptions in which a relative of the birth parents adopts the child. (p. 366)

Adrenal Cortex: the part of the adrenal gland that secretes corticoids. (p. 24)

Adrenal Medulla: the inner portion of the adrenal gland that secretes catecholamines. (p. 25)

Adrenocorticotropic Hormone (ACTH): activates the adrenal cortex to secrete corticoid hormones. (p. 23)

Aerobic Exercise: exercise of relatively long duration, using large muscle groups, that does not require more oxygen than can be inhaled. (p. 233)

Ageism: prejudice based on a person's age. (p. 388)

Agency Adoptions: adoptions in which the birth parents relinquish the baby to an adoption agency. (p. 366)

Aggressive: acting in a way to get what one is entitled to, one's rights, but at the expense of someone else's rights. (p. 99)

AIDS: acquired immune deficiency syndrome. (p. 287)

Aldosterone: the primary mineralocorticoid. (p. 24)

Anaerobic Exercise: exercise of short duration that requires more oxygen than can be inhaled. (p. 233)

Anal Opening: the exit point for unusable food substances. (p. 31)

Anapanasati: a Zen practice that involves counting breaths as the object of focus during meditation. (p. 170)

Antibodies: substances produced by the body to fight antigens. (p. 50)

Antigen: a foreign substance irritating to the body. (p. 50)

Anxiety: an unrealistic fear that manifests itself in physiological arousal and behaviors to avoid or escape the anxiety-provoking stimulus. (p. 131)

Apoplexy: a lack of oxygen to the brain resulting from a blockage or rupture of a blood vessel; also called stroke. (p. 44)

Aqua Dynamics: a program consisting of structured exercises conducted in limited water areas. (p. 244)

Armchair Desensitization: a form of systematic desensitization in which the stimulus is imagined. (p. 135)

Aromatherapy: the use of plant material added to massage oil thought to have pharmacological qualities that improve health. (p. 215)

Arteriosclerosis: loss of elasticity of the coronary arteries. (p. 45)

Asanas: body positions used during the practice of yoga. (p. 216)

Assertive: acting in a way to get what one is entitled to, one's rights, but not at the expense of someone else's rights. (p. 100)

Atherosclerosis: clogging of the coronary arteries. (p. 45)

Attitude of Gratitude: focusing on things about which to be grateful. (p. 123)

Autogenic Meditation: visualization of relaxing images used during autogenic training. (p. 185)

Autogenic Training: a relaxation technique that involves a sensation of heaviness, warmth, and tingling in the limbs. (p. 5)

Autogenic Training: a relaxation technique that involves imagining one's limbs to be heavy, warm, and tingling. (p. 181)

Autohypnosis: being able to place oneself in a hypnotic state. (p. 181)

Autoimmune Response: a physiological response in which the body turns on itself. (p. 51)

Autonomic Nervous System: controls such body processes as hormone balance, temperature, and width of blood vessels. (p. 21)

B

B Cells: a type of lymphocyte that produces antibodies. (p. 41)

Barriers: reasons given or situations that interfere with someone engaging in behaviors that he or she wishes to engage in. (p. 260)

Biofeedback: the use of instrumentation to measure psychophysiological processes and a means of reporting that measurement back to the person being monitored. (p. 209)

Body Scanning: a relaxation technique that searches for relaxed body parts and transports that sensation to less relaxed areas. (p. 214)

Boomerang Children: children who leave home to live elsewhere but subsequently return to live with the parents. (p. 357)

Bracing: the contraction of muscles for no obvious purpose. (p. 5)

Bracing: Unnecessary muscle tension. (p. 32)

Burnout: an adverse stress reaction to work with psychological, psychophysiological, and behavioral components. (p. 312)

C

Carcinogens: cancer-causing agents. (p. 49)

Caregivers: people who provide care for children, elders, or the disabled. (p. 390)

Cerebellum: part of the subcortex responsible for coordination. (p. 21)

Cerebral Cortex: the upper part of the brain responsible for thinking functions. (p. 21)

Cerebral Hemorrhage: a rupture of a blood vessel in the brain. (p. 44)

Closed Adoption: adoptions in which there is no contact between the birth parents and the adoptive parents. (p. 365)

Cocreator Perception Deficiency (CCPD): the belief that one is either the victim of circumstances or the master of circumstances, each of which is erroneous. (p. 130)

Cognitive Appraisal: interpretation of a stressor. (p. 64)

Cohabitation: romantically involved couples living together although not married. (p. 358)

Cold Turkey: stopping a behavior all at once. (p. 264)

Corticotropin Releasing Factor (CRF): released by hypothalamus and results in the release of adrenocorticotropic hormone. (p. 23)

Cortisol: the primary glucocorticoid. (p. 24)

Course Overload: Having too many courses or courses too difficult to complete well during one semester. (p. 333)

D

DESC Form: a formula for verbally expressing assertiveness consisting of a description of the situation, expression of feelings, specification of preferred change, and consequences of whether or not a change is made. (p. 101)

Developmental Tasks: a series of life tasks that need to be achieved at various stages of life in order for the next stage of life to be happy and successful. (p. 385)

Diaphragmatic Breathing: deep breathing that expands the belly rather than just the chest. (p. 213)

Diastolic Blood Pressure: the pressure of the blood against the arterial walls when the heart is relaxed. (p. 43)

Diencephalon: part of the subcortex responsible for regulation of the emotions. (p. 21)

Distress: stress that results in negative consequences such as decreased performance growth. (p. 68)

Distress: bad things to which one has to adapt and that can lead to a stress reaction. (p. 3)

Double-Blind Studies: research investigations in which neither the research subjects nor the data collectors are aware of who is in the control group and who is in the experimental group. (p. 158)

Dual-Career Family: a family in which both spouses work outside the home with careers of their own. (p. 363)

E

Electromyographic (EMG) Biofeedback: biofeedback that measures muscle contraction. (p. 210)

Emotion-Focused Coping: the use of activities to feel better about the task. (p. 320)

Endocrine System: comprised of hormones that regulate physiological functions. (p. 23)

Endorphins: brain neurotransmitters that decrease pain and produce feelings of well-being. (p. 237)

Epinephrine: a catecholamine secreted by the adrenal medulla. (p. 25)

Erotic Love (eros): a passionate, all-enveloping type of love recognized by the heart racing and other signs of excitement. (p. 335)

Esophagus: the food pipe. (p. 31)

Essential Hypertension: hypertension with no known cause. (p. 43)

Ethnicity: a group of people having a common heritage such as common customs, characteristics, language, and history. (p. 280)

Eustress: stress that results in positive consequences such as enhanced performance or personal growth. (p. 68)

Eustress: good things to which one has to adapt and that can lead to a stress reaction. (p. 3)

Extended Family: relatives other than spouses and children. (p. 355)

External Locus of Control: the perception that one has little control over events that affect one's life. (p. 130)

F

Fear Hierarchy: a list of small steps through an anxiety-provoking stimulus. (p. 134)

Fight-or-Flight Response: the body's stress reaction that includes an increase in heart rate, respiration, blood pressure, and serum cholesterol. (p. 3)

Flextime: scheduling work at irregular times to meet one's lifestyle. (p. 304)

Foster Care: an arrangement in which temporary care for a child is provided by someone other than the birth parents. (p. 367)

G

Galvanic Skin Response (GSR): the electrodermal response or the electrical conductance of the skin. (p. 32)

Gastrointestinal (GI) System: the body system responsible for digestion. (p. 31)

General Adaptation Syndrome: the three stages of stress reaction described by Hans Selye. (p. 3)

Glucocorticoids: regulate metabolism of glucose. (p. 24)

Gluconeogenesis: the producing of glucose from amino acids by the liver. (p. 24)

Gray Matter: the cerebral cortex. (p. 22)

Grief: the sad feelings associated with the death of a loved one. (p. 393)

H

Hardy: a state of mind and body that includes three factors: commitment, control, and challenge. (p. 137)

Hassles: daily interactions with the environment that are essentially negative. (p. 90)

Hate Crimes: crimes against people based on their race, ethnicity, sexual orientation, or religion. (p. 283)

Health Behavior: activities that are taken by people who believe themselves to be healthy and that are designed to maintain health, a subclass of lifestyle behaviors. (p. 259)

Hippocampus: part of the brain that "sounds the alarm" that stress is present. (p. 24)

Hot Reactors: people who react to stress with an all-out physiological reaction. (p. 39)

Human Immunodeficiency Virus (HIV): the virus that causes AIDS. (p. 287)

Human Immunodeficiency Virus: the virus that causes acquired immune deficiency syndrome (AIDS). (p. 338)

Hydrochloric Acid: a substance found in the digestive system that helps break down food for digestion. (p. 31)

Hypoglycemia: a condition of low blood sugar. (p. 86)

Hypothalamus: part of the diencephalon that activates the autonomic nervous system. (p. 21)

I

Independent Adoption: adoptions in which the birth parents select the adoptive parents and relinquish the baby to their care. (p. 366)

Infant Mortality: death of infants before one year of age. (p. 285)

Instant Calming Sequence (ICS): a relaxation technique that elicits relaxation quickly in a five-step approach. (p. 217)

Intercessory Prayer: prayers that seek divine intervention either to prevent an occurrence or to help overcome it. (p. 156)

Internal Locus of Control: the perception that one has control over events that affect one's life. (p. 130)

Interventions: activities to prevent a stressor from resulting in negative consequences. (p. 64)

In Vivo Desensitization: a form of systematic desensitization in which the stimulus is actually encountered. (p. 135)

J

Jacobsonian Relaxation: a relaxation technique involving contracting and relaxing muscle groups throughout the body; also called progressive relaxation or neuromuscular relaxation. (p. 196)

Jealousy: fear of losing one's property, such as a lover, friend, status, or power. (p. 341)

K

Koans: Unanswerable, illogical riddles used as the object of focus during meditation. (p. 170)

L

Large Intestine: part of the digestive system that receives unusable food substances from the small intestine. (p. 31)

Life Expectancy: the number of years a person is expected to live when born. (p. 286)

Lifestyle Behaviors: all of the activities in which people engage. (p. 259)

Limbic System: produces emotions, the "seat of emotions." (p. 22)

Living Will: instructions regarding the type of medical care wanted in the case of being incapacitated with a terminal disease or being in a vegetative state. (p. 396)

Locus of Control: the perception of the amount of control one has over events that affect one's life. (p. 260)

Ludic Love (Ludus): a playful, flirtatious type of love involving no long commitment. (p. 335)

M

Mandala: a geometric figure used as the object of focus during meditation. (p. 170)

Manic Love (Mania): a combination of passionate love (eros) and flirtatious playing love characterized by jealousy and irrational joy that usually does not result in a long commitment. (p. 335)

Mantra: a word that is the focus of meditation. (p. 87)

Mantra: a word used as the object of focus during meditation. (p. 170)

Massage: a relaxation technique that involves manipulating points in the body that are muscularly tense. (p. 215)

Material Reinforcement: rewarding a behavior with a tangible object. (p. 262)

Medulla Oblongata: part of the subcortex responsible for the regulation of the heartbeat and breathing. (p. 21)

Memory T and B Cells: cells left in the bloodstream and the lymphatic system to recognize and respond to future attacks to the body by the same invader. (p. 41)

Mindfulness: focusing attention on the present moment to relax. (p. 217)

Mineralocorticoids: regulate the balance between sodium and potassium. (p. 24)

Motivational Factors: variables associated with job satisfaction; includes working on stimulating tasks, being recognized for work well done, and positive relationships with work colleagues. (p. 309)

Myocardial Infarction: when a part of the heart dies because of a lack of oxygen. (p. 44)

N

Nadam: imagined sounds used as the object of focus during meditation. (p. 170)

Neuromuscular Relaxation: a relaxation technique involving contracting and relaxing muscle groups throughout the body; also called progressive relaxation or Jacobsonian relaxation. (p. 196)

Neuromuscular Relaxation: another term for progressive relaxation. (p. 5)

Nonassertive: giving up what one is entitled to, one's rights, in order not to upset another person. (p. 99)

Norepinephrine: a catecholamine secreted by the adrenal medulla. (p. 25)

Nuclear Family: a married couple and their children. (p. 355)

O

Occupational Stress: the combination of sources of stress at work, individual characteristics, and extraorganizational stressors. (p. 300)

Open Adoption: adoptions where there is contact between the birth parents and the adoptive parents. (p. 365)

Oxytocin: a hormone secreted by the pituitary gland. (p. 23)

P

Panic Disorder: a condition in which feelings of terror arise from unrealistic fear, resulting in symptoms such as feeling numb, sweaty, weak, and faint. (p. 132)

Parasympathetic Nervous System: part of the autonomic nervous system responsible for conserving energy. (p. 28)

Perceptions: a person's cognitive interpretation of events. (p. 119)

Phagocytes: a type of white blood cell whose purpose is to destroy substances foreign to the body. (p. 41)

Physical Fitness: ability to do one's work and have energy remaining for recreational activities. Consists of muscular strength, muscular endurance, cardiorespiratory endurance, flexibility, body composition, and agility. (p. 234)

Plaque: debris that clogs coronary arteries. (p. 44)

Pons: part of the subcortex responsible for regulating sleep. (p. 21)

Pranayama: a Hindu practice that involves breathing as the object of focus during meditation. (p. 170)

Preattack: synonymous with prodrome. (p. 47)

Primary Control: attempts to change a situation; similar to problem-focused coping. (p. 156)

Problem-Focused Coping: the use of activities specific to getting a task done. (p. 320)

Prodrome: the constriction phase of a migraine headache; also called preattack. (p. 47)

Progressive Relaxation: a relaxation technique involving contracting and relaxing muscle groups throughout the body; also called neuromuscular relaxation or Jacobsonian relaxation. (p. 196)

Progressive Relaxation: a relaxation technique that involves contracting and relaxing muscle groups throughout the body. (p. 5)

Pseudostressors: food substances that produce a stresslike response; also called sympathomimetics. (p. 84)

Psychogenic: a physical disease caused by emotional stress without a microorganism involved. (p. 40)

Psychoneuroimmunology: the study of the illness-causing and healing effects of the mind on the body. (p. 40)

Psychophysiological: synonymous with psychosomatic. (p. 39)

Psychosomatic: conditions that have a mind and body component. (p. 39)

Q

Quieting Reflex (QR): a six-step relaxation technique that results in relaxation in seconds. (p. 216)

R

Race: a group of people with similar physical traits, blood types, genetic patterns, and inherited characteristics. (p. 280)

Reflective Listening: paraphrasing the speaker's words and feelings; also called active listening. (p. 104)

Reflexology: a massage technique that massages a "reflex zone" in the foot in which damage to body parts is thought to be manifested. (p. 214)

Relaxation Response: a series of bodily changes that are the opposite of the stress reaction. (p. 5)

Relaxation Response: the physiological state achieved when one is relaxed; also called the trophotropic response. (p. 172)

Religion: an organized entity in which people have common beliefs and engage in common practices relevant to spiritual matters. (p. 154)

Reminder System: a means of reminding oneself to perform a particular behavior. (p. 264)

Reticular Activating System (RAS): a network of nerves that connects the mind and the body. (p. 22)

Rheumatoid Factor: a blood protein associated with rheumatoid arthritis. (p. 51)

S

Saliva: substance in the mouth that starts to break down food. (p. 31)

Secondary Control: attempts to control oneself or one's emotional reactions; similar to emotion-focused coping. (p. 156)

Self-Contracting: making a contract with oneself to change a behavior. (p. 263)

Self-Esteem: how highly one regards oneself. (p. 129)

Self-Monitoring: the process of observing and recording behavior. (p. 261)

Sexual Harassment: unwelcome sexually related actions that interfere with work performance. (p. 316)

Sexually Transmitted Infections (STIs): diseases such as syphilis, gonorrhea, chlamydia, and genital warts that are transmitted through sexual activity. (p. 339)

Shaping: changing a behavior a little bit at a time. (p. 264)

Shiatsu: acupressure massage. (p. 215)

Shyness: to be afraid of people and being worried of what strangers and powerful others think of oneself. (p. 340)

Significant Other: another person who is important to an individual. (p. 263)

Single-Parent Families: families in which the father or the mother is absent because of divorce, marital separation, out-of-wedlock pregnancy, or death. (p. 360)

Skeletal Muscles: muscles attached to bones. (p. 32)

Small Intestine: part of the digestive system into which the esophagus empties. (p. 31)

Smooth Muscles: muscles that control the contraction of internal organs. (p. 32)

Social Phobia: overwhelming fear and excessive self-consciousness in everyday situations; a chronic fear of being watched by others and not performing well. Fear of public speaking is an example. (p. 132)

Social Reinforcement: rewarding a behavior with social approval by someone else. (p. 262)

Social Support: the presence of significant others with whom to discuss stressors. (p. 89)

Somatogenic: a psychosomatic disease that results from the mind increasing the body's susceptibility to disease-causing microbes or natural degenerative processes. (p. 40)

Specific Phobia: an intense fear of a specific situation that poses little or no actual danger. Fear of elevators is an example. (p. 133)

Sphygmomanometer: an instrument used to measure blood pressure. (p. 43)

Spiritual Disease: a condition in which people are not true to their spiritual selves and are living a "life story" that is inconsistent with their beliefs and values. (p. 162)

Spiritual Health: adherence to religious doctrine; the ability to discover and express one's purpose in life; to experience love, joy, peace, and fullfillment; or to achieve and help others to achieve full potential. (p. 153)

Spirituality: a person's view of life's meaning, direction, purpose, and connectedness to other things, other people, and the past and future. (p. 154)

State Anxiety: anxiety that is either temporary in nature or specific to a particular stimulus. (p. 131)

Storgic Love (Storge): a calm, companionate type of love conceiving of a long commitment. (p. 335)

Stressor: something with the potential to cause a stress reaction. (p. 3)

Stroke: a lack of oxygen to the brain resulting from a blockage or rupture of a blood vessel; also called apoplexy. (p. 44)

Subcortex: the lower part of the brain responsible for various physiological processes necessary to stay alive. (p. 21)

Suppressor T Cells: cells whose purpose is to halt the immune response. (p. 41)

Sympathetic Nervous System: part of the autonomic nervous system responsible for expending energy. (p. 28)

Sympathomimetics: synonymous with pseudostressors. (p. 84)

Systematic Desensitization: either imagining or encountering an anxiety-provoking stimulus while practicing relaxation. (p. 134)

Systolic Blood Pressure: the pressure of the blood as it leaves the heart. (p. 43)

T

T Cells: a type of lymphocyte whose purpose is to destroy substances foreign to the body by puncturing invaded body cells and killing the cells and foreign substances. (p. 41)

T-Lymphocytes: a part of the immune system that destroys mutant cells. (p. 49)

Tai Chi: an exercise and relaxation technique developed in China that involves focused, slow, rhythmic movement. (p. 219)

Tailoring: making a behavior change program specific to the life of the individual. (p. 262)

Target Heart Rate Range: the maximal heart rate while exercising. (p. 240)

Temporomandibular (TMJ) Syndrome: the interference with the smooth functioning of the jaw. (p. 52)

Thalamus: part of the diencephalon that relays sensory impulses to the cerebral cortex. (p. 21)

Thermal Biofeedback: biofeedback that measures temperature. (p. 210)

Thyroid Gland: an endocrine gland that secretes the hormone thyroxin. (p. 26)

Thyrotropic Hormone (TTH): stimulates the thyroid gland to secrete thyroxin. (p. 23)

Thyrotropic Hormone Releasing Factor (TRF): released by hypothalamus and stimulates the pituitary gland to secrete thyrotropic hormone. (p. 23)

Trait Anxiety: a general sense of anxiety not specific to a particular stimulus. (p. 131)

Transcendental Meditation (TM): a relaxation technique involving the use of a sanskrit word as the object of focus. (p. 170)

Trophotropic Response: the physiological state achieved when one is relaxed; also called the relaxation response. (p. 172)

Type A Behavior Pattern: a cluster of behaviors associated with the development of coronary heart disease. (p. 125)

Type A: a behavior pattern associated with the development of coronary heart disease. (p. 45)

Type B Behavior Pattern: behavior pattern that is not excessively competitive, no free-floating hostility and no sense of time urgency. Also develops coronary heart disease. (p. 126)

U

Uplifts: positive events that make us feel good. (p. 90)

V

Vasopressin (ADH): a hormone secreted by the pituitary gland. (p. 23)

W

Workaholic: immersing oneself excessively in work at the expense of nonwork activities. (p. 310)

Y

Years of Potential Life Lost: the number of years between when a person is expected to live and the age of death; a measure of premature death. (p. 286)

Yoga: a set of Hindu relaxation techniques. (p. 216)

Abrams, David B., et al. "Integrating Individual and Public Health Perspectives for Treatment of Tobacco Dependence Under Managed Health Care: A Combined Stepped-Care Matching Model." *Annals of Behavioral Medicine* 18(1996): 290–304.

Adams, Patch. "Humour and Love: The Origination of Clown Therapy." *Postgraduate Medical Journal* 78(2002): 447–48.

Ader, R., D. L. Felten, and N. Cohen (ed.). *Psychoneuroimmunology,* 3rd ed. (San Diego: Academic Press, 2001).

Adler, Ronald B. *Confidence in Communication: A Guide to Assertive and Social Skills.* New York: Holt, Rinehart & Winston, 1977.

Administration on Aging. *A Profile of Older Americans: 2001.* Washington, DC: U.S. Department of Health and Human Services, 2001.

Administration on Aging. *A Profile of Older Americans: 2002.* Washington, DC: Department of Health and Human Services, 2005. http://www.aoa.gov/prof/Statistics/profile/4_pf.asp

Administration on Aging. *Elder Rights & Resources, Elder Abuse: Elder Abuse Is a Serious Problem* (Washington, DC: Department of Health and Human Services, 2005). http://www.aoa.gov/eldfam/elder_rights/elder_abuse/elder_abuse.asp

"Aerobic Instructor Burnout." *Reebok Instructor News* 1(1988): 1, 4–5.

Agardh, E. E., A. Ahlbom, T. Andersson, S. Efendic, V. Grill, J. Hallqvist, A. Norman, and C. G. Ostenson. "Work Stress and Low Sense of Coherence Is Associated with Type 2 Diabetes in Middle-Aged Swedish Women." *Diabetes Care* 26(2003): 719–24.

"Ageless Sex." *Psychology Today,* March 1989, 62.

Aiken, L. *Later Life.* Philadelphia: W. B. Saunders Co., 1978.

Ajzen, Icek. "The Theory of Planned Behavior." *Organizational Behavior and Human Decision Process* 50(1991): 179–211.

Ajzen, Icek, and Martin Fishbein. *Understanding Attitudes and Predicting Social Behavior.* Englewood Cliffs, NJ, Prentice-Hall, 1980.

Alexander, C., G. Swanson, M. Rainforth, T. Carlisle, C. Todd, and R. Oates. "Effects of the Transcendental Meditation Program on Stress Reduction, Health, and Employee Development: A Prospective Study in Two Occupational Settings." *Anxiety, Stress, Coping* 6(1993): 245–62.

Allen, A. M., D. N. Allen, and G. Sigler. "Changes in Sex-Role Stereotyping in Caldecott Medal Award Picture Books 1938–1988." *Journal of Research in Childhood Education* 7(1993): 67–73.

Allen, K., B. E. Shykoff, and J. L. Izzo, Jr. "Pet Ownership, but Not ACE Inhibitor Therapy, Blunts Home Blood Pressure Responses to Mental Stress." *Hypertension* 38(2001): 15–20.

Allen, Karen, Jim Blascovich, and Wendy B. Mendes, "Cardiovascular Reactivity and the Presence of Pets, Friends, and Spouses: The Truth About Cats and Dogs." *Psychosomatic Medicine* 64(2002): 727–39.

Allen, Karen, Jim Blascovich, Joe Tomaka, and Robert M. Kelsey. "Presence of Human Friends and Pet Dogs as Moderators of Autonomic Responses to Stress in Women." *Journal of Personality and Social Psychology* 61(1991): 582–89.

Allen, Mike. "With Adoption Push, Bush Adopts a Clinton Tactic." *Washington Post,* 24 July 2002, A2.

Allen, Roger J. *Human Stress: Its Nature and Control.* Minneapolis: Burgess, 1983.

Allen, Roger J., and David Hyde. *Investigations in Stress Control.* Minneapolis: Burgess, 1980.

Allen, W. R. "Class, Culture, and Family Organization: The Effects of Class and Race on Family Structure in Urban America." *Journal of Comparative Family Studies* 10(1979): 301–12.

Allison, J. "Respiratory Changes During Transcendental Meditation." *Lancet* no. 7651(1970): 833–34.

Aloma, J., et al., "Fertility, Family Planning and Women's Health: New Data from the 1995 Survey of Family Growth. Vital Health Statistics 23(1997).

Altschuler, E. L. "Pet-Facilitated Therapy for Posttraumatic Stress Disorder." *Annals of Clinical Psychiatry* 11(1999): 29–30.

Alzheimer's Association. *Caregiver Stress* (Chicago: Alzheimer's Association, 2005). http://www.alz.org/care/coping/caregiverstress.asp

American Academy of Family Physicians. *A Report on Lifestyles/Personal Health Care in Different Occupations.* Kansas City: American Academy of Family Physicians, 1979.

American Association of University Women. *Shortchanging Girls, Shortchanging America.* Washington, DC: American Association of University Women, 1991.

American Cancer Society. *American Cancer Society Guidelines on Diet and Cancer Prevention.* http://www.cancer.org/docroot/MED/content/MED_2_1X_American_Cancer_Society_guidelines_on_diet_and_cancer_prevention.asp

American Cancer Society. *Cancer Facts and Figures—2002.* Atlanta: American Cancer Society, 2002.

American Cancer Society. *Nutrition and Cancer Risk.* http://www.cancer.org/docroot/NWS/content/NWS_2_1X_Nutririon_and_Cancer_Risk.asp

American College Health Association. *Acquaintance Rape.* Baltimore, MD: American College Health Association, 1992.

American College of Sports Medicine. "ACSM Position Stand on the Recommended Quantity and Quality of Exercise for Developing and Maintaining Cardiorespiratory and Muscular Fitness, and Flexibility in Healthy Adults." *Medicine and Science in Sports and Exercise* 30(1998): 975–91.

———. "AHA/ACSM Joint Statement: Recommendations for Cardiovascular Screening, Staffing, and Emergency Policies at Health Fitness Facilities." *Medicine and Science in Sports and Exercise* 30(1998): 1–19.

———. *Guidelines for Exercise Testing and Prescription.* 3rd ed. Philadelphia: Lea and Febiger, 1986.

———. "Nutrition and Athletic Performance." *Medicine and Science in Sports and Exercise* 32(2000): 2130–45.

American Podiatry Association. *Jogging Advice from Your Podiatrist.* Washington, DC: American Podiatry Association, n.d.

American Psychiatric Association. *Diagnostic and Statistical Manual of Mental Disorders.* 4th ed. Washington, DC: American Psychiatric Association, 1994.

Anand, B. K., G. S. Chhina, and B. Singh. "Some Aspects of Electroencephalographic Studies in Yogis." *Electroencephalography and Clinical Neurophysiology* 13(1961): 452–56.

Anand, B. K., et al. "Studies on Shri Ramananda Yogi During His Stay in an Air-Tight Box." *Indian Journal of Medical Research* 49(1961): 82–89.

Anbar, R. D. "Stressors Associated with Dyspnea in Childhood: Patients' Insights and a Case Report." *American Journal of Clinical Hypnosis* 47(2004): 93–101.

Andersen, B. L., W. B. Farrar, D. Golden-Kreutz, L. A. Kutz, R. MacCallum, M. E. Courtney, and R. Glaser. "Stress and Immune Responses Following Surgical Treatment of Regional Breast Cancer." *Journal of the National Cancer Institute* 90(1998): 30–36.

Anderson, G. E. "College Schedule of Recent Experience." Master's thesis, North Dakota State University, 1972.

Anderson, Jack. "Whistleblower Stress." *Washington Post*, 24 March 1985, C7.

Anderson, J. R., and I. Waldon. "Behavioral and Content Components of the Structured Interview Assessment of the Type A Behavior Pattern in Women." *Journal of Behavioral Medicine* 6(1983): 123–34.

Anderson, M. B., and J. M. Williams. "A Model of Stress and Athletic Injury: Prediction and Prevention." *Journal of Sport Psychology of Injury* 10(1988): 294–306.

Anderson, N. B. "Racial Differences in Stress-Induced Cardiovascular Reactivity and Hypertension: Current Status and Substantive Issues." *Psychological Bulletin* 105(1989): 89–105.

Anderson, N. B., et al. "Race, Parental History of Hypertension, and Patterns of Cardiovascular Reactivity in Women." *Psychophysiology* 26(1989): 39–47.

Annenberg Public Policy Center. "American Public Remains Opposed to Same-Sex Marriages as They Begin in Massachusetts, Annenberg Data Show." *National Annenberg Election Survey.* http://www. annnenbergpublicpolicy center.org

Anthony, J. "Psychological Aspects of Exercise." *Clinics in Sports Medicine* 10(1991): 171–80.

Arafat, I., and W. L. Cotton. "Masturbation Practices of Males and Females." *Journal of Sex Research* 10(1974): 293–307.

Arambula, P., E. Peper, M. Kawakami, and K. H. Gibney. "The Physiological Correlates of Kundalini Yoga Meditation: A Study of a Yoga Master." *Applied Psychophysiology and Biofeedback* 26(2001): 147–53.

Argetsinger, Amy. "Colleges Brace for Baby Boom Echo, More Adults." *Washington Post*, 8 July 2000, B-5.

Arling, G. "Strain, Social Support, and Distress in Old Age." *Journal of Gerontology* 42(1987): 107–13.

Armstead, Cheryl A., K. A. Lawler, G. Gordon, J. Cross, and J. Gibbons. "Relationship of Racial Stressors to Blood Pressure Responses and Anger Expression in Black College Students." *Health Psychology* 8(1989): 541–56.

Arnow, B. A. "Why Are Empirically Supported Treatments for Bulimia Nervosa Underutilized and What Can We Do About It?" *Journal of Clinical Psychology* 55(1999): 769–79.

Astin, A. W., L. J. Sax, and J. Avalos. "Long-Term Effects of Volunteerism During the Undergraduate Years." *Review of Higher Education* 22(1999): 187–202.

———. AVMA Group Health and Life Insurance Trust. "Laugh Yourself Healthy: Studies Show Humor-Health Link." *Journal of the American Veterinary Medical Association* 226(2005):1970–71.

Bagchi, B. K., and M. A. Wengor. "Electrophysiological Correlates of Some Yogi Exercises." In *Electroencephalography, Clinical Neurophysiology and Epilepsy,* edited by L. van Bagaert and J. Radermecker. First International Congress of Neurological Sciences, vol. 3. London: Pergamon, 1959.

Baird, C. L. and L. Sands. "A Pilot Study of the Effectiveness of Guided Imagery with Progressive Muscle Relaxation to Reduce Chronic Pain and Mobility Difficulties of Osteoarthritis." *Pain Management Nursing* 5(2004): 97–104.

Baker, D. B. "The Study of Stress at Work." *Annual Review of Public Health* 6(1985): 367–81.

Ballenger, J. C., et al. "Consensus Statement on Posttraumatic Stress Disorder from the International Consensus Group on Depression and Anxiety." *Journal of Clinical Psychiatry* 61(2000): 60–66.

Band, E., and J. Weisz. "How to Feel Better When It Feels Bad: Children's Perpectives on Coping with Everyday Stress." *Developmental Psychology* 24(1988): 247–53.

Bandura, A. "Moving into Forward Gear in Health Promotion and Disease Prevention." *Proceedings of the Society of Behavioral Medicine's 16th Annual Scientific Sessions* (1995): 17, 28.

———. *Self-Efficacy: The Exercise of Control.* New York: W. H. Freeman, 1997.

Bankole, Akinrinola, Jacqueline E. Darroch, and Susheela Singh. "Determinants of Trends in Condom Use in the United States, 1988–1995." *Family Planning Perspectives* 31(1999): 264–71.

Barakat, Matthew. "Women Narrow the Salary Gap." *Washington Post*, 4 July 2000, E3.

Barefoot, J. C., W. G. Dahlstrom, and W. B. Williams. "Hostility, CHD Incidence, and Total Mortality: A 25-Year Follow-Up Study of 255 Physicians." *Psychosomatic Medicine* 45(1985): 59–64.

Barling, J., S. D. Bluen, and V. Moss. "Dimensions of Type A Behavior and Marital Dissatisfaction." *Journal of Psychology* 124(1990): 311–19.

Barling, Julian. "Interrole Conflict and Marital Functioning Amongst Employed Fathers." *Journal of Occupational Behaviour* 7(1986): 1–8.

Barnes, Patricia M., Eve Powell-Griner, Kim McFann, and Richard L. Nahin. "Complementary and Alternative Medicine Use Among Adults: United States, 2002." *Advance Data* 343(2004).

Barr, Stephen. "Elder Care Becoming Major Issue for Many Workers." *Washington Post,* 20 August 2002, B2.

Bartone, P. T. "Hardiness Protects Against War-Related Stress in Army Reserve Forces." *Consulting Psychology Journal* 51(1999): 72–83.

Bassuk, E. L., and L. Rosenberg. "The Psychosocial Characteristics of Homeless and Housed Children." *Pediatrics* 85(1990): 257–61.

Bassuk, E. L., and L. Rubin. "Homeless Children: A Neglected Population." *American Journal of Orthopsychiatry* 57(1987): 279–86.

Bassuk, E. L., R. W. Carmen, and L. F. Weinreb. *Community Care for Homeless Families: A Program Design Manual.* Newton Center, MA: The Better Homes Foundation, 1990.

Becker, Marshall H., and Lawrence W. Green. "A Family Approach to Compliance with Medical Treatment—A Selective Review of the Literature." *International Journal of Health Education* 18(1975): 1–11.

Beckett, L. A., et al. "Anlaysis of Change in Self-Reported Physical Function Among Older Persons in Four Population Studies." *American Journal of Epidemiology* 143(1996): 766–78.

Beehr, V. A., and J. E. Newman. "Job Stress, Employee Health, and Organizational Effectiveness: A Facet Analysis, Model, and Literature Review." *Personnel Psychology* 31(1978): 665–99.

Belisle, Marc, Ethel Roskies, and Jean-Michel Levesque. "Improving Adherence to Physical Activity." *Health Psychology* 6(1987): 159–72.

Benavidesa, F. G., J. Benacha, A. V. Diez-Rouxb, and C. Romana. "How Do Types of Employment Relate to Health Indicators? Findings from the Second European Survey on Working Conditions." *Journal of Epidemiology and Community Health* 54(2000): 494–501.

Benezra, E. Eliot. "Personality Factors of Individuals Who Survive Traumatic Experiences Without Professional Help," *International Journal of Stress Management* 3(1996): 147–53.

Bennett, M. P., J. M. Zeller, L. Rosenberg, and J. McCann. "The Effect of Mirthful Laughter on Stress and Natural Killer Cell Activity." *Alternative Therapeutic Health Medicine* 9(2003): 38–45.

Benson, Herbert, and Miriam Z. Klipper. *The Relaxation Response.* New York: William Morrow, 2000.

Benson, Herbert, and William Proctor. *Beyond the Relaxation Response.* East Rutherford, NJ: Berkley Publishing Group, 1985.

Benson, Herbert, and Marg Stark. *Timeless Healing: The Power and Biology of Belief.* New York: Simon & Schuster, 1996.

Benson, Herbert, and Eileen M. Stuart. *The Wellness Book: The Comprehensive Guide to Maintaining Health and Treating Stress-Related Illness.* New York: Simon & Schuster, 1992.

Berger, Richard A. *Applied Exercise Physiology.* Philadelphia: Lea and Febiger, 1982.

Bernhard, J. D., J. Kristeller, and J. Kabat-Zinn. "Effectiveness of Relaxation and Visualization Techniques as an Adjunct to Phototherapy and Photochemotherapy of Psoriasis." *Journal of the American Academy of Dermatology* 19(1988): 573–74.

Bickel, C., J. W. Ciarrocchi, W. J. Sheers, B. K. Estadt, D. A. Powell, and K. I. Pargament. "Perceived Stress, Religious Coping Styles, and Depressive Affect." *Journal of Psychology and Christianity* 17(1998): 33–42.

Biondi, D. M. "Physical Treatments for Headache: A Structured Review." *Headache* 45(2005): 738–46.

Black, A. R., J. L. Cook, V. M. Murry, and C. E. Cutrona. "Ties that Bind: Implications of Social Support for Rural, Partnered African American Women's Health Functioning." *Womens Health Issues* 15(2005): 216–23.

Blakeslee, Sandra. "Study Links Emotions to Second Heart Attack." *New York Times,* 20 September 1990, B8.

Blanchard, E. B. and M. Kim. "The Effect of the Definition of Menstrually-Related Headache on the Response to Biofeedback Treatment." *Applied Psychophysiology and Biofeedback* 30(2005): 53–63.

Blanchard, Edward, et al. "Three Studies of the Psychologic Changes in Chronic Headache Patients Associated with Biofeedback and Relaxation Therapies." *Psychosomatic Medicine* 48(1986): 73–83.

Blanchard, Edward B., and Leonard H. Epstein. *A Biofeedback Primer.* Reading, MA: Addison-Wesley, 1978.

Blanchard, Edward B., et al. "Two, Three, and Four Year Follow-Up on the Self-Regulatory Treatment of Chronic Headache." *Journal of Consulting and Clinical Psychology* 55(1987): 257–59.

Bloom, B., and D. Dawson, "Family Structure and Child Health." *American Journal of Public Health* 81(1991): 1526–27.

Bluen, S. D., J. Barling, and W. Burns. "Predicting Sales Performance, Job Satisfaction, and Depression by Using the Achievement Strivings and Impatience-Irritability Dimensions of Type A Behavior." *Journal of Applied Psychology* 75(1990): 212–16.

Blumenstein, B., I. Breslav, M. Bar-Eli, G. Tenenbaum, and Y. Weinstein. "Regulation of Mental States and Biofeedback Techniques: Effects on Breathing Pattern." *Biofeedback Self Regulation* 20(1995): 155–67.

Blumenthal, J. A., M. M. Burg, J. Barefoot, R. B. Williams, T. Haney, and G. Zimet. "Social Support, Type A Behavior, and Coronary Artery Disease." *Psychosomatic Research* 49(1987): 331–40.

Bobak, M., and M. Marmot. "East-West Mortality Divide and Its Potential Explanations: Proposed Research Agenda." *British Medical Journal* 312(1996): 421–25.

Boller, Jon D., and Raymond P. Flom. "Behavioral Treatment of Persistent Post-traumatic Startle Response." *Journal of Behavior Therapy and Experimental Psychiatry* 12(1981): 321–24.

Bond, J. T., E. Galinsky, and J. E. Swanberg. *The 1997 National Study of the Changing Workforce.* New York: Families and Work Institute, 1998.

Border, Laura L. B., and Nancy Van Note Chism, "Teaching for Diversity," *New Directions for Teaching and Learning* 49(1992): 12.

Boudarene, M., J. J. Legros, and M. Timsit-Berthier. "Study of the Stress Response: Role of Anxiety, Cortisol and DHEAs." *Encephale* 28(2002): 139–46.

Bourdon, K. H., J. H. Boyd, D. S. Rae, et al. "Gender Differences in Phobias: Results of the ECA Community Survey." *Journal of Anxiety Disorders* 2(1988): 227–41.

Boyd, J. H., D. S. Rae, J. W. Thompson, et al. "Phobia: Prevalence and Risk Factors." *Social Psychiatry and Psychiatric Epidemiology* 25(1990): 314–23.

Boyle, G. J., and J. M. Joss-Reid. "Relationship of Humor to Health: A Psychometric Investigation." *British Journal of Health Psychology* 9(2004): 51–66.

Bramston, P., H. Chipuer, and G. Pretty. "Conceptual Principles of Quality of Life: An Empirical Exploration." *Journal of Intellectual Disability Research* 49(2005): 728–33.

Braverman, Eric R. *The Amazing Way to Reverse Heart Disease: Beyond the Hypertension Hype: Why Drugs are Not the Answer.* North Bergen, NJ: Basic Health Publications, 2004.

Braza, Jerry F. *Moment by Moment.* Salt Lake City: Healing Resources, 1993.

Brody, Jane E. "Effects of Beauty Found to Run Surprisingly Deep." *New York Times,* 1 September 1981, C1–C3.

Brody, L. "Come to Your Senses." *Shape,* October 1993, 84–89.

Brosse, Therese. "A Psychophysiological Study of Yoga." *Main Currents in Modern Thought* 4(1946): 77–84.

Brouha, Lucien. "The Step Test: A Simple Method of Testing the Physical Fitness of Boys." *Research Quarterly* 14(1943): 23.

Brown, Barbara B. "Recognition Aspects of Consciousness Through Association with EEG Alpha Activity Represented by a Light Signal." *Psychophysiology* 6(1970): 442–52.

———. *Stress and the Art of Biofeedback.* New York: Harper & Row, 1977.

Brown, R. P. and P. L. Gerbarg. "Sudarshan Kriya Yogic Breathing in the Treatment of Stress, Anxiety, and Depression: Part II—Clinical Applications and Guidelines." *Journal of Alternative and Complementary Medicine* 11(2005): 711–17.

Brownell, K. D., et al. "The Effect of Couples Training and Partner Cooperativeness in the Behavior Treatment of Obesity." *Behavior Research Therapy* 16(1978): 323–33.

Bruess, Clint E., and Jerrold S. Greenberg. *Sexuality Education: Theory and Practice.* New York: Macmillan, 1988.

Brunner, E., G. Davey Smith, M. Marmot, R. Canner, M. Bekinska, and J. O'Brien. "Childhood Social Circumstances and Psychosocial and Behavioural Factors as Determinants of Plasma Fibrinogen." *Lancet* 347(1996): 1008–13.

Brush, Stephen G. "Neither Reasonable nor Fair: SAT Discriminates Against Women, Rewards Coaching." *The Faculty Voice* 4(May–June 1990): 4.

Bryant, Anne L. "Hostile Hallways: The AAUW Survey on Sexual Harassment in America's Schools." *Journal of School Health* 63(1993): 355–57.

Brzowsky, Sara. "How to Be Stress-Resilient." *Parade,* October 12, 2003, 10–12.

Buckworth, Rod, and Janet Dishman. *Exercise Psychology.* Champaign, IL: Human Kinetics, 2000.

Budzynski, Thomas H., et al. "EMG Biofeedback and Tension Headache: A Controlled Outcome Study." *Psychosomatic Medicine* 35(1973): 484–96.

Buhr, T. A., D. B. Chaffin, and B. J. Martin. "EMG Biofeedback as a Tool for Simulating the Effects of Specific Leg Muscle Weakness on a Lifting Task." *Journal of Occupational Rehabilitation* 9(1999): 247–66.

Bureau of the Census. *Poverty in the United States: 1991.* Washington, DC: U.S. Department of Commerce, September 1992, Series P-60, no. 181.

Burke, R. J. "Work and Non-Work Stressors and Well-Being Among Police Officers: The Role of Coping." *Anxiety, Stress and Coping* 14(1998): 1–18.

Burke, R. J. "Workaholism in Organizations: Measurement Validation and Replication." *International Journal of Stress Management* 6(1999): 45–55.

Burke, R. J., and M. P. Leiter. "Contemporary Organizational Realities and Professional Efficacy: Downsizing, Reorganization, and Transition." In *Coping, Health and Organizations,* edited by P. Deue, M. P. Leiter, and T. Cox. London: Taylor and Francis, 2000, 237–56.

Burke, R. J., and D. L. Nelson. "Mergers and Acquisitions, Downsizing, and Privatization: A North American Perspective." In *The New Organizational Reality,* edited by M. K. Gowing, J. D. Kraft, and J. C. Quick. Washington, DC: American Psychological Association, 1998, 21–54.

Burke, Ronald J. "Beliefs and Fears Underlying Type A Behavior: What Makes Sammy Run So Fast and Aggressively?" *Journal of Human Stress* 10(1984): 174–82.

Burks, Nancy, and Barclay Martin. "Everyday Problems and Life Change Events: Ongoing Versus Acute Sources of Stress." *Journal of Human Stress* 11(1985): 27–35.

Byrd, Robert. "Job-Stress Illness Up, Report Says; More Injury Claims Cite Mental Anxiety." *Washington Post,* 3 October 1986, F2.

Cady, Steven H., and Gwen E. Jones. "Massage Therapy as a Workplace Intervention for Reduction of Stress." *Perceptual and Motor Skills* 84(1997): 157–58.

Cairns, D., and J. A. Pasino. "Comparison of Verbal Reinforcement and Feedback in the Operant Treatment of Disability due to Chronic Low Back Pain." *Behavior Therapy* 8(1977): 621–30.

Callon, Eleanor W., et al. "The Effect of Muscle Contraction Headache Chronicity on Frontal EMG." *Headache* 26(1986): 356–59.

Cannon, Walter B. *The Wisdom of the Body.* New York: W. W. Norton, 1932.

Caplan, G. *Support Systems and Community Mental Health.* New York: Behavioral Publications, 1974.

Cappelleri, J. C., J. Eckenrode, and J. L. Powers. "The Epidemiology of Child Abuse: Findings from the Second National Incidence and Prevalence Study of Child Abuse and Neglect." *American Journal of Public Health* 83(1993): 1622–24.

"Caregiving." *AARP Webplace.* Washington, DC: American Association of Retired Persons, 1995.

Carlisle, Dafoni. "A Pet for Life." *Pets & Health,* 2004. http://www.hda-online. org.uk/hdt/0802/pets.html

Carlson, C., P. Bacaseta, and D. Simanton. "A Controlled Evaluation of Devotional Meditation and Progressive Relaxation." *Journal of Psychology and Theology* 16(1988): 362–68.

Carkcl, M. R. "Grades and Racism Linked in Report." *The Diamondback,* 11 October 1993, 1, 7.

Carrington, J. *The Book of Meditation.* Boston: Element, 1998.

Carruthers, Malcomb. "Autogenic Training." *Journal of Psychosomatic Research* 23(1979): 437–40.

Case, R. B., et al. "Type A Behavior and Survival After Acute Myocardial Infarction." *New England Journal of Medicine* 312(1985): 737–41.

Cauthen, N. R., and C. A. Prymak. "Meditation Versus Relaxation: An Examination of the Physiological Effects with Transcendental Meditation." *Journal of Consulting and Clinical Psychology* 45(1977): 496–97.

CCH Inco. *2004 CCH Unscheduled Absence Survey.* Riverside, CA: CCH Inco., 2004.

Celso, B. G., D. J. Ebener, and E. J. Burkhead. "Humor Coping, Health Status, and Life Satisfaction Among Older Adults Residing in Assisted Living Facilities." *Aging Mental Health* 7(2003): 438–45.

Center on Child Abuse Prevention Research. *Current Trends in Child Abuse Reporting and Fatalities: The Results of the 1997 Annual 50 State Survey.* Chicago: National Committee to Prevent Child Abuse, 1998.

Centers for Disease Control. "Weapon-Carrying Among High School Students—United States, 1990." *MMWR* 40(1991): 681–84.

Centers for Disease Control and Prevention. "Cases of HIV Infection and AIDS in the United States, by Race/Ethnicity, 1998–2002." *HIV/AIDS Surveillance Supplemental Report* 10(2002): 12.

———. "AIDS Cases, Deaths, and Persons Living with AIDS by Year, 1985–2002—United States." *HIV/AIDS Surveillance Report,* 14(2002): 16.

Centers for Disease Control and Prevention. *HIV/AIDS Surveillance Report, 2003.* 12, 2005.

Centers for Disease Control and Prevention. "Sexual Behavior and Selected Health Measures: Men and Women 15–44 Years of Age, United States, 2002." *Advance Data* 352(2005): 21–22, 25.

Cervantes, R. C., A. M. Padilla, and V. N. Salgado de Snyder. "The Hispanic Stress Inventory: A Culturally Relevant Approach to Psychosocial Assessment." *Psychosocial Assessment* 3(1991): 438–47.

Cha, Ariana Eunjung. "ISO Romance? Online Matchmakers Put Love to the Test." *Washington Post,* 4 May 2003, pp. A1, A14–A15.

Chadwick, J., et al. "Psychological Job Stress and Coronary Heart Disease." NIOSH report under contract no. CDC-99-74-42, National Institute for Occupational Safety and Health, 1979.

Chang, Elizabeth. "Absence-Minded." *Washington Post,* 9 April 2000, 9.

Chapman, Larry S. "Developing a Useful Perspective on Spiritual Health: Well-Being, Spiritual Potential, and the Search for Meaning," *American Journal of Health Promotion,* Winter 1987, 31–39.

Chapman, Stanley L. "A Review and Clinical Perspective on the Use of EMG and Thermal Biofeedback for Chronic Headaches." *Pain* 27(1986): 1–43.

Charlesworth, Edward A., and Ronald G. Nathan. *Stress Management: A Comprehensive Guide to Wellness.* Houston: Biobehavioral Publishers, 1982.

Charlesworth, Georgina. "Older Adults Who Reported Strain When Caring for a Spouse with Disabilities Had Increased Mortality." *Evidence Based Medicine* 5(2000): 128.

Chase, Anne. "Police Psychologist: Post Remains Vacant for 9 Months Despite Growing Stress in Department." *Prince George's Journal,* 14 March 1980, A4.

Chen, W. W. "Enhancement of Health Locus of Control Through Biofeedback." *Perceptual Motor Skills* 80(1995): 466.

Cherlin, A. "Remarriage as an Incomplete Institution." *American Journal of Sociology* 84(1978): 634.

Cheung, Y. L., Molassiotis, A., and Chang, A. M. "The Effect of Progressive Muscle Relaxation Training on Anxiety and Quality of Life After Stoma Surgery in Colorectal Cancer Patients." *Psychooncology* 12(2003): 254–66.

Chickering, A., and R. Havighurst. "The Life Cycle." In *The Modern American College* edited by A. Chickering et al. San Francisco: Jossey-Bass, 1988.

Children's Bureau, Administration for Children and Families. *Child Maltreatment 1996: Reports from the States to the National Child Abuse and Neglect Data System.* Washington, DC: Department of Health and Human Services, 1998.

Children's Bureau, Administration on Children, Youth, and Families, National Clearinghouse on Child Abuse and Neglect Information. "Summary of Key Findings from Calendar Year 2000." www.calib. com/nccanch/pubs/factsheets/ canstats.cfm, April 2002.

Choudhury, Bikram. *Bikram's Beginning Yoga Class.* Los Angeles: J. P. Tarcher, 1978.

Christie, M. D. and K. S. Schultz. "Gender Differences on Coping with Job Stress and Organizational Outcomes." *Work Stress* 12(1998): 351–61.

Christie, W. and C. Moore. "The Impact of Humor on Patients with Cancer." *Clinical Journal of Oncological Nursing* 9(2005): 211–18.

Clarke, D. "Motivational Differences Between Slot Machine and Lottery Players." *Psychological Reports* 96(2005): 843–48.

Clarke, D. and R. Singh. "Life Events, Stress Appraisals, and Hospital Doctors' Mental Health." *New Zealand Medical Journal* 117(2004): U1121.

Clark, N., E. Arnold, and E. Foulds. "Serum Urate and Cholesterol Levels in Air Force Academy Cadets." *Aviation and Space Environmental Medicine* 46(1975): 1044–48.

Clays, Els, Dirk, De Bacquer, Joris, Delanghe, France, Kittel, Lieve, Van Renterghem, and Guy. De Backer. "Associations Between Dimensions of Job Stress and Biomarkers of Inflammation and Infection." *Journal of Occupational & Environmental Medicine* 47(2005): 878–83.

Cleveland Clinic Heart Center. "Angry Young Men Become Angry Older Men—With Heart Attacks." *Health Extra* (November 2002). http://www.clevelandclinic.org/heartcenter/pub/guide/prevention/ stress/anger.htm

Cobb, Kevin. "Managing Your Mileage—Are You Feeling Groovy or Burning Out?" *American Health,* October 1989, 78–84.

Cobb, S., and R. M. Rose. "Hypertension, Peptic Ulcer, and Diabetes in Air Traffic Controllers." *Journal of the American Medical Association* 224(1973): 489–92.

Cohen, S., J. E. Schwartz, E. J. Bromet, and D. K. Parkinson. "Mental Health, Stress, and Poor Behaviours in Two Community Samples." *Preventive Medicine* 20(1991): 306–15.

Cohen, Sheldon. "Sound Effects on Behavior." *Psychology Today,* October 1981, 38–49.

Colburn, D., and A. Trafford. "Guns at Home: Doctors Target Growing Epidemic." *Washington Post Health,* 12 October 1993, 12–15.

Colburn, Don. "When Violence Begins at Home." *Washington Post Health,* 15 March 1994, 7.

College Board. "2003–2004 College Costs." *CollegeBoard.com for Students,* 2004. http://www.collegeboard.com

Collet, L. "MMPI and Headache: A Special Focus on Differential Diagnosis, Prediction of Treatment Outcome and Patient: Treatment Matching." *Pain* 29(1987): 267–68.

Collet, L., J. Cottraux, and C. Juenet. "GSR Feedback and Schultz Relaxation in Tension Headaches: A Comparative Study. *Pain* 25(1986): 205–13.

Colling, K. B. "Caregiver Interventions for Passive Behaviors in Dementia: Links to the NDB Model." *Aging and Mental Health* 8(2004): 117–25.

Comfort, Alex. *A Good Age.* New York: Crown Publishers, 1976.

The Commonwealth Fund, *A Comparative Survey of Minority Health,* New York: The commonwealth Fund. *www.cmwf.org:80/ minhltm. html.*

"Communication/Cultural Barriers May Affect Receipt of Cardiovascular Procedures Among Hispanics." *Research Activities* 261(2002): 3–4.

Connolly, C. "Report Says Minorities Get Lower-Quality Health Care." *Washington Post,* March 21, 2002, A2.

Consumer Action. *Budgeting and Planning: Building a Better Future.* www.consumer-action.org/Library/English/Money_Mgt/MM-I-1_EN/MM-I-01_EN.html.

Consumers Union. *Holiday Shopping and Credit Tips.* www.consumersunion. org/finance/ holiday2wc1198.html

Coon, Vicki S., Jeffrey C. Valentine, and Harris M. Cooper. "Interventions to Increase Physical Activity Among Aging Adults." *Annals of Behavioral Medicine* 24(2002): 190–200.

Cooper, Kenneth H. *The Aerobics Way: New Data on the World's Most Popular Exercise Program.* New York: M. Evans, 1977.

Coopersmith, Stanley. *The Antecedents of Self-Esteem.* San Francisco: W. H. Freeman, 1967.

"Coping with Stress." *Washington Post Health,* 8 September 1998, 5.

Corbett, Ann. "Too Stressed for Sex: The Decline and Fall of Married Love." *Washington Post,* 8 October 1985, B5.

Corbin, Charles B., and Ruth Lindsey. *Concepts of Physical Fitness with Laboratories.* 6th ed. Dubuque, IA: Wm. C. Brown Communications, 1988.

Cory, Christopher T. "The Stress-Ridden Inspection Suite and Other Jittery Jobs." *Psychology Today,* January 1979, 13–14.

Costa A. J., S. Labuda Schrop, G. McCord, and C. Ritter. "Depression in Family Medicine Faculty." *Family Medicine* 37(2005): 271–75.

Cotman, C. W., and C. Engesser, "Exercise Enhances and Protects Brain Function." *Exercise and Sports Sciences Reviews* 30(2002): 75–79.

Counsell, C. M., J. Abram, and M. Gilbert. "Animal Assisted Therapy and the Individual with Spinal Cord Injury." *SCI Nursing* 14(1997): 52–55.

Courneya, Kerry S., Paul A. Estabrooks, and Claudio R. Nigg. "A Simple Reinforcement Strategy for Increasing Attendance at a Fitness Facility." *Health Education and Health Behavior* 2(1997): 708–15.

Cowing, Patricia S. "Reducing Motion Sickness: A Comparison of Autogenic-Feedback Training and an Alternative Cognitive Task." *Aviation, Space, and Environmental Medicine* 53(1982): 449–53.

Coyle, C. T., and R. D. Enright. "Forgiveness Intervention with Post-Abortion Men." *Journal of Consulting and Clinical Psychology* 65(1998): 1042–46.

Crittendon, Ann. "We 'Liberated' Mothers Aren't." *Washington Post,* 5 February 1984, D4.

Cunningham, W. E., et al. "Participation in Research and Access to Experimental Treatments for HIV-Infected Patients." *Research Activities* 261(2002): 5.

Curtis, John D., and Richard A. Detert. *How to Relax: A Holistic Approach to Stress Management.* Palo Alto, CA: Mayfield, 1981.

Curtis, John D., Richard A. Detert, Jay Schindler, and Kip Zirkel. *Teaching Stress Management and Relaxation Skills: An Instructor's Guide.* La Crosse, WI: Coulee Press, 1985.

Curtis, J. R., and D. L. Patrick. "Race and Survival Time with AIDS: A Synthesis of the Literature." *American Journal of Public Health* 83(1993): 1425–28.

Danskin, David G., and Mark A. Crow. *Biofeedback: An Introduction and Guide.* Palo Alto, CA: Mayfield, 1981.

Dato, Robert. "Letter to the Editor: The Law of Stress." *International Journal of Stress Management* 3(1996): 181–82.

Davidson, J. R., V. M. Payne, K. M. Connor, E. B. Foa, B. O. Rothbaum, M. A. Hertzberg, and R. H. Weisler. "Trauma, Resilience and Saliostasis: Effects of Treatment in Post-Traumatic Stress Disorder." *International Clinical Psychopharmacology* 20(2005): 43–48.

Davidson, M. J., and C. L. Cooper. *Shattering the Glass Ceiling: The Woman Manager.* London: Paul Chapman, 1992.

Davidson, M. J., and S. Fielden, "Stress and the Working Woman." In *Handbook of Gender and Work,* edited by G. N. Powell. Thousand Oaks, CA: Sage, 1999.

Davis, G. C. "Post Traumatic Stress Disorder in Victims of Civilian Trauma and Criminal Violence," *Psychiatric Clinics of North America* 17(1994): 289–99.

Davis, Martha, Matthew McKay, and Elizabeth Robbins Eshelman. *The Relaxation and Stress Reduction Workbook.* Richmond, CA: New Harbinger Publications, 1980.

Davis, S. K., and V. Chavez. "Hispanic Househusbands." *Hispanic Journal of Behavioral Sciences* 7(1985): 317–32.

Deahl, M., M. Srinivasan, N. Jones, J. Thomas, C. Neblett, and A. Jolly. "Preventing Psychological Trauma in Soldiers: The Role of Operational Stress Training and Psychological Debriefing." *British Journal of Medical Psychology* 73(2000): 77–85.

Dean, Dwight. "Alienation: Its Meaning and Measurement." *American Sociological Review* 26(1961): 753–58.

Dean, R. A. "Humor and Laughter in Palliative Care." *Journal of Palliative Care* 13(1997): 34–39.

DeLamater, John, and Patricia MacCorquodale. *Premarital Sexuality: Attitudes, Relationships, Behavior.* Madison: University of Wisconsin Press, 1979.

DeLongis, Anita, et al. "Relationship of Daily Hassles, Uplifts, and Major Life Events to Health Status." *Health Psychology* 1(1982): 119–36.

Dennis, Dixie L., and Brent G. Dennis. "Spirituality@Work.Health." *American Journal of Health Education* 34(2003): 297–301.

de Vries, Aiko P., et al. "Looking Beyond the Physical Injury: Posttraumatic Stress Disorder in Children and Parents After Pediatric Traffic Injury." *Pediatrics* 104(1999): 1293–99.

Devineni, T., and E. B. Blanchard. "A Randomized Controlled Trial of an Internet-Based Treatment for Chronic Headache." *Behaviour Research and Therapy* 43(2005): 277–92.

DiCara, L. V., and Neal E. Miller. "Instrumental Learning of Vasomotor Responses by Rats: Learning to Respond Differentially in the Two Ears." *Science* 159(1968): 1485.

Dillbeck, M. C. "The Effect of the Transcendental Meditation Technique on Anxiety Levels." *Journal of Clinical Psychology* 33(1977): 1076–78.

Dillon, K. M., F. Minchoff, and K. H. Baker. "Positive Emotional States and Enhancement of the Immune System." *International Journal of Psychiatry in Medicine* 15(1985): 13–18.

Dinoff, M., N. C. Rickard, and J. Colwick. "Weight Reduction Through Successive Contracts." *American Journal of Orthopsychiatry* 42(1972): 110–13.

Dintiman, George B., and Jerrold S. Greenberg. *Health Through Discovery.* 4th ed. New York: Random House, 1989.

Dintiman, George B., et al. *Discovering Lifetime Fitness: Concepts of Exercise and Weight Control.* St. Paul: West, 1984.

Dion, Maureen. "A Study of the Effects of Progressive Relaxation Training on Changes in Self-Concepts in Low Self-Concept College Students." *Dissertation Abstracts International* 37(1977): 4860.

Doan, T., T. Plante, G. Manuel, and M. DiGregorio. "The Influence of Aerobic Exercise and Relaxation Training on Coping with Test-Taking Anxiety." *Anxiety, Stress, and Coping* 8(1995): 101–11.

Donatelle, Rebecca J., and Lorraine G. Davis. *Access to Health.* 6th ed. Boston: Allyn & Bacon, 2000, 567.

Donatelle, Roberta J., and M. J. Hawkins. "Employee Stress Claims: Increasing Implications for Health Promotion Programming." *American Journal of Health Promotion* 3(1989): 19–25.

Dorey, G., M. J. Speakman, R. C. Feneley, A. Swinkels, and C. D. Dunn. "Pelvic Floor Exercises for Erectile Dysfunction." *BJU International* 96(2005): 595–97.

Dowd, J. J., and V. L. Bengston, "Aging in Minority Populations: An Examination of the Double Jeopardy Hypothesis." In *Aging, the Individual, and Society: Readings in Social Gerontology,* edited by J. S. Quadargo. New York: St. Martin's Press, 1984.

Downing, G. *Massage Book.* Berkeley, CA: Book Works Publishing Co., 1972. Distributed by Random House, Inc.

"The Dream Is Danger, Roper Starch Worldwide Inc. Report." *Wall Street Journal,* 29 November 1994, B1.

Drehle, David Von. "Gay Marriage Is a Right, Massachusetts Court Rules." *Washington Post,* 19 November 2003, A1.

Dreyfuss, F., and J. Czaczkes. "Blood Cholesterol and Uric Acid of Healthy Medical Students Under Stress of an Examination." *Archives of Internal Medicine* 103(1959): 708–11.

Duhamel, Meredith. "Rising Above Stress: Staying Hardy." *Medical Selfcare,* January/February 1989, 26–29, 59.

Dunbar, Flanders. *Psychosomatic Diagnosis.* New York: Harper, 1943.

Dunn, T. "The Practice and Spirit of T'ai Chi Chuan." *Yoga Journal* (1987): 62–68.

Dustmann, R. E., R. Emmerson, and D. Shearer. "Physical Activity, Age, and Cognitive-Neuropsychological Function," *Journal of Aging and Physical Activity* 2(1994): 143–181.

Eaton, W. W., J. C. Anthony, W. Mandel, and R. Garrison. "Occupations and the Prevalence of Major Depressive Disorder." *Journal of Occupational Medicine* 32(1990): 1079–86.

Edelman, Marion Wright. *The Measure of Our Success: A Letter to My Children and Yours.* Boston: Beacon Press, 1992.

Editors of the *Ladies' Home Journal* and the Harvard School of Public Health's Center for Communication. "Your Body, Your Health." *Ladies' Home Journal,* February 1988, 91–93, 134–36.

Egdahl, R., and D. Walsh. *Mental Wellness Programs for Employees.* New York: Springer-Verlag, 1980.

Eldridge, William, Stanley Blostein, and Virginia Richardson. "A Multidimensional Model for Assessing Factors Associated with Burnout in Human Service Organizations." *Public Personnel Management* 12(1983): 315.

Elias, Marilyn. "Type A's: Like Father, like Son." *USA Today,* 7 August 1985, D1.

Elkins, G., M. H. Rajab, and J. Marcus. "Complementary and Alternative Medicine Use by Psychiatric Inpatients." *Psychological Reports* 96(2005): 163–66.

Ellis, Albert and Catharine MacLaren. *Rational Emotive Behavior Therapy: A Therapist's Guide* (Atascadero, CA: Impact Publishers, 2004).

Ellis, Albert, and Robert Harper. *A New Guide to Rational Living.* Englewood Cliffs, NJ: Prentice-Hall, 1979.

Engel, George L. "Studies of Ulcerative Colitis. III. The Nature of the Psychological Processes." *American Journal of Medicine,* August 1955.

Enright, R. D., and the Human Development Study Group. "Counseling Within the Forgiveness Triad: On Forgiving, Receiving Forgiveness, and Self-Forgiveness." *Counseling and Values* 40(1996): 107–26.

Epstein, M. *Thoughts Without a Thinker.* New York: HarperCollins, 1995.

Erdman, L. "Laughter Therapy for Patients with Cancer." *Oncology Nursing Forum* 18(1991): 1359–63.

Erikson, Erik H. *Childhood and Society.* New York: W. W. Norton, 1963.

Etnier, J. L., W. Salazar, D. M. Landers, S. J. Pertruzello, M. Han, and P. Nowell. "The Influence of Physical Fitness and Exercise Upon Cognitive Functioning: A Meta-Analysis," *Journal of Sport and Exercise Psychology* 19(1997): 249–77.

Everly, George S., and Daniel A. Girdano. *The Stress Mess Solution: The Causes of Stress on the Job.* Bowie, MD: Robert J. Brady, 1980.

Everson, Susan A., George A. Kaplan, Riitta Salonen, and Jukka T. Salonen. "Does Low Socioeconomic Status Potentiate the Effects of Heightened Cardiovascular Responses to Stress on the Progression of Carotid Atherosclerosis?" *American Journal of Public Health* 88(1998): 389–94.

Exline, J., A. M. Yali, and M. Lobel. "When God Disappoints: Difficulty Forgiving God and Its Role in Negative Emotion." *Journal of Health Psychology* 4(1999): 365–79.

Eysenck, Hans J. "Health's Character." *Psychology Today,* December 1988, 28–35.

Federal Bureau of Investigation. "Crime in the United States." *Uniform Crime Reports,* 2002.

———. "The Structure of Family Violence: An Analysis of Selected Incidents." *Uniform Crime Reports 2000.* www.fbi.gov/ucr/nibrs/famvio21.pdf.

Federal Bureau of Investigation. *Hate Crime Statistics, 2003.* Washington, DC: U.S. Department of Justice, 2004.

Federal Interagency Forum on Child and Family Statistics. *America's Children: Key National Indicators of Well-Being.* Washington, DC: Federal Interagency Forum on Child and Family Statistics, 1997.

Feiner, R. D., S. S. Farber, and J. Primavera. "Transitions in Stressful Life Events: A Model of Primary Prevention." In *Prevention Psychology: Theory, Research and Practice,* edited by R. D. Feiner, L. A. Jason, J. N. Moritsugu, and S. S. Farber. New York: Plenum, 1983.

Feingold, C., and L. J. Perlich. "Teaching Critical Thinking Through a Health-Contract," *Nurse Education* 24 (1999): 42–44.

Feist, Jess, and Linda Brannon. *Health Psychology: An Introduction to Behavior and Health.* Belmont, CA: Wadsworth, 1988.

Feldman, Robert H. L. "The Assessment and Enhancement of Health Compliance in the Workplace." In *Occupational Health Promotion: Health Behavior in the Workplace,* edited by George S. Everly and Robert H. L. Feldman. New York: John Wiley & Sons, 1985, 33–46.

Fenell, D. L. "Characteristics of Long-Term First Marriages." *Journal of Mental Health Counseling* 15(1993): 446–60.

Fennell, R. "Evaluating the Effectiveness of a Credit Semester Course on AIDS Among College Students." *Journal of School Health* 22(1991): 35–41.

Fenster, L., et al. "Psychological Stress in the Workplace and Spontaneous Abortion." *American Journal of Epidemiology* 142(1995): 1176–83.

Ferguson, P., and J. Gowan. "TM—Some Preliminary Findings." *Journal of Humanistic Psychology* 16(1977): 51–60.

Feuerstein, Georg, Larry Payne, and Lilias Folan. *Yoga for Dummies.* Foster City, CA: IDG Books Worldwide, 1999.

Feynman, R. P. *Surely You're Joking, Mr. Feynman!: Adventures of a Curious Character.* New York: W. W. Norton, 1985.

Field, Tiffany M. "Massage Therapy Effects." *American Psychologist* 53(1998): 1270–81.

Field, Tiffany, Maria Hernandez-Reif, and Olga Quintino. "Elder Retired Volunteers Benefit from Giving Massage Therapy to Infants." *Journal of Applied Gerontology* 17(1998): 229–39.

Field, Tiffany, Olga Quintino, and Maria Hernandez-Reif. "Adolescents with Attention Deficit Hyperactivity Disorder Benefit from Massage Therapy." *Adolescence* 33(1998): 103–8.

Field, Tiffany, Saul Schanberg, and Cynthia Kuhn. "Bulimic Adolescents Benefit from Massage Therapy." *Adolescence* 33(1998): 555–63.

Fier, B. "Recession Is Causing Dire Illness." *Moneysworth,* 23 June 1975.

Finger, Alan, and Al Bingham. *Yoga Zone Introduction to Yoga: A Beginner's Guide to Health, Fitness, and Relaxation.* Three Rivers, CA: Three Rivers Press, 2000.

Fink, N. "Jewish Meditation: An Emerging Spiritual Practice." *Tikkun* 13(1998): 60–61.

Fisher, S. *Stress in Academic Life.* Buckingham, England: Open University Press, 1994.

Fisher, S., and B. Hood. "The Stress of the Transition to University: A Longitudinal Study of Vulnerability to Psychological Disturbance and Homesickness." *British Journal of Psychology* 78(1987): 425–41.

Fishman, Ricky. "Headache Cures." *Medical Selfcare,* November/December 1989, 24–29, 64.

Florian, V., M. Mikulincer, and O. Taubman. "Does Hardiness Contribute to Mental Health During a Stressful Real-Life Situation? The Roles of Appraisal and Coping." *Journal of Personality and Social Psychology* 68(1995): 687–95.

Flynn, L. "PC Software Turns Bosses into Snoops." *Washington Post,* 28 June 1993, 21, 28.

Fontana, Alan, Linda Spoonster Schwartz, and Robert Rosenheck. "Posttraumatic Stress Disorder Among Female Vietnam Veterans: A Causal Model of Epidemiology." *American Journal of Public Health* 87(1997): 169–75.

Forman, Jeffrey W., and Dave Myers. *The Personal Stress Reduction Program.* Englewood Cliffs, NJ: Prentice Hall, 1987.

Forney, Deanna S., Fran Wallace-Schutzman, and T. Thorn Wiggers. "Burnout Among Career Development Professionals: Preliminary Findings and Implications." *Personnel and Guidance Journal* 60(1982): 435–39.

Frankenhauser, M. "The Psychophysiology of Workload, Stress, and Health: Comparison Between the Sexes." *Annals of Behavioral Medicine* 13(1991): 197–204.

Frankenhauser, M., and B. Gardell. "Underload and Overload in Working Life: Outline of a Multidisciplinary Approach." *Journal of Human Stress* 2(1976): 35–46.

Franklin, Neshama. "Massage—a Happy Medium." *Medical Selfcare,* September/October 1989, 71–73.

Frazier, T. W. "Avoidance Conditioning of Heart Rate in Humans." *Psychophysiology* 3(1966): 188–202.

Freedman, Vicki A., and Linda G. Martin. "Understanding Trends in Functional Limitations Among Older Americans." *American Journal of Public Health* 88(1998): 1457–62.

French, J. R. P., and R. D. Caplan. "Psychosocial Factors in Coronary Heart Disease." *Industrial Medicine* 39(1970): 383–97.

Freudenberger, Herbert J., and Gail North. *Women's Burnout.* New York: Doubleday & Co., 1985.

Friedman, Howard S., and Stephanie Booth-Kewley. "The 'Disease-Prone Personality': A Meta-Analytic View of the Construct." *American Psychologist* 42(1987): 539–55.

Friedman, L. C., A. E. Brown, C. Romero, M. F. Dulay, L. E. Peterson, P. Wehrma, D. J. Whisnand, L. Laufman, and J. Lomax. "Depressed Mood and Social Support as Predictors of Quality of Life in Women Receiving Home Health Care." *Quality of Life Research* 14(2005): 1925–29.

Friedman, Meyer, A. E. Brown, and Ray Rosenman. "Voice Analysis Test for Detection of Behavior Pattern: Responses of Normal Men and Coronary Patients." *Journal of the American Medical Association* 208(1969): 828–36.

Friedman, Meyer, and Ray H. Rosenman. "Association of Specific Overt Behavior Pattern with Blood and Cardiovascular Findings: Blood Clotting Time, Incidence of Arcus Senilis, and Clinical Coronary Artery Disease." *Journal of the American Medical Association* 169(1959): 1286–96.

———. *Type A Behavior and Your Heart.* Greenwich, CT: Fawcett, 1974.

Friedman, Meyer, Ray Rosenman, and V. Carroll. "Changes in the Serum Cholesterol and Blood Clotting Time in Men Subjected to Cycle Variation of Occupational Stress." *Circulation* 17(1958): 852–64.

Friedman, Meyer, and Diane Ulmer. *Treating Type A Behavior and Your Heart.* New York: Alfred A. Knopf, 1984.

Friedman, S. D., and J. H. Greenhaus. *Allies or Enemies? How Choices About Work and Family Affect the Quality of Men's and Women's Lives.* New York: Oxford University Press, 2000.

Fujii, T., T. Torisu, and S. Nakamura. "A Change of Occlusal Conditions After Splint Therapy for Bruxers With and Without Pain in the Masticatory Muscles." *Craniology* 23(2005): 113–18.

Fuller, George D. *Biofeedback: Methods and Procedures in Clinical Practice.* San Francisco: Biofeedback Press, 1977.

Funk, Steven C., and Kent B. Houston. "A Critical Analysis of the Hardiness Scale's Validity and Utility." *Journal of Personality and Social Psychology* 53(1987): 572–78.

Gafni, M. "My Unique Pathology." *Tikkun* 15(2000): 8–9.

Galambos, S. A., P. C. Terry, G. M. Moyle, S. A. Locke, and A. M. Lane. "Psychological Predictors of Injury Among Elite Athletes." *British Journal of Sports Medicine* 39(2005): 351–54.

Galway, W. Timothy. *The Inner Game of Tennis.* New York: Random House, 1997.

Ganesh-Kumar, A. E., John Bienenstock, Edward J. Goetzl, and Michael G. Blennerhassett. *Autonomic Neuroimmunology.* London: Taylor & Francis, 2003.

Ganguli, M., M. E. Lytle, M. D. Reynolds, and H. H. Dodge. "Random Versus Volunteer Selection for a Community-Based Study." *Journal of Gerontology* 53A(1998): M39–M46.

Gans, J., and D. Blyth. *America's Adolescence: How Healthy Are They?* Chicago, IL: American Medical Association, 1990.

Garrity, T. F., J. M. Kotchen, H. E. McKean, D. Gurley, and M. McFadden. "The Association Between Type A Behavior and Change in Coronary Risk Factors Among Young Adults." *American Journal of Public Health* 80(1990): 1354–57.

Gartner, J. "Religious Commitment, Mental Health, and Prosocial Behavior: A Review of the Empirical Literature." In *Religion and the Clinical Practice of Psychology,* edited by E. P. Shafranske. Washington, DC: American Psychological Association, 1996, 187–214.

Gates, Rolf and Katrina Kenison. *Meditations from the Mat: Daily Reflections on the Path of Yoga.* Peterborough, Canada: Anchor Books, 2002.

Gerschman, Jack A., et al. "Hypnosis in the Control of Gagging." *Australian Journal of Clinical and Experimental Hypnosis* 9(1981): 53–59.

Getchel, Bud. *Physical Fitness: A Way of Life.* New York: John Wiley, 1983.

Giga, Sabir I., Cary L. Cooper, and Brian Faragher. "The Development of a Framework for a Comprehensive Approach to Stress Management Interventions at Work." *International Journal of Stress Management* 10(2003): 280–96.

Gillespie, David F. "Correlates for Active and Passive Types of Burnout." *Journal of Social Service Research* 4(Winter 1980–81): 1–16.

Gilman, L. "Elder Abuse." *American Health,* September 1993, 84.

Girdano, Daniel A., and George S. Everly. *Controlling Stress and Tension: A Holistic Approach.* Englewood Cliffs, NJ: Prentice Hall, 1986.

Girdano, Daniel A., George S. Everly, and Dorothy E. Dusek. *Controlling Stress and Tension.* Boston: Allyn & Bacon, 1997, 39.

Girdano, Daniel S., George S. Everly, and Dorothy E. Dusek. *Controlling Stress and Tension.* Boston: Allyn & Bacon, 2001.

Glanz, K., R. T. Coyne, V. Y. Chollette, and V. W. Pinn. "Cancer-Related Health Disparities in Women." *American Journal of Public Health* 93(2003): 292–98.

Glanz, Karen, Barbara K. Rimer, and Frances Marcus Lewis (Editors). *Health Behavior and Health Education.* San Francisco: Jossey-Bass, 2002.

Glass, David C. "Stress Behavior, Patterns, and Coronary Disease." *American Scientist* 65(1977): 177–87.

Golding, J. M., and M. A. Burnam. "Stress and Social Support as Predictors of Depressive Symptoms in Mexican American and Non-Hispanic Whites." *Journal of Social and Clinical Psychology* 9(1990): 268–87.

Goldstein, Amy, and Roberto Suro. "A Journey of Stages: Assimilation's Pull Is Still Strong, but Its Pace Varies." *Washington Post,* 16 January 2000, A1.

Goleman, Daniel, and Gary E. Schwartz. "Meditation as an Intervention in Stress Reactivity." *Journal of Consulting and Clinical Psychology* 44(1976): 456–66.

Gordon, J. S., J. K. Staples, A. Blyta, and M. Bytyqi. "Treatment of Posttraumatic Stress Disorder in Postwar Kosovo High School Students Using Mind-Body Skills Groups: A Pilot Study." *Journal of Traumatic Stress* 17(2004): 143–47.

Gorton, B. "Autogenic Training." *American Journal of Clinical Hypnosis* 2(1959): 31–41.

Grant, Eleanor. "The Housework Gap." *Psychology Today* 22(1988): 8.

Greeff, A. P. and W. S. Conradie. "Use of Progressive Relaxation Training for Chronic Alcoholics with Insomnia." *Psychological Reports* 82(1998): 407–12.

Green, B. L., M. C. Grace, D. J. Lindy, and A. C. Leonard. "Race Differences in Response to Combat Stress." *Journal of Traumatic Stress* 3(1990): 379–93.

Green, Elmer E., A. M. Green, and E. D. Walters. "Voluntary Control of Internal States: Psychological and Physiological." *Journal of Transpersonal Psychology* 2(1970): 1–26.

Green, Lawrence W., David M. Levine, and Sigrid Deeds. "Clinical Trials of Health Education for Hypertensive Outpatients: Design and Baseline Data." *Preventive Medicine* 4(1975): 417–25.

Green, Tim. "My Favorite Routine: Chair Aerobics." *Shape,* June 1986, 150–53.

Greenberg, E. R., and C. Canzoneri. *Organizational Staffing and Disability Claims.* New York: American Management Association Report, 1996.

Greenberg, Jerrold S. "The Masturbatory Behavior of College Students." *Psychology in the Schools* 9(1972): 427–32.

———. *Student-Centered Health Instruction: A Humanistic Approach.* Reading, MA: Addison-Wesley, 1978.

———. "A Study of Stressors in the College Student Population." *Health Education* 12(1981): 8–12.

———. "A Study of the Effects of Stress on the Health of College Students: Implications for School Health Education." *Health Education* 15(1984): 11–15.

———. *Health Education: Learner-Centered Instructional Strategies.* Boston, MA: WCB/McGraw-Hill, 1998.

———. *Health Education and Health Promotion.* New York: McGraw-Hill, 2004.

Greenberg, Jerrold S., Clint E. Bruess, and Debra W. Haffner. *Exploring the Dimensions of Human Sexuality.* 2nd ed. Sudbury, MA: Jones and Bartlett, 2004.

Greenberg, Jerrold S., Clint E. Bruess, and Doris Sands. *Sexuality: Insights and Issues.* Dubuque, IA: Wm. C. Brown Communications, 1986.

Greenberg, Jerrold S., Clint E. Bruess, Kathleen Mullen, and Doris Sands. *Sexuality: Insights and Issues.* 2nd ed. Dubuque, IA: Wm. C. Brown Communications, 1989.

Greenberg, Jerrold S., George B. Dintiman, and Barbee Myers Oakes. *Physical Fitness and Wellness.* 3rd ed. Champaign, IL: Human Kinetics, 2004.

Greene, W. A. "Operant Conditioning of the GSR Using Partial Reinforcement." *Psychological Reports* 19(1976): 571–78.

Greenfeld, Lawrence A., et al. "Violence by Intimates: Analysis of Data on Crimes by Current or Former Spouses, Boyfriends, and Girlfriends." *Bureau of Justice Statistics Factbook,* March 1998.

Greenway, F. L., G. A. Bray, and R. L. Marlin. "Methods to Maximize Retention in Weight Loss Studies." *Obesity Research* 7(1999): 593–96.

Greenwood, James W. "Management Stressors." *NIOSH Proceeding: Reducing Occupational Stress.* Cincinnati: National Institute for Occupational Safety and Health, April 1978, 41.

Griest, J. H., et al. "Running as Treatment for Depression." *Comparative Psychiatry* 20(1979): 41–54.

Grimsley, Kirstin Downey. "A Little Baby Powder on the Bottom Line." *Washington Post,* 17 July 1998, F1, F5.

———. "At Work-Site Schools, Kids Learn While Parents Earn." *Washington Post,* 8 September 1998, A1, A8.

———. "Companies See Results After 6 Years of Unusual Alliance on Work-Life Issues." *Washington Post,* 23 November 1997, H1.

———. "Message Overload Taking Toll on Workers." *Washington Post,* 5 May 1998, C13.

———. "Family a Priority for Young Workers." *Washington Post,* 3 May 2000, E1, E2.

Guitar, B. "Reduction of Stuttering Frequency Using Analogue Electromyographic Feedback." *Journal of Speech and Hearing Research* 18(1975): 672–85.

Hall, Holly. "A Woman's Place . . ." *PsychologyToday* 22(1988): 28–29.

Hansen, A., C. Edlund, and I. B. Branholm. "Significant Resources Needed for Return to Work After Sick Leave." *Work* 25(2005): 231–40.

Hanser, Suzanne B., and Larry W. Thompson. "Effects of a Music Therapy Strategy on Depressed Older Adults." *Journal of Gerontology* 49 (1994): 265–69.

Harenstam, A. B., and T. P. G. Theorell. "Work Conditions and Urinary Excretion of Catecholamines—A Study of Prison Staff in Sweden." *Scandinavian Journal of Work and Environmental Health* 14(1988): 257–64.

Hargrave, T. D., and J. N. Sells. "The Development of a Forgiveness Scale." *Journal of Marital and Family Therapy* 23(1997): 41–62.

Harrington, Walt W. "Seeing the Light." *Washington Post Magazine,* 13 December 1993, 10–15, 22–25.

Harris, A. H. S., C. E. Thoresen, M. E. McCullough, and D. B. Larson. "Spirituality and Religiously Oriented Health Interventions." *Journal of Health Psychology* 4(1999): 413–33.

Harris, Louis. *Harris Poll.* Washington, DC: National Council on the Aging, 1975.

Hart, Elizabeth A., Mark R. Leary, W. Jack Rejeski. "The Measurement of Social Physique Anxiety." *Journal of Sport and Exercise Physiology* 11(1989): 94–104.

Hashmonai, M., D. Kopelman, and A. Assalia. "The Treatment of Primary Palmar Hyperhidrosis: A Review." *Surgery Today* 30(2000): 211–18.

Hasslebring, Bobbie. "Health and Fitness According to Robert Cooper." *Medical Selfcare,* September/October 1989, 52–56, 69–70.

Hathaway, W. L., and K. I. Pargament. "Intrinsic Religiousness, Religious Coping, and Psychological Competence: A Covariance Structure Analysis." *Journal for the Scientific Study of Religion* 29(1992): 423–41.

Hatta, T., and M. Nakamura. "Can Antistress Music Tapes Reduce Mental Stress?" *Stress Medicine* 7(1991): 181–84.

Haugland, S., B. Wold, and T. Torsheim. "Relieving the Pressure? The Role of Physical Activity in the Relationship Between School-Related Stress and Adolescent Health Complaints." *Research Quarterly for Exercise and Sport* 74(2003): 127–35.

Havighurst, Robert J. *Developmental Tasks and Education.* New York: David McKay Company, 1972.

Hawkes, Steven R., Melisa L. Hull, Rebecca L. Thulman, and Paul M. Richins. "Review of Spiritual Health: Definition, Role, and Intervention Strategies in Health Promotion," *American Journal of Health Promotion* 9(1995): 371–78.

Haynes, S. G., and M. Feinleib. "Women at Work and Coronary Heart Disease: Prospective Findings from the Framingham Heart Study." *American Journal of Public Health* 70(1980): 133–41.

Haynes, Suzanne G., M. Feinleib, and W. B. Kannel. "The Relationship of Psychosocial Factors to Coronary Heart Disease in the Framingham Study III. Eight Year Incidence of Coronary Heart Disease." *American Journal of Epidemiology* 3(1980): 37–58.

Head, Jenny, Stephen A. Stansfeld, and Johannes Siegrist. "The Psychosocial Work Environment and Alcohol Dependence: A Prospective Study." *Occupational and Environmental Medicine* 61(2004): 219–24.

Heide, E. J., and T. D. Borkovec. "Relaxation-Induced Anxiety: Mechanisms and Theoretical Implications." *Behaviour Research and Therapy* 22(1984): 1–12.

Helman, C. *Culture, Health and Illness.* Bristol, England: John Wright, 1986.

Helmreich, R. L., J. T. Spence, and R. S. Pred. "Making It Without Losing It: Type A, Achievement Motivation, and Scientific Attainment Revisited." *Personality and Social Psychology Bulletin* 14(1988): 495–504.

Help End Domestic Violence. National Resource Center on Domestic Violence, undated.

Helsing, Knud J., Moyses Szklo, and George W. Comstock. "Factors Associated with Mortality After Widowhood." *American Journal of Public Health* 71(1981): 802–9.

Henig, Robin Marantz. "The Jaw out of Joint." *Washington Post, Health,* 9 February 1988, 16.

Herholtz, K., W. Buskies, M. Rist, G. Pawlik, W. Hollman, and W. D. Heiss. "Regional Cerebral Blood Flow in Man at Rest and During Exercise," *Journal of Neurology* 234(1987): 9–13.

Herron, R. E., S. L. Hillis, J. V. Mandarino, D. W. Orme-Johnson, and K. G. Walton. "The Impact of the Transcendental Meditation Program on Government Payments to Physicians in Quebec." *American Journal of Health Promotion* 10(1996): 208–16.

Hidalgo, R. B., and J. R. Davidson. "Posttraumatic Stress Disorder: Epidemiology and Health-Related Considerations." *Journal of Clinical Psychiatry* 61(2000): 5–13.

Hidderley, M. and M. Holt. "A Pilot Randomized Trial Assessing The Effects of Autogenic Training in Early Stage Cancer Patients in Relation to Psychological Status and Immune System Responses." *European Journal of Oncology Nursing: The Official Journal of European Oncology Nursing Society* 8(2004): 61–65.

———. "Is There a Clown in the House? The Art of Medical Slapstick." *Washington Post Magazine,* 9 May 2004, 13.

Hill, C., Z. Rubin, and L. Peplau. "Breakups Before Marriage: The End of 103 Affairs." In *Divorce and Separation,* edited by G. Levinger and O. Moles. New York: Basic Books, 1979.

Hixson, K. A., H. W. Gruchow, and D. W. Morgan. "The Relation Between Religiosity, Selected Health Behaviors, and Blood Pressure Among Adult Females." *Preventive Medicine* 27(1998): 545–52.

Hjelle, L. A. "Transcendental Meditation and Psychological Health." *Perceptual and Motor Skills* 39(1974): 623–28.

Hobfoll, S. E., C. L. Dunahoo, Y. Ben-Porath, and J. Monnier. "Gender and Coping: The Dual-Axis Model of Coping." *Journal of Community Psychology* 22 (1994): 49–82.

Hobson, Charles J., and Linda Delunas. "National Norms and Life-Event Frequencies for the Revised Social Readjustment Rating Scale." *International Journal of Stress Management* 8(2001): 299–314.

Hochwald, Lambeth. "The Top 10 Healthiest Companies for Women." *Health,* July/August 2003, 148–155, 202.

Hoeymans, Nancy, et al. "Age Time, and Cohort Effects on Functional Status and Self-Rated Health in Elderly Men." *American Journal of Public Health* 87(1997): 1620–25.

Holahan, C. K., C. J. Holohan, and S. S. Belk. "Adjustment in Aging: The Roles of Life Stress, Hassles, and Self-Efficacy." *Health Psychology* 3(1984): 315–28.

Holmes, Thomas H., and Richard H. Rahe. "The Social Readjustment Rating Scale." *Journal of Psychosomatic Research* 11(1967): 213–18.

Holtrop, J., and A. Slonim. "Sticking to It: A Multifactor Cancer Risk-Reduction Program for Low-Income Clients." *Journal of Health Education* 31(2000): 122–27.

Hospice Foundation of America. *What Is Hospice?* Hospice Foundation of America, 2004. http://www.hospicefoundation.org/ what_is/

———. *Shattering Eight Myths About Grief.* Hospice Foundation of America, 2004. http://www.hospicefoundation.org/grief/8myths.htm

House, J. S. *Work Stress and Social Support.* Reading, MA: Addison-Wesley, 1981, 39.

Houston, B. Kent, and C. R. Snyder, eds. *Type A Behavior Pattern: Research, Theory and Intervention.* New York: John Wiley & Sons, 1988.

Hovell, Melbourne F., Beverly Calhoun, and John P. Elder. "Modification of Students' Snacking: Comparison of Behavioral Teaching Methods." *Health Education* 19(1988): 26–37.

Howard, Jane. *Families.* New York: Simon & Schuster, 1978.

Howard, John H., David A. Cunningham, and Peter A. Rechnitzer. "Personality (Hardiness) as a Moderator of Job Stress and Coronary Risk in Type A Individuals: A Longitudinal Study." *Journal of Behavioral Medicine* 9(1986): 229–44.

"How to Prevent Back Trouble." *U. S. News & World Report,* 14 April 1975, 45–48.

Hull, Jay G., Ronald R. Van-Treuren, and Suzanne Virnelli. "Hardiness and Health: A Critique and Alternative Approach." *Journal of Personality and Social Psychology* 53(1987): 518–30.

Humphrey, James H. *Childhood Stress in Contemporary Society.* New York: The Haworth Press, 2004.

Humphrey, R., and P. McCarthy. "High Debt and Poor Housing: A Taxing Life for Contemporary Students." *Youth and Policy* 56(1997): 55–64.

Humphrey, Robin, et al. "Stress and the Contemporary Student." *Higher Education Quarterly* 52(1998): 221–42.

Hunt, Morton. *Sexual Behavior in the 1970s.* Chicago: Playboy Press, 1974.

Hurrell, J. J., and M. J. Colligan. "Psychological Job Stress." In *Environmental and Occupational Medicine,* edited by W. N. Rom. Boston: Little, Brown, 1982, 425–30.

Hurrell, Joseph. "An Overview of Organizational Stress and Health." In *Stress Management in Work Settings,* edited by Lawrence R. Murphy and Theodore F. Schoenborn. Washington, DC: National Institute for Occupational Safety and Health, 1987, 31–45.

Hypertension Update. Chicago: Abbott Laboratories, 1976.

"In the Company of (Few) Women." *Washington Post,* 20 November 1 997, D1.

"An Interview with Larry Dossey." *Tikkun* 15(2000): 11–16.

Iribarren, Carlos, Stephen Sidney, Diane E. Bild, Kiang Liu, Jerome H. Markovitz, Jeffrey M. Roseman, and Karen Matthews. "Association of Hostility with Coronary Artery Calcification in Young Adults." *Journal of the American Medical Association* 283(2000): 2546–51.

Irujo, Suzzane. "An Introduction to Intercultural Differences and Similarities in Nonverbal Communication." In *Toward Multiculturalism,* edited by J. Wurzl. Yarmouth: Intercultural Press, 1988, 142–50.

Ivancevich, John M., Michael T. Matteson, and Edward P. Richards III. "Who's Liable for Stress on the Job?" *Harvard Business Review,* March–April 1985, 66.

Iwasaki, Yoshi, Kelly J. MacKay, and Janice Ristock. "Gender-Based Analysis of Stress Among Professional Managers: An Exploratory Qualitative Study." *International Journal of Stress Management* 11(2004): 56–79.

Iyengar, B. K. S. *Light on Yoga.* New York: Schocken Books, 1965.

Jacobson, Edmund. *Progressive Relaxation.* 2nd ed. Chicago: University of Chicago Press, 1938.

———. *You Must Relax.* New York: McGraw-Hill Book Co., 1970.

Jacobson, N. S., J. M. Gottman, E. Gortner, S. Burns, and J. W. Shortt. "Psychological Factors in the Longitudinal Course of Battering: When Do the Couples Split Up? When Does the Abuse Decrease?" *Violence and Victims* 11(1996): 71–88.

Jamal, M. "Relationship of Job Stress and Type A Behavior to Employees' Job Satisfaction, Organizational Commitment, Psychosomatic Health Problems, and Turnover Motivation." *Human Relations* 43(1990): 727–38.

Jamal, Muhammad, and Vishwanath V. Baba. "Type-A Behavior, Its Prevalence and Consequences Among Woman Nurses." *Human Relations* 44(1991): 1213–28.

———. "Type-A Behavior, Job Performance and Well-Being in College Teachers." *International Journal of Stress Management* 8(2001): 231–40.

———. "Type-A Behavior, Components, and Outcomes: A Study of Canadian Employees." *International Journal of Stress Management* 10(2003): 39–50.

Jaynes, G. D., and R. N. Williams. *A Common Destiny: Blacks and American Society.* Washington, DC: National Academy Press, 1989.

Jennings, Charles, and Mark J. Tager. "Good Health Is Good Business." *Medical Self-Care,* Summer 1981, 14.

Johnson, Jeffrey V., Walter Stewart, Ellen M. Hall, Peeter Fredlund, and Tores Theorell. "Long-Term Psychosocial Work Environment and Cardiovascular Mortality Among Swedish Men." *American Journal of Public Health* 86(1996): 324–31.

Johnston, Derek W., Marie Johnston, Beth Pollard, Ann-Louise Kinmonth, and David Mant. "Motivation Is Not Enough: Prediction of Risk Behavior Following Diagnosis of Coronary Heart Disease from the Theory of Planned Behavior." *Health Psychology* 23(2004): 533–38.

Jones, John W. "A Measure of Staff Burnout Among Health Professionals." Paper presented at the annual meeting of the American Psychological Association, Montreal, September 1980.

Jones, M. A., and J. Emmanuel. "Stages and Recovery Steps of Teacher Burnout." *Education Digest* 45(1981): 9–11.

Jones, Nancy Aaron, and Tiffany Field. "Massage and Music Therapies Attenuate Frontal EEG Asymmetry in Depressed Adolescents." *Adolescence* 34(1999): 529–34.

Jones, R. L., ed. *Black Adult Development and Aging.* Berkeley, CA: Cobb and Henry, 1989.

Jorgensen, L. G., M. Perko, B. Hanel, T. V. Schroeder, N. H. Secher. "Middle Cerebral Arterial Flow Velocity and Blood Flow During Exercise and Muscle Ischemia in Humans." *Journal of Applied Physiology* 72(1992): 1123–32.

Jorm, A. F., H. Christensen, K. M. Griffiths, R. A. Parslow, B. Rodgers, and K. A. Blewitt. "Effectiveness of Complementary and Self-Help Treatments for Anxiety Disorders." *Medical Journal of Australia* 181(2004):S29–46.

Joyce, A. "At the Breaking Point, Passing up Vacation." *Washington Post,* 22 May 2005a, F6.

———. "Fast Food, If Any at All." *Washington Post,* 17 April 2005b, F5.

Jung, J., and H. K. Khalsa. "The Relationship of Daily Hassles, Social Support, and Coping to Depression in Black and White Students." *Journal of General Psychology* 116(1989): 407–17.

Kabat-Zinn, Jon, et al. "Clinical Use of Mindfulness Meditation for the Self-Regulation of Chronic Pain." *Journal of Behavioral Medicine* 8(1985): 163–90.

———. "Four-Year Follow-Up of a Meditation-Based Program for the Self-Regulation of Chronic Pain: Treatment Outcomes and Compliance." *The Clinical Journal of Pain* 2(1987): 154–73.

———. "Effectiveness of Meditation-Based Stress Reduction Program in the Treatment of Anxiety Disorders." *American Journal of Psychiatry* 149(1992): 936–43.

Kahn, J. A., G. B. Slap, D. I. Bernstein, L. M. Kollar, A. M. Tissot, P. A. Hillard, and S. L. Rosenthal. "Psychological, Behavioral, and Interpersonal Impact of Human Papillomavirus and Pap Test Results." *Journal of Women's Health* 14(2005): 650–59.

Kamiya, J. "Conscious Control of Brain Waves." *Psychology Today* 1(1978): 57–60.

Kanji, N., A. R. White, and E. Ernst. "Autogenic Training Reduces Anxiety After Coronary Angioplasty: A Randomized Clinical Trial." *American Heart Journal* 147(2004): E10.

Kanner, A. D., et al. "Comparison of Two Modes of Stress Management: Daily Hassles and Uplifts Versus Major Life Events." *Journal of Behavioral Medicine* 4(1981): 1–39.

Karasek, Robert A., et al. "Job Characteristics in Relation to the Prevalence of Myocardial Infarction in the U.S. Health Examination Survey (HES) and the Health and Nutrition Examination Survey (HANES)." *American Journal of Public Health* 78(1988): 190–98.

Karasek, R. A., J. Schwartz, and T. Theorell. *Job Characteristics, Occupation, and Coronary Heart Disease.* Final report on contract no. R-01-0H00906. Cincinnati: National Institute for Occupational Safety and Health, 1982.

Kasamatsu, A., and T. Hirai. "Studies of EEG's of Expert Zen Meditators." Folia *Psychiatrica Neurologica Japonica* 28(1966): 315.

Kasl, S. V. "The Influence of the Work Environment on Cardiovascular Health: A Historical, Conceptual, and Methodological Perspective." *Journal of Occupational Health Psychology* 1(1996): 42–56.

Kasl, Stanislav V., and Sidney Cobb. "Health Behavior, Illness Behavior, and Sick-Role Behavior." *Archives of Environmental Health* 12(1966): 246–66.

Katz, Jane. "The W.E.T. Workout: A Swimmer's Guide to Water Exercise Techniques." *Shape,* June 1986, 82–88+.

Kaushik, R., R. M., Kaushik, S. K. Mahajan, and V. Rajesh. "Biofeedback Assisted Diaphragmatic Breathing and Systematic Relaxation Versus Propranolol in Long Term Prophylaxis of Migraine." *Complementary Therapies in Medicine* 13(2005): 165–74.

Kaye, W. H., K. L. Klump, G. K. Frank, and M. Strober. "Anorexia and Bulimia Nervosa." *Annual Review of Medicine* 51(2000): 299–313.

Keen, Sam, and Ofer Zur. "Who Is the New Ideal Man?" *Psychology Today* 23(November 1989): 54–60.

Kelly, Colleen. *Assertion Training: A Facilitator's Guide.* LaJolla, CA: University Associates, 1979.

Kendler, K. S., E. E. Walters, K. R. Truett, et al. "A Twin-Family Study of Self-Report Symptoms of Panic-Phobia and Somatization." *Behavior Genetics* 25(1995): 499–515.

Keppel, K. G., J. N. Pearcy, and D. K. Wagener. "Trends in Racial and Etnic-Specific Rates for the Health Status Indicators: United States, 1990–98." *Healthy People 2000 Statistical Notes,* no. 23. (Hyattsville, MD: National Center for Health Statistics, 2002).

Kern-Buell, C. L., A. V. McGrady, P. B. Conran, and L. A. Nelson. "Asthma Severity, Psychophysiological Indicators of Arousal, and Immune Function in Asthma Patients Undergoing Biofeedback-Assisted Relaxation." *Applied Psychophysiology and Biofeedback* 25(2000): 79–91.

Kessler, Marcia. "Preventing Burnout: Taking the Stress out of the Job." *The Journal of Volunteer Administration* 9(1991): 15–20.

Kessler, R. C. "Posttraumatic Stress Disorder: The Burden to the Individual and to Society." *Journal of Clinical Psychiatry* 61(2000): 4–12.

Kessler, R. K., and H. W. Neighbors. "A New Perspective on the Relationship Among Race, Social Class, and Psychological Distress." *Journal of Health and Social Behavior* 27(1986): 107–15.

Khasky, Amy D., and Jonathan C. Smith. "Stress, Relaxation States, and Creativity." *Perceptual and Motor Skills* 88(April 1999): 409–16.

Kiecolt-Glaser, J. K., R. Glaser, D. Williger, J. Stout, G. Messick, S. Sheppard, D. Ricker, S. C. Romisher, W. Briner, G. Bonnell, and R. Donnerberg. "Psychosocial Enhancement of Immunocompetence in a Geriatric Population." *Health Psychology* 4(1990): 25–41.

Kiesling, Stephen. "Loosen Your Hips: Walkshaping." *American Health,* October 1986, 62–67.

Kiesling, Stephen, and T. George Harris. "The Prayer War." *Psychology Today* 23(October 1989): 65–66.

Kimmel, H. D. "Instrumental Conditioning of Autonomically Mediated Behavior." *Psychological Bulletin* 67(1967): 337–45.

Kimmel, H. D., and F. A. Hill. "Operant Conditioning of the GSR." *Psychological Reports* 7(1960): 555–62.

King, Tracey, and Ellynne Bannon. *The Burden of Borrowing: A Report on the Rising Rates of Student Loan Debt.* The State PIRG's Higher Education Project, 2002. http://www.pirg.org/highered

Kittleson, Mark J., and Becky Hageman-Righey. "Wellness and Behavior Contracting." *Health Education* 19(1988): 8–11.

Klausner, T. I. "The Best Kept Secret. Pelvic Floor Muscle Therapy for Urinary Incontinence." *Advance for Nurse Practitioners* 13(2005): 43–46, 48.

Kobasa, Suzanne C. "Stressful Life Events, Personality, and Health: An Inquiry into Hardiness." *Journal of Personality and Social Psychology* 37(1979): 1–11.

Kobasa, Suzanne C., Salvatore R. Maddi, and Mark C. Puccetti. "Personality and Exercise as Buffers in the Stress-Illness Relationship." *Journal of Behavioral Medicine* 5(1982): 391–404.

Kobasa, Suzanne C., Salvatore R. Maddi, and Marc A. Zola. "Type A and Hardiness." *Journal of Behavioral Medicine* 6(1983): 41–51.

Kobasa, Suzanne C., et al. "Effectiveness of Hardiness, Exercise, and Social Support as Resources Against Illness." *Journal of Psychosomatic Research* 29(1985): 525–33.

Kobayashi, Y., T. Hirose, Y. Tada, A. Tsutsumi, and N. Kawakami. "Relationship Between Two Job Stress Models and Coronary Risk Factors Among Japanese Part-Time Female Employees of a Retail Company." *Journal of Occupational Health* 47(2005): 201–10.

Koenig, H. G. *Is Religion Good for Your Health? The Effects of Religion on Physical and Mental Health.* New York: Haworth Pastoral Press, 1997.

Kolander, Cheryl A., Danny J. Ballard, and Cynthia K. Chandler. *Contemporary Women's Health* (New York: McGraw-Hill, 2005).

Koop, C. Everett. *Understanding AIDS: A Message from the Surgeon General.* Washington, DC: Department of Health and Human Services, 1988.

Koskenvuo, Markku, Jaakko Kaprio, Richard J. Rose, Antero Kesaniemi, and Seppo Sarna. "Hostility as a Risk Factor for Mortality and Ischemic Heart Disease in Men." *Psychosomatic Medicine* 50(1988): 330–40.

Krause, N. "Stress in Racial Differences in Self-Reported Health Among the Elderly." *Gerontologist* 27(1987): 72–76.

Krenz, Eric W., and Keith P. Henschen. "The Effects of Modified Autogenic Training on Stress in Athletic Performance." In *Human Stress: Current Selected Research,* Vol. I, edited by James H. Humphrey. New York: AMS Press, 1986, 199–205.

Kristeller, J. L., and C. B. Hallett. "An Exploratory Study of a Meditation-Based Intervention for Binge Eating Disorder." *Journal of Health Psychology* 4(July 1999): 357–63.

Kriyananda. *Yoga Postures for Self-Awareness.* San Francisco: Ananda Publications, 1967.

Krucoff, Carol. "Cash for Working Out: Exercise Pays Off at Companies with Financial Incentive Programs," *Washington Post,* 4 November 1997, 24.

Krucoff, Carol, and Mitchell Krucoff. *Healing Moves: How to Cure, Relieve, and Prevent Common Ailments with Exercise.* New York: Harmony Books, 2000.

Kübler-Ross, Elisabeth. *On Death and Dying.* New York: Simon and Schuster, 1970.

Kukla, Kenneth J. "The Effects of Progressive Relaxation Training upon Athletic Performance During Stress." *Dissertation Abstracts International* 37(1977): 6392.

Kumanyika, Shiriki K. "Maintenance of Dietary Behavior Change." *Health Psychology* 14(2000): 42–56.

Kunde, Diana. "When the Massage Is the Message." *Washington Post,* 24 May 1998, H6.

Kurl, Sudhir, Jari A. Laukkanen, Rainer Rauramaa, Timo A. Lakka, Juhani Sivenius, and Jukka T. Salonen, "Cardiorespiratory Fitness and the Risk of Stroke in Men." *Archives of Internal Medicine* 163(2003): 1682–88.

Labbe, E. E. "Treatment of Childhood Migraine with Autogenic Training and Skin Temperature Biofeedback: A Component Analysis." *Headache* 35(1995): 10–13.

Labott, Susan M., and Randall B. Martin. "The Stress-Moderating Effects of Weeping and Humor." *Journal of Human Stress* 13(1987): 159–64.

Lacroix, J. Michael, Melissa A. Clarke, J. Carson Bock, and Neville C. Doxey. "Physiological Changes After Biofeedback and Relaxation Training for Multiple-Pain Tension-Headache Patients." *Perceptual and Motor Skills* 63(1986): 139–53.

Landrine, H., and E. Klonoff. *African American Acculturation: Deconstructing Race and Reviving Culture.* Thousand Oaks, CA: Sage, 1996.

Lane, Charles. "States' Recognition of Same-Sex Unions May Be Tested." *Washington Post,* 19 November 2003, A8.

Lange, Nancy. "How Did September 11th Affect Students?" *About Campus* 7(2002): 21–24.

Laumann, Edward O., John H. Gagnon, Robert T. Michaels, and Stuart Michaels. *The Social Organization of Sexuality: Sexual Practices in the United States.* Chicago: University of Chicago Press, 1994.

Lauver, P. J., and R. M. Jones. "Factors Associated with Perceived Career Options in American Indian, White, and Hispanic Rural High School Students." *Journal of Counseling Psychology* 38(1991): 159–66.

Lavanco, G. "Burnout Syndrome and Type-A Behavior in Nurses and Teachers in Sicily." *Psychological Reports* 81(1997): 523–28.

Lazarus, Richard S. *Psychological Stress and the Coping Process.* New York: McGraw-Hill Book Co., 1966.

———. "Puzzles in the Study of Daily Hassles." *Journal of Behavioral Medicine* 7(1984): 375–89.

Lazarus, Richard S., and A. DeLongis. "Psychological Stress and Coping in Aging." *American Psychologist* 38(1983): 245–54.

Lazarus, Richard S., and Susan Folkman. *Stress, Appraisal, and Coping.* New York: Springer, 1984.

Lear, Martha Weinman. "How Many Choices Do Women Really Have?" *Woman's Day,* 11 November 1986, 109–11, 180–83.

Lee, Martin, Emily Lee, Melinda Lee, Joyce Lee, and T. C. Master. *The Healing Art of Tai Chi: Becoming One with Nature.* New York: Sterling Publications, 1996.

Lehrer, P. M. "Varieties of Relaxation Methods and Their Unique Effects." *International Journal of Stress Management* 3(1996): 1–15.

Lehrer, P. M., and R. L. Woolfolk. "Are Stress Reduction Techniques Interchangeable, or Do They Have Specific Effect?: A Review of the Comparative Empirical Literature." In *Principles and Practice of Stress Management,* edited by R. L. Woolfolk and P. M. Lehrer. New York: Guilford, 1984.

Leigh, B. C., M. T. Temple, and K. F. Trocki. "The Sexual Behavior of U.S. Adults: Results from a National Survey." *American Journal of Public Health* 83(1993): 1400–08.

Leiter, M. P. "Coping Patterns as Predictors of Burnout: The Function of Control and Escapist Coping Patterns." *Journal of Organizational Behavior* 12(1991): 123–144.

LeShan, Lawrence. "An Emotional Life-History Pattern Associated with Neoplastic Disease." *Annals of the New York Academy of Sciences,* 1966.

LeShan, Lawrence, and R. E. Worthington. "Some Recurrent Life-History Patterns Observed in Patients with Malignant Disease." *Journal of Nervous and Mental Disorders* 124(1956): 460–65.

Levin, J. S., and P. L. Schiller. "Is There a Religious Factor in Health?" *Journal of Religion and Health* 26(1987): 9–36.

Levin, J. S., and H. Vanderpool. "Is Religious Attendance Really Conducive to Better Health? Toward an Epidemiology of Religion." *Social Science and Medicine* 24(1987): 589–600.

Levine, A. *When Dreams and Heroes Died.* San Francisco: Jossey-Bass, 1983.

Levine, Susan. "One in Four U.S. Families Cares for Aging Relatives." *Washington Post,* 24 March 1997, A13.

Liebert, R. M., and L. W. Morris. "Cognitive and Emotional Components of Test Anxiety: A Distinction and Some Initial Data." *Psychological Reports* 20(1967): 975–78.

Light, K. C., C. A. Dolan, M. R. Davis, and A. Sherwood. "Cardiovascular Responses to an Active Coping Challenge as Predictors of Blood Pressure Patterns 10 to 15 Years Later." *Psychosomatic Medicine* 54(1992): 217–30.

Lindemann, Erich. "Symptomatology and Management of Acute Grief." In *Stress and Coping: An Anthology,* edited by Alan Monet and Richard S. Lazarus. New York: Columbia University Press, 1977.

Linden, W. "Practicing of Meditation by School Children and Their Levels of Field Independence-Dependence, Test Anxiety, and Reading Achievement." *Journal of Consulting and Clinical Psychology* 41(1973): 139–43.

Linton, Steven J. "Behavioral Remediation of Chronic Pain: A Status Report." *Pain* 24(1986): 125–41.

Locke, Steven E., and Douglas Colligan. "Tapping Your Inner Resources: A New Science Links Your Mind to Your Health." *Shape,* May 1988, 112–14.

Logue, B. J. "Women at Risk: Predictors of Financial Stress for Retired Women Workers." *Gerontologist* 31(1991): 657–65.

London, K. A. "Cohabitation, Marriage, Marital Dissolution, and Remarriage: United States, 1988, Data from the National Survey of Family Growth." *Advance Data* (From the National Center for Health Statistics), No. 194, 4 January 1991.

Long, B. C. "Relationship Between Coping Strategies, Sex-Typed Traits and Environmental Characteristics: A Comparison of Male and Female Managers." *Journal of Counseling Psychology* 37(1990): 185–94.

Long, Nicholas J., and Jody Long. *Conflict and Comfort in College.* Belmont, CA: Wadsworth, 1970.

Lowis, Michael J., and Jenny Hughes. "A Comparison of the Effects of Sacred and Secular Music on Elderly People." *Journal of Psychology* 131 (1997): 45–55.

Luskin, F. M., K. A. Newell, M. Griffith, M. Holmes, S. Telles, E. DiNucci, F. F. Marvasti, M. Hill, K. R. Pelletier, and W. L. Haskell. "A Review of Mind/Body Therapies in the Treatment of Musculoskeletal Disorders with Implications for the Elderly." *Alternative Therapies in Health and Medicine* 6(2000): 46–56.

Luthe, Wolfgang. "Method, Research and Application of Autogenic Training." *American Journal of Clinical Hypnosis* 5(1962): 17–23.

———, ed. *Autogenic Training.* New York: Grune & Stratton, 1965.

———, ed. *Autogenic Therapy.* Vols. 1–6. New York: Grune & Stratton, 1969.

Lutz, A., L. L. Greischar, N. B. Rawlings, M. Ricard, and R. J. Davidson. "Long-Term Meditators Self-Induce High-Amplitude Gamma Synchrony During Mental Practice." *Proceedings of the National Academy of Sciences* 101(2004):16369–73.

Lynch, D. J., A. McGrady, E. Alvarez, and J. Forman. "Recent Life Changes and Medical Utilization in an Academic Family Practice." *Journal of Nervous and Mental Disorders* 193(2005): 633–35.

Lynch, John W., Susan A. Everson, George A. Kaplan, Riitta Salonen, and Jukka T. Salonen. "Progression of Carotid Atherosclerosis?" *American Journal of Public Health* 88(1998): 389–94.

MacBride-King, J., and H. Paris. "Balancing Work and Family Responsibilities." *Canadian Business Review* 16(1989): 17–21.

MacDonald, C. M. "A Chuckle a Day Keeps the Doctor Away: Therapeutic Humor and Laughter." *Journal of Psychosocial Nursing Mental Health Services* 42(2004): 18–25.

Machlowitz, Marilyn. *Workaholics: Living with Them, Working with Them.* Reading, MA: Addison-Wesley, 1980.

MacKinnon, Catherine. *Sexual Harassment of Working Women.* New Haven, CT: Yale University Press, 1979.

MacLean, C., et al. "Altered Responses of Cortisol, GH, TSH and Testosterone to Acute Stress After Four Months' Practice of Transcendental Meditation." *Annals of the New York Academy of Science* 746(1994): 381–84.

Macleod, John, Scott Beach, and Richard Schulz. "Mortality Among Elderly Caregivers." *Journal of the American Medical Association* 283(2000): 2105–6.

Maddi, Salvatore R. "Personality as a Resource in Stress Resistance: The Hardy Type." Paper presented in the symposium on "Personality Moderators of Stressful Life Events" at the annual meeting of the American Psychological Association, Montreal, September 1980.

Mahony, D. L., W. J. Burroughs, and L. G. Lippman. "Perceived Attributes of Health-Promoting Laughter: A Cross-Generational Comparison." *Journal of Psychology* 136(2002): 171–81.

Mahoney, M. J., and C. E. Thoresen. *Self-Control: Power to the Person.* Monterey, CA: Brooks/Cole, 1974.

Maier, Steven F., and Mark Laudenslager. "Stress and Health: Exploring the Links." *Psychology Today,* August 1985, 44–49.

Makara, G., M. Palkovits, and J. Szentagothal. "The Endocrine Hypothalamus and the Hormonal Response to Stress." In *Selye's Guide to Stress Research,* edited by Hans Selye. New York: Van Nostrand Reinhold, 1980.

Mann, R. A. "The Behavior-Therapeutic Use of Contingency Contracting to Control an Adult-Behavior Problem: Weight Control." *Journal of Applied Behavioral Analysis* 5(1972): 99–109.

Mansfield, P. K., P. B. Koch, J. Henderson, J. R. Vicary et al. "The Job Climate for Women in Traditionally Male Blue-Collar Occupations." *Sex Roles* 25(1991): 63–79.

Manuck, S. B., et al. "Does Cardiovascular Reactivity to Mental Stress Have Prognostic Value in Post-Infarction Patients? A Pilot Study." *Psychosomatic Medicine* 54(1992): 102–8.

Manuck, S. B., A. L. Kasprowicz, and M. F. Muldoon. "Behaviorally-Evoked Cardiovascular Reactivity and Hypertension: Conceptual Issues and Potential Association." *Annals of Behavioral Medicine* 12(1990): 17–29.

Manuso, J. S. J. "Stress Management in the Workplace." In *Health Promotion in the Workplace,* edited by M. P. O'Donnell and T. Ainsworth. New York: John Wiley & Sons, 1984, 362–90.

Margolis, B. L., W. H. Kroes, and R. P. Quinn. "Job Stress: An Unlisted Occupational Hazard." *Journal of Occupational Medicine* 16(1974): 654–61.

Marieb, Elaine N. *Human Anatomy and Physiology.* Redwood City, CA: Benjamin/Cummings, 1989, 555.

Marin, H. and M. A. Menza. "The Management of Fatigue in Depressed Patients." *Essential Psychopharmacology* 6(2005): 185–92.

Marlin Company. *Attitudes in the American Workplace VII.* North Haven, CT: Marlin Company, 2001.

Marwick, Charles. "Music Hath Charms for Care of Preemies." *Journal of the American Medical Association* 283(2000): 468.

Maslach, C., and W. B. Schaufeli. "Historical and Conceptual Development of Burnout." In *Professional Burnout: Recent Developments in Theory and Research,* edited by W. B. Schaufeli, C. Maslach, and T. Marck. Washington, DC: Taylor & Francis, 1993, 1–16.

Mason, H. J., E. Serrano-Ikkos, and M. A. Kamm. "Psychological State and Quality of Life in Patients Having Behavioral Treatment (Biofeedback) for Intractable Constipation." *American Journal of Gastroenterology* 97(2002): 3154–59.

Mason, James W. "A Historical View of the Stress Field." *Journal of Human Stress* 1(1975): 22–36.

Massage Therapy Journal. Available from the American Massage Therapy Association, P.O. Box 1270, Kingsport, TN 37662.

Matich, J., and L. Sims. "A Comparison of Social Support Variables Between Women Who Intend to Breast or Bottle Feed." *Social Science Medicine* 34(1992): 919–27.

Matsumoto, M. and J. C. Smith. "Progressive Muscle Relaxation, Breathing Exercises, and ABC Relaxation Theory." *Journal of Clinical Psychology* 57(2001): 1551–57.

Matsunaga, S., K. Hayashi, T. Naruo, S. Nozoe, and S. Komiya. "Psychologic Management of Brace Therapy for Patients with Idiopathic Scoliosis." *Spine* 30(2005): 547–50.

Matthews, Karen A. "Psychological Perspective on Type A Behavior Pattern." *Psychological Bulletin* 91(1982): 293–323.

Matthews, Karen A., and Suzanne G. Haynes. "Reviews and Commentary: Type A Behavior Pattern and Coronary Disease Risk. Update and Critical Evaluation." *American Journal of Epidemiology* 123(1986): 923–60.

Mauger, P. A., J. E. Perry, T. Freeman, D. C. Grove, A. G. McBride, and K. E. McKinney. "The Measurement of Forgiveness: Preliminary Research." *Journal of Psychology and Christianity* 11(1992): 170–80.

Mayo Foundation for Medical Education and Research. *The Health Benefits of Caring for a Pet.* http://www.mayoclinic.com

McCaffery, M., N. Smith, and N. Oliver. "Is Laughter the Best Medicine?" *American Journal of Nursing* 98(1998): 12–14.

McCarthy, P., and R. Humphrey. "Debt: The Reality of Student Life." *Higher Education* Quarterly 49(1995): 78–86.

McCraty, R., M. Atkinson, and G. Rein. "Music Enhances the Effects of Positive Emotional States on Salivary IgA." *Stress Medicine* 12(1996): 167–75.

McCraty, R., M. Atkinson, and W. A. Tiller. "New Electrophysiological Correlates Associated with Intentional Heart Focus." *Subtle Energies* 4(1995): 251–62.

McCurdy, Mindy. "Cool Water Workout." *Shape,* August 1990, 64–73.

McEwen, B. S. "Protective and Damaging Effects of Stress Mediators." *The New England Journal of Medicine* 338(1998): 171–78.

McFarlane, D., E. M. Duff, and E. Y. Bailey. "Coping with Occupational Stress in an Accident and Emergency Department." *Western Indian Medical Journal* 53(2004): 242–47.

McFarlane, Stewart, and Mew Hong Tan. *Complete Book of T'ai Chi.* London: DK Publishing, 1997.

McGinnis, R. A., A. McGrady, S. A. Cox, and K.A. Grower-Dowling. "Biofeedback-Assisted Relaxation in Type 2 Diabetes." *Diabetes Care* 28(2005): 2145–49.

McGuigan, F. J. "Stress Management Through Progressive Relaxation." *International Journal of Stress Management* 1(1994): 205–14.

McLaughlin, Christine R. "Furry Friends Can Aid Your Health." *Discovery Health Channel,* 2004. http://www.health.discovery.com/centers/aging/powerofpets/powerofpets_print.html

McLean, Alan A. *Work Stress.* Reading, MA: Addison-Wesley, 1979.

McLeroy, K. R., Lawrence W. Green, K. D. Mullen, and V. Foshee. "Assessing the Health Effects of Health Promotion in Worksites: A Review of the Stress Program Evaluations." *Health Education Quarterly* 11(1984): 379–401.

McMillan, Lynley H. W., Michael P. O'Driscoll, Nigel V. Marsh, and Elizabeth C. Brady. "Understanding Workaholism: Data Synthesis, Theoretical Critique, and Future Design Strategies." *International Journal of Stress Management* 8(2001): 69–91.

McNeil, Kevin, et al. "Measurement of Psychological Hardiness in Older Adults." *Canadian Journal on Aging* 5(1986): 43–48.

McNeilly, M., and A. Zeichner. "Neuropeptide and Cardiovascular Response to Intravenous Catheterization in Normotensive and Hypertensive Blacks and Whites." *Health Psychology* 8(1989): 487–501.

McQuade, Walter, and Ann Aikman. *Stress.* New York: Bantam Books, 1974.

McTiernan, Anne, Charles Kooperberg, Emily White, Sara Wilcox, Ralph Coates, Lucile L. Adams-Campbell, Nancy Woods, and Judith Ockene. "Recreational Physical Activity and the Risk of Breast Cancer in Postmenopausal Women: The Women's Health Initiative Study." *Journal of the American Medical Association* 290(2003): 1331–36.

Mehling, W. E., K. A. Hamel, M. Acree, N. Byl, and F.M. Hecht. "Randomized, Controlled Trial of Breath Therapy for Patients with Chronic Low-Back Pain." *Alternative Therapies in Health and Medicine* 11(2005): 44–52.

Melchior, A. *National Evaluation of Learn and Serve America School and Community-Based Programs.* Washington, DC: The Corporation for National Service, 1997.

Mental Health Service. "Freshman: Aiding the Transition." *Mental Health Update* 8(1990): 1–2.

Merit System Protection Board report on sexual harassment in the workplace given before the Subcommittee on Investigations, Committee on the Post Office and Civil Service, U.S. House of Representatives, September 1980.

Metcalf, C. W., and R. Felible. *Lighten Up: Survival Skills for People Under Pressure.* Reading, MA: Addison-Wesley, 1992.

Michael, R. T., J. H. Gagnon, E. O. Laumann, and G. Kolata. *Sex in America.* New York: Little, Brown, 1994.

Midlarsky, E., and E. Kahana. "Predictors of Helping and Well-Being in Older Adults: A Cross-Sectional Survey Research Project." In *Altruism in Later Life.* Thousand Oaks, CA: Sage, 1994, 126–88.

Mikevic, P. "Anxiety, Depression and Exercise." *Quest* 33(1982): 140–53.

Miller, J. J., K. Fletcher, and J. Kabat-Zinn. "Three-Year Follow-Up and Clinical Implications of a Mindfulness Meditation-Based Stress Reduction Intervention in the Treatment of Anxiety Disorders." *General Hospital Psychiatry* 17(1995): 192–200.

Miller, M., and D. Solot. *Organization for Unmarried People Condemns Cohabitation Report,* 8 February 1999.

Miller, Neal E. "Learning of Visceral and Glandular Response." *Science* 163(1969): 434–45.

———. "RX: Biofeedback." *Psychology Today,* February 1985, 54–59.

Mishra, K. D., R. J. Gatchel, and M. A. Gardea. "The Relative Efficacy of Three Cognitive-Behavioral Treatment Approaches to Temporomandibular Disorders." *Journal of Behavioral Medicine* 23(2000): 293–309.

Mitchell, J. B., M. G. Flynn, A. H. Goldfarb, V. Ben-Ezra, and T. L. Copmann. "The Effect of Training on the Norepinephrine Response at Rest and During Exercise in 5° and 20° C Environments." *Journal of Sports Medicine and Physical Fitness* 30(1990): 235–40.

Miyai, N., M. Arita, I. Morioka, S. Takeda, and K. Miyashita. "Ambulatory Blood Pressure, Sympathetic Activity, and Left Ventricular Structure and Function in Middle-Aged Normotensive Men with Exaggerated Blood Pressure Response to Exercise." *Medical Science Monitor* 11(2005): CR478–84.

Mohren, D. C., G. M. Swaen, I. Kant, C. P. van Schayck, and J. M. Galama. "Fatigue and Job Stress as Predictors for Sickness Absence During Common Infections." *International Journal of Behavioral Medicine* 12(2005): 11–20.

Monastra, V. J., S. Lynn, M. Linden, J. F. Lubar, J. Gruzelier, and T. J. LaVaque. "Electroencephalographic Biofeedback in the Treatment of Attention-Deficit/Hyperactivity Disorder." *Applied Psychophysiology and Biofeedback* 30(2005): 95–114.

Monat, Alan, and Richard S. Lazarus, (Editors). *Stress and Coping: An Anthology.* New York: Columbia University Press, 1985.

Moos, R. H., and George F. Solomon. "Psychologic Comparisons Between Women with Rheumatoid Arthritis and Their Nonarthritic Sisters." *Psychosomatic Medicine* 2(1965): 150.

Morgan, Janet DiVittorio. "I Work Because I Have To." In *The Mothers' Book: Shared Experiences,* edited by Ronnie Friedland and Carol Kort. Boston: Houghton Mifflin, 1981, 96.

Morgan, K., S. Dixon, N. Mathers, J. Thompson, and M. Tomeny. "Psychological Treatment for Insomnia in the Regulation of Long-Term Hypnotic Drug Use." *Health Technology Assessment* 8(2004): iii–iv, 1–68.

Morin, Richard. "Who's Sexually Harassing America's Fighting Men?" *Washington Post,* 16 November 1997, C5.

Moskowitz, Daniel B. "Workers' Compensation Awards for Job Stress on the Rise." *Washington Post, Business,* 14 October 1985, 39.

Moss, G. E. *Illness, Immunity and Social Interaction.* New York: John Wiley & Sons, 1973.

Murphy, J. K., B. S. Alpert, E. S. Willey, and G. W. Somes. "Cardiovascular Reactivity to Psychological Stress in Healthy Children." *Psychophysiology* 25(1988): 144–52.

Nabi, H., S. M. Consoli J. F. Chastang M. Chiron, S. Lafont, and E. Lagarde. "Type A Behavior Pattern, Risky Driving Behaviors, and Serious Road Traffic Accidents: A Prospective Study of the GAZEL Cohort." *American Journal of Epidemiology* 161(2005): 864–70.

Nagengast, S. L., M. M. Baun, M. Megel, and J. M. Leibowitz. "The Effects of the Presence of a Companion Animal on Physiological Arousal and Behavioral Distress in Children During a Physical Examination." *Journal of Pediatric Nursing* 12(1997): 323–30.

Nakamura, Raymond. *Health in America: A Multicultural Perspective.* Dubuque, IA: Kendall Hunt, 2003.

Narrow, W. E., D. S. Rae, and D. A. Regier. *NIMH Epidemiology Note: Prevalence of Anxiety Disorders. One-Year Prevalence Best Estimates Calculated from ECA and NCS Data. Population Estimates Based on U.S. Census Estimated Residential Population Age 18 to 54 on July 1, 1998.* Unpublished.

National Alliance for Caregiving and AARP. *Caregiving in the United States.* Bethesda, MD: National Alliance for Caregiving, 2004.

National Center for Complementary and Alternative Medicine. "Major Domains of Complementary and Alternative Medicine." *nccam.nih.gov.*

National Center for Health Statistics. "Advance Report of Final Divorce Statistics, 1985." *Monthly Vital Statistics Report* 36 (7 December 1987).

———. "Advance Report of Final Divorce Statistics, 1987." *Monthly Vital Statistics Report* 38(15 May 1990): 1.

———. "Advance Report of Final Marriage Statistics, 1985." *Monthly Vital Statistics Report* 37(29 April 1988).

———. "Advance Report of Final Marriage Statistics, 1987." *Monthly Vital Statistics Report* 38(3 April 1990): 3–4.

———. "Aging in the Eighties: Functional Limitations of Individuals Age 65 Years and Over." *Advance Data,* 10 June 1987.

———. "Aging in the Eighties, People Living Alone—Two Years Later." *Advance Data,* 4 April 1988.

———. "Annual Summary of Births, Marriages, Divorces, and Deaths: United States, 1986." *Monthly Vital Statistics Report* 35(24 August 1987).

———. "Annual Summary of Births, Marriages, Divorces, and Deaths: United States, 1992." *Monthly Vital Statistics Report* 41(28 September 1993).

———."Births, Marriages, Divorces, and Deaths: Provisional Data for October 2001," *National Vital Statistics Report* 50(26 June 2002), 1.

———. "Blood Pressure Levels and Hypertension in Persons Ages 6–74 Years: United States, 1976–80." *Advance Data,* 8 October 1982.

———. *Health, United States,* 1996. Hyattsville, MD: Public Health Service, 1993.

———. *Health, United States, 1967–97 and Injury Chartbook.* Hyattsville, MD: Public Health Service, 1997.

———. *Health, United States, 2003.* Hyattsville, MD: National Center for Health Statistics, 2003.

———. *Healthy People 2000 Review. Health, United States,* 1992. Hyattsville, MD: Public Health Service, 1993.

———. *1985 National Health Interview Survey.* Washington, DC: U.S. Department of Health and Human Services, 1985.

———. *1992 Statistical Abstract of the United States.*

———. "Use of Nursing Homes by the Elderly: Preliminary Data from the 1985 National Nursing Home Survey." *Advance Data,* 14 May 1987.

———. *Health, United States, 2004.* Hyattsville, MD: National Center for Health Statistics, 2004.

———. "Sexual Behavior and Selected Health Measures: Men and Women 15–44 Years of Age, United States, 2002." *Advance Data* 32(2005).

National Clearinghouse on Child Abuse and Neglect Information. *Child Maltreatment 2002: Summary of Key Findings.* http://www.nccanch. acf.hhs.gov

National Coalition for the Homeless. *Homelessness in America: Unabated and Increasing.* Washington, DC: National Coalition for the Homeless, 1997.

National Coalition for Homelessness. "How Many People Experience Homelessness?" *NCH Fact Sheet* 2(2002).

———. "Who Is Homeless?" *NCH Fact Sheet* 3(2005).

National Coalition for the Homeless. *Who Is Homeless? NCH Fact Sheet #3.* Washington, DC: National Coalition for the Homeless, 2005.

National Family Caregivers Association. *Caregiving Statistics.* Kensington, MD: National Family Caregivers Association, 2005. http://www. thefamilycaregiver.org/who/stats.cfm#2

National Heart, Lung, and Blood Institute. "Aim for a Healthy Weight." *Patient and Public Education Materials,* 2000. www.nhlbi.nih.gov/ health/public/heart/ obesity/lose_wt/risk.htm.

———. "Hypertension Prevalence and the Status of Awareness, Treatment, and Control in the United States: Final Report of the Subcommittee on Definition and Prevalence of the 1984 Joint National Committee." *Hypertension* 7(1985): 457–68.

National Hospice Organization. *The Basics of Hospice.* Arlington, VA: National Hospice Organization, undated.

National Hospice and Palliative Care Organization. *NHPCO Facts and Figures.* Alexandria, VA: National Hospice and Palliative Care Organization, 2004.

National Institute of Mental Health. "Family Process and Social Networks." In National Institute of Mental Health. *Basic Behavioral Science Research for Mental Health.* Washington, DC: National Institute of Mental Health, updated 1 June 1999. http://www.nimh.nih.gov/ publicat/ baschap6.cfm

National Institute of Mental Health. *Anxiety Disorder.* http://www.nimh. gov/publicat/anxiety.cfm

———. *Retirement: Patterns and Predictions.* Washington, DC: National Institute of Mental Health, 1975.

National Institute of Mental Health Genetics Workgroup. *Genetics and Mental Disorders.* NIH Publication No. 98-4268. Rockville, MD: National Institute of Mental Health, 1998.

National Law Center on Homelessness and Poverty. *Out of Sight—Out of Mind? A Report on Anti-Homeless Laws, Litigation, and Alternatives* in *50 United States Cities*. Washington, DC: National Law Center on Homelessness and Poverty, 1999.

———. "Poverty in America: Overview." 25 July 2002. http://www.nlchp.org/FA_HAPIA/.

National Low Income Housing Coalition. *Out of Reach: Rental Housing at What Cost?* Washington, DC: National Low Income Housing Coalition, 1998.

National Safety Council Report. *Stress Management.* Boston: Jones & Bartlett, 1995.

Naughton, T. J. "A Conceptual View of Workaholism and Implications for Career Counseling and Research." *The Career Development Quarterly* 14(1987): 180–87.

Navarette S. "An Empirical Study of Adult Children of Workaholics: Psychological Functioning and Intergenerational Transmission," Doctoral diss., California Graduate Institute, 1998.

Naveen, K. V., R. Nagarathna, and H. R. Nagendra. "Yoga Breathing Through a Particular Nostril Increases Spatial Memory Scores Without Lateralized Effects." *Psychological Reports* 81(1997): 555–61.

Neugebauer, R., et al. "Association of Stressful Life Events with Chromosomally Normal Spontaneous Abortion." *American Journal of Epidemiology* 143(1996): 588–96.

Newmark, T. S. and D. F. Bogacki. "The Use of Relaxation, Hypnosis, and Imagery in Sport Psychiatry." *Clinics in Sports Medicine* 24(2005): 973–77.

Ng, Franklin (ed.). *Asian American Issues Relating to Labor, Economics, and Socioeconomic Status (Asians in America: The Peoples of East, Southeast, and South Asia in American Life and Culture).* Berlin, Germany: Garland Publishing, 1998.

Niedhammer, Isabelle, Marcel Goldberg, Annette Leclerc, Simone David, Isabelle Bugel, and Marie-France Landre. "Psychosocial Work Environment and Cardiovascular Risk Factors in an Occupational Cohort in France." *Journal of Epidemiology and Community Health* 52(1998): 93–100.

"1992 Baxter Survey of American Health Habits." In *How Employers Are Saving Through Wellness and Fitness Programs,* edited by B. Kerber. Wall Township, NJ: American Business Publishing, 1994, 32.

Noland, Melody P., and Robert H. L. Feldman. "An Empirical Investigation of Exercise Behavior in Adult Women." *Health Education* 16(1985): 29–33.

Nordentoft, M., et al. "Intrauterine Growth Retardation and Premature Delivery: The Influence of Maternal Smoking and Psychological Factors." *American Journal of Public Health* 86(1996): 347–54.

Northwestern National Life Insurance Company. *Employee Burnout: America's Newest Epidemic.* Minneapolis: Northwestern National Life Insurance Company, 1991.

Nowack, Kenneth M. "Coping Style, Cognitive Hardiness, and Health Status." *Journal of Behavioral Medicine* 12(1989): 145–58.

———. "Type A, Hardiness, and Psychological Distress." *Journal of Behavioral Medicine* 9(1986): 537–48.

Nutting, P. A., W. L. Freeman, D. R. Risser, S. D. Helgerson, R. Paisano, J. Hisnanick, S. K. Beaver, I. Peters. J. P. Carney, and M. A. Speers. "Cancer Incidence Among Indians and Alaska Natives, 1980 Through 1987." *American Journal of Public Health* 83(1993): 1589–98.

O'Brien, F., and K. Sothers. "The UW-SP Stress Management Program." *Health Values* 8(1984): 35–40.

Ockene, J. K., et al. "Relapse and Maintenance Issues for Smoking Cessation." *Health Psychology* 19(2000): 17–31.

O'Driscoll, Michael P., Steven Poelmans, Paul E. Spector, Thomas Kalliath, Tammy D. Allen, Cary L. Cooper, and Juan I. Sanchez. "Family-Responsive Interventions, Perceived Organizational and Supervisor Support, Work-Family Conflict, and Psychological Strain." *International Journal of Stress Management,* 10(2003): 326–44.

"Of Rats and Men." *Psychology Today,* July 1985, 21.

Office of Disease Prevention and Health Promotion. "Exercise for Older Americans." *Healthfinder.* Washington, DC: Office of Disease Prevention and Health Promotion National Health Information Center, November 1987.

———. *Healthy People 2010.* Washington, DC: Department of Health and Human Services, 2000.

Office of Policy Development and Research. *Housing Our Elders: A Report Card on the Housing Conditions and Needs of Older Americans.* Washington, DC: U.S. Department of Housing and Urban Development, 1999.

Okamura, J. and A. Agbayani. "Filipino Americans." In *Handbook of Social Services for Asians and Pacific Islanders,* edited by Noreen Mokuau. New York: Greenwood Press, 1991, 97–115.

Oldenburg, D. "Getting a Life: The Movement Takes a Pragmatic Turn." *Washington Post,* 12 October 1993, C5.

Oleckno, W. A., and M. J. Blacconiere. "Wellness of College Students and Differences by Gender, Race, and Class Standing." *College Student Journal* 24(1990): 421–29.

Oman, D., and D. Reed. "Religion and Mortality Among the Community-Dwelling Elderly." *American Journal of Public Health* 88(1998): 1469–75.

Oman, D., C. E. Thoresen, and K. McMahon. "Volunteerism and Mortality Among the Community-Dwelling Elderly." *Journal of Health Psychology* 4(1999): 301–16.

"On the Pulse." *Washington Post,* 6 February 1985, 5.

Ong, A. D., C. S. Bergeman, and T. L. Bisconti. "The Role of Daily Positive Emotions During Conjugal Bereavement." *The Journals of Gerontology. Series B, Psychological Sciences and Social Sciences* 59(2004): P168–76.

Orme-Johnson, D. W. "Medical Care Utilization and the Transcendental Meditation Program." *Psychosomatic Medicine* 49(1987): 493–507.

Ornish, Dean. *Dr. Dean Ornish's Program for Reversing Heart Disease: The Only System Scientifically Proven to Reverse Heart Disease Without Drugs or Surgery.* New York: Ballantine Books, 1996.

Ornstein, Robert, and David Sobel. *The Healing Brain: A New Perspective on the Brain and Health.* New York: Simon & Schuster, 1987.

Osipow, Samuel H., and Arnold R. Spokane. "Occupational Environment Scales." Unpublished scales, University of Maryland, 1980.

Ossebaard, H. C. "Stress Reduction by Technology? An Experimental Study into the Effects of Brainmachines on Burnout and State Anxiety." *Applied Psychophysiology and Biofeedback* 25 (2000): 93–101.

Ostelo, R. W., M. W. van Tulder, J. W. Vlaeyen, S. J. Linton, S. J. Morley, and W. J. Assendelft. "Behavioural Treatment for Chronic Low-Back Pain." *Cochrane Database of Systematic Reviews* 1(2005): CD002014.

Ott, M. J. "Mindfulness Meditation: A Path of Transformation and Healing." *Journal of Psychosocial Nursing and Mental Health Services* 42(2004): 22–29.

Ouchi, W. *Theory Z.* Reading, MA: Addison-Wesley, 1981.

Overholser, J. C., W. H. Norman, and I. W. Miller. "Life Stress and Support in Depressed Patients." *Behavioral Medicine,* Fall 1990, 125–31.

Pae, P. "In Area Homes, Businesses Are Booming: Thousands Seek a Balance Between Work and Family Life." *Washington Post,* 24 October 1993, B1, B6.

Paludi, M. A., and R. B. Barickman. "In Their Own Voices: Responses from Individuals Who Have Experienced Sexual Harassment and Supportive Techniques for Dealing with Victims of Sexual Harassment." In *Academic and Workplace Sexual Harassment: A Resource Manual.* Albany, NY: State University of New York Press, 1991, 29–30.

Pargament, K. I., B. Cole, L. Vandecreek, T. Belavich, C. Brant, and L. Perez. "The Vigil: Religion and the Search for Control in the Hospital Waiting Room." *Journal of Health Psychology* 4(1999): 327–41.

Pargament, K. I., D. S. Ensing, K. Falgout, H. Olsen, B. Reilly, K. Van Haitsma, and R. Warren. "God Helps Me: Religious Coping Efforts as Predictors of the Outcomes of Significant Negative Life Events." *American Journal of Community Psychology* 18(1990): 793–825.

Pargament, K. I., J. Kennel, W. Hathaway, N. Grevengoed, J. Newman, and W. Jones. "Religion and the Problem-Solving Process: Three Styles of Coping." *Journal of the Scientific Study of Religion* 27(1988): 90–104.

Parker, S. J., and D. E. Barnett. "Maternal Type A Behavior During Pregnancy, Neonatal Crying, and Early Infant Temperament: Do Type A Women Have Type A Babies?" *Pediatrics* 89(1992): 474–79.

Pasquali, E. A. "Humor: An Antidote for Terrorism." *Journal of Holistic Nursing* 21(2003): 398–414.

Pasupathy, S., K. M. Naseem, and S. Homer-Vanniasinkam. "Effects of Warm-Up on Exercise Capacity, Platelet Activation and Platelet-Leucocyte Aggregation in Patients with Claudication." *British Journal of Surgery* 92(2005): 50–55.

Patel, D. R., E. L. Phillips, and H. D. Pratt. "Eating Disorders." *Indian Journal of Pediatrics* 65(1998): 487–94.

Paternak, C. A. "Molecular Biology of Environmental Stress." *Impact of Science on Society* 41(1991): 49–57.

Patlak, Marjie. "Eating to Avoid Cancer Gets More Complicated." *Washington Post, Health,* 2 April 1986, 16–17.

Patrick, Pamela K. S. *Health Care Worker Burnout: What It Is, What to Do About It.* Chicago: Blue Cross Association, Inquiry Books, 1981.

Pavot, W. and E. Deiner. "Review of the Satisfaction with Life Scale." *Psychological Assessment* 5(1993): 164–72.

Pawlow, L. A., P. M. O'Neil, and R. J. Malcolm. "Night Eating Syndrome: Effects of Brief Relaxation Training on Stress, Mood, Hunger, and Eating Patterns." *International Journal of Obesity and Related Metabolic Disorders* 27(2003): 970–78.

Payne, J. W. "What Really Works? Forget Hearsay. Here's How Science Sizes up Some Therapies." *Washington Post,* 12 July 2005, HE01.

Peavey, B., F. Lawlis, and A. Goven. "Biofeedback-Assisted Relaxation: Effective on Phagocytic Capacity." *Biofeedback and Self-Regulation* 11(1985): 33–47.

Pelletier, K. R. *Healthy People in Unhealthy Places: Stress and Fitness at Work.* New York: Delacorte Press/Seymour Lawrence, 1984.

Pelletier, Kenneth. *Mind as Healer-Mind as Slayer: A Holistic Approach to Preventing Stress Disorders.* New York: Bantam Doubleday Dell, 1984.

Penk, W. E., et al. "Ethnicity: Post-Traumatic Stress Disorder (PTSD) Differences Among Black, White, and Hispanic Veterans Who Differ in Degree of Exposure to Combat in Vietnam." *Journal of Clinical Psychology* 45(1989): 729–35.

Peters, Ruanne K., Herbert Benson, and John M. Peters. "Daily Relaxation Response Breaks in a Working Population: II. Effects on Blood Pressure." *American Journal of Public Health* 67(1977): 954–59.

Peterson, J., et al. "The Playboy Reader's Sex Survey, Part 2." *Playboy.* March 1983, 90–92, 178–84.

Peterson, Michael, and John F. Wilson. "Work Stress in America." *International Journal of Stress Management,* 11(2004): 91–113.

Phillips, M., R. G. A. Feachem, C. J. L. Murray, M. Over, and T. Kjellstrom. "Adult Health: A Legitimate Concern for Developing Countries." *American Journal of Public Health* 83(1993): 1527–30.

Phua, D. H., H. K. Tang, and K. Y. Tham, "Coping Responses of Emergency Physicians and Nurses to the 2003 Severe Acute Respiratory Syndrome Outbreak."*Academic Emergency Medicine* 12(2005): 322–28.

Piccinino, Linda J., and William D. Mosher. "Trends in Contraceptive Use in the United States: 1982–1995." *Family Planning Perspectives* 30(1998): 4–10, 46.

Pinkham, J. R., P. S. Casamassimo, and S. M. Levy. "Dentistry and the Children of Poverty." *Journal of Dentistry for Children* 55(1988): 17–24.

Planned Parenthood of America. www.plannedparenthood.org/WOMENS HEALTH/what if pregnant. htm#Adoption?

Plante, Thomas G., and Maire Ford. "The Association Between Cardiovascular Stress Responsivity and Perceived Stress Among Subjects with Irritable Bowel Syndrome and Temperomandibular Joint Disorder: A Preliminary Study." *International Journal of Stress Management* 7(2000): 103–19.

Plante, Thomas G., David Marcotte, Gerdenio Manuel, and Eleanor Willemsen. "The Influence of Brief Episodes of Aerobic Exercise Activity, Soothing Music-Nature Scenes Condition, and Suggestion on Coping with Test-Taking Anxiety." *International Journal, of Stress Management* 3(1996): 155–66.

Pollock, Susan E. "Human Response to Chronic Illness: Physiologic and Psychosocial Adaptation." *Nursing Research* 35(1986): 90–95.

Pond, Jim. "Survey Shows Studying Freshmen's Top Worry." *The Diamondback,* 15 April 1985, 1, 3.

Poppen, Roger. *Behavioral Relaxation Training and Assessment.* New York: Pergamon Press, 1988, 66.

Potter, B. A. *Preventing Job Burnout.* Palo Alto, CA: Consulting Psychologists Press, 1987.

Potter, G. "Intensive Therapy: Utilizing Hypnosis in the Treatment of Substance Abuse Disorders." *American Journal of Clinical Hypnosis* 47(2004): 21–28.

Powell, D. H. "Behavioral Treatment of Debilitating Test Anxiety Among Medical Students." *Journal of Clinical Psychology* 60(2004): 853–65.

Powers, S. W. and F. Andrasik. "Biobehavioral Treatment, Disability, and Psychological Effects of Pediatric Headache." *Pediatric Annals* 34(2005): 461–65.

Prado-Leon, L. R., A. Celis, and R. Avila-Chaurand. "Occupational Lifting Tasks as a Risk Factor in Low Back Pain: A Case-Control Study in a Mexican Population." *Work* 25(2005): 107–14.

Pred, R. S., J. T. Spence, and R. L. Helmreich. "The Development of New Scales for the Jenkins Activity Survey Measure of the Type A Construct." *Social and Behavioral Sciences Documents* 16, no. 2679 (1986).

President's Council on Physical Fitness and Sports. *An Introduction to Running: One Step at a Time.* Washington, DC: President's Council on Physical Fitness and Sports, 1980.

———. *Aqua Dynamics.* Washington, DC: President's Council on Physical Fitness and Sports, 1981.

———. *Building a Healthier Company.* Washington, DC: President's Council on Physical Fitness and Sports, n.d.

Priest, Dana. "Hill-Thomas Legacy May Be Challenges to Old Workplace Patterns." *Washington Post,* 12 March 1992, A8.

"Princeton Study: Student Stress Lowers Immunity." *Brain Mind Bulletin* 14(1989): 1, 7.

Prochaska, James, C. C. DiClemente, and J. D. Norcross. "In Search of How People Change: Applications to Addictive Behaviors." *American Psychologist* 47(1992): 1102–14.

Public Health Service. *Healthy People: The Surgeon General's Report on Health Promotion and Disease Prevention.* Washington, DC: U.S. Government Printing Office, 1999.

"Putting the Heart in Cardiac Care." *Psychology Today,* April 1986, 18.

Quinn, S. C. "Perspective: AIDS and the African-American Woman: The Triple Burden of Race, Class, and Gender." *Health Education Quarterly* 20(1993): 305–20.

Rabkin, S., and F. Matthewson. "Chronobiology of Cardiac Sudden Death in Men." *Journal of the American Medical Association* 244(1980): 1357–58.

Ragland, David R., and Richard J. Brand, "Type A Behavior and Mortality from Coronary Heart Disease." *New England Journal of Medicine* 318(1988): 65–69.

Raina, Parminder, D. Waltner-Toews, B. Bonnett, C. Woodward, and T. J. Abernathy. "Influence of Companion Animals on the Physical and Psychological Health of Older People: An Analysis of a One-Year Longitudinal Study." *American Geriatric Society* 47(1999): 323–29.

Randall-Davis, E. *Strategies for Working with Culturally Diverse Communities and Clients.* Washington, DC: Association for the Care of Children's Health, 1989.

Rani, N. Jhansi, and P. V. Krishna Rao. "Body Awareness and Yoga Training." *Perceptual and Motor Skills* 79(1994): 1103–6.

Rathus, Spencer A. "A 30-Item Schedule for Assessing Assertive Behavior." *Behavior Therapy* 4(1973): 398–406.

Redd, Kenneth E. "Why Do Students Borrow So Much? Recent National Trends in Student Loan Debt." *ERIC Digest,* 2001. http://www.ericfacility.net/ericdigests/ed451759.html

Reed, S. and P. R. Giacobbi. "The Stress and Coping Responses of Certified Graduate Athletic Training Students." *Journal of Athletic Training* 39(2004): 193–200.

Reigel, B., et al. "Psychogenic Cough Treated with Biofeedback and Psychotherapy: A Review and Case Report." *American Journal of Physical Medicine and Rehabilitation* 74(1995): 155–58.

Rein, Glen, Mike Atkinson, and Rollin McCraty. "The Physiological and Psychological Effects of Compassion and Anger: Part 1 of 2." *Journal of Advancement in Medicine* 8(1995): 87–105.

Rennison, Callie Marie. "Intimate Partner Violence, 1993–2001." *Bureau of Justice Statistics: Crime Data Brief,* February 2003.

Rice, Philip L. *Stress and Health* (Monterey, CA: Brooks/Cole, 1999).

Rice, Phillip L. *Stress and Health: Principles and Practice for Coping and Wellness.* Monterey, CA: Brooks/Cole, 1987.

Rich, Spencer. "Study Details Income Lost in Giving Birth." *Washington Post,* 15 March 1988, A21.

Richards, P. S., and A. E. Bergin. *A Spiritual Strategy for Counseling and Psychotherapy.* Washington, DC: American Psychological Association, 1997.

Richburg, Keith B. "College Students' Average Age Rises." *Washington Post,* 14 August 1985, A4.

Riddle, Patricia, and Geraldine A. Johnson. "Sexual Harassment: What Role Should Educators Play?" *Health Education* 14(1983): 20–23.

Rider, M. S., and J. Achterberg. "Effects of Music-Assisted Relaxation: Effects on Phagocytic Capacity." *Biofeedback and Self-Regulation* 14(1989): 247–57.

Riese, H., L. J. Van Doornen, I. L. Houtman, and E. J. De Geus. "Job Strain in Relation to Ambulatory Blood Pressure, Heart Rate, and Heart Rate Variability Among Female Nurses." *Scandinavian Journal of Work, Environment & Health* 30(2004): 477–85.

Riley, V. "Mouse Mammary Tumors: Alternation of Incidence as Apparent Function of Stress." *Science* 189(1975): 465–67.

Roberts, Diane. "Sexual Harassment in the Workplace: Considerations, Concerns, and Challenges." *SIECUS Report* 28(2000): 8–11.

Robins, L. N. and D. A. Regier (eds). *Psychiatric Disorders in America: The Epidemiologic Catchment Area Study* (New York: Free Press, 1991).

Robinson B. E. *Chained to the Desk: A Guidebook for Workaholics, Their Partners and Children, and the Clinicians Who Treat Them* (New York: New York University Press, 1998).

Robinson, Bryan E., Claudia Flowers, and Jane Carroll. "Work Stress and Marriage: Examining the Relationship Between Workaholism and Marital Cohesion." *International Journal of Stress Management* 8(2001): 165–75.

Robinson, B. E. and L. Kelley. "Adult Children of Workaholics: Self-Concept, Locus of Control, Anxiety, and Depression." *American Journal of Family Therapy* 26(1998): 223–38.

Robinson, B. E. and P. Post. "Risk of Addiction to Work and Family Functioning." *Psychological Reports* 81(1997): 91–95.

Robinson, Joe. "Ahh, Free at La—Oops! Time's Up," *Washington Post,* 27 July 2003, B1, B3.

Robinson, P. H. "Review Article: Recognition and Treatment of Eating Disorders in Primary and Secondary Care." *Alimentary Pharmacological Therapy* 14(2000): 367–77.

Robinson, Vera M. "Humor in Nursing." In *Behavioral Concepts and Nursing Intervention,* 2nd ed., edited by C. Carlson and B. Blackwell. Philadelphia: Lippincott, 1978.

———. "Humor and Health." In *Handbook of Humor Research,* edited by Paul E. Mcghee and Jeffrey H. Goldstein. New York: Springer-Verlag, 1983.

Roman, J. A. "Cardiorespiratory Functioning in Flight." *Aerospace Medicine* 34(1963): 322–37.

Roper, W. L. "Current Approaches to Prevention of HIV Infections." *Public Health Reports* 106(1991): 111–15.

Rosato, Frank D. *Fitness and Wellness: The Physical Connection.* St. Paul: West, 1986.

Rosch, Paul J., and Kenneth R. Pelletier. "Designing Worksite Stress Management Programs." In *Stress Management in Work Settings,* edited by Lawrence R. Murphy and Theodore F. Schoenborn. Washington, DC: National Institute for Occupational Safety and Health, 1987, 69–91.

———. G. D. Rose and J. G. Carlson, "The Behavioral Treatment of Raynaud's Disease: A Review," *Biofeedback and Self-Regulation* 12(1987): 257–72.

Rosenbaum, Jean. "Aerobics Without Injury." *Medical Self-Care,* Fall 1984, 30–33.

Rosenbaum, Jean, and Veryl Rosenbaum. *Living with Teenagers.* New York: Stein & Day, 1980.

Rosenfeld, J. P., G. Cha, T. Blair, and I. H. Gotlib. "Operant (Biofeedback) Control of Left-Right Frontal Alpha Power Differences: Potential Neurotherapy for Affective Disorders." *Biofeedback Self Regulation* 20(1995): 241–58.

Rosenlund, M., N. Berglind, G. Pershagen, L. Jarup, and G. Bluhm. "Increased Prevalence of Hypertension in a Population Exposed to Aircraft Noise." *Occupational and Environmental Medicine* 58(2001): 769–773.

Rosenman, Ray H., Richard Brand, and C. David Jenkins. "Coronary Heart Disease in the Western Collaborative Group Study: Final Follow-Up Experience of 8 1/2 Years." *Journal of the American Medical Association* 223(1975): 872–77.

Rosenman, Ray H., Meyer Friedman, and Reuban Strauss. "A Predictive Study of Coronary Heart Disease: The Western Collaborative Group Study." *Journal of the American Medical Association* 189(1964): 15–22.

Rotter, Julian B. "Generalized Expectancies for Internal vs. External Control of Reinforcement." *Psychological Monographs* 80(1966): whole no. 609.

Rotter, J. B., "Internal Versus External Control of Reinforcement: A Case History of a Variable." *American Psychologist* 45(1990): 489–93.

Rovner, Sandy. "Learning Ways to Beat Stress." *Washington Post, Health,* 22 September 1987, 16.

Rowe, J. L., G. H. Montgomery, P. R. Duberstein, and D. H. Bovbjerg. "Health Locus of Control and Perceived Risk for Breast Cancer in Healthy Women." *Behavioral Medicine* 31(2005): 33–40.

Rowlands, Peter. *Saturday Parent.* New York: Continuum, 1980.

Rubenstein, Carin, and Carol Tavris. "Special Survey Results: 26,000 Women Reveal the Secrets of Intimacy." *Redbook,* September 1987, 147–49, 214–15.

Rubin, J. B. *Psychotherapy and Buddhism: Toward an Integration.* New York: Plenum Press, 1996.

Rubin, R. T. "Biochemical and Endocrine Responses to Severe Psychological Stress." In *Life Stress and Illness,* edited by E. K. E. Gunderson and Richard H. Rahe. Springfield, IL: Charles C. Thomas, 1974.

Rush, M. C., W. A. Schoel, and S. M. Barnard. "Psychological Resiliency in the Public Sector: 'Hardiness' and Pressure for Change." *Journal of Vocational Behavior* 46(1995): 17–39.

Russek, Henry I., and Linda G. Russek. "Is Emotional Stress an Etiological Factor in Coronary Heart Disease?" *Psychosomatics* 17(1976): 63.

Sadker, Myra, and David Sadker. "Sexism in the Schools of the '80s." *Psychology Today,* March 1985, 54–57.

Safran, Claire. "What Men Do to Women on the Job: A Shocking Look at Sexual Harassment." *Redbook,* November 1976, 149, 217–24.

Salameh, Waleed Anthony. "Humor in Psychotherapy: Past Outlooks, Present Status, and Future Frontiers." In *Handbook of Humor Research,* edited by Paul E. Mcghee and Jeffrey H. Goldstein. New York: Springer-Verlag, 1983, 75–108.

Salgado de Snyder, V. N. "Factors Associated with Acculturative Stress and Depressive Symptomatology Among Married Mexican Immigrant Women." *Psychology of Women Quarterly* 11(1987): 475–88.

Salgado de Snyder, V. N., R. C. Cervantes, and A. M. Padilla. "Gender and Ethnic Differences in Psychosocial Stress and Generalized Distress Among Hispanics." *Sex Roles* 22(1990): 441–53.

Salzberg, Sharon, and Joseph Goldstein, *Insight Meditation: A Step-By-Step Course on How to Meditate.* Gilroy, CA: Sounds True, 2002.

Sanchez, Rene. "Oregon Ignites Revolution in Adoption." *Washington Post,* 26 November 1998, A1.

Sandlund, Erica S., and Torsten Norlander. "The Effects of Tai Chi Chuan Relaxation and Exercise on Stress Responses and Well-Being: An Overview of Research." *International Journal of Stress Management* 7(2000): 139–49.

Sandor, P. S. and J. Afra. "Nonpharmacologic Treatment of Migraine." *Current Pain and Headache Report* 9(2005): 202–5.

Sands, Steven. "The Use of Humor in Psychotherapy." *Psychoanalytic Review* 71(1984): 458.

Schaufeli, Wilmar B., and Maria C. W. Peeters. "Job Stress and Burnout Among Correctional Officers: A Literature Review." *International Journal of Stress Management* 7(2000): 19–48.

Schecter, Janet, Lawrence W. Green, Lise Olsen, Karen Kruse, and Margaret Cargo. "Application of Karasek's Demand/Control Model in a Canadian Occupational Setting Including Shift Workers During a Period of Reorganization and Downsizing." *American Journal of Health Promotion* 11(1997): 394–99.

Schleifer, Steven, et al. "Suppression of Lymphocyte Stimulation Following Bereavement." *JAMA* 250(1983): 374–77.

Schmied, Lori A., and Kathleen A. Lawler. "Hardiness, Type A Behavior, and the Stress-Illness Relation in Working Women." *Journal of Personality and Social Psychology* 51(1985): 1218–23.

Schnall, P. L., et al. "The Relationship Between Job Strain, Workplace Diastolic Blood Pressure, and Left Ventricular Mass Index." *Journal of the American Medical Association* 263(1990): 1929–35.

Schneider, R., F. Staggers, C. Alexander, W. Sheppard, M. Rainforth, and C. King. "A Randomized Controlled Trial of Stress Reduction for the Treatment of Hypertension in Older African Americans." *Hypertension* 26(1995): 820–27.

Schneider, R. H., C. N. Alexander, F. Staggers, D. W. Orme-Johnson, M. Rainforth, J. W. Salerno, W., Sheppard, A. Castillo-Richmond, V. A. Barnes, and S. I. Nidich. "A Randomized Controlled Trial of Stress Reduction in African Americans Treated for Hypertension for Over One Year." *American Journal of Hypertension* 18(2005): 88–98.

Schoenbeorn, C. A. "Marital Status and Health: United States, 1999–2002." *Advance Data from the Vital and Health Statistics* 351(2004): 1.

Schultz, Johannes. *Das Autogene Training.* Stuttgart, Germany: Geerg-Thieme Verlag, 1953.

Schultz, Johannes, and Wolfgang Luthe. *Autogenic Training: A Psychophysiologic Approach to Psychotherapy.* New York: Grune & Stratton, 1959.

Schultz, V. "Reconceptualizing Sexual Harassment." *Yale Law Journal* 107(1998): 1683.

Schulz, Richard, and Scott Beach. "Caregiving as a Risk Factor for Mortality: The Caregiver Health Effects Study." *Journal of the American Medical Association* 282(1999): 2215–19.

Schwinn, Beth. "Burned in Pursuit of the Burn." *Washington Post, Health,* 14 August 1986, 12.

Scott, K. S., K. S. Moore, and M. P. Miceli. "An Exploration of the Meaning and Consequences of Workaholism." *Human Relations* 50(1997): 287–314.

Scott, S. "A Great Deal for Mall Employees." *Lexington Herald-Leader* 8 June 2002, E3.

Scott, W. C., D. Kaiser, S. Othmer, and S. I. Sideroff. "Effects of an EEG Biofeedback Protocol on a Mixed Substance Abusing Population." *American Journal of Drug and Alcohol Abuse* 31(2005): 455–69.

Seeley, Rod R., Trent D. Stephens, and Philip Tate. *Anatomy & Physiology.* Boston: McGraw-Hill, 2003, 190–9.

Seeman, Teresa E., Tina M. Lusignolo, Marilyn Albert, and Lisa Beckman. "Social Relationships, Social Support, and Patterns of Cognitive Aging in Healthy, High-Functioning Older Adults: MacArthur Studies of Successful Aging." *Health Psychology* 20 (2001): 243–55.

Segell, Michael. "The American Man in Transition." *American Health,* January/February 1989, 59–61.

Seigel, D. "A Cold Day in Rochester." *Tikkun* 15(2000): 61.

Sells, J. N., and T. D. Hargrove. "Forgiveness: A Review of the Theoretical and Empirical Literature." *Journal of Family Therapy* 20(1998): 21–36.

Selye, Hans. *The Stress of Life.* New York: McGraw-Hill Book Co., 1956.

———. *Stress Without Distress.* New York: J. B. Lippincott, 1974.

Seo, J. T., J. H. Choe, W. S. Lee, and K. H. Kim. "Efficacy of Functional Electrical Stimulation-Biofeedback with Sexual Cognitive-Behavioral Therapy as Treatment of Vaginismus." *Urology* 66(2005): 77–81.

Shapiro, D. H., and D. Giber. "Meditation and Psychotherapeutic Effects." *Archives of General Psychiatry* 35(1978): 294–302.

Shapiro, Shoshana, and Paul M. Lehrer. "Psychophysiological Effects of Autogenic Training and Progressive Relaxation." *Biofeedback and Self-Regulation* 5(1980): 249–55.

Shappell, Stephen D. "Health Benefits of Pets." *HealthCenterOnline,* 2004. http:www.healthcenteronline.com/Health_Benefits_of_Pets.html

Sharpley, C. F., J. K. Dua, R. Reynolds, and A. Acosta. "The Direct and Relative Efficacy of Cognitive Hardiness: A Behavior Pattern, Coping Behavior and Social Support as Predictors of Stress and Ill-Health." *Scandinavian Journal of Behavior Therapy* 1 (1999): 15–29.

Shearn, D. W. "Operant Conditioning of Heart Rate." Science 137(1962): 530–31.

Sheftell, F. D., S. D. Silberstein, A. M. Rapoport, and R. W. Rossum, "Migraine and Women: Diagnosis, Pathophysiology, and Treatment." *Journal of Women's Health* 1(1992): 5–19.

Shekelle, R. B., et al. "The MRFIT Behavior Pattern Study II. Type A Behavior and Incidence of Coronary Heart Disease." *American Journal of Epidemiology* 122(1985): 559–70.

Sheth, R. D., C. E. Stafstrom, and D. Hsu. "Nonpharmacological Treatment Options for Epilepsy." *Seminars in Pediatric Neurology* 12(2005): 106–13.

Shinn, Marybeth, and Beth Weitzman. "Homeless Families Are Different." In *Homelessness in America,* edited by Jim Baumohl. Washington, DC: National Coalition for Homelessness, 1996, 109–22.

Shiriki, K. K. "Maintenance of Dietary Behavior Change." *Health Psychology* 19(2000): 42–56.

Shostak, Arthur B. *Blue-Collar Stress.* Reading, MA: Addison-Wesley, 1980.

Shulman, Karen R., and Gwen E. Jones. "The Effectiveness of Massage Therapy Intervention on Reducing Anxiety in the Workplace." *Journal of Applied Behavioral Science* 32 (1996): 160–73.

Siegel, J. M. "Stressful Life Events and Use of Physician Services Among the Elderly: The Moderating Role of Pet Ownership." *Journal of Personality and Social Psychology* 58(1990): 1081–86.

Simeons, A. T. W. *Man's Presumptuous Brain: An Evolutionary Interpretation of Psychosomatic Disease.* New York: E. P. Dutton, 1961.

Simon, A. "The Neurosis, Personality Disorders, Alcoholism, Drug Use and Misuse, and Crime in the Aged." In *Handbook of Mental Health and Aging,* edited by J. E. Birren and R. B. Sloane. Englewood Cliffs, NJ: Prentice-Hall, 1980, 653–70.

Simon, Cheryl. "A Care Package." *Psychology Today,* April 1988, 44–49.

Singer, Jefferson A., Michael S. Neale, and Gary E. Schwartz. "The Nuts and Bolts of Assessing Occupational Stress: A Collaborative Effort with Labor." In *Stress Management in Work Settings,* edited by Lawrence R. Murphy and Theodore F. Schoenborn. Washington, DC: National Institute for Occupational Safety and Health, 1987, 3–29.

Siniatchkin, M., A. Hierundar, P. Kropp, R. Kuhnert, W. Gerber, and U. Stephani. "Self-Regulation of Slow Cortical Potentials in Children with Migraine: An Exploratory Study." *Applied Psychophysiology and Biofeedback* 25(2000): 13–32.

"Sleeping with the Boss." *Forum,* December 1979, 7.

Smith, H. P. R. "Heart Rate of Pilots Flying Aircraft on Scheduled Airline Routes." *Aerospace Medicine* 38(1967): 1117–19.

Smith, Jonathan C. *Relaxation Dynamics: Nine World Approaches to Self-Relaxation.* Champaign, IL: Research Press, 1985.

Smith R. E., F. L. Smoll, and J. T. Ptacek. "Conjunctive Moderator Variables in Vulnerability and Resiliency Research: Life Stress, Social Support and Coping Skills, and Adolescent Sport Injuries." *Journal of Personality and Social Psychology* 58(1990): 360–69.

Smith, D. "Stressed at School." *Washington Post,* 9 September 2000, A14.

Smith, R. E., J. T. Ptacek, and F. L Smoll. "Sensation Seeking, Stress, and Adolescent Injuries: A Test of Stress-Buffering, Risk-Taking, and Coping Skills Hypotheses." *Journal of Personality and Social Psychology* 62(1992): 1016–24.

Sobel, D. S., and R. Ornstein (eds.). *The Healthy Body and Healthy Mind Handbook.* New York: Patient Education Media, 1996.

Solcava, I., and J. Sykora. "Relation Between Psychological Hardiness and Physiological Response." *Homeostasis in Health and Disease* 36(1995): 30–34.

Solomon, Z., M. Mikulincer, and S. E. Hobfoll. "Objective Versus Subjective Measurement of Stress and Social Support: Combat Related Reactions." *Journal of Consulting and Clinical Psychology* 55(1987): 557–83.

Somer, E. "Biofeedback-Aided Hypnotherapy for Intractable Phobic Anxiety." *American Journal of Clinical Hypnosis* 37(1995): 54–64.

Sonenstein, Freya L., Leighton Ku, Laura Duberstein Lindberg, Charles F. Turner, and Joseph H. Pleck. "Changes in Sexual Behavior and Condom Use Among Teenaged Males: 1988 to 1995." *American Journal of Public Health* 88(1998): 956–59.

Sorenson, Jacki. *Aerobic Dancing.* New York: Rawson, Wade, 1979.

Sothers, K., and K. N. Anchor. "Prevention and Treatment of Essential Hypertension with Meditation-Relaxation Methods." *Medical Psychotherapy* 2(1989): 137–56.

Sparacino, Jack. "The Type A Behavior Pattern: A Critical Assessment." *Journal of Human Stress* 10(1984): 174–82.

Spence, J. T., and A. S. Robbins. "Workaholism: Definition, Measurement, and Preliminary Results." *Journal of Personality Assessment* 58(1992): 160–78.

Sprecher, Susan. "Two Sides of the Breakup of Dating Relationship." *Personal Relationships* 1(1994): 199–222.

Sprecher, Susan, Diane Felmlee, Sandra Metts, Beverley Fehr, and Debra Vanni. "Factors Associated with Distress Following the Breakup of a Close Relationship." *Journal of Social and Personal Relationships* 15(1998): 791–809.

Stang, Paul, Michael Von Korff, and Bradley S. Galer. "Reduced Labor Force Participation Among Primary Care Patients with Headache." *Journal of General Internal Medicine* 13(1998): 296–302.

Statistics Canada. *2001 Census.* Ottawa, 2001.

"Statistics on Sexual Harassment." Capstone Communications, 1999. www.capstn.com/stats.htm.

Stellnam, Jeanne, and Mary Sue Henifer, *Office Work Can Be Dangerous to Your Health* New York: Panthcon, 1983.

Steptoe, A. "Impact of Job and Marital Strain on Ambulatory Blood Pressure." *American Journal of Hypertension* 18(2005): 1138.

Stich, S. "Together, They Laugh Stress Away." *Parade Magazine,* 21 April 2002, 22.

Stockholm MUSIC Study. *Data from a Cross-Sectional Study of Ergonomic and Psychosocial Exposure and Morbidity: Function of the Musculoskeletal System.* Stockholm, Sweden: MUSIC Books, 1991.

Stone, William J. *Adult Fitness Programs: Planning, Designing, Managing, and Improving Fitness Programs.* Glenview, IL: Scott, Foresman and Company, 1987.

Stoney, Catherine M. "Plasma Homocysteine Levels Increase in Women During Psychological Stress." *Life Sciences* 64(1999): 2359–65.

Stoney, Catherine M., and Tilmer O. Engebretson. "Plasma Homocysteine Concentrations are Positively Associated with Hostility and Anger." *Life Sciences* 66(2000): 2267–75.

Straus, Stephen E. Statement by Stephen E. Straus, M.D., Director, National Center for Complementary and Alternative Medicine Before the Senate Appropriations Subcommittee on Labor, HHS, Education, and Related Agencies, 28 March 2000. *nccam.nih.gov*

Strawbridge, W. J., R. D. Cohen, S. J. Shema, and G. A. Kaplan. "Frequent Attendance at Religious Services and Mortality over 28 Years." *American Journal of Public Health* 87(1997): 957–61.

Strawbridge, W.J.,S. Deleger, R.E. Roberst, and G. A. Kaplan. "Physical Activity Reduces the Risk of Subsequent Depression for Older Adults." *American Journal of Epidemiology* 156(2002): 328–34.

"Strength Training Among Adults Aged >65 Years—United States, 2001." *Morbidity and Mortality Weekly Report* 53(2004): 25–28.

"Stress." *Newsweek,* 14 June 1999, 61.

"Stress and the Common Cold." *Washington Post,* 10 December 1996, 10–15.

"Stress Reduction May Speed Healing." *Washington Post, Health,* 21 November 1995, 5.

Strickland, B. "Internal-External Control Expectancies: From Contingency to Creativity." *American Psychologist* 27(1963): 282.

Stritof, Sheri and Bob Stritof. "Marriage Qualities Survey Results." *Your Guide to Marriage,* June 2005. http://marriage.about.com/od/keysforsuccess/a/qualresults.htm

Stroebel, Charles F. *QR: The Quieting Reflex.* New York: Berkley Books, 1983.

Strohl, Lydia. "Faith: The Best Medicine." *The Washingtonian,* December 2000: 63–65, 138–140.

"Student Finances, by the Numbers." *Chronicle of Higher Education,* 49(2002): 13.

Suenaga, H., R. Yamashita, Y. Yamabe, T. Torisu, T. Yoshimatsu, and H. Fujii. "Regulation of Human Jaw Tapping Force with Visual Biofeedback." *Journal of Oral Rehabilitation* 27(2000): 355–60.

Suplee, Curt. "Stressed Women Turn to Mother Nurture, Study Says." *Washington Post,* 9 May 2000, A2.

Sutherland, G., M. B. Andersen, and T. Morris. "Relaxation and Health-Related Quality of Life in Multiple Sclerosis: The Example of Autogenic Training." *Journal of Behavioral Medicine* 28(2005): 249–56.

Sutton, Nigel. *Applied Tai Chi Chuan.* Tokyo: Charles E. Tuttle, 1998.

Swoboda, F. "Employers Recognizing What Stress Costs Them, U.N. Report Suggests." *Washington Post,* 28 March 1992, H2.

Szekely, Barbara. "Nonpharmacological Treatment of Menstrual Headache: Relaxation-Biofeedback Behavior Therapy and Person-Centered Insight Therapy." *Headache* 26(1986): 86–92.

Taub, E., S. Steiner, E. Weingarten, and K. Walton. "Effectiveness of Broad Spectrum Approaches to Relapse Prevention in Severe Alcoholism: A Long-Term, Randomized, Controlled Trial of Transcendental Meditation, EMG, Biofeedback, and Electronic Neurotherapy." *Alcohol Treatment Quarterly* 11 (1994): 187–220.

Tauber, C.M. *Sixty-Five Plus in America.* Washington, DC: Census Bureau, 1992.

Taylor, Shelly E. *Health Psychology.* New York: Random House, 1986.

Taylor, Shelly E., Laura Cousino Klein, Brian P. Lewis, Tara L. Gruenewald, Regan A. Gurung, and John A. Updegraff. "Biobehavioral Response to Stress in Females: Tend-and-Befriend, Not Fight-or-Flight." *Psychological Review* 107(2000): 411–29.

"Teenagers and Sexuality: When Unmarried Adolescents Become Sexually Active." *Washington Post,* 10 March 1991, A3.

Telles, S., S. Narendran, and P. Raghuraj. "Comparison of Changes in Autonomic and Respiratory Parameters of Girls After Yoga and Games at a Community Home." *Perceptual Motor Sports* 84(1997): 251–57.

Telljohann, Susan K., and Jans H. Price, "A Preliminary Investigation of Inner City Primary Grade Students' Perceptions of Guns." *Journal of Health Education* 25(1994): 41–46.

Theorell, T., L. Alfredsson, P. Westerholm, and B. Falck. "Coping with Unfair Treatment at Work—What Is the Relationship Between Coping and Hypertension in Middle-Aged Men and Women?" *Psychotherapy and Psychosomatics* 69(2000): 86–94.

Theorell, T., and B. Floderus-Myrhed. "Workload and Myocardial Infarction—A Prospective Psychosocial Analysis." *International Journal of Epidemiology* 6(1977): 17–21.

Theorell, T. and A. Harenstam. "Influence of Gender on Cardiovascular Disease. In *Handbook of Gender, Culture, and Health,* edited by R. M. Eisler and M. Herson. (Mahwah, NJ: Erlbaum, 2000.

Theorell, T., and R. Rahe. "Life-Change Events, Ballistocardiography and Coronary Death." *Journal of Human Stress* 1(1975): 18–24.

Theorell, T., and T. Akerstedt. "Day and Night Work: Changes in Cholesterol, Uric Acid, Glucose, and Potassium in Serum and in Circadian Patterns of Urinary Catecholamine Excretion—a Longitudinal Cross-Over Study of Railroad Repairmen." *Acta Medicine Scandinavia* 200(1976): 47–53.

Thomas, D., and K. A. Abbas. "Comparison of Transcendental Meditation and Progressive Relaxation in Reducing Anxiety." *British Medical Journal* no. 6154(1978): 1749.

Thomson, W. C., and J. C. Wendt. "Contribution of Hardiness and School Climate to Alienation Experienced by Student Teachers." *Journal of Educational Research* 88(1995): 269–74.

Tobias, Maxine, and Mary Stewart. *Stretch and Relax: A Day by Day Workout and Relaxation Program.* Tucson, AZ: The Body Press, 1975.

Toffler, Alvin. *Future Shock.* New York: Random House, 1970.

———. *The Third Wave.* New York: William Morrow & Co., 1980.

Towbes, L. C., and L. H. Cohen. "Chronic Stress in the Lives of College Students: Scale Development and Prospective Prediction of Distress." *Journal of Youth and Adolescence* 25(1996): 199–217.

Trunnell, Eric P., and Jerry F. Braza. "Mindfulness in the Workplace." *Journal of Health Education* 26(1995): 285–91.

Tsutsumi, Akizumi, Tores Theorell, Johan Hallqvist, Christina Reuterwall, and Ulf de Faire. "Association Between Job Characteristics and Plasma Fibrinogen in a Normal Working Population: A Cross Sectional Analysis in Referents of the SHEEP Study." *Journal of Epidemiology and Community Health* 53(1999): 348–54.

Tucker, Larry A., Galen E. Cole, and Glenn M. Friedman. "Stress and Serum Cholesterol: A Study of 7,000 Adult Males." *Health Values* 11(1987): 34–39.

Turhan H., A. R. Erbay, A. S. Yasar, A. Bicer, O. Sahin, N. Basar, and E. Yetkin. "Plasma Homocysteine Levels in Patients with Isolated Coronary Artery Ectasia." *International Journal of Cardiology* 104(2005): 158–62.

Turk, D. C., Donald H. Meichenbaum, and W. H. Berman. "Application of Biofeedback for the Regulation of Pain: A Critical Review." *Psychological Bulletin* 86(1979): 1322–38.

Turk, M. "The Grim Reaper of Youth." *American Health,* October 1993, 14.

Turnbull, G. J. "A Review of Post-Traumatic Stress Disorder. Part I: Historical Development and Classification." *Injury* 29(1998): 87–91.

Ulbrich, P. M., and G. J. Warheit. "Social Support, Stress, and Psychological Distress Among Older Black and White Adults." *Journal of Aging and Health* 1(1989): 286–305.

Ulbrich, P. M., G. J. Warheit, and R. S. Zimmerman. "Race, Socioeconomic Status, and Psychological Distress: An Examination of Differential Vulnerabilities." *Journal of Health and Social Behavior* 30(1989): 131–46.

U.S. Bureau of the Census. *Current Population Reports, Population Characteristics, Series P-20, No. 417. Households, Families, Marital Status, and Living Arrangements: March 1987. Advance Report.* Washington, DC: U.S. Government Printing Office, 1987.

———. *Current Population Reports, Series P-20, No. 419. Household and Family Characteristics: March 1986.* Washington, DC: U.S. Government Printing Office, 1987.

———. *Current Population Reports, P20–467. Household and Family Characteristics: March, 1992.* Washington, DC: U.S. Government Printing Office, 1993.

———. *Current Population Reports, Series P-23, No. 150. Population Profile of the United States: 1984–85.* Washington, DC: U.S. Government Printing Office, 1987.

———. *Current Population Reports, Series P-23, No. 159, Population Profile of the United States: 1989.* Washington, DC: U.S. Government Printing Office, 1989.

———. *Current Population Reports, Series P-23, No. 162, Studies in Marriage and the Family.* Washington, DC: U.S. Government Printing Office, 1989, 1.

———. *Current Population Reports, Series P-23, No. 163, Changes in American Family Life.* Washington, D.: U.S. Government Printing Office, 1989, 13.

———. *Current Population Reports, P-23, No. 173. Population Profile of the United States: 1991.* Washington, DC: U.S. Government Printing Office, 1991.

———. *Current Population Reports, Special Studies, P-23–190, 6+ in the United States.* Washington, DC: U.S. Government Printing Office, 1996.

———. *Current Population Reports, Series P-70, No. 10. Male-Female Differences in Work Experience, Occupations, and Earnings: 1984.* Washington, DC: U.S. Government Printing Office, 1987.

———. *Current Population Survey* (March 1997).

———. "How We're Changing, Demographic State of the Nation." *Current Population Reports* P-23–193 (March 1997).

U.S. Census Bureau. "America's Families and Living Arrangements, 2000." *Current Population Reports,* 2001.

U.S. Census Bureau. *Statistical Abstracts of the United States, 2004–2005.* Washington, DC: U.S Government Printing Office, 2005.

U.S. Census Bureau. *Statistical Abstracts of the United States: 2006.* Washington, DC: U.S. Government Printing Office, 2005.

———. "Household and Family Characteristics March 1998 (Update)." *Current Population Reports,* 1998.

———. "Marital Status and Living Arrangements: March 1998 (Update)." *Current Population Reports,* P20–514. Washington, DC: U.S. Department of Commerce, 1998.

———. "Married-Couple and Unmarried-Partner Households: 2000." *Census 2000 Special Reports,* 2003.

———. "Population Profile of the United States, 2000." *Current Population Reports,* 2001.

U.S. Census Bureau. *Statistical Abstract of the United States: 2002.* Washington, DC: U.S. Census Bureau, 2002.

U.S. Conference of Mayors. *17th Annual Conference Survey of Hunger, Homelessness Documents Increase in Current Demands.* 17 December 2001. http://www.usmayors.org/uscm/us_mayor_newspaper/documents/12_17_01/hunger_homelessness.asp.

U.S. Department of Agriculture. *Expenditures on Children by Families, 2001 Annual Report.* Washington, DC: U.S. Department of Agriculture, 2002.

U.S. Department of Health and Human Services. *Healthy People 2010: Understanding and Improving Health.* 2nd ed. Washington, DC: U.S. Government Printing Office, 2000.

———. "1992 National Survey of Worksite Health Promotion Activities: Summary." *American Journal of Health Promotion* 7(1993): 452–64.

———. *HIV/AIDS Surveillance Report.* Washington, DC: U.S. Department of Health and Human Services, 1996.

U. S. Department of Labor, Bureau of Labor Statistics. "Time-Use Survey—First Results Announced by BLS." *News,* 14-September 2004. http://www.bls.gov/tus

U.S. Department of Labor. *Employment and Earnings.* Washington, DC: United States Department of Labor, August 1997.

U.S. General Accounting Office. *Children and Youths: Report to Congressional Committees.* Washington, DC: U.S. Government Printing Office, 1989.

U.S. National Center for Health Statistics. "Fertility, Family Planning, and Women's Health: New Data from the 1995 National Survey of Family Growth." *Vital and Health Statistics,* Ser. 23, no. 19 (1997).

"U.S. Nurses Overworked, Overstressed, but Help May Be on the Way." *The Nation's Health.* February 1993, 4.

U.S. Public Health Service. *Healthy People 2000: National Health Promotion and Disease Objectives.* Washington, DC: U.S. Department of Health and Human Services, September 1992.

———. *Healthy People: The Surgeon General's Report on Health Promotion and Disease Prevention.* Washington, DC: U.S. Government Printing Office, 1999.

———. *Physical Activity and Health: A Report of the Surgeon General.* Washington, DC: U.S. Department of Health and Human Services, 1996.

"U.S. Seniors: The New Boom Generation." *Washington Post,* 15 September 1992, 5.

University of Michigan. "U.S. Husbands Are Doing More Housework While Wives Are Doing Less." *News and Information Services,* 12 March 2002.

Vagg, Peter R., Charles D. Spielberger, and Carol F. Wasala. "Effects of Organizational Level and Gender on Stress in the Workplace." *International Journal of Stress Management* 9(2002): 243–61.

van de Putte, E. M., R. H. Engelbert, W. Kuis, G. Sinnema, J. L. Kimpen, and C. S. Uiterwaal. "Chronic Fatigue Syndrome and Health Control in Adolescents and Parents." *Archives of Disease in Childhood* 90(2005): 1020–24.

van Doornen, L., and K. Orlebeke. "Stress, Personality and Serum Cholesterol Level." *Journal of Human Stress* 8(1982): 24–29.

Vega, W. A., and R. G. Rumbaut. "Ethnic Minorities and Mental Health." *Annual Review of Sociology* 17(1991): 351–83.

Vickers, Andrew, and Catherine Zollman. "ABC of Complementary Medicine: Massage Therapies." *British Medical Journal* 319(1999): 1254–57.

Violante, F. S., F. Graziosi, R. Bonfiglioli, S. Curti, and S. Mattioli. "Relations Between Occupational, Psychosocial and Individual Factors and Three Different Categories of Back Disorder Among Supermarket Workers." *International Archives of Occupational and Environmental Health* (2005): 1–12.

Vissing, Yvonee. *Out of Sight, Out of Mind: Homeless Children and Families in Small Town America.* Lexington, KY: University Press of Kentucky, 1996.

Vobejda, Barbara. "Web Site to List Foster Children for Adoption." *Washington Post,* 25 November 1998, A5.

Vyas, R. and N. Dikshit. "Effect of Meditation on Respiratory System, Cardiovascular System and Lipid Profile." *Indian Journal of Physiological Pharmacology* 46(2002): 487–91.

Wahlund, K., List, T., and Larsson, B. "Treatment of Temporomandibular Disorders among Adolescents: A Comparison Between Occlusal Appliance, Relaxation Training, and Brief Information." *Acta Odontology Scandinavia* (2003): 203–11.

Waite, P. J., S. R. Hawks, and J. A. Gast. "The Correlation Between Spiritual Well-Being and Health Behaviors." *American Journal of Health Promotion* 13(1999): 159–62.

Wallace, Robert Keith. "Physiological Effects of Transcendental Meditation." *Science* 167(1970): 1751–54.

Wallace, Robert Keith, and Herbert Benson. "The Physiology of Meditation." *Scientific American* 226(1972): 84–90.

Walling, Anne. D. "Update on the Management of Migraine Headaches," *American Family Physician.* October 1, 2004. http://www.findarticles.com/p/articles/mi_m3225/is_7_70/ai_n8570254

Wallston, Kenneth A., Barbara S. Wallston, and Robert DeVellis. "Development of the Multidimensional Health Locus of Control (MHLC) Scales." *Health Education Monographs* 6(1978): 160–70.

Walsh, Sharon Warren. "Confronting Sexual Harassment at Work." *Washington Post, Business,* 21 July 1986, 16–17.

Walster, Elaine, and G. William Walster. *A New Look at Love.* Reading, MA: Addison-Wesley, 1978.

Walters, K. L. and J. M. Simoni. "Reconceptualizing Native Women's Health: An "Indigent" Stress-Coping Model." *American Journal of Public Health* 92(2002): 520–24.

Wamala, Sarah P., Murray A. Mittleman, Karen Schenck-Gustafson, and Kristina Orth-Gomer. "Potential Explanations for the Educational Gradient in Coronary Heart Disease: A Population-Based Case-Control Study of Swedish Women." *American Journal of Public Health* 89(1999): 315–21.

Waters, W. F., M. J. Hurry, P. G. Binks, C.E. Carney, L. E. Lajos, K. H. Fuller, B. Betz, J. Johnson, T. Anderson, and J. M. Tucci. "Behavioral and Hypnotic Treatments for Insomnia Subtypes." *Behavioral Sleep Medicine* 1(2003): 81–101.

Weber, Tricia R. "Humor as a Stress Management Strategy." *The Health Education Monograph Series* 16(1998): 35–39.

Webster, D. W., P. S. Gainer, and H. R. Champion. "Weapon Carrying Among Inner-City Junior High School Students: Defensive Behavior vs. Aggressive Delinquency." *American Journal of Public Health* 83(1993): 1604–8.

Webster's New World College Dictionary. 4th ed. New York: Macmillan, 1999.

Wee, Eric L. "More College Students Live, Then Learn." *Washington Post,* 5 March 1996, A1, A7.

Weiman, Clinton G. "A Study of the Occupational Stressor and the Incidence of Disease/Risk." *Journal of Occupational Medicine* 19(1977): 119–22.

———. "A Study of the Occupational Stressor and the Incidence of Disease/Risk." *NIOSH Proceeding: Reducing Occupational Stress.* Cincinnati: National Institute for Occupational Safety and Health, April 1978, 55.

Weldon, Gail. "The ABC's of Aerobics Injuries." *Shape,* September 1986, 86–90+.

White, Louise M. "Attention Type A's! You May Be 'Talking Yourself into' Coronary Heart Disease." *The University of Maryland Graduate School Chronicle* 19(1985): 6–7.

White-Corey, Shelley. "Five-Star Instructors—Choosing a Fitness Instructor." *American Fitness,* January/February 1996. Available at http://www.findarticles.com/p/articles/mi_m0675/is_n1_v14/ai_17793077#continue

Wiley, D. C., and D. J. Ballard. "How Can Schools Help Children from Homeless Families?" *Journal of School Health* 63(1993): 291–93.

Will, G. F. "The Tragedy of Illegitimacy." *Washington Post,* 31 October 1993, C7.

Wing, R. R., and R. W. Jeffrey. "Benefits of Recruiting Participants with Friends and Increasing Social Support for Weight Loss and Maintenance." *Journal of Consulting and Clinical Psychology* 67(1999): 132–38.

Winship, M. *CDC Seoprevalence Study.* Unpublished raw data.

Winstead-Fry, P., C. G. Hernandez, G. M. Colgan, et al. "The Relationship of Rural Persons' Multidimensional Health Locus of Control to Knowledge of Cancer, Cancer Myths, and Cancer Danger Signs." *Cancer Nursing* 22(1999): 456–62.

Wolf, A. N., S. L. Gortmaker, L. Cheung, H. M. Gray, D. B. Herzog, and G. A. Colditz. "Activity, Inactivity, and Obesity: Racial, Ethnic, and Age Differences Among Schoolgirls." *American Journal of Public Health* 83(1993): 1625–27.

Wolf, Stewart. *The Stomach.* Oxford: Oxford University Press, 1965.

Wolf, Stewart, and Harold G. Wolff. *Headaches: Their Nature and Treatment.* Boston: Little, Brown, 1953.

Wolff, Harold G. *Stress and Disease.* Springfield, IL: Charles C. Thomas, 1953.

Wolpe, Joseph. *The Practice of Behavior Therapy.* 2nd ed. New York: Pergamon, 1973.

Women on Words & Images. *Dick and Jane as Victims.* Princeton, NJ: Women on Words & Images, 1975.

Women's Bureau. *Facts on Women Workers.* Washington, DC: U.S. Department of Labor, 1984.

"Women's Health: More Sniffles in Splitsville." *American Health,* July/August 1986, 96, 98.

Wooten, P. "Humor: An Antidote for Stress." *Holistic Nursing Practice* 10(1996): 49–56.

Worthington, E. L., T. A. Kurusu, M. E. McCullough, and S. J. Sandage. "Empirical Research on Religion and Psychotherapeutic Processes and Outcomes: A 10-Year Review of Research Prospectus." *Psychological Bulletin* 119(1996): 448–87.

Wright, L. "The Type A Behavior Pattern and Coronary Artery Disease." *American Psychologist* 453 (1988): 2–14.

Yamada, Y., K. Tatsumi, T. Yamaguchi, N. Tanabe, Y. Takiguchi, T. Kuriyama, and R. Mikami. "Influence of Stressful Life Events on the Onset of Sarcoidosis." *Respirology* 8(2003): 186–91.

Yoo, H. J., S. H. Ahn, S. B. Kim, W. K. Kim, and O. S. Han. "Efficacy of Progressive Muscle Relaxation Training and Guided Imagery in Reducing Chemotherapy Side Effects in Patients with Breast Cancer and in Improving Their Quality of Life." *Supportive Care in Cancer* 13(2005): 826–33.

Yorko, Karen H., Leslie R. Martin, Howard S. Friedman, Christopher Peterson, and Martin E. P. Seligman. "Catastrophizing and Untimely Death." *Psychological Science* 9(1998): 127–30.

Young, F. W., and N. Glasgow. "Voluntary Social Participation and Health." *Research on Aging* 20(1998): 339–62.

"Youth Risk Behavior Surveillance—United States, 1999." *Mortality and Morbidity Weekly Report* 49(2000): 1–96.

Yu, S., J. W. G. Yarnell, P. M. Sweetnam, and L. Murray. "What Level of Physical Activity Protects Against Premature Cardiovascular Death? The Caerphilly Study." *Heart* 89(2003): 502–6.

Zarski, J. J. "Hassles and Health: A Replication." *Health Psychology* 3(1984): 243–51.

Zich, J., and L. Temoshok. "Perceptions of Social Support in Men with AIDS and ARC: Relationships with Distress and Hardiness." *Journal of Applied Social Psychology* 17(1987): 193–215.

Zimbardo, Philip G. *Shyness: What It Is and What to Do About It.* Reading, MA: Addison-Wesley, 1977.

Zimmerman, Tansella, "Preparation Courses for Childbirth in Primipara: A Comparison." *Journal of Psychosomatic Research* 23(1979): 227–33.

Page 7: © Keith Brofsky/Getty Images;

Page 14: © Digital Vision/PunchStock;

Page 40: © Stockbyte/PunchStock;

Page 49: Amos Morgan/Getty Images;

Page 68: PhotoDisc/Getty Images;

Page 71: Karl Weatherly/Getty Images;

Page 89: Jack Star/PhotoLink/Getty Images;

Page 103: © image100/PunchStock;

Page 107: PhotoLink/Getty Images;

Page 112: Royalty-Free/CORBIS;

Page 124: Monica Lau/Getty Images;

Page 125: Keith Brofsky/Getty Images;

Page 126: Steve Mason/Getty Images;

Page 128: Ryan McVay/Getty Images;

Page 132: The McGraw-Hill Companies, Inc./Gary He, photographer;

Page 137: The McGraw-Hill Companies, Inc./Jill Braaten, photographer;

Pages 154, 156,158: Royalty-Free/CORBIS;

Page 160: The McGraw-Hill Companies, Inc./Gary He, photographer;

Page 171: Joaquin Palting/Getty Images;

Page 172: S. Solum/PhotoLink/Getty Images;

Page 173: Royalty-Free/CORBIS;

Page 183: Colin Paterson/Getty Images;

Page 187: © Digital Vision/PunchStock;

Page 196: Getty Images;

Page 198: Royalty-Free/CORBIS;

Page 214: Digital Vision/Getty Images;

Page 215: Ryan McVay/Getty Images;

Page 216: © Brand X Pictures/PunchStock;

Page 218: Getty Images;

Page 219: © Digital Vision;

Page 220: © Creatas/PunchStock;

Page 233: © Royalty-Free/CORBIS;

Page 234: © PhotoLink/Photodisc/Getty Images;

Page 238: JupiterImages;

Page 240: PhotoLink/Getty Images;

Page 245: Getty Images;

Page 246: StockTrek/Getty Images;

Page 249: Keith Brofsky/Getty Images;

Page 264: Getty Images;

Page 281: Ryan McVay/Getty Images;

Page 283: Rim Light/PhotoLink/Getty Images;

Page 285: Digital Vision/Getty Images;

Page 290: Getty Images;

Pages 301, 308, 313, 314: Royalty-Free/CORBIS;

Page 318: Ryan McVay/Getty Images;

Page 332: (top) Ryan McVay/Getty Images, (bottom) Getty Images;

Page 334: Andrew Ward/Life File/Getty Images;

Page 335: Getty Images;

Page 341: David Buffington/Getty Images;

Page 342: Amos Morgan/Getty Images;

Pages 346, 356: Steve Cole/Getty Images;

Page 358: Courtesy of the author;

Page 362: Digital Vision/Getty Images;

Page 363: Keith Brofsky/Getty Images;

Page 364: © SW Productions/Getty Images;

Page 367: The McGraw-Hill Companies, Inc./Jill Braaten, photographer;

Page 369: Ryan McVay/Getty Images;

Page 371: Don Farrall/Getty Images;

Pages 373, 374, 376: Royalty-Free/CORBIS;

Page 384: Getty Images;

Page 386: Royalty-Free/CORBIS;

Pages 387, 389: Keith Brofsky/Getty Images;

Page 391: Kent Knudson/PhotoLink/Getty Images;

Page 394: Karl Weatherly/Getty Images;

Page 399: Getty Images